W9-ARY-774

Frederic S. Mishkin
Columbia University

The Economics of Money, Banking, and Financial Markets

Third Edition

HarperCollinsPublishers

Sponsoring Editor: Bruce Kaplan
Development Editor: Jane Tufts
Project Coordination, Text and Cover Design: York Production Services
Production Manager: Michael Weinstein
Compositor: York Graphic Services, Inc.
Printer and Binder: Arcata Graphics/Hawkins
Cover Printer: The Lehigh Press, Inc.
Cover Photos: "Whole World in the Hand," © Gary Landsman Studio/Uniphoto;
"Currency," J. R. Bale/Index Stock; "Coins," SuperStock Inc.; "Coins," Four by Five;
"Buildings, Irvine California," SuperStock Inc.

For permission to use copyrighted material, grateful acknowledgment is made to the copyright holders on pp. A-17–A-18, which are hereby made part of this copyright page.

The Economics of Money, Banking, and Financial Markets, Third Edition
Copyright © 1992 by Mishkin Economics, Inc.

All rights reserved. Printed in the United States of America. No part of this book may be used or reproduced in any manner whatsoever without written permission, except in the case of brief quotations embodied in critical articles and reviews. For information address HarperCollins Publishers Inc., 10 East 53rd Street, New York, NY 10022.

Library of Congress Cataloging-in-Publication Data

Mishkin, Frederic S.
   The economics of money, banking, and financial markets / Frederic
S. Mishkin. — 3rd ed.
     p.   cm.
   Includes bibliographical references and index.
   ISBN 0-673-52141-9 (student edition)   ISBN 0-673-52174-5 (instructor's edition)
    1. Finance. 2. Money. 3. Banks and banking.   I. Title.
HG173.M632 1992
332—dc20   91-24472
                                                   CIP

92 93 94 9 8 7 6 5 4 3 2

To Sally

//// Brief Contents

Detailed Contents

*Summary, Key Terms, and Questions and Problems appear at the end of every chapter.

PART II
FUNDAMENTALS OF INTEREST RATES

PART IV
THE MONEY SUPPLY PROCESS

PART VI
INTERNATIONAL FINANCE

PART VII
MONETARY THEORY

Preface

In recent years, the field of money, banking, and financial markets has become one of the most exciting in all of economics. Financial markets are changing rapidly, with new financial instruments appearing almost every day; the once staid banking industry is now highly dynamic and is continually featured in the media as a result of the crisis in the savings-and-loan and commercial banking industries; well-functioning international financial markets and trade have created an integrated world economy in which events in one country's financial markets have a major impact on financial markets in other countries; the conduct of monetary policy is at center stage in debates about economic policy; and new developments in monetary theory have changed the way we think about the role of money in the economy.

This third edition of *The Economics of Money, Banking, and Financial Markets* is a major revision that conveys these exciting developments in the money, banking, and financial markets field.

BASIC FEATURES

In writing this edition, I have continued to be guided by four basic features that have always distinguished this book from its competitors: stress on the economic way of thinking, a modern approach to the subject, flexibility, and numerous pedagogical aids.

The Economic Way of Thinking

An important problem in teaching money, banking, and financial markets is that students often memorize a mass of facts that are forgotten after the final exam and that soon become obsolete because of the rapid pace of financial innovation. To keep students from falling into this trap, this book continually stresses the economic way of thinking by focusing on a few basic economic principles that students can use to understand the structure of financial markets and institutions, bank management, the operation of financial markets both here and abroad, and the role of money in the economy. These principles include a simplified approach to portfolio choice (what I call the Theory of Asset Demand), the concept of equilibrium, supply and demand analysis, profit maximization, asymmetric information (adverse selection and moral hazard), and aggregate demand and supply analysis.

This new edition pushes the economic way of thinking even further than previous editions by presenting a thorough economic analysis of financial markets and institutions in Part III. This analysis allows the student to have a whole new understanding of why financial markets and institutions are set up the way they are and of how they operate to promote economic efficiency.

To help students apply these economic principles, the text adopts an approach found in the best principles of economics books: simple models are constructed in which the variables being held constant are carefully delineated, and the models are then used to explain important economic phenomena by focusing on the appropriate change in variables, *ceteris paribus*. In order to make the subject matter exciting for students, this edition continues to emphasize the interaction between economic theory and empirical data. Throughout the text—in over twenty major applications and over fifty special interest boxes—evidence is presented that supports or casts doubt on the economic propositions being discussed. This exposure to real-life events and data dissuades students from thinking that economists merely make abstract assumptions and develop theories that have nothing to do with actual behavior.

A Modern Approach

As with previous editions, this edition also seeks to present a contemporary approach to money, banking, and financial markets that enables students to understand important and relevant policy debates. It uses a modern asset-market approach to interest rate and exchange rate determination instead of the older approaches used in other textbooks, which stress flows rather than stocks of assets. The modern asset-market approaches are much better suited to explaining the high volatility we see in asset prices such as interest rates and exchange rates and have thus been adopted by the economics profession when discussing current policy debates. To keep the discussion of monetary theory modern, this book contains an extensive treatment of the role of expectations in current policy debates. The theory of rational expectations receives special attention in the final two chapters. Also included is new material on such topics as real business cycle theory and hysteresis.

The third edition provides a completely updated theory of financial markets and institutions based on recently developed literature on asymmetric information and financial structure. The new material, which is unique to this book, provides the student with a modern approach to understanding financial markets and institutions and allows an in-depth analysis of the current crisis in banking regulation. It also enables the student to better understand the role of financial crises in aggregate economic activity, a topic in monetary theory that is currently receiving a great deal of research attention.

Flexibility

In using previous editions, adopters, reviewers, and survey respondents have continually praised this text's flexibility. There are as many ways to teach money, banking, and financial markets as there are instructors. To satisfy the diverse needs of instructors, the text achieves its flexibility as follows: Core chapters provide the basic analysis used throughout the book, and other chapters, or sections of chapters, can be used or omitted according to the instructor's preference. For example, Chapter 3 provides an introductory overview of the financial system, which allows the instructor to then choose any of a number of different paths to follow in covering financial markets and institutions. The text has also been designed to allow instructors to cover the most important issues in monetary theory and policy without having to use the ISLM model, while more complete treatments of monetary theory make use of the ISLM chapters. Similarly, instructors can teach the course without including the chapters on foreign exchange rate determination and international finance, although instructors who want their course to have more of an international orientation can teach these chapters early in the course. (More detailed information about how the text can be used flexibly in your course is available in the *Instructor's Manual.*)

NEW TO THE THIRD EDITION

Although the basic features and material of the previous edition have been retained, the third edition represents a major revision.

A New Approach to Teaching Financial Markets and Institutions

This edition departs from the previous edition and other textbooks in the field by developing a comprehensive economic framework for analyzing financial markets and institutions. The framework makes use of economic concepts such as transactions costs, adverse selection, moral hazard, and the principal-agent problem to provide a new way of organizing the teaching of financial markets and institutions. It also provides a unifying economic framework to organize students' thinking about financial markets and institutions so that they can make sense of, rather than be confused by, all the facts about our financial system. Furthermore, this economic framework, in contrast to a set of facts about financial institutions, will not go out of date; it will allow instructors to discuss the latest developments in financial markets and institutions, thus making it easier for them to keep their teaching current.

An entirely new Chapter 8, An Economic Analysis of Financial Structure, begins with a discussion of eight basic puzzles about financial structure and then goes on to provide solutions to these puzzles by analyzing the impact of transaction costs and asymmetric information on financial markets. Students are surprised by some of these puzzles—the relative unimportance of the stock market as a source of finance for corporations, for example—and find understanding why they occur to be fascinating.

The adverse selection, moral hazard, and principal-agent concepts are then applied in the remaining chapters in Part III to develop a deeper knowledge of financial institutions. They are used in a new section, Principles of Loan Management, in Chapter 9, The Banking Firm and Bank Management (Chapter 8 in the previous edition) and in two new sections, Principles of Insurance Management and Government Financial Intermediation, in Chapter 12, Nonbank Financial Institutions (Chapter 10 in the previous edition). An entirely new chapter, Chapter 11, The Crisis in Banking Regulation, again uses these concepts to take an in-depth look at why the current crisis in banking regulation and the savings-and-loan industry has occurred and what might be done to prevent such crises in the future.

Because this new approach to teaching financial markets and institutions stresses lasting economic concepts, it will work especially well with the latest articles on financial markets and institutions. To make it easier for instructors to keep their courses up to date, an annual reader especially for this text, edited by James Eaton of Bridgewater College and myself, will be sold with the text at a particularly low price. This reader will enable instructors to keep their course especially current during the three-year life of this edition, something that no other textbook in the field can provide.

The stress on flexibility has continued in the writing of this new material on financial markets and institutions. Because not all instructors will want to teach Chapter 8, the concepts of adverse selection, moral hazard, and the principal-agent problem are explained briefly in the later chapters that make use of them: Chapters 9, 11, and 12. These chapters are thus self-contained so that Chapter 8 does not have to be covered in order to teach them. This presentation allows instructors to cover different amounts of material according to their preference.

A Thorough Integration of International Topics Throughout the Text

To meet the growing interest in international trade and financial markets of students and their instructors, the third edition thoroughly integrates international topics throughout the text. One vehicle for doing this is a new set of over twenty special interest boxes, unique to this text, that are called A Global Perspective. These boxes give students an international perspective at an early stage in the text by continually comparing the financial system and monetary policy in the United States to that of other countries.

In addition, the chapters on foreign exchange rate determination and international finance have been moved into the body of the text, immediately after the chapters on the Federal Reserve System and the conduct of monetary policy. The chapters on foreign exchange rates and international finance are best taught at this point in the course because later chapters that look at how aggregate economic activity is determined can examine the role of international factors more effectively. International trade flows (net exports) are now included in the definition of aggregate demand in the text of the ISLM Chapters 24 and 25 (rather than in an appendix), which allows the instructor to discuss more directly how exchange rates and international trade flows influence interest rates and aggregate output in the ISLM model. International trade flows are given a full treatment in the analysis of aggregate demand and supply in Chapter 26 and in the discussion of monetary transmission mechanisms in Chapter 28.

The approach to internationalizing the text in this edition using both the global perspective boxes and the placement of the international finance chapters in the middle of the text is comprehensive and yet is quite flexible. Although many instructors will teach the text using all of this material, others will choose not to. Instructors who wish to stay with a closed-economy framework can easily do so by skipping the international finance chapters and by skipping the material in the monetary theory chapters that deal with net exports and international trade. Because this material does not affect the basic monetary theory analysis, all of the monetary theory chapters can be taught without it. In addition, because the global perspective boxes are self-contained, they can also be skipped without any loss of continuity.

A More Modern Asset-Market Approach to Exchange Rate Determination

Although the asset-market approach to exchange rate determination is similar in this and the previous edition, Chapters 21 and 22 have been revised to model exchange rate determination using the interest parity equilibrium condition. This leads to a more modern approach that follows closely the current literature on exchange rate determination. Not only does this lead to pedagogical improvements, but it also allows analysis of such phenomena as exchange rate overshooting and the different effects from sterilized and unsterilized exchange rate intervention.

New Appendixes for Teaching Finance-Oriented Courses

Two new appendixes have been included that are particularly useful in teaching courses that have a financial markets and institutions orientation or that are taught in finance departments in business schools (as is the case for the course I teach using this book). A mathematical appendix to Chapter 5, placed at end of the text, provides a far more extensive treatment of theories of portfolio choice than is contained in the chapter. It makes clear the distinction between systematic and nonsystematic risk, and it lays out both the capital asset pricing model and arbitrage pricing theory.

An appendix to Chapter 8 carries the analysis of financial structure further by examining the corporate finance topic of why corporations have been restructured in the 1980s to have an increased level of debt relative to equity. The appendix makes use of principal-agent analysis (a particular example of moral hazard) and Jensen's free cash flow theory to explain the increase in corporate leverage. It also focuses on the currently controversial (and heated!) policy debate on whether the resulting increase in corporate debt has been bad for the economy and should thus be stopped by government restrictions on takeovers and leveraged buyouts.

Expositional Changes, New Boxes, and Updating

As a result of comments from reviewers and users of the text, the exposition has been improved at many points in the text. Chapter 13 on financial innovation has been tightened up. Chapters 15 and 16 have been simplified by including the excess reserves-checkable deposits ratio in the money multiplier and by eliminating discussion of the time deposits-checkable deposits ratio (since reserve requirements on time deposits have been eliminated). Chapter 26, Aggregate Demand and Supply Analysis, now downplays the Keynesian-Monetarist debate and leaves the activist/nonactivist debate to the chapter on money and inflation (Chapter 28). New summary tables have been added at several points to clarify and provide study aids to the student. In addition to the new global perspective boxes, there are also new special interest boxes to keep the text both lively and current. These include boxes on monetary union in Germany and Europe, international policy coordination, Donald Trump and his financial difficulties, Japanese and German banking arrangements, the Keating savings-and-loan scandal, the failure of the Bank of New England, junk bonds, and the rise and fall of Michael Milken and Drexel, Burnham. The discussion of the empirical evidence on the demand for money in the appendix to Chapter 23 has been updated as have many boxes in the text. All figures and data in the text have also been thoroughly updated through the end of 1990 (except in rare instances when this was not possible).

PEDAGOGICAL AIDS

A textbook must be a solid motivational teaching tool. To this end, a wide variety of pedagogical features are incorporated into my presentation.

These include:

1. **Chapter Previews** at the beginning of each chapter that tell students where the chapter is heading, why specific topics are important, and how they relate to other topics in the book;

2. **Special Interest Boxes** that highlight dramatic historical episodes, interesting ideas, or interesting facts related to the subject matter;

3. **Following the Financial News** boxes, which introduce students to relevant news articles and data that are reported in the press;

4. **Study Guides,** which are highlighted statements scattered throughout the text that provide hints on how to think about or approach a topic as students work their way through it;

5. **Key Statements,** which are important points that are set in boldface type so that students can easily find them for later reference;

6. **Captioned Graphs** whose captions help students clearly understand the interrelationship of the variables plotted and the principles of analysis;

7. **Summary Tables** that provide a useful study aid in reviewing material;

8. **Summary** at the end of each chapter that lists the main points;

9. **Key Terms,** which are important words or phrases appearing in boldface type when they are defined for the first time and which are listed at the end of the chapter;

10. **End-of-Chapter Questions and Problems,** numbering over 400, which help students learn the subject matter by applying economic concepts, including a special class of problems that students find particularly relevant, entitled *Using Economic Analysis to Predict the Future;*

11. **Glossary** at the back of the book that provides the definitions for all the key terms;

12. **Solutions to Problems** at the back of the book, which provides the solutions to half of the questions and problems (marked by *).

SUPPLEMENTARY MATERIALS

The Economics of Money, Banking, and Financial Markets, third edition, includes the most comprehensive package of supplementary materials of any money, banking, and financial markets textbook. These include:

1. **Study Guide and Workbook,** prepared by John McArthur of Wofford College and myself, which includes chapter synopses/completions, exercises, self-tests and answers to the exercises and self-tests.

2. **Instructor's Manual/Test Bank,** prepared by John McArthur and myself, which includes sample course outlines, answers to questions and problems in the text, additional suggested readings, essay and discussion questions, and 2,000 multiple-choice questions, many with graphs.

3. **Computer Software,** prepared for IBM PCs by Richard Alston and Wan Fu Chi of Weber State College, which provides students with hands-on experience with the analytic concepts in the text.

4. **Computer Exercise Book,** which provides students with exercises to be used with the computer software.

5. **Reader,** edited by James W. Eaton of Bridgewater College and myself, which will be updated annually to enable instructors to keep the content of their course current throughout the three-year life of an edition of the text, and which will be sold with the text at a low price.

6. **Transparencies** for *all* of the figures, tables, and summary tables.

7. **Computerized Test Bank** available on diskettes, which has been substantially expanded to roughly twice the size with this edition to include over 2,000 multiple-choice test items, many with graphs, enabling the instructor to produce exams automatically.

ACKNOWLEDGMENTS

As always in so large a project, there are many people to thank. Special thanks go to Bruce Kaplan, economics editor at HarperCollins, who is a thoroughgoing professional, and to Jane Tufts, development editor, who is the best in the business. I also have been assisted by comments from my colleagues at Columbia University—Frank Edwards, Alberto Giovannini, Glenn Hubbard, and Bob Shay—and from my students.

I have also been helped in this and earlier editions by outside reviewers as well as correspondents who have made this a better book. I thank the following:

Avner Bar-Ilan	Dartmouth College
Willie Belton	Georgia Institute of Technology
Ben Bernanke	Princeton University
Charles Britton	University of Arkansas
Kathleen Brook	New Mexico State University
Kevin Calandri	California State University, Sacramento
John Campbell	Princeton University
Steven Cobb	Xavier University
John Cooper	Moorehead University
Dean Croushore	Pennsylvania State University
Nicholas DeLeonardis	DePaul University
John Domonkos	Cleveland State University
Donald Dutkowsky	Syracuse University
James Eaton	Bridgewater College
Martin Eichenbaum	Northwestern University
Robert Eisenbeis	University of North Carolina, Chapel Hill
Robert Eisner	Northwestern University

Gregory Falls	Central Michigan University
Mary Gade	Oklahoma State University
Patrick Gaughan	Fairleigh Dickinson University
Mark Gertler	New York University
Frank Gery	Saint Olaf College
Oliver Guinn	Washburn University of Topeka
Mark Haggerty	Washington State University
William Holahan	University of Wisconsin, Milwaukee
S. Hussain Jafri	Tarleton State University
Frederick Joutz	George Washington University
John Kaatz	Georgia Institute of Technology
Hugo Kaufman	Queens College
Richard Keehn	University of Wisconsin, Parkside
Nicholas Kontos	Marshall University
John Knudsen	University of Idaho
Kishore Kulkarni	Metropolitan State College of Denver
Beverly Lapham	University of Minnesota
K. T. Liaw	Saint John's University
David Macpherson	Miami University
Nelson Mark	Ohio State University
Thomas Mayer	University of California, Davis
W. Douglas McMillin	Louisiana State University
Patricia Mosser	Columbia University
Gerard O'Boyle	Saint John's University
Masao Ogaki	University of Rochester
Ronnie Phillips	Colorado State University
Dean Popp	San Diego State University
Gary Quinlivan	Saint Vincent College
Duane Rosa	West Texas State University
Daniel Rubenson	Southern Oregon State College
Dawn Saunders	College of Saint Joseph
Zena Seldon	University of Wisconsin, La Crosse
Charles Staley	State University of New York, Stony Brook
Duane Stock	University of Oklahoma
Kay Unger	University of Montana
R. Vaitheswaran	Coe College
Howard Wall	State University of New York at Buffalo
John Wassom	Western Kentucky University
Eugene White	Rutgers University
Paul Wolfson	University of Wisconsin, Milwaukee
Robert Zimmerman	Xavier University

Finally, I want to thank my wife Sally and my son Matthew, who provide me with a warm and happy environment that enables me to do my work, and my father, Sidney, who a long time ago put me on the path that led to this book.

Frederic S. Mishkin

PART I

Introduction

CHAPTER 1

Why Study Money, Banking, and Financial Markets?

PREVIEW On the evening news you have just heard that the money supply has declined by $4 billion. What effect might this have on the interest rate of an automobile loan when you finance your purchase of a sleek new sports car? Does it mean that a house will be more or less affordable in the future? Will it make it easier or harder for you to get a job next year?

   This book will provide answers to these questions by exploring the role of money in the economy and by examining how financial institutions (banks, insurance companies, mutual funds, and so on) and financial markets (such as those for bonds, stocks, and foreign exchange) work. Financial markets and institutions not only affect your everyday life, but also involve the movement of huge flows of funds (trillions of dollars) throughout our economy, which affect the profits of businesses, the goods and services that are produced, and even the economic well-being of countries other than the United States. What happens to money, financial institutions, and financial markets is of great concern to our politicians and can even have a major impact on our elections. The study of money, banking, and financial markets will reward you with an understanding of many exciting issues. In this chapter we outline what these issues are and why they are worth studying.

WHY STUDY MONEY?

Money or the **money supply** is defined as anything that is generally accepted in payments for goods or services or in the repayment of debts. Money is linked to changes in economic variables that affect all of us and that are important to the health of the economy.

Money and Inflation

Thirty years ago the six-dollar movie you might have seen last week would have set you back only one or two dollars. In fact, for six dollars you probably could have had dinner, seen the movie, and bought yourself a big bucket of hot buttered popcorn. As seen in Figure 1.1, which illustrates the movement of average prices in the economy from 1950 to 1990, the prices of most items are quite a bit higher now than they were then. The average price of goods and services in an economy is called the **aggregate price level** or, more simply, the price level (a more precise definition is found in the appendix to this chapter). From 1950 to 1990, the price level has more than quintupled. **Inflation** is a condition of a continually rising price level, and it affects individuals, businesses, and the government. Inflation is generally regarded as an important problem to be solved and has often been a primary concern of politicians and policymakers. How to solve the inflation problem requires that we know something about its causes.

What explains inflation? One clue to answering this question is found in Figure 1.1, which plots the money supply and the price level. As we can see, the price level and the money supply generally move closely together. These

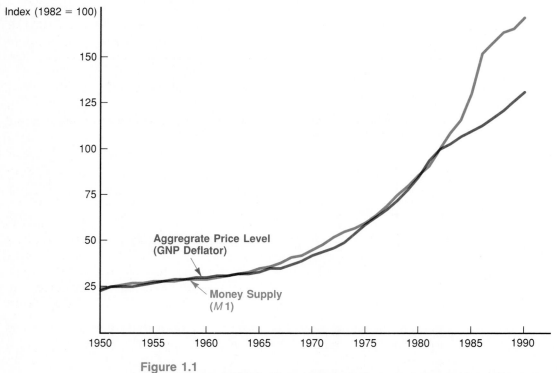

Figure 1.1
Aggregate Price Level and the Money Supply in the United States: 1950–1990
Source: *Economic Report of the President.*

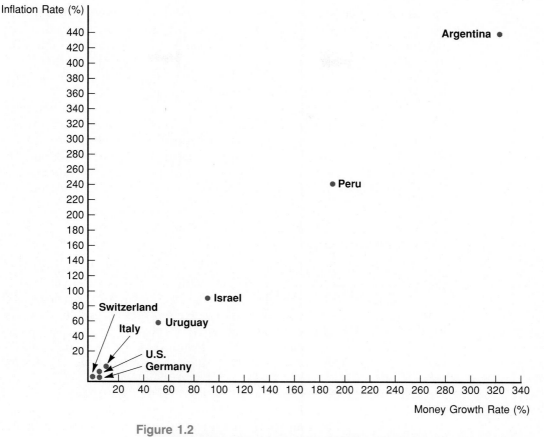

Figure 1.2
Average Inflation Rate Versus Average Rate of Money Growth for a Number of Countries: 1980–1990 Source: *International Financial Statistics.*

data seem to indicate that a continuing increase in the money supply might be an important factor in causing inflation, that is, a continuing increase in the price level.

Further evidence that inflation may be tied to continuing increases in the money supply is found in Figure 1.2. For a number of countries, it plots the average **inflation rate** (the rate of change of the price level, usually measured as a percentage change per year) over the ten-year period, 1980–1990, against the average rate of money growth over the same period.[1] As you can see, there is a positive association between inflation and the growth

---

[1]If the aggregate price level at time t is denoted by P_t, the inflation rate from time $t - 1$ to t (π_t) is defined as

$$\pi_t = \frac{(P_t - P_{t-1})}{P_{t-1}}$$

rate of the money supply: Those countries with the highest inflation rates are also the ones with the highest money growth rates. Peru and particularly Argentina, for example, have recently been experiencing very high inflations and their rates of money growth have been high. On the other hand, Switzerland and Germany have had very low inflation rates over the same period, and their rates of money growth have been low.

Such evidence has led Milton Friedman, a Nobel laureate in economics, to make his famous statement, "Inflation is Always and Everywhere a Monetary Phenomenon."[2] This statement suggests a good reason for studying money because its rate of growth may be a driving force behind inflation. We look at money's role in creating inflation by studying **monetary theory,** the theory that relates changes in the quantity of money to changes in economic activity and the price level.

Money and Business Cycles

In 1981–1982 total production of goods and services (called **aggregate output**) in the economy fell, the number of people out of work rose to more than 10 million (over 10% of the labor force), and better than 25,000 businesses failed. After 1982, the economy began to expand rapidly, and by 1989, the **unemployment rate** (the percentage of the available labor force unemployed) had declined from over 10% to around the 5% level. In 1990, the eight-year expansion came to an end and the economy began to decline again.

Why did the economy contract in 1981–1982, boom thereafter, and begin to contract again in 1990? Evidence suggests that money plays an important role in generating **business cycles,** that is, the upward and downward movement of aggregate output produced in the economy. Business cycles affect all of us in very immediate and important ways. When output is rising, for example, it is easier to find a good job; and when output is falling, finding a good job might be quite difficult. Figure 1.3 shows the movements of the rate of growth of money over the 1951–1990 period, with the shaded areas representing **recessions** or periods when aggregate output is declining. What we see is that the rate of money growth has declined before every recession. In fact, every recession in the twentieth century has been preceded by a decline in the rate of money growth, indicating that changes in money might also be a driving force behind business cycle fluctuations. However, not every decline in the rate of money growth is followed by a recession.

We explore how money might affect aggregate output when we study monetary theory and examine with empirical evidence the link between money and business cycles.

---

[2]Milton Friedman, *Dollars and Deficits* (Englewood Cliffs, N.J.: Prentice-Hall, 1968), p. 39.

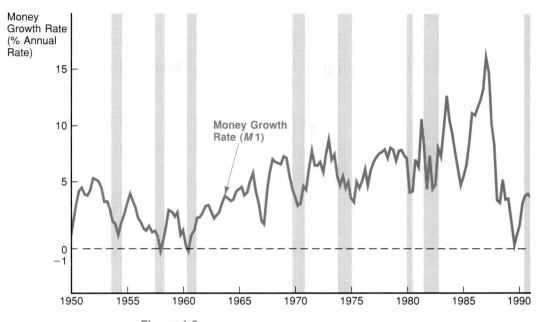

Figure 1.3
Money Growth (*M*1 Annual Rate) and the Business Cycle in the United States: 1951–1990 Shaded areas represent recessions. Sources: Federal Reserve *Bulletin* and Citibase databank.

Money and Interest Rates

An **interest rate** is the cost of borrowing or the price paid for the rental of funds (usually expressed as a percentage of the rental of $100 per year). We see many interest rates in the economy—mortgage interest rates, car loan rates, and interest rates on many different types of bonds. Interest rates are important variables to you because they affect so many personal decisions. High interest rates could deter you from buying a house or a car because the cost of financing them would be high. On the other hand, high interest rates could encourage you to save. You can earn more interest income by putting your savings into an account at the bank when interest rates are high.

Interest rates have an impact on the overall health of the economy because they affect not only consumers' willingness to spend or save, but also businesses' investment decisions. High interest rates, for example, may cause a corporation to postpone building a new plant that would ensure more jobs.

Economists frequently talk about "the interest rate" because most interest rates move together. So it is important to explain the common fluctuations in interest rates that have been substantial in the past twenty-five years. As a matter of fact, interest rate fluctuations in no other period of United States history have been as great. For example, the interest rate on long-term

U.S. Treasury bonds was about 4% in 1965, rose to close to 15% in 1981, and was below 9% in 1990. In the previous twenty-five-year period, from 1940 to 1965, the rate fluctuated between 2% and 5%.

What do these fluctuations mean and what causes them? In addition to other factors, money plays an important role in interest rate fluctuations. Figure 1.4 shows the changes in the interest rate on long-term Treasury bonds and the rate of money growth. As the money growth rate rose in the 1960s and 1970s, the long-term bond rate rose with it. However, the relationship between money growth and interest rates is less clear-cut in the 1980s. We analyze the relationship between money and interest rates when we examine the behavior of interest rates.

Conduct of Monetary Policy

Because money can affect many economic variables that are important to the well-being of our economy, politicians and policymakers in the federal government care about the conduct of **monetary policy,** the management of money and interest rates. The organization responsible for the conduct of

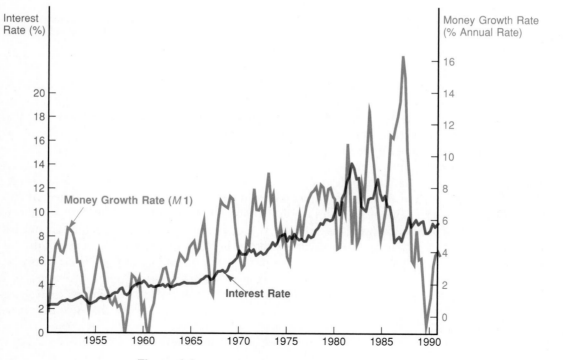

Figure 1.4
Money Growth (M1 Annual Rate) and Interest Rates (Long-term U.S. Treasury Bonds): 1951–1990 Sources: Federal Reserve *Bulletin* and Citibase databank.

monetary policy in the United States is the Federal Reserve System. In later chapters we will study how the Federal Reserve System can affect the quantity of money in the economy and then look at how monetary policy is actually conducted.

Budget Deficits and Monetary Policy

The **budget deficit** is the excess of government expenditures over tax revenues, a deficit that the government must finance by borrowing. As Figure 1.5 shows, in 1983 budget deficits peaked relative to the size of our economy (as calculated by the GNP measure of aggregate output), but have declined since then. However, budget deficits still exceed $200 billion per year and have been the subject of legislation (Gramm-Rudman) and bitter battles between the president and the Congress in recent years. You may have seen or heard statements in newspapers or on TV that such deficits are undesirable because they will ultimately lead to inflation. We will explore the validity (or invalidity) of such statements by first examining the impact the financing of these deficits has on the conduct of monetary policy and thereafter by exploring why these deficits might lead to a higher rate of money growth, a higher rate of inflation, and higher interest rates.

WHY STUDY BANKING? _____

The second major topic of this book is the business of banking. **Banks** are financial institutions that accept deposits and make loans. Included in the term *banks* are such firms as commercial banks, savings and loan associations,

Figure 1.5
Government Budget Surplus (+) or Deficit (−), as Percentage of GNP: 1950–1990
Source: *Economic Report of the President.*

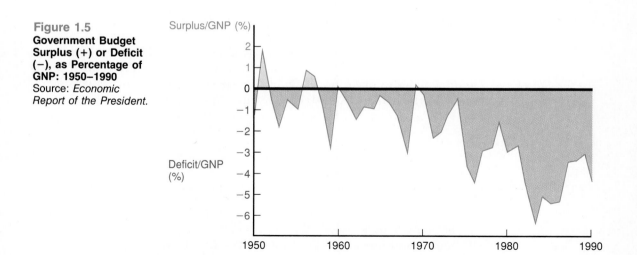

mutual savings banks, and credit unions. The banking industry has been much in the news lately. Failures of commercial banks have been running at the highest rates since the Great Depression and the savings and loan industry has required a massive bailout, costing taxpayers over $100 billion. Banks are important to our study of money and the economy because:

1. They provide a channel for linking those who want to save with those who want to invest.
2. They play an important role in determining the quantity of money in the economy.
3. They have been one source of the rapid financial innovation that is currently expanding the ways that we can invest our savings.

Financial Intermediation

If you wanted to make a loan to IBM or General Motors, you would not go directly to the president of the company and offer him a loan. Instead, most of us make loans to such companies by using the middlemen known as **financial intermediaries:** institutions such as commercial banks, savings and loan associations, mutual savings banks, credit unions, insurance companies, mutual funds, pension funds, and finance companies, which borrow funds from those who have saved and, in turn, make loans to others.

Banks are the financial intermediaries that the average person interacts with most frequently. When a person needs a loan to buy a house or a car, he usually obtains it from his local bank. Most Americans keep a large proportion of their financial wealth in banks in the form of checking accounts, savings accounts, or some other type of bank deposit.

Financial intermediation is an important activity in the economy because it allows funds to be channeled from those who might otherwise not put them to productive use to those who will. In this way financial intermediaries can help promote a more efficient and dynamic economy.

Since banks are the largest financial intermediaries in our economy, they deserve careful study. We will examine how they manage their assets and liabilities to make profits, how they are regulated by the government, and why the banking industry is currently in such a sorry state. In addition, we will discuss the operation and regulation of other financial intermediaries such as insurance companies, pension funds, and mutual funds.

Banking and the Money Supply

Banks play a critical role in the creation of money, not by printing twenty-dollar bills, but by lending; a bank's loans create checking account deposits, a component of money. We will study how banks decide to make loans in order to understand how the money supply is determined and why conducting monetary policy may be a complicated task.

Financial Innovation

In our economy it used to be that you had to have considerable wealth to obtain high interest rates on your savings. If you were an average wage earner with only a small amount of savings, you could only put it in a savings account at a low interest rate. Nowadays, small savers have a number of options for what they can do with their savings. For example, they can put their funds in NOW (negotiable order of withdrawal) accounts and money market mutual funds, both of which allow them to write checks on their accounts and yet earn higher rates of interest. To see why these options have been developed, we will study why and how financial innovation takes place.

We will also study financial innovation because it shows us how creative thinking on the part of financial institutions can lead to higher profits. By seeing how and why financial institutions have been creative in the past, we will obtain a better grasp of how they may be creative in the future. This knowledge will provide us with useful clues about how the financial system may change over time.

The rapid pace of financial innovation has meant that many regulations imposed on the banking system by government have become obsolete, or even worse, damaging to the health of the financial system. Rapid changes in the regulatory environment have accompanied rapid financial innovation. Understanding the how and why of regulations allows us to understand how banks may evolve in the future and keeps our knowledge about banks and their role in determining the money supply from becoming obsolete.

WHY STUDY FINANCIAL MARKETS? ─────────────────────

Financial markets are ones in which funds are transferred from those who have excess funds available to those who have a shortage. Financial markets like the bond and stock markets can be important in channeling funds from those who do not have a productive use for them to those who do, thereby resulting in higher economic efficiency. Activities in financial markets also have direct effects on how rich we are and on the behavior of business firms.

Bond Market

The bond market is especially important to economic activity because it is where interest rates are determined. Because different interest rates have a tendency to move in unison, economists frequently lump interest rates together and refer to "*the* interest rate." However, as we can see in Figure 1.6, interest rates on several types of bonds do sometimes differ substantially. The interest rate on three-month Treasury bills, for example, fluctuates more than the other interest rates and is lower on average. The interest rate on Baa corporate bonds (a medium-quality corporate bond) is higher on

Interest Rate (%)

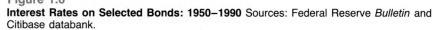

Figure 1.6
Interest Rates on Selected Bonds: 1950–1990 Sources: Federal Reserve *Bulletin* and Citibase databank.

average than the other interest rates, and the spread between it and the other rates became larger in the 1970s.

We will study how the common movements in these interest rates come about and why interest rates on different bonds vary.

Stock Market

As evidenced by the fact that it is referred to as "the market," the stock market, in which claims on the earnings of corporations (shares of stock) are traded, is the most widely followed financial market in America. A big swing in the prices of shares in the stock market is always a big story on the evening news. People often express their opinion on where the market is heading and will frequently tell you about their latest "big killing" (although you seldom hear about their latest "big loss"!). The attention that the market receives can probably be best explained by one simple fact: It is a place where people can get rich quickly.

As Figure 1.7 indicates, stock prices have been extremely volatile. They climbed substantially in the 1950s, reached a peak in 1966, then fluctuated up and down until 1973, when they fell sharply. Stock prices had recovered substantially by the early 1980s when a major stock market boom began, sending the Dow Jones Industrial Average to a peak of 2722 on August 25, 1987. After a 17% decline over the next month and a half, the stock market experienced its worst one-day drop in its entire history on "Black Monday," October 19, 1987, when the Dow Jones Industrial Average fell by over 500

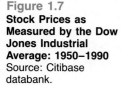

Figure 1.7
Stock Prices as Measured by the Dow Jones Industrial Average: 1950–1990
Source: Citibase databank.

points, a 22% decline. These considerable fluctuations in stock prices affect the size of people's wealth and as a result may affect their willingness to spend.

The stock market is also an important factor in business firms' investment decisions because the price of shares affects the amount of funds that can be raised by selling newly issued stock to finance investment spending. A higher price for a firm's shares means that it can raise a larger amount of funds, which can be used to buy plant and equipment.

We will explore how stock prices behave and respond to information in the marketplace. We will also see that monetary policy can affect stock prices, which, in turn, can have an effect on the business cycle.

Foreign Exchange Market

The price of one country's currency in terms of another's is called the **foreign exchange rate.** Figure 1.8 shows the exchange rate for the U.S. dollar

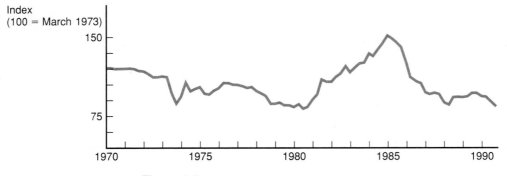

Figure 1.8
Exchange Rate of the U.S. Dollar: 1970–1990 Sources: Federal Reserve *Bulletin* and Citibase databank.

from 1970 to 1990 (measured as the value of the American dollar in terms of a basket of foreign currencies). The fluctuations in prices in this market have also been substantial: The dollar weakened considerably from 1971 to 1973, rose slightly in value until 1976, and then reached a low point in the 1978–1980 period. From 1980 to early 1985 the dollar dramatically appreciated in value, but since then has fallen substantially.

What have these fluctuations in the exchange rate meant to the American public and businesses? A change in the exchange rate has a direct effect on American consumers because it affects the cost of foreign goods. When in 1985 a British pound cost approximately $1.30, £100 of British goods (say Shetland sweaters) would cost $130. With a weaker dollar that raised the cost of a pound to $1.90 in 1990, the same £100 of Shetland sweaters cost $190. Thus we see that a weaker dollar leads to more expensive foreign goods, makes vacationing in England more expensive, and makes it harder for you to indulge in your yen for imported French cheese. The result is that Americans will decrease their purchases of foreign goods and will increase their consumption of domestic goods (e.g., travel in the United States, or American sweaters).

On the other hand, a strong dollar means that U.S. goods exported abroad will cost more in foreign countries and foreigners will buy fewer of them. Exports of steel, for example, declined sharply when the dollar strengthened in the 1980–1985 period. A strong dollar benefited American consumers by making foreign goods cheaper, but hurt American businesses and eliminated some jobs by cutting both domestic and foreign sales of their products. The recent weakness of the dollar has had the opposite effect: It has made foreign goods more expensive but has made American businesses more competitive. Fluctuations in the foreign exchange markets have major consequences for the American economy.

We will study how exchange rates are determined in the foreign exchange market in which dollars are bought and sold for foreign currencies. Finally, we will see how the foreign exchange rate can affect the money supply in the United States and how U.S. monetary policy can affect the foreign exchange rate.

CONCLUDING REMARKS

The field of money, banking, and financial markets is an exciting one. We not only will discuss issues that directly affect your life—interest rates on loans and on your savings and how monetary policy may affect your job prospects and the price of goods in the future—but we will gain a clearer understanding of economic phenomena you frequently hear about in the news media. Our study of money, banking, and financial markets will also introduce you to many of the controversies about the conduct of economic policy that are currently being hotly debated in the political arena.

SUMMARY

1. Money appears to be a major influence on inflation, business cycles, and interest rates. Because these economic variables are so important to the health of the economy, we need to understand how monetary policy is and should be conducted. We also need to study government budget-making because it can be an influential factor in the conduct of monetary policy.

2. Banks are the most important of a number of financial intermediaries that channel funds from those who otherwise might not put them to productive use to those who can. Banks also play a critical role in the creation of money and have been important in the rapid pace of recent financial innovation.

3. Activities in financial markets have direct effects on individuals' wealth, on the behavior of business firms, and on the efficiency of our economy. Three financial markets deserve particular attention: the bond market (where interest rates are determined); the stock market (which has a major effect on people's wealth); and the foreign exchange market (because fluctuations in the foreign exchange rate have such major consequences for the American economy).

KEY TERMS

money (money supply)	monetary theory	recessions	banks
aggregate price level	aggregate output	interest rate	financial intermediaries
inflation	unemployment rate	monetary policy	financial markets
inflation rate	business cycles	budget deficit	foreign exchange rate

QUESTIONS AND PROBLEMS

1. Has the inflation rate in the United States increased or decreased in the past few years? How about interest rates?

* 2. If history repeats itself and we see a decline in the rate of money growth, what might you expect to happen to:
   a) real output
   b) the inflation rate
   c) interest rates

3. When was the most recent recession?

* 4. When interest rates fall, how might you change your economic behavior?

5. Can you think of any financial innovation in the past ten years that has affected you personally? Has it made you better or worse off? Why?

* 6. Is everybody worse off when interest rates rise?

7. Explain the effect of a fall in stock prices on consumers' decisions to spend and firms' decisions to invest in new plants and equipment.

* 8. Looking at Figure 1.8, in what years would you have chosen to visit the Grand Canyon in Arizona rather than the Tower of London?

9. When the dollar is worth more in relation to currencies of other countries, are you more likely to buy American-made or French-made jeans? Are U.S. companies that make jeans happier when the dollar is strong or when it is weak? What about an American company that is in the business of importing jeans into the United States?

---

*Questions marked with * are answered at the end of the book in an appendix, "Answers to Selected Questions and Problems."

Defining Aggregate Output, Income, and the Price Level

Because these terms are used so frequently throughout the text, we need to have a clear understanding of the definitions of aggregate output, income, and the price level.

AGGREGATE OUTPUT AND INCOME

The most commonly reported measure of aggregate output, **gross national product (GNP),** is defined as the value of all final goods and services produced in an economy during the course of the year. This measure of GNP is careful to exclude two sets of items that at first glance you might mistakenly think would be included in GNP. Purchases of goods that have been produced in the past, whether a Rembrandt painting or a house built twenty years ago, are not counted as part of GNP, nor are purchases of stocks or bonds. None of these enter into GNP because they are not goods and services produced in the course of the year. Intermediate goods, which are used up in producing final goods and services, such as the sugar in a candy bar or the energy used to produce steel, are also not counted separately as part of GNP. They are not counted separately because to do so would be double counting, since the value of the final goods already includes the value of the intermediate goods.

Aggregate income, which is the total income of factors of production (land, labor, and capital) from producing goods and services in the economy during the course of the year, is best thought of as being equal to aggregate output. Because the payments for final goods and services eventually must flow back to the owners of the factors of production as income, income payments equal payments for final goods and services. If, for example, the economy has an aggregate output of $5 trillion, then total income payments in the economy (aggregate income) also equals $5 trillion.

DISTINCTION BETWEEN REAL AND NOMINAL MAGNITUDES

When the total value of final goods and services is calculated using current prices, the resulting GNP measure is referred to as nominal GNP. The word *nominal* indicates that values are measured using current prices. If all prices doubled but actual production of goods and services remained the same, then nominal GNP would double even though people do not enjoy the benefits of twice as many goods and services. As a result nominal variables can be misleading measures of economic well-being.

A more reliable measure of economic well-being measures values in terms of prices for an arbitrary base year, currently 1982. GNP measured with constant prices is referred to as real GNP, with the word *real* indicating that values are measured in terms of fixed prices. Real variables thus measure the quantities of goods and services and do not change because prices have changed but only if actual quantities have changed.

A brief example will make the distinction clearer. Suppose that you have a nominal income of $30,000 in 1992 while you had a nominal income of $15,000 in 1982. If all prices doubled from 1982 until 1992, are you better off? The answer is "no" because, although your income has doubled, your $30,000 will buy you only the same amount of goods (but at double the price). A real income measure would indicate that your income in terms of the goods it can buy is the same. Measured in 1982 prices, the $30,000 of nominal income in 1992 turns out to be only $15,000 of real income. Since your real income is actually the same in the two years, you are no better or worse off in 1992 than you were in 1982.

Because real variables measure quantities in terms of real goods and services, they are typically of more interest than nominal variables. In this text, discussions of aggregate output or aggregate income will always refer to real measures (such as real GNP).

AGGREGATE PRICE LEVEL

In the chapter we defined the aggregate price level as a measure of average prices in the economy. Two measures of the aggregate price level are commonly met in economic data. The first is the GNP deflator, which is defined as

$$\text{GNP deflator} = \frac{\text{nominal GNP}}{\text{real GNP}}$$

If 1992 nominal GNP is $6 trillion, but 1992 real GNP in 1982 prices is $4 trillion, the GNP deflator is

$$\frac{\$6 \text{ trillion}}{\$4 \text{ trillion}} = 1.50$$

The GNP deflator indicates that, on average, prices have risen 50% since 1982. Typically measures of the price level are expressed as a price index, which expresses the price level for the base year (in our example, 1982) as 100. Thus the GNP deflator for 1992 would be written down as 150.

Another popular measure of the aggregate price level (and the one that is most frequently reported in the press) is the consumer price index (CPI). The CPI is measured by pricing a "basket" list of goods and services bought by a typical urban household over a given period, say one month. If over the course of the year the cost of this basket of goods and services rises from $500 to $600, then the CPI has risen by 20%. The CPI is also expressed as a price index with the base year equal to 100.

Both the CPI and GNP deflator measures of the price level can be used to convert or deflate a nominal magnitude into a real magnitude. This is accomplished by dividing the nominal magnitude by the price index. In our example, in which the GNP deflator for 1992 is 1.50 (expressed as an index of 150), real GNP for 1992 equals

$$\frac{\$6 \text{ trillion}}{1.50} = \$4 \text{ trillion in 1982 prices}$$

which corresponds to the real GNP figure for 1992 mentioned above.

CHAPTER 2

What Is Money?

PREVIEW   If you had lived in America before the Revolutionary War, your money might have primarily consisted of Spanish doubloons (silver coins which were also called "pieces of eight"). Before the Civil War, the principal forms of money in the United States were not only gold and silver coins, but also notes issued by private banks called banknotes. Today, not only do you use coins and dollar bills issued by the government as money, but also checks written on accounts held at banks. Money has been different things at different times—however, it has *always* been important to people and to the economy.

In order to understand the effects of money on the economy, we must understand exactly what money is. In this chapter we develop precise definitions by exploring the functions of money, by looking at why and how it promotes economic efficiency, by examining how its forms have evolved over time, and by examining how money is currently measured.

MEANING OF "MONEY"

As the word *money* is used casually in everyday conversation, it can mean many things, but to economists it has a very specific meaning. To avoid confusion, we must clarify how economists' use of the word *money* differs from conventional usage.

Economists define money (or equivalently, the money supply) as anything that is generally accepted in payment for goods or services or in the repayment of debts. **Currency,** which is dollar bills and coins, clearly fits this definition and is one type of money. When most people talk about "money," they're talking about currency. If, for example, someone comes up to you and says "Your money, or your life," you should quickly hand over all your currency rather than engage in a philological discussion by asking "What exactly do *you* mean by money?"

To define money merely as currency is much too narrow for economists. Since checks are also accepted as payment for purchases, checking account deposits are considered to be money as well. An even broader definition of

20

money is often needed because other items such as traveler's checks or savings deposits can sometimes be used to pay for goods or can effectively function as money if they can be quickly and easily converted into currency or checking account deposits. As you can see, there is no single, precise definition of money or the money supply, even for economists. We will frequently run into this problem throughout our study of money and banking.

To complicate matters further, the word *money* is frequently used synonymously with *wealth*. When people say "Joe sure is rich, he has an awful lot of money," they probably mean that Joe not only has a lot of currency and a high balance in his checking account, but that he also has stocks, bonds, four cars, three houses, and a yacht. Thus, while currency is too narrow a definition of money, this other popular usage is much too broad. Economists make a distinction between money in the form of currency, demand deposits, and other items that are used to make purchases and **wealth,** the total collection of pieces of property that are a store of value. Wealth includes not only money, but also anything subject to ownership (called **assets**), such as bonds, common stock, art, land, furniture, cars, or houses.

It is also usual for people to use the word *money* to describe what economists call "income," as in the sentence, "Sheila would be a wonderful catch; she has a good job and earns a lot of money." **Income** is a flow of earnings per unit of time. Money, on the other hand, is a stock; that is, it is a certain amount at a given point in time. If someone tells you that he has an income of $1000, you cannot tell whether he earned a lot or a little without knowing whether this $1000 is earned per year, per month, or even per day. On the other hand, if someone tells you that she has $1000 in her pocket, you know exactly how much this is.

To reemphasize, always keep in mind that the money discussed in this book refers to anything that is generally accepted in payment for goods and services or in the repayment of debts and is distinct from "income" and "wealth."

FUNCTIONS OF MONEY

Whether money is shells or rocks or gold or paper, in any economy it has three primary functions: It is a medium of exchange, a unit of account, and a store of value. Of the three functions, its function as a medium of exchange is what distinguishes money from other assets such as stocks, bonds, or houses.

Medium of Exchange

In almost all market transactions in our economy, money in the form of currency or checks is a **medium of exchange;** that is, it is used to pay for goods and services. The use of money as a medium of exchange promotes economic efficiency by eliminating much of the time spent in exchanging goods and services. To see why, let's look at a barter economy, one without money in which goods or services are exchanged directly for other goods or services.

Take the case of Ellen the Economics Professor who can do just one thing well: give brilliant economics lectures. In a barter economy, if Ellen wants to eat, she must find a farmer who not only produces the food she likes, but also wants to learn economics. As you might expect, this search will be difficult and time consuming, and Ellen may spend more time looking for such an economics-hungry farmer than she will teaching. It is even possible that she will have to quit lecturing and go into farming herself. Even so, she may still starve to death.

The time spent trying to exchange goods and services is called a **transactions cost.** In a barter economy, transactions costs are high because people have to satisfy a double coincidence of wants; that is, they have to find someone who has a good or service they want and who also wants the good or service they have to offer.

Let's see what happens if we introduce money into Ellen the Economics Professor's world. Ellen can teach anyone who is willing to pay money to hear her lecture. She can then go to any farmer (she probably would not deal directly with the farmer but would go to the supermarket instead) and buy the food she needs with the money she has been paid. The problem of the double coincidence of wants is avoided, and Ellen saves a lot of time, which she may spend doing what she does best: teach.

We see money promotes economic efficiency by eliminating much of the time spent exchanging goods and services. It also promotes efficiency by allowing people to specialize in what they do best. We see, therefore, that money is an essential item in an economy. It acts as a lubricant that allows the economy to run more smoothly by lowering transactions costs, thereby encouraging specialization and the division of labor.

The need for money is so strong that almost every society, except the most primitive, invents it. For a commodity to function effectively as money, it has to meet several criteria: (1) it must be easily standardized, making it simple to ascertain its value; (2) it must be widely accepted; (3) it must be divisible so that it is easy to "make change"; (4) it must be easy to carry; and (5) it must not deteriorate quickly. Forms of money that have satisfied these criteria have taken many unusual forms throughout human history, ranging from wampum (strings of beads) used by American Indians, to tobacco and whiskey used by the early American colonists, to cigarettes used in prisoner-of-war camps during World War II or currently in the Soviet Union.[1] The

---

[1]An extremely entertaining article on the development of money in a prisoner-of-war camp during World War II is R. A. Radford, "The Economic Organization of a P.O.W. Camp," *Economica*, vol. 12 (November 1945), pp. 189–201.

diversity of forms of money that have been developed over the years is as much a testament to the inventiveness of the human race as is the development of tools and language.

Unit of Account

The second role of money is to provide a **unit of account;** that is, it is used to measure value in the economy. We measure the values of goods and services in terms of money, just as we measure weight in terms of pounds or distance in terms of miles. To see why this function is important, let's look again at a barter economy where money does not perform this function. If the economy has only 3 goods, say peaches, economics lectures, and movies, then we only need to know 3 prices to tell us how to exchange one for another: the price of peaches in terms of economics lectures (that is, how many economics lectures you have to pay for a peach), the price of peaches in terms of movies, and the price of economics lectures in terms of movies. If there were 10 goods, we would need to know 45 prices in order to exchange one good for another; with 100 goods, we would need 4950 prices; and with 1000 goods, 499,500 prices.[2]

Think of how hard it would be to shop in a supermarket with 1000 different items on its shelves; deciding whether chicken or fish is cheaper would be difficult if the price of a pound of chicken were quoted as four pounds of butter while the price of a pound of fish were quoted as eight pounds of tomatoes. To make sure that you can compare the prices of all items, the price tags of each item would have to list up to 999 different prices and the time spent reading them would result in very high transactions costs.

The solution to the problem is to introduce money into the economy and have all prices quoted in terms of units of money, enabling us to quote the price of economics lectures, peaches, and movies in terms of dollars. If there were only three goods in the economy, this would not be a great advantage over the barter system because we still would need three prices to conduct transactions. On the other hand, for 10 goods we now need only 10 prices; 100 goods, 100 prices; and so on. At the 1000-good supermarket, there are now only 1000 prices to look at, not 499,500!

---

[2]The formula for telling us the number of prices we need when we have N goods is the same formula that tells us the number of pairs when there are N items. It is

$$\frac{N(N-1)}{2}$$

In the case of 10 goods, for example, we would need

$$\frac{10(10-1)}{2} = \frac{90}{2} = 45$$

prices.

Table 2.1 **Number of Prices in a Barter versus a Money Economy**

No. of Goods	No. of Prices in a Barter Economy	No. of Prices in a Money Economy
3	3	3
10	45	10
100	4950	100
1000	499,500	1000
10,000	49,995,000	10,000

We can see that using money as a unit of account reduces transactions costs in an economy by reducing the number of prices that need to be considered. The benefits of this function of money grow as the economy becomes more complex, as shown in Table 2.1, which compares the number of prices required in a barter versus a money economy given a specific number of goods.

Store of Value

Money also functions as a **store of value;** that is, it is a store of purchasing power over time. A store of value is used to separate the time when income is received from when it is spent. This function of money is useful because most of us do not want to spend our income immediately upon receipt of it, but rather want to wait until we have the time or desire to shop.

Money is not unique as a store of value because any asset, whether it be money, stocks, bonds, land, houses, art, or jewelry, is a means of storing wealth. Many of these assets have advantages over money as a store of value: They often pay the owner a higher interest rate than money, experience price appreciations, and deliver services such as providing a roof over one's head. If these assets are a more desirable store of value than money, then why do people hold money at all?

The answer to this question relates to an important economic concept called **liquidity,** which is the relative ease and speed with which an asset can be converted into a medium of exchange, and it is a very desirable feature. Money is the most liquid asset of all because it *is* the medium of exchange; that is, unlike other assets, it does not have to be converted into anything else in order to make purchases. Other assets involve transactions costs when they are converted into money. When you sell your house, for example, you have to pay a brokerage commission (usually 6 to 7% of the sales price), and if you need cash immediately to pay some pressing bills, you might have to settle for a lower price in order to sell the house quickly. The fact that money is the most liquid asset, then, explains why people are willing to hold it even if it is not the most attractive store of value.

How good a store of value money is depends on the price level, since its value is fixed in terms of the price level. A doubling of all prices, for example, means that the value of money has dropped in half, while a halving of all prices means that the value of money has doubled. In an inflation, when the price level is increasing rapidly, money loses value rapidly and people will be more reluctant to hold their wealth in this form. This is especially true during periods of extreme inflation, known as **hyperinflation,** in which the inflation rate exceeds 50% per month.

An example of such a hyperinflation occurred in Germany after World War I, with inflation rates sometimes exceeding 1000% per month. By the end of the hyperinflation in 1923, the price level had risen to over 30 billion times what it had been just two years before. The quantity of money needed to purchase even the most basic items became excessive. There are stories, for example, that near the end of the hyperinflation, a wheelbarrow of cash would be required to pay for a loaf of bread. Money was losing its value so rapidly that workers were paid and given time off several times during the day to spend their wages before the money became worthless. No one wanted to hold on to money and so the use of money to carry out transactions declined and barter became more and more dominant. Transactions costs skyrocketed, and as we would expect, output in the economy fell sharply.

EVOLUTION OF THE PAYMENTS SYSTEM

We can obtain a better picture of the functions of money and what forms money has taken over time by looking at the evolution of the **payments system,** the method of conducting transactions in the economy. The payments system has been evolving over centuries, and with it the form of money. At one point, precious metals such as gold were used as the principal means of payment and were the main form of money. Later, paper assets such as checks and currency began to be used in the payments system and viewed as money. Where the payments system is heading has an important bearing on how money will be defined in the future.

To obtain perspective on where the payments system is heading, it is worth exploring how it has evolved. In order for some object to function as money, it must be universally acceptable, that is, everyone must be willing to accept it in payment for goods and services. An object that clearly has value to everyone is a likely candidate to serve as money, and a natural choice is a precious metal such as gold or silver. From ancient times until several hundred years ago, these metals functioned as the medium of exchange in all but the most primitive societies. The problem with a payments system based exclusively on precious metals is that such a form of money is very heavy and is hard to transport from one place to another. Imagine the holes you'd wear in your pockets if you had to buy things only with coins! Indeed, for large purchases such as a house, you'd have to rent a truck to transport the money payment.

The next development in the payments system was paper currency (pieces of paper that function as a medium of exchange). Initially, paper currency had a promise to be convertible into coins or into a quantity of precious metal. In most countries, however, it has evolved into **fiat money,** paper currency that governments make legal tender (i.e., legally it must be accepted as payment for debts) and yet is not convertible into coins or precious metal. Paper currency has the advantage of being much lighter than coins or precious metal; but it can be accepted as a medium of exchange only if there is some trust in the authorities (usually governments) who issue it and when printing has reached a sufficiently advanced stage that counterfeiting becomes extremely difficult. Since paper currency has evolved into a legal arrangement, countries can change the currency that they use at will. Indeed, this is exactly what has happened recently in Germany and it may even occur in all of Europe at some point in the future (see Box 2.1).

Box   2.1   **A Global Perspective**

Monetary Union in Germany, 1990: With Europe 1992, Will Europe Be Far Behind?

Monetary union—the adoption of a common currency by two regions or countries—is often thought of as the last stage of political and economic integration. Advocates of monetary union point to the advantages that a single currency has in eliminating the transactions costs involved with having to exchange the currency of one region for the currency of another. As the extraordinary recent events in Europe indicate, there may be other important reasons to put the economic cart before the political horse and proceed with monetary union first. With the tidal wave of emigration from East to West Germany in 1989 and early 1990 (which continued even after the fall of East Germany's communist regime), rapid integration of the two economies became imperative even before political union could take place to slow the emigration from the East. To hasten economic integration, the two Germanies took the radical step in July 1990 of adopting the West German deutsche mark as the common currency, allowing East Germans to ex-

change one East German mark for one West German mark.

Monetary union in Germany may be only the beginning of further monetary union throughout Europe. As part of the Europe 1992 initiative to promote one integrated market in the twelve European Community (EC) countries by the end of 1992, the European Economic Commission (EEC) has outlined a plan to achieve the creation of a single European currency based on the ECU, the European currency unit. Again, the motive behind monetary union is not just gains in efficiency resulting from lower transaction costs; but it is also the push such a monetary union gives toward the integration of Europe's different economies. Because of the controversy surrounding the EEC plan for a single European currency, no one knows for sure whether the monetary union in Europe will occur in the near future. For the first time in history, however, a single European currency is now a distinct possibility.

Major drawbacks of paper currency and coins are that they are easily stolen and can be expensive to transport because of their bulk. To combat this problem, another step in the evolution of the payments system occurred with the development of modern banking: the invention of checks. Checks are a type of IOU payable on demand that allows transactions to take place without the need to carry around large amounts of currency. The introduction of checks was a major innovation improving the efficiency of the payments system. Frequently payments are made back and forth which cancel each other; without checks this would involve the movement of a lot of currency. With checks, payments that cancel each other can be settled by canceling the checks, and no currency need be moved. The use of checks thus reduces the transportation costs associated with the payments system and improves economic efficiency. Another advantage of checks is that they can be written for any amount up to the balance in the account, making transactions for large amounts much easier. Checks are advantageous in that loss from theft is greatly reduced, and they provide convenient receipts for purchases.

There are, however, two problems with a payments system based on checks. First, it takes time to get checks from one place to another, which is particularly serious if you are paying someone in a different location who needs to be paid quickly. In addition, if you have a checking account, you know it takes several business days before a bank will credit your account with a check that you have deposited. If your need for cash is urgent, this feature of paying by check can be frustrating, indeed. Second, all the paper shuffling required to process checks is costly; there are estimates that it currently costs well over $5 billion per year to process all the checks written in the United States.

With the development of the computer and advanced telecommunications technology, there would seem to be a better way to organize our payments system. All paperwork could be eliminated by converting completely to what is known as an electronic funds transfer system (EFTS), that is, a system in which all payments are made using electronic telecommunications. Let's see how such a system might work.

The store of the future would have a computer terminal [typically referred to as a point-of-sale (POS) system] that would allow you to make your purchases without cash or checks. When you have selected your purchase, say, a new pair of jeans, you would just sit down at the terminal, punch in your secret code number, and be able to move funds from your bank account to the store's. When the store verified that this had happened, you would be given the jeans and leave. If you had a bill to pay, you would just turn on your personal computer and dial into a special electronic network where you could transfer funds from your bank account to the account of the person or firm whom you owed. These transactions would occur instantaneously and no humans would be required to process any paper.

Does EFTS sound farfetched? It isn't, because to a great extent this kind of system is already in operation. The Federal Reserve has a telecommunications system, called Fedwire, that allows all financial institutions that maintain accounts with the Federal Reserve to wire (transfer) funds to each other without having to send checks. In addition, CHIPS (Clearing House Interbank Payment System), a private electronic funds transfer system, is used to wire funds among banks internationally. Now banks, money market mutual funds, securities dealers, and corporations can wire funds using these systems. Wire transfers typically are for amounts greater than $1 million, so that although less than 1% of the number of transactions use electronic funds transfers, over 80% of the dollar value of transactions are conducted electronically. Indeed, when we say that a corporation is paying for something with a check, it is frequently paying by an electronic wire transfer.

Lately, EFTS has been touching the lives of the public-at-large directly. Certain recurrent debts such as utility bills and mortgage payments can now be paid automatically every month out of one's checking account. Many companies pay salaries by wiring them directly into their employees' bank accounts. Some banks offer their customers a service whereby they can plug their personal computers into a network that allows them to conduct certain transactions such as moving funds from their savings accounts into their checking accounts.

Although it has been predicted that checks will soon disappear from America's economy, the movement to a checkless society has been far slower than many expected. While EFTS may be more efficient than a payments system based on paper, several things work against the complete disappearance of the paper system. Paper has advantages because it provides receipts and because it may make it harder to commit fraud. We often read in newspapers that an unauthorized person has been able to "access" a computer database and has been able to alter information entered there. The fact that this has been a frequent occurrence means that unscrupulous persons might be able to access bank accounts in an electronic payments system and steal funds by moving them from someone else's account into their own. The prevention of this activity is no easy task, and there is a whole new field developing to improve computer security. Another problem with the electronic payments system is that there are still many tricky legal issues that need to be sorted out. For example, can you stop payment on a wire transfer the way you can with checks? Who is responsible if someone gets access to your secret code number and removes funds illegally from your account?

The conclusion from this discussion seems to be that we are moving toward a payments system in which the use of paper will diminish, although the development of new forms of electronic money may be a gradual process because of obstacles such as the provision of adequate security.

MEASURING MONEY

The definition of money as anything that is generally accepted in payment for goods and services tells us that money is defined by people's behavior.

What makes an asset money is that people believe it will be accepted by others when making payment. As we have seen, many different assets have performed this role over the centuries, ranging from gold to paper currency to checking accounts. For that reason, this behavioral definition does not tell us exactly what assets in our economy should be considered money.

In order to measure money, we need a precise definition that tells us exactly what assets should be included. There are two ways of obtaining a precise definition of money: the theoretical approach and the empirical approach.

Theoretical and Empirical Definitions of Money

The theoretical approach defines money by using economic theory to decide which assets should be included in its measure. As we have seen, the key feature of money is that it is used as a medium of exchange. Therefore, the theoretical approach focuses on this aspect and suggests that only assets that clearly act as a medium of exchange belong in a measure of the money supply. Currency, checking account deposits, and traveler's checks can all be used to pay for goods and services and clearly function as a medium of exchange. The theoretical approach suggests that a measure of the money supply should include only these assets.

Unfortunately, the theoretical approach is not as clear-cut as we would like. Other assets besides those listed above function somewhat like a medium of exchange but are not quite as liquid as currency and checking account deposits. Customers of brokerage firms, for example, can write checks against the value of the securities held for them by the firm. (Because there are often restrictions on the check-writing privilege—for example, a minimum amount for which you can write a check—it is not clear whether these accounts really function as a medium of exchange.) Similarly, there are other assets (savings accounts at banks) that can be turned quickly into cash without incurring appreciable costs.

The ambiguities inherent in the theoretical approach in determining which assets should be included in a measure of money have led many economists to suggest that money should be defined with a more empirical approach; that is, the decision about what to call money should be based on which measure of money works best in predicting movements of variables that money is supposed to explain. For example, we might look at which measure of money does the best job of predicting the inflation rate or the business cycle and then officially designate it as the preferred measure of the money supply. Unfortunately, the empirical evidence on which measure of money is best is mixed; a measure that predicts well in one period may not predict well in another; and a measure that predicts inflation may not be the best predictor of the business cycle.

As you can see, neither approach to choosing an exact definition of money is entirely satisfactory. The theoretical approach is not specific enough to tell us which assets should be included in or excluded from the appropriate measure of money. The empirical approach encounters difficulties because the evidence on which is the preferred measure of money is mixed, and even if it weren't, we could not be sure that a measure that has worked well in the past would work well in the future. The ambiguity about precisely what money is, is not a very satisfactory state of affairs because policymakers who are responsible for managing the economy need to know exactly what the components of the money supply are if they are to conduct policy by trying to control it.

The Federal Reserve's Monetary Aggregates

The **Federal Reserve System** (also known as the **Fed**), the central banking authority responsible for monetary policy in the United States, has conducted many studies on how to best define money. The problem of defining money has become especially crucial because extensive financial innovation has produced new types of assets which might properly belong in a measure of money. Since 1980, the Fed has modified its definitions of money several times and has settled on the following measures of the money supply, which

Following the Financial News

The Monetary Aggregates

Data for the Federal Reserve's monetary aggregates (*M*1, *M*2, and *M*3) are published every Friday. In the *Wall Street Journal* the data are found in the Federal Reserve Data column, an example of which is found to the right.

The first entry indicates that the money supply (*M*1) averaged $839.0 billion for the week ending February 18, 1991. The "sa" for this entry indicates that the data are seasonally adjusted; that is, seasonal movements, such as those associated with the Christmas shopping season, have been removed from the data.

Source: *Wall Street Journal* (Friday, March 1, 1991).

FEDERAL RESERVE DATA

MONETARY AGGREGATES
(daily average in billions)

	One week ended:	
	Feb. 18	Feb. 11
Money supply (M1) sa	839.0	836.5
Money supply (M1) nsa	824.3	828.7
Money supply (M2) sa	3359.8	3353.0
Money supply (M2) nsa	3348.7	3348.3
Money supply (M3) sa	4167.0	4161.6
Money supply (M3) nsa	4153.2	4157.0
	Four weeks ended:	
	Feb. 18	Jan. 21
Money supply (M1) sa	834.7	825.0
Money supply (M1) nsa	821.5	846.9
Money supply (M2) sa	3349.2	3330.3
Money supply (M2) nsa	3338.2	3353.1
Money supply (M3) sa	4154.4	4115.8
Money supply (M3) nsa	4141.4	4134.8
	Month	
	Jan.	Dec.
Money supply (M1) sa	826.7	825.4
Money supply (M2) sa	3332.5	3330.5
Money supply (M3) sa	4125.4	4112.6

nsa-Not seasonally adjusted. sa-Seasonally adjusted.

Table 2.2   **Measures of the Monetary Aggregates: December 1990**

	Billions of Dollars
$M1 =$	
Currency	249.6
+ Traveler's checks	7.8
+ Demand deposits	289.9
+ Other checkable deposits	297.0
Total = $M1$	844.3
$M2 =$	
$M1$	
+ Small-denomination time deposits	1161.1
+ Savings deposits	407.3
+ Money market deposit accounts	510.3
+ Money market mutual fund shares (noninstitutional)	347.8
+ Overnight repurchase agreements	54.2
+ Overnight Eurodollars	19.4
+ Consolidation adjustment[a]	−0.1
Total = $M2$	3344.3
$M3 =$	
$M2$	
+ Large-denomination time deposits	506.3
+ Money market mutual fund shares (institutional)	127.0
+ Long-term repurchase agreements	89.7
+ Term Eurodollars	72.7
+ Consolidation adjustment[a]	−13.7
Total = $M3$	4126.3
$L =$	
$M3$	
+ Short-term Treasury securities	355.3
+ Commercial paper	349.2
+ Savings bonds	125.0
+ Bankers acceptances	34.5
Total = L	4990.3

Source: Board of Governors of the Federal Reserve System, "Money Stock Revisions," February 1991, mimeo.

[a]An adjustment to avoid double counting. For example, the $M2$ consolidation adjustment subtracts short-term repurchase agreements and Eurodollars held by money market mutual funds (which are already included in money market mutual fund balances).

are also referred to as **monetary aggregates** (Table 2.2). (The assets listed in Table 2.2 will be described in more detail in Chapter 3.)

The narrowest definition of money that the Fed reports is **$M1$,** which corresponds to the definition proposed by the theoretical approach and includes currency, checking account deposits, and traveler's checks. These assets are clearly money because they can be used directly as a medium of exchange. Until the middle 1970s, only commercial banks were permitted to establish checking accounts, and they were not allowed to pay any interest on them. With the financial innovation that has occurred (discussed more extensively in Chapter 13), regulations have changed so that other types of banks such as savings and loan associations, mutual savings banks, and credit unions also can issue checking accounts. In addition, banking institutions can issue other checkable deposits such as NOW (negotiated order of withdrawal) accounts, super-NOW accounts, and ATS (automatic transfer from savings) accounts that do pay interest on their balances. Table 2.2 lists the assets included in the measures of the monetary aggregates; both demand deposits (checking accounts that pay no interest) and these other checkable deposits are included in the $M1$ measure.

The **$M2$** monetary aggregate adds to $M1$ other assets that have check-writing features (money market deposit accounts and money market mutual fund shares) and other assets (small-denomination time deposits, savings deposits, overnight repurchase agreements, and overnight Eurodollars) that are extremely liquid because they can be turned into cash quickly at very little cost.

The **$M3$** monetary aggregate adds to $M2$ somewhat less liquid assets such as large-denomination time deposits, long-term repurchase agreements, term Eurodollars, and institutional money market mutual fund shares.

The final measure, **L,** which is really not a measure of money at all but is rather a measure of highly liquid assets, adds to $M3$ several types of securities that are essentially highly liquid bonds, such as short-term Treasury securities, commercial paper, savings bonds, and bankers acceptances.

Because we cannot be sure which of the monetary aggregates is closest to the true measure of money, it is logical to wonder if their movements closely parallel each other. If they do, then using one monetary aggregate to conduct policy will be the same as using another, and the fact that we are not sure of the appropriate definition of money (for a given policy decision) is then not too costly. On the other hand, if the monetary aggregates do not move together, then what one monetary aggregate tells us is happening to "money" might be quite different from what another monetary aggregate would tell us. The conflicting stories might present a confusing picture that will make it hard for policymakers to decide on the right course of action.

Figure 2.1 plots the growth rates $M1$, $M2$, and $M3$ over the 1960–1990 period. The growth rates of these three monetary aggregates do have some tendency to move together; the timing of their rises and falls is roughly similar, and all of them show a higher rate of growth on average in the 1970s than in the 1960s and a slowdown in the late 1980s.

There are, however, some glaring discrepancies in the movements of these aggregates. According to $M1$, the growth rate of money did not accelerate from 1968, when it was in the 6 to 7% range, to 1971, when it was at a similar level. In the same period, the $M2$ and $M3$ measures tell a different

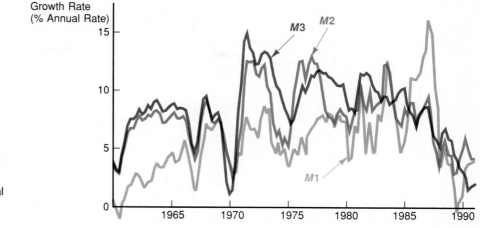

Figure 2.1
Growth Rates of the Three Money Aggregates: 1960–1990 Sources: Federal Reserve *Bulletin* and Citibase databank.

story; they show a marked acceleration from the 8 to 10% range to the 12 to 15% range. Similarly, while the growth rate of $M1$ actually increased from 1971 to 1987, the growth rates of $M2$ and $M3$ in this same period instead had a downward trend. To this extent, the different measures of money tell a different story about the course of monetary policy from the 1970s to the 1980s.

From the data in Figure 2.1, you can see that obtaining a single precise, correct definition of money does seem to matter and that it *does* make a difference which monetary aggregate policymakers and economists choose as the true measure of money.

Money as a Weighted Aggregate

The measures of the money supply listed in Table 2.2 make a black-and-white decision about whether an asset is money by including it totally or not including it at all. This distinction, however, is not always so clear-cut. Since all assets have some degree of "moneyness," that is, some degree of liquidity, we might want to say that some fraction of any asset functions as money. For example, a share in a money market fund that allows you to write checks with some restrictions against your shares might be viewed as being 60% like money, while a savings account deposit is viewed as 40% like money. Then, you might want to define the money supply to include not only the items in $M1$, but also 60% of money market fund shares and 40% of savings deposits:

$$M1 + .60(\text{money market fund shares}) + .40(\text{savings deposits})$$

A measure of the money supply using the above approach is called a weighted monetary aggregate because each asset receives different weights (for example, 1 for $M1$, .60 for the money market fund shares, and .40 for savings deposits) when added together. Fed research along these lines has produced measures of money that seem to predict inflation and business cycles somewhat better than more conventional measures.[3] How successful the monetary aggregates created by this approach will be in the future, only time will tell.

HOW RELIABLE ARE THE MONEY DATA?

The difficulties of measuring money arise not only because it is hard to decide what is the best definition of money, but also because the Fed frequently revises earlier low estimates of the monetary aggregates by large amounts later on. There are two reasons why the Fed revises its figures. First, because small depository institutions need only report the amounts of their deposits infrequently, the Fed has to estimate these amounts until the small depository institutions provide the actual figures at some future date. Second, the adjustment of the data for seasonal variation is revised substantially as more data become available. To see why this happens, let's look at an example of the seasonal variation of the money data around Christmastime. The monetary aggregates always rise around Christmas because of increased spending during the holiday season; the rise is greater in some years than in others. This means the factor that adjusts the data for the seasonal variation due to Christmas must be estimated from several years of data, and the estimates of this seasonal factor become more precise only as more data become available. When the data on the monetary aggregates are revised, it often means that the seasonal adjustments change dramatically from the initial calculation.

Table 2.3 shows how severe a problem data revisions can be. It provides the rates of money growth from one-month periods calculated from initial estimates of the $M2$ monetary aggregate, along with the rates of money growth calculated from a major revision of the $M2$ numbers published in February of 1991. As the table shows, for one-month periods the initial versus the revised data can give a different picture of what is happening to monetary policy. For May 1990, for example, the initial data indicated that the growth rate of $M2$ at an annual rate was -2.9%, while the revised data indicate a much higher growth rate of 1.1%.

A distinctive characteristic shown in Table 2.3 is that the differences between the initial and revised $M2$ series tend to cancel out. You can see this by looking at the last row of the table, which shows the average rate of $M2$ growth for the two series and the average difference between them. The average $M2$ growth for the initial calculation of $M2$ is 2.9%, while the revised number is 3.3%, a difference of only 0.4%. The conclusion that we can draw

---

[3]William Barnett, Edward Offenbacher, and Paul Spindt, "New Concepts of Aggregate Money," *Journal of Finance*, vol. 36 (May 1981), pp. 487–505.

Table 2.3   **Growth Rate of _M_2: Initial and Revised Series (compounded annual rates in %)**

Period	Initial	Revised	Difference (Revised − Initial)
Jan 1990	4.0	3.9	−0.1
Feb 1990	9.4	7.9	−1.5
March 1990	5.1	5.4	0.3
April 1990	2.3	3.8	1.5
May 1990	−2.9	1.1	4.0
June 1990	1.9	2.8	0.9
July 1990	1.5	1.5	0.0
Aug 1990	6.7	5.1	−1.6
Sept 1990	5.7	4.5	−1.2
Oct 1990	0.3	1.4	1.1
Nov 1990	−1.4	0.3	1.7
Dec 1990	2.0	1.7	−0.3
Average	2.9	3.3	+0.4

Source: Federal Reserve _Bulletin,_ various issues; Board of Governors of the Federal Reserve System, "Money Stock Revisions," February 1991, mimeo.

is that the initial data on the monetary aggregates reported by the Fed are not a reliable guide to what is happening to "short-run" movements in the money supply, such as the one-month growth rates. On the other hand, the initial money data are reasonably reliable for "longer-term" periods, such as a year. _**The moral of the story is that we probably should not pay very much attention to short-run movements in the money supply numbers, but rather should only be concerned with longer-run movements.**_

SUMMARY

1. To economists, the word _money_ has a different meaning from _income_ or _wealth_. Money is anything that is generally accepted as payment for goods or services or in the repayment of debts.

2. There are three primary functions of money: (1) a medium of exchange, (2) a unit of account, and (3) a store of value. Money as a medium of exchange avoids the problem of double coincidence of wants that arises in a barter economy by lowering transactions costs and encouraging specialization and the division of labor: Money as a unit of account reduces the number of prices needed in the economy, which also reduces

transactions costs. Money also functions as a store of value, but performs this role poorly if it is rapidly losing value in an inflation.

3. The payments system has evolved over time. Until several hundred years ago, the payments system in all but the most primitive societies was primarily based on precious metals. The introduction of paper currency lowered the cost of transporting money. The next major advance was the introduction of checks, which lowered transactions costs still further. We currently are moving toward an electronic payments system where the paper system is eliminated and all

transactions are handled by computers. Despite the potential efficiency of such a system, there are obstacles that are slowing the movement to the checkless society and the development of new forms of electronic money.

4. There are two approaches to the measurement of money: theoretical and empirical. The theoretical approach defines the money supply by using economic reasoning, whereas the empirical approach decides on the best measure of money by seeing which measure best predicts inflation and business cycles. Neither approach is completely adequate: the theoretical is not specific enough while the empirical suffers from the problem that a measure that predicts well in one period will not necessarily continue to predict well in the future. The Federal Reserve System has defined three different measures of the money supply—$M1$, $M2$, and $M3$—and a measure of liquid assets—L. These measures are not equivalent and do not always move together, so they cannot be used interchangeably by policymakers. Obtaining the precise, correct definition of money does seem to matter and has implications for how monetary policy is conducted.

5. Another problem in the measurement of money is that the data are not always as accurate as we would like. Substantial revisions in the data do occur, which indicate that initially released money data are not a reliable guide to short-run (for example, month to month) movements in the money supply, although they are more reliable over longer periods of time, such as a year.

KEY TERMS

currency	transactions cost	payments system	$M1$
wealth	unit of account	fiat money	$M2$
assets	store of value	Federal Reserve System	$M3$
income	liquidity	(Fed)	L
medium of exchange	hyperinflation	monetary aggregates	

QUESTIONS AND PROBLEMS

1. Which of the following three expressions uses economists' definition of "money"?
   a) "How much money did you earn last week?"
   b) "When I go to the store, I always make sure that I have enough money."
   c) "The love of money is the root of all evil."
* 2. There are three goods produced in an economy by three individuals:

Good	Producer
Apples	Apple-orchard owner
Bananas	Banana grower
Chocolate	chocolatier

   If the apple-orchard owner only likes bananas, the banana grower only likes chocolate, and the chocolatier only likes apples, will any trade between these three persons take place in a barter economy? How will introducing money into the economy benefit these three producers?

3. Why did cavemen not need money?
* 4. Was money a better store of value in the United States in the 1950s than it was in the 1970s? Why or why not? In which period would you have been more willing to hold money?
5. Rank the following assets from most liquid to least liquid:
   a) checking account deposits
   b) houses
   c) currency
   d) washing machines
   e) savings deposits
   f) common stock

* 6. Why have some economists described money during a hyperinflation as a "hot potato" that is quickly passed from one person to another?

7. In Brazil, a country that has been undergoing a rapid inflation, many transactions are conducted in dollars rather than in the cruzados, the domestic currency. Why?

* 8. Suppose a researcher discovers that a measure of the total amount of debt in the U.S. economy is better able to predict inflation and the business cycle over the past twenty years than is $M1$, $M2$, or $M3$. Does this discovery mean that we should define money to equal the total amount of debt in the economy?

9. Look up the $M1$, $M2$, and $M3$ numbers in the Federal Reserve *Bulletin* for the most recent one-year period. Have their growth rates been similar? What implications do their growth rates have for the conduct of monetary policy?

*10. Which of the Federal Reserve's measures of the monetary aggregates, $M1$, $M2$, or $M3$, is composed of the most liquid assets? Which is the largest measure?

11. In a weighted monetary aggregate, which of the following assets would probably receive the highest weights? which would receive the lowest weights?

a) currency

b) savings account deposits

c) NOW accounts

d) U.S. savings bonds

e) houses

f) furniture

*12. Why are revisions of monetary aggregates less of a problem for measuring long-run movements of the money supply than they are for short-run movements?

13. In ancient Greece, why was gold a more likely candidate for use as money than was wine?

*14. Why were people in the United States in the nineteenth century sometimes willing to be paid by check rather than with gold, even though they knew that there was a possibility that the check might bounce?

15. Would you be willing to give up your checkbook and instead use an electronic funds transfer system if it were made available? Why or why not?

CHAPTER 3

An Overview of the Financial System

PREVIEW   Inez the Inventor has designed a low-cost robot that cleans house (even does windows), mows the lawn, and washes the car, but she has no funds to put her wonderful invention into production. Walter the Widower has plenty of savings, which he and his wife accumulated over the years. If we could get Inez and Walter together so Walter could provide funds to Inez, then Inez's robot would see the light of day and the economy would be better off: we would have cleaner houses, shinier cars, and more beautiful lawns.

Financial markets (bond and stock markets) and financial intermediaries (banks, insurance companies, pension funds) have the basic function of getting people such as Inez and Walter together by moving funds from those who have surplus funds (Walter) to those who have a shortage of funds (Inez). More realistically, when IBM invents a better computer, it may need funds to bring it to market, or alternatively, a local government may need funds to build a road or a school. Well-functioning financial markets and financial intermediaries are needed to improve our economic well-being and are crucial to our economic health.

To study the effects of financial markets and financial intermediaries on the economy, we first must acquire an understanding of their general structure and operation. In this chapter, which is an introduction to the topic, we will learn about the major financial intermediaries and the instruments that are traded in financial markets. In addition, we will begin to explore how and why they are regulated.

This chapter is meant to be a preliminary overview of the fascinating study of financial markets and institutions. We will return to a more detailed treatment of the regulation, structure, and evolution of financial markets in Chapters 8 through 13.

FUNCTION OF FINANCIAL MARKETS

Financial markets perform the essential economic function of channeling funds from those who have saved surplus funds, because they spend less than their income, to those who have a shortage of funds, because they wish

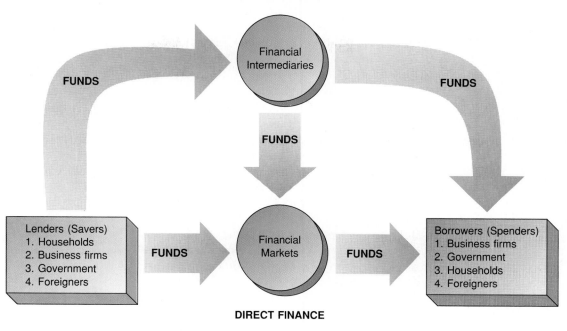

Figure 3.1
Flows of Funds Through the Financial System

to spend more than their income. This function is shown schematically in Figure 3.1. Those who have saved and are lending funds, the lenders-savers, are on the left, and those who must borrow funds to finance their spending, the borrowers-spenders, are on the right. The principal lenders-savers are households, but business firms and the government (particularly state and local government) as well as foreigners and their governments sometimes also find themselves with excess funds and so lend them out. The most important borrowers-spenders are business firms and the government, but households and foreigners also borrow to finance their purchases of cars, furniture, and houses. The arrows show that funds flow from lenders-savers to borrowers-spenders via two routes.

In direct finance (the route at the bottom of Figure 3.1) borrowers borrow funds directly from lenders in financial markets by selling them **securities** (also called financial instruments), which are claims on the borrower's future income or assets. While securities are assets for the person who buys them, they are **liabilities** (an IOU or a debt) for the individual or firm that sells (issues) them. For example, if General Motors needs to borrow funds to pay for a new factory to manufacture front-wheel-drive cars, it might borrow the funds from a saver by selling him a **bond,** a security that promises to make payments periodically for a specified period of time.

Why is this channeling of funds from savers to spenders so important to the economy? The answer is that those who save are frequently not the same people (the entrepreneurs) who have profitable investment opportunities available to them. Let's first think about this on a personal level. Suppose you have saved $1000 this year, but there is no borrowing and lending because there are no financial markets. If you do not have an investment opportunity in which you could earn income with these savings, you will just hold on to the $1000 and will earn no interest. On the other hand, Carl the Carpenter has a productive use for your $1000: He can use it to purchase a new tool that will shorten the time it takes him to build a house, thereby earning an extra $200 per year. If you could get in touch with Carl, then you could lend him the $1000 at a rental fee (interest) of $100 per year and both of you would be better off. You would earn $100 per year on your $1000, instead of the zero amount that you earned otherwise, while Carl would earn $100 more income per year (the $200 extra earnings per year minus the $100 rental fee for the use of the funds).

In the absence of financial markets, you and Carl the Carpenter might not ever get together. Without financial markets it is hard to transfer funds from a person without investment opportunities to one who has them; both of you would be worse off.

The existence of financial markets is also beneficial even if someone borrows for a purpose other than increasing production in a business. Say, for example, that you are recently married, have a good job, and want to buy a house. You earn a good salary, but since you have just started to work, you have not yet saved much. Over time you would have no problem saving enough to buy the house of your dreams, but by then you would be old and gray and would not be able to get full enjoyment from it. Without financial markets, you are stuck; you cannot buy the house and will continue to live in your tiny apartment.

If a financial market were set up so that people who had built up savings could lend you the money to buy the house, you would be more than happy to pay them some interest in order to own a home while you are still young enough to enjoy it. Then, when you had saved up enough funds, you would pay back your loan. The overall outcome would be such that you would be better off, as would the persons who made you the loan. They would now earn some interest, whereas they would not if the financial market did not exist.

Now we can see why financial markets have such an important function in the economy. They allow funds to move from those without productive investment opportunities to those who have such opportunities. By so doing, financial markets contribute to higher production and efficiency in the overall economy. They also directly improve the well-being of consumers by allowing them to time their purchases better. They provide funds to young people to buy what they need and can eventually afford, without forcing them to wait until they have saved up the entire purchase price. Financial markets that are operating efficiently improve the economic welfare of everyone in the society.

STRUCTURE OF FINANCIAL MARKETS

Now that we understand the basic function of financial markets, we will look more closely at their structure. Following are several different classifications, each of which illustrates essential features of these markets.

Debt and Equity Markets

There are two ways that a firm or an individual can obtain funds in a financial market. The most common method is to issue a debt instrument, such as a bond or a mortgage, which is a contractual agreement by the borrower to pay the holder of the instrument fixed dollar amounts at regular intervals (interest payments) until a specified date (the maturity date) when a final payment is made. The **maturity** of a debt instrument is the time (term) to that instrument's expiration date. A debt instrument is **short term** if its maturity is a year or less and is **long term** if its maturity is ten years or longer. Debt instruments with a maturity between one and ten years are said to be **intermediate term.**

The second method of raising funds is by issuing **equities,** such as common stock, which are claims to share in the net income (income after expenses and taxes) and the assets of a business firm. If you own one share of common stock in a company that has issued one million shares, then you are entitled to one one-millionth of the firm's net income and one one-millionth of the firm's assets. Equities usually make periodic payments (**dividends**) to their shareholders and are considered to be long-term securities because they have no maturity date.

The main disadvantage of owning a corporation's equities rather than its debt is that an equity holder is a residual claimant, that is, the corporation must pay all its debt holders before it pays its equity holders. The advantage of holding equities is that equity holders benefit directly from any increases in the corporation's profitability and/or asset value, since equities confer ownership rights on the equity holders. Debt holders will not share in this benefit because their dollar payments are fixed. We will examine the pros and cons of debt versus equity instruments in more detail when we come to Chapter 8, which provides an economic analysis of financial structure.

The total value of equities in the United States has typically fluctuated between $1 and $5 trillion during the past twenty years, depending on the prices of shares. Although the average person is more aware of the stock market than any other financial market, the size of the debt market greatly exceeds that of the equities market: The value of debt instruments ($11.1 trillion at the end of 1990) is more than two times larger than the value of equities ($4.2 trillion at the end of 1990).

Primary and Secondary Markets

A **primary market** is a financial market in which new issues of a security, such as a bond or a stock, are sold to initial buyers by the corporation or government agency borrowing the funds. A **secondary market** is a financial market in which the securities that have been previously issued (and are thus secondhand) can be resold.

The primary markets for securities are not well known to the public because the selling of securities to initial buyers takes place behind closed doors. The New York and American Stock Exchanges, in which previously issued stocks are traded, are the best-known examples of secondary markets, although the bond markets, in which previously issued bonds of major corporations and the U.S. government are bought and sold, actually have larger trading volume. Other examples of secondary markets are foreign exchange markets, futures markets, and options markets. When an individual buys a security in the secondary market, the person who has sold the security receives money in exchange for the security, but the corporation which issued the security acquires no new funds. A corporation acquires new funds only when its securities are first sold in the primary market.

Secondary markets serve two functions. First, they make it easier to sell these financial instruments in order to raise cash, that is, they make the financial instruments more liquid. The increased liquidity of these instruments then makes them more desirable and thus easier for the issuing firm to sell in the primary market. Second, they determine the price of the security that the issuing firm sells in the primary market. The firms that buy securities in the primary market will pay the issuing corporation only the price they think the secondary market will set for this security: The higher the security prices in the secondary market, the higher will be the price that an issuing firm will receive for its security in the primary market and, hence, the greater the amount of capital it can raise. Conditions in the secondary market are therefore the most relevant to the corporation issuing securities. It is for this reason that books like this one, which deal with financial markets, focus on the behavior of secondary markets rather than primary markets.

Exchanges and Over-the-Counter Markets

Secondary markets can be organized in two ways. One is to organize **exchanges,** where buyers and sellers of securities (or their agents or brokers) meet in one central location to conduct trades. The New York and American Stock Exchanges for stocks and the Chicago Board of Trade for commodities (wheat, corn, silver, etc.) are examples of organized exchanges.

The other method of organizing a secondary market is to have an **over-the-counter (OTC) market,** in which dealers at different locations who have an inventory of securities stand ready to buy and sell securities "over-the-counter" to anyone who comes to them and is willing to accept their prices. Because over-the-counter dealers are in computer contact with each other and know the prices set by each other, the OTC market is very competitive and not very different from a market with an organized exchange.

Many common stocks are traded over-the-counter, although the largest corporations have their shares traded at organized stock exchanges such as the New York Stock Exchange. On the other hand, the U.S. government bond market, with a larger trading volume than the New York Stock Exchange, is set up as an over-the-counter market. Forty or so dealers establish a "market" in these securities by standing ready to buy and sell U.S. government bonds. Other over-the-counter markets include those that trade negotiable certificates of deposit, federal funds, bankers acceptances, and foreign exchange.

Money and Capital Markets

Another way of making a distinction between markets is on the basis of the maturity of the securities traded in that market. The **money market** is a financial market in which only short-term debt instruments (maturity less than one year) are traded, while the **capital market** is the market in which longer-term debt (maturity greater than one year) and equity instruments are traded. Money market securities are usually more widely traded than longer-term securities and so tend to be more liquid. In addition, as we will see in Chapter 4, short-term securities have smaller fluctuations in prices than long-term securities, making them safer investments. As a result, corporations and banks actively use this market to earn interest on surplus funds that they expect to have only temporarily. Capital market securities, such as stocks and long-term bonds, are often held by financial intermediaries such as insurance companies and pension funds, which have little uncertainty about the amount of funds they will have available in the future.

FUNCTION OF FINANCIAL INTERMEDIARIES

As shown in Figure 3.1, funds can move from lenders to borrowers by a second route, called indirect finance because it involves a middleman: a financial intermediary that stands between the lenders-savers and the borrowers-spenders and helps transfer funds from one to the other. A financial intermediary does this by borrowing funds from the lenders-savers and then, in turn, makes loans to borrowers-spenders. A bank, for example, might acquire funds by issuing a liability to the public in the form of savings deposits and then use the funds to acquire an asset by making a loan to General Motors or by buying a GM bond in the financial market. The ultimate result is that funds have been transferred from the public (the lenders-savers) to GM (the borrower-spender) with the help of the financial intermediary (the bank).

Financial intermediaries are not in the business of moving funds from lenders-savers to borrowers-spenders for the fun of it. They are in it to get rich. By charging a higher interest rate on loans than they pay on the funds they have acquired from lenders-savers, financial intermediaries, such as banks, make a profit. Nonetheless, by engaging in the process of indirect finance, called **financial intermediation,** financial intermediaries can improve the lot of small savers by providing them with high-interest income and can help small borrowers who can now get loans they otherwise would not obtain. Large borrowers also benefit because the process of financial intermediation means that more funds are made available to borrowers in the financial markets. Without financial intermediation, the full benefits of a financial market cannot be achieved.

The reason why financial intermediaries are needed to obtain the full benefits of financial markets is that there are substantial information costs and transactions costs in the economy. For lenders to identify potential borrowers and for borrowers to identify potential lenders is a costly process. Once a lender finds a potential borrower, he has the additional problem of having to spend time and money on a credit check to find out if the borrower is likely to repay his debts. In addition to these information costs, the actual process of making a loan or buying a security involves transactions costs; in the case of a loan, an appropriate loan contract must be written up, or in the case of purchasing a security, brokerage commissions must be paid. To see why these costs require financial intermediaries to play an essential role in channeling of funds from lenders-savers to borrowers-spenders, let's look at some examples.

With direct finance, borrowers and lenders always deal directly with each other, which works well up to a point. For a well-known company, such as American Telephone and Telegraph (AT&T), it is easy to sell bonds in an open market to other firms and individuals because everyone knows that AT&T is a solid company. But what happens when Carl the Carpenter needs to borrow to buy a tool that increases his productivity? He will not be able to sell bonds because no one knows who he is and if he is a good credit risk. Thus, in a world with direct finance only, he may not be able to borrow.

Conversely, people who have small amounts of savings are wary of buying securities because it is costly to collect information on which is the best to buy. The transactions costs of purchasing securities might also be very high for a small saver because the transactions costs (primarily brokerage commissions) for each security bought declines with the amount purchased. Consequently, only if you have a large amount of funds with which to purchase a large number of securities could you take advantage of the declining transactions costs.

The transactions costs of making a loan for an individual are even greater: Few of us have the legal expertise to draw up an ironclad loan contract, and hiring a lawyer to do so is very expensive, making it unprofitable for small savers to make loans. In this way, many small savers and borrowers limited to direct finance will be frozen out of the market and will not be able to share many of the benefits provided by the existence of financial markets.

Let's see what happens when financial intermediaries are introduced into the economy. With them, small savers can now provide their funds to the financial markets by lending these funds to a trustworthy intermediary, the Honest John Bank, which in turn lends the funds out either by making loans or by buying securities such as stocks or bonds. Financial intermediaries have higher earnings on their investments because they are experts in regard to who to lend to (especially on small borrowers) or what securities to buy, and they can take advantage of lower transaction costs by purchasing securities in large quantities. They can afford to pay the lenders-savers interest or provide substantial services and still earn a profit.

The success of financial intermediaries is evidenced by the fact that most Americans invest their savings with them and also obtain their loans from them. Indeed, although the media focus much of their attention on securities markets, particularly the stock market, financial intermediaries are a far more important source of finance for corporations than are securities markets. This is true not only for the United States but for other industrialized countries as well (see Box 3.1). We will further explore the role of financial intermediaries in the economy, why they are so important and how they operate, in Chapters 8 through 13.

B o x   3 . 1   **A Global Perspective**

How Important Are Financial Intermediaries Relative to Securities Markets: An International Comparison

The pattern of the financing of corporations differs across countries, but one key fact emerges. Studies of the major developed countries, including the United States, Canada, Great Britain, Japan, Italy, Germany, and France, show that when businesses go looking for funds to finance their activities they usually obtain these funds from financial intermediaries.* Not surprisingly, the United States and Canada, which have the most developed securities markets in the world, also make the greatest use of them in financing corporations. Even so, in the United States loans from financial intermediaries are almost twice as important for corporate finance as are securities markets. The countries that have made least use of securities markets are Germany and Japan; in these two countries finance from financial intermediaries has been almost ten times greater than that from securities markets. However, with the deregulation of Japanese securities markets in recent years, the share of corporate financing by financial intermediaries has been declining relative to the use of securities markets.

Although the dominance of financial intermediaries over securities markets is clear in all countries, the relative importance of bond versus stock markets differs widely across countries. In the United States, the bond market is far more important as a source of corporate finance: On average, the amount of new financing raised using bonds is ten times the amount using stocks. On the other hand, countries such as France and Italy make use of equities markets more than the bond market to raise capital. (Explanations for why financial intermediaries play a more important role in financing businesses than do securities markets and what factors in different countries influence the choice between bond and equity financing are discussed in Chapter 8.)

*See, for example, Colin Mayer, "Financial Systems, Corporate Finance, and Economic Development," in R. Glenn Hubbard, ed., *Asymmetric Information, Corporate Finance, and Investment* (Chicago: University of Chicago Press, 1990), pp. 307–332.

FINANCIAL INTERMEDIARIES

We have seen why financial intermediaries play such an important role in the economy. Now we look at the principal financial intermediaries and how they perform the intermediation function. There are three categories: (1) depository institutions (banks), (2) contractual savings institutions, and (3) investment intermediaries. Table 3.1 provides a guide to the discussion of the financial intermediaries that fit into these three categories by describing their primary liabilities (sources of funds) and assets (uses of funds). The relative size of these intermediaries in the United States is indicated by Table 3.2, which lists the amount of their assets at the end of 1970, 1980, and 1990.

Depository Institutions (Banks)

Depository institutions (which, for simplicity, we will refer to as "banks" throughout this text) are financial intermediaries that accept deposits from individuals and institutions and make loans. The study of money and banking focuses special attention on this group of financial institutions (which include commercial banks, savings and loan associations, mutual savings banks, and credit unions) because they are involved in the creation of depos-

Table 3.1   Primary Assets and Liabilities of Financial Intermediaries

Intermediary	Primary Liabilities (Sources of Funds)	Primary Assets (Uses of Funds)
Depository Institutions		
Commercial banks	Deposits	Business and consumer loans, mortgages, U.S. government securities and municipal bonds
Savings and loan associations	Deposits	Mortgages
Mutual savings banks	Deposits	Mortgages
Credit unions	Deposits	Consumer loans
Contractual savings institutions		
Life insurance companies	Premiums from policies	Corporate bonds and mortgages
Pension funds	Employer and employee contributions	Corporate bonds and stock
Fire and casualty insurance companies	Premiums from policies	Municipal bonds, corporate bonds and stock, and U.S. government securities
Investment intermediaries		
Mutual funds	Shares	Stocks and bonds
Money market mutual funds	Shares	Money market instruments
Finance companies	Commercial paper, stocks, and bonds	Consumer and business loans

Table 3.2 **Principal Financial Intermediaries**

Type of Financial Intermediaries	Value of Assets (billions of $, end of year)		
	1970	1980	1990
Depository institutions (banks)			
Commercial banks	517	1357	3356
Savings and loan associations	171	614	1098
Mutual savings banks	79	170	264
Credit unions	18	67	215
Contractual savings institutions			
Life insurance companies	201	464	1409
Fire and casualty insurance companies	50	174	528
Pension funds (private)	112	470	1169
State and local government retirement funds	60	198	806
Investment intermediaries			
Finance companies	64	202	574
Mutual funds	47	62	609
Money market mutual funds	0	76	499

Source: Federal Reserve Flow of Funds.

its, an important component of the money supply. Their behavior plays an important role in how the money supply is determined.

Commercial Banks These financial intermediaries primarily raise funds by issuing checkable deposits (deposits on which checks can be written), savings deposits (deposits that are payable on demand but do not allow their owner to write checks), and time deposits (deposits with fixed terms to maturity). They then use these funds to make commercial, consumer, and mortgage loans and to buy U.S. government securities and municipal bonds. There are approximately 12,000 commercial banks in the United States, and as a group, they are the largest of the financial intermediaries and have the most diversified portfolios (collections) of assets.

Savings and Loan Associations Savings and loan associations' (S&Ls) primary sources of funds are savings deposits (often called shares), time, and checkable deposits. The acquired funds have traditionally been used to make mortgage loans. Savings and loans are the next largest group of financial intermediaries, numbering around 2500. In the 1950s and 1960s, S&Ls grew much more rapidly than commercial banks, but when interest rates climbed sharply from the late 1960s to the early 1980s, S&Ls encountered difficulties which slowed their rapid growth. Because mortgages are long-term loans, with the most common maturity being twenty-nine years, many in existence today were made years ago when interest rates were substantially lower. When interest rates rose, savings and loans frequently found that the income from their mortgages was well below the cost of acquiring funds. Many of them began to suffer large losses and many have gone out of business.

Until 1980, savings and loans were restricted to making mortgage loans and could not establish checking accounts. Their troubles encouraged Congress to include provisions in the Depository Institutions Deregulation and Monetary Control Act of 1980 allowing savings and loans to issue checking accounts, make consumer loans, and pursue many activities previously restricted to commercial banks. The Garn-St Germain Act of 1982 further expanded the allowable activities for savings and loans. In addition, they are now subject to the same requirements regarding deposits at the Federal Reserve as the commercial banks. The net result of this legislation is that the distinction between savings and loans and commercial banks is being blurred, and these intermediaries will become more competitive with each other in the future.

Mutual Savings Banks Mutual savings banks are very similar to savings and loans. They raise funds by accepting deposits and use them primarily to make mortgage loans. Their corporate structure is somewhat different from that of S&Ls in that they are always structured as "mutuals," which means that they function as cooperatives where the depositors own the bank. There are around 500 of these institutions, and they are located primarily in New York state and New England. Like savings and loans, until 1980 they were restricted to making mortgage loans, and they suffered similar problems when interest rates rose from the late 1960s to the early 1980s. They were similarly affected by the banking legislation in the 1980s and now can issue checkable deposits and make loans other than mortgages.

Credit Unions These financial institutions, numbering about 15,000, are very small cooperative lending institutions organized around a particular societal group: union members, employees of a particular firm, and so forth. They acquire funds from deposits and primarily make consumer loans. With the banking legislation in the 1980s, credit unions too are allowed to issue checkable deposits and can make mortgage loans in addition to consumer loans.

Contractual Savings Institutions

Contractual savings institutions, such as insurance companies and pension funds, are financial intermediaries that acquire funds at periodic intervals on a contractual basis. Because they can predict reasonably accurately how much they will have to pay out in benefits in the coming years, they do not have to worry as much as depository institutions about losing funds. As a result, the liquidity of assets is not as important a consideration for them as it is for depository institutions, and they tend to invest their funds primarily in long-term securities such as corporate bonds, stocks, and mortgages.

Life Insurance Companies   Life insurance companies insure people against financial hazards following a death and sell annuities (annual income payments upon retirement). They acquire funds from the premiums that people pay to keep their policies in force and use them mainly to buy corporate bonds and mortgages. They also purchase stocks but are restricted in the amount that they can hold. Currently, with over $1.4 trillion of assets, they are the largest of the contractual savings institutions.

Fire and Casualty Insurance Companies   These companies insure their policyholders against loss from theft, fire, and accidents. They are very much like life insurance companies, receiving funds through premiums for their policies, but they have a greater possibility of loss of funds if major disasters occur. For this reason, they use their funds to buy more liquid assets than life insurance companies do. Their largest holding of assets is municipal bonds, as well as corporate bonds and stocks and U.S. government securities.

Pension Funds (Private) and State and Local Retirement Funds   These financial institutions provide retirement income in the form of annuities to employees who are covered by a pension plan. Funds are acquired by contributions from employers or from the employees who either have a contribution automatically deducted from their paychecks or voluntarily contribute. The largest asset holdings of pension funds are corporate bonds and stocks. The establishment of pension funds has been actively encouraged by the federal government both through legislation requiring pension plans and through tax incentives to encourage contributions.

Investment Intermediaries

This category of financial intermediaries includes finance companies, mutual funds, and money market mutual funds.

Finance Companies   Finance companies raise funds by selling commercial paper and by issuing stocks and bonds. They lend these funds to consumers who make purchases of such items as furniture, automobiles, and home improvements and to small businesses. Some finance companies are organized by a parent corporation to help sell its product. Ford Motor Credit Company, for example, makes loans to consumers who purchase Ford automobiles.

Mutual Funds   These financial intermediaries acquire funds by selling shares to many individuals and use the proceeds to purchase diversified portfolios of stocks and bonds. Mutual funds allow shareholders to pool their resources so that they can take advantage of the lower transactions costs when buying large blocks of stocks or bonds. In addition, mutual funds allow shareholders to hold more diversified portfolios than they otherwise would. Shareholders can sell (redeem) shares at any time, but the value of these shares will be determined by the value of the mutual fund's holdings of securities. Since these fluctuate greatly, the value of mutual fund shares will too; therefore, investments in mutual funds can be a risky business.

Money Market Mutual Funds These are relatively new financial institutions, which have the characteristics of a mutual fund but also function to some extent as a depository institution because they, in effect, offer a kind of deposit. Like most mutual funds, they sell shares to acquire funds that are then used to buy money market instruments that are both safe and very liquid. The interest on these assets is then paid out to the shareholders.

A key feature of these funds is that shareholders can write checks against the value of their shareholdings. There generally are, however, restrictions on the use of the check-writing privilege; checks frequently cannot be written for amounts less than a set minimum, such as $500, and a substantial amount of money is required initially to open an account. In effect, shares in a money market mutual fund function like checking account deposits that pay interest, but with some restrictions on the check-writing privilege. Money market mutual funds have undergone extraordinary growth since 1971 when they first appeared. By 1990 their assets had climbed to close to $500 billion.

FINANCIAL MARKET INSTRUMENTS

To complete our understanding of how financial markets perform the important role of channeling funds from lenders-savers to borrowers-spenders, we need to examine the securities (instruments) traded in financial markets. We first focus on the instruments traded in the money market and then turn to those traded in the capital market.

Money Market Instruments

Because of their short terms to maturity, the debt instruments traded in the money market undergo the least price fluctuations and so are the least risky investments. The principal money market instruments are listed in Table 3.3 along with the amount outstanding at the end of 1970, 1980, and 1990.

United States Treasury Bills These short-term debt instruments of the U.S. government are issued in three-, six-, and twelve-month maturities. They pay a set amount at maturity and have no interest payments, but they effectively pay interest by initially selling at a discount, that is, at a price lower than

Table 3.3 **Principal Money Market Instruments**

Type of Instrument	Amount Outstanding (billions of $, end of year)		
	1970	1980	1990
Negotiable bank certificates of deposit (large denomination)	55	317	543
U.S. Treasury bills	81	216	527
Commercial paper	33	122	557
Bankers' acceptances	7	42	52
Repurchase agreements	3	57	144
Eurodollars	2	55	92
Federal funds	16	18	61

Sources: Federal Reserve Flow of Funds Accounts: Federal Reserve *Bulletin: Banking and Monetary Statistics 1945–1970, Annual Statistical Digest 1971–1975: Economic Report of the President;* Board of Governors of the Federal Reserve System, "Money Stock Revisions," February 1991, mimeo. Note that the figures for federal funds after 1970 are for large banks only.

the set amount paid at maturity. For instance, you might buy a one-year Treasury bill in May of 1992 for $9,000 that can be redeemed for $10,000 in May of 1993.

U.S. Treasury bills are the most liquid of all the money market instruments because they are the most actively traded. They also are the safest of all money market instruments because there is no possibility of **default,** a situation where the party issuing the debt instrument (the federal government in this case) is unable to make interest payments or pay off the amount owed when the instrument matures. The federal government is always able to meet its debt obligations because it can raise taxes or issue currency to pay off its debts. Treasury bills are held mainly by banks, although small amounts are held by households, corporations, and other financial intermediaries.

Negotiable Bank Certificates of Deposit (CDs) A certificate of deposit (CD) is a debt instrument sold by a bank to depositors that pays annual interest of a given amount and at maturity pays back the original purchase price. Before 1961, CDs were nonnegotiable; that is, they could not be sold to someone else and could not be redeemed from the bank before maturity without paying a substantial penalty. In 1961, in order to make CDs more liquid and more attractive to investors, Citibank introduced the first negotiable CD in large denominations (over $100,000) that could be resold in a secondary market. This instrument is now issued by almost all the major commercial banks and has been extremely successful, with the amount outstanding currently exceeding the amount of U.S. Treasury bills. They are an extremely important source of funds to commercial banks, from corporations, money market mutual funds, charitable institutions, and government agencies.

Commercial Paper   Commercial paper is a short-term debt instrument issued by large banks and well-known corporations, such as General Motors or AT&T. Before the 1960s, corporations usually borrowed their short-term funds from banks, but since then they have come to rely more heavily on selling commercial paper to other financial intermediaries and corporations for their immediate borrowing needs; that is, they engage in direct finance. The growth of the commercial paper market has been substantial: The amount of commercial paper outstanding has increased by over fifteen hundred percent (from $33 billion to $557 billion) in the period 1970–1990.

Bankers' Acceptances   These money market instruments are created in the course of carrying out international trade and have been in use for hundreds of years. A banker's acceptance is a bank draft (a promise of payment similar to a check) issued by a firm, payable at some future date, and guaranteed for a fee by the bank who stamps it as "accepted." The firm issuing the instrument is required to deposit the required funds into its account to cover the draft. If the firm fails to do so, the bank's guarantee means that it is obligated to make good on the draft. The advantage to the firm is that the draft is more likely to be accepted when purchasing goods abroad because the foreign exporter knows that even if the company purchasing the goods goes bankrupt, the bank draft will still be paid off. These "accepted" drafts are often resold in a secondary market at a discount and so are similar in function to Treasury bills. Typically, they are held by many of the same parties that hold Treasury bills, and the amount outstanding also has had substantial growth, rising by six hundred percent ($7 billion to $52 billion) from 1970 to 1990.

Repurchase Agreements (RPs)   Repurchase agreements are effectively short-term loans (usually with a maturity of less than two weeks) in which Treasury bills serve as collateral, an asset that the lender receives if the borrower does not pay back the loan. RPs are made as follows: A large corporation, such as General Motors, may have some idle funds in their bank account, say, $1 million, which they would like to lend overnight. GM uses this excess $1 million to buy Treasury bills from a bank, which agrees to repurchase them the next morning at a price slightly above GM's purchase price. The effect of this agreement is that GM makes a loan of $1 million to the bank and holds $1 million of the bank's Treasury bills until the bank repurchases the bills to pay off the loan. RPs are a fairly recent (1969) innovation in financial markets. Repurchase agreements are now an important source of funds to banks (over $140 billion), and the most important lenders in this market are large corporations.

Federal (Fed) Funds   These are typically overnight loans between banks of their deposits at the Federal Reserve. The "federal funds" designation is somewhat confusing because these loans are not made by the federal government or by the Federal Reserve but are made by banks to other banks.

Following the Financial News

Money Market Rates

The *Wall Street Journal* publishes daily a listing of interest rates on many different financial instruments in its Money Rates column. (See "Today's Contents" on page 1 of the *Journal* for the location.)

The interest rates in the Money Rates column that are discussed most frequently in the media are:

Prime rate: the interest rate charged preferred corporate customers on bank loans, an indicator of the cost of business borrowing from banks.

Federal funds rate: the interest rate charged on overnight loans in the federal funds market, a sensitive indicator of the cost to banks of borrowing funds.

Treasury bill rate: the interest rate on Treasury bills, an indicator of general interest rate movements.

Federal Home Loan Mortgage Corp. rates: interest rates on "Freddie Mac" guaranteed mortgages, an indicator of the cost of financing residential housing purchases.

Source: *Wall Street Journal* (Friday, March 1, 1991).

MONEY RATES

Thursday, February 28, 1991

The key U.S. and foreign annual interest rates below are a guide to general levels but don't always represent actual transactions.

PRIME RATE: 8¾%–9%. The base rate on corporate loans at large U.S. money center commercial banks.

FEDERAL FUNDS: 10% high, 6⅜% low, 7% near closing bid, 8% offered. Reserves traded among commercial banks for overnight use in amounts of $1 million or more. Source: Babcock Fulton Prebon (U.S.A.) Inc.

DISCOUNT RATE: 6%. The charge on loans to depository institutions by the New York Federal Reserve Bank.

CALL MONEY: 8½% to 9%. The charge on loans to brokers on stock exchange collateral.

COMMERCIAL PAPER placed directly by General Motors Acceptance Corp.: 6.10% 25 to 33 days; 6.65% 34 to 59 days; 6.60% 60 to 89 days; 6.55% 90 to 119 days; 6.50% 120 to 149 days; 6.475% 150 to 179 days; 6.35% 180 to 270 days.

COMMERCIAL PAPER: High-grade unsecured notes sold through dealers by major corporations in multiples of $1,000: 6.80% 30 days; 6.70% 60 days; 6.65% 90 days.

CERTIFICATES OF DEPOSIT: 6.31% one month; 6.36% two months; 6.35% three months; 6.35% six months; 6.60% one year. Average of top rates paid by major New York banks on primary new issues of negotiable C.D.s, usually on amounts of $1 million and more. The minimum unit is $100,-000. Typical rates in the secondary market: 6.85% one month; 6.70% three months; 6.70% six months.

BANKERS ACCEPTANCES: 6.68% 30 days; 6.53% 60 days; 6.48% 90 days; 6.43% 120 days; 6.40% 150 days; 6.38% 180 days. Negotiable, bank-backed business credit instruments typically financing an import order.

LONDON LATE EURODOLLARS: 7% – 6⅞% one month; 6 15/16% – 6 13/16% two months; 6⅞% – 6¾% three months; 6⅞% – 6¾% four months; 6⅞% – 6¾% five months; 6⅞% – 6¾% six months.

LONDON INTERBANK OFFERED RATES (LIBOR): 7% one month; 6⅞% three months; 6⅞% six months; 7 1/16% one year. The average of interbank offered rates for dollar deposits in the London market based on quotations at five major banks. Effective rate for contracts entered into two days from date appearing at top of this column.

FOREIGN PRIME RATES: Canada 11–11.25%; Germany 10.50%; Japan 8.25%; Switzerland 10.25%; Britain 13%. These rate indications aren't directly comparable; lending practices vary widely by location.

TREASURY BILLS: Results of the Tuesday, February 25, 1991, auction of short-term U.S. government bills, sold at a discount from face value in units of $10,000 to $1 million: 6.01% 13 weeks; 6.01% 26 weeks.

FEDERAL HOME LOAN MORTGAGE CORP. (Freddie Mac): Posted yields on 30-year mortgage commitments for delivery within 30 days. 9.44%, standard conventional fixed-rate mortgages; 7.625%, 2% rate capped one-year adjustable rate mortgages. Source: Telerate Systems Inc.

FEDERAL NATIONAL MORTGAGE ASSOCIATION (Fannie Mae): Posted yields on 30 year mortgage commitments for delivery within 30 days (priced at par). 9.37%, standard conventional fixed rate-mortgages; 7.35%, 6/2 rate capped one-year adjustable rate mortgages. Source: Telerate Systems Inc.

MERRILL LYNCH READY ASSETS TRUST: 6.48%. Annualized average rate of return after expenses for the past 30 days; not a forecast of future returns.

One reason why a bank might borrow in the federal funds market is that it might find the deposits it has at the Fed do not meet the amount required by regulation. It can then borrow these deposits from another bank, which transfers them to the borrowing bank using the Fed's wire transfer system. This market is very sensitive to the credit needs of the banks, so that the interest rate on these loans, called the **federal funds rate,** is a closely watched barometer of the tightness of credit market conditions in the banking system; when it is high, it indicates that the banks are strapped for funds, whereas when it is low, banks' credit needs are low.

Eurodollars U.S. dollars deposited in foreign banks outside the United States or in foreign branches of U.S. banks are called **Eurodollars.** American banks can borrow these deposits from other banks or from their own foreign branches when they need funds. Eurodollars have become an important source of funds for banks (over $90 billion).

The money market has undergone great changes in the past thirty years, with new financial instruments increasing at a far more rapid rate than others. Why this has been happening is a fascinating topic which we will discuss in Chapter 13, where we will examine the forces that have been driving the rapid pace of financial innovation in recent years.

Capital Market Instruments

Capital market instruments are debt and equity instruments with maturities of over one year. They have far wider price fluctuations than money market instruments and are considered to be fairly risky investments. The principal capital market instruments are listed in Table 3.4, with the amount outstanding at the end of 1970, 1980, and 1990.

Stocks Stocks are equity claims on the net income and assets of a corporation. Their value of over $4 trillion at the end of 1990 exceeds that of any other type of security in the capital market. The amount of new stock issues in any given year is typically quite small, being less than 1% of the total value of shares outstanding. Individuals hold over 60% of the value of stocks with the rest being held by pension funds, mutual funds, and insurance companies.

Mortgages Mortgages are loans to individuals or business firms to purchase housing, land, or other real structures, where the structure or land serves as collateral for the loan. The mortgage market is the largest debt market in the United States, with the amount outstanding of residential mortgages (used to purchase residential housing) more than triple the amount outstanding of commercial and farm mortgages. Savings and loan associations and mutual savings banks have been the primary lenders in the residential mortgage

Table 3.4   Principal Capital Market Instruments: Amount Outstanding

Type of Instrument	Amount Outstanding (billions of $, end of year)		
	1970	1980	1990
Corporate stocks (market value)	906	1634	4165
Residential mortgages	355	1099	2924
Corporate bonds	167	366	987
U.S. government securities (marketable long-term)	160	407	1653
State and local government bonds	146	279	640
U.S. government agency securities	51	193	412
Bank commercial loans	152	457	815
Consumer loans	134	355	809
Commercial and farm mortgages	116	353	846

Sources: Federal Reserve Flow of Funds Accounts, Federal Reserve *Bulletin,* and *Banking and Monetary Statistics 1941–1970.*

market, although commercial banks have started to enter this market more aggressively. The majority of commercial and farm mortgages are made by commercial banks and life insurance companies. The federal government has played an active role in the mortgage market via the three government agencies (FNMA, GNMA, and FHLMC) that provide funds to the mortgage market by selling bonds and using the proceeds to buy mortgages.

Corporate Bonds   These are long-term bonds issued by corporations with very strong credit ratings. The typical corporate bond sends the holder an interest payment twice a year and pays off the face value when the bond matures. Some corporate bonds, called convertible bonds, also have the additional feature of allowing the holder to convert them into a specified number of shares of stock at any time up to the maturity date. This feature makes these convertible bonds more desirable to prospective purchasers than bonds without it and allows the corporation to reduce its interest payments because these bonds can increase in value if the price of the stock appreciates sufficiently. Because the outstanding amount of both convertible and nonconvertible bonds for any given corporation is small, they are not nearly as liquid as other securities such as U.S. government bonds.

Although the size of the corporate bond market is substantially smaller than the stock market, with the amount of corporate bonds outstanding less than one-quarter that of stocks, the volume of new corporate bonds issued each year is substantially greater than the volume of new stock issues. Thus, the behavior of the corporate bond market is probably far more important to a firm's financing decisions than the behavior of the stock market. The principal buyers of corporate bonds are life insurance companies, with pension funds and households the other large holders.

U.S. Government Securities These long-term debt instruments are issued by the U.S. Treasury to finance the deficits of the federal government. Because they are the most widely traded bonds in the United States (the volume of transactions on average exceeds $100 billion daily), they are the most liquid security traded in the capital market. They are held by the Federal Reserve, banks, households, and foreigners.

U.S. Government Agency Securities These are long-term bonds issued by various government agencies. Many of these securities are guaranteed by the federal government and so they function much like U.S. government bonds; they are held by similar parties.

State and Local Government Bonds State and local bonds, also called municipal bonds, are long-term instruments issued by state and local governments to finance expenditures on schools, roads, and so on. An important feature of these bonds is that their interest payments are exempt from federal income tax and generally from state taxes in the issuing state. Commercial banks, with their high income tax rate, are the biggest buyers of these securities, owning over one-half the total amount outstanding. The next biggest group of holders are wealthy individuals in high-income tax brackets, followed by insurance companies.

Consumer and Bank Commercial Loans These are loans to consumers and business firms made principally by banks, but in the case of consumer loans, also by finance companies. There are often no secondary markets in these loans and so they are the least liquid of the capital market instruments listed in Table 3.4.

REGULATION OF THE FINANCIAL SYSTEM

The financial system is among the most heavily regulated sectors of the American economy. (This is also the case in foreign countries: see Box 3.2.) Political forces have encouraged the government to play such a strong role in order to accomplish the following: (1) provide information to investors, (2) ensure the soundness of the financial system, (3) improve control of monetary policy, and (4) encourage home ownership. We will examine how these four concerns have led to the present regulatory environment. As a study aid, the principal regulatory agencies of the U.S. financial system are listed in Table 3.5.

Providing Information to Investors

A particular problem faced by an investor in a financial market is to know whether a potential investment is safe. Often an individual can evaluate the

B o x   3 . 2   **A Global Perspective**

Financial Regulation Abroad

Given that political forces are not too different here and in other industrialized countries, financial regulation in Japan, Canada, and Europe has similar characteristics to financial regulation in the United States. The provision of information is improved by requiring corporations issuing securities to report information about assets and liabilities, earnings, and sales of stock and by prohibitions on insider trading. The soundness of intermediaries is ensured by licensing and periodic inspection of financial intermediaries' books and by the provision of deposit insurance (although its coverage is smaller and its existence is often purposely not advertised). Monetary control is enhanced by requiring depository institutions to keep a fraction of their deposits in the central bank. Although encouragement of home ownership is typically not pursued as strongly in regulation abroad, maximum ceilings on interest rates both for deposits and bonds have

been very common. Recently, however, many of these ceilings have been removed as has occurred in the United States.

The major differences between financial regulation in the United States and abroad relate to bank regulation. Only the United States currently prevents a national banking system by restricting branches across regions. Indeed, this difference between the United States and Europe will widen because new banking directives for the European Economic Commission (EEC) will enable a bank licensed in one EEC country to offer a full range of services in all other EEC countries. U.S. banks are also the most restricted from engaging in a full range of financial services and in the assets they can hold. Banks abroad frequently hold shares in commercial firms, and in Japan and Germany, often hold sizable stakes in such firms.

quality of a product by buying it and trying it. For example, you can find out about the quality of the meat at your local butcher by buying a steak and eating it. If the quality does not suit you, then you will look for another butcher. On the other hand, some products are harder to evaluate, and the securities traded in financial markets are an example. An ordinary investor cannot tell whether a security issued by a firm is a safe investment or not. Private firms, such as Standard and Poor's Corporation or Moody's Investor Service, which rate the quality of bonds, may spring up to provide information about the quality of some financial securities. However, the public may feel that not enough information is supplied to investors by the private market and that investors require protection. They therefore may encourage the government to step in to ensure that more information about securities is provided.

As a result of the stock market crash in 1929 and revelations of massive frauds in the aftermath, political demands for regulation culminated in The Securities Act of 1933 and the establishment of the Securities and Exchange Commission (SEC). The SEC requires corporations issuing securities to disclose certain information about their sales, assets, and earnings to the public and restricts trading by the largest stockholders (known as "insiders") in the corporation. By requiring disclosure of this information and by discourag-

Table 3.5 Principal Regulatory Agencies of the U.S. Financial System

Regulatory Agencies	Who They Regulate	Nature of Regulations
Securities and Exchange Commission (SEC)	Organized exchanges and financial markets	Requires disclosure of information, restricts "insider" trading
Commodities Futures, Trading Commission (CFTC)	Futures markets exchanges	Regulates procedures for trading in futures markets
Office of the Comptroller of the Currency	Federally chartered commercial banks	Charters and examines books of federally chartered commercial banks and imposes restrictions on assets they can hold
National Credit Union Administration (NCUA)	Federally chartered credit unions	Charters and examines books of federally chartered credit unions and imposes restrictions on assets they can hold
State Banking and Insurance Commissions	State chartered banks (depository institutions) and insurance companies	Charters and examines books of state chartered banks and insurance companies; imposes restrictions on assets they can hold; imposes restrictions on branching
Federal Deposit Insurance Corporation (FDIC)	Commercial banks, mutual savings banks, and savings and loan associations	Provides insurance of up to $100,000 for each depositor at a bank; examines books of insured banks and imposes restrictions on assets they can hold
Federal Reserve System	All banks (depository institutions)	Examines books of commercial banks who are members of the system; sets reserve requirements for all banks; imposes restrictions on interest payments on deposits
Office of Thrift Supervision	Savings and loan associations	Examines books of savings and loan associations; imposes restrictions on assets they can hold

ing insider trading, which could be used to manipulate security prices, the SEC hopes investors will be better informed and be protected from some of the abuses in financial markets that occurred before 1933. Indeed, in recent years the SEC has been particularly active in prosecuting those involved in insider trading, Ivan Boesky, for example (see Box 29.1 in Chapter 29).

Ensuring the Soundness of Financial Intermediaries

The government tries to protect investors and depositors by ensuring the safety of the funds they have provided to financial intermediaries. This protection is provided by six different types of regulations.

1. State banking and insurance commissions, as well as the Office of the Comptroller of the Currency (an agency of the federal government), have created very tight regulations as to who is allowed to set up a financial intermediary. Individuals or groups that want to establish a financial intermediary, such as a bank or an insurance company, must obtain a charter from the state or the federal government. Only if they are upstanding citizens with impeccable credentials and a large amount of initial funds will they be given a charter.

2. There are stringent reporting requirements for financial intermediaries. Their bookkeeping must follow certain strict principles, their books are subject to periodic inspections, and they must make certain information available to the public.

3. There are restrictions on what financial intermediaries are allowed to do and what assets they can hold. Before you put your funds into a bank or some other such institution, you would want to know that your funds are safe and that the bank or other financial intermediary will be able to meet its obligations to you. One way of doing this is to restrict the financial intermediary from engaging in certain risky activities. Legislation passed in 1933 separates commercial banking from the securities industry so that banks do not engage in risky ventures associated with this industry. Another way is to restrict financial intermediaries from holding certain risky assets, or at least from holding a greater quantity of these risky assets than is prudent. Commercial banks and other depository institutions, for example, are effectively not allowed to hold any common stock because stock prices have substantial fluctuations. Insurance companies are allowed to hold common stock, but their holdings cannot exceed a certain fraction of their total assets.

4. The government can insure those providing funds to a financial intermediary from any financial loss if the financial intermediary should fail. The most important government agency that provides this type of insurance is the Federal Deposit Insurance Corporation (FDIC), which insures each depositor at a commercial bank or mutual savings bank up to losses of $100,000. All commercial and mutual savings banks, with a few minor exceptions, make contributions into the FDIC, which are used to pay off depositors in the case of a bank's failure. The FDIC was created in 1934 after the massive bank failures of 1930–1933 in which the savings of many depositors at commercial banks were wiped out. Similar government agencies exist for other depository institutions: The Savings Association Insurance Fund (part of the FDIC) provides deposit insurance for savings and loan associations and the National Credit Union Share Insurance Fund (NCUSIF) for credit unions.

5. Politicians have often declared that unbridled competition among financial intermediaries promotes failures that will harm the public. Although the evidence that competition does this is extremely weak, it has not stopped the state and federal governments from imposing many restrictive regulations. These regulations have taken two forms. First are the restrictions on the opening of additional locations (branches). Banks are often not allowed to open up branches in other states, and in some states banks are not allowed to open any additional locations.

6. In addition, competition has been inhibited by regulations that impose restrictions on interest rates that can be paid on deposits. After 1933, banks were prohibited from paying interest on checking accounts. In addition, until 1986 the Federal Reserve System had the power under **Regulation Q** to set maximum interest rates that banks could pay on savings deposits. These regulations were instituted because of the widespread belief that unrestricted interest rate competition helped encourage bank failures during the Great Depression. Later evidence does not seem to support this view.

Improving Control of Monetary Policy

Banks play a very important role in determining the supply of money: Much regulation of these financial intermediaries is intended to improve its control. One such rule is the requirement that all depository institutions keep a certain fraction of their deposits in accounts at the Federal Reserve System (the Fed), the central bank in the United States, which allows the Fed to exercise more precise control over the money supply. Deposit insurance regulation can also be rationalized along these lines: The FDIC gives depositors confidence in the banking system and eliminates widespread bank failures which can, in turn, cause large, uncontrollable fluctuations in the quantity of money.

Encouraging Home Ownership

The encouragement of home ownership is one of the most popular positions that any American politician can take. Home ownership is viewed as fostering a more politically involved electorate, more responsible citizens, and hence a more stable society. Home ownership is as much a part of the American consumer's dream as baseball and apple pie. The Congress has passed many laws that encourage home ownership. One such example is the deductibility of interest payments on mortgages in calculating federal income taxes. Another example is the creation by Congress of federal agencies whose purpose is to make mortgages more readily available to people who want to purchase homes.

Regulations have also been imposed on financial intermediaries to encourage home ownership. Until 1980, financial intermediaries such as savings and loan associations and mutual savings banks were restricted from making loans other than mortgages. It was felt that by forcing savings and loans and mutual savings banks to make mortgage loans, more mortgages would be made available and this would encourage the purchase of houses. As we will see in coming chapters, this view made less and less sense in the 1970s, and with the banking legislation in 1980, known as the Depository Institutions Deregulation and Monetary Control Act, savings and loans and mutual savings banks are now allowed to make many other kinds of loans. However, the quantity of these other loans is still restricted.

Regulations restricting interest payments on deposits, such as Regulation Q, have also been used to encourage home ownership by allowing mortgage-issuing institutions (such as savings and loans and mutual savings banks) to pay slightly higher interest rates on deposits than commercial banks. Since this would attract more funds into mortgage-issuing institutions, the view was that more mortgages would be made available. The financial innovations that occurred in the 1970s made this view less and less tenable because these regulations made it harder for mortgage-issuing institutions to acquire funds when interest rates on bonds and other debt instruments rose. As a result, the Depository Institutions Deregulation and Monetary Control Act of 1980 set in motion a gradual elimination of the Regulation Q interest rate ceilings.

Now, a larger segment of the public questions whether the mass of regulations described above achieves its intended goals. In later chapters we will discuss whether these regulations have been beneficial and we will see that market forces and legislation since 1980 have encouraged a more competitive financial system.

INTERNATIONALIZATION OF FINANCIAL MARKETS

The growing internationalization of financial markets has become an important trend. Before the 1980s, U.S. financial markets were much larger than financial markets outside the United States, but in recent years the dominance of U.S. markets has been disappearing. The extraordinary growth of foreign financial markets has been the result of large increases in the pool of savings in foreign countries such as Japan and of the deregulation of foreign financial markets, which has enabled them to expand their activities. American corporations and banks are now more likely to tap international capital markets to raise needed funds, while American investors often seek investment opportunities abroad. Similarly, foreign corporations and banks raise funds from Americans, while foreigners are becoming important investors in the United States. A look at international bond markets and world stock markets will give us a picture of how this globalization of financial markets is taking place.

The International Bond Market and Eurobonds

The more traditional instruments in the international bond market are known as **foreign bonds.** Foreign bonds are sold in a foreign country and are denominated in that country's currency. For example, if the Swedish automaker Volvo sells a bond in the United States, denominated in U.S. dollars, it is classified as a foreign bond. Foreign bonds have been an important instrument in the international capital market for centuries. In fact, a large percentage of U.S. railroads built in the nineteenth century were financed by sales of foreign bonds in Britain.

A more recent innovation in the international bond market is the **Eurobond,** a bond denominated in a currency other than that of the country in which it is sold—for example, a bond denominated in U.S. dollars sold in London. Currently, over 80% of the new issues in the international bond market are Eurobonds, and the market for these securities has grown very rapidly: at over a 40% annual rate since 1980. With new issues of Eurobonds in the neighborhood of $200 billion per year, the Eurobond market has passed the U.S. corporate bond market as a source of new funds.

World Stock Markets

Until quite recently, the U.S. stock market was by far the largest in the world; but foreign stock markets have been growing in importance. Now, the United States is not always number one: Starting in the mid 1980s, the value of stocks traded in Japan has at times exceeded the value of stocks traded in the United States. The increased interest in foreign stocks has prompted the development in the United States of mutual funds specializing in trading in foreign stock markets. American investors now not only pay attention to the Dow Jones Industrial Average, but also to stock price indices for foreign stock markets such as The Nikkei Average (Tokyo) and the Financial Times–Stock Exchange 100-share Index (London).

Following the Financial News

Foreign Stock Market Indexes

Foreign Stock Market indexes are published daily in the *Wall Street Journal* next to the "World Markets" column which reports developments in foreign stock markets.

Source: *Wall Street Journal* (Friday, March 1, 1991).

Stock Market Indexes

EXCHANGE	2/28/91 CLOSE	NET CHG	PCT CHG
Tokyo Nikkei Average	26409.22 +	314.97 +	1.21
Tokyo Topix Index	1960.32 +	24.95 +	1.29
London FT 30-share	1910.7 +	32.9 +	1.75
London 100-share	2380.9 +	32.9 +	1.40
London Gold Mines	137.7 +	3.3 +	2.46
Frankfurt DAX	1542.09 −	23.43 −	1.50
Zurich Credit Suisse	539.5 −	1.0 −	0.19
Paris CAC 40	1759.79 +	28.77 +	1.66
Milan Stock Index	1115 +	1.0 +	0.09
Amsterdam ANP-CBS General	182.5 +	2.1 +	1.16
Stockholm Affarsvarlden	1070.1 +	9.0 +	0.85
Brussels Stock Index	5613.78 +	79.99 +	1.41
Australia All Ordinaries	1405.6 +	15.4 +	1.11
Hong Kong Hang Seng	3552.14 +	39.35 +	1.12
Singapore Straits Times	1459.57 +	16.22 +	1.12
Johannesburg J'burg Gold	1067 +	38.0 +	3.69
Madrid General Index	264.13 +	0.05 +	0.02
Toronto 300 Composite	3462.37 +	17.31 +	0.50
Euro, Aust, Far East MSCI-p	898.0 +	11.1 +	1.25

p-Preliminary
na-Not available

The internationalization of financial markets is having profound effects on the United States. Foreigners, particularly the Japanese, are not only providing funds to corporations in the United States, but they are also helping to finance a significant fraction of the federal government's huge budget deficit. Without these foreign funds, the U.S. economy would have grown far less rapidly. The internationalization of financial markets is also leading the way to a more integrated world economy in which flows of goods and technology between countries are more commonplace. In later chapters we will examine many examples of how international factors play an important role in our economy.

SUMMARY

1. The basic function of financial markets is to channel funds from savers who have excess funds to spenders who have a shortage of funds. This improves the economic welfare of everyone in the society because it allows funds to move from those without productive investment opportunities to those who have such opportunities, thereby contributing to increased efficiency in the economy. In addition, it benefits consumers directly by allowing them to make purchases when they need them most.

2. Financial markets can be classified as debt and equity markets, primary and secondary markets, exchanges and over-the-counter markets, and money and capital markets.

3. Financial intermediaries are financial institutions with the distinguishing characteristic that they acquire funds by issuing liabilities and then, in turn, use the funds to acquire assets by purchasing securities or making loans. They allow small savers and borrowers to benefit from the existence of financial markets, thus increasing the benefits of these markets to the economy.

4. The principal financial intermediaries fall into three categories: (a) banks—commercial banks, savings and loan associations, mutual savings banks, credit unions, and money market mutual funds; (b) contractual savings institutions—life insurance companies, pension funds, and fire and casualty insurance companies; and (c) investment intermediaries—finance companies, mutual funds, and money market mutual funds.

5. The principal money market instruments (debt instruments with maturities of less than one year) are U.S. Treasury bills, negotiable bank certificates of deposit, commercial paper, bankers' acceptances, repurchase agreements, federal funds, and Eurodollars. The principal capital market instruments (debt and equity instruments with maturities greater than one year) are stocks, mortgages, corporate bonds, U.S. government securities, U.S. government agency securities, state and local government bonds, and consumer and bank commercial loans.

6. Political forces have encouraged the government to regulate financial markets and financial intermediaries for four reasons: (a) to provide information to investors, (b) to ensure a sound financial system, (c) to improve control of monetary policy, and (d) to encourage home ownership. Regulations include requiring disclosure of information to the public, restrictions on who can set up a financial intermediary, restrictions on what assets financial intermediaries can hold, the provision of deposit insurance, the requirement that depository institutions keep a certain fraction of their deposits in accounts at the Federal Reserve, and the setting of maximum interest rates that can be paid on checking accounts and savings deposits.

7. An important trend in recent years is the growing internationalization of financial markets. Eurobonds, which are denominated in a currency other than that of the country in which they are sold, are now the dominant security in the international bond market and have passed U.S. corporate bonds as a source of new funds.

KEY TERMS

securities	intermediate term	over-the-counter market	federal funds rate
liabilities	equities	money market	Eurodollars
bond	dividends	capital market	Regulation Q
maturity	primary market	financial intermediation	foreign bonds
short term	secondary market	default	Eurobond
long term	exchanges		

QUESTIONS AND PROBLEMS

* 1. Why is a share of IBM common stock an asset for its owner and a liability for IBM?

  2. If I can buy a car today for $5000 and it is worth $10,000 in extra income next year to me because it enables me to get a job as a traveling anvil salesperson, should I take out a loan from Larry the Loan Shark at a 90% interest rate if no one else will give me a loan? Will I be better or worse off as a result of taking out this loan? Can you make a case for legalizing loan sharking?

* 3. Some economists suspect that one of the reasons that economies in developing countries grow so slowly is that they do not have well-developed financial markets. Does this argument make sense?

  4. The U.S. economy borrowed heavily from the British in the nineteenth century to build a railroad system. What was the principal debt instrument used? Why did this make both countries better off?

* 5. Why might you be willing to make a loan to your neighbor by putting funds in a savings account earning a 5% interest rate at the bank and having the bank loan her the funds at a 10% interest rate, rather than loan her the funds yourself?

  6. Answer the following true, false, or uncertain: "In a world without information and transactions costs, financial intermediaries would not exist." Explain.

* 7. Why might an unregulated financial market not provide enough information to investors?

  8. Do firms issuing securities benefit from the existence of regulatory agencies, such as the SEC, even though complying with disclosure regulations is costly?

* 9. Are restrictions on the types of assets financial intermediaries can hold a good thing? Discuss the costs and benefits of these restrictions.

  10. Should there be more government regulation to encourage home ownership? Why or why not?

*11. Why are regulations that restrict competition considered to be undesirable? How would the economy suffer as a result?

  12. If you suspect that a company will go bankrupt next year, which would you rather hold: bonds issued by the company or equities issued by the company? Why?

*13. "Since corporations do not actually raise any funds in secondary markets, they are less important to the economy than are primary markets." Comment.

  14. In two lists, rank the following money market instruments in terms of their liquidity and their safety:
  a) U.S. Treasury bills
  b) negotiable CDs
  c) repurchase agreements
  d) commercial paper

*15. Discuss some of the manifestations of the globalization of world capital markets.

PART II

Fundamentals of Interest Rates

CHAPTER 4

Understanding Interest Rates

PREVIEW   Interest rates are among the most closely watched variables in the economy. Their movements are reported almost daily by the news media because they directly affect our everyday lives and have important consequences for the health of the economy. They affect such personal decisions as whether to consume or save, whether to buy a house, and whether to purchase bonds or put funds into a savings account. Interest rates also affect the economic decisions of businesses or households, such as whether to use their funds to invest in new equipment for factories or to save their money in a bank.

Before we can go on with the study of money, banking, and financial markets, we must understand exactly what the phrase *interest rates* means. We will see that a concept called the "yield to maturity" is the most accurate measure of interest rates; the yield to maturity is what economists mean when they use the term *interest rates*. We will discuss how the yield to maturity is measured on many of the credit market instruments mentioned in the previous chapter and will examine alternative (but less accurate) ways in which interest rates are quoted. We will also see that a bond's interest rate will not necessarily indicate how good an investment the bond is because what it earns (its rate of return) can differ from its interest rate. Finally, we will explore the distinction between real interest rates, which are adjusted for changes in the price level, and nominal interest rates, which are not.

Although learning definitions is not always the most exciting of pursuits, it is important to read carefully and understand the concepts presented in this chapter. Not only are they continually used throughout the remainder of this text, but a clear grasp of these terms will help you better understand the role that interest rates play in your life as well as in the general economy.

MEASURING INTEREST RATES

In Chapter 3 you were introduced to a number of credit market instruments, which fall into four types:

1. Simple loan. A **simple loan** provides the borrower with an amount of funds (principal) which at the maturity date must be repaid to the lender along with an additional amount known as an interest payment. If, for example, a bank made you a simple loan of $100 for one year, you would have to repay the principal of $100 in one year's time along with an additional interest payment of, let's say, $10. Commercial loans to businesses are often of this type.

2. Fixed payment loan. A **fixed payment loan** provides a borrower with an amount of funds that he is to repay by making the same payment every month, consisting of part of the principal and interest for a set number of years. For example, if you borrowed $1000, a fixed payment loan might require you to pay $126 every year for twenty-five years. Installment loans (auto loans, for example) and mortgages are frequently of the fixed payment type.

3. Coupon bond. A **coupon bond** pays the owner of the bond a fixed interest payment (coupon payment) every year until the maturity date, when a specified final amount **(face or par value)** is repaid. The coupon payment is so named because the bond holder often receives the coupon payment by clipping a coupon off the bond and sending it to the bond issuer, who then sends the payment to the holder. For example, a coupon bond with $1000 face value might pay you a coupon payment of $100 per year for ten years and at the maturity date repay you the face value amount of $1000. (The face or par value of a bond is usually in $1000 increments.)

A coupon bond is identifiable in three ways. First is the corporation or governmental agency that issues the bond. Second is the maturity date of the bond. Third is the bond's **coupon rate,** the dollar amount of the yearly coupon payment expressed as a percentage of the face value of the bond. In our example, the coupon bond has a yearly coupon payment of $100 and a face value of $1000. The coupon rate is then $100/$1000 = .10, or 10%. Treasury bonds and notes and corporate bonds are examples of coupon bonds.

4. Discount bond. A **discount bond** is bought at a price below its face value (at a discount), and the face value is repaid at the maturity date. Unlike a coupon bond, a discount bond does not make any interest payments; it just pays off the face value. For example, a discount bond with a face value of $1000 might be bought for $900 and in a year's time the owner would be repaid the face value of $1000. U.S. Treasury bills, U.S. savings bonds, and so-called zero-coupon bonds are examples of discount bonds.

These four types of instruments require payments at different times: Simple loans and discount bonds make payment only at their maturity dates, while fixed payment loans and coupon bonds have payments periodically until maturity. How would you decide which of these instruments provides you with more income? After all, they all seem so different because they make payments at different times. To solve this problem, the concept of present value was invented to provide us with a procedure for measuring interest rates on these different types of instruments. We turn to it now.

Concept of Present Value

The concept of **present value** is based on the common-sense notion that a dollar paid to you one year from now is less valuable to you than a dollar today, because you can deposit the dollar in a savings account and have more than a dollar in one year. We will now define this concept more formally.

In the case of a simple loan, the interest payment divided by the amount of the loan is a natural and sensible way to measure the cost of borrowing funds: The measure of the cost is the "simple interest rate." In the example we used to describe the simple loan, a loan of $100 today requires the borrower to repay the $100 a year from now and to make an additional interest payment of $10. Hence, using the definition above, the simple interest rate (i) is

[handwritten: interest rate $= \dfrac{\text{interest payment}}{\text{principle}}$]

$$i = \frac{\$10}{\$100} = .10 = 10\%$$

If you make this $100 loan, at the end of the year you would receive $110, which can be rewritten as

[handwritten: principle + principle × interest rate] $\$100 \times (1 + .10) = \$110$

If you then loaned out the $110, at the end of two years you would receive

$$\$110 \times (1 + .10) = \$121$$

or equivalently,

$$\$100 \times (1 + .10) \times (1 + .10) = \$100 \times (1 + .10)^2 = \$121$$

Continuing with the loan again, you would receive at the end of three years

$$\$121 \times (1 + .10) = \$100 \times (1 + .10)^3 = \$133.10$$

These calculations of the proceeds from a simple loan can be generalized as follows: If the simple interest rate i is expressed as a decimal fraction (such as .10 for the 10% interest rate in our example), then after making these loans for n years, you will receive a total payment of

$$\$100 \times (1 + i)^n$$

We can also work these calculations backwards. Since $100 today will turn into $110 next year when the simple interest rate is 10%, we could say that the $110 next year is worth only $100 today. Or we could say that no one would pay more than $100 to get $110 next year. Similarly, we could say that $121 two years from now or $133.10 three years from now is worth only $100 today. This process of calculating what dollars received in the future are worth today is called discounting the future. We have been implicitly solving the forward-looking equations above for today's value of a future dollar amount. For example, in the case of the $133.10 received three years from now, when $i = .10$,

$$\$100 \times (1 + i)^3 = \$133.10$$
$$\text{(current)} \qquad \text{(future)}$$

so that

$$\$100 = \frac{\$133.10}{(1 + i)^3}$$

More generally, we can solve this equation to tell us the present value or **present discounted value (PV)** of the future $1, that is, today's value of a $1 payment received n years from now when the simple interest rate is i:

$$\text{PV of future } \$1 = \frac{\$1}{(1 + i)^n} \tag{4.1}$$

Intuitively, what Equation (4.1) tells us is that if you are promised $1 for certain ten years from now, this dollar would not be as valuable to you as $1 is today because you can earn interest on the dollar.

The concept of present value is extremely useful (see Box 4.1) because it allows us to figure out today's value of a credit market instrument at a given simple interest rate (i) by just adding up the present value of all the future payments received. This allows us to compare the value of two instruments with very different timing of their payments, such as a discount bond and a coupon bond. As we will see, this concept also allows us to obtain an equivalent measure of the interest rate on all four types of credit market instruments discussed here.

B o x   4 . 1

Is the Cost of the S&L Bailout Really Over $500 Billion? An Application of the Present Value Concept

The government bailout of the savings and loan industry was one of the major news stories of the past decade. Statements frequently appeared in the press that the cost of the bailout to taxpayers would exceed $500 billion, more than $2,000 for every man, woman, and child in the United States. The over $500 billion figure makes for wonderful political rhetoric, but is the cost really this high?

The answer is "no," and the concept of present value tells us why. The $500 billion figure includes bond payments over the *next forty years*. The pres-

ent value concept tells us that to figure out the cost of these payments in today's dollars we have to discount them back to the present. When we do this, the present value of these payments is on the order of $150 billion, not $500 billion. It is still true that a present value of the bailout of $150 billion is nothing to sneeze at, but it is not quite as scary as a figure more than three times this size. (Chapter 11 contains an extensive discussion of the S&L crisis and bailout.)

Yield to Maturity

Although there are several common ways of calculating interest rates, the most important is the **yield to maturity,** the interest rate that equates the present value of payments received from a debt instrument with its value today. Because the concept behind the calculation of the yield to maturity makes good economic sense, economists consider it to be the most accurate measure of interest rates. We now calculate the yield to maturity for the four types of credit market instruments.

Simple Loan   Using the concept of present value, the yield to maturity on a simple loan is easy to calculate. For the one-year loan we discussed, today's value is $100 and the payments in one year's time would be $110 (the repayment of $100 plus the interest payment of $10). We can use this information to solve for the yield to maturity (i) by recognizing that the present value of the future payments must equal today's value of a loan. Making today's value of the loan ($100) equal to the present value of the $110 payment in a year [using Equation (4.1)] gives us

$$\$100 = \frac{\$110}{1 + i}$$

Solving for i,

$$i = \frac{\$110 - \$100}{\$100} = \frac{\$10}{\$100} = .10 = 10\%$$

This calculation of the yield to maturity should look familiar because it equals the interest payment of $10 divided by the loan amount of $100; that is, it equals the simple interest rate on the loan. An important point to recognize is that *for simple loans, the simple interest rate equals the yield to maturity.* Thus the same term (i) is used to denote both the yield to maturity and the simple interest rate.

Study Guide

The key to understanding the calculation of the yield to maturity is the equating of today's value of the debt instrument with the present value of all of its future payments. The best way to learn this principle is to apply it to other specific examples of the four types of credit market instruments in addition to those which we will discuss here. See if you can develop the equations that would allow you to solve for the yield to maturity in each case.

Fixed Payment Loan   As you recall, this type of loan has the same payment every year throughout the life of the loan. On a fixed-rate mortgage, for example, the borrower makes the same payment to the bank every month until the maturity date, when the loan will be completely paid off. To calculate the yield to maturity for a fixed payment loan, we follow the same strategy we used for the simple loan—we equate today's value of the loan with its present value. Because the fixed payment loan involves more than one payment, the present value of the fixed payment loan is calculated as the sum of the present values of all payments [using Equation (4.1)].

In the case of our earlier example, the loan is $1000 and the yearly payment is $126 for the next twenty-five years. The present value (PV) is calculated as follows. At the end of one year there is a $126 payment with a PV of $\$126/(1 + i)$; at the end of two years there is another $126 payment with a PV of $\$126/(1 + i)^2$; and so on until at the end of the twenty-fifth year the last payment of $126 with a PV of $\$126/(1 + i)^{25}$ is made. Making today's value of the loan ($1000) equal to the sum of the present values of all the yearly payments gives us

$$\$1000 = \frac{\$126}{1 + i} + \frac{\$126}{(1 + i)^2} + \frac{\$126}{(1 + i)^3} + \cdots + \frac{\$126}{(1 + i)^{25}}$$

More generally, for any fixed payment loan,

$$LOAN = \frac{FP}{1 + i} + \frac{FP}{(1 + i)^2} + \frac{FP}{(1 + i)^3} + \cdots + \frac{FP}{(1 + i)^N} \qquad (4.2)$$

where $LOAN$ = amount of the loan
$\quad FP$ = fixed yearly payment
$\quad N$ = number of years until maturity

For a fixed payment loan amount, the fixed yearly payment and the number of years until maturity are known quantities, and only the yield to maturity is not. So we can solve this equation for the yield to maturity, i. Because this calculation is not easy, tables have been created that allow you to find i given the loan's values for $LOAN$, FP, and N. For example, in the case of the twenty-five-year loan with yearly payments of $126, the yield to maturity taken from the table that solves the above equation is 12%. Real estate brokers always have such a table handy (or a pocket calculator that can solve such an equation) so that they can immediately tell the prospective house buyer exactly what his yearly payments will be if he finances the house purchase by taking out a mortgage (Figure 4.1).[1]

Coupon Bond To calculate the yield to maturity for a coupon bond, follow the same strategy used for the fixed payment loan: Equate today's value of the bond with its present value. Because coupon bonds also have more than one payment, the present value of the bond is calculated as the sum of the

---

[1] The calculation with a pocket calculator programmed for this purpose just requires you to enter the amount of the loan (*LOAN*), the number of years to maturity (*N*), and the interest rate (*i*) and then to run the program.

12%		**Monthly Payment Necessary to Amortize a Loan**					
Term	19	20	21	22	23	24	25
Amount	Years	Years	Years	Years	Years	Years	Years
$ 25	.28	.28	.28	.27	.27	.27	.27
50	.56	.56	.55	.54	.54	.54	.53
75	.84	.83	.82	.81	.81	.80	.79
100	1.12	1.11	1.09	1.08	1.07	1.07	1.06
200	2.24	2.21	2.18	2.16	2.14	2.13	2.11
300	3.35	3.31	3.27	3.24	3.21	3.19	3.16
400	4.47	4.41	4.36	4.32	4.28	4.25	4.22
500	5.58	5.51	5.45	5.39	5.35	5.31	5.27
600	6.70	6.61	6.54	6.47	6.42	6.37	6.32
700	7.81	7.71	7.63	7.55	7.48	7.43	7.38
800	8.93	8.81	8.71	8.63	8.55	8.49	8.43
900	10.04	9.91	9.80	9.71	9.62	9.55	9.48
1000	11.16	11.02	10.89	10.78	10.69	10.61	10.54
2000	22.31	22.03	21.78	21.56	21.38	21.21	21.07
3000	33.47	33.04	32.67	32.34	32.06	31.82	31.60
4000	44.62	44.05	43.55	43.12	42.75	42.42	42.13
5000	55.77	55.06	54.44	53.90	53.43	53.02	52.67

Figure 4.1
A Mortgage Payments Table For a $1000, twenty-five-year, fixed payment loan with a 12% interest rate, the table indicates that the monthly payment is $10.54 ($126 per year).

present values of all the coupon payments plus the present value of the final payment of the face value of the bond.

The present value of a $1000 face value bond with ten years to maturity and yearly coupon payments of $100 (a 10% coupon rate) can be calculated as follows. At the end of one year there is a $100 coupon payment with a *PV* of $100/(1 + i); at the end of the second year there is another $100 coupon payment with a *PV* of $100/(1 + i)^2; and so on until at maturity there is a $100 coupon payment with a *PV* of $100/(1 + i)^{10} plus the repayment of the $1000 face value with a *PV* of $1000/(1 + i)^{10}. Setting today's value of the bond (its current price, denoted by P_B) equal to the sum of the *PV*'s of all the payments for this bond gives us

$$P_B = \frac{\$100}{1 + i} + \frac{\$100}{(1 + i)^2} + \frac{\$100}{(1 + i)^3} + \cdots + \frac{\$100}{(1 + i)^{10}} + \frac{\$1000}{(1 + i)^{10}}$$

More generally, for any coupon bond,[2]

$$P_B = \frac{C}{1 + i} + \frac{C}{(1 + i)^2} + \frac{C}{(1 + i)^3} + \cdots + \frac{C}{(1 + i)^N} + \frac{F}{(1 + i)^N} \quad (4.3)$$

---

[2]Most coupon bonds actually make coupon payments on a semiannual basis rather than once a year as assumed here. The effect on the calculations is only very slight and will be ignored here.

10.00%				**Bond Values Per $100 of Face Value**						
				Years to Maturity						
Yield	1 yr	2 yr	3 yr	4 yr	5 yr	6 yr	7 yr	8 yr	9 yr	10 yr
10.00	100.00	100.00	100.00	100.00	100.00	100.00	100.00	100.00	100.00	100.00
10.25	99.77	99.56	99.37	99.20	99.04	98.90	98.77	98.66	98.55	98.46
10.50	99.54	99.12	98.74	98.40	98.09	97.82	97.56	97.34	97.13	96.95
10.75	99.31	98.68	98.12	97.61	97.16	96.75	96.38	96.04	95.74	95.47
11.00	99.08	98.25	97.50	96.83	96.23	95.69	95.21	94.77	94.38	94.02
11.25	98.85	97.82	96.89	96.06	95.32	94.65	94.05	93.52	93.04	92.61
11.50	98.62	97.39	96.28	95.30	94.41	93.63	92.92	92.29	91.72	91.22
11.75	98.39	96.96	95.68	94.54	93.52	92.61	91.80	91.08	90.44	89.86
12.00	98.17	96.53	95.08	93.79	92.64	91.62	90.71	89.89	89.17	88.53
12.25	97.94	96.11	94.49	93.05	91.77	90.63	89.62	88.73	87.93	87.23
12.50	97.72	95.69	93.90	92.31	90.91	89.66	88.56	87.58	86.72	85.95
12.75	97.49	95.28	93.32	91.59	90.06	88.71	87.51	86.46	85.52	84.70

Figure 4.2
A Bond Table For a ten-year, 10.00% coupon rate bond, the table indicates that a yield to maturity of 11.75% corresponds to a price of $89.86 per $100 of face value (i.e., a $1000 face value bond sells for approximately $900).

where C = yearly coupon payment
F = face or par value of the bond
N = years to maturity date
P_B = price of coupon bond

In Equation (4.3), the coupon payment, the face value, the years to maturity, and the price of the bond are known quantities, and only the yield to maturity is not. Thus we can solve this equation for the yield to maturity, i.[3] Just as in the case of the fixed payment loan, this calculation is not easy, so that bond tables (Figure 4.2) have been created which allow you to read off the yield to maturity for a bond given its coupon rate, its years to maturity, and its price. Some business-oriented pocket calculators have built-in programs that solve this equation for you.[4]

Let's look at several examples of the solution for the yield to maturity on our 10% coupon rate bond which matures in ten years. If the purchase price of the bond is $1000, then, either using a pocket calculator with the built-in program or by looking at a bond table, we will find that the yield to maturity is 10%. If the price is $900, then we find that the yield to maturity is 11.75%. Table 4.1 shows the yields to maturity calculated for several different bond prices.

---

[3]In other contexts, it is also called the internal rate of return.

[4]The calculation of a bond's yields to maturity with the programmed pocket calculator just requires you to enter the amount of the yearly coupon payment (C), the face value (F), the number of years to maturity (N), and the price of the bond (P_B) and then to run the program.

Table 4.1   **Yields to Maturity on a 10% Coupon Rate Bond Maturing in Ten Years (face value = $1000)**

Price of Bond	Yield to Maturity
$1200	7.13%
$1100	8.48%
$1000	10.00%
$ 900	11.75%
$ 800	13.81%

Three interesting facts are illustrated by Table 4.1:

1. When the coupon bond is priced at its face or par value, the yield to maturity equals the coupon rate.
2. The price of a coupon bond and the yield to maturity are negatively related; that is, as the yield to maturity rises, the price of the bond falls. If the yield to maturity falls, the price of the bond rises.
3. The yield to maturity is greater than the coupon rate when the bond price is below the par value.

These three facts are true for any coupon bond and are really not that surprising if you think about the reasoning behind the calculation of the yield to maturity. When you put $1000 in a bank account with an interest rate of 10%, you can take out $100 every year and you will be left with the $1000 at the end of ten years. This is similar to buying the $1000 bond with a 10% coupon rate analyzed in Table 4.1, which pays a $100 coupon payment every year and then repays $1000 at the end of ten years. If the bond is purchased at the par value of $1000, its yield to maturity must equal the interest rate of 10%, which is also equal to the coupon rate of 10%. The same reasoning applied to any coupon bond demonstrates that, if the coupon bond is purchased at its par value, the yield to maturity and the coupon rate must be equal.

It is straightforward to show that the bond price and the yield to maturity are negatively related. As i, the yield to maturity, rises, all denominators in the bond-price formula must necessarily rise. Thus a rise in the interest rate as measured by the yield to maturity means that the price of the bond must fall. Another way to explain why the bond price falls when the interest rises is that a higher interest rate implies that the future coupon payments and final payment are worth less when discounted back to the present; hence the price of the bond must be lower.

There is one special case of a coupon bond that is worth discussing because its yield to maturity is particularly easy to calculate. This bond is called a **consol;** it is a perpetual bond with no maturity date and no repayment of principal that makes fixed coupon payments of $C forever. Consols were first sold by the British Treasury during the Napoleonic Wars and still are traded today; however, they are quite rare in American capital markets. The formula in Equation (4.3) for the price of the consol (P_c) simplifies to the following:[5]

$$P_c = \frac{C}{i} \qquad (4.4)$$

One nice feature of consols is that you can immediately see that as i goes up, the price of the bond falls. For example, if a consol pays $100 per year forever and the interest rate is 10%, its price will be $1000 = $100/.10. If the interest rate rises to 20%, then its price will fall to $500 = $100/.20. We can also rewrite this formula as

$$i = \frac{C}{P_c} \qquad (4.5)$$

We see then that it is also easy to calculate the yield to maturity for the consol (despite the fact that it never matures). For example, with a consol that pays $100 yearly and a price of $2000, the yield to maturity is easily calculated to be 5% (= $100/$2000).

Discount Bond   The yield to maturity calculation for a discount bond is similar to that for the simple loan. Let us consider a discount bond such as a one-year U.S. Treasury bill, which pays off a face value of $1000 in one year's

---

[5]The bond-price formula for a consol is

$$P_c = \frac{C}{1 + i} + \frac{C}{(1 + i)^2} + \frac{C}{(1 + i)^3} + \cdots$$

which can be written as

$$P_c = C(x + x^2 + x^3 + \cdots)$$

in which

$$x = \frac{1}{1 + i}$$

From your high school algebra you might remember the formula for an infinite sum:

$$1 + x + x^2 + x^3 + \cdots = \frac{1}{1 - x} \quad \text{for } x < 1$$

and so,

$$P_c = C\left(\frac{1}{1 - x} - 1\right) = C\left(\frac{1}{1 - \dfrac{1}{1 + i}} - 1\right)$$

which by suitable algebraic manipulation becomes

$$P_c = C\left(\frac{1 + i}{i} - \frac{i}{i}\right) = \frac{C}{i}$$

time. If the current purchase price of this bill is $900, then equating this price to the present value of the $1000 received in one year, using Equation (4.1), gives us

$$\$900 = \frac{\$1000}{1 + i}$$

and solving for i,

$$i = \frac{\$1000 - \$900}{\$900} = .111 = 11.1\%$$

More generally, for any one-year discount bond, the yield to maturity can be written as

$$i = \frac{F - P_d}{P_d} \tag{4.6}$$

where F = the face or par value of the discount bond
$\quad P_d$ = the current price of the discount bond

In other words, the yield to maturity equals the increase in price over the year ($F - P_d$) divided by the initial price (P_d).

An important feature of this equation is that it indicates that for a discount bond, the yield to maturity is negatively related to the current bond price. This is the same conclusion that we reached for a coupon bond. For example, Equation (4.6) above shows that a rise in the bond price from $900 to $950 means that the bond will have a smaller increase in its price over its lifetime, so that the yield to maturity falls from 11.1 to 5.3%. Similarly, a fall in the yield to maturity means that the price of the discount bond has risen.

Summary The concept of present value tells you that a dollar in the future is not as valuable to you as a dollar today because you can earn interest on this dollar: Specifically a dollar received n years from now is only worth $\$1/(1 + i)^n$ today. The present value of a set of future payments on a debt instrument equals the sum of the present values of each of the future payments. The yield to maturity for an instrument is the interest rate that equates the present value of the future payments on that instrument to its value today. Because the procedure for calculating the yield to maturity is based on sound economic principles, this is the measure that economists think most accurately describes the interest rate.

Our calculations of the yield to maturity for a variety of bonds reveal the important fact that **current bond prices and interest rates are negatively related: When the interest rate rises, the price of the bond falls and vice versa.**

OTHER MEASURES OF INTEREST RATES

The yield to maturity is the most accurate measure of interest rates and is what economists mean when they use the term *interest rates*. Unless otherwise specified, the terms *interest rate* and *yield to maturity* will be used synonymously in this book. However, because the yield to maturity is sometimes difficult to calculate, other, less accurate, measures of interest rates have come into common use in bond markets. You will frequently encounter two of these measures, the "current yield" and the "yield on a discount basis," when reading the newspaper, and it is important for you to understand what they mean and how they differ from the more accurate measure of interest rates, the yield to maturity.

Current Yield

The **current yield** is an approximation for the yield to maturity on coupon bonds that is often reported because in contrast to the yield to maturity, it is easily calculated. It is defined as the yearly coupon payment divided by the price of the security,

$$i_c = \frac{C}{P_B} \tag{4.7}$$

where i_c = the current yield
P_B = the price of the coupon bond
C = the yearly coupon payment

This formula is identical to the formula in Equation (4.5), which describes the calculation of the yield to maturity for a consol. Hence, for a consol, the current yield is an exact measure of the yield to maturity. When a coupon bond has a long time (or term) to maturity (say, twenty years or more), it is very much like a consol, which pays coupon payments forever. Thus you would expect the current yield to be a rather close approximation of the yield to maturity for a long-term coupon bond, and you can safely use the current yield calculation instead of looking up the yield to maturity in a bond table. However, as the time to maturity of the coupon bond shortens (say, it becomes less than five years), it behaves less and less like a consol and so the approximation afforded by the current yield becomes worse and worse.

We have also seen that when the bond price equals the par value of the bond, the yield to maturity is equal to the coupon rate (the coupon payment divided by the par value of the bond). Because the current yield equals the coupon payment divided by the bond price, the current yield is also equal to the coupon rate when the bond price is at par. This logic leads us to the conclusion that, when the bond price is at par, the current yield equals the yield to maturity. This means that the nearer the bond price is to the bond's par value, the better will the current yield approximate the yield to maturity.

The current yield is negatively related to the price of the bond. In the case of our 10% coupon rate bond, when the price rises from $1000 to $1100, the current yield falls from 10% (= $100/$1000) to 9.09% (= $100/$1100). As Table 4.1 indicates, the yield to maturity is also negatively related to the price of the bond; when the price rises from $1000 to $1100, the yield to maturity falls from 10 to 8.48%. In this we see an important fact: The current yield and the yield to maturity always move together; a rise in the current yield always signals that the yield to maturity has also risen.

The general characteristics of the current yield (the yearly coupon payment divided by the bond price) can be summarized as follows: The current yield is a better approximation for the yield to maturity, the nearer the bond's price is to the bond's par value and the longer the maturity of the bond. It becomes a worse approximation, the further the bond's price is from the bond's par value and the shorter the bond's maturity. Regardless of whether or not the current yield is a good approximation of the yield to maturity, a change in the current yield *always* signals a change in the same direction of the yield to maturity.

Yield on a Discount Basis

Before the advent of calculators and computers, dealers in U.S. Treasury bills found it difficult to calculate interest rates as a yield to maturity. Instead, they quoted the interest rate on bills as a **yield on a discount basis or discount yield** and they still do so today. Formally, the yield on a discount basis is defined by the following formula:

$$i_{db} = \frac{(F - P_d)}{F} \times \frac{360}{\text{(number of days to maturity)}} \tag{4.8}$$

where i_{db} = yield on a discount basis
F = face value of the discount bond
P_d = purchase price of the discount bond

There are two peculiarities of this method for calculating interest rates. First, it uses the percentage gain on the face value of the bill, $(F - P_d)/F$, rather than the percentage gain on the purchase price of the bill, $(F - P_d)/P_d$, used in calculating the yield to maturity. Second, it puts the yield on an annual basis by taking the year to be 360 days long rather than 365 days.

Because of these peculiarities, the discount yield understates the interest rate on bills as measured by the yield to maturity. On our one-year bill, which is selling for $900 and has a face value of $1000, the yield on a discount basis would be

$$i_{db} = \frac{\$1000 - \$900}{\$1000} \times \frac{360}{365} = .099 = 9.9\%$$

while the yield to maturity for this bill, which we calculated before, is 11.1%. The discount yield understates the yield to maturity by a factor of over 10%. A little over 1% of the understatement is because the length of the year is understated by a factor of a little greater than 1%; when the bill has one year to maturity, the second term on the right-hand side of the formula is .986 rather than 1.0, as it should be.

The more serious source of the understatement, however, is the use of the percentage gain on the face value rather than on the purchase price. Since, by definition, the purchase price of a discount bond is always less than the face value, the percentage gain on the face value is necessarily smaller than the percentage gain on the purchase price. The greater the difference between the purchase price and the face value of the discount bond, the greater the discount yield's understatement of the yield to maturity. Since the difference between the purchase price and the face value gets larger the longer the maturity, we can draw the following conclusion about the relation of the yield on a discount basis to the yield to maturity: The yield on a discount basis always understates the yield to maturity, and this understatement becomes more severe, the longer the maturity of the discount bond.

Another important feature of the discount yield is that, like the yield to maturity, it is negatively related to the price of the bond. For example, when the price of the bond rises from $900 to $950, the formula indicates that the yield on a discount basis declines from 9.9 to 4.9%. At the same time, the yield to maturity declines from 11.1 to 5.3%. Here we see another important factor about the relationship of yield on a discount basis to yield to maturity: They always move together; that is, a rise in the discount yield always means that the yield to maturity has risen, and a decline in the discount yield means that the yield to maturity has declined as well.

The characteristics of the yield on a discount basis can be summarized as follows: Yield on a discount basis understates the more accurate measure of the interest rate, the yield to maturity; and the longer the maturity of the discount bond, the greater this understatement becomes. However, even though the discount yield is a somewhat misleading measure of the interest rates, a change in the discount yield always indicates a change in the same direction for the yield to maturity.

APPLICATION
READING THE BOND PAGE OF THE NEWSPAPER

Now that we understand the different interest rate definitions, let's apply our knowledge and take a look at what kind of information appears on the bond page of a typical newspaper. Bond prices and yields are quoted in three different ways in the newspaper. The "Following the Financial News" box contains the *Wall Street Journal*'s listing for three different types of bonds on Friday, March 1, 1991. Panel (a) contains the information on U.S. Treasury bonds and notes. Both are coupon bonds, with the only difference being their time to maturity from when they were originally issued: Notes have a time to maturity of less than ten years, while bonds have a time to maturity of more than ten years.

The pieces of information found in the "Rate" and "Maturity" columns identify the bond by giving the coupon rate and the maturity date. For example, T-bond #1 has a coupon rate of 6½% indicating that it pays out $65 per year on a $1000 face value bond, and a maturity date of November 1991. Notice that T-bond #3 has two dates under the "Mat. Date" column. These dates indicate that the bond is callable: that is, the Treasury has the option of redeeming the bond and paying off the face value before the maturity date. T-bond #3 matures in November 2014, but between November of 2009 and the maturity date, the Treasury can call the bond and pay it off early at the face value of $1000.

The next three pieces of information tell us about the bond's price. By convention, all prices in the bond market are quoted per $100 of face value. Furthermore, the numbers after the colon point represent 32nds. In the case of T-bond #1, the first price of 99:31 represents 99 and $^{31}/_{32}$ = 99.969, or an actual price of $999.69 for a $1000 face value bond. The bid price tells you what price you will receive if you sell the bond, while the asked price tells you what you must pay for the bond. (You might want to think of the bid price as the "wholesale" price and the asked price as the "retail" price.) The "Chg." column indicates how much the bid price has changed from the previous trading day.

Notice that for all the bonds and notes the asked price is more than the bid price. Can you guess why this happens? The difference between the two (the "spread") provides the bond dealer who trades these securities with a profit. For T-bond #1, when the dealer buys it at $99^{31}/_{32}$ and sells it for $100^{1}/_{32}$, he makes a profit of $^{2}/_{32}$. This profit is what enables the dealer to make a living and provide the service of allowing you to buy and sell bonds at will.

The "Ask Yld." column provides the yield to maturity, which is 6.45% for T-bond #1. It is calculated with the method described earlier in this chapter using the asked price as the price of the bond. The asked price is used in the calculation because the yield to maturity is most relevant to a person who is going to buy and hold the security, and thus earn the yield. The person selling the security, on the other hand, is not going to be holding it and is thus less concerned with the yield.

The figure for the current yield is not usually included in the newspaper's quotations for the Treasury securities, but it is included in panel (a) to give you some real-world examples of how well the current yield approximates the yield to maturity. Our previous discussion provided us with some

Following the Financial News

Bond Prices and Interest Rates

Bond prices and interest rates are published daily. In the *Wall Street Journal* they can be found in the NYSE/AMEX Bonds, Treasury Issues, and Govt/Agency Issues section of the paper. Three basic formats for quoting bond prices and yields are illustrated below in a section from the *Wall Street Journal*.

Thursday, February 28, 1991

Representative Over-the-Counter quotations based on transactions of $1 million or more.

Treasury bond, note and bill quotes are as of mid-afternoon. Colons in bid-and-asked quotes represent 32nds; 101:01 means 101 1/32. Net changes in 32nds. n-Treasury note. Treasury bill quotes in hundredths, quoted on terms of a rate of discount. Days to maturity calculated from settlement date. All yields are to maturity and based on the asked quote. For bonds callable prior to maturity, yields are computed to the earliest call date for issues quoted above par and to the maturity date for issues below par. *-When issued.

Source: Federal Reserve Bank of New York.

(a) Treasury Bonds and Notes

GOVT. BONDS & NOTES

Rate	Maturity	Bid	Asked	Chg.	Ask Yld.	
T-bond #1 ▶ 6½	Nov 91n	99:31	100:01	− 1	6.45	◀ Current Yield = 6.49%
8½	Nov 91n	101:11	101:13	....	6.42	
T-bond #2 ▶ 14¼	Nov 91n	105:10	105:14	− 1	6.20	◀ Current Yield = 13.52%
T-bond #3 ▶ 11¾	Nov 09-14	131:09	131:13	− 13	8.39	◀ Current Yield = 8.94%
11¼	Feb 15	129:29	130:01	− 15	8.33	
10⅝	Aug 15	123:20	123:24	− 15	8.33	
9⅞	Nov 15	115:30	116:02	− 16	8.33	
9¼	Feb 16	109:18	109:22	− 14	8.32	
T-bond #4 ▶ 7¼	May 16	88:31	89:03	− 13	8.29	◀ Current Yield = 8.14%

(b) Treasury Bills

TREASURY BILLS

Maturity	Days to Mat.	Bid	Asked	Chg.	Ask Yld.	Maturity	Days to Mat.	Bid	Asked	Chg.	Ask Yld.
Apr 04 '91	31	5.63	5.61	− 0.05	5.72	Jul 11 '91	129	6.05	6.03	+ 0.01	6.25
Apr 11 '91	38	5.67	5.65	+ 0.01	5.76	Jul 18 '91	136	6.05	6.03	+ 0.01	6.26
Apr 18 '91	45	5.72	5.70	+ 0.02	5.82	Jul 25 '91	143	6.05	6.03	+ 0.01	6.26
Apr 25 '91	52	6.03	6.01	− 0.01	6.15	Aug 01 '91	150	6.05	6.03	+ 0.02	6.27
May 02 '91	59	6.04	6.02	+ 0.01	6.16	Aug 08 '91	157	6.05	6.03	+ 0.02	6.28
May 09 '91	66	6.04	6.02	+ 0.01	6.17	Aug 15 '91	164	6.05	6.03	+ 0.02	6.29
May 16 '91	73	6.04	6.02	....	6.18	Aug 22 '91	171	6.03	6.01	+ 0.02	6.27
May 23 '91	80	6.04	6.02	....	6.19	Aug 29 '91	178	6.04	6.02	+ 0.03	6.29
May 30 '91	87	6.04	6.02	+ 0.01	6.19	Sep 26 '91	206	5.98	5.96	+ 0.02	6.23
Jun 06 '91	94	6.06	6.04	+ 0.03	6.22	Oct 24 '91	234	6.06	6.04	+ 0.04	6.33
Jun 13 '91	101	6.05	6.03	+ 0.02	6.22	Nov 21 '91	262	6.06	6.04	+ 0.04	6.34
Jun 20 '91	108	6.05	6.03	+ 0.04	6.23	Dec 19 '91	290	6.01	5.99	+ 0.04	6.31
Jun 27 '91	115	6.01	5.99	+ 0.02	6.19	Jan 16 '92	318	6.02	6.00	+ 0.04	6.34
Jul 05 '91	123	6.06	6.04	+ 0.02	6.25	Feb 13 '92	346	6.03	6.01	+ 0.04	6.37

(c) New York Stock Exchange Bonds

CORPORATION BONDS
Volume, $95,320,000

Bonds	Cur Yld	Vol	Close	Net Chg.	
Bond #1 ▶ ATT 5⅝95	6.2	7	91¼	...	◀ Yield to Maturity = 8.24%
ATT 6s00	7.3	36	82¼ −	1¼	
ATT 8¾00	8.7	399	100⅞ −	¼	
ATT 7s01	7.9	217	88⅝ +	½	
ATT 8.80s05	8.8	221	100¼ +	⅛	
ATT 8⅝s07	8.9	149	97⅜ −	⅝	
Bond #2 ▶ ATT 8⅝26	9.2	209	94¼ +	¼	◀ Yield to Maturity = 9.18%

Source: *Wall Street Journal* (Friday, March 1, 1991).

rules to decide when the current yield is likely to be a good approximation and when it is not.

T-bonds #3 and #4 mature in over twenty years, meaning that their characteristics are like those of a consol. The current yields should then be a good approximation of the yields to maturity, and they are: The current yields are within six-tenths of a percentage point of the values for the yields to maturity. This approximation is reasonable even for T-bond #3, which has a price more than 30% above its face value.

Now let's take a look at T-bonds #1 and #2, which have a much shorter time to maturity. The current yield is a good approximation when the price is very near the par price of 100, as it is for T-bond #1. However, the price of T-bond #2 differs by only 5% from the par value, and look how poor an approximation the current yield is for the yield to maturity; it overstates the yield to maturity by over 7 percentage points. This bears out what we learned earlier about the current yield: It can be a very misleading guide to the value of the yield to maturity for a short-term bond if the bond price is not very close to par.

Two other categories of bonds are reported much like the Treasury bonds and notes in the newspaper. Government agency and miscellaneous securities include securities issued by U.S. government agencies such as the Government National Mortgage Association, which makes loans to savings and loan institutions, and international agencies such as the World Bank. Tax-exempt bonds are the other category reported in a manner similar to panel (a), except that yield to maturity calculations are not usually provided. Tax-exempt bonds include bonds issued by local government and public authorities whose interest payments are exempt from federal income taxes.

Panel (b) quotes yields on U.S. Treasury bills, which, as we have seen, are discount bonds. Since there is no coupon, these securities are identified solely by their maturity dates, which you can see in the first column. The next column "Days to Mat." provides the number of days to maturity of the bill. Dealers in these markets always refer to prices by quoting the yield on a discount basis. The "Bid" column gives the discount yield for those selling the bills to dealers, while the "Asked" column gives the discount yield for those buying the bills from the dealer. As with bonds and notes, the dealers' profits are made by the asked price being higher than the bid price, leading to the asked discount yield being lower than the bid discount yield.

As we learned earlier, the yield on a discount basis understates the yield to maturity which is reported in the last column of panel (b). This is evident from a comparison of the "Yield" and the "Asked Discount" columns. As we would also expect from our discussion of the calculation of yields on a discount basis, the understatement grows as the maturity of the bill lengthens.

Panel (c) has quotations for corporate bonds traded on the New York Stock Exchange. Corporate bonds traded on the American Stock Exchange are reported in a like manner. The first column identifies the bond by telling us who is the corporation issuing it. The bonds we are looking at all have been issued by American Telephone and Telegraph (AT&T). The next column tells the coupon rate and the maturity date (5⅝ and 1995 for Bond #1). The "Cur Yld" column reports the current yield (6.2%), and "Vol" gives the volume of trading in that bond (7 bonds of $1000 face value traded that day). The "Close" price is the last traded price that day per $100 of face value. The price of 91¼ represents $912.50 for a $1000 face value bond. The "Net Chg" is the change in the closing price from the previous trading day.

The yield to maturity is also shown for two bonds. This information is not usually provided in the newspaper, but it is included here because it shows how misleading the current yield can be for a short maturity bond such as the 5⅝ of 1995. The current yield of 6.2% is a misleading measure of the interest rate because the yield to maturity is actually 8.24%.

THE DISTINCTION BETWEEN INTEREST RATES AND RETURNS

Many persons think that the interest rate on a bond tells them all they need to know about how well off they are as a result of owning it. If Irving the Investor thinks that he is better off when he owns a long-term bond yielding a 10% interest rate and the interest rate rises to 20%, he will have a rude awakening: As we will shortly see, Irving has lost his shirt! How well a person does by holding a bond or any other security over a particular time period is accurately measured by the **return** or, in more precise terminology, the **rate of return.** For any security, the rate of return is defined as the payments to the owner plus the change in its value, expressed as a ratio to its purchase price. To make this definition clearer, let us see what the return would look like for a $1000 face value coupon bond with a coupon rate of 10%, which is bought for $1000 and is then held for one year, when it is sold for $1200. The payments to the owner are the yearly coupon payments of $100, and the change in its value is $1200 − $1000 = $200. Adding these together and expressing them as a ratio to the purchase price of $1000 gives us the one-year holding period return for this bond:

$$\frac{\$100 + \$200}{\$1000} = \frac{\$300}{\$1000} = .30 = 30\%$$

You might have noticed something quite surprising about the return that we have just calculated: It equals 30%, yet as Table 4.1 indicates, initially the yield to maturity was only 10%. This demonstrates that *the return on a bond will not necessarily equal the interest rate on that bond.* We now see that the distinction between interest rate and return can be important, although in many cases the interest rate and the return on a security are closely related.

Study Guide

The concept of return discussed here is an extremely important one because it is used continually throughout the book. Make sure that you understand how a return is calculated and why it can differ from the interest rate. This will make the material presented later in the book easier to follow.

More generally, the return on a bond held from t to $t + 1$ can be written as

$$RET = \frac{C + P_{t+1} - P_t}{P_t} \tag{4.9}$$

where RET = return from holding the bond from t to $t + 1$
P_t = price of the bond at time t
P_{t+1} = price of the bond at time $t + 1$
C = coupon payment

A convenient way to rewrite the return formula above is to recognize that it can be split up into two separate terms. The first is the current yield, i_c (the coupon payment over the purchase price):

$$\frac{C}{P_t} = i_c$$

The second term is the **rate of capital gains,** or the change in the bond's price relative to the initial purchase price:

$$\frac{P_{t+1} - P_t}{P_t} = g$$

where g = rate of capital gains
Equation (4.9) can then be rewritten as

$$RET = i_c + g \tag{4.10}$$

which shows that the return on a bond is the current yield (i_c) plus the rate of capital gains (g). This rewritten formula illustrates the point that we just discovered. Even for a bond for which the current yield, i_c, is an accurate measure of the yield to maturity, the return can differ substantially from the interest rate. This will occur if there are sizable fluctuations in the price of the bond that produce substantial capital gains or losses.

An interesting case to look at is what happens to the returns on bonds of different maturities when interest rates rise. Table 4.2 calculates the one-year return on several 10% coupon rate bonds all purchased at par when interest rates on all these bonds rise from 10 to 20%. There are several key findings in this table that are generally true of all bonds:

Table 4.2 **One-Year Returns on Different Maturity 10% Coupon Rate Bonds When Interest Rates Rise**

(1) Years to Maturity When Bond Is Purchased	(2) Initial Yield to Maturity	(3) Initial Price	(4) Yield to Maturity Next Year	(5) Price Next Year[a]	(6) Initial Current Yield	(7) Rate of Capital Gain	(8) Rate of Return = 6 + 7
30	10%	1000	20%	503	10%	−49.7%	−39.7%
20	10%	1000	20%	516	10%	−48.4%	−38.4%
10	10%	1000	20%	597	10%	−40.3%	−30.3%
5	10%	1000	20%	741	10%	−25.9%	−15.9%
2	10%	1000	20%	917	10%	−08.3%	+01.7%
1	10%	1000	20%	1000	10%	0	+10.0%

[a]Calculated from Equation (4.3).

1. The only bond whose return equals the initial yield to maturity is one whose time to maturity is the same as the holding period (see the last bond in Table 4.2).

2. A rise in interest rates is associated with a fall in bond prices, resulting in capital losses on bonds whose term to maturities are longer than the holding period.

3. The longer a bond's maturity, the greater is the size of the price change associated with an interest rate change.

4. The longer a bond's maturity, the lower is the rate of return that occurs as a result of the increase in the interest rate.

5. Even though a bond has a substantial initial interest rate, its return can turn out to be negative if interest rates rise.

At first it frequently puzzles students that a rise in interest rates can mean that a bond has been a poor investment (as it puzzles poor Irving the Investor). The trick to understanding this is to recognize that a rise in the interest rate means that the price of a bond has fallen. A rise in interest rates therefore means that a capital loss has occurred, and if this loss is large enough, the bond can be a poor investment indeed.[6] For example, we see in Table 4.2 that the bond which, when purchased, has thirty years to maturity has a capital loss of 49.7% when the interest rate rises from 10 to 20%. This loss is so large that it exceeds the current yield of 10%, resulting in a negative return (loss) of −39.7%.

---

[6]If Irving does not sell the bond, then his capital loss is often referred to as a "paper loss." This is a loss nonetheless because if he had not bought this bond and instead had put his money in the bank, he would now be able to buy more bonds than he presently owns.

The finding that longer-maturity bonds have a greater response of their prices to a change in interest rates helps explain an important fact about the behavior of bond markets. *Prices and returns for long-term bonds are more volatile than those for shorter-term bonds.* Price changes of + and −20% within a year, with corresponding variations in their returns, are common for bonds with over twenty years to maturity (the AT&T 8⅝'s of 2007 in Box 4.2 for example).

For coupon bonds with a maturity that is as short as the holding period (for example, the last bond in Table 4.2), the yield to maturity and the rate of return are equal. The key to understanding why the yield to maturity is equal to the return for any bond whose time to maturity matches the holding period is to recognize that (in this case) the price at the end of the holding period is already fixed at the face value. The change in interest rates can then have no effect on the price at the end of the holding period for these bonds and, therefore, the return will be equal to the yield to maturity.

Summary   The return on a bond, which tells you how good an investment it has been over the holding period, is equal to the yield to maturity in only one special case: when the holding period and the maturity of the bond are identical. For bonds whose maturity is greater than the holding period, capital gains and losses can lead to substantial differences between the return

B o x   4 . 2

Should Retirees Invest in "Gilt-Edged" Long-Term Bonds?

A common bit of conventional wisdom is that retirees should invest their money in "gilt-edged" securities like long-term bonds issued by a solid corporation such as American Telephone and Telegraph (AT&T) because this will provide them with a safe return. Is this good advice given today's financial markets? The table at the right provides the prices and one-year returns on AT&T's 8⅝'s of 2007 from 1980 to 1990.

As you can see, there have been big swings in the returns on this supposedly "safe" investment, with low returns and even losses occurring in several years. If retirees at times need to sell bonds to pay bills, they may find themselves in financial difficulties when the bonds decline in value. Conclusion: retirees beware!

Prices and One-Year Returns on AT&T's 8⅝'s of 2007: 1980–1990

Year	Price at End of Year	Return
1980	70¾	
1981	61¾	−0.5%
1982	77⅝	+39.7%
1983	71⅛	+2.7%
1984	73¼	+15.1%
1985	88⅞	+33.1%
1986	99⅝	+21.89%
1987	91	0.0%
1988	89¼	+7.55%
1989	98½	+20.03%
1990	96⅛	+6.35%

and the interest rate as measured by the yield to maturity. It is especially important for long-term bonds, where the capital gains and losses can be substantial. This is why long-term bonds are not considered to be safe assets with a sure return over short holding periods.

THE DISTINCTION BETWEEN REAL AND NOMINAL _____
INTEREST RATES

So far in our discussion of interest rates we have ignored the effects of inflation on the cost of borrowing. What we have up to now been calling the interest rate makes no allowance for inflation, and it is more precisely referred to as the **nominal interest rate,** which is to distinguish it from the **real interest rate,** the interest rate that is adjusted for expected changes in the price level so that it more accurately reflects the true cost of borrowing.[7] The real interest rate is more accurately defined by the Fisher equation, named after Irving Fisher, one of the great monetary economists of the twentieth century. The Fisher equation states that the nominal interest rate (i) equals the real interest rate (i_r) plus the expected rate of inflation (π^e).[8]

$$i = i_r + \pi^e \tag{4.11}$$

Rearranging terms, we find that the real interest rate equals the nominal interest rate minus the expected inflation rate:

$$i_r = i - \pi^e \tag{4.12}$$

To see why this definition makes sense, let us first consider a situation in which you have made a one-year simple loan with a 5% interest rate ($i = 5\%$) and you expect the price level to stay constant over the course of the year ($\pi^e = 0\%$). As a result of making the loan, at the end of the year you will have 5% more in **real terms,** that is, in terms of real goods and services you can

_____

[7]The real interest rate defined in the text is more precisely referred to as the "ex ante real interest rate" because it is adjusted for *expected* changes in the price level. This is the real interest rate that is most important to economic decisions, and typically, it is what economists mean when they use the phrase *the real interest rate.* The interest rate which is adjusted for *actual* changes in the price level is called the "ex post real interest rate." It describes how well a lender has done in real terms *after the fact.*

[8]A more precise formulation of the Fisher equation is

$$i = i_r + \pi^e + (i_r \times \pi^e)$$

because

$$1 + i = (1 + i_r)(1 + \pi^e) = 1 + i_r + \pi^e + (i_r \times \pi^e)$$

and subtracting 1 from both sides gives us the equation above. For small values of i_r and π^e the term $i_r \times \pi^e$ is very small so that we ignore it as in the text.

buy. In this case, the interest rate you have earned in terms of real goods and services is 5%, that is,

$$i_r = 5\% - 0\% = 5\%$$

as indicated by the Fisher definition.

Now what if the interest rate rises to 10%, but you expect the inflation rate to be 20% over the course of the year. Although you will have 10% more dollars at the end of the year, you will be paying 20% more for goods; the result is that you will be able to buy 10% less goods at the end of the year and you are 10% worse off *in real terms*. This is also exactly what the Fisher definition tells us because

$$i_r = 10\% - 20\% = -10\%$$

As a lender, you are clearly less anxious to make a loan in this case because in terms of real goods and services you have actually earned a negative interest rate of 10%. On the other hand, the borrower fares quite well

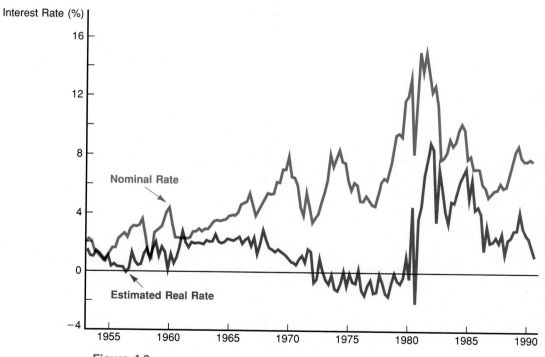

Figure 4.3

Real and Nominal Interest Rates (Three-month Treasury Bill): 1953–1990 Source: Constructed by the author using the procedure outlined in Frederic S. Mishkin, "The Real Interest Rate: An Empirical Investigation," *Carnegie-Rochester Conference Series on Public Policy,* vol. 15 (1981), pp. 151–200.

because at the end of the year, the amounts he will have to pay back will be worth 10% less in terms of goods and services—the borrower will be ahead by 10% in real terms. ***As you would expect, when the real interest rate is low, there are greater incentives to borrow and less to lend.***

A similar distinction can be made between nominal returns and real returns. Nominal returns, which do not allow for inflation, are what we have been referring to as returns. When inflation is subtracted from a nominal return, we have the real return which indicates the amount of extra goods and services that can be purchased as a result of holding the security.

The distinction between real and nominal interest rates is important, because the real interest rate, which reflects the real cost of borrowing, is likely to be a better indicator of the incentives to borrow and lend. It appears to be a better guide to how people will be affected by what is happening in credit markets. Figure 4.3 on page 89, which presents estimates from 1953 to 1990 of the real and nominal interest rates on three-month U.S. Treasury bills, shows us that nominal and real rates often do not move together. (This is also true for nominal and real interest rates in the rest of the world—see Box 4.3.) In particular, when nominal rates in the United States were high in the 1970s, real rates were actually extremely low, often negative. By the standard of nominal interest rates you would have thought that credit market conditions were tight in this period because it was expensive to borrow. However, the estimates of the real rates indicate that you would have been mistaken. In real terms, the cost of borrowing actually was quite low.[9]

---

[9]Since most interest income in the United States is subject to federal income taxes, the true earnings in real terms from holding a bond is not the real interest rate defined by the Fisher equation. Instead, it equals the *after-tax real interest rate*, which equals the nominal interest rate *after income tax payments have been subtracted*, minus the expected inflation rate. For a person facing a 30% tax rate, the after-tax interest rate earning on a bond yielding 10% is only 7% because 30% of the interest income must be paid to the IRS. Thus the after-tax real interest rate on this bond when expected inflation is 20% equals -13% ($= 7\% - 20\%$). More generally, the after-tax real interest rate can be expressed as

$$i \times (1 - \tau) - \pi^e$$

where τ = the income tax rate.

This formula for the after-tax real interest rate also provides a better measure of the effective cost of borrowing for many corporations and individuals in the United States, because in calculating income taxes they can deduct interest payments on loans from their income. Thus, if you face a 30% tax rate and take out a mortgage loan with a 10% interest rate, you are able to deduct the 10% interest payment and thus lower your taxes by 30% of this amount. Your after-tax nominal cost of borrowing is then 7% (10% minus 30% of the 10% interest payment), and when the expected inflation rate is 20%, the effective cost of borrowing in real terms is again -13% ($= 7\% - 20\%$).

As the example (and the formula above) indicate, after-tax real interest rates are always below the real interest rate defined in the Fisher equation. For a further discussion of measures of after-tax real interest rates, see Frederic S. Mishkin, "The Real Interest Rate: An Empirical Investigation," *Carnegie-Rochester Conference Series on Public Policy*, vol. 15 (1981), pp. 151–200.

B o x   4 . 3   **A Global Perspective**

Nominal and Real Interest Rates in Foreign Industrialized Countries

The graph shows the trade-weighted average of real and nominal three-month interest rates for nine major foreign industrialized countries. Just as in the United States, real and nominal interest rates do not move together. Real interest rates in these foreign countries had an upward trend from 1973 to 1990; this was not true for nominal interest rates. The general conclusion that movements in nominal interest rates are not a good indicator of movements in real interest rates appears to be generally true throughout the world.

Trade-Weighted Real and Nominal Interest Rates in Nine Foreign Industrialized Countries: 1973–1990.

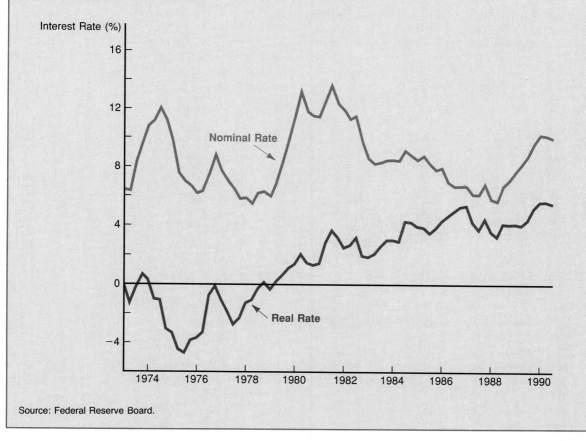

Source: Federal Reserve Board.

SUMMARY

1. The yield to maturity, which is the measure that most accurately describes interest rates, is the interest rate that equates the present value of future payments of a debt instrument with its value today. Application of this principle reveals that bond prices and interest rates are negatively related: When the interest rate rises, the price of the bond must fall, and vice versa.

2. There are two less accurate measures of interest rates that are commonly used to quote interest rates on coupon and discount bonds. The current yield, which equals the coupon payment divided by the price of a coupon bond, is a less accurate measure of the yield to maturity the shorter the maturity of the bond and the further away the price is from the par value. The yield on a discount basis (also called a discount yield) understates the yield to maturity on a discount bond, and the understatement worsens the longer the maturity of the discount security.

Even when either of these measures is a misleading guide to the size of the interest rate, a change always signals a change in the same direction for the yield to maturity.

3. The return on a security, which tells you how well you have done by holding this security over a stated period of time, can differ substantially from the interest rate as measured by the yield to maturity. Long-term bond prices have substantial fluctuations when interest rates change. Capital gains and losses can then be large, which is why long-term bonds are not considered to be safe assets with a sure return.

4. The real interest rate is defined as the nominal interest rate minus the expected rate of inflation. It is a better measure of the incentives to borrow and lend than is the nominal interest rate, and it is a more accurate indicator of the tightness of credit market conditions than is the nominal interest rate.

KEY TERMS

simple loan

fixed payment loan

coupon bond

face or par value

coupon rate

discount bond

present value or present
   discounted value

yield to maturity

consol

current yield

yield on a discount basis
   or discount yield

return or rate of return

rate of capital gains

nominal interest rate

real interest rate

real terms

QUESTIONS AND PROBLEMS

* 1. Would a dollar tomorrow be worth more or less to you today when the interest rate is 20% or when it is 10%?

2. You have just won a $20 million state lottery, which promises to pay you $1 million (tax free) every year for the next twenty years. Have you really won $20 million?

* 3. If the interest rate is 10%, what is the present value of a security that pays you $1100 next year, $1210 the year after, and $1331 the year after that?

4. If the same security sold for $4000, is the yield to maturity greater or less than 10%? Why?

* 5. Write down the formula that is used to calculate the yield to maturity on a twenty-year 10% coupon bond with $1000 face value that sells for $2000.

6. What is the yield to maturity on a $1000 face value discount bond maturing in one year, which sells for $800?

* 7. What is the yield to maturity on a simple loan for $1 million that requires a repayment of $2 million in five years' time?

8. To pay for college, you have just taken out a $1000 government loan that makes you pay $126 per year for 25 years. However, you don't

have to start making these payments until you graduate from college two years from now. Why is the yield to maturity necessarily less than 12%, the yield to maturity on a normal $1000 fixed payment loan in which you pay $126 per year for 25 years?

* 9. Which $1000 bond has the higher yield to maturity: a twenty-year bond selling for $800 with a current yield of 15% or a one-year bond selling for $800 with a current yield of 5%?

10. Pick five U.S. Treasury bonds from the bond page of the newspaper and calculate the current yield. Notice when the current yield is a good approximation to the yield to maturity.

*11. You are offered two bonds: a one-year U.S. Treasury bond with a yield to maturity of 9% and a one-year U.S. Treasury bill with a yield on a discount basis of 8.9%. Which would you rather own?

12. Which would you rather be holding if there is a decline in interest rates: long-term bonds or short-term bonds? Why?

*13. Francine the Financial Advisor has just given you the following advice, "Long-term bonds sure are a great investment because their interest rate is over 20%." Is Francine necessarily right?

14. If mortgage rates rise from 5 to 10% but the expected rate of increase in housing prices rises from 2 to 9%, are people more or less likely to buy houses?

*15. Interest rates were lower in the mid-1980s than they were in the late 1970s, yet many economists have commented that real interest rates were actually much higher in the mid-1980s than in the late 1970s. How does this make sense? Do you think that these economists are right?

CHAPTER 5

A Simple Approach to Portfolio Choice: The Theory of Asset Demand

PREVIEW   Suppose you suddenly struck it rich! Maybe you've just won $25 million in the lottery and your first payment of $600,000 has arrived. Or your dear departed Aunt Thelma has remembered you with a $200,000 bequest. There are a lot of things you might want to do with this windfall: put a down payment on a mansion, buy a Ferrari, or invest in gold coins, land, Treasury bills, or IBM stock. How will you decide what collection (portfolio) of assets you should hold to store your newfound wealth? What criteria should you use to decide among these different stores of wealth? Should you buy only one type of asset or several different types?

This chapter helps answer these questions by developing an economic theory known as the *theory of asset demand* (or the *theory of portfolio choice*). This theory—one of the basic analytical tools for the study of money, banking, and financial markets—outlines criteria that are important when deciding which assets are worth buying. In addition it gives us an idea why it is good to diversify and not to put all our eggs in one basket.

In later chapters, we use the theory of asset demand to examine many economic phenomena, such as the behavior of interest rates, bank asset and liability management, the money supply process, the evolution of the banking system, financial innovation, the demand for money, and theories of financial market behavior.

DETERMINANTS OF ASSET DEMAND

An asset is a piece of property that is a store of value. Items such as money, bonds, stocks, art, land, houses, farm equipment, manufacturing machinery, and so on are all assets. Faced with the question of whether to buy and hold an asset or whether to buy one asset rather than another, an individual must consider the following factors:

1. Wealth, the total resources available to the individual
2. Expected return on one asset relative to the expected return on alternative assets
3. Degree of uncertainty or risk associated with the return on one asset relative to alternative assets
4. Liquidity of one asset relative to alternative assets; that is, how quickly and easily it can be turned into cash

---

Study Guide

As we discuss each factor that influences asset demand, remember that we are always holding all the other factors constant. Also, think of additional examples of how changes in each factor would influence your decision to purchase a particular asset, say a house or a share of common stock. This intuitive approach will help you understand how the theory works in practice.

Wealth

When a person finds that his wealth has increased, he has more resources available with which to purchase assets and so, not surprisingly, the quantity of assets he demands increases.[1] The demands for different assets do have different responses to changes in wealth, however, with the quantity demanded of some assets growing more rapidly with a rise in wealth than the quantity demanded of others. The degree of this response is measured by a concept called the **wealth elasticity of demand** (which is similar to the concept of income elasticity of demand that you learned in your economics principles course). The wealth elasticity of demand measures how much, with everything else unchanged, the quantity demanded of an asset changes in percentage terms in response to a percentage change in wealth:

$$\frac{\% \text{ change in quantity demanded}}{\% \text{ change in wealth}} = \text{wealth elasticity of demand}$$

If, for example, the quantity of currency demanded increases only by 50% when wealth increases by 100%, we say that currency has a wealth elasticity of demand of ½. If, for a common stock, the quantity demanded increases by 200% when wealth increases by 100%, then the wealth elasticity of demand becomes 2.

---

[1] Although it is possible that some assets (called "inferior assets") might have the property that the quantity demanded does not increase as wealth increases, such assets are rare. Thus, for our purposes, we will always assume that demand for an asset increases as wealth increases.

Assets can be sorted into two categories depending on the value of their wealth elasticity of demand. An asset is a **necessity** if there is only so much that people want to hold, so that as wealth grows, the percentage increase in the quantity demanded of the asset is less than the percentage increase in wealth—in other words, its wealth elasticity is less than 1. Since the quantity demanded of a necessity does not grow proportionally with wealth, the amount of this asset that people want to hold relative to their wealth falls as wealth grows. An asset is a **luxury** if its wealth elasticity is greater than 1, and as wealth grows, the quantity demanded of this asset grows more than proportionally and the amount that people hold relative to their wealth grows. Common stocks and municipal bonds are examples of luxury assets, and currency and checking account deposits are necessities.

The effect of changes in wealth on the quantity demanded of an asset can be summarized: *Holding everything else constant, an increase in wealth raises the quantity demanded of an asset, and the increase in the quantity demanded is greater if the asset is a luxury rather than a necessity.*

Expected Returns

In the preceding chapter we saw that the return on an asset measures how much we gain from holding that asset. When we make a decision to buy an asset, then we are influenced by what we expect the return on that asset to be. If a Mobil Oil Corporation bond, for example, has a return of 15% half of the time and 5% the other half of the time, then its expected return (which you can think of as the average return) is 10%.[2] If the expected return on the Mobil Oil bond rises relative to expected returns on alternative assets, holding everything else constant, then it becomes more desirable to purchase it and the quantity demanded increases. This can occur in either of two ways: (1) when the expected return on the Mobil Oil bond rises while the return on an alternative asset—say, stock in American Broadcasting Corporation—remains unchanged, or (2) when the return on the alternative asset, the ABC stock, falls while the return on the Mobil Oil bond remains unchanged. To summarize: *An increase in an asset's expected return relative to that of an*

---

[2]More generally, the expected return equals a weighted sum of each possible realized return multiplied by the probability of its occurring:

$$RET^e = \Sigma p_i \times RET_i$$

where RET^e = expected return
p_i = probability of getting the realization RET_i
RET_i = realization of the return

For a Mobil Oil bond,

$$RET^e = \frac{1}{2} \times 15\% + \frac{1}{2} \times 5\% = 10\%$$

alternative asset, holding everything else unchanged, raises the quantity demanded of the asset.

Risk

The degree of risk or uncertainty of an asset's returns also affects the demand for the asset. Consider two assets: stock in Fly-by-Night Airlines and stock in Feet-on-the-Ground Bus Company. Suppose Fly-by-Night Airlines stock has a return of 15% half the time and 5% the other half of the time, making its expected return 10%, while stock in Feet-on-the-Ground Bus Company has a fixed return of 10%. Fly-by-Night Airlines stock has uncertainty associated with its returns and so has greater risk than stock in Feet-on-the-Ground Bus Company, whose return is a sure thing.[3]

A *risk-averse* person prefers stock in Feet-on-the-Ground Bus Company (the sure thing) to Fly-by-Night Airlines stock (the riskier asset), even though the stocks have the same expected return, 10%. On the other hand, a person who prefers risk is a *risk preferrer* or *risk lover*. Most people are risk averse since, everything else being equal, they will prefer to hold the less risky asset. *Hence, holding everything else constant, if an asset's risk rises relative to that of alternative assets, its quantity demanded will fall.*

Liquidity

Another factor that affects the demand for an asset is its liquidity, that is, how quickly it can be converted into cash without incurring large costs. A house, for example, is not a very liquid asset, because to sell a house quickly in order to pay bills, it might have to be sold for a much lower price. Also the transactions costs in selling a house (broker's commissions, lawyer's fees, etc.) are substantial. A U.S. Treasury bill, on the other hand, is a highly liquid asset. It can be sold with low transactions costs in a well-organized market where there are many buyers, so it can be sold quickly with low cost. *The more liquid an asset is relative to alternative assets, holding everything else unchanged, the more desirable it is and the greater will be the quantity demanded.*

---

[3]One frequently used, formal measure of risk is the standard deviation σ:

$$\sigma = \sqrt{\Sigma p_i \times (RET_i - RET^e)^2}$$

where all the variables are as defined in the previous footnote. For Fly-by-Night Airlines stock it equals $\sqrt{.5 \times (15\% - 10\%)^2 + .5 \times (5\% - 10\%)^2} = 5\%$, while for stock in Feet-on-the-Ground Bus Company it is $\sqrt{1 \times (10\% - 10\%)^2} = 0\%$. As you would expect, Fly-by-Night Airlines stock, the riskier asset, has a higher standard deviation of its returns. If there is another asset, such as High Flyer Incorporated stock with a return of 0% half the time and 20% the other half the time, its expected return is also 10%. This asset is riskier than either of the other two assets and the standard deviation of its returns demonstrates this. For High Flyer stock the standard deviation is $\sqrt{.5 \times (0\% - 10\%)^2 + .5 \times (20\% - 10\%)^2} = 10\%$, which is higher than the standard deviations for stock in Fly-by-Night Airlines or Feet-on-the-Ground Bus Company.

THEORY OF ASSET DEMAND

All the determining factors we have just discussed can be assembled together into the **theory of asset demand,** which states that, holding all of the other factors constant:

1. The quantity demanded of an asset is usually positively related to wealth, with the response being greater if the asset is a luxury rather than a necessity.
2. The quantity demanded of an asset is positively related to its expected return relative to alternative assets.
3. The quantity demanded of an asset is negatively related to the risk of its returns relative to alternative assets.
4. The quantity demanded of an asset is positively related to its liquidity relative to alternative assets.

These results are summarized in Table 5.1.

BENEFITS OF DIVERSIFICATION

Our discussion of the theory of asset demand indicates that most people like to avoid risk; that is, they are risk averse. Why, then, do many investors hold many risky assets rather than just one? Doesn't holding many risky assets expose the investor to more risk?

The old warning about not putting all your eggs in one basket holds the key to the answer: Because holding many risky assets (called **diversification**) reduces the overall risk an investor faces, diversification is beneficial. To see why this is so, let's look at some specific examples of how an investor fares on his investments when he is holding two risky securities.

Table 5.1 **Summary: Response of the Demand for an Asset to Changes in Income or Wealth, Expected Returns, Risk, and Liquidity**

Change in Variable		Change in Quantity Demanded
Wealth	↑	↑
Expected Return Relative to Other Assets	↑	↑
Risk Relative to Other Assets	↑	↓
Liquidity Relative to Other Assets	↑	↑

Note: Only increases (↑) in the variables are shown. The effect of decreases in the variables on the change in demand would be the opposite of those indicated in the second column.

Consider two assets: common stock of Frivolous Luxuries, Inc. and common stock of Bad Times Products, Unlimited. When the economy is strong, which we'll assume is one-half of the time, Frivolous Luxuries has high sales and the return on the stock is 15%; when the economy is weak, the other half of the time, sales are low and the return on the stock is 5%. On the other hand, suppose that Bad Times Products thrives when the economy is weak so that its stock has a return of 15%, but it earns less when the economy is strong and has a return on the stock of 5%. Since both these stocks have a return of 15% half the time and 5% the other half of the time, both have an expected return of 10%. However, both stocks carry a fair amount of risk because there is uncertainty about their actual returns.

Suppose, however, that instead of buying one stock or the other, Irving the Investor puts half his savings in Frivolous Luxuries stock and the other half in Bad Times Products stock. When the economy is strong, Frivolous Luxuries stock has a return of 15%, while Bad Times Products has a return of 5%. The result is that Irving earns a return of 10% (the average of 5% and 15%) on his holdings of the two stocks. When the economy is weak, Frivolous Luxuries has a return of only 5% and Bad Times Products has a return of 15%, so Irving still earns a return of 10%. If Irving diversifies by buying both stocks, he earns a return of 10% regardless of whether the economy is strong or weak. Irving is better off from this strategy of diversification because his expected return is 10%, the same as from holding either Frivolous Luxuries or Bad Times Products alone, and yet he is not exposed to *any* risk.

Although the case we have described demonstrates the benefits of diversification, it is somewhat unrealistic. It is quite hard to find two securities with the characteristic that when the return of one is high, the return of the other is always low.[4] In the real world we are more likely to find at best returns on securities that are independent of each other; that is, when one is high, the other is just as likely to be high as to be low.

Suppose that both securities have an expected return of 10%, with a return of 5% half the time and 15% the other half the time. Sometimes both securities will earn the higher return and sometimes both will earn the lower return. In this case if Irving holds equal amounts of each security, he will on average earn the same return as if he had just put all his savings into one of the securities. However, because the returns on these two securities are independent, it is just as likely that when one earns the high 15% return, the other earns the low 5% return and vice versa, giving Irving a return of 10% (equal to the expected return). Because Irving is more likely to earn what he expected to earn when he holds both securities instead of just one.

---

[4]Such a case is described by saying that the returns on the two securities are perfectly *negatively* correlated.

we can see that Irving has again reduced his risk through diversification.[5]

The one case in which Irving will not benefit from diversifying occurs when the returns on the two securities move perfectly together. In this case, when the first security has a return of 15%, the other also has a return of 15% and holding both securities results in a return of 15%. When the first security has a return of 5%, the other has a return of 5% and holding both results in a return of 5%. The result of diversifying by holding both securities is a

---

B o x   5 . 1

Dangers of Not Diversifying: Trump—The Fall

The saga of Donald Trump, a symbol of arrogant wealth in the 1980s, illustrates the dangers of not diversifying. Trump, the author of the best-seller, *Trump: The Art of the Deal,* made one deal too many in real estate. Trump's real estate holdings included the Plaza Hotel, a 74-acre plot of undeveloped land on Manhattan's West Side, and two casinos in Atlantic City, at which point he plunged further into the real estate market and borrowed heavily to buy and refurbish another casino in Atlantic City, the Taj Mahal, at a cost of $1 billion.

With Trump's lack of diversification, any softening of the real estate and casino markets could prove disastrous, and this is exactly what happened. With the weakening of the real estate market in the Northeast beginning in the late 1980s and lower revenues than expected in Atlantic City casinos, Trump found himself unable to meet his debt payments by mid-1990. Only with a $65 million bailout loan from four New York City banks and a group of seventy other banks that had pieces of his loans was Trump able to avoid bankruptcy. Continuing troubles at his prize casino, the Taj Mahal, forced Trump to give up half his stake in the casino in late 1990.

Under the arrangements with the banks, Trump had to give up much of his autonomy in running his businesses; and what's worse, he was even put on a budget. His personal spending was restricted to $450,000 *a month* in 1990, $375,000 a month in 1991, and $300,000 a month in 1992 and thereafter. Although these restrictions would not be a hardship for you or me, the free-spending Trump may find them a serious hindrance to his life-style. The 110-room mansion in Florida, the $29 million yacht, and the helicopter may all have to go. What may even be more galling to "the Donald," as he is called by those close to him, is that the magic of the Trump name may be no more. In 1989, Trump's net worth was reported to be $1.7 billion, while in August 1990 the New Jersey Casino Control Commission disclosed that he might have a *negative* net worth of $294 million.

---

[5]We can also see that diversification in the example above leads to lower risk by examining the standard deviation of returns when Irving diversifies and when he doesn't. The standard deviation of returns if Irving holds only one of the two securities is $\sqrt{.5 \times (15\% - 10\%)^2 + .5 \times (5\% - 10\%)^2} = 5\%$. When Irving holds equal amounts of each security, there is a probability of $\frac{1}{4}$ that he will earn 5% on both (for a total return of 5%), a probability of $\frac{1}{4}$ that he will earn 15% on both (for a total return of 15%), and a probability of $\frac{1}{2}$ that he will earn 15% on one and 5% on the other (for a total return of 10%). The standard deviation of returns when Irving diversifies is thus $\sqrt{.25 \times (15\% - 10\%)^2 + .25 \times (5\% - 10\%)^2 + .5 \times (10\% - 10\%)^2} = 3.5\%$. Since the standard deviation of returns when Irving diversifies is lower than when he holds only one security, we can see that diversification has reduced risk.

return of 15% half of the time and 5% the other half of the time, which is exactly the same set of returns that are earned by holding only one of the securities. Consequently, diversification in this case does not lead to any reduction of risk.

The examples we have just examined illustrate the following important points about diversification:

1. Diversification is almost always beneficial to the risk-averse investor since it reduces risk unless returns on securities move perfectly together (which is an extremely rare occurrence).

2. The less the returns on two securities move together, the more benefit (risk reduction) there is from diversification.

For a real-world perspective on diversification, see Box 5.1.

With our understanding of the factors that influence investors' decisions to buy and hold different assets, we are ready to explore in the next chapter how the price of a particular asset—bonds—is determined.

SUMMARY

1. The theory of asset demand tells us that the quantity demanded of an asset is (a) positively related to wealth, (b) positively related to the expected return on the asset relative to alternative assets, (c) negatively related to the riskiness of the asset relative to alternative assets, and (d) positively related to the liquidity of the asset relative to alternative assets.

2. Diversification (the holding of more than one asset) benefits investors because it reduces the risk they face, and the benefits are greater the less returns on securities move together.

KEY TERMS

wealth elasticity of demand

necessity

luxury

theory of asset demand

diversification

QUESTIONS AND PROBLEMS

1. In terms of the theory of asset demand, explain why you would be more or less willing to buy a share of Polaroid stock in the following situations:
   a) your wealth falls
   b) you expect it to appreciate in value
   c) the bond market becomes more liquid
   d) you expect gold to appreciate in value
   e) prices in the bond market become more volatile

* 2. In terms of the theory of asset demand, explain why you would be more or less willing to buy a house under the following circumstances:
   a) you just inherited $100,000
   b) real estate commissions fall from 6% of the sales price to 4% of the sales price
   c) you expect Polaroid stock to double in value next year
   d) prices in the stock market become more volatile

  e) you expect housing prices to fall
3. In terms of the theory of asset demand, explain why you would be more or less willing to buy gold under the following circumstances:
   a) gold again becomes acceptable as a medium of exchange
   b) prices in the gold market become more volatile
   c) you expect inflation to rise and gold prices tend to move with the aggregate price level
   d) you expect interest rates to rise
* 4. In terms of the theory of asset demand, explain why you would be more or less willing to buy AT&T bonds under the following circumstances:
   a) trading in these bonds increases so that they are easier to sell
   b) you expect a "bear market" in stocks (i.e., stock prices are expected to decline)

  c) brokerage commissions on stocks fall
  d) you expect interest rates to rise
  e) brokerage commissions on bonds fall
5. True, false, or uncertain: "The more risk averse someone is, the more likely they are to diversify." Explain.
* 6. Suppose that I own a pro football team and I plan to diversify by purchasing shares in either
   a) a company that owns a pro basketball team, or
   b) a pharmaceutical company
   Which of these two investments is more likely to reduce the overall risk I face? Why?
7. True, false, or uncertain: "No one who is risk averse will ever buy a security that has a lower expected return, more risk, and less liquidity than another security." Explain.

CHAPTER 6

The Behavior of Interest Rates

PREVIEW   In the early 1950s nominal interest rates on three-month Treasury bills were about 1% at an annual rate, by 1981 they had reached a level of over 15%, then fell to below 6% in the mid-1980s and by 1990 rose above 7%. What explains these substantial fluctuations in interest rates? One reason why we study money, banking, and financial markets is to provide some answers to this question.

In this chapter we examine how nominal interest rates are determined and the factors that influence their behavior. Since we know that interest rates are negatively related to the price of bonds, if we can explain why bond prices change, we can also explain why interest rates fluctuate. Here we will apply supply and demand analysis to examine how bond prices and interest rates change.

THE LOANABLE FUNDS FRAMEWORK: SUPPLY AND _____ DEMAND IN THE BOND MARKET

We first approach the analysis of interest rate determination by studying the supply and demand for bonds. The first step in the analysis is to use the theory of asset demand discussed in Chapter 5 to obtain a **demand curve,** which is the relationship between the quantity demanded and the price when all other economic variables are held constant (i.e., values of other variables are taken as given). You may recall from previous economics courses that the assumption that all other economic variables are held constant is called *ceteris paribus*, which means "everything else equal" in Latin.

The Demand Curve

To clarify our analysis, let us consider the demand for one-year discount bonds, which make no coupon payments but which pay the owner the $1000 face value in a year. If the holding period is one year, then as we have seen in

Chapter 5, the return on the bonds is known absolutely and is equal to the interest rate as measured by the yield to maturity. This means that the expected return on this bond is equal to the interest rate i, which, using Equation (4.6) in Chapter 4, is

$$i = RET^e = \frac{(F - P_d)}{P_d}$$

where i = interest rate = yield to maturity
   RET^e = expected return
    F = face value of the discount bond
    P_d = initial purchase price of the discount bond

This formula shows that a particular value of the interest rate corresponds to each bond price. If the bond sells for $950, the interest rate and expected return is

$$\frac{(\$1000 - \$950)}{\$950} = .053 = 5.3\%$$

At this interest rate and expected return, let us assume that the quantity of bonds demanded is 100, which is plotted as point A in Figure 6.1. At a price of $900, the interest rate and expected return equal

$$\frac{(\$1000 - \$900)}{\$900} = .111 = 11.1\%$$

Since the expected return on these bonds is higher, with all other economic variables (such as income, expected returns on other assets, risk, and liquidity) held constant, the quantity demanded of bonds will be higher as predicted by the theory of asset demand. Point B in Figure 6.1 shows that the quantity of bonds demanded at the price of $900 has risen to 200. Continuing with this reasoning, if the bond price is $850 (interest rate and expected return = 17.6%), the quantity of bonds demanded (point C) will be greater than at point B. Similarly, at the lower prices of $800 (interest rate = 25%) and $750 (interest rate = 33.3%), the quantity of bonds demanded will be even higher (points D and E). The curve B^d which connects these points is the demand curve for bonds. It has the usual downward slope, indicating that at lower prices of the bond (everything else equal), the quantity demanded is higher.[1]

---

[1]Note that although our analysis indicates that the demand curve is downward sloping, it does not imply that the curve is a straight line. For ease of exposition, however, we will draw demand curves and supply curves as straight lines.

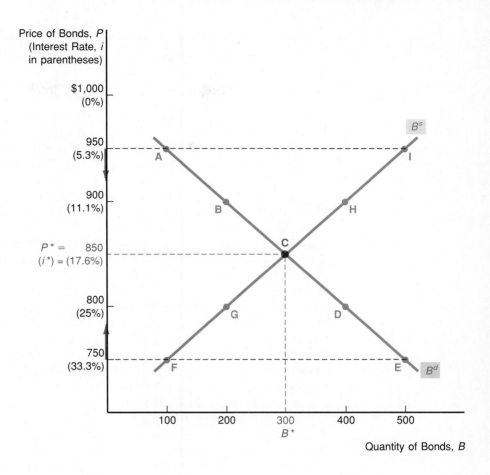

Figure 6.1
Supply and Demand for Bonds

The Supply Curve

An important assumption behind the demand curve for bonds in Figure 6.1 is that all other economic variables besides the bond's price and interest rate are held constant. We use the same assumption in deriving a **supply curve,** the relationship between the quantity supplied and the price when all other economic variables are held constant.

When the price of the bonds is $750 (interest rate = 33.3%), point F shows that the quantity of bonds supplied is 100. If the price is at $800, the interest rate is at the lower rate of 25%. Since at this interest rate it is now less costly to borrow by issuing bonds, firms will be willing to borrow more through bond issues and the quantity of bonds supplied is at the higher level of 200 (point G). An even higher price of $850 corresponding to a lower interest rate of 17.6% results in a larger quantity of bonds supplied of 300 (point C). Higher prices of $900 and $950 result in even greater quantities of bonds supplied (points H and I). The B^s curve which connects these points is the supply curve for bonds. It has the usual upward slope found in supply curves, indicating that as the price increases (everything else being equal), the quantity supplied increases.

Market Equilibrium

In economics, **market equilibrium** occurs when the amount that people are willing to buy (*demand*) equals the amount that people are willing to sell (*supply*) at a given price. In the bond market this is achieved when the quantity of bonds demanded equals the quantity of bonds supplied:

$$B^d = B^s \tag{6.1}$$

In Figure 6.1, equilibrium occurs at point C, where the demand and the supply curves intersect at a bond price of $850 (interest rate of 17.6%) and a quantity of bonds of 300. The price of $P^* = \$850$, where the quantity demanded equals the quantity supplied, is called the equilibrium or market-clearing price. Similarly, the interest rate of $i^* = 17.6\%$ that corresponds to this price is called the equilibrium or market-clearing interest rate.

The concepts of market equilibrium and equilibrium price or interest rate are useful because there is a tendency for the market to head toward them. We can see that it does in Figure 6.1 by first looking at what happens when we have a bond price that is above the equilibrium price. When the price of bonds is set too high, let's say at $950, then the quantity of bonds supplied at point I is greater than the quantity of bonds demanded at point A. A situation like this in which the quantity of bonds supplied exceeds the quantity of bonds demanded is called a condition of **excess supply.** Since people want to sell more bonds than others want to buy, the price of the bonds will fall, and this is why the downward arrow is drawn in the figure at the bond price of $950. As long as the bond price remains above the equilibrium price, there will continue to be an excess supply of bonds and the price will continue to fall. This will stop only when the price has reached the equilibrium price of $850 where the excess supply of bonds has been eliminated.

Now let's look at what happens when the price of bonds is below the equilibrium price. If the price of the bonds is set too low at $750, the quantity demanded at point E is greater than the quantity supplied at point F. This is called a condition of **excess demand.** People now want to buy more bonds than others are willing to sell and so the price of bonds will be driven up. This is illustrated by the upward arrow drawn in the figure at the bond price of $750. Only when the excess demand for bonds is eliminated by the price rising to the equilibrium level of $850 is there no further tendency for the price to rise.

We can see that the concept of equilibrium price is a useful one because it indicates where the market will settle. Because each price on the vertical axis of Figure 6.1 corresponds to a value of the interest rate, the same diagram also shows us that the interest rate will head toward the equilibrium interest rate of 17.6%. When the interest rate is below the equilibrium interest rate, as it is when it is at 5.3%, the price of the bond is above the equilibrium price and there will be an excess supply of bonds. The price of the bond then falls, leading to a rise in the interest rate toward the equilibrium level. Similarly, when the interest rate is above the equilibrium level, as it is when it is at 33.3%, there is excess demand for bonds and the bond price will rise, driving the interest rate back down to the equilibrium level of 17.6%.

Supply and Demand Analysis

Our Figure 6.1 is a conventional supply and demand diagram with price on the vertical axis and quantity on the horizontal axis. Because the interest rate that corresponds to each bond price is also marked on the vertical axis, this diagram allows us to read the equilibrium interest rate, giving us a model that describes the determination of interest rates. However, it does have the disadvantage of having interest rates run the wrong way on the vertical axis. Moreover, because economists are more concerned with the value of interest rates rather than the price of bonds, it is somewhat cluttered by the presence of the bond price.

The solution to the problem is to plot the supply and demand for bonds on a diagram where the vertical axis provides the values of the interest rate only and where the interest rates run in the right direction, that is, rise as we go up the axis. Such a diagram is found in Figure 6.2(a), where points A through I match the corresponding points in Figure 6.1. It is important to recognize that a supply and demand diagram like Figure 6.2(a) can be drawn *for any type of bond* because the interest rate and the price of a bond are always negatively related for any type of bond, whether it be a discount bond or a coupon bond.

This figure looks somewhat peculiar since the demand curve for bonds is upward sloping and the supply curve for bonds is downward sloping. However, the curves having these slopes are completely consistent with our usual supply and demand analysis because they are plotted against interest rates rather than bond prices.

To make the demand curve have the usual downward slope and the supply curve the usual upward slope, the horizontal axis and the demand and supply curves can be renamed. Because a firm supplying bonds is in fact taking out a loan from a person buying a bond, "supplying a bond" is equivalent to "demanding a loan." Thus the supply curve for bonds can be reinterpreted as indicating the quantity of loans demanded for each value of the interest rate. If we rename the horizontal axis to be **loanable funds,** defined as the quantity of loans, the supply of bonds can be renamed the *demand for loanable funds*. Similarly, the demand curve for bonds can be renamed the *supply of loanable funds*, because buying (demanding) a bond is equivalent to supplying a loan. Figure 6.2(b) reproduces the curves in Figure 6.2(a), but relabels them and the horizontal axis using the loanable funds terminology. The renamed demand and supply curves have the usual slopes.

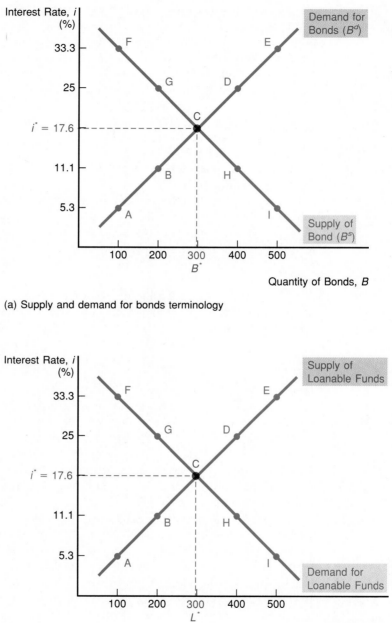

(a) Supply and demand for bonds terminology

Figure 6.2
Supply and Demand for Bonds with the Interest Rate on the Vertical Axis

(b) Loanable funds terminology

Since supply and demand diagrams that explain how interest rates are determined in the bond market most commonly use the loanable funds terminology, this analysis is known as the **loanable funds framework.** Because in later chapters describing the conduct of monetary policy we focus on how the demand and supply of bonds is affected, we will continue to conduct supply and demand analysis in terms of bonds rather than loanable funds. Whether the analysis is done in terms of loanable funds or in terms of the demand and supply for bonds, the results are the same and are equivalent ways of analyzing the determination of interest rates.[2]

CHANGES IN EQUILIBRIUM INTEREST RATES

In this section we will see how we can use the supply and demand framework for bonds to analyze why interest rates change. To avoid confusion, it is important to make the distinction between *movements along a demand (or supply) curve* and *shifts in a demand (or supply) curve*. When quantity demanded (or supplied) changes as a result of a change in the price of the bond (or equivalently, of a change in the interest rate), we have a *movement along the demand (or supply) curve*. The change in the quantity demanded when we move from point A to B to C, and so on in Figures 6.1 or 6.2 is, for example, a movement along a demand curve. A *shift in the demand (or supply) curve,* on the other hand, occurs when the quantity demanded (or supplied) changes *at each given price (or interest rate) of the bond* in response to a change in some other factor besides the bond's price or interest rate. When one of these factors changes so that we have a shift in the demand or supply curve, there will be a new equilibrium value for the interest rate.

In the following pages we will look at how the supply and demand curves shift in response to changes in variables, such as expected inflation and wealth, and what effects these changes have on the equilibrium value of interest rates.

Shifts in the Demand for Bonds

The theory of asset demand developed in Chapter 5 provides a framework for deciding what factors cause the demand curve for bonds to shift. These factors include changes in

_____

[2]An important feature of the analysis here is that supply and demand are always in terms of *stocks* (an amount at a given point in time) of assets, not in terms of flows. This approach is somewhat different from certain loanable funds analyses which are conducted in terms of flows (loans per year). The asset market approach (i.e., one that emphasizes stocks of assets rather than flows) is now the dominant methodology used by economists because correctly conducting analyses in terms of flows is very tricky, especially when we encounter inflation.

1. Wealth
2. Expected returns on bonds relative to alternative assets
3. Risk of bonds relative to alternative assets
4. Liquidity of bonds relative to alternative assets

To see how a change in each of these curves (holding all other factors constant) can shift the demand curve, let us look at some examples.

Wealth   When the economy is growing rapidly so that wealth is increasing, the quantity of bonds demanded at each bond price (or interest rate) increases as shown in Figure 6.3. To see how this works, consider point B on the initial demand curve for bonds, B_1^d. At an interest rate of 11.1%, it tells us that the quantity of bonds demanded is 200. With higher wealth, the quantity of bonds demanded at the same interest rate must rise, say, to 400 (point B'). Similarly, the higher wealth causes the quantity demanded at an interest rate of 25% to rise from 400 to 600 (point D to D'). Continuing with this reasoning for every point on the initial demand curve, B_1^d, we can see that the demand curve shifts to the right from B_1^d to B_2^d as is indicated by the arrows.

The conclusion we have reached is that *in an expanding economy with growing wealth, the demand for bonds rises and the demand curve for bonds shifts to the right.* However, how much demand will shift (increase) will depend on the extent to which bonds are luxuries rather than necessities. Using the same reasoning, *in a recession when income and wealth are falling, the demand for bonds falls and the demand curve shifts to the left.*

Expected Returns   For a one-year discount bond and a one-year holding period, the expected return and the interest rate are identical. Here there is no component of its expected return that is unrelated to the bond price or interest rate.

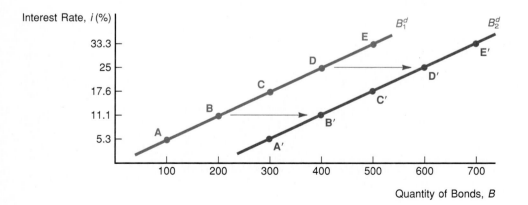

Figure 6.3
Shift in the Demand Curve for Bonds   When the demand for bonds increases, the demand curve shifts to the right as shown above.

For bonds with maturities greater than one year, the expected return may differ greatly from the interest rate. For example, we saw in Chapter 4, Table 4.2, that a rise in the interest rate on a long-term bond from 10 to 20% would lead to a sharp decline in price and a very negative return. Hence, if people begin to think that interest rates will be higher next year than they had originally anticipated, the expected return on long-term bonds would fall and the quantity demanded would fall at each interest rate. ***Higher expected interest rates in the future decrease the demand for long-term bonds and shift the demand curve to the left.***

A revision downward of expectations of future interest rates, on the other hand, would mean that long-term bond prices would be expected to rise more than originally anticipated and the resulting higher expected return would raise the quantity demanded at each interest rate. ***Lower expected interest rates in the future increase the demand for long-term bonds and shift the demand curve to the right*** (Figure 6.3).

Changes in expected returns on other assets can also shift the demand curve for bonds. If people suddenly became more optimistic about the stock market and began to expect higher stock prices in the future, then expected capital gains and expected returns on stocks would rise. With the expected return on bonds held constant, the expected return on bonds relative to stocks would fall, lowering the demand for bonds and shifting the demand curve to the left.

A change in expected inflation is likely to alter expected returns on physical assets (also called real assets) such as automobiles and houses, which affect the demand for bonds. Since movements in the price of real assets are tied to the movements of the general price level, an increase in expected inflation from, say, 5 to 10%, will lead to expectations of a faster rate of increase of prices on cars and houses and hence higher nominal capital gains. The resulting rise in the expected returns on these real assets will lead to a fall in the expected return on bonds relative to the expected return on real assets. ***An increase in the expected rate of inflation will cause the demand for bonds to decline and the demand curve to shift to the left.***

Risk If prices in the bond market become more volatile, the risk associated with bonds increases and bonds become a less attractive asset. ***An increase in the riskiness of bonds causes the demand for bonds to fall and the demand curve to shift to the left.***

On the other hand, an increase in the volatility of prices in another asset market, such as the stock market, would make bonds more attractive. ***An increase in the riskiness of alternative assets causes the demand for bonds to rise and the demand curve to shift to the right*** (Figure 6.3).

Liquidity If more people started trading in the bond market and as a result it became easier to sell bonds quickly, the increase in their liquidity would cause the quantity of bonds demanded at each interest rate to rise. ***Increased liquidity of bonds results in an increased demand for bonds and the demand*** *curve shifts to the right* (Figure 6.3). *Similarly, increased liquidity of alternative assets lowers the demand for bonds and shifts the demand curve to the left.* The reduction of brokerage commissions for trading common stocks that occurred when the fixed rate commission structure was abolished in 1975, for example, increased the liquidity of stocks relative to bonds and the resulting lower demand for bonds shifted the demand curve to the left.

Shifts in the Supply of Bonds

The factors that can cause the supply curve for bonds to shift include

1. Expected profitability of investment opportunities
2. Expected inflation
3. Government activities

We will look at how the supply curve shifts when each of these factors changes (when all others remain constant).

Expected Profitability of Investment Opportunities   The more profitable investments that a firm expects it can make, the more willing it will be to borrow and increase the amount of its outstanding debt in order to finance these investments. When the economy is growing rapidly, as in a business cycle expansion, investment opportunities that are expected to be profitable abound and the quantity of bonds supplied at any given interest rate will increase (shown in Figure 6.4). *Therefore, in a business cycle expansion, the supply of bonds increases and the supply curve shifts to the right. Likewise, in a recession, there are far fewer expected profitable investment opportunities so the supply of bonds falls and the supply curve shifts to the left.*

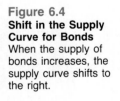

Figure 6.4
Shift in the Supply Curve for Bonds
When the supply of bonds increases, the supply curve shifts to the right.

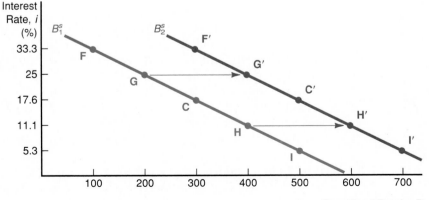

Expected Inflation   As we saw in Chapter 4, the real cost of borrowing is more accurately measured by the real interest rate, which equals the (nominal) interest rate minus the expected inflation rate. For a given interest rate, when expected inflation increases, the real cost of borrowing falls and the quantity of bonds supplied increases at any given interest rate. ***An increase in expected inflation causes the supply of bonds to increase and the supply curve to shift to the right*** (Figure 6.4).

Government Activities   The activities of the government can influence the supply of bonds in several ways. The U.S. Treasury issues bonds in order to finance government deficits, that is, the difference between the expenditures of the government and its revenues. When these deficits are large, as they have been recently, the Treasury sells more bonds and the quantity of bonds supplied at each interest rate increases. ***Higher government deficits increase the supply of bonds and shift the supply curve to the right*** (Figure 6.4).

State and local governments and other government agencies also issue bonds to finance their expenditures and this can also affect the supply of bonds. We will see in later chapters that the conduct of monetary policy involves the purchase and sale of bonds, which in turn influences the supply of bonds.

Changes in the Equilibrium Interest Rate

We now can use our knowledge of how supply and demand curves shift to analyze how the equilibrium interest rate can change. The best way to do this is to pursue several applications that are particularly relevant to our understanding of how monetary policy affects interest rates.

Study Guide

Supply and demand analysis for the bond market is best learned by practicing applications. When there is an application in the text and we look at how the interest rate changes because some economic variable increases, see if you can draw the appropriate shifts in the supply and demand curves when this same economic variable decreases. While you are practicing applications, keep two things in mind:

1. When you examine the effect of a variable change, remember that we are assuming that all other variables are unchanged; that is, we are making use of the *ceteris paribus* assumption.

2. The bond supply and demand curves in the diagrams have the *opposite* slopes to the ones you are used to: the demand curve slopes *up* and the supply curve slopes *down*. This occurs because the curves are plotted against the interest rate, which is inversely related to the bond price.

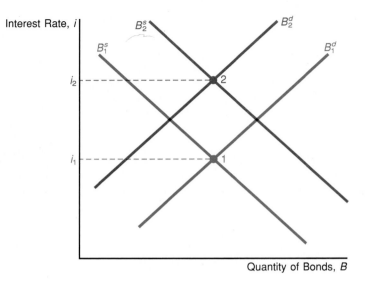

Interest Rate, i

Quantity of Bonds, B

Figure 6.5
Response to a Change in Expected Inflation
When expected inflation rises, the supply curve shifts out from B_1^s to B_2^s and the demand curve shifts from B_1^d to B_2^d. The equilibrium moves from point 1 to point 2 and the equilibrium interest rate rises from i_1 to i_2.

Changes in Expected Inflation: The Fisher Effect   We have already done most of the work to evaluate how a change in expected inflation affects the nominal interest rate, because we have already analyzed how a change in expected inflation shifts the supply and demand curves. Figure 6.5 shows the effect on the equilibrium interest rate of an increase in expected inflation.

Suppose expected inflation is initially at 5% and the initial supply and demand curves, B_1^s and B_1^d, intersect at point 1, where the equilibrium interest rate is i_1. If expected inflation rises to 10%, the expected return on bonds relative to real assets falls for any given interest rate. As a result, the demand for bonds falls and the demand curve shifts to the left from B_1^d to B_2^d. The rise in expected inflation also shifts the supply curve. At any given interest rate, the real cost of borrowing has declined, causing the quantity of bonds supplied to increase, and the supply curve shifts to the right from B_1^s to B_2^s.

When the demand and supply curves shift in response to the change in expected inflation, the equilibrium moves from point 1 to point 2, which is the intersection of B_2^d and B_2^s. Also, the equilibrium interest rate has risen from i_1 to i_2. Note that Figure 6.5 has been drawn so that the equilibrium quantity of bonds remains the same for both point 1 and point 2. However, depending on the size of the shifts in the supply and demand curves, the equilibrium quantity of bonds could either rise or fall when expected inflation rises.

Our supply and demand analysis has generated an important result. **When expected inflation rises, interest rates will rise.** This result has been named the **Fisher effect,** after Irving Fisher, the economist who first pointed out the relation of expected inflation to interest rates. The accuracy of this prediction is shown in Figure 6.6. The interest rate on three-month Treas-

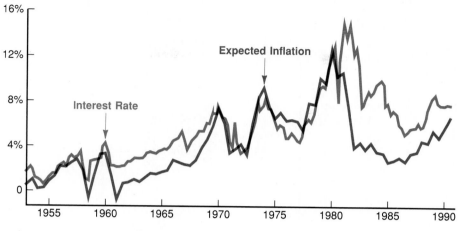

Figure 6.6
Expected Inflation and Interest Rates (Three-Month Treasury Bills): 1953–1990 Source:
Calculated by the author using procedures outlined in Frederic S. Mishkin, "The Real
Interest Rate. An Empirical Investigation," *Carnegie-Rochester Conference Series on Public
Policy,* vol. 15 (1981), pp. 151–200.

ury bills has usually moved along with the expected inflation rate (a phenomenon true in other countries as well, as shown in Box 6.1). Consequently, it is understandable that many economists recommend that the
fight against inflation must be won if we want to lower interest rates.

A Business Cycle Expansion   Figure 6.7 analyzes the effects of a business
cycle expansion on interest rates. In a business cycle expansion, the amount
of goods and services being produced in the economy rises so that national

Figure 6.7
**Response to a
Business Cycle
Expansion**   In a
business cycle
expansion when
income and wealth are
rising, the demand
curve shifts out from
B_1^d to B_2^d and the
supply curve shifts out
from B_1^s to B_2^s. If the
supply curve shifts out
more than the demand
curve, as is drawn in
this figure, the
equilibrium moves up
from point 1 to point 2,
where the equilibrium
interest rate has risen
from i_1 to i_2.

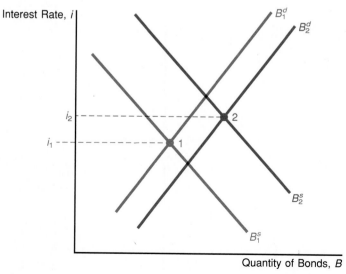

B o x   6 . 1      **A Global Perspective**

Expected Inflation and Interest Rates in Foreign Industrialized Countries

The graph shows the trade-weighted average of three-month interest rates and expected inflation for nine major foreign industrialized countries. Interest rates and expected inflation in these countries do move in tandem, particularly before 1980,

just as we find for the United States. The conclusion that there is a Fisher effect—so that when expected inflation rises, interest rates rise—is equally valid in foreign countries as it is in the United States.

Trade-Weighted Three-Month Nominal Interest Rates and Expected Inflation in Nine Foreign Industrialized Countries: 1973–1990

Source: Federal Reserve.

income increases. When this occurs, business firms will be more willing to borrow because they are likely to have many profitable investment opportunities for which they need financing. Hence, at a given interest rate, the quantity of bonds that firms want to sell (that is, the supply of bonds) will increase. This means that in a business cycle expansion, the supply curve for bonds shifts to the right (shown in Figure 6.7) from B_1^s to B_2^s.

The expanding economy will also affect the demand for bonds. The theory of asset demand tells us that as the business cycle expands and wealth increases, the demand for bonds will rise as well. We see this in Figure 6.7, where the demand curve has shifted to the right from B_1^d to B_2^d.

Given that both the supply and demand curves have shifted to the right, we know that the new equilibrium reached at the intersection of B_2^d and B_2^s also must move to the right. However, depending on whether the supply curve shifts more than the demand curve or vice versa, the new equilibrium interest rate can either rise or fall.

The supply and demand analysis used here gives us an ambiguous answer to the question of what will happen to interest rates in a business cycle expansion. The figure has been drawn so that the shift in the supply curve is greater than the shift in the demand curve, causing the equilibrium interest rate reached at point 2 to rise to i_2, which is greater than the initial equilibrium interest rate of i_1. The reason the figure has been drawn so that a business cycle expansion and a rise in income lead to a higher interest rate is because this is the outcome we actually see in the data.

Figure 6.8 plots the movement of the interest rate on three-month U.S. Treasury bills from 1951 to 1990 and indicates when the business cycle is undergoing recessions (shaded areas). As you can see, the interest rate rises during business cycle expansions and falls during recessions, which is what the supply and demand diagram indicates.

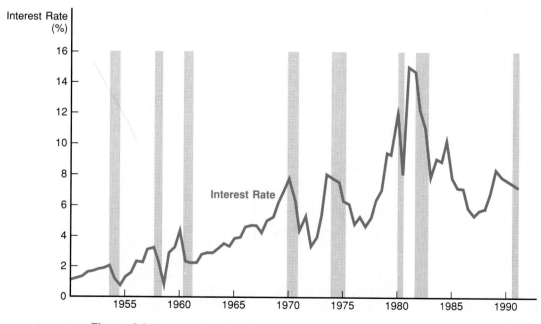

Figure 6.8
Business Cycle and Interest Rates (Three-Month Treasury Bills): 1951–1990   Shaded areas indicate periods of recession. Sources: Federal Reserve *Bulletin* and Citibase databank.

THE LIQUIDITY PREFERENCE FRAMEWORK: —————————
SUPPLY AND DEMAND IN THE MONEY MARKET

Whereas the loanable funds framework determines the equilibrium interest rate using the supply and demand for bonds, an alternative model developed by John Maynard Keynes and known as the **liquidity preference framework** determines the equilibrium interest rate in terms of the supply and demand for money. Although the two frameworks look different, the liquidity preference analysis is closely related to the loanable funds framework.

The starting point of Keynes' analysis is his assumption that there are two main categories of assets that people use to store their wealth: (1) money and (2) bonds. Therefore, total wealth in the economy must equal the total quantity of bonds plus money in the economy, which equals the quantity of bonds supplied (B^s) plus the quantity of money supplied (M^s). The quantity of bonds and money that people want to hold and thus demand (B^d and M^d) must also equal the total amount of wealth, since people will not be able to purchase more assets than their available resources allow. The conclusion is that the quantity of bonds and money supplied must equal the quantity of bonds and money demanded:

$$B^s + M^s = B^d + M^d \qquad (6.2)$$

Collecting the bond terms on one side of the equation and the money terms on the other, this equation can be rewritten as

$$B^s - B^d = M^d - M^s \qquad (6.3)$$

The rewritten equation tells us that if the money market is in equilibrium ($M^s = M^d$), then the right-hand side of equation (6.3) equals zero, implying that $B^s = B^d$, so that the bond market is also in equilibrium.

Thus it is the same to think about determining the equilibrium interest rate by equating the supply and demand for bonds or by equating the supply and demand for money. In this sense, the liquidity preference framework, which analyzes the money market, is equivalent to the loanable funds framework, which analyzes the bond market. In practice, the approaches differ because by assuming that there are only two kinds of assets, money and bonds, the liquidity preference approach implicitly ignores any effects on interest rates that arise from changes in the expected returns on real assets such as automobiles and houses. In most instances, both frameworks yield the same predictions.

The reason that we approach the determination of interest rates with both frameworks is that the loanable funds framework is easier to use when analyzing the effects from changes in expected inflation, while the liquidity preference framework provides a simpler analysis of the effects from changes in income, the price level, and the supply of money.

Since the definition of money that Keynes used includes currency (which earns no interest) and checking account deposits (which in his time typically earned only low interest if any), he assumed that money has a zero rate of return. Bonds, the only alternative asset to money in Keynes' framework, have an expected return equal to the interest rate i.[3] As this interest rate rises (holding everything else unchanged), the expected return on money falls relative to the expected return on bonds, and as the theory of asset demand tells us, this causes the demand for money to fall.

We can also see that the demand for money and the interest rate should be negatively related by using the concept of **opportunity cost,** the amount of interest (expected return) sacrificed by not holding the alternative asset, in this case a bond. As the interest rate on bonds, i, rises, the opportunity cost of holding money rises and so money is less desirable and the quantity of money demanded must fall.

Figure 6.9 shows the quantity of money demanded at a number of interest rates, with all other economic variables such as income and the price level held constant. At an interest rate of 25%, point A shows that the quantity of money demanded is $100 billion. If the interest rate is at the lower rate of 20%, the opportunity cost of money is lower and the quantity of money demanded rises to $200 billion, as indicated by the move from point A to

---

[3]Keynes did not actually assume that the expected returns on bonds equaled the interest rate, but rather argued that they were closely related (see Chapter 23). This distinction makes no appreciable difference in the analysis above.

Figure 6.9
Equilibrium in the Money Market

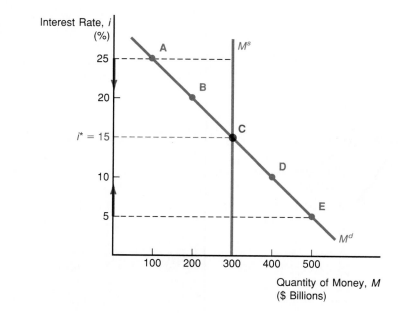

point B. If the interest rate is even lower, the quantity of money demanded is even higher, as is indicated by points C, D, and E. The curve connecting these points, M^d, is the demand curve for money, and it is downward sloping.

At this point in our analysis, we will assume that a central bank controls the amount of money supplied at a fixed quantity of $300 billion, so the supply curve for money drawn in the figure, M^s, is a vertical line at $300 billion. The equilibrium where the quantity of money demanded equals the quantity of money supplied occurs at the intersection of the supply and demand curves at point C, where

$$M^d = M^s \tag{6.4}$$

The resulting equilibrium interest rate is at $i^* = 15\%$.

We can again see that there is a tendency to approach this equilibrium by first looking at the relationship of money demand and supply when the interest rate is above the equilibrium interest rate. When the interest rate is at 25%, the quantity of money demanded at point A is $100 billion, yet the quantity of money supplied is $300 billion. The excess supply of money means that people are holding more money than they desire, so they will try to get rid of their excess money balances by trying to buy bonds. Accordingly, they will bid up the price of bonds, and as it rises, the interest rate will fall toward the equilibrium interest rate of 15%. This tendency is shown by the downward arrow drawn at the interest rate of 25%.

Likewise, if the interest rate is at 5%, then the quantity of money demanded at point E is $500 billion, yet the quantity of money supplied is only $300 billion. There is now an excess demand for money because people want to hold more money than they currently have. To try to get the money, they will sell their only other asset—bonds—and their price will fall. As the price of bonds falls, the interest rate will rise toward the equilibrium rate of 15%. Only when the interest rate is at its equilibrium value will there be no tendency for it to move further, and the interest rate will settle to its equilibrium value.

CHANGES IN EQUILIBRIUM INTEREST RATES

Analyzing how the equilibrium interest rate changes using the liquidity preference framework requires that we understand what causes the demand and supply curves for money to shift.

Study Guide
Learning the liquidity preference framework also requires practicing applications. When there is an application in the text to examine how the interest rate changes because some economic variable increases, see if you can draw

the appropriate shifts in the supply and demand curves when this same economic variable decreases. And remember to use the *ceteris paribus* assumption: When examining the effect of a change in one variable, hold all other variables constant.

Shifts in the Demand for Money

In Keynes' liquidity preference analysis, there are two factors that cause the demand curve for money to shift: (1) income and (2) the price level.

Income Effect   In Keynes' view there were two reasons why income would affect the demand for money. First, as an economy expands and income rises, wealth increases and people will want to hold more money as a store of value. Second, as the economy expands and income rises, people will want to carry out more transactions using money, with the result that they will also want to hold more money. The conclusion is that **a higher level of income causes the demand for money to increase and the demand curve to shift to the right.**

Price Level Effect   Keynes took the view that people care about the amount of money they hold *in real terms,* that is, in terms of the goods and services that it can buy. When the price level rises, the same nominal quantity of money is no longer as valuable; it cannot be used to purchase as many real goods or services. In order to restore their holdings of money in real terms to its former level, people will want to hold a greater nominal quantity of money, so **a rise in the price level causes the demand for money to increase and the demand curve to shift to the right.**

Shifts in the Supply of Money

We will assume that the supply of money is completely controlled by the central bank, which in the United States is the Federal Reserve. (Actually, the process that determines the money supply is substantially more complicated and involves banks, depositors, and borrowers from banks. We will study it in more detail later in the book.) For now, all we need to know is that **an increase in the money supply engineered by the Federal Reserve will shift the supply curve for money to the right.**

Changes in the Equilibrium Interest Rate

To see how the liquidity preference framework can be used to analyze the movement of interest rates, we will again look at several applications that will be useful in evaluating the effect of monetary policy on interest rates.

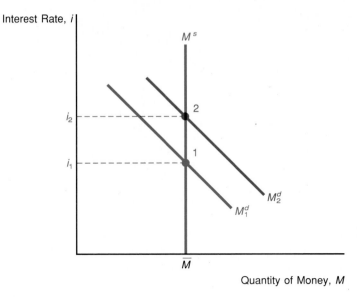

Figure 6.10

Response to a Change in Income
In a business cycle expansion when income is rising, the demand curve shifts out from M_1^d to M_2^d. The supply curve is fixed at $M^s = \overline{M}$. The equilibrium interest rate rises from i_1 to i_2.

Changes in Income When income is rising during a business cycle expansion, we have seen that the demand for money will rise. It is shown in Figure 6.10 by the shift rightward in the demand curve from M_1^d to M_2^d. The new equilibrium is reached at point 2 at the intersection of the M_2^d curve with the money supply curve, M^s. As you can see, the equilibrium interest rate rises from i_1 to i_2. The liquidity preference framework thus generates the conclusion that *when income is rising during a business cycle expansion (holding other economic variables constant), interest rates will rise.* This conclusion is unambiguous when contrasted to the conclusion reached about the effects of a change in income on interest rates using the loanable funds framework.

Changes in the Price Level When the price level rises, the value of money in terms of what it can purchase is lower. In order to restore their money holdings in real terms to its former level, people will want to hold a greater nominal quantity of money. A higher price level shifts the demand curve for money to the right from M_1^d to M_2^d (Figure 6.11). The equilibrium moves from point 1 to point 2, where the equilibrium interest rate has risen from i_1 to i_2, illustrating that *when the price level increases, with the supply of money and other economic variables held constant, interest rates will rise.*

Changes in the Money Supply An increase in the money supply due to expansionary monetary policy by the Federal Reserve implies that the supply curve for money shifts to the right. As is shown in Figure 6.12 by the movement of the supply curve from M_1^s to M_2^s, the equilibrium moves from point 1 down to point 2, where the M_2^s supply curve intersects with the de-

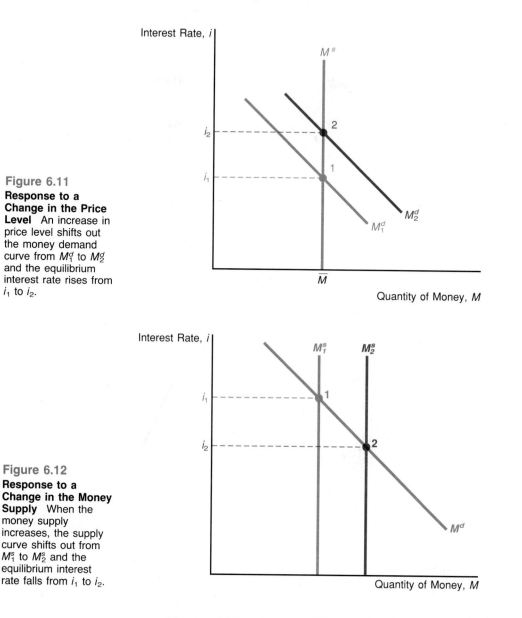

Figure 6.11

Response to a Change in the Price Level An increase in price level shifts out the money demand curve from M_1^d to M_2^d and the equilibrium interest rate rises from i_1 to i_2.

Figure 6.12

Response to a Change in the Money Supply When the money supply increases, the supply curve shifts out from M_1^s to M_2^s and the equilibrium interest rate falls from i_1 to i_2.

mand curve, M^d, and the equilibrium interest rate has fallen from i_1 to i_2. *When the money supply increases (everything else remaining equal), interest rates will decline.*[4]

---

[4]This same result can be generated using the loanable funds framework. As we will see in Chapters 14 and 15, the primary way that a central bank produces an increase in the money supply is by buying bonds and thereby decreasing the supply of bonds to the public. The resulting shift to the left of the supply curve for bonds will lead to a decline in the equilibrium interest rate.

APPLICATION
MONEY AND INTEREST RATES //////////////////////////////

The liquidity preference analysis in Figure 6.12 seems to lead to the conclusion that an increase in the money supply will lower interest rates. This conclusion has important policy implications, because is has frequently caused politicians to call for a more rapid growth of the money supply in order to drive down interest rates.

But is this conclusion that money and interest rates should be negatively related correct? Might there be other important factors left out of the liquidity preference analysis in Figure 6.12 that would reverse this conclusion? We will provide answers to these questions by applying the supply and demand analysis we have learned in this chapter to obtain a deeper understanding of the relationship between money and interest rates.

An important criticism of the conclusion that a rise in the money supply lowers interest rates has been raised by Milton Friedman, a Nobel laureate in economics. He acknowledges that the liquidity preference analysis is correct and calls the result that an increase in the money supply (*everything else remaining equal*) lowers interest rates the "liquidity effect." However, he views the liquidity effect as merely part of the story: An increase in the money supply might not leave "everything else equal" and will have other effects on the economy that may make interest rates rise. If these effects are substantial, then it is entirely possible that when the money supply rises, interest rates too may rise.

We have already laid the groundwork to discuss these other effects because we have shown how changes in income, the price level, and expected inflation affect the equilibrium interest rate.

Study Guide
To get further practice with the loanable funds and liquidity preference frameworks, show how the effects discussed here work by drawing the supply and demand diagrams that explain each effect. This exercise will also help you to better understand the effect of money on interest rates.

1. Income Effect. Because an increasing money supply is an expansionary influence on the economy, it should raise national income and wealth. Both the liquidity preference and loanable funds frameworks indicate that interest rates will then rise (see Figures 6.7 and 6.10). ***Thus the "income effect" of an increase in the money supply is a rise in interest rates in response to the higher level of income.***

2. Price Level Effect. An increase in the money supply can also cause the overall price level in the economy to rise. The liquidity preference framework predicts that this will lead to a rise in interest rates. ***So the "price level effect" from an increase in the money supply is a rise in interest rates in response to the rise in the price level.***

Following the Financial News

Forecasting Interest Rates

Forecasting interest rates is a time-honored profession. Economists are hired (sometimes at very high salaries) to forecast interest rates because businesses need to know what they will be to plan their future spending, while banks and investors require interest rate forecasts in order to decide which assets to buy. Interest rate forecasters predict what will happen to the factors that affect the supply and demand for bonds and for money—factors such as the strength of the economy, the profitability of investment opportunities, the expected inflation rate, and the size of government budget deficits and borrowing. They then use the supply and demand analysis we have outlined in this chapter to come up with their interest rate forecasts.

The *Wall Street Journal* reports on interest rate forecasts from leading forecasters twice a year (early January and July) in its "Economy" column or in its "Credit Markets" column, which surveys developments in the bond market daily. Forecasting interest rates is a perilous business. To their embarrassment, even the top forecasters are frequently far off in their forecasts.

A Sampling of Interest-Rate, Economic and Currency Forecasts
(In percent except for the dollar vs. yen)

	JUNE 1990 SURVEY					NEW FORECASTS FOR 1991									
	3-MO. TREASURY BILLS[1] 12/31	30-YR. BONDS 12/31	GNP[2] 2nd HALF 1990	CPI[3] 2nd HALF 1990	DLR. vs. YEN 12/31	3-MONTH TREASURY BILLS[1] 6/30	12/31	30-YEAR TREASURY BONDS 6/30	12/31	GNP[2] 1st HALF	2nd HALF	INFLATION RATE[3] 1st HALF	2nd HALF	DOLLAR vs. YEN 6/30	12/31
Robert Barbera, Lehman Brothers	7.40	8.00	1.2	3.8	140	4.90	5.60	6.80	7.40	-2.4	5.4	2.6	2.7	126	130
David Berson, Fannie Mae	7.75	8.30	1.7	4.9	152	6.48	6.95	7.70	7.92	-0.1	2.4	3.5	4.3	140	145
Paul Boltz, T. Rowe Price	8.25	8.75	2.3	4.5	150	6.50	7.30	8.00	8.80	-0.6	2.4	4.7	5.0	125	135
Philip Braverman, DKB Securities	7.00	7.75	0.5	3.5	140	6.00	5.00	7.40	6.90	-2.5	-2.5	4.0	3.5	125	140
Dewey Daane, Vanderbilt Univ.	7.75	9.00	1.8	5.0	140	6.00	6.50	8.00	8.50	-2.5	-0.5	5.0	5.5	130	125
Robert Dederick, Northern Trust	8.00	8.50	2.2	4.0	145	6.00	6.25	7.85	8.20	-1.0	3.0	3.8	4.0	130	125
Gail Fosler, Conference Board	8.30	8.60	3.3	5.3	155	6.00	6.50	8.50	8.60	1.6	1.7	4.4	4.9	140	155
Lyle Gramley, Mortg. Bankers Assn.	8.00	8.50	1.8	4.4	150	6.80	8.00	8.10	8.20	-0.6	2.1	3.5	4.2	128	130
Maury Harris, PaineWebber Inc.	7.50	8.25	2.0	3.9	150	6.00	6.50	7.50	8.00	-1.0	3.5	2.0	2.0	130	140
Richard Hoey, Barclays de Zoete	7.50	8.25	-1.5	4.4	148	6.35	6.45	7.90	8.00	-2.2	3.7	4.2	3.8	120	135
Stuart G. Hoffman, PNC Fin'l Corp.	7.63	8.25	1.4	4.1	153	6.35	6.80	7.80	8.15	-1.8	1.2	4.5	4.2	133	138
Edward Hyman, C.J. Lawrence	7.25	8.00	1.0	3.0	158	6.20	6.20	7.20	7.20	-2.0	0.5	3.5	3.0	140	150
Saul Hymans, Univ. of Michigan	8.13	8.76	3.4	4.3	152	7.03	7.18	8.41	8.42	1.6	3.4	5.1	4.5	127	127
David Jones, Aubrey G. Lanston	7.75	8.25	1.2	4.5	152	6.50	6.00	7.75	7.50	-2.0	-1.0	5.8	5.3	130	135
Jerry Jordan, First Interstate	7.25	8.00	2.5	3.7	145	6.30	6.60	7.80	8.00	1.2	2.9	3.7	4.1	128	137
Samuel Kahan, Fuji Securities	7.50	8.00	1.7	3.8	145	6.50	6.25	8.00	7.75	0.0	1.5	2.0	3.5	145	135
Irwin Kellner, Manufacturers Hanover	7.50	8.25	0.9	3.5	140	5.25	5.50	8.50	9.00	-1.5	1.5	4.5	3.0	125	120
Lawrence Kudlow, Bear Stearns	7.10	7.30	1.3	3.0	160	6.10	6.40	7.63	7.61	0.8	2.1	4.0	3.8	140	150
Carol Leisenring, CoreStates Fin'l	7.30	8.10	1.9	4.2	145	6.20	6.70	7.80	8.00	-0.7	2.0	4.5	2.7	140	150
Alan Lerner, Bankers Trust Co.	7.50	7.85	1.5	4.5	145	6.25	6.65	7.75	8.15	0.5	1.5	3.5	4.3	150	160
Mickey Levy, CRT Govt. Securities	7.45	8.00	0.8	3.8	160	6.50	6.40	7.50	7.60	0.6	1.7	3.0	3.5	138	140
William Melton, IDS	7.65	8.60	1.0	3.9	149	6.00	6.40	7.90	8.20	-0.2	3.1	3.7	2.7	125	122
Lynn Michaelis, Weyerhaeuser Co.	7.80	8.40	1.5	4.6	145	6.50	6.00	7.70	7.30	0.0	0.8	4.8	4.0	130	125
Arnold Moskowitz, Moskowitz Capital	8.05	8.70	1.9	4.8	165	5.80	4.80	7.60	7.20	-2.9	1.1	3.8	3.0	136	141
Elliott Platt, Donaldson Lufkin	7.23	7.88	1.3	4.0	148	6.18	6.15	7.50	7.50	-1.0	2.5	3.5	4.0	127	127
Donald Ratajczak, Georgia State Univ.	7.83	8.55	2.1	3.9	148	6.46	6.69	7.68	7.93	-1.8	1.6	3.6	3.5	136	140
David Resler, Nomura Securities Int'l	7.25	7.75	1.8	3.6	155	5.90	6.10	6.90	7.30	-2.0	1.7	2.6	3.0	135	140
Alan Reynolds, Hudson Institute	7.50	7.80	2.7	3.6	149	6.00	6.60	7.80	7.80	-1.4	2.7	3.0	3.4	143	140
Richard Rippe, Dean Witter	7.50	7.75	1.7	3.8	142	6.45	6.65	7.50	7.80	0.6	2.4	3.1	4.1	130	125
Norman Robertson, Mellon Bank	7.60	8.30	1.9	4.0	148	6.20	6.30	7.50	7.80	-1.1	1.7	4.3	3.0	126	131
Francis Schott, Equitable Life	7.70	8.20	1.8	4.3	150	6.30	6.40	7.90	8.10	-1.8	1.2	4.9	4.2	128	123
A. Gary Shilling, Shilling & Co.	6.00	7.25	-2.4	2.7	170	5.00	3.00	6.00	4.00	-4.5	-2.5	3.0	2.0	170	190
Allen Sinai, Boston Co.	7.50	7.92	0.8	3.8	141	5.93	5.75	7.83	7.22	-2.8	2.0	4.5	3.7	125	137
James F. Smith, Univ. of N.C.	6.75	7.75	3.7	2.9	158	6.45	5.65	7.60	6.95	2.7	4.2	2.3	3.6	143	157
Neal Soss, First Boston Corp.	7.50	8.00	1.3	4.5	145	5.75	6.00	7.00	7.25	-2.0	1.5	4.5	4.2	140	150
Donald Straszheim, Merrill Lynch	7.49	8.10	1.7	4.4	150	5.75	6.15	7.50	7.75	-2.0	1.7	4.3	3.8	120	130
Joseph Wahed, Wells Fargo Bank	7.50	8.00	2.0	3.7	150	6.00	5.50	7.50	7.60	-1.6	1.0	3.2	3.9	137	140
Raymond Worseck, A.G. Edwards	8.50	8.80	2.3	4.2	145	6.30	6.10	7.70	7.80	-0.8	0.5	4.7	4.1	145	135
David Wyss, DRI/McGraw-Hill	7.95	8.75	1.9	3.8	148	6.25	7.10	8.15	8.90	-1.2	2.2	4.0	3.5	120	130
Edward Yardeni, Prudential-Bache	7.75	7.75	2.0	3.5	165	6.25	6.25	7.50	7.00	2.0	2.0	3.0	3.5	140	150
Average[4]	7.56	8.16	1.6	4.0	150	6.14	6.23	7.65	7.73	-0.9	1.7	3.8	3.7	134	138
Actual closing rates as of 12/31/90[5]	6.62	8.24	N.A.	N.A.	135										

N.A.-Not available. [1]Treasury bill rates are on a bond-equivalent basis. [2]Gross national product, adjusted for inflation. Seasonally adjusted annual rate. [3]Consumer price index, annual rate. [4]Averages for the mid-1990 survey, published July 5, are for the analysts polled at that time. [5]The government will estimate second-half GNP later this month.

Source: *Wall Street Journal* (Wednesday, January 2, 1991), p. 2.

3. Expected Inflation Effect. The rising price level, that is, the higher inflation rate, that results from an increase in the money supply also affects interest rates by affecting the expected inflation rate. Specifically, an increase in the money supply may lead people to expect a higher price level in the future—hence the expected inflation rate will be higher. The loanable funds framework has shown us that this increase in expected inflation will lead to a higher level of interest rates. ***Therefore, the "expected inflation effect" of an increase in the money supply is a rise in interest rates in response to the rise in the expected inflation rate.***

At first glance it would appear as though the price level effect and expected inflation effect are the same thing. They both indicate that increases in the price level induced by an increase in the money supply will raise interest rates. However, there is a subtle difference between the two, and this is why they are discussed as two separate effects.

Suppose there is a one-time increase in the money supply today that leads to a rise in prices to a permanently higher level by next year. As the price level rises over the course of this year, the interest rate will rise via the price level effect. Only at the end of the year when the price level has risen to its peak will the price level effect be at a maximum.

The rising price level will also raise interest rates via the expected inflation effect because people will expect that inflation will be higher over the course of the year. However, when the price level stops rising next year, inflation and the expected inflation rate will fall back down to zero. Any rise in interest rates as a result of the earlier rise in expected inflation will then be reversed. We thus see that, in contrast to the price level effect that reaches its greatest impact next year, the expected inflation effect will have its smallest impact (that is, zero) next year. The basic difference between the two effects is then that the price level effect remains even after prices have stopped rising, while the expected inflation effect does not.

An important point is that the expected inflation effect will only continue as long as the price level continues to rise. As we will see in our discussion of monetary theory in subsequent chapters, a one-time increase in the money supply will not produce a continually rising price level, only a higher rate of money supply growth will. Thus a higher rate of money supply growth is needed if the expected inflation effect is to persist.

Does a Higher Rate of Growth of the Money Supply Lower Interest Rates?

We can now put together all the effects we have discussed to help us decide whether our analysis supports the politicians who advocate a greater rate of growth of the money supply when they feel that interest rates are too high. Of all the effects, only the liquidity effect indicates that a higher rate of money growth will cause a decline in interest rates. In contrast, the income, price level, and expected inflation effects indicate that interest rates will rise when money growth is higher. Which of these effects are largest and how quickly do they take effect? The answer to this question is critical in determining whether interest rates will rise or fall when money supply growth is increased.

Generally, the liquidity effect from the greater money growth takes effect immediately because the rising money supply leads to an immediate decline in the equilibrium interest rate. The income and price level effects take time to work because the increasing money supply takes time to raise the price level and income, which in turn raise interest rates. The expected inflation effect, which also raises interest rates, can be slow or fast depending on whether people adjust their expectations of inflation slowly or quickly when the money growth rate is increased.

Three possibilities are outlined in Figure 6.13; each shows how interest rates respond over time to an increased rate of money supply growth starting at time T. Panel (a) shows a case in which the liquidity effect dominates the other effects so that the interest rate falls from i_1 at time T to a final level of i_2. The liquidity effect operates quickly to lower the interest rate, but as time goes by, the other effects start to reverse some of the decline. Because the liquidity effect is larger than the others, however, the interest rate never rises back to its initial level.

Panel (b) has a lesser liquidity effect than the other effects, with the expected inflation effect operating slowly because expectations of inflation are slow to adjust upward. Initially, the liquidity effect drives down the interest rate. Then the income, price level, and expected inflation effects begin to raise it. Since these effects are dominant, the interest rate eventually rises above its initial level to i_2. In the short run, lower interest rates result from increased money growth, but eventually they end up climbing above the initial level.

Panel (c) has the expected inflation effect dominating as well as operating rapidly, because people quickly raise their expectation of inflation when the rate of money growth is increased. The expected inflation effect begins immediately to overpower the liquidity effect, so the interest rate immediately starts to climb. Over time, as income and price level effects start to take hold, the interest rate rises even higher and the eventual outcome is an interest rate that is substantially above the initial interest rate. The result shows clearly that increasing money supply growth is not the answer to reducing interest rates but, rather, money growth should be reduced in order to lower interest rates!

An important issue for economic policymakers is which of these three scenarios is closer to reality. If a decline in interest rates is desired, then an increase in money supply growth is called for when the liquidity effect dominates the other effects [panel (a)]. A decrease in money growth is appropriate if the other effects dominate the liquidity effect and expectations of inflation adjust rapidly [panel (c)]. If the other effects dominate the liquidity effect but expectations of inflation only adjust slowly [panel (b)], then

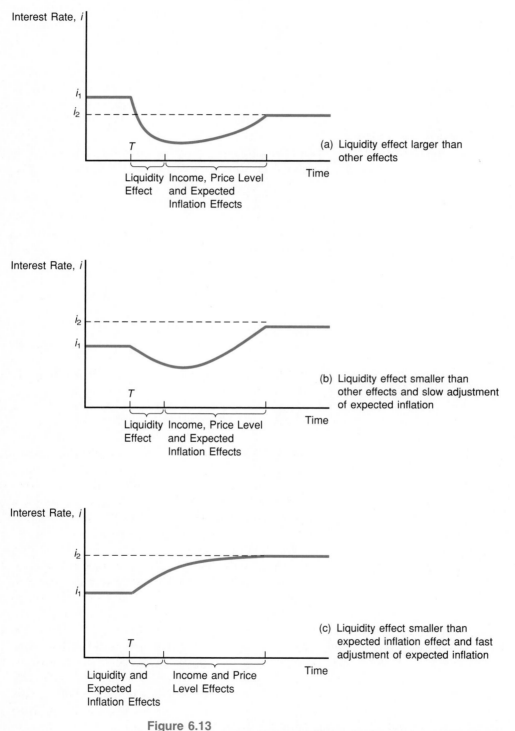

Interest Rate, i

i_1
i_2

T

(a) Liquidity effect larger than other effects

Time

Liquidity Effect   Income, Price Level and Expected Inflation Effects

Interest Rate, i

i_2
i_1

T

(b) Liquidity effect smaller than other effects and slow adjustment of expected inflation

Time

Liquidity Effect   Income, Price Level and Expected Inflation Effects

Interest Rate, i

i_2
i_1

T

(c) Liquidity effect smaller than expected inflation effect and fast adjustment of expected inflation

Time

Liquidity and Expected Inflation Effects   Income and Price Level Effects

Figure 6.13
Response Over Time to an Increase in Money Supply Growth

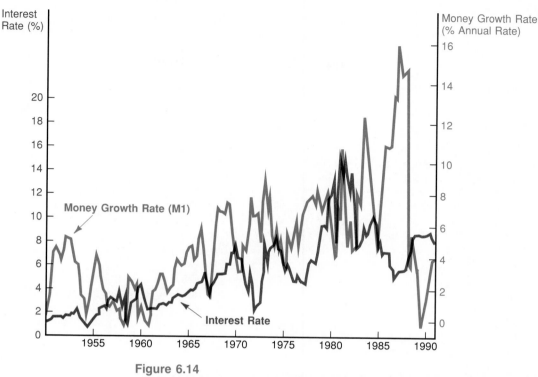

Figure 6.14
Money Growth (*M*1 Annual Rate) and Interest Rates (Three-Month Treasury Bills):
1951–1990 Sources: Federal Reserve *Bulletin* and Citibase databank.

whether you want to increase or decrease money growth depends on whether you care more about what happens in the short run or the long run.

Which scenario is supported by the evidence? The relationship of interest rates and money growth from 1951 to 1990 is plotted in Figure 6.14. When the rate of money supply growth began to climb in the mid-1960s, interest rates rose, indicating that the liquidity effect was dominated by the price level, income, and expected inflation effects. By the 1970s, interest rates reached levels unprecedented in the period after World War II, as did the rate of money supply growth.

The scenario depicted in panel (a) of Figure 6.13 seems doubtful, and the case for lowering interest rates by raising the rate of money growth is much weakened. Looking back at Figure 6.6, which shows the relationship between interest rates and expected inflation, you should not find this too surprising. The rise in the rate of money supply growth in the 1960s and 1970s is matched by a large rise in expected inflation, which would lead us to predict that the expected inflation effect would be dominant. It is the most plausible explanation for why interest rates rose in the face of higher money growth. However, Figure 6.14 does not really tell us which one of the two scenarios in panels (b) and (c) of Figure 6.13 is more accurate. It depends critically on how fast people's expectations about inflation adjust. How expectations are formed and whether they adjust rapidly is an important topic, which is currently being actively studied by economists and is dealt with in Chapter 29.

SUMMARY

1. The supply and demand analysis for bonds, known as the loanable funds framework, provides one theory of how interest rates are determined. It predicts that interest rates will change when there is a change in demand because of changes in income (or wealth), expected returns, risk and/or liquidity, or when there is a change in supply because of changes in the attractiveness of investment opportunities, the real cost of borrowing, and/or government activities.

2. An alternative theory of how interest rates are determined is provided by the liquidity preference framework which analyzes the supply and demand for money. It shows that interest rates will change when there is a change in the de-

mand for money because of changes in income or the price level, or when there is a change in the supply of money.

3. There are four possible effects of an increase in the money supply on interest rates: (a) the liquidity effect, (b) the income effect, (c) the price level effect, and (d) the expected inflation effect. The liquidity effect indicates that a rise in money supply growth will lead to a decline in interest rates, while the other effects work in the opposite direction. The evidence seems to indicate that the income, price level, and expected inflation effects dominate the liquidity effect so that an increase in money supply growth leads to higher rather than lower interest rates.

KEY TERMS

demand curve

supply curve

market equilibrium

excess supply

excess demand

loanable funds

loanable funds
  framework

Fisher effect

liquidity preference
  framework

opportunity cost

QUESTIONS AND PROBLEMS

In all the problems, answer the questions by drawing the appropriate supply and demand diagrams.

* 1. As we will see in Chapter 15, an important way that the Federal Reserve decreases the money supply is by selling bonds to the public. Using the loanable funds framework, show what effect this action has on interest rates. Is your answer consistent with what you would expect to find with the liquidity preference framework?

2. Using both the liquidity preference and loanable funds frameworks, show why interest rates are *procyclical* (that is, rise when the economy is expanding and fall during recessions).

* 3. Why should a rise in the price level (but *not* in expected inflation) cause interest rates to rise when the nominal money supply is fixed?

4. Look up the column "Credit Markets" in the *Wall Street Journal*. Underline the statements in the column that explain bond price movements, and

draw the appropriate supply and demand diagrams that support these statements.

5. What effect will a sudden increase in the volatility of gold prices have on interest rates?

* 6. How might a sudden increase in people's expectations of future real estate prices affect interest rates?

7. Explain what effect a large federal deficit might have on interest rates.

* 8. Using both the loanable funds and liquidity preference frameworks, show what the effect is on interest rates when the riskiness of bonds rises. Are the results the same in the two frameworks?

9. If the price level falls next year, remaining fixed thereafter, and the money supply is fixed, what is likely to happen to interest rates over the next two years? (Hint: Take account of both the price level effect and the expected inflation effect.)

*10. Will there be an effect on interest rates if brokerage commissions on stocks fall? Why?

Using Economic Analysis to Predict the Future

11. The president of the United States announces in his press conference that he will fight the higher inflation rate with a new anti-inflation program. Predict what will happen to interest rates if the public believes him.

*12. Suppose the chairman of the Fed announces that interest rates will rise sharply next year and the market believes him. What will happen to today's interest rate on AT&T bonds, such as the 8 ⅝s of 2007?

13. Predict what will happen to interest rates if the public suddenly expects a large increase in stock prices.

*14. Predict what will happen to interest rates if prices in the bond market become more volatile.

15. If a new chairman of the Federal Reserve Board is appointed who has a reputation for advocating even a slower rate of money growth than his predecessor, what will happen to interest rates? Discuss the possible resulting situations.

CHAPTER 7

The Risk and Term Structure of Interest Rates

PREVIEW   In our supply and demand analysis of interest rate behavior in Chapter 6, we examined the determination of just one interest rate. Yet we saw earlier that there are enormous numbers of bonds, and their interest rates can and do differ. In this chapter we complete the interest rate picture by examining the relationship of the various interest rates to each other. Understanding why they differ from bond to bond can help business firms, banks, insurance companies, and private investors decide which bonds to purchase as investments or which ones they should sell.

We first look at why bonds with the same term (length of time) to maturity have different interest rates. The relationship among these interest rates is called the **risk structure of interest rates,** although risk, liquidity, *and* income tax rules all play an important role in determining the risk structure. A bond's term to maturity also affects its interest rate, and the relationship among interest rates on bonds with different terms to maturity is called the **term structure of interest rates.** In this chapter we will examine the sources and causes of fluctuations in interest rates relative to one another and will look at a number of theories that explain these fluctuations.

RISK STRUCTURE OF INTEREST RATES

Figure 7.1 shows the yields to maturity for several different categories of long-term bonds from 1919 to 1990. It shows us two important features of interest rate behavior for bonds of the same maturity: Interest rates on different categories of bonds differ from each other in any given year, and the spread (that is, the difference) between the interest rates varies over time. The interest rates on municipal bonds, for example, are above those on U.S. government bonds in the late 1930s but are lower thereafter. In addition, the spread between the interest rates on Baa corporate bonds (riskier than

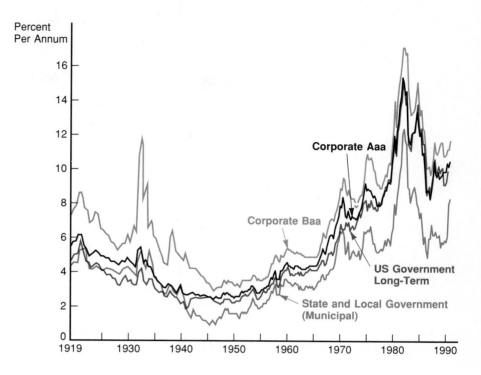

Figure 7.1
Long-Term Bond Yields: 1919–1990
Sources: Board of Governors of the Federal Reserve System, *Banking and Monetary Statistics,* and Federal Reserve *Bulletin.*

Aaa corporate bonds) and U.S. government bonds is very large during the Great Depression years 1930–1933, is smaller during the 1940s, 1950s, and 1960s, and then widens again in the 1970s and 1980s. What factors are responsible for these phenomena?

Default Risk

One attribute of a bond that influences its interest rate is its **default risk,** the chance that the issuer of the bond will default, that is, be unable to make interest payments or pay off the face value when the bond matures. A corporation suffering big losses, such as the Chrysler Corporation did in the 1970s, might be more likely to suspend interest payments on its bonds.[1] The default risk on its bonds would therefore be quite high. On the other hand, U.S. government bonds have no default risk because the federal government can always increase taxes or even print money to pay off its obligations. Bonds with no default risk, such as U.S. government bonds, are called **default-free bonds.** The spread between the interest rates on bonds with de-

---

[1]Chrysler did not default on its loans in this period, but it would have if not for a government bailout plan intended to preserve jobs, which, in effect, provided Chrysler with funds that were used to pay off creditors.

fault risk and default-free bonds, called the **risk premium,** indicates how much additional interest people must earn in order to be willing to hold a risky bond. Our supply and demand analysis of the bond market, developed in the preceding chapter, can be used to explain why a bond with default risk always has a positive risk premium and why the higher the default risk is, the larger the risk premium will be.

Study Guide

Two exercises will help you better understand the risk structure:

1. Put yourself in the shoes of an investor—see how your purchase decision would be affected by changes in risk and liquidity.

2. Practice drawing the appropriate shifts in the supply and demand curves when risk and liquidity change. For example, see if you can draw the appropriate shifts in the supply and demand curves when, in contrast to the examples in the text, a corporate bond has a decline in default risk or an improvement in its liquidity.

In order to examine the effect of default risk on interest rates, let us look at the supply and demand diagrams for the default-free (U.S. government) and corporate long-term bond markets in Figure 7.2. To make the diagrams

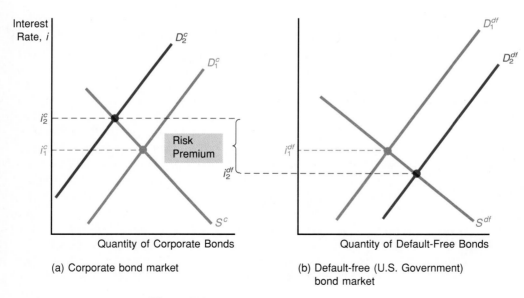

(a) Corporate bond market

(b) Default-free (U.S. Government) bond market

Figure 7.2

Response to an Increase in Default Risk on Corporate Bonds An increase in default risk on corporate bonds lowers the demand from D_1^c in to D_2^c. Simultaneously, it raises the demand for default-free bonds from D_1^{df} to D_2^{df}. The equilibrium rate for corporate bonds rises from i_1^c to i_2^c, while it falls from i_1^{df} to i_2^{df} in the default-free bond market.

somewhat easier to read, let's assume that initially there is no possibility of default on the corporate bonds, so they are default-free like U.S. government bonds. In this case, these two bonds have the same attributes (identical risk and maturity) and their equilibrium interest rates will initially be equal ($i_1^c = i_1^{df}$) and the risk premium on corporate bonds ($i_1^c - i_1^{df}$) will be zero.

If the possibility of a default increases because a corporation begins to suffer large losses, then the default risk on corporate bonds will increase and the expected return on these bonds will decrease. In addition, the corporate bond's return will be more uncertain as well. The theory of asset demand predicts that because the expected return on the corporate bond falls relative to the expected return on the default-free (U.S. government) bond while its relative riskiness rises, the corporate bond is less desirable (holding everything else equal) and the demand for it will fall. The demand curve for corporate bonds in Figure 7.2, panel (a), then shifts in from D_1^c to D_2^c.

At the same time, the expected return on default-free (U.S. government) bonds increases relative to the expected return on corporate bonds while their relative riskiness declines. The default-free bonds thus become more desirable, and the demand rises [as shown in panel (b) by the outward shift in the demand curve for these bonds from D_1^{df} to D_2^{df}].

The equilibrium interest rate for corporate bonds rises from i_1^c to i_2^c, while the default-free bond equilibrium interest rate falls from i_1^{df} to i_2^{df}. The spread between the interest rates on corporate and default-free bonds, that is, the risk premium on corporate bonds, has risen from zero to $i_2^c - i_2^{df}$. We can now conclude the following: ***A bond with default risk will always have a positive risk premium, and an increase in its default risk will raise the risk premium.***

Because default risk is so important to the size of the risk premium, purchasers of bonds need to have information on whether a corporation is likely to default on its bonds. Two major investment advisory firms, Moody's Investors Service and Standard and Poor's Corporation, provide default risk information by rating the quality of corporate and municipal bonds in terms of the probability of default. The different ratings and their description are contained in Table 7.1. Bonds with relatively low risk of default are called "investment grade" securities and have a rating of Baa (or BBB) and above. Bonds with ratings below Baa (or BBB) have higher default risk and have been aptly dubbed **junk bonds.**

Next, let's look back at Figure 7.1 and see if we can explain the relationship between interest rates on corporate and U.S. government bonds. Corporate bonds always have higher interest rates than U.S. government bonds because they always have some risk of default whereas U.S. government bonds do not. Because Baa-rated corporate bonds have a greater default risk than the higher-rated Aaa bonds, their risk premium is greater and, therefore, the Baa rate always exceeds the Aaa rate.

We also can use the same analysis to explain the huge jump in the risk

Table 7.1   **Bond Ratings by Moody's and Standard and Poor's**

Moody's	Standard and Poor's	Descriptions	Examples of Corporations with Bonds Outstanding in 1991
Aaa	AAA	Highest quality (lowest default risk)	General Electric; IBM; Shell Oil
Aa	AA	High quality	Mobil; Coca-Cola; Toys "R" Us; General Motors
A	A	Upper medium grade	Westinghouse; Sears; Xerox; PepsiCo; Colgate-Palmolive
Baa	BBB	Medium grade	Chrysler; Columbia Pictures; Honeywell; Texaco
Ba	BB	Lower medium grade	Union Carbide; Wendy's; Black and Decker; RJR-Nabisco
B	B	Speculative	Chock Full O'Nuts; Fruit of the Loom; Mattel; Atari
Caa	CCC-CC	Poor; high default risk	
Ca	C	Highly speculative	
C	D	Lowest grade	

premium on Baa corporate bond rates during the Great Depression years 1930–1933 and the rise in the risk premium in the 1970s and 1980s (see Figure 7.1). The Great Depression period saw a very high rate of business failures and defaults. As we would expect, these factors led to a substantial increase in default risk for bonds issued by vulnerable corporations, and the risk premium for Baa bonds reached unprecedentedly high levels. The 1970s and 1980s again saw higher levels of business failures and defaults, although they were still well below the Depression levels. Again, as expected, default risks and risk premiums for corporate bonds rose, widening the spread between interest rates on corporate and government bonds. Our analysis also explains the sharp rise in the spread between interest rates on junk bonds and government bonds after the stock market crash in October 1987 (Box 7.1).

Liquidity

Another attribute of a bond that influences its interest rate is its liquidity. As we learned in Chapter 5, a liquid asset is one that can be quickly and cheaply converted into cash if the need arises. The more liquid an asset is, the more

B o x   7 . 1

The Stock Market Crash of 1987 and the Junk Bond–Treasury Spread

The stock market crash of October 19, 1987, had a major impact on bond markets that is well explained by the supply and demand analysis in Figure 7.2. As a consequence of the Black Monday crash, many investors began to doubt the financial health of corporations with lower credit ratings that had issued junk bonds. The increase in default risk for junk bonds made them less desirable at any given interest rate, decreased the quantity demanded, and shifted the demand curve for junk bonds to the left. As shown in the left-hand panel of Figure 7.2, the interest rate on junk bonds should have risen, which is indeed what happened: interest rates on junk bonds shot up by about one percentage point. On the other hand, the increase in the perceived default risk for junk bonds after the crash made default-free U.S. Treasury bonds relatively more attractive and shifted the demand curve for these securities to the right—an outcome described by some analysts as a "flight to quality." Just as our analysis predicts in Figure 7.2, interest rates on Treasury securities fell by about one percentage point. The overall outcome was that the spread between interest rates on junk bonds and government bonds rose by two percentage points, from 4% before the crash to 6% immediately after.

desirable it is (holding everything else constant). U.S. government bonds are the most liquid of all bonds because they are so widely traded that they are the easiest to sell quickly and the cost of selling them is low. Corporate bonds, on the other hand, are not as liquid because fewer bonds for any one corporation are traded; thus it can be costly to sell these bonds in an emergency because it may be hard to find buyers quickly.

How does the less liquid attribute of corporate bonds affect their interest rates relative to the interest rate on U.S. government bonds? By using our supply and demand analysis, we can show that the less liquid a bond is, everything else equal, the higher its interest rate will be relative to more liquid securities. Therefore, the lower liquidity of corporate bonds relative to U.S. government bonds increases the spread between the interest rates on these two bonds.

The analysis shown in Figure 7.3 is similar to the default-risk analysis in Figure 7.2. If two bonds, A and B, initially are equally liquid and all their other attributes are the same, then their equilibrium interest rates will initially be equal: $i_1^A = i_1^B$. If bond A now becomes less liquid because it becomes less widely traded, then, as the theory of asset demand indicates, its demand will fall, shifting its demand curve in from D_1^A to D_2^A as in panel (a). The other bond, bond B, becomes relatively more liquid in comparison to bond A, so its demand curve shifts out from D_1^B to D_2^B as in panel (b). We can see in Figure 7.3 that the equilibrium interest rate on the less liquid asset, bond A, rises, while the equilibrium interest rate on the more liquid asset, bond B, falls, increasing the spread between them. Therefore, the differences among the various bond rates (that is, the risk premiums) reflect not only a bond's de-

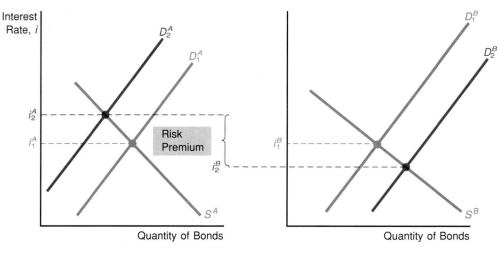

Figure 7.3
Response to a Change in Liquidity When bond A becomes less liquid, the demand for bond A shifts in from D_1^A to D_2^A and the demand for bond B shifts out from D_1^B to D_2^B. The equilibrium rate for bond A rises from i_1^A to i_2^A, while it falls from i_1^B to i_2^B for bond B.

fault risk, but its liquidity too. This is why a risk premium is sometimes called a "liquidity premium." Most accurately, it should be called a risk *and* liquidity premium, but convention dictates that it be called a risk premium.

Income Tax Considerations

Referring back to Figure 7.1, we are still left with one puzzle—the behavior of municipal bond rates. Municipal bonds are certainly not default-free: State and local governments have defaulted on the municipal bonds they have issued in the past—particularly during the Great Depression of 1929–1933 and even more recently in the case of the Washington State Public Power Supply System in 1983. Also, municipal bonds are not as liquid as U.S. government bonds.

Why is it, then, that these bonds have had lower interest rates than U.S. government bonds for the past forty years, as indicated in Figure 7.1? The explanation for the lower interest rates lies in the fact that interest payments on municipal bonds are exempt from income taxes, a factor that has the same effect on the demand for municipal bonds as an increase in their expected return.

Let us imagine that you are lucky enough to have a high income to put you in a 31% income tax bracket, where for every extra dollar of income you have to pay 31 cents to the government. If you own a \$1000 face value U.S. government bond that sells for \$1000 and has a coupon payment of \$100, you get to keep only $69 of the payment after taxes. Although the bond has a 10% interest rate, you actually earn only 6.9% after taxes.

Suppose, however, that you put your savings into a $1000 face value municipal bond that sells for $1000 and pays only $80 of coupon payments. Its interest rate is only 8%, but because it is a tax-exempt security, you pay no taxes on the $80 coupon payment and you earn 8% after taxes. Clearly, you earn more on the municipal bond after taxes, so you are willing to hold the riskier and less liquid municipal bond even though it has a lower interest rate than the U.S. government bond. (This was not true before World War II as explained in Box 7.2.)

Another way of understanding why municipal bonds have lower interest rates than U.S. government bonds makes use of the supply and demand analysis we conducted in Figure 7.3. The tax advantages of municipal bonds which raise their after-tax expected return relative to U.S. government bonds make them more desirable. The result is that the demand for them increases and lowers their interest rates, as occurs in Figure 7.3(b). On the other hand, U.S. government bonds become less desirable because their after-tax expected return relative to that of municipal bonds decreases. Hence, the demand for U.S. government bonds decreases and raises their interest rates as in Figure 7.3(a). The resulting lower interest rates for municipal bonds and higher interest rates for U.S. government bonds, then, explains why municipal bonds can have interest rates below that of U.S. government bonds.

Another tax consideration is important to holders of U.S. government and corporate bonds. Some U.S. government bonds have an extra provision that allows them to be cashed in at par value to pay off estate taxes when their holder dies. For example, the U.S. Treasury 3s of February 1995 (that is, the bond maturing in February of 1995 with a coupon rate of 3%) was selling for $969 on March 7, 1991. However, if its owner dies on that day, then the bond

B o x   7 . 2

Interest Rates on Municipal and U.S. Government Bonds Before World War II

As you can see in Figure 7.1, municipal bonds had higher interest rates than U.S. government bonds before World War II. At first glance this might appear to be a contradiction because of the tax-exempt status of these bonds, which would lower their interest rates relative to taxable U.S. government bonds according to the analysis in the text. The contradiction is resolved by recognizing that the tax-exempt status of municipal bonds did not convey much of an advantage before World War II because income tax rates were extremely low in that period.

can be cashed in at the par value of $1000 to pay estate taxes. (Such bonds are irreverently called "flower bonds.")

Recognizing this tax consideration explains another seeming contradiction found on the bond page of the newspaper. There are cases where two government bonds with the same maturity date have very different yields. For example, the 3s of February 1995 had a yield of 3.85% on March 7, 1991, while the 10½s of February 1995 had a yield of 7.59%. Both these securities should have the same yields because they have the same risk characteristics (they are default-free). The yields differ because the 3s of February 1995 are flower bonds, while the 10½s of February 1995 are not. Suppose that an aging Richie Rich expects to die in the near future and has a substantial amount of wealth that will be subject to estate taxes. If he buys the flower bonds (the 3s of February 1995) for $969 today and dies six months from now, then the bond will be worth $1000 at his death. The return on the bond over six months equals the sum $15 (half the annual sum of $30 coupon payment) plus the $31 increase in its value ($46), divided by the initial purchase price, $969. Thus although the yield to maturity on this bond is only 3.85%, the six-month return for Richie's estate is 4.75% (9.50% at an annual rate). This bond is therefore an attractive security for Richie to buy, despite its low yield.

To summarize, the risk structure of interest rates (the relationship among interest rates on bonds with the same maturity) is explained by three factors: default risk, liquidity, and the income tax treatment of the bond. As a bond's default risk increases, the risk premium on that bond (the spread between its interest rate and the interest rate on a default-free bond) rises. As a bond's liquidity improves, its interest rate will fall. If a bond has favorable tax treatment—for example, its coupon payments are exempt from income taxes or it is a flower bond—then its interest rate will be lower than comparable bonds without these tax benefits.

TERM STRUCTURE OF INTEREST RATES

We have seen how risk, liquidity, and tax considerations (collectively embedded in the risk structure) can influence interest rates. Another factor that influences the interest rate on a bond is its term to maturity: Bonds with identical risk, liquidity, and tax characteristics may have different interest rates because the terms to maturity are different. A plot of the yields on bonds with differing terms to maturity, but with the same risk, liquidity, and tax considerations, is called a **yield curve,** and it describes the term structure of interest rates for a particular type of bonds, say government bonds. The "Following the Financial News" box shows several yield curves for Treasury securities which were published in the *Wall Street Journal*. Yield curves can be classified as upward sloping, flat, and downward sloping. When yield

Following the Financial News

Yield Curves

The *Wall Street Journal* publishes a plot of the yield curves for Treasury securities, an example of which is found here. It is typically found next to the "Credit Markets" column on a daily basis.

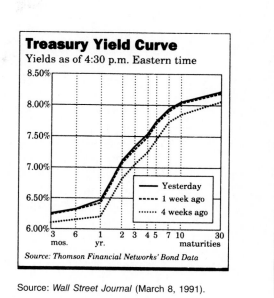

Treasury Yield Curve

Yields as of 4:30 p.m. Eastern time

Legend:
— Yesterday
---- 1 week ago
······ 4 weeks ago

Source: Thomson Financial Networks' Bond Data

Source: *Wall Street Journal* (March 8, 1991).

curves are upward sloping, as in the "Following the Financial News" box, the long-term interest rates are above the short-term interest rate; when yield curves are flat, short- and long-term interest rates are the same; and when yield curves are downward sloping, long-term interest rates are below the short-term interest rate. Yield curves can also have more complicated shapes in which they first slope up and then down, or vice versa. Typically, yield curves are upward sloping, as in the "Following the Financial News" box, but at times they have different shapes. Why do we most often see upward sloping yield curves but sometimes see other shapes?

Three theories have been put forth to explain the term structure of interest rates, that is, the relationship among interest rates on bonds of different maturities reflected in yield curve patterns. Although the expectation hypothesis and the segmented markets theory do not explain the empirical facts very well, we discuss them first for two reasons. First, the ideas in these two theories provide the groundwork for the most widely accepted theory, the preferred habitat theory, which does a far better job of explaining the empirical facts. Second, it is important to see how economists modify theories to improve them when they find that they are inconsistent with available empirical evidence.

Expectations Hypothesis

The **expectations hypothesis** of the term structure states the following common-sense proposition: The interest rate on a long-term bond will equal an average of short-term interest rates that people expect to occur over the life of the long-term bond. For example, if people expect that short-term interest rates will be 10% on average over the coming five years, then the expectations hypothesis predicts that the interest rate on bonds with five years to maturity will be 10% too. If short-term interest rates were expected to rise even higher after this five-year period, so that the average short-term interest rate over the coming twenty years is 11%, then the interest rate on twenty-year bonds would equal 11% and would be higher than the interest rate on five-year bonds. We can see that the explanation provided by the expectations hypothesis for why interest rates on bonds of different maturities differ is that short-term interest rates are expected to have different values at future dates.

The starting point of this theory is that buyers of bonds do not prefer bonds of one maturity over another, so that they will not hold any quantity of a bond if its expected return is less than that of another bond with a different maturity. Bonds that have this characteristic are said to be perfect substitutes. What this means in practice is that if bonds of different maturity are perfect substitutes, then the expected return on these bonds must be equal.

To see how the view that bonds of different maturity are perfect substitutes leads to the expectations hypothesis, let us consider the following two investment strategies:

1. The purchase of a one-year bond and then, when it matures in one year, the purchase of another one-year bond

2. The purchase of a two-year bond which is held until maturity

Because both strategies must have the same expected return if people are holding both one- and two-year bonds, then the interest rate on the two-year bond must equal the average of the two one-year interest rates. For example, let's say that the current interest rate on the one-year bond is 9% and you expect the interest rate on the one-year bond next year to be 11%. If you pursue the first strategem of buying the two one-year bonds, then the expected return over the two years will average out to be (9% + 11%)/2 = 10% per year. You will only be willing to hold both the one- and two-year bonds if the expected return per year of the two-year bond equals this. Therefore, the interest rate on the two-year bond must equal 10%, the average interest rate on the two one-year bonds.

We can make this argument more general. Consider the choice of holding for two periods a two-period bond versus two one-period bonds. With the following definitions,

i_t = today's (time t) interest rate on a one-period bond

i_{t+1}^e = the interest rate on a one-period bond expected for next period (time $t + 1$)

i_{2t} = today's (time t) interest rate on the two-period bond

The expected return over the two periods from buying and holding the two-period bond is

$$(1 + i_{2t})(1 + i_{2t}) - 1 = 1 + 2(i_{2t}) + (i_{2t})^2 - 1$$

Because $(i_{2t})^2$ is extremely small [if $i_{2t} = 10\% = .10$, then $(i_{2t})^2 = .01$], we can simplify this to

$$2(i_{2t})$$

When one-period bonds are bought, the expected return over the two periods is

$$(1 + i_t)(1 + i_{t+1}^e) - 1 = 1 + i_t + i_{t+1}^e + i_t(i_{t+1}^e) - 1$$

Because $i_t(i_{t+1}^e)$ is also extremely small [if $i_t = i_{t+1}^e = .10$, then $i_t(i_{t+1}^e) = .01$], we can simplify this to

$$i_t + i_{t+1}^e$$

Both bonds will be held only if these expected returns are equal, that is, when

$$2(i_{2t}) = i_t + i_{t+1}^e$$

Solving for i_{2t} in terms of the one-period rates, we have

$$i_{2t} = \frac{i_t + i_{t+1}^e}{2} \tag{7.1}$$

which tells us that the two-period rate must equal the average of the two one-period rates. We can conduct the same steps for bonds with a longer maturity so that we can examine the whole term structure of interest rates. Doing so, we will find that the interest rate of i_{nt} on an n-period bond must equal[2]

$$i_{nt} = \frac{i_t + i_{t+1}^e + i_{t+2}^e + \cdots + i_{t+n-1}^e}{n} \tag{7.2}$$

Equation (7.2) states that the n-period interest rate equals the average of the one-period interest rates expected to occur over the n-period life of the bond. This is a restatement of the expectations hypothesis in more precise terms.

----

[2]The analysis here has been conducted for discount bonds. Formulas for interest rates on coupon bonds would differ slightly from those above, but would convey the same principle.

The expectations hypothesis is an elegant theory that provides an explanation of why the term structure of interest rates (as represented by yield curves) changes at different times. When the yield curve is upward sloping, the expectations hypothesis suggests that short-term interest rates are expected to rise in the future. In the case in which the long-term rate is currently above the short-term rate, the average of future short-term rates is expected to be higher than the current short-term rate, which can occur only if short-term interest rates are expected to rise. We have already seen this in our concrete example where the two-year rate of 10% is above the current one-year rate of 9%. This means that the one-year rate is expected to rise next year to the 11% level. When the yield curve slopes down, then the average of future short-term interest rates is expected to be below the current short-term rate, implying that short-term interest rates are expected to fall, on average, in the future. Only when the yield curve is flat does the expectations hypothesis suggest that short-term interest rates are not expected to change, on average, in the future.

The expectations hypothesis also explains why, as we see in Figure 7.4, interest rates on bonds of different maturity move together over time. Historically, short-term interest rates have the characteristic that if they increase today, they will tend to be higher in the future. Hence, a rise in short-term rates will raise people's expectations of future short-term rates. Since long-term rates are related to the average of expected future short-term rates, a

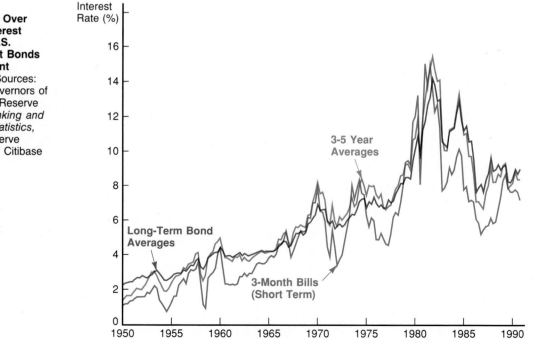

Figure 7.4
Movements Over Time of Interest Rates on U.S. Government Bonds with Different Maturities Sources: Board of Governors of the Federal Reserve System, *Banking and Monetary Statistics,* Federal Reserve *Bulletin,* and Citibase databank.

rise in short-term rates also will raise long-term rates, causing short- and long-term rates to move together.

The expectations hypothesis is an attractive theory because it provides a simple explanation of the behavior of the term structure, but unfortunately, it has a major shortcoming. There is one important empirical fact that is inconsistent with this theory. Yield curves are *usually* upward sloping, implying that short-term interest rates are usually expected to rise in the future. In actual practice, short-term interest rates are just as likely to fall as they are to rise. If the expectations hypothesis is a complete theory, then the market's expectations about movements in short-term interest rates are inconsistent with the actual movements. This makes economists uncomfortable because they find it hard to believe that the bond market is that foolish. The expectations hypothesis has been modified to account for this inconsistency, as we will see when we discuss the preferred habitat theory.

Segmented Markets Theory

As the name suggests, the **segmented markets theory** of the term structure sees markets for different maturity bonds as completely separate and segmented. The interest rate for each maturity bond is then determined by the supply and demand for that maturity bond with no effects from expected returns on other maturity bonds.

The segmented markets theory starts with the premise that bonds of different maturities are not substitutes at all, so that the expected return from holding a bond of one maturity has no effect on the demand for a bond of another maturity. This theory of the term structure is then at the opposite extreme to the expectations hypothesis, which assumes that bonds of different maturity are perfect substitutes.

The argument for why bonds of different maturities are not substitutes is that investors have strong preferences for bonds of one maturity but not for another, and so they will only be concerned with the expected returns for bonds of the maturity they prefer. This might occur because they have a particular holding period in mind, and if they match the maturity of the bond to the desired holding period, then they can obtain a certain return with no risk at all. (We have seen in Chapter 4 that if the term to maturity equals the holding period, the return is known for certain because it just equals the yield.) For example, people who have a short holding period would prefer to hold short-term bonds. On the other hand, if you were putting funds away for your young child to go to college, your desired holding period might be much longer and you would want to hold longer-term bonds.

In the segmented markets theory, differing yield curve patterns are accounted for by differing supply and demand for bonds of different maturities. The yield curve slopes upward because, according to the segmented markets theory, the demand for short-term bonds is relatively higher than for longer-term bonds, with the result that short-term bonds have a higher price and a lower interest rate. A downward-sloping yield curve would indicate that the demand for long-term bonds is relatively higher and their yields will then be lower. Since yield curves are usually upward sloping, the theory indicates that, on average, people usually prefer to hold short-term bonds rather than long-term bonds.

Although the segmented markets theory can explain why yield curves usually tend to slope upward, it still has a major flaw. Because it sees bond markets for different maturities as completely segmented, there is no reason for a rise in interest rates on a bond of one maturity to affect the interest rate on a bond of another maturity. Therefore, it cannot explain the empirical fact that interest rates on bonds of different maturities tend to move together.

We are then in the unsatisfactory position of having two important empirical facts to explain, although each of our two theories of the term structure is able to explain one but not the other. A logical step to solve this problem is to combine both theories, which leads us to the preferred habitat theory.

Preferred Habitat Theory

The **preferred habitat theory** of the term structure states the following: The interest rate on a long-term bond will equal an average of short-term interest rates expected to occur over the life of the long-term bond plus a term premium that responds to supply and demand conditions for that bond.

The theory takes the view that bonds of different maturities are substitutes so that the expected return on one bond *does* influence the expected return on a bond of a different maturity, but it also allows investors to prefer one bond maturity over another. We might then think of investors as having a preference for bonds of one maturity over another, thus having a bond market where they are more comfortable to reside; we then might say that they have a preferred habitat. Investors still care about the expected returns on bonds with a maturity other than their preferred maturity, and so they will not allow expected returns on one bond to get too far out of line with that on another bond with a different maturity. Since they prefer bonds of one maturity over another, they will be willing to buy bonds that do not have the preferred maturity only if they earn a somewhat higher expected return.

If investors prefer the habitat of short-term bonds over longer-term bonds, for example, they might be willing to hold short-term bonds even though they have a lower expected return. This means that investors would have to be paid a positive term premium to be willing to hold a long-term bond. Such an outcome would modify the expectations hypothesis story by adding a positive term premium term to the equation which describes the relationship between long- and short-term interest rates. The preferred habitat theory is thus written down as

$$i_{nt} = k_{nt} + \frac{i_t + i_{t+1}^e + i_{t+2}^e + \cdots + i_{t+n-1}^e}{n} \tag{7.3}$$

where k_{nt} = term premium for the n-period bond at time t.

Let us see if the preferred habitat theory is consistent with the two empirical facts we have discussed. It explains why interest rates on different maturity bonds move together over time: A rise in short-term interest rates indicates that short-term interest rates will, on average, be higher in the future and that long-term interest rates will rise along with them.

The preferred habitat theory also explains why yield curves are usually upward sloping by recognizing that the term premium is likely to be positive as a result of people's preference for holding short-term bonds. Even if short-term interest rates are usually expected to stay the same on average in the future, long-term interest rates will still be above short-term rates. Therefore, yield curves that slope upward should be the norm.

How can the theory explain the appearance of downward-sloping yield curves if the term premium is positive? It must be that short-term interest rates are expected to fall so much in the future that the average of the expected short-term rates is well below the current short-term rate. Then, even when the positive term premium is added to this average, the resulting long-term rate will still be below the current short-term interest rate.

There is one final empirical fact about yield curves that can be explained by the preferred habitat theory. Yield curves tend to have an especially steep upward slope when short-term interest rates are low and a downward slope when short-term rates are high. When short-term rates are low, people generally expect them to rise to some normal level in the future, and the average of future expected short-term rates is high relative to the current short-term rate. With the additional boost of a positive term premium, long-term interest rates will be substantially above current short-term rates and the yield curve would then have a steep upward slope. Conversely, if short-term rates are high, people usually expect them to come back down. Long-term rates would then drop below short-term rates because the average of expected future short-term rates would be so far below current short-term rates that, despite positive term premiums, the yield curve would slope down.

As our discussion indicates, a particularly attractive feature of the preferred habitat theory is that it tells you what the market is predicting about future short-term interest rates by just looking at the slope of the yield curve. A steeply rising yield curve [as in panel (a) of Figure 7.5] indicates that short-term interest rates are expected to rise in the future. A moderately steep yield curve [as in panel (b)] indicates that short-term interest rates are not expected to rise or fall much in the future. A flat yield curve [as in panel (c)] indicates that short-term rates are expected to fall moderately in the future. Finally, a downward-sloping yield curve [as in panel (d)] indicates that short-term interest rates are expected to fall sharply in the future. See Box 7.3 for

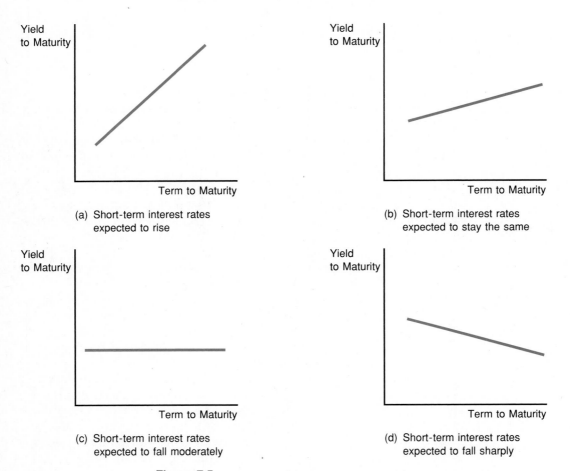

Figure 7.5
Yield Curves and the Market's Expectations of Future Short-Term Interest Rates

the evidence on what the slope of the yield curve tells us about future movements of short-term interest rates.

Summary The preferred habitat theory is the most widely accepted theory of the term structure of interest rates because it explains the major empirical facts about the term structure so well. It combines the features of both the expectations hypothesis and the segmented markets theory by asserting that a long-term interest rate will be the sum of a term premium (which is determined by the supply and demand for bonds of different maturities) and of the average of the short-term interest rates that are expected to occur over the life of the bond.

This theory explains the following facts: (1) interest rates on bonds of different maturities tend to move together over time; (2) yield curves usually

B o x   7 . 3

Recent Evidence on the Term Structure

Some researchers examining the term structure of interest rates in the 1980s questioned whether the slope of the yield curve provides information about movements of future short-term interest rates.* They found that the spread between long- and short-term interest rates does not always help predict future short-term interest rates, a finding that may stem from substantial fluctuations in the term premium for long-term bonds. More recent research, however, by Eugene Fama, Robert Bliss, John Campbell, and Robert Shiller, which uses more sophisticated tests, finds that the term structure contains information about the future movements of interest rates.†

---

*Robert J. Shiller, John Y. Campbell, and Kermit L. Schoenholtz, "Forward Rates and Future Policy: Interpreting the Term Structure of Interest Rates," *Brookings Papers on Economic Activity* 1 (1983), pp. 173–217; and N. Gregory Mankiw and Lawrence H. Summers, "Do Long-Term Interest Rates Overreact to Short-Term Interest Rates?" *Brookings Papers on Economic Activity* 1 (1984), pp. 243–247.

†Eugene Fama, "The Information in the Term Structure," *Journal of Financial Economics* 13 (1984), pp. 509–528; Eugene Fama and Robert Bliss, "The Information in Long-Maturity Forward Rates," *American Economic Review* 77 (September 1987), pp. 680–692; and John Y. Campbell and Robert J. Shiller, "Cointegration and Tests of the Present Value Models," *Journal of Political Economy* 95 (October 1987), pp. 1062–1088.

---

slope upward; and (3) when short-term interest rates are low, yield curves are more likely to have a steep upward slope, whereas when short-term interest rates are high, yield curves are more likely to slope downward.

The theory also shows how to tell what the market is predicting for the movement of short-term interest rates in the future. A steep upward slope of the yield curve means that short rates are expected to rise; a mild upward slope means that short rates are expected to remain the same; a flat slope means that short rates are expected to fall moderately; and a downward slope means that short rates are expected to fall sharply.

APPLICATION
INTERPRETING YIELD CURVES, 1980–1991 /

Figure 7.6 illustrates several different yield curves that have appeared for U.S. government bonds in recent years. What do these yield curves tell us about the public's expectations of future movements of short-term interest rates?

Study Guide
Try to answer the above question before reading further in the text. If you have trouble answering it with the preferred habitat theory, first try answer-

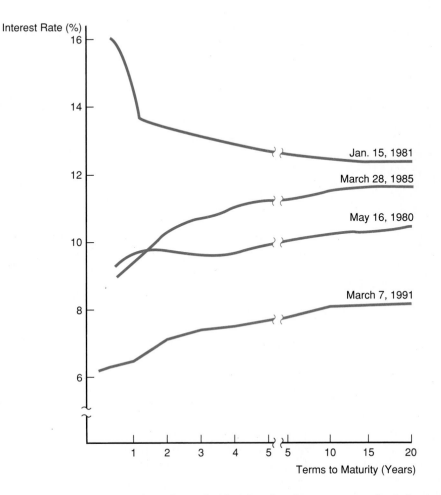

Figure 7.6
Yield Curves for U.S. Government Bonds
Sources: Federal Reserve Bank of St. Louis; *U.S. Financial Data,* various issues; and the *Wall Street Journal.*

ing it with the expectations hypothesis (simpler, because you don't have to worry about the term premium). When you understand what the expectations of future interest rates are in this case, modify your analysis by taking account of the term premium.

The steep downward-sloping yield curve that occurred on January 15, 1981, indicates that short-term interest rates were expected to decline sharply in the future. In order for longer-term interest rates with their positive term premium to be well below the short-term interest rate, short-term interest rates must be expected to decline so sharply that their average is far below the current short-term rate. Indeed, the public's expectations of sharply lower short-term interest rates evident in the yield curve were realized soon after January 15; by March, three-month Treasury bill rates had declined from the 16% level to the 13% level.

The steep upward-sloping yield curves on March 28, 1985, and March 7, 1991, indicated that short-term interest rates would climb in the future.

The long-term interest rate is above the short-term interest rate when short-term interest rates are expected to rise because their average plus the term premium will be above the current short-term rate. The moderately upward-sloping yield curve on May 16, 1980, indicated that short-term interest rates were expected to neither rise nor fall in the future. In this case, their average remains the same as the current short-term rate and the positive term premium for longer-term bonds explains the moderate upward slope of the yield curve.

SUMMARY

1. Bonds with the same maturity will have different interest rates because of three factors: (a) default risk, (b) liquidity, and (c) tax considerations. The more default risk a bond has, the higher will be its interest rate relative to other bonds. The more liquid a bond is, the lower will be its interest rate. Bonds with tax-exempt status will have lower interest rates than they otherwise would. The relationship among interest rates on bonds with the same maturity that arise because of these three factors is known as the risk structure of interest rates.

2. There are three theories of the term structure that provide explanations of how interest rates on bonds with different terms to maturity are related. The expectations hypothesis views long-term interest rates as equaling the average of future short-term interest rates expected to occur over the life of the bond, while the segmented markets theory treats the determination of interest rates for each bond's maturity as the outcome of supply and demand in that market only. Neither of these theories can explain both the fact that interest rates on bonds of different maturities move together over time and that yield curves are usually upward sloping.

3. The preferred habitat theory combines the features of the other two theories and by so doing is able to explain the facts just mentioned. It views long-term interest rates as equaling the average of future short-term interest rates expected to occur over the life of the bond, plus a term premium that reflects the supply and demand for bonds of different maturities. This theory allows us to infer the market's expectations about the movement of future short-term interest rates from the yield curve. A steeply upward-sloping curve indicates that future short-term rates are expected to rise; a mildly upward-sloping curve indicates that short-term rates are expected to stay the same; a flat curve indicates that short-term rates are expected to decline slightly; and a downward-sloping curve indicates that a substantial decline in short-term rates is expected in the future.

KEY TERMS

risk structure of interest rates

term structure of interest rates

default risk

default-free bonds

risk premium

junk bonds

yield curve

expectations hypothesis

segmented markets theory

preferred habitat theory

QUESTIONS AND PROBLEMS

1. Which should have the higher risk premium on its interest rates: a corporate bond with a Moody's Baa rating or a corporate bond with a C rating? Why?

* 2. Why do U.S. Treasury bills have lower interest rates than large denomination negotiable bank CDs?

3. Risk premiums on corporate bonds are usually anticyclical; that is, they decrease during business cycle expansions and increase during recessions. Why is this so?

* 4. Answer true, false, or uncertain: "If bonds of different maturities are close substitutes, their interest rates are more likely to move together." Explain.

5. If yield curves, on average, were flat, what would this say about the term premiums in the term structure? Would you be more or less willing to accept the expectations hypothesis?

* 6. Assuming that the expectations hypothesis is the correct theory of the term structure, calculate the interest rates in the term structure for maturities of one to five years and plot the resulting yield curves for the following series of one-year interest rates over the next five years:
   a) 5%, 7%, 7%, 7%, 7%
   b) 5%, 4%, 4%, 4%, 4%
   How would your yield curves change if people preferred shorter-term bonds over longer-term bonds?

7. Assuming that the expectations hypothesis is the correct theory of the term structure, calculate the interest rates in the term structure for maturities of one to five years and plot the resulting yield curves for the following path of one-year interest rates over the next five years:
   a) 5%, 6%, 7%, 6%, 5%
   b) 5%, 4%, 3%, 4%, 5%
   How would your yield curves change if people preferred shorter-term bonds over longer-term bonds?

* 8. If the yield curve looks like the following, what is the market predicting about the movement of future short-term interest rates? What might the yield curve indicate about the market's predictions about the inflation rate in the future?

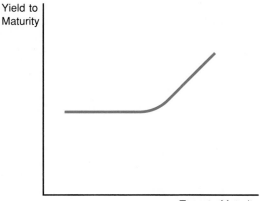

9. If the yield curve looks like the following, what is the market predicting about the movement of future short-term interest rates? What might the yield curve indicate about the market's predictions about the inflation rate in the future?

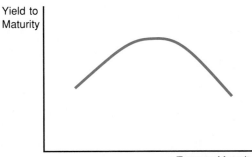

*10. What effect would reducing income tax rates have on the interest rates on municipal bonds? Would interest rates on Treasury securities be affected, and if so, how?

Using Economic Analysis to Predict the Future

11. Predict what will happen to interest rates on a corporation's bonds if the federal government guarantees that it will pay creditors if the corpo-

ration goes bankrupt. What will happen to the interest rates on Treasury securities?

*12. Predict what would happen to the risk premiums on corporate bonds if brokerage commissions were lowered in the corporate bond market.

13. If the income tax exemption on municipal bonds were abolished, what would happen to the interest rates on these bonds? What effect would it have on interest rates on U.S. Treasury securities?

*14. What effect would the abolition of estate taxes have on interest rates on "flower bonds"? on interest rates on other U.S. Treasury securities?

15. If expectations of future short-term interest rates suddenly rise, what would happen to the slope of the yield curve?

PART III

Financial Institutions

CHAPTER 8

An Economic Analysis of Financial Structure

PREVIEW   A healthy and vibrant economy requires a financial system that moves funds from people who save to people who have productive investment opportunities. But how does the financial system make sure that your hard-earned savings get channeled to Paula the Productive Investor rather than to Benny the Bum?

This chapter answers this question by providing an economic analysis of how our financial structure is designed to promote economic efficiency. The analysis focuses on a few simple but powerful economic concepts that enable us to explain features of our financial markets such as why financial contracts are written as they are, why financial intermediaries are more important for getting funds to borrowers than are securities markets, and why financial crises occur and have such severe consequences for the health of the economy.

BASIC PUZZLES ABOUT FINANCIAL STRUCTURE

Our financial system is complex in structure and function. There are many different types of institutions: banks, insurance companies, mutual funds, stock and bond markets, and so on—all of which are regulated by government. The financial system channels billions of dollars per year from savers to those with productive investment opportunities. If we take a close look at our financial structure, we find eight basic puzzles which we need to solve in order to understand how our financial system works.

The pie chart in Figure 8.1 indicates how American businesses financed their activities using external funds (those obtained from outside the business itself) in the period 1970–1985. The *loans* category is primarily made up of bank loans, but it also includes loans made by other financial intermediaries; the *bonds* category includes marketable debt securities such as corporate bonds and commercial paper; *stock* includes stock market shares; and *other* includes other loans such as government loans, loans by foreigners, and

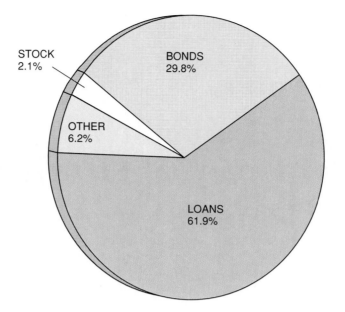

Figure 8.1

Sources of External Funds for Nonfinancial Businesses in the United States The categories of external funds are as follows: *Loans* is made up primarily of bank loans, but it also includes loans made by other financial intermediaries. *Bonds* includes marketable debt securities such as corporate bonds and commercial paper. *Stock* includes stock market shares. *Other* includes other loans such as government loans, loans by foreigners, and trade debt (loans made by businesses to other businesses when they purchase goods). Source: Colin Mayer, "Financial Systems, Corporate Finance, and Economic Development," in R. Glenn Hubbard, ed., *Asymmetric Information, Corporate Finance, and Investment* (Chicago: University of Chicago Press, 1990), p. 312.

trade debt (loans made by businesses to other businesses when they purchase goods).

Puzzle 1: Stocks are not an important source of finance for American businesses. Because so much attention in the media is focused on the stock market, many people have the impression that stocks are one of the most important sources of finance for American corporations. However, as we can see in the pie chart, the stock market accounted for only a small fraction of the financing of American businesses in the 1970–1985 period, 2.1%. Indeed, starting in 1984 American corporations on average have not issued shares to finance their activities at all; instead, they have repurchased large numbers of shares so that the stock market actually has been a *negative* source of corporate finance in recent years.[1] Why is the stock market such an unimportant source of finance in the United States?

---

[1] Why stocks have been repurchased to such a great extent in recent years is a topic analyzed in the appendix on corporate restructuring, which follows this chapter.

Puzzle 2: Issuing marketable securities is not the primary way businesses finance their operations. Figure 8.1 shows that bonds are a far more important source of finance than are stocks in the United States (29.8% versus 2.1%). However, stocks and bonds combined (31.9%), which make up the total share of marketable securities, still supply less than one-third of the external funds corporations need to finance their activities. As we can see in Box 8.1, the fact that issuing marketable securities is not the most important source of finance is true elsewhere in the world as well. Indeed, most countries, with the exception of Canada, have a much smaller share of external finance supplied by marketable securities than does the United States. Why are marketable securities not used more extensively to finance corporate activities?

B o x   8 . 1   **A Global Perspective**

Sources of External Finance for Nonfinancial Businesses: A Comparison of the United States and Five Industrialized Countries

The bar chart compares the sources of external financing for businesses in the United States to those in five other developed countries: the United Kingdom, France, Germany, Japan, and Canada. The definitions of the categories are identical to those used in Figure 8.1.

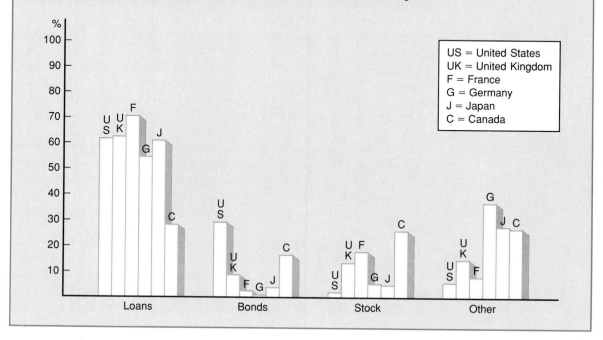

Puzzle 3: Indirect finance, which involves the activities of financial intermediaries, is many times more important than direct finance, in which businesses raise funds directly from lenders in financial markets. Direct finance involves the sale to households of marketable securities such as stocks and bonds. The 31.9% share of stocks and bonds as a source of external finance for American businesses actually greatly overstates the importance of direct finance in our financial system. Since 1970, less than 5% of newly issued corporate bonds and commercial paper and around 50% of stocks have been sold directly to American households. The rest of these securities have been bought primarily by financial intermediaries such as insurance companies, pension funds, and mutual funds. These figures indicate that direct finance is used in less than 5% of the external financing of American business. Since in most countries marketable securities are an even less important source of finance than in the United States, direct finance is also far less important than indirect finance in the rest of the world. Why are financial intermediaries and indirect finance so important in financial markets?

Puzzle 4: Banks are the most important source of external funds to finance businesses. As we can see in Figure 8.1 and in Box 8.1, with the exception of Canada, the primary sources of external funds for business are loans (61.9% in the United States). Most of these loans are bank loans, so the data suggest that banks have the most important role in financing business activities. An extraordinary fact that surprises most people is that bank loans in the United States provide *twenty-five times* more financing of corporate activities than does the stock market. What makes banks so important to the workings of the financial system?

Puzzle 5: The financial system is among the most heavily regulated sectors of the economy. You learned in Chapter 3 that the financial sector is heavily regulated, not only in the United States but in all other developed countries as well. Governments regulate financial markets to promote the provision of information and to ensure the soundness of the financial system. Why are financial markets so extensively regulated throughout the world?

Puzzle 6: Only large, well-established corporations have access to securities markets to finance their activities. Individuals and smaller businesses that are not well established almost never raise funds by issuing marketable securities. Instead, they obtain their financing from banks. Why do only large, well-known corporations have the ability to raise funds in the securities markets?

Puzzle 7: Collateral is a prevalent feature of debt contracts for both households and business. **Collateral** is property that is pledged to the lender if a borrower cannot make his or her debt payments. Collateralized debt is the predominant form of household debt contract and is widely used in business borrowing as well. Over 85% of the household debt in the United States consists of collateralized loans: your automobile is collateral for an auto loan while your house is collateral for your mortgage. Commercial and farm mortgages, in which property is pledged as collateral, make up one-quarter of borrowing by nonfinancial business; corporate bonds and other bank loans also often involve pledges of collateral. Why is collateral such an important feature of debt contracts?

Puzzle 8: Debt contracts are typically extremely complicated legal documents that place substantial restrictions on the behavior of the borrower. Many students think about debt contracts as a simple IOU that can be written on a single piece of paper. The reality of debt contracts is far different, however. Bond or loan contracts, are typically lengthy legal documents with provisions (called **restrictive covenants**) that restrict and specify certain activities that the borrower can engage in. Restrictive covenants are not just a feature of debt contracts for businesses; automobile loans and residential mortgages, which most of us come into contact with at some point in our lives, have, for example, restrictive covenants that require the borrower to have sufficient insurance on the automobile or house purchased with the loan. Why are debt contracts so complex and restrictive?

As you might recall from Chapter 3, an important feature of financial markets is that they have substantial transactions and information costs. An economic analysis of how these costs affect financial markets will provide us with solutions to the eight puzzles, which, in turn, will provide us with a much deeper understanding of how our financial system works. In the next section we examine the impact of transactions costs on the structure of our financial system. Then we turn to how information costs affect financial structure.

HOW TRANSACTIONS COSTS INFLUENCE FINANCIAL STRUCTURE

Transactions costs are a major problem for people who have excess funds to lend. Suppose you are approached by Paula the Productive Investor who needs $5,000 to set up her business, which you think is a surefire investment opportunity. You have the cash and would like to lend her the money, but in order to protect your investment, you have to hire a lawyer to write up the loan agreement and that will cost you $1,000. When you figure in this transactions cost for making the loan, you realize that you can't make enough from the deal and reluctantly tell Paula she will have to look elsewhere.

You still have $5,000 that you would like to invest, and so you think about investing in the stock market. However, you are again faced with high transactions costs. Since you only have $5,000, you can only buy a small number of shares. The stockbroker tells you that your purchase is so small that the brokerage commission for buying the stock you picked will be a large percentage of the purchase price of the shares. If instead you decide to buy a bond, the problem is even worse because the smallest denomination for a bond is typically $10,000 and you do not have that much to invest. Indeed, the broker may not even be interested in your business at all because the small size of your account doesn't make it worthwhile. Again you are disappointed and realize that you will not be able to use financial markets to earn a return on your hard-earned savings. You can take some consolation, however, in the fact that you are not alone in being stymied by high transactions costs. This is a fact of life for most of us since most American households never own any securities.

You also face another problem because of transactions costs. Since you have only a small amount of funds available, you can only make a small number of investments. That is, you have to put all your eggs in one basket, and your inability to diversify will subject you to a lot of risk.

How Financial Intermediaries Reduce Transactions Costs

These examples of the problems posed by transactions costs illustrate that small savers like you or borrowers like Paula might be frozen out of financial markets and thus be unable to benefit from them. Is there anyone who can come to the rescue? The answer is "yes." Financial intermediaries, an important part of the financial structure, have evolved to reduce transactions costs and allow small savers and borrowers to benefit from the existence of financial markets.

Economies of Scale   One solution to the problem of high transactions costs is to bundle the funds of many investors together so that they can take advantage of **economies of scale,** that is, the decrease in transactions costs per dollar of investment as the size (scale) of transactions increases. By bundling investors' funds together, transactions costs for each individual investor are far smaller. Economies of scale exist because the total cost of carrying out a transaction in financial markets increases only a little as the size of the transaction grows. For example, the cost of arranging a purchase of 10,000 shares of stock is not all that much greater than the cost of arranging a purchase of 50 shares of stock.

The presence of economies of scale in financial markets helps explain why financial intermediaries developed and are such an important part of our financial structure. The clearest example of a financial intermediary that arose because of economies of scale is a mutual fund. A mutual fund is a financial intermediary that sells shares to individuals and then invests the proceeds in bonds or stocks. Because it buys large blocks of stocks or bonds, a mutual fund can take advantage of lower transactions costs. These cost savings are then passed on to individual investors after the mutual fund has taken its cut in the form of management fees for administering their accounts. An additional benefit for individual investors is that a mutual fund is large enough to purchase a widely diversified portfolio of securities. The increased diversification for individual investors reduces their risk, thus making them better off.

Development of Expertise to Lower Transactions Costs   Financial intermediaries also arise because they are better able to develop expertise to lower transactions costs. Banks (depository institutions) and other financial intermediaries that make loans become experts at acquiring appropriate legal advice so that they can inexpensively write ironclad loan contracts. Similarly, they develop expertise in computer technology so that they can cheaply provide convenient services such as one-statement checking or automatic teller machines. Economies of scale are important factors in lowering the costs to financial intermediaries for such things as lawyers and computer technology. For example, once a bank has invested a lot of money in paying a lawyer to produce a good legal loan contract, it can use this contract over and over again in its loan transactions, thus lowering the legal cost per transaction. Instead of a loan contract costing $1,000 as in our earlier example, a bank might pay a lawyer $5,000 to draw up a good loan agreement which it will use for 2,000 loans, at a cost of $2.50 per loan.

An important outcome of a financial intermediary's low transactions costs is that it can provide its customers with liquidity services, that is, services that make it easier for customers to conduct transactions. Banks, for example, provide depositors with checking accounts that enable them to pay their bills easily. In addition, depositors can earn interest on checking and savings accounts, yet still have a liquid store of value that can be converted into goods and services whenever necessary.

ASYMMETRIC INFORMATION: ADVERSE SELECTION AND MORAL HAZARD

The presence of transactions costs in financial markets explains, in part, why financial intermediaries and indirect finance play such an important role in financial markets (Puzzle 3). To obtain a fuller understanding of financial structure, however, we turn to the role of information in financial markets.[2]

In transactions that take place in financial markets, one party often does not know all that he or she needs to know about the other party to make correct decisions. The inequality of the information that each party has is called **asymmetric information.** For example, a borrower who takes out a

---

[2] An excellent survey of the literature on information and financial structure that expands on the topics discussed in the rest of this chapter is contained in Mark Gertler, "Financial Structure and Aggregate Economic Activity: An Overview," *Journal of Money, Credit and Banking* 20 (August 1988, part 2), pp. 559–588.

loan usually has better information about the potential returns and risk associated with the investment projects he plans to undertake than does the lender. Lack of information creates problems in the financial system on two fronts: before the transaction is entered into and after the transaction is entered into.

Adverse selection is the problem created by asymmetric information *before* the transaction occurs. Adverse selection in financial markets occurs when the potential borrowers who are the most likely to produce an undesirable *(adverse)* outcome—the bad credit risks—are the ones who most actively seek out a loan and are thus most likely to be *selected*. Since adverse selection makes it more likely that loans might be made to bad credit risks, lenders may decide not to make any loans even though there are good credit risks in the marketplace.

To understand why adverse selection occurs, suppose that you have two aunts to whom you might make a loan—Aunt Sheila and Aunt Louise. Aunt Louise is a conservative type who only borrows when she has an investment that she is quite sure will pay off. Aunt Sheila, on the other hand, is an inveterate gambler who has just come across a get-rich-quick scheme that will make her a millionaire if she can just borrow $1,000 to invest in it. Unfortunately, as with most get-rich-quick schemes, there is a high probability that the investment won't pay off and that Aunt Sheila will lose the $1,000.

Which of your aunts is most likely to call you to ask for a loan? Aunt Sheila, of course, because she has so much to gain if the investment pays off. You, however, would not want to make a loan to her because there is a high probability that her investment will turn sour and she will be unable to pay you back.

If you knew both your aunts very well—that is, if information was not asymmetric—then you wouldn't have a problem, because you would know that Aunt Sheila is a bad risk and so you would not lend to her. Suppose, though, that you don't know your aunts well (does anyone *really* know their relatives well enough?). You are more likely to lend to Aunt Sheila than to Aunt Louise because it would be Aunt Sheila who would be hounding you for the loan. Because of the possibility of adverse selection you might decide not to lend to either of your aunts, even though there are times when Aunt Louise, who is an excellent credit risk, might need a loan for a worthwhile investment.

Moral hazard is the problem created by asymmetric information *after* the transaction occurs. Moral hazard in financial markets occurs when the lender is subjected to the *hazard* that the borrower has incentives to engage in activities that are undesirable *(immoral)* from the lender's point of view, because these activities make it less likely that the loan will be paid back. Since moral hazard lowers the probability that the loan will be repaid, lenders may decide that they would rather not make a loan.

As an example of moral hazard, suppose you made a $1,000 loan to another relative, Uncle Melvin, who needs the money to purchase a word processor so he can set up a business typing students' term papers. Once you have made the loan, however, Uncle Melvin is more likely to slip off to the track and play the horses. If he bets on a twenty to one long shot and wins, he is able to pay you back your $1,000 and live high on the hog with the remaining $19,000. On the other hand, if he loses, as is likely, then you don't get paid back and all he has lost is his reputation as a reliable, upstanding uncle. Uncle Melvin therefore has an incentive to go to the track, since his gains ($19,000) if he bets correctly may be much greater than the cost to him (his reputation) if he bets incorrectly. *If you knew* what Uncle Melvin was up to, you would prevent him from going to the track and he would not be able to engage in moral hazard. However, because it is hard for you to keep informed about his whereabouts—that is, information is asymmetric—there is a good chance that Uncle Melvin will go to the track and you will not get paid back. The possibility of moral hazard might therefore discourage you from making the $1,000 loan to Uncle Melvin, even if you were sure that you would be paid back if he used it to set up his business.

Study Guide

Because the concepts of adverse selection and moral hazard are extremely useful in understanding the economic behavior we examine in this and later chapters, you need to understand them fully. One way to distinguish between them is to remember that adverse selection is a problem of asymmetric information *before* entering into a transaction, whereas moral hazard is an asymmetric information problem *after* the transaction has occurred. A helpful way to nail down these concepts is to think of other examples, whether for financial or other types of transactions, in which an adverse selection or moral hazard problem occurs.

HOW ADVERSE SELECTION ("LEMONS PROBLEM") INFLUENCES FINANCIAL STRUCTURE

A particular characterization of the adverse selection problem and how it interferes with the efficient functioning of a market was outlined in a famous article by George Ackerloff. It is referred to as the "lemons problem" since it resembles the problem of lemons in the used car market.[3] A potential buyer of a used car frequently is unable to assess the quality of the car; that is, he

---

[3] George Ackerloff, "The Market for 'Lemons': Quality, Uncertainty and the Market Mechanism," *Quarterly Journal of Economics 84* (August 1970) pp. 488–500. Two important papers that have applied the lemons problem analysis to financial markets are Stewart Myers and N.S. Majluf, "Corporate Financing and Investment Decisions When Firms Have Information that Investors Do Not Have," *Journal of Financial Economics* 13 (June 1984) pp. 187–221 and Bruce Greenwald, Joseph E. Stiglitz, and Andrew Weiss, "Information Imperfections in the Capital Market and Macroeconomic Fluctuations," *American Economic Review* 74 (May 1984) pp. 194–199.

can't tell whether a used car is a good car that will run well or is a lemon that will continually give him grief. The price that the buyer will pay therefore needs to reflect the *average* quality of the cars in the market, so that the price lies somewhere in between the low value of a lemon and the high value of a good car.

The owner of a used car, on the other hand, is more likely to know whether the car is good or a lemon. If the car is a lemon, the owner is more than happy to sell it at the price the buyer is willing to pay which (at somewhere between the value of a lemon and a good car) is greater than the lemon's value. However, if the car is a good car, the owner knows that the car is undervalued by the price the buyer is willing to pay and so the owner may not want to sell it. As a result of this adverse selection, very few good used cars will come to the market. Since the average quality of a used car available in the market will be low and since very few people want to buy a lemon, there will be few sales. The used car market will then function poorly and, indeed, may not function at all.

Lemons in the Stock and Bond Markets

A similar lemons problem arises in securities markets, that is, the debt (bond) and equity (stock) markets. Suppose our friend Irving the Investor, a potential buyer of securities such as common stock, can't distinguish between good firms with high expected profits and low risk and bad firms with low expected profits and high risk. In this situation, Irving will only be willing to pay a price that reflects the *average* quality of firms issuing securities—a price that lies between the value of securities from bad firms and those from good firms. If the owners or managers of a good firm have better information than Irving and *know* that they are a good firm, then they know that their securities are undervalued and will not want to sell them to Irving at the price he is willing to pay. The only firms willing to sell Irving securities will be bad firms (because the price is higher than the securities are worth). Our friend Irving is not stupid: He does not want to hold securities in bad firms and thus he will decide not to purchase securities in the market. In an outcome similar to that in the used car market, this securities market will not work very well because few firms will sell securities in it to raise capital.

The analysis is similar if Irving considers purchasing a corporate debt instrument in the bond market rather than an equity share. Irving will buy a bond only if its interest rate is high enough to compensate him for the average default risk of the good and bad firms trying to sell the debt. The knowledgeable owners of a good firm realize that they will be paying a higher interest rate than they should and so they are unlikely to want to borrow in this market. Only the bad firms will be willing to borrow and since investors like Irving are not anxious to buy bonds issued by bad firms, they will probably not buy any bonds at all. Few bonds are then likely to sell in this market and so it will not be a good source of finance.

The adverse selection (lemons problem) analysis that we have just conducted explains Puzzle 2—why in no country in the world are marketable securities the primary source of finance for business firms. It also helps partially explain Puzzle 1—why stocks are not an important source of finance for American business. The presence of the lemons problem keeps securities markets such as the stock and bond markets from being effective in channeling funds from savers to borrowers.

Solutions to Adverse Selection Problems

In the absence of asymmetric information, the lemons (adverse selection) problem would go away. If a buyer knows as much about the quality of a used car as the seller so that she too can tell a good car from a lemon, then the buyer will be willing to pay full value for a good used car. Since the owners of good used cars can now get a fair price, they will be willing to sell them in the market. The market will have many transactions and will do its intended job: channeling good cars to people who want them. Similarly, if purchasers of securities can distinguish good from bad firms, they will pay the full value of securities issued by good firms, and good firms will sell their securities in the market. The securities market will then be able to move funds to the good firms that have the most productive investment opportunities.

Private Production and Sale of Information   The solution to the adverse selection (lemons) problem in financial markets is to produce information that eliminates asymmetric information and allows people supplying funds to have full information about the individuals or firms who need to finance their investment activities. One way to get this information to savers-lenders is to have private companies collect and produce information that distinguishes good from bad firms and then sell it to purchasers of securities. In the U.S. companies such as Standard and Poor's, Moody's, and Value Line gather information on firms' balance sheet positions and their investment activities, publish this data, and sell it to subscribers (individuals, libraries, and financial intermediaries involved in purchasing securities).

The system of private production and sale of information does not, however, completely solve the adverse selection problem in securities markets because of the so-called **free-rider problem.** The free-rider problem occurs when people who do not pay for information can take advantage of the information that other people have paid for. The free-rider problem suggests that the private sale of information will only be a partial solution to the lemons problem. To see why, suppose that you have just purchased information that tells you which firms are good and which are bad. You believe this purchase is worthwhile because you can make up the cost of acquiring this information, and then some, by purchasing the securities of good firms that are undervalued. However, when our savvy (freeloading) investor Irving sees you buying certain securities, he buys right along with you even though he has not paid for this information. If many other investors act as Irving does, the increased demand for the undervalued good securities will cause their low price to be bid up immediately to reflect the securities' true value. As a result of all these free riders, you can no longer buy the securities for less than their true value. Now since you will not gain any extra profits from purchasing the information, you realize that you never should have paid for this information in the first place. If other investors come to the same realization, private firms and individuals may not be able to sell enough of this information to make it worth their while to gather and produce it. The weakened ability of private firms to profit from selling information will mean that less information is produced in the marketplace, and so the adverse selection (lemons) problem will still interfere with the efficient functioning of securities markets.

Government Regulation to Increase Information in Securities Markets The free-rider problem prevents the private market from producing enough information to eliminate asymmetric information that leads to adverse selection. Could financial markets benefit from government intervention? The government could, for instance, produce information to help investors distinguish good from bad firms and provide it to the public for free. This solution, however, would involve the government in releasing negative information about firms, a practice that might be politically difficult. A second possibility (and one followed by the United States and most governments throughout the world) is for the government to regulate securities markets in a way that encourages firms to reveal information about themselves, so that investors can determine how good or bad the firm is. In the United States, the Securities and Exchange Commission is the government agency that requires firms selling their securities in public markets to adhere to standard accounting principles and to disclose information about their sales, assets, and earnings. Similar regulations are found in other countries.

The problem of asymmetric information and adverse selection in financial markets thus helps explain why financial markets are among the most heavily regulated sectors in the economy (Puzzle 5). Government regulation to increase information for investors is needed to reduce the adverse selection problem, which interferes with the efficient functioning of securities (stock and bond) markets.

Although government regulation lessens the adverse selection problem, it does not eliminate it. Even when firms provide information to the public about their sales, assets, or earnings, they *still* have more information than investors: There is a lot more to knowing the quality of a firm than is provided by information on sales or earnings. Furthermore, bad firms have an incentive to make themselves look like good firms since this would enable them to fetch a higher price for their securities. Bad firms will therefore slant the information they are required to transmit to the public, thus making it harder for investors to sort out the good firms from the bad.

Financial Intermediation   So far we have seen that private production of information and government regulation to encourage provision of information do not eliminate the adverse selection problem in financial markets. How, then, can the financial structure help promote the flow of funds to those with productive investment opportunities when there is asymmetric information? A clue is provided by the structure of the used car market.

An important feature of the used car market is that most used cars are not sold directly by one individual to another. An individual considering buying a used car might pay for privately produced information by subscribing to a magazine like *Consumer Reports* to find out if a particular make of car has a good repair record. Nevertheless, reading *Consumer Reports* does not solve the adverse selection problem, because even if a particular make of car has a good reputation, the actual car someone is trying to sell could be a lemon. The prospective buyer might also bring the used car to a mechanic for a once-over. But what if the prospective buyer doesn't know a mechanic that he can trust, or what if the mechanic would charge a high fee to evaluate the car?

Because these roadblocks make it hard for individuals to acquire enough information about used cars, most used cars are not sold directly by one individual to another. Instead, they are sold by an intermediary—a used-car dealer who purchases used cars from individuals and resells them to other individuals. Used-car dealers produce information in the market by becoming experts in determining whether a car is a good car or a lemon. Once they know a car is good, they can sell it with some form of a guarantee: either a guarantee that is explicit, such as a warranty, or an implicit guarantee in which they stand by their reputation for honesty. People are more likely to purchase a used car because of a dealer's guarantee, and the dealer is able to make a profit on her production of information about automobile quality by being able to sell the used car at a higher price than she paid for it. If the dealer purchases and then resells a particular car on which she has produced information, she avoids the problem of someone else free riding off the information she produced.

Just as used-car dealers help to solve adverse selection problems in the automobile market, financial intermediaries play a similar role in financial markets. A financial intermediary such as a bank becomes an expert in the production of information about firms so that it can sort out good credit risks from bad ones. Then it can acquire funds from depositors and lend them to the good firms. Because the bank is able to lend mostly to good firms, it is able to earn a higher return on its loans than the interest it has to pay to its depositors. As a result, the bank earns a profit, which allows it to engage in this information production activity.

An important element in the ability of the bank to profit from the information it produces is that it avoids the free-rider problem by primarily making private loans, rather than by purchasing securities that are traded in the open market. Because a private loan is not traded, other investors cannot watch what the bank is doing and bid up the loan's price so that the bank receives no compensation for the information it has produced. The bank's role as an intermediary that holds mostly nontraded loans is the key to its success in reducing asymmetric information in financial markets.

Our analysis of adverse selection indicates that financial intermediaries in general, and banks in particular because they hold a large fraction of nontraded loans, should play a greater role in moving funds to corporations than do securities markets. Our analysis thus explains Puzzles 3 and 4: why indirect finance is so much more important than direct finance and why banks are the most important source of external funds to finance business.

Our analysis of adverse selection also explains which firms are more likely to obtain funds from banks and financial intermediaries rather than from the securities markets. The better known a corporation is, the more information about its activities is available in the marketplace. Thus it is easier for investors to evaluate the quality of the corporation and determine whether it is a good or bad firm. Because investors have fewer worries about adverse selection with well-known corporations, they will be willing to invest directly in their securities. We thus have an explanation for Puzzle 6: The larger and more mature a corporation is, the more information investors have about it and the more likely it is that the corporation can raise funds in securities markets.

Collateral and Net Worth   Adverse selection only interferes with the functioning of financial markets if a lender suffers a loss when a borrower is unable to make loan payments and thereby defaults. Collateral, which is property promised to the lender if the borrower defaults, reduces the consequences of adverse selection because it reduces the lender's losses in the case of a default. If a borrower defaults on a loan, the lender can sell the collateral and use the proceeds to make up for the losses on the loan. For example, if you fail to make your mortgage payments, the lender can take title to your house, auction it off, and use the receipts to pay off the loan. Lenders are thus more willing to make loans secured by collateral, and borrowers are willing to supply collateral because the reduced risk for the lender makes it more likely they will get the loan in the first place and perhaps at a better loan rate. The presence of adverse selection in credit markets thus provides an explanation for why collateral is an important feature of debt contracts (Puzzle 7).

Net worth (also called **equity capital**), the difference between a firm's assets (what it owns or is owed) and its liabilities (what it owes), can perform a similar role to collateral. If a firm has a high net worth, then even if it engages in investments that cause it to have negative profits and so defaults on its debt payments, the lender can take title to the firm's net worth, sell it off, and use the proceeds to recoup some of the losses from the loan. In addition, the more net worth a firm has in the first place, the less likely it is to default because the firm has a cushion of assets that it can use to pay off its loans.

Hence, when firms seeking credit have high net worth, the consequences of adverse selection are less important and lenders will be more willing to make loans. This analysis lies behind the often-heard lament, "only those who don't need money can borrow it."

Summary   So far we have used the concept of adverse selection to explain seven of the eight puzzles about financial structure introduced earlier: the first four, which emphasize the importance of financial intermediaries and the relative unimportance of securities markets for the financing of corporations; the fifth, that financial markets are among the most heavily regulated sectors of the economy; the sixth, the fact that only large, well-established corporations have access to securities markets; and the seventh, that collateral is an important feature of debt contracts. In the next section, we will see that the other asymmetric information concept of moral hazard provides additional reasons for the importance of financial intermediaries and the relative unimportance of securities markets for the financing of corporations, the prevalence of government regulation, and the importance of collateral in debt contracts. In addition, the concept of moral hazard can be used to explain our final puzzle (Puzzle 8) of why debt contracts are complicated legal documents that place substantial restrictions on the behavior of the borrower.

HOW MORAL HAZARD AFFECTS THE CHOICE BETWEEN DEBT AND EQUITY CONTRACTS

Moral hazard occurs after the financial transaction takes place, when the seller of a security has incentives to hide information and engage in activities that are undesirable for the purchaser of the security. Moral hazard has important consequences for whether a firm finds it easier to raise funds with debt rather than equity contracts.

Moral Hazard in Equity Contracts: The Principal-Agent Problem

Equity contracts, such as common stock, are claims to a share in the profits and assets of a business firm. Equity contracts are subject to a particular example of moral hazard called the **principal-agent problem.** When managers own only a small fraction of the firm they work for, the stockholders who own most of the firm's equity (called the *principals*) are separate from the managers of the firm who are the *agents* of the owners. This separation of ownership and control leads to moral hazard in which the managers in control (the agents) may act in their own interest rather than in the interest of the stockholders-owners (the principals) because the managers have less incentive to maximize profits than the stockholders-owners do.

To fully understand the principal-agent problem, suppose that your friend Steve asks you to become a silent partner in his ice cream store. The store requires an investment of $10,000 to set up, but Steve only has $1,000. So you purchase an equity stake (stock shares) for $9,000 which entitles you to 90% of the ownership of the firm, while Steve owns only 10%. If Steve works hard to make tasty ice cream, keeps the store clean, smiles at all the customers, and hustles to wait on tables quickly, after all expenses (including Steve's salary) the store will have $50,000 in profits per year of which Steve receives 10% ($5,000) and you receive 90% ($45,000).

On the other hand, if Steve doesn't provide quick and friendly service to his customers, uses the $50,000 in income to buy art works for his office, and even sneaks off to the beach while he should be at the store, the store will not earn any profit. Steve can only earn the additional $5,000 (his 10% share of the profits) over his salary if he works hard and forgoes unproductive investments (e.g., art for his office). Steve might decide that an extra $5,000 just isn't enough to make him want to expend the effort to be a good manager; he might decide it would only be worth his while if he earned an extra $10,000. If Steve feels this way, he does not have enough incentive to be a good manager and will end up with a beautiful office, a good tan, and a store that doesn't show any profits. Because the store won't show any profits, Steve's decision not to act in your interest will cost you $45,000 (your 90% of the profits if he had chosen to be a good manager instead).

The moral hazard arising from the principal-agent problem might be even worse if Steve were not totally honest. Because his ice cream store is a cash business, Steve has the incentive to pocket $50,000 in cash and tell you that the profits were zero. He now gets a return of $50,000, but you get nothing.

Further indications that the principal-agent problem created by equity contracts can be severe are provided by examples of managers who build luxurious offices for themselves or have high-priced cars as their corporate automobiles. (For a graphic example of such behavior, see the appendix at the end of this chapter.) Besides pursuing personal benefits, managers might also pursue corporate strategies (such as the acquisition of other firms) that enhance their personal power but do not increase the corporation's profitability.

The principal-agent problem would not arise if the owners of a firm had complete information about what the managers were up to and could prevent wasteful expenditures or fraud. The principal-agent problem, which is an example of moral hazard, only arises because a manager, say Steve, has more information about his activities than does the stockholder—that is, because there is asymmetric information. The principal-agent problem would also not arise if Steve alone owned the store and there was no separation of ownership and control. If this were the case, Steve's hard work and avoidance of unproductive investments would yield him a profit (and extra income) of $50,000, an amount that would make it worth his while to be a good manager.

Solutions to the Principal-Agent Problem

Production of Information: Monitoring   You have seen that the principal-agent problem arises because managers have more information about their activities and the actual profits than do stockholders. One way for stockholders to reduce this moral hazard problem is for them to engage in a particular type of information production, the monitoring of the firm's activities: auditing the firm frequently and checking on what the management is doing. The problem is that the monitoring process can be expensive in terms of time and money, as reflected in the name economists give it—**costly state verification.** Costly state verification makes the equity contract less desirable and it explains, in part, why equity is not a more important element in our financial structure.

As with adverse selection, the free-rider problem decreases the amount of information production that would reduce the moral hazard (principal-agent) problem. In this example, the free-rider problem decreases monitoring. If you know that other stockholders are paying to monitor the activities of the company you hold shares in, you can take a free ride on their activities. Then you can use the money you save by not engaging in monitoring to vacation on a Caribbean island. If you can do this, though, so can other stockholders. Perhaps all the stockholders will go to the islands and no one will spend any resources on monitoring the firm. The moral hazard problem for shares of common stock will then be severe, making it hard for firms to issue them to raise capital.

Government Regulation to Increase Information   As with adverse selection, the government has an incentive to try to reduce the moral hazard problem created by asymmetric information. Governments everywhere have laws to force firms to adhere to standard accounting principles which make profit verification easier. They also pass laws to impose stiff criminal penalties on those who commit the fraud of hiding and stealing profits. However, these measures will only be partially effective. Catching this kind of fraud is not easy: Fraudulent managers have the incentive to make it very hard for government agencies to find or prove fraud.

Financial Intermediation   Financial intermediaries have the ability to avoid the free-rider problem when there is moral hazard. One financial intermediary in our financial structure that helps reduce the moral hazard arising from the principal-agent problem is the **venture capital firm.** Venture capital firms pool the resources of their partners and use the funds to help budding entrepreneurs start new businesses. In exchange for the use of the venture capital, the firm receives an equity share in the new business. Because verification of earnings and profits is so important to prevent moral hazard, venture capital firms usually insist on having several people on the managing body of the firm, the board of directors, so that they can keep a close watch on the firm's activities. When a venture capital firm supplies start-up funds, the equity in the firm is not marketable to anyone *but* the venture capital firm. Thus, other investors are unable to free ride off of the verification activities of the venture capital firm. As a result of this arrangement, the venture capital firm is able to garner the full benefits of its verification activities so that it is given the appropriate incentives to minimize the moral hazard problem.

Debt Contracts   Moral hazard arises with an equity contract, which is a claim on profits in all situations, whether the firm is making or losing money. If a contract could be structured so that moral hazard would only occur in certain situations, then there would be a reduced need to monitor managers and the contract would be more attractive than the equity contract. The debt contract has exactly these attributes because it is a contractual agreement by the borrower to pay the lender *fixed* dollar amounts at periodic intervals. When the firm has high profits, the lender receives the contractual payments and does not need to know the exact profits of the firm. If the managers are hiding profits or are pursuing activities that are personally beneficial but that don't increase profitability, the lender doesn't care as long as these activities do not interfere with the ability of the firm to make the debt payments on time. Only when the firm cannot meet its debt payments, thereby being in a state of default, is there a need for the lender to verify the state of the firm's profits. Only in this situation do lenders involved in debt contract need to act more like equity holders; now they need to know how much income the firm has in order to get their fair share of the proceeds.

The advantage of a less frequent need to monitor the firm, and thus a lower cost of state verification, helps explain why debt contracts are used so much more frequently to raise capital than are equity contracts. As mentioned in the discussion of Puzzle 1, equity shares account for only a small fraction of external funds raised by American businesses, 2%. All the other sources of external funds involve debt contracts. The concept of moral hazard thus helps explain the puzzle of why debt contracts are so much more prevalent than equity contracts in our financial system.[4]

HOW MORAL HAZARD INFLUENCES FINANCIAL STRUCTURE IN DEBT MARKETS

Even with the advantages just described, debt contracts are still subject to moral hazard. Because a debt contract requires the borrowers to only pay out a fixed amount and lets them keep any profits above this amount, the

---

[4] Another factor that encourages the use of debt contracts rather than equity contracts in the United States is our tax code. Debt interest payments are a deductible expense for American firms, whereas dividend payments to equity shareholders are not. The increased incentive for American corporations to use debt instruments rather than equity to raise funds is discussed further in the appendix to this chapter.

borrowers have an incentive to take on investment projects that are riskier than the lenders would like.

As an example, suppose that because you are concerned about the problem of verifying the profits of Steve's ice cream store, you decide not to become an equity partner. Instead, you lend Steve the $9,000 he needs to set up his business and have a debt contract that pays you an interest rate of 10%. As far as you are concerned, this is a surefire investment because there is a strong and steady demand for ice cream in your neighborhood. However, once you give Steve the funds, he might, just like Uncle Melvin earlier, use them for purposes other than you intended. Instead of opening up the ice cream store, Steve might use your $9,000 loan to invest in chemical research equipment because he thinks he has a one-in-ten chance of inventing a diet ice cream that tastes every bit as good as the premium brands, but has no calories.

Obviously, this is a very risky investment, but if Steve is successful he will become a multimillionaire. He has a strong incentive to undertake the riskier investment because the gains to him would be so large if he succeeded. You clearly would be very unhappy if Steve used your loan for the riskier investment, because if he is unsuccessful, which is highly likely, you would lose most, if not all, the money you gave him. On the other hand, if he were successful, you wouldn't share in his success: You would still get only a 10% return on the loan since the principal and interest payments are fixed. Because of the potential for moral hazard (Steve might use your money to finance a very risky venture), you probably would not make the loan to Steve, even though an ice cream store in the neighborhood is a good investment that would provide benefits for everyone.

Solutions to Moral Hazard in Debt Contracts

Net Worth When a borrower has more at stake because his net worth (the difference between his assets and liabilities) is high, his incentives to commit moral hazard will be greatly reduced because he has a lot to lose. To see this, let's again return to Steve and his ice cream business. Suppose that the cost of setting up either the ice cream store or the research equipment is $100,000 instead of $10,000. So Steve needs to put $91,000 of his own money into the business (instead of $1,000) in addition to the $9,000 supplied by your loan. Now if Steve is unsuccessful in inventing the no-calorie premium ice cream, he has a lot to lose, the $91,000 of net worth (the $100,000 in assets minus the $9,000 loan). He will think twice about undertaking the riskier investment and is more likely to invest in the ice cream store which is more of a sure thing. Hence, when Steve has more of his money (net worth) in the business, you are more likely to make him the loan.

One way of describing the solution that high net worth provides to the moral hazard problem is to say that it makes the debt contract **incentive**

compatible; that is, it aligns the incentives of the borrower to that of the lender. The more net worth a borrower has, the more he has the incentive to behave in the way that the lender expects and desires. Therefore, the greater a borrower's net worth, the smaller the moral hazard problem in the debt contract, and the easier it is for the firm to borrow. Alternatively, with a lower net worth, the moral hazard problem is greater and it is harder for the firm to borrow.

Monitoring and Enforcement of Restrictive Covenants As the example of Steve and his ice cream store shows, if you could make sure that Steve doesn't invest in anything riskier than the ice cream store, then it would be worth your while to make him the loan. You can ensure that Steve uses your money for the purpose *you* want it to be used for by writing provisions (called restrictive covenants) into the debt contract that restrict his firm's activities. By monitoring Steve's activities to see whether he is complying with the restrictive covenants and enforcing the covenants if he is not, you can make sure that he will not take on risks at your expense.

Restrictive covenants are directed at reducing moral hazard by either ruling out undesirable behavior or by encouraging desirable behavior. There are four types of restrictive covenants that achieve this objective.

1. Covenants can be designed to prevent moral hazard by keeping the borrower from engaging in the undesirable behavior of undertaking risky investment projects. Some types of this covenant mandate that a loan can only be used to finance specific activities such as the purchase of particular equipment or inventories. Other types restrict a firm from engaging in certain risky business activities such as purchasing other businesses.

2. Restrictive covenants can encourage the borrower to engage in desirable activities that make it more likely that the loan will be paid off. One restrictive covenant of this type requires the breadwinner in a household to carry life insurance that pays off the mortgage upon his or her death. Restrictive covenants of this type for businesses focus on encouraging the borrowing firm to keep its net worth high, since higher borrower net worth reduces moral hazard and makes it less likely that lender will suffer losses. These restrictive covenants typically specify that the firm must maintain minimum holdings of certain assets relative to the firm's size.

3. Because collateral is an important protection for the lender, restrictive covenants can encourage the borrower to keep the collateral in good condition and make sure that it stays in the possession of the borrower. This is the type of covenant that people like you and I encounter most often. Automobile loan contracts, for example, require the car owner to have a minimum amount of collision and theft insurance and prevent the sale of the car unless the loan is paid off. Similarly, the recipient of a home mortgage must have adequate insurance on the home and must pay off the mortgage when the property is sold.

4. Restrictive covenants also require a borrowing firm to provide information about its activities periodically in the form of quarterly accounting and income reports, thereby making it easier for the lender to monitor the firm and prevent moral hazard. This type of convenant also may stipulate that the lender has the right to audit and inspect the firm's books at any time.

We now see why debt contracts are often complicated legal documents with numerous restrictions on the borrower's behavior—Puzzle 8: debt contracts need to have complicated restrictive covenants to minimize moral hazard.

Financial Intermediation   Although restrictive covenants help reduce the moral hazard problem, they do not eliminate the problem completely. It is almost impossible to write covenants that rule out *every* risk-taking activity. Furthermore, borrowers may be clever enough to find loopholes in the restrictive covenants that make them ineffective.

Another problem with restrictive covenants is that they must be monitored and enforced. A restrictive covenant is meaningless if the borrower can violate it because he knows the lender is not checking up on him or is unwilling to pay for legal proceedings started if the covenant is violated. Because monitoring and enforcement of restrictive covenants are costly, the free-rider problem arises in the debt securities (bond) market just as it does in the stock market. If you know that other bond holders are monitoring and enforcing the restrictive covenants, then you can free ride on their monitoring and enforcement. But other bond holders can do the same thing, so the likely outcome is that not enough resources are devoted to monitoring and enforcing the restrictive covenants. Moral hazard, therefore, continues to be a severe problem for marketable debt.

As we have seen before, financial intermediaries, particularly banks, have the ability to avoid the free-rider problem as long as they primarily make private loans. Private loans are not traded so no one else can free ride off of the intermediary's monitoring and enforcement of the restrictive covenants. The intermediary making private loans thus receives the benefits of monitoring and enforcement and will work to shrink the moral hazard problem inherent in debt contracts. The concept of moral hazard has provided us with additional reasons why financial intermediaries play a more important role in channeling funds from savers to borrowers than do marketable securities, as described in Puzzles 1 through 4.

Summary   The presence of asymmetric information in financial markets leads to adverse selection and moral hazard problems that interfere with the efficient functioning of financial markets. Solutions to these problems involve the private production and sale of information, government regulation to increase information in financial markets, the importance of collateral and net worth to debt contracts, and the use of monitoring and restrictive covenants. A key finding from our analysis is that the existence of the free-rider problem for traded securities such as stocks and bonds indicates that financial intermediaries, particularly banks, should play a greater role than securities markets in financing the activities of businesses. Economic analysis of the consequences of adverse selection and moral hazard has helped explain the basic features of our financial system. Thereby it has also provided solutions to the eight puzzles about our financial structure outlined at the beginning of this chapter.

APPLICATION
FINANCIAL CRISES AND AGGREGATE/ /
ECONOMIC ACTIVITY

Our economic analysis of the effects of adverse selection and moral hazard can help us understand **financial crises,** major disruptions in financial markets that are characterized by sharp declines in asset prices and the failures of many financial and nonfinancial firms. Financial crises have been common in most countries throughout history. The United States has had major financial crises in 1819, 1837, 1857, 1873, 1884, 1893, 1907, and 1929–1933, but none since then.[5] Studying financial crises is worthwhile because they have led to severe economic downturns in the past and have the potential for doing so in the future.

Financial crises occur when adverse selection and moral hazard problems in financial markets become much worse, so that financial markets are unable to efficiently channel funds from savers to those who have productive investment opportunities. As a result of the inability of financial markets to function efficiently, there is a sharp contraction in economic activity.

Factors Causing Financial Crises

Five factors in the economic environment can lead to substantial worsening of adverse selection and moral hazard problems in financial markets, which then cause a financial crisis: (1) increases in interest rates, (2) stock market declines, (3) unanticipated declines in the aggregate price level, (4) increases in uncertainty, and (5) bank panics.

Increases in Interest Rates   As we saw earlier, individuals and firms with the riskiest investment projects are exactly those who are willing to pay the high-

---

[5] Although we in the United States have not experienced any financial crises since the Great Depression, we have had several close calls—the October 1987 stock market crash, for example. An important reason why we have escaped financial crises is the timely action of the Federal Reserve to prevent crises during episodes like that in October 1987. We look at the issue of the Federal Reserve's role in preventing financial crises in Chapter 19.

est interest rates. If market interest rates are driven up sufficiently because of increased demand for credit or because of a decline in the money supply, good credit risks are less likely to want to borrow while bad credit risks are still willing to borrow. Because of the resulting increase in adverse selection, lenders will no longer want to make loans. The substantial decline in lending will lead to a substantial decline in investment and aggregate economic activity.

Stock Market Declines   A sharp decline in the stock market can increase adverse selection and moral hazard problems in financial markets and create a financial crisis. A decline in the stock market means that the net worth of corporations has fallen, because share prices are the valuation of a corporation's net worth. The decline in net worth as a result of a stock market decline makes lenders less willing to lend because, as we have seen, the net worth of a firm has a similar role to collateral. When the value of collateral declines, it provides less protection to lenders so that losses from loans are likely to be more severe. Because lenders are now less protected against the consequences of adverse selection, they decrease their lending, which in turn causes investment and aggregate output to decline.

In addition, the decline in corporate net worth as a result of a stock market decline increases moral hazard incentives for borrowing firms to make risky investments, because they now have less to lose if their investments go sour. The resulting increase in moral hazard makes lending less attractive—another reason why a stock market decline and hence a decline in net worth leads to decreased lending and economic activity.

Unanticipated Declines in the Price Level   Unanticipated declines in the price level also decrease the net worth of firms. Because debt payments are contractually fixed in nominal terms, an unanticipated decline in the price level raises the value of firms' liabilities in *real* terms (increases the burden of the debt), but does not raise the real value of firms' assets. The result is that net worth in *real* terms (the difference between assets and liabilities in *real* terms) declines. A sharp drop in the price level, therefore, causes a substantial decline in real net worth and an increase in adverse selection and moral hazard problems facing lenders. An unanticipated decline in the price level thus leads to the outcome described above in which lending and economic activity falls.

Increases in Uncertainty   A dramatic increase in uncertainty in financial markets, due perhaps to the failure of a prominent financial or nonfinancial institution, a recession, or a stock market crash, makes it harder for lenders to screen good from bad credit risks. The resulting inability of lenders to solve the adverse selection problem, makes them less willing to lend, which leads to a decline in lending, investment, and aggregate activity.

Bank Panics Banks perform an important financial intermediation role by engaging in information-producing activities that facilitate productive investment for the economy. Thus a financial crisis in which many banks go out of business (called a **bank panic**) reduces the amount of financial intermediation undertaken by banks and so leads to a decline in investment and aggregate economic activity. A decrease in the number of banks during a financial crisis also decreases the supply of funds to borrowers, which in turn leads to higher interest rates. Since a rise in interest rates also increases adverse selection in credit markets, bank panics further intensify the decrease in economic activity through this channel as well.

Anatomy of a Financial Crisis

Now that we have examined the five factors that can produce serious disruptions in financial markets, we are ready to look at the anatomy of a financial crisis.

Study Guide

To fully understand what takes place in a financial crisis, make sure that you can state the reasons why each of the five factors—(1) increases in interest rates, (2) stock market declines, (3) unanticipated declines in the aggregate price level, (4) increases in uncertainty, and (5) bank panics—increases adverse selection and moral hazard problems, which in turn lead to a decline in economic activity. To help you with the anatomy of a financial crisis described below, you might want to refer to Figure 8.2—a diagram that traces the sequence of events in a financial crisis.

Most financial crises in the United States have begun with a sharp rise in interest rates, a steep stock market decline, and an increase in uncertainty resulting from a failure of major financial or nonfinancial firms (the Ohio Life Insurance & Trust Co. in 1857, the Northern Pacific Railroad and Jay Cooke & Co. in 1873, Grant & Ward in 1884, the National Cordage Co. in 1893, the Knickerbocker Trust Company in 1907, and the Bank of United States in 1930). During these crises, the increase in uncertainty, the rise in interest rates, and the stock market decline increased the severity of adverse selection problems in credit markets; the stock market decline also increased moral hazard problems. The increase in adverse selection and moral hazard problems then made it less attractive for lenders to lend and led to a decline in investment and aggregate economic activity.

Because of the worsening business conditions and uncertainty about their bank's health (perhaps banks would go broke), depositors began to withdraw their funds from banks. As we will see in Chapters 10 and 16, such massive withdrawal of deposits led to bank panics. The resulting decline in

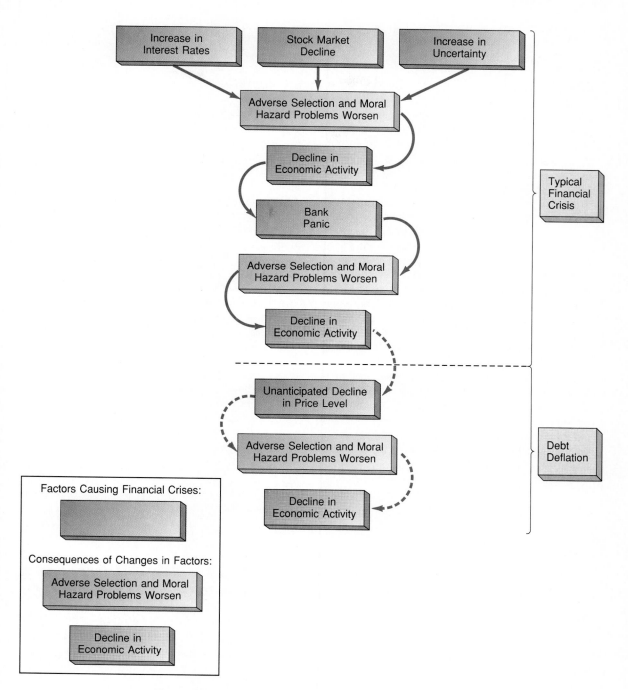

Figure 8.2
Anatomy of a Financial Crisis   Solid line arrows trace the sequence of events in a typical financial crisis; dotted line arrows show the additional set of events if the financial crisis develops into a debt-deflation.

B o x   8 . 2

Case Study of a Financial Crisis: The Great Depression

Federal Reserve officials viewed the stock market boom of 1928 and 1929, in which stock prices doubled, as excessive speculation. In order to curb it, they pursued a tight monetary policy to raise interest rates. The Fed got more than it bargained for with the stock market crash in October 1929.

Although the 1929 crash had a great impact on the minds of a whole generation, most people forget that by the middle of 1930 over half of the stock market decline had been reversed. What might have been a normal recession turned into something far different, however, with adverse shocks to the agricultural sector, a continuing decline in the stock market after the middle of 1930, and a sequence of bank failures from October 1930 until March 1933 in which over one-third of the banks in the United States went out of business (described in more detail in Chapter 16).

The continuing decline in stock prices after mid-1930 (by mid-1932 stocks had declined to 10% of their value at the 1929 peak) and the increase in uncertainty from the unsettled business conditions created by the economic contraction made adverse selection and moral hazard problems worse in the credit markets. The loss of one-third of the banks reduced the amount of financial intermediation. This intensified adverse selection and moral hazard problems, thereby decreasing the ability of financial markets to channel funds to firms with productive investment opportunities. As our analysis predicts, the amount of outstanding commercial loans fell by half from 1929 to 1933 and investment spending collapsed, declining by 90% from its 1929 level.

The short-circuiting of the recovery process that kept the economy from recovering quickly, which it does in most recessions, occurred because of a fall in the price level by 25% in the 1930–1933 period. This huge decline in prices triggered the process of debt-deflation in which net worth fell because of the increased burden of indebtedness borne by firms. The decline in net worth and the resulting increase in adverse selection and moral hazard problems in the credit markets led to a prolonged economic contraction in which unemployment rose until it reached 25% of the labor force. The financial crisis in the Great Depression was the worst ever experienced in the United States, and it explains why this economic contraction was also the most severe one ever experienced in the United States.*

---

*See Ben Bernanke, "Nonmonetary Effects of the Financial Crisis in the Propagation of the Great Depression," *American Economic Review* 73 (June 1983), pp. 257–276, for a discussion of the role of asymmetric information problems in the Great Depression period.

the number of banks raised interest rates even further and decreased the amount of financial intermediation by banks. Worsening of the problems created by adverse selection and moral hazard led to further economic contraction.

Finally, there was a sorting out of insolvent (truly bankrupt) firms from healthy firms by bankruptcy proceedings. The same process occurred for banks, often with the help of public and private authorities. Once this sorting out was complete, uncertainty in financial markets declined, the stock market underwent a recovery, and interest rates fell. The overall result was that adverse selection and moral hazard problems diminished and the financial crisis subsided. With the financial markets able to operate well again, the stage was set for the recovery of the economy.

If, however, the economic downturn led to a sharp decline in prices, the recovery process was short-circuited. In this situation, a process called **debt-deflation** occurred in which a substantial decline in the price level set in, leading to a further deterioration in firms' net worth because of the increased burden of indebtedness. When debt-deflation set in, the adverse selection and moral hazard problems continued to increase so that lending, investment spending, and aggregate economic activity remained depressed for a long time. The most important example of a financial crisis that included debt-deflation is the Great Depression, the worst economic contraction in U.S. history (Box 8.2).

SUMMARY

1. There are eight basic puzzles about our financial structure: the first four emphasize the importance of financial intermediaries and the relative unimportance of securities markets for the financing of corporations; the fifth recognizes that financial markets are among the most heavily regulated sectors of the economy; the sixth states that only large, well-established corporations have access to securities markets; the seventh indicates that collateral is an important feature of debt contracts; and the eighth presents debt contracts as complicated legal documents that place substantial restrictions on the behavior of the borrower.

2. Transactions costs freeze many small savers and borrowers out of direct involvement with financial markets. Financial intermediaries can take advantage of economies of scale and are better able to develop expertise to lower transactions costs, thus enabling their savers and borrowers to benefit from the existence of financial markets.

3. Asymmetric information results in two problems: adverse selection, which occurs before the transaction, and moral hazard, which occurs after the transaction. Adverse selection occurs when bad credit risks are the ones most likely to be lent to, and moral hazard occurs when the borrower has incentives to engage in activities that are undesirable from the lender's point of view.

4. Adverse selection interferes with the efficient functioning of financial markets. Solutions to the adverse selection problem include private production and sale of information, government regulation to increase information, financial intermediation, and collateral and net worth. The free-rider problem occurs when people who do not pay for information take advantage of the information other people have paid for. This problem explains why financial intermediaries and particularly banks play a more important role in financing the activities of businesses than do securities markets.

5. Moral hazard in equity contracts is known as the principal-agent problem because the manager (the agent) has less incentive to maximize profits than the stockholders (the principals). The principal-agent problem explains why debt contracts are so much more prevalent in financial markets than are equity contracts. Solutions to the principal-agent problem include monitoring, government regulation to increase information, and financial intermediation.

6. Solutions to the moral hazard problem in debt contracts include net worth, monitoring and enforcement of restrictive covenants, and financial intermediaries.

7. Financial crises are major disruptions in financial markets. The disruptions are caused by increases in adverse selection and moral hazard problems which prevent financial markets from channeling funds to those with productive investment opportunities, thereby leading to a

sharp contraction in economic activity. There are five factors that lead to financial crises: (1) increases in interest rates, (2) stock market declines, (3) unanticipated declines in the aggregate price level, (4) increases in uncertainty, and (5) bank panics.

KEY TERMS

collateral

restrictive covenants

economies of scale

asymmetric information

adverse selection

moral hazard

free-rider problem

net worth (equity capital)

principal-agent problem

costly state verification

venture capital firm

incentive compatible

financial crises

bank panic

debt-deflation

QUESTIONS AND PROBLEMS

1. How can economies of scale help explain the existence of financial intermediaries?

* 2. Describe two ways in which financial intermediaries help to lower transactions costs in the economy.

3. Would moral hazard and adverse selection still arise in financial markets if information was not asymmetric? Explain.

* 4. How do standard accounting principles required by the government help financial markets work more efficiently?

5. Do you think the lemons problem would be more severe for stocks listed on the New York Stock Exchange or those listed over-the-counter? Explain.

* 6. Which firms are most likely to use bank financing rather than to issue bonds or stocks to finance their activities? Why?

7. How can the existence of asymmetric information provide a rationale for government regulation of financial markets?

* 8. Would you be more willing to lend to someone who has put all of her life savings into her business than if she hasn't? Why?

9. Rich people often worry that someone will marry them for their money. Is this an example of an adverse selection problem?

*10. True, false or uncertain: "The more collateral backing a loan, the less the lender has to worry about adverse selection."

11. How does the free-rider problem make adverse selection and moral hazard problems worse in financial markets?

*12. Explain how the separation of ownership and control in American corporations might lead to poor management.

13. Is a financial crisis more likely to occur when the economy is experiencing deflation or inflation? Explain.

*14. How can a stock market crash help provoke a financial crisis?

15. How can a sharp rise in interest rates help provoke a financial crisis?

Corporate Restructuring: An Economic Analysis

An important feature of the financial structure in the United States is the degree to which businesses are financed with debt versus equity contracts. In the 1980s, there was a major transformation in this aspect of our financial structure. Beginning in 1984, new issues of equity shares were no longer being used to fund investment activities in the U.S. economy; instead, equity shares were being repurchased at a rapid rate by American corporations. In every year from 1984 to 1990, net issues of equity shares were negative, with net equity repurchases averaging over $75 billion per year.

As they undertook these equity repurchases, American corporations began to greatly increase their indebtedness. In 1984, the increase in nonfinancial corporate debt jumped to over $150 billion per year; in previous years it had risen at rates nearer $50 billion per year. In every year from 1984 to 1990, the rate of increase remained in excess of $100 billion. This growth in corporate indebtedness is visible in Figure 8A.1, which shows the level of nonfinancial corporate indebtedness relative to GNP since 1970. From 1970 to 1983, corporate debt grew at a rate somewhat slower than GNP, and the ratio of corporate debt to GNP declined to around 31%. Beginning in 1984, however, the debt-GNP ratio began to rise sharply and climbed to close to 40% by 1990.

What explains this important change in financial structure in the United States? Why did it occur in the 1980s? Is the increase in corporate indebtedness a good thing for the American economy? To answer these questions, in this appendix we conduct an economic analysis of corporate restructuring.

MERGERS, TAKEOVERS, AND LEVERAGED BUYOUTS IN THE CORPORATE RESTRUCTURING PROCESS

A major factor driving the dramatic increases in corporate indebtedness in the 1980s was the restructuring of the management of American corporations through **mergers,** in which two corporations combine to make one larger corporation, or by **acquisitions** (also called **takeovers**), in which a group of investors or a corporation purchases another corporation. Activity

$$\frac{\text{Corporate Debt}}{\text{GNP}}$$

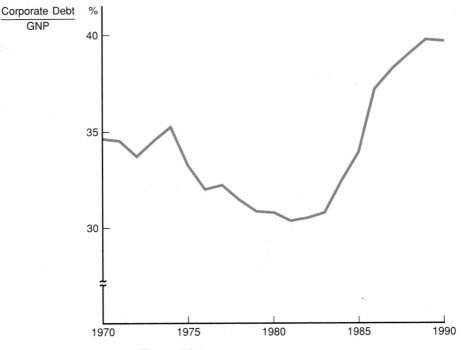

Figure 8A.1

Nonfinancial Corporate Debt Relative to GNP: 1970–1990 Source: Federal Reserve Flow of Funds Accounts and *Economic Report of the President.*

in this market reached record levels in the mid-1980s—close to $200 billion a year, and of the 100 largest mergers and acquisitions ever, 90 occurred since 1979.

The principal method of financing takeovers and mergers in the 1980s was the use of debt. For example, the $25 billion takeover of RJR-Nabisco in February 1989, the largest takeover ever in the United States, was financed using over $20 billion in debt, with over half coming from banks throughout the world. To understand why corporate indebtedness jumped in the 1980s, we need answers to two questions: Why did merger and acquisition activity increase so much in the 1980s and why was this activity financed primarily with new issues of debt?

To answer these two questions, we first examine theories of how merger and acquisition activity and increasing indebtedness might be beneficial. Then we look at some of the negative aspects of corporate restructuring when we examine whether the increase in corporate debt has been good for the economy.

The Principal-Agent Problem and Free Cash Flow Theory

The large American corporation is characterized by the separation of ownership and control. Managers own only a small fraction of the total equity shares in their firm, typically less than 5%. As we saw in the chapter, separation of ownership and control leads to a particular example of moral hazard, the principal-agent problem: Managers in control (the agent) may act in their own interest rather than in the interest of the stockholders-owners (the principals) because they have less incentive to maximize profits than the owners do.

The principal-agent problem can lead to poor management because the agent (the managers) may not put in enough effort to make the firm as profitable as it should be. Alternatively, managers might engage in activities that benefit them personally but do not benefit the stockholders. Managers might have the company pay for fancy corporate jets, ritzy apartments, or personal maids, which benefit the managers but do not increase profits (see Box 8A.1). Or in order to enhance their prestige, managers might find it

Box   8 A . 1

F. Ross Johnson and the RJR-Nabisco Takeover

The saga of F. Ross Johnson and the RJR-Nabisco takeover shows that high free cash flow and a small ownership share can produce managerial incentives to pursue personal goals at the expense of the stockholders.

RJR-Nabisco, a cigarette and food company, had substantial cash flow. Yet the continuing decline in the cigarette industry left it with few profitable investment opportunities within the industry, resulting in high free cash flow. As free cash flow theory predicts, the managers of RJR-Nabisco pursued unprofitable investments to increase the size of their business, spending hundreds of millions on development of a smokeless cigarette that was a huge flop. What is striking about the RJR-Nabisco example is the tendency for its chief operating officer, F. Ross Johnson, to spend excessive sums on personal perks. An associate at RJR-Nabisco described Johnson as suffering from "a corporate royalty complex" and that he "had trouble remembering what was his and what was the company's."

He had the company pay for two personal maids, more than a dozen houses and apartments, two dozen country club memberships, and a fleet of ten corporate airplanes, called unofficially the RJR air force. F. Ross Johnson's behavior was an example of the principal-agent problem in practice.

The huge free cash flow and the resulting incentives for managers to waste it by having the firm engage in nonprofitable activities made RJR-Nabisco ripe for a takeover. After Johnson and his company's top executives tried to engineer a purchase of the firm for $17 billion in October 1988, a group led by Henry Kravis finally bought it for $25 billion in February 1989. After this takeover, the largest in U.S. history, Johnson was fired and the new management sold many of his corporate toys just as our analysis would predict. Johnson lost out in the bid for RJR-Nabisco, but we shouldn't feel sorry for him: His severance package left him with $53 million!

personally worthwhile to expand the company, even if it means going into unprofitable operations.

Michael Jensen of the Harvard Business School has developed a theory to explain when the principal-agent problem is most likely to lead to poor managerial performance. His theory is based on the concept of **free cash flow.**[1] Cash flow is the difference between cash receipts and cash expenditures (which includes interest and dividends),[2] while *free* cash flow is the amount of cash flow that *exceeds* the amount of profitable investment opportunities open to the firm. If Steve's ice cream store yielded a cash flow of $25,000 and yet enlarging the ice cream store would not be profitable, then the free cash flow would be $25,000. If a $10,000 renovation to enlarge the store would be profitable, then the free cash flow would be $15,000 ($25,000 of cash flow minus the $10,000 profitable investment opportunity).

The higher is free cash flow, the greater are the amounts of funds that a manager has to waste. Just as Steve was willing to lower his store's profits to pursue personal goals because of the principal-agent problem, managers with large amounts of free cash flow under their control are more likely to pursue their personal goals at the expense of the stockholders. High free cash flow, therefore, makes poor managerial performance more likely.

Takeovers as a Solution to the Principal-Agent Problem

If a corporation has incompetent managers or managers who spend company funds in ways that do not benefit the stockholders because free cash flow is high, then stockholders can benefit by "throwing the bums out." One method of doing this is to fire the managers and bring in a new set of managers. You might think that shareholders could simply effect the necessary change in management, but such a change is not easy. First, the shareholders would have to spend their time and money to monitor the managers of the firm to ascertain if they are incompetent or not. The free-rider problem, however, makes it unlikely that the shareholders will monitor the managers' performance. Also, the legal structure of how the corporation is governed may make it quite difficult for the shareholders to vote current management out. In addition, the shareholders' representatives on the board of directors may be too reluctant or slow to fire bad managers. Outright firing of the highest-level corporate managers, for example, is extremely rare. Because

---

[1] Michael Jensen, "Agency Costs of Free Cash Flow, Corporate Finance and Takeovers," *American Economic Review* 76 (May 1986) pp. 323–329, and "Takeovers: Their Causes and Consequences," *Journal of Economic Perspectives* (Winter 1988), pp. 21–48.

[2] Cash flow differs from profits because it subtracts out dividend payments and tax payments, while profits do not. Profits, on the other hand, do subtract depreciation expenses, while cash flow does not.

of all these difficulties, the principal-agent problem will probably not be solved by internal changes in management.

If bad managers cannot be removed by firing, they can be removed by the process of takeovers. A group of investors led by a takeover specialist such as a Henry Kravis, a Carl Icahn, or a T. Boone Pickens can try to buy the firm at a price greater than the current market price. If they succeed in taking over the firm, they can put in new, more efficient managers, thereby increasing profits. As a result of these higher profits, the firm's shares will increase in price and the takeover group will have earned a profit as long as the shares after the takeover increase to a price greater than the takeover purchase price.

While actual takeovers can increase economic efficiency if they replace poor managers with better managers, just the threat of takeovers may remove conflicts of interest between owners and managers and help solve the principal-agent problem. If a manager who performs poorly is more likely to be thrown out of her job because her firm is more likely to be taken over, she has a greater incentive to be a good manager. As long as there are enough takeovers to make the threat of takeovers a serious one, then the threat alone will often be enough to promote good management.

Increased Indebtedness as a Solution to the Principal-Agent Problem

Increasing a firm's indebtedness can give managers better incentives to act in the interest of the stockholders-owners, and so indebtedness provides another way of solving the principal-agent problem. To see how, let's return to our example of your partnership with Steve. Recall that of the $10,000 investment in Steve's store, you have put up $9,000 and own 90% of the business while Steve has put up $1,000 and owns only 10%. The problem facing Steve is that if he works hard and is a good manager so that the store earns profits of $50,000, he only receives $5,000, his 10% share. Because he only finds it worth his while to be a good manager if he earns an extra $10,000 over his salary, his incentives to be a good manager aren't strong enough and so he chooses to be a poor manager instead and the store earns no profits.

Now suppose that Steve is able to borrow $9,000 from a bank at a 10% interest rate and buys your shares in his business. You are happy to sell, because the firm wasn't earning any profits anyway. The result is that the finances of the firm have been restructured so that equity (ownership shares) has been swapped for debt (Steve's bank loan). Now when Steve asks himself whether he should put in the effort to be a good manager, the answer is "yes." He now owns 100% of the equity in the firm and if he is a good manager, he keeps the $49,100 in profits ($50,000 less the $900, 10% interest payment on the $9,000 bank loan)—a sum that makes it worth his while to perform his manager's role properly. *The restructuring of the firm's finances has enabled Steve, the manager, to increase his share of the profits,* thereby promoting better managerial incentives and eliminating the principal-agent problem.

The corporate restructuring we have just described is one that increases the **leverage** of the firm, the ratio of debt to equity. The debt-equity ratio, which was zero (there was $10,000 of equity, 90% owned by you and 10% owned by Steve, and no debt), now rises to nine ($9,000 of debt owed to the bank and $1,000 of equity owned by Steve). A corporate restructuring in which equity is replaced by debt and so leverage increases, as in the example here, is called a **leveraged buyout (LBO).** If the manager of the firm, as in our example, is the one who engineers the deal and so ends up owning a greater share of the firm, then it is called a management leveraged buyout.

Alternatively, an outsider could restructure Steve's ice cream business by borrowing $9,000, putting up $1,000, and buying both you and Steve out. In this case, the restructuring is a takeover. Nonetheless, the managerial incentives for this outsider are exactly the same as they were for Steve when he arranged the restructuring. The outsider who has taken over the firm now has a claim to all the profits of the firm, thereby reducing the principal-agent problem. LBO restructuring can also occur as part of a merger arrangement. The crucial point here is that whether a leveraged buyout occurs as a result of a management buyout, a merger, or a takeover, the increase in leverage (the ratio of debt to equity), reduces the principal-agent problem and leads to improved performance of the firm.

When Are Corporate Restructuring Most Likely to Occur?

We have seen that takeovers can be profitable for takeover specialists (sometimes pejoratively called corporate raiders) when higher profits can be earned by installing better management after the takeover. Free cash flow theory tells us when this is most likely to occur because it suggests that managers will perform worse when free cash flow is high. High free cash flow means that managers have greater incentives to engage in wasteful spending and so they are more likely to perform badly. In such a situation, the gains to a takeover will be high and thus it is more likely to occur.

The takeover specialist is also likely to restructure the finances of the firm with a high free cash flow to increase its indebtedness when bidding for it. As we saw in Steve's ice cream store, the increased indebtedness (leverage) improves managerial incentives and increases the potential profitability of the firm. Indeed, an entrenched management, possibly in response to a takeover threat, might do the corporate restructuring itself and try to undertake a management leveraged buyout of the firm. If it does this, the management will have better incentives to maximize profits because they will get a larger share of the profits.

Jensen's analysis of free cash flow provides an explanation of which firms are most likely to be taken over. Free cash flow will be highest for firms in profitable industries with high cash flow, but which have low growth prospects and hence poor investment opportunities. These firms are most likely to be taken over and restructured with LBOs. Indeed, if a profitable industry needs to shrink, firms in this industry are especially likely to have high free cash flow and be threatened by takeovers. The tobacco industry with its shrinking cigarette market is just such an industry—a fact that helps explain the largest LBO takeover to date, that of RJR-Nabisco described in Box 8A.1.

Why Did Corporate Restructuring Occur in the 1980s?

Free cash flow theory also helps explain why the takeovers and LBO boom and the resulting increase in corporate indebtedness occurred in the 1980s. As a result of increased foreign competition, the maturing of American industries, and deregulation in the 1980s, many firms in the United States experienced slower growth and even shrinkage. The dearth of investment opportunities in such industries as oil, tobacco, broadcasting, and food processing, increased their free cash flow and increased the principal-agent problem, making takeovers and LBOs more profitable. Not surprisingly, the resulting boom in takeovers and LBOs made many takeover specialists extremely rich.

Additional political and institutional factors also fueled the takeover and LBO boom of the 1980s. Lax enforcement of antitrust laws restrictions during the Reagan years removed barriers to mergers and takeovers. Also improvements in the technology of conducting takeovers and LBOs made them easier and less costly to execute. These included the development of increasingly sophisticated investment bankers and legal advisors, and financial innovations such as the development of the junk bond market which made financing takeovers and LBOs easier.

The collapse in the late 1980s of the junk bond market and the demise of Drexel Burnham (an investment banking firm that was a major player in the takeover-LBO game), the troubles of Donald Trump, and the bankruptcy of celebrated companies such as the Campeau Corporation that restructured with LBOs, all may lead to decreased leverage and a decline in takeover activity in the future. In addition, many state legislatures have passed anti-takeover legislation, for example, New York, New Jersey, Maryland, Pennsylvania, Connecticut, Illinois, Kentucky, Michigan, Ohio, Indiana, and Minnesota; also, the Federal Reserve in 1987 implemented new restrictions on the use of debt in certain takeovers. The likelihood is that the 1990s will see substantially less merger and takeover activity than the 1980s and a slower growth in corporate indebtedness. As an investment banker stated recently, "Debt is becoming a four letter word."[3]

---

[3] As quoted from Richard L. Kauffman, director of equity capital markets at the First Boston Corporation, in Wayne Leslie, "Balance Sheets in 90's: Less Debt," *New York Times* July 23, 1990.

APPLICATION
RESTRUCTURING OF THE OIL INDUSTRY IN THE 1980s/ / / / / / / / / / / / / /

The roles of the principal-agent problem and free cash in stimulating take-overs and LBOs can be used to explain why merger and takeover activity was greater in the oil industry in the 1980s than in any other industry.

By the 1980s, the OPEC oil price increases in 1973 and 1979 had led to huge cash flows for this industry. For example, in 1984 the cash flows of the ten largest oil companies were $48.5 billion, over 25% of the total cash flows of the largest 200 firms in the United States. At the same time, the oil industry was experiencing excess capacity in its refining and distribution operations, and the increasing difficulty of discovering oil in the United States made oil exploration and drilling activity unprofitable. The resulting paucity of investment opportunities in this industry and its huge cash flows meant that the oil industry had the highest free cash flow of any industry in the United States.

Consistent with our principal-agent analysis, managers, with their small ownership in the firm, added to their personal power and glory by expanding their size of firms with heavy spending on oil exploration and development that had little or no payoff. The high free cash flow also caused the managers of oil companies to pursue growth by investing funds outside their industry. Mobil bought Marcor, the parent company of Montgomery Ward; Exxon purchased Reliance Electric and Vydec, manufacturing and office equipment firms, respectively; and several oil companies acquired mining firms (Sohio bought Kennecott, ARCO purchased Anaconda Minerals, and Amoco bought Cyprus Mines). None of these acquisitions was successful. Although some of the failures can be attributed to bad luck (the collapse of minerals prices in the 1980s), the facts indicate that oil company management had little expertise outside its own industry.

Oil company management was clearly not operating in the interests of the stockholders, and yet changes in management were not forthcoming from stockholders or boards of directors. The gains from restructuring these oil firms and making them more efficient were colossal, and T. Boone Pickens of Mesa Petroleum spotted a golden opportunity. Oil companies fought the attempts of Pickens to take over their companies by merging. In the process they increased their debt and paid out large amounts of capital to stockholders. In addition, they cut back expenditures on exploration and development and reduced excess capacity in refining and distribution. Because wasteful spending was reduced, the payouts to stockholders increased and the resulting gains to stockholders were substantial: The mergers of Gulf-Chevron, Getty-Texaco, and Du Pont-Conoco yielded increases in the values of these firms collectively by over $17 billion. Other oil companies such as Phillips, Unocal, and Arco restructured themselves by purchasing their own stock using debt and cash, increases in dividends, and reductions in exploration and development. The gains in market value of these firms from these restructurings was over $5 billion.

Although his activities produced enormous gains for oil company stock-holders, Pickens was not successful in taking over any major oil company. However, we need not pity him—his holdings of oil company shares acquired during his takeover bids increased tremendously in value when oil company restructuring made these firms leaner and more efficient. As a result, T. Boone Pickens became one of the richest men in America.

IS THE INCREASE IN CORPORATE DEBT GOOD FOR THE ECONOMY?

As Figure 8A.1 shows, takeovers and LBOs led to a dramatic increase in the indebtedness of American corporations. One consequence of the increased debt-service burden has been a disturbingly high rate of business failures in recent years. Surprisingly, the rate of bankruptcies kept rising for four years after the end of the 1981–1982 recession. Even in the late 1980s, a period of economic expansion, bankruptcies were running at more than double the average rate in the 1953–1980 period. Has the increased indebtedness resulting from takeovers and LBOs been good for the economy? Our principal-agent analysis has so far stressed the benefits of takeovers and LBOs that increase corporate indebtedness. Takeovers and LBOs have the economic rationale that they increase economic efficiency by improving managerial incentives. To examine whether increased indebtedness is a good thing, however, we need to move beyond principal-agent analysis.

In the chapter we saw that the principal-agent problem is not the only form of moral hazard. Debt contracts lead to another type in which borrowers take on too much risk. Because debt requires the firm to pay out only a fixed amount and lets it keep any profits above this amount, the firm and its managers have much to gain if a risky investment turns out to be successful, while the lender does not. (Recall that this was the case for Steve's investment in inventing a no-calorie ice cream). Managers of firms with a large amount of debt after an LBO or takeover therefore have an incentive to choose investment projects that are too risky. This moral hazard problem may lead to more risk taking than is healthy for the economy.

With its increased indebtedness after an LBO or takeover, a firm is also more likely to suffer bankruptcy. A bad shock may make it impossible for the firm to pay the now extremely high interest payments to the lenders. Unfortunately, bankruptcy has substantial costs, only one of which is high legal costs. Once a company goes into bankruptcy court, there are strong conflicts of interest between creditors (debt holders) and equity holders which make operations of the company very difficult. In addition, the company's suppliers may be reluctant to ship goods because they are not sure they will be paid, which further cripples the firm's operations. Difficulties of this type have been experienced by Campeau, a Canadian company that owns such famous department stores as Bloomingdale's, Jordan Marsh, and Burdine's, which entered bankruptcy in 1989 after a leveraged buyout led to much higher debt payments. The jewel of the Campeau department store crown, Bloomingdale's, suffered because shoppers experienced a shortage of merchandise.

Even if a leveraged company is not in bankruptcy, its high indebtedness may hinder it in long-term agreements with suppliers, customers, and workers who fear the possibility of bankruptcy. Managers of a firm with high interest payments after an LBO or takeover may also be more likely to manage for the short-term rather than the long-term; for example, they may not invest in items like research and development (R&D) that have long-term payoffs. The problem of short-sightedness in its operations can become especially severe when a firm with high debt is facing financial distress. Then it may cut production, sell valuable assets, and forego profitable investment opportunities. For example, if after a leveraged buyout Steve became worried that he couldn't meet his firm's interest payments, he might cut costs by lowering the butterfat content of his ice cream, hoping that his customers wouldn't notice, at least in the short run.

Another important consideration is that even if increased indebtedness improves the performance of individual firms, it could lead to adverse consequences for the economy as a whole. As described in the chapter (the application on financial crises), a bankruptcy of one firm may lead to a cutback of production and employment which then leads to financial troubles at another firm. A more highly leveraged economy with greater indebtedness may thus make a series of escalating bankruptcies more likely, with potential serious repercussions for the economy. Increased leverage may also make a financial breakdown of the type that occurred in the Great Depression more probable. A series of escalating bankruptcies might threaten the health of the banking system and this could be disastrous for the economy (see Box 8.2 in the chapter). Indeed, many economists worry that increased corporate indebtedness might make it harder for the Federal Reserve to contain financial crises like the one we almost experienced after the Penn Central Bankruptcy in 1970. Increased leverage as a result of takeovers and LBOs may make our economy more fragile and inherently more unstable, an unhappy thought.

Evidence on the Benefits and Costs of Takeovers and LBOs

The controversy surrounding takeovers and LBOs led to research about whether corporate restructuring is beneficial.[4] Here, we will examine the evidence, both pro and con, on the desirability of corporate restructuring.

---

[4] Much of the evidence discussed here is surveyed in Ben Bernanke, "Is There Too Much Corporate Debt?" *Federal Reserve Bank of Philadelphia Quarterly Review* (September/October 1989), pp. 3–13; and the "Symposium on Takeovers" in the *Journal of Economic Perspectives* 2 (Winter 1988).

Evidence in Favor   The first piece of evidence usually cited by those who believe that takeovers and LBOs improve economic performance is that takeovers definitely benefit the shareholders of the target companies. The premiums over the market price paid for shares in hostile takeovers have averaged on the order of 30% (i.e., an offer of $130 for a share originally selling at $100), but recently they have been an even higher 50%. The simplest explanation for this finding is that a takeover makes the operation of the firm more efficient because it improves management and managerial incentives. The resulting expectations of future higher profits of the restructured company then lead to the higher price for its shares. Because the higher share price reflects increased managerial efficiency, it indicates that the takeover is good for the economy.

There are two other pieces of evidence that lend some support to the view that takeovers increase economic efficiency by improving management. First, takeover targets are usually firms with very poor performance, just as we would expect if takeovers occur in order to improve management. Second, several studies have found that productivity does rise on average in firms that have been taken over.

Evidence Against   Critics of takeovers respond that there are other explanations for the increase in the value of firms when taken over. One possibility is that the rise in the market value of target firms is a mistake and does not reflect expectations of higher future profits of these firms. Although this is a possibility, it does imply that stock market prices are unrelated to future firm profitability, an implication with which economists are not entirely comfortable.

More serious critics of the view that the higher value of the target firm after a takeover implies an improvement in economic efficiency agree that takeovers lead to higher future profitability of the target firm. They argue, however, that the higher profits occur not because of increased efficiency but because other parties—the government, workers, customers, and bond holders—lose when the firm is taken over. Particularly important is the fact that the tax code in the United States favors debt over equity, since interest payments to debt holders are tax deductible for the corporation whereas dividend payments are not. Thus, the government loses tax revenue when debt is swapped for equity as in most takeovers.

Other research has found that as a result of some takeovers, wage concessions are wrung from the workers, decreasing their income. For example, one study has found that wage concessions granted by the TWA unions were larger than the premiums paid to TWA shareholders by Carl Icahn. If a takeover results in increased monopolization of a market and hence higher prices for the company's goods, then customers suffer losses. Bond holders can also come out big losers, as occurred in the RJR-Nabisco LBO, because the higher leverage of the firm after the takeover increases the default risk on previously issued bonds and results in a price decline. The key point here is that the increased future profits of the takeover target may in reality be paid for by other participants in the economy and may not indicate increased economic efficiency.

Critics of takeovers and LBOs blame the decline in the growth rate of research and development (R&D) since 1984 on the wave of takeovers and LBOs that occurred in the early 1980s. They claim that the increased indebtedness after a corporate restructuring makes management more short-sighted, so that it does not invest sufficiently in R&D, which has long-term payoffs. They view the potential consequences of takeovers and LBOs for the U.S. economy to be disastrous because a decline in R&D may make it harder for us to compete with countries like Japan.

Does the evidence support an increase in management shortsightedness when indebtedness of the firm increases after corporate restructuring? Although there is some evidence that increased indebtedness after corporate restructuring leads to a decline in R&D, the actual effects of takeovers and LBOs on American R&D is quite small.[5] Corporate restructuring is more likely to occur in older, low-tech industries which are the industries with the highest free cash flow. Thus, LBOs and takeovers have taken place in industries in which R&D is relatively unimportant. Evidence suggests that takeovers and LBOs are not the cause of the decline in R&D growth in the United States.

Even if, on balance, one views the evidence discussed so far as supporting the view that takeovers and LBOs promote more efficient management, the jury would still be out on the desirability of takeovers and LBOs. We still need to consider evidence on how the resulting increased indebtedness might affect the overall economy. Studies of the Great Depression and of other periods in which financial crises have occurred indicate that increased indebtedness can greatly increase the severity of recessions.[6] Furthermore, studies suggest that a severe recession might interact with a high level of corporate indebtedness to trigger a serious crisis of escalating bankruptcies.[7] The evidence therefore suggests that increased indebtedness makes the economy more fragile and thus could prove dangerous.

---

[5] See Bronwyn Hall, "The Impact of Corporate Restructuring on Industrial Research and Development," National Bureau of Economic Research Working Paper No. 3216, December 1989.

[6] See, for example, Ben Bernanke, "Nonmonetary Effects of the Financial Crisis in the Propagation of the Great Depression," *American Economic Review* 73 (June 1983), pp. 257–276; and Frederic S. Mishkin, "Asymmetric Information and Financial Crises: A Historical Perspective," in R. Glenn Hubbard, ed., *Financial Markets and Financial Crises* (Chicago: University of Chicago Press, 1991).

[7] Ben S. Bernanke and John Y. Campbell, "Is There a Corporate Debt Crisis?" *Brookings Papers on Economic Activity* (1988:1), pp. 83–125; and Ben Bernanke, John Y. Campbell, and Toni M. Whited, "U.S. Corporate Leverage: Developments in 1987 and 1988," *Brookings Papers on Economic Activity* (1990:1), pp. 255–286.

What Should Policymakers Do About LBOs and Takeovers?

Our discussion has shown us that takeovers and LBOs can improve managerial incentives and so increase economic efficiency. The evidence provides some support for this position, although it also suggests that takeovers and LBOs may result in some corporate shortsightedness. Because increasing efficiency in American corporations is especially important in today's economic environment of heightened international competition, most economists would not support an outright ban on takeovers or LBOs.

On the other hand, we have seen that takeovers and LBOs may result from biases toward debt in our tax code, and that resulting high indebtedness may make the overall economy more fragile. There are thus good reasons to think that there is too much indebtedness in the U.S. economy. The economy might be better off if policymakers reduced the incentives for leverage by reducing the tax advantages of debt over equity. Policymakers might also try to change the rules of corporate governance to make it easier for stockholders to change management or to write management contracts that give managers better incentives to perform in the stockholders' interest. The result would be a reduced need to use increased leverage to ensure better management.

CHAPTER 9

The Banking Firm and Bank Management

PREVIEW   Because banks (depository institutions) play such an important role in channeling funds to borrowers with productive investment opportunities, they play an important role in ensuring that the economy runs smoothly and efficiently. In the United States, banks supply over $5 trillion of credit: They provide loans to businesses, help us finance our college educations or the purchase of a new car or home, and provide us with checking and savings accounts.

In this chapter, we examine how banks, the most important of the financial intermediaries, operate to earn the highest profits possible: how and why they make loans, how they acquire funds and manage their assets and liabilities (debts), and how they earn income. Although we will focus on commercial banks because they hold over two-thirds of the assets in the banking system, the principles are just as applicable to other types of banking institutions, such as savings and loans, mutual savings banks, and credit unions.

THE BANK BALANCE SHEET

To understand how a bank operates, first we need to examine the bank **balance sheet,** which lists its assets and liabilities. As the name implies, this list balances; that is, it has the characteristic that

$$\text{Total assets} = \text{total liabilities} + \text{capital}$$

Furthermore, a bank's balance sheet lists *sources* of bank funds (liabilities) and *uses* to which they are put (assets). Banks obtain funds by borrowing and by issuing other liabilities such as deposits. They then use these funds to acquire assets such as securities and loans. The revenue that banks receive from their holdings of securities and loans covers the expenses of issuing liabilities and ideally yields a profit. The balance sheet of all commercial banks at the end of 1990 appears in Table 9.1.

Table 9.1   **Balance Sheet of All Commercial Banks, End of 1990 (Items as % of Total)**

Assets (Uses of Funds)		Liabilities (Sources of Funds)	
(In order of decreasing liquidity)			
Reserves	2	Checkable deposits	18
Cash items in process of collection	3	Nontransaction deposits	
Deposits with other banks	2	Savings deposits	17
Securities		Small denomination (<$100,000) time deposits	19
U.S. government and agency	13	Large denomination time deposits	15
State and local government and other securities	6	Borrowings	24
Loans		Bank capital	7
Commercial and industrial	19		
Real estate	24		
Consumer	11		
Interbank	6		
Other loans	7		
Other assets (for example, physical capital)	7		
TOTAL	100	TOTAL	100

Source: Federal Reserve *Bulletin.*

Liabilities

A bank acquires funds by issuing (selling) liabilities (sources of funds), which can then be used to purchase income-earning assets.

Checkable Deposits   These are accounts at a bank that entitle the owner(s) of the account to write checks to third parties. Checkable deposits include all types of accounts on which checks can be drawn: non-interest-bearing checking accounts (demand deposits), interest-bearing NOW (negotiable order of withdrawal) accounts, super-NOW accounts, and the money market deposit accounts (MMDAs) introduced in 1982. Table 9.1 depicts checkable deposits as an important source of bank funds, making up 18% of bank liabilities. Once they were the most important source of bank funds (over 60% of bank liabilities in 1960), but their share of bank liabilities has shrunk over time.

Checkable deposits are payable on demand; that is, if a depositor shows up at the bank and requests payment by making a withdrawal, the bank will pay the depositor immediately. Similarly, if a person receives a check written on an account from a bank, when the bank is presented with the check it must transfer funds immediately to that person's account.

A checkable deposit is an asset for the depositor because it is part of his wealth. Conversely, because the depositor can withdraw funds from his account that the bank is obligated to pay, checkable deposits are a liability of the bank. They are usually the lowest-cost source of bank funds because depositors are willing to forgo some interest in order to have access to a liquid asset that can be used to make purchases. The bank's costs of maintaining checkable deposits include interest payments as well as the costs incurred in servicing these accounts [processing and storing of canceled checks, preparing and sending out monthly statements, providing efficient tellers (human or otherwise), maintaining an impressive building, and advertising/marketing to entice customers to deposit their funds with a given bank]. In recent years interest paid on deposits (checkable and time) have been around 50% of total bank operating expenses, while the costs involved in servicing accounts (employee salaries, building rent, etc.) have been approximately 35% of operating expenses.

Nontransaction Deposits Nontransaction deposits are the primary source of bank funds (51% of bank liabilities in Table 9.1). Characteristically, they earn interest and do not allow their owner to write checks. Their interest rates are usually higher than those on checking accounts because the depositor is not provided with nearly as many services. There are two basic types of nontransaction deposits: savings accounts and time deposits (also called certificates of deposits, CDs).

Savings accounts were once the most common type of nontransaction deposit. In these accounts, to which funds can be added or withdrawn any time, transactions and interest payments are recorded in a small book (the passbook) held by the owner of the account or in a monthly statement. Technically, this form of deposit is not payable on demand (the bank *can* wait up to thirty days to pay); however, because of competition for deposits, banks allow depositors to make withdrawals from their savings accounts without delay.

Time deposits have a fixed maturity length ranging from several months to over five years and have substantial penalties for early withdrawal (the forfeit of several months' interest). Small denomination time deposits (deposits of less than $100,000) are less liquid for the depositor than passbook savings, they earn higher interest rates and are a more costly source of funds for the banks.

Large-denomination time deposits (CDs) are available in denominations of $100,000 or over and are typically bought by corporations or other banks. Large-denomination CDs are negotiable, so that, like a bond, they can be resold in a secondary market before they mature. For this reason, negotiable CDs are held by corporations, money market mutual funds, and other financial institutions as alternative assets to Treasury bills and other short-term bonds. Since 1961, when they first appeared, negotiable CDs have become an important source of bank funds (15%).

Borrowings   Banks obtain funds by borrowing from the Federal Reserve System, other banks, and corporations. Borrowings from the Fed are called **discount loans** (also known as an "advance"). Banks also borrow reserves overnight in the federal (Fed) funds market from other U.S. banks and financial institutions. Other sources of borrowed funds are loans made to banks by their parent companies (bank holding companies), loan arrangements with corporations (such as repurchase agreements), and borrowings of Eurodollars (deposits denominated in U.S. dollars residing in foreign banks or foreign branches of U.S. banks). Borrowings have become a more important source of bank funds over time: In 1960, they comprised only 2% of bank liabilities, while currently they exceed 20% of bank liabilities.

Bank Capital   The final category on the liabilities side of the balance sheet is bank capital, the bank's net wealth, which equals the difference between total assets and liabilities (7% of total bank assets in Table 9.1). The funds are raised by selling new equity (stock) or from retained earnings. Bank capital is a cushion against a drop in the value of its assets, which could force the bank into insolvency (where the value of bank assets falls below its liabilities so that the bank is bankrupt). One important component of bank capital is loan loss reserves which are described in Box 9.1.

B o x   9 . 1

Understanding Loan Loss Reserves

Perhaps you have seen headlines in the press about banks' large increases in loan loss (bad debt) reserves. Often there is much confusion about loan loss reserves, probably because they have a similar-sounding name to the reserves item in a bank's balance sheet. Actually, loan loss reserves have nothing to do with the reserves asset item in the balance sheet, instead they are a component of bank capital.

To see how loan loss reserves work, suppose that a bank suspects that some of its loans, say, $1 million worth, might prove to be bad debts which will have to be written off (valued at zero) in the future. The bank can set aside $1 million of its earnings and put it into its loan loss reserves ac-

count, and so the $1 million is counted as part of its capital. As a result of adding to loan loss reserves, the bank reduces its reported earnings by the $1 million, in effect, taking its lumps even before the bad debt is written off. When the bank determines that the $1 million loan will never be paid back and formally writes it off, the loan loss reserves account will drop by $1 million, the amount of the bad loan. Now the bank's assets are lowered by $1 million, as is bank capital. At this time, however, reported earnings are unaffected by the loan write-off. Adding to loan loss reserves at an earlier date provides a cushion to absorb the loan write-off when it occurs.

Assets

The assets of a bank constitute the uses of bank funds. The income-earning assets, which yield interest payments, enable banks to make profits.

Reserves All banks hold some of the funds they acquire as deposits in an account at the Fed. **Reserves** are these deposits plus currency that is physically held by banks (called **vault cash** because it is stored in bank vaults overnight). Although reserves currently do not pay any interest, banks hold them for two reasons. First, some reserves, called **required reserves,** are held because, by law, the Fed requires that for every dollar of deposits at a bank, a certain fraction (ten cents, for example) must be kept as reserves. This fraction (10% in the example) is called the **required reserve ratio.** Additional reserves, called **excess reserves,** are held because they are the most liquid of all bank assets and can be used by a bank to meet its obligations when funds are withdrawn—either directly by a depositor or indirectly when a check is written on an account.

Cash Items in Process of Collection Suppose a check written on an account at another bank is deposited in your bank and the funds for this check have not yet been received (collected) from the other bank. The check is classified as a cash item in process of collection, which is an asset for your bank because it has a claim on the other bank and will be paid these funds within a few days.

Deposits at Other Banks Many small banks hold deposits in larger banks in exchange for a variety of services, including check collection, foreign exchange transactions, and help with securities purchases. This is an aspect of a system called "correspondent banking."

Collectively, reserves, cash items in process of collection, and deposits at other banks are often referred to as "cash items." In Table 9.1 they constitute only 7% of total assets and their importance has been shrinking over time: In 1960, for example, they were 20% of total assets.

Securities A bank's holdings of securities are an important income-earning asset: Securities (made up entirely of debt instruments for commercial banks since they are not allowed to hold stock) are 19% of bank assets in Table 9.1, and they provide commercial banks with about 15% of their revenue. These securities can be classified into three categories: (1) U.S. government and agency, (2) state and local government, and (3) other securities. U.S. government and agency securities are the most liquid because they can be easily traded and converted into cash with low transactions costs. Because of their high liquidity, short-term U.S. government securities are called **secondary reserves.**

State and local government securities are desirable for banks to hold not only because of their tax advantages (their interest payments are tax deductible for federal and sometimes state income taxes), but also because state and local governments are more likely to do business with banks that hold their securities. State and local government and other securities are less marketable (hence less liquid) and are also riskier than U.S. government securities, primarily because of default risk: There is some possibility that the issuer of the securities may not be able to make its interest payments or pay back the face value of the securities when they mature. Because these securities are less liquid and riskier than U.S. government and agency ones, their expected returns (after taxes) are higher, as the theory of asset demand predicts.

Loans   Banks principally make their profits by issuing loans. In Table 9.1, 67% of bank assets are in the form of loans and in recent years produce over 60% of the bank revenues. A loan is a liability for the individual or corporation receiving it but an asset for a bank because it provides income to the bank. Loans are typically less liquid than other assets because they cannot be turned into cash until the loan matures. If the bank makes a one-year loan, for example, it cannot get its funds back until the loan comes due in one year. Loans also have a higher probability of default than other assets. Because of the lack of liquidity and higher default risk, the bank earns its highest return on loans.

As you can see in Table 9.1, the largest categories of loans for commercial banks are commercial and industrial loans made to businesses and real estate loans. Commercial banks also make consumer loans and lend to each other. The bulk of these interbank loans are overnight loans lent in the federal funds market. The major difference in the balance sheets of the various depository institutions is primarily in the type of loan in which they specialize. Savings and loans and mutual savings banks, for example, specialize in residential mortgages, while credit unions tend to make consumer loans.

Other Assets   The physical capital (bank buildings, computers, and other equipment) owned by the banks is included in this category.

BASIC OPERATION OF A BANK

Before proceeding to more detailed study of how a bank manages its assets and liabilities in order to make the highest profit, you should understand the basic operation of a bank.

In general terms, banks make profits by selling liabilities with one set of characteristics (a particular combination of liquidity, risk, and return) and using the proceeds to buy assets with a different set of characteristics. Banks thus provide a service to the public of transforming one type of asset into another. Instead of making a mortgage loan to a neighbor, a person can hold a savings deposit that enables a bank to make the loan to the neighbor. The bank has, in effect, transformed the savings deposit into a mortgage loan.

The process of transforming assets and providing a set of services (check clearing, record keeping, credit analysis, etc.) is like any other production process in a business firm. If the bank produces desirable services at low cost and earns substantial income on its assets, then it earns profits; if not, the bank suffers losses.

To make our analysis of the operation of a bank more concrete, we will use a tool called a **T-account.** A T-account is a simplified balance sheet (which looks like a T) that lists only the changes that occur in balance sheet items starting from some initial balance sheet position. Let's say, for example, that Jane Brown has heard that the First National Bank provides excellent service, so she opens a checking account with a $100 bill. She now has a $100 checkable deposit at the bank, which shows up as a $100 liability in the bank's balance sheet. On the other hand, the bank now puts her $100 bill into its vault so that the bank's assets rise by the $100 increase in vault cash. The T-account for the bank looks as follows:

First National Bank			
Assets		Liabilities	
Vault cash	+ $100	Checkable deposits	+ $100

Since vault cash is also part of the bank's reserves, we can rewrite the T-account as follows:

Assets		Liabilities	
Reserves	+ $100	Checkable deposits	+ $100

Note that Jane Brown's opening of a checking account leads to an *increase in the bank's reserves equal to the increase in checkable deposits.*

If Jane had opened her account with a $100 check written from an account at another bank, say, the Second National Bank, we would get the same result. The initial effect on the T-account of the First National Bank is as follows:

Assets		Liabilities	
Cash items in process of collection	+ 100	Checkable deposits	+ 100

Checkable deposits increase by $100 as before, but now the First National Bank is owed $100 by the Second National Bank. This asset for the First National Bank is entered in the T-account as $100 of "cash items in process of collection" because the First National Bank will now try to collect the funds that it is owed. It could go directly to the Second National Bank and ask for payment of the funds, but if the two banks are in separate states, this would be a time-consuming and costly process. Instead, the First National Bank deposits the check in its account at the Fed, and the Fed collects the funds from the Second National Bank. The result is that the Fed transfers $100 of reserves from the Second National Bank to the First National Bank, and the final balance sheet positions of the two banks are as follows:

First National Bank		Second National Bank	
Assets	Liabilities	Assets	Liabilities
Reserves + $100	Checkable deposits+ $100	Reserves − $100	Checkable deposits −$100

The process initiated by Jane Brown can be summarized as follows: When a check written on an account at one bank is deposited in another, the bank receiving the deposit gains reserves equal to the amount of the check, while the bank on which the check is written sees its reserves fall by the same amount. *Therefore, when a bank receives additional deposits, it gains an equal amount of reserves; when it loses deposits, it loses an equal amount of reserves.*

Study Guide

T-accounts are used to study various topics throughout this text. Whenever you see a T-account, try to analyze what would happen if the opposite action were taken; for example, what would happen if Jane Brown decided to close her $100 account at the First National Bank by writing a $100 check and depositing it in a new checking account at the Second National Bank?

Now that you understand how banks gain and lose reserves, we can examine how a bank will rearrange its balance sheet to make a profit when it experiences a change in its deposits. Let's return to the situation where the First National Bank has just received the extra $100 of checkable deposits. As you know, the bank is required to keep a certain fraction of its checkable deposits as required reserves. If the fraction (the required reserve ratio) is 10%, the First National Bank's required reserves have increased by $10 and we can rewrite its T-account as follows:

First National Bank

Assets		Liabilities	
Required reserves	+ $10	Checkable deposits	+ $100
Excess reserves	+ $90		

Let's see how well the bank is doing as a result of the additional checkable deposits. Because reserves pay no interest, it has no income from the additional $100 of assets. On the other hand, servicing the extra $100 of checkable deposits is costly, because the bank must keep records, pay tellers, return canceled checks, pay for check clearing, and so forth. The bank is making a loss! The situation is even worse if the bank makes interest payments on the deposits, as with NOW accounts. If it is to make a profit, the bank must put to productive use all, or part, of the $90 of excess reserves it has available.

Let us assume that the bank chooses not to hold any excess reserves but to make loans instead. The T-account looks then like this:

Assets		Liabilities	
Required reserves	+ $10	Checkable deposits	+ $100
Loans	+ $90		

The bank is now making a profit because it holds short-term liabilities such as checkable deposits and uses the proceeds to buy longer-term assets such as loans with higher interest rates. This process of asset transformation is frequently described by saying that banks are in the business of "borrowing short and lending long." For example, if the loans have an interest rate of 10% per year, the bank earns $9 in income from its loans over the year. If the $100 of checkable deposits is in a NOW account with a 5% interest rate and it costs another $3 per year to service the account, the cost per year of these deposits is $8. The bank's profit on the new deposits is then $1 per year (a 1% return on assets).

GENERAL PRINCIPLES OF BANK ASSET AND LIABILITY MANAGEMENT

Now that you have some idea of how a bank operates, let's look at how a bank manages its assets and liabilities in order to earn the highest possible profit. The bank manager has three primary concerns: First is to make sure that the bank has enough ready cash to pay its depositors when there are **deposit outflows,** that is, when deposits are lost because depositors make withdrawals and demand payment. To keep enough cash on hand, the bank must engage in **liquidity management,** the acquisition of sufficiently liquid assets to meet the obligations of the bank to depositors. Second is to minimize risk by acquiring assets that have a low rate of default risk and by diversifying asset holdings (asset management). Third is to acquire funds at low cost (liability management).

To fully understand bank management, we need to go beyond the general principles of bank asset and liability management described immediately below and look in more detail at how a bank manages its assets. The two sections following this one provide an in-depth discussion of how a bank manages its loan assets and how it minimizes **interest-rate risk,** the riskiness of earnings and returns on its assets that results from interest rate changes.

Liquidity Management and the Role of Reserves

Let us see how a typical bank, the First National Bank, can deal with deposit outflows that occur when its depositors withdraw cash from checking or savings accounts or write checks that are deposited in other banks. In the example that follows we assume that the bank has ample excess reserves and that all deposits have the same required reserve ratio of 10% (the bank is required to keep 10% of its time and checkable deposits as reserves). Suppose the First National Bank's initial balance sheet is as follows:

Assets		Liabilities	
Reserves	$20 million	Deposits	$100 million
Loans	$80 million	Bank capital	$ 10 million
Securities	$10 million		

The bank's required reserves are 10% of $100 million, or $10 million. Since it holds $20 million of reserves, the First National Bank has excess reserves of $10 million. If a deposit outflow of $10 million occurs, the bank's balance sheet becomes

Assets		Liabilities	
Reserves	$10 million	Deposits	$90 million
Loans	$80 million	Bank capital	$10 million
Securities	$10 million		

The bank loses $10 million of deposits *and* $10 million of reserves, but since its required reserves are now 10% of only $90 million ($9 million), its reserves still exceed this amount by $1 million. ***In short, if a bank has ample reserves, a deposit outflow does not necessitate changes in other parts of its balance sheet.***

The situation is quite different when a bank holds insufficient excess reserves. Let's assume that instead of initially holding $10 million in excess reserves, the First National Bank makes loans of $10 million, so that it holds no excess reserves. Its initial balance sheet would be

Assets		Liabilities	
Reserves	$10 million	Deposits	$100 million
Loans	$90 million	Bank capital	$ 10 million
Securities	$10 million		

When it suffers the $10 million deposit outflow, its balance sheet becomes

Assets		Liabilities	
Reserves	$ 0 million	Deposits	$90 million
Loans	$90 million	Bank capital	$10 million
Securities	$10 million		

After $10 million has been withdrawn from deposits and hence reserves, the bank has a problem: It has a reserve requirement of 10% of $90 million, or $9 million, but it has no reserves! To eliminate this shortfall, the bank can do a number of different things. It can, for example, obtain $9 million by reducing its loans by this amount and depositing the $9 million it then receives at the Fed, thereby increasing its reserves by $9 million. This transaction changes the balance sheet as follows:

Assets		Liabilities	
Reserves	$ 9 million	Deposits	$90 million
Loans	$81 million	Bank capital	$10 million
Securities	$10 million		

The First National Bank is once again in good shape because its $9 million of reserves satisfies the reserve requirement.

However, this process of reducing its loans can be quite costly. If the First National Bank has numerous short-term loans renewed at fairly short intervals, it can reduce its total amount of loans outstanding fairly quickly by "calling in" loans—that is, by not renewing some loans when they come due.

Unfortunately for the bank, this is likely to antagonize the customers whose loans are not being renewed, because they have not done anything to deserve this treatment. Indeed, they are likely to take their business elsewhere in the future, a costly occurrence for the bank.

A second method for reducing its loans is for the bank to sell them off to other banks. Again, this can be quite costly, since other banks do not personally know the customers who have taken out the loans and so may not be willing to buy the loans at their full value.

Another alternative is for the bank to sell some of its securities to help meet the deposit outflow. For example, it might sell $9 million of its securities and deposit the proceeds at the Fed, resulting in the following balance sheet:

Assets		Liabilities	
Reserves	$ 9 million	Deposits	$90 million
Loans	$90 million	Bank capital	$10 million
Securities	$ 1 million		

Although there are no disgruntled loan customers or a loss from the sale of loans, the bank incurs some brokerage and other transactions costs when it sells the securities. The U.S. government securities that are classified as secondary reserves are very liquid and so the transactions costs of selling them are quite modest. However, the other securities the bank holds are less liquid and the transactions costs can be appreciably higher. Even so, the cost of selling the $9 million of securities is likely to be far less than the cost of calling in $9 million of loans.

A fourth way that the bank can meet a deposit outflow is to acquire reserves by borrowing from the Fed. In our example, the First National Bank could leave its security and loan holdings the same and borrow $9 million in discount loans from the Fed. Its balance sheet would be

Assets		Liabilities	
Reserves	$ 9 million	Deposits	$90 million
Loans	$90 million	Discount loans	
Securities	$10 million	from the Fed	$ 9 million
		Bank capital	$10 million

There are two costs associated with discount loans. First is the interest rate that must be paid the Fed (called the **discount rate**). The second is a nonpecuniary cost resulting from the Fed's discouragement of too much borrowing from it. If a bank takes out too many discount loans, the Fed may refuse to let it borrow further. In popular parlance, the Fed can "close down the discount window" for that bank.

Finally, a bank can acquire reserves to meet a deposit outflow by borrowing them from other banks or corporations. If the First National Bank acquires the $9 million shortfall in reserves by borrowing it from corporations or from other banks (typically through the Federal Funds market),[1] then its balance sheet becomes

Assets		Liabilities	
Reserves	$ 9 million	Deposits	$90 million
Loans	$90 million	Borrowings from	
Securities	$10 million	other banks or	
		corporations	$ 9 million
		Bank capital	$10 million

The cost to this activity is the interest rate on these loans.

The preceding discussion explains why banks hold excess reserves even though loans or securities earn a higher return. When a deposit outflow occurs, holding excess reserves allows the bank to escape the costs of (1) calling in or selling off loans, (2) selling securities, (3) borrowing from the Fed, or (4) borrowing from other banks or corporations. ***Excess reserves are insurance against the costs associated with deposit outflows. The higher the costs associated with deposit outflows, the more excess reserves banks will want to hold.***

Just as you and I would be willing to pay an insurance company to insure us against a casualty loss such as theft of a car, a bank is willing to pay the cost of holding excess reserves (the opportunity cost, which is the earnings forgone by not holding income-earning assets such as loans or securities) in order to insure against losses due to deposit outflows. Since excess reserves—like insurance—have a cost, banks also take other steps to protect themselves; for example, they might shift their holdings of assets to more liquid securities (secondary reserves).

Study Guide

Bank management is easier to grasp if you put yourself in the banker's shoes and imagine what you would do in the situations described. To understand a bank's possible responses to deposit outflows, imagine how you as a banker might respond to two successive deposit outflows of $10 million.

---

[1]One way that the First National Bank can borrow from other banks and corporations is by selling negotiable certificates of deposit. This method for obtaining funds is discussed later in the section on liability management.

Prevention of Bank Failure   Banks also hold excess and secondary reserves to prevent a **bank failure,** a situation in which a bank cannot satisfy its obligations to pay its depositors and have enough reserves to meet its reserve requirements. To see how a bank failure could happen, let's suppose the bank's initial balance sheet position is as follows:

Assets		Liabilities	
Reserves	$10 million	Deposits	$100 million
Loans	$90 million	Bank capital	$ 10 million
Securities	$10 million		

Suppose a rumor is circulating that the president of the bank has just absconded to the Bahamas with a substantial amount of bank funds and, as a result, the bank suffers a $20 million deposit outflow when depositors hastily withdraw $20 million. If the bank sells $10 million of securities to obtain $10 million of reserves, its balance sheet is

Assets		Liabilities	
Reserves	$ 0 million	Deposits	$80 million
Loans	$90 million	Bank capital	$10 million

The bank is now $8 million short of reserves (required reserves are $8 million, 10% of $80 million). It if does not have any loans to call in, the bank might try to sell off its loans to other banks in order to acquire the $8 million of reserves it needs. The proceeds from the distress sale of loans, however, will be lower than the value of the loans; the resulting loss for the bank may be greater than the initial amount of its bank capital. In this situation, the value of bank assets may fall below its liabilities, causing the bank to become **insolvent** (bankrupt). Other banks will be unwilling to make loans to this bank because they cannot be sure of getting paid back.

If the Fed is unwilling to make unrestricted loans to the bank because it views the bank's balance sheet as unsound, the Federal Deposit Insurance Corporation (FDIC) classifies the bank as "failed." The FDIC now has the legal right to take over the bank, dismiss its management, and sell off its assets.[2]

Since the owners of the bank will be almost entirely wiped out by this occurrence, they would clearly like to prevent it. This emergency could have

---

[2]The Fed may make loans to the bank while the FDIC is taking over the bank. In this case, the bank still has failed and the Fed makes the loans in order to keep the doors of the bank open while the FDIC arranges with other bank regulatory authorities to close the bank or to merge it into another bank. The FDIC's role when a bank fails is described in Chapter 10.

been averted if the First National Bank had held $8 million more in excess or secondary reserves or if it had a larger cushion of bank capital to absorb the losses resulting from the deposit outflow. *A bank holds excess reserves, secondary reserves, and bank capital because they provide insurance against the highest cost of a deposit outflow—bank failure.*

Asset Management

Now that you understand why a bank has a need for liquidity, we can examine the basic strategy a bank pursues in managing its assets. In order to maximize its profits, a bank must seek the highest returns possible on loans and securities, at the same time trying to minimize risk and making adequate provisions for liquidity by holding liquid assets.

First, banks try to find borrowers who will pay high interest rates and are unlikely to default on their loans. They seek out loan business by advertising their borrowing rates and by approaching corporations directly to solicit loans. It is up to the bank's loan officer to decide if potential borrowers are good credit risks who will make interest and principal payments on time. Typically, banks are conservative in their loan policies; the default rate is usually less than 1%. It is, however, important that banks not be so conservative that they miss out on attractive lending opportunities that earn high interest rates.

Second, banks try to purchase securities with high returns and low risk. Third, in managing their assets, banks must attempt to minimize risk by diversifying. They accomplish this by purchasing many different types of assets (short- and long-term, U.S. Treasury, and municipal bonds) and approving many types of loans to a number of customers. Banks that have not sufficiently sought the benefits of diversification often come to regret it later. For example, banks that had overspecialized in making loans to energy companies, real estate developers, or farmers suffered huge losses in the 1980s with the slump in energy, property, and farm prices. Indeed, many of these banks went broke because they had "put too many rotten eggs in one basket."

Finally, the bank must manage the liquidity of its assets so that it can satisfy its reserve requirements without bearing huge costs: This means that it will hold liquid securities even if they earn a somewhat lower return than other assets. The bank must decide, for example, how much excess reserves must be held to avoid costs from a deposit outflow. In addition, it will want to hold U.S. government securities as secondary reserves so that even if a deposit outflow forces some costs on the bank, these will not be terribly high. Again, it is not wise for a bank to be too conservative. If it avoids all costs associated with deposit outflows by holding only excess reserves, losses are suffered because reserves earn no interest, while the bank's liabilities are costly to maintain. The bank must balance its desire for liquidity against the increased earnings that can be obtained from less liquid assets such as loans.

Liability Management

Before the 1960s, liability management was a staid affair: For the most part, banks took their liabilities as fixed and spent their time trying to achieve an optimal mix of assets. There were two main reasons for the emphasis on asset management. First, over 60% of the sources of bank funds were obtained through checkable (demand) deposits that by law could not pay any interest. Thus banks could not actively compete with each other for these deposits and so their amount was effectively a given for an individual bank. Second, because the markets for making overnight loans between banks were not well developed, banks rarely borrowed from other banks to meet their reserve needs.

Starting in the 1960s, however, large banks (called **money center banks**) in key financial centers began to explore ways in which the liabilities on their balance sheets could provide them with reserves and liquidity. This led to an expansion of overnight loans markets, such as the federal funds market, and the development of new financial instruments such as negotiable CDs (first developed in 1961), which enabled money center banks to quickly acquire funds.[3]

This new flexibility in liability management meant that banks could take a different approach to bank management. They no longer needed to depend on checkable deposits as the primary source of bank funds and as a result no longer treated their sources of funds (liabilities) as given. Instead, they aggressively set target goals for their asset growth and tried to acquire funds (by issuing liabilities) as they were needed.

For example, today when a money center bank finds an attractive loan opportunity, it can acquire funds by selling a negotiable CD. Or if it has a reserve shortfall, funds can be borrowed from another bank in the federal funds market without incurring high transactions costs. The federal funds market also can be used to finance loans.

The emphasis on liability management explains some of the important changes over the past thirty years in the composition of banks' balance sheets. While negotiable CDs and bank borrowings have greatly increased in importance as a source of bank funds in recent years (rising from 2% of bank liabilities in 1960 to 39% by the end of 1990), checkable deposits have decreased in importance (from 61% of bank liabilities in 1960 to 18% by the end of 1990). Newfound flexibility in liability management and the search for higher profits also has stimulated banks to increase the proportion of their assets held in loans, which earn higher income (from 46% of bank assets in 1960 to 67% by the end of 1990).

---

[3]Because small banks are not as well known as money center banks and so might be a higher credit risk, they find it harder to raise funds in the negotiable CD market. Thus they do not engage nearly as actively in liability management.

PRINCIPLES OF LOAN MANAGEMENT

As is clear from our discussion of general principles of asset management, to earn high profits, banks need to make successful loans that are paid back in full. The economic concepts of adverse selection and moral hazard, which were introduced in the previous chapter, provide a framework for understanding the principles banks need to follow in order to make successful loans.[4]

Adverse selection in loan markets occurs because bad credit risks (those most likely to default on their loans) are the ones who usually line up for loans: In other words, those who are most likely to produce an *adverse* outcome are the most likely to be *selected*. Borrowers with very risky investment projects have much to gain if their projects are successful, and so they are the most anxious to obtain loans. Clearly, however, they are the least desirable borrowers because of the greater possibility that they will be unable to pay back their loans.

Moral hazard occurs in loan markets because borrowers have incentives to engage in undesirable (*immoral*) activities from the lender's point of view. In such situations it is more likely that the lender will be subjected to the *hazard* of default. Once borrowers have a loan, they are more likely to invest in high-risk investment projects—projects that pay high returns to the borrowers if successful. The high risk, however, makes it less likely that they will be able to pay the loan back.

To be profitable, banks must overcome the adverse selection and moral hazard problems that make loan defaults more likely. The attempts of banks to solve these problems help explain the following loan management principles: screening and monitoring, establishment of long-term customer relationships and lines of credit, collateral and compensating balance requirements, and credit rationing.

Screening and Monitoring

Asymmetric information is present in loan markets because lenders have less information about the investment opportunities and activities of borrowers than borrowers do. This situation leads to two information-producing activities by banks, screening and monitoring. Indeed, Walter Wriston, a former head of Citicorp, the largest bank corporation in the United States, often stated that the business of banking is the production of information.

Screening   Adverse selection in loan markets requires that banks screen out the good credit risks from the bad so that loans are profitable to the banks. In

---

[4]Other financial intermediaries such as insurance companies, pension funds, and finance companies also make private loans, and the management principles we outline here apply to them as well.

order to accomplish effective screening, banks must collect reliable information from prospective borrowers. Effective screening and information collection together form an important principle of loan management.

When you go into a bank to apply for a consumer loan (e.g., a car loan or a mortgage to purchase a house), the first thing you are asked to do is to fill out forms that seek a great deal of information about your personal finances. You are asked about your salary, bank accounts, other assets (such as cars, insurance policies, furnishings), outstanding loans, your record of loan, credit card and charge account repayments, the number of years you've worked, and who your employers have been. You also are asked personal questions such as your age, marital status, and number of children. The bank uses this information to evaluate how good a credit risk you are by calculating your "credit score," a statistical measure derived from your answers that predicts whether you are likely to have trouble making your loan payments. Deciding on how good a risk you are cannot be entirely scientific, so the bank must also use judgment. The loan officer, whose job is to decide whether you should be given the loan, might call your employer or talk to some of the personal references you supplied. She might even make a judgment based on your demeanor or your appearance. (This is why you should dress neatly and conservatively when you go to the bank to apply for a loan.)

The process of screening and collecting information is similar when a bank makes a business loan. It collects information about the company's profits and losses (income) and about its assets and liabilities. The bank also needs to evaluate the likely future success of the business. So in addition to obtaining information on such items as sales figures, a loan officer might ask questions about the company's future plans, the way the loan will be used, and the competition in the industry. She may even visit the company to obtain a firsthand look at its operations. The bottom line is that, whether for personal or business loans, bankers need to be nosy.

The Role of Specialization in Lending One puzzling feature of bank lending is that a bank often specializes by lending to local firms or by lending mainly to firms in particular industries, say energy. In one sense, this behavior appears surprising because it means that the bank is not diversifying its portfolio of loans and thus is exposing itself to more risk. But from another perspective such specialization makes perfect sense. Remember, the adverse selection problem requires the bank to screen out good from bad credit risks. It is easier for the bank to collect information about local firms and determine their creditworthiness than to collect similar information for firms that are far away. Similarly, by specializing its lending to firms in specific industries, the bank becomes more knowledgeable about these industries and is therefore able to better predict whether the firms it lends to will be able to make timely payments on their debt.

Monitoring and Enforcement of Restrictive Covenants Once a loan is made, the borrower has an incentive to take on risky activities that make it less likely that the loan will be paid off. To reduce the likelihood of such moral hazard, banks must adhere to the loan management principle that a bank should write provisions (called restrictive covenants) into loan contracts that restrict borrowers from engaging in risky activities. By monitoring borrowers' activities to see whether they are complying with the restrictive covenants and by enforcing the covenants if they are not, banks can make sure that borrowers are not taking on risks at the bank's expense. The need for banks to engage in screening and monitoring explains why successful banks spend so much money on auditing and information-collecting activities.

Long-Term Customer Relationships and Lines of Credit

An additional way for banks to obtain information about their borrowers is through long-term customer relationships—another important principle of bank management.

If a prospective borrower has had a checking or savings account or other loans with the bank over a long period of time, a loan officer can look at past activity on the accounts and learn quite a bit about the borrower. The balances in the checking and savings accounts tell the banker how liquid the potential borrower is and at what time of year the borrower has a strong need for cash. A review of the checks the borrower has written reveals the borrower's suppliers. If the borrower has borrowed previously from the bank, then the bank has a record of the loan payments. Thus, long-term customer relationships reduce the costs of information collection and make it easier to screen out good from bad credit risks.

The need for monitoring by banks adds to the importance of long-term customer relationships. If the borrower has borrowed from the bank before, the bank has already established procedures for monitoring that customer. Therefore the costs of monitoring long-term customers will be lower than those for new customers.

Long-term relationships benefit the customers as well as the bank. A firm with a previous relationship will find it easier to obtain a loan at a low interest rate, because the bank has an easier time determining if the prospective borrower is a good credit risk and has fewer costs to monitoring the borrower.

A long-term customer relationship has another advantage for the bank. No bank can think of every contingency when it writes a restrictive covenant into a loan contract; there will always be risky borrower activities that are not ruled out by a restrictive covenant. However, what if borrowers want to preserve a long-term relationship with a bank because it will be easier for them to get future loans at low interest rates? The borrower then has the incentive to avoid risky activities that would upset the bank, even if restrictions on these risky activities are not specified in the loan contract. Indeed, if a bank doesn't like what a borrower is doing even when the borrower isn't violating any restrictive covenants, it has some power to discourage the borrower from such activity: The bank can threaten not to let the borrower have new loans in the future. Long-term customer relationships, therefore, enable banks to deal with moral hazard contingencies even if they didn't think of them ahead of time.

The advantages of establishing long-term customer relationships suggest that closer ties between corporations and banks might be beneficial to both. One way to create these ties is for banks to hold equity stakes in companies they lend to and for banks to have memberships on the boards of directors that manage these companies. Currently, such financial arrangements do not exist in the United States. They were outlawed by legislation passed in the 1930s. They are, however, an important feature of the Japanese and the German financial systems. Box 9.2 discusses how financial ties work in these countries to help banks cope with asymmetric information.

Banks also create long-term relationships and gather information by issuing a **line of credit** to a commercial customer. A line of credit is a bank's

---

B o x   9 . 2   **A Global Perspective**

Japanese and German Banking Arrangements: A Better Way to Deal with Asymmetric Information?

An important feature of the Japanese economic system is the *keiretsu,* or industrial group. Each keiretsu is made up of a core group of banks and other financial intermediaries which are linked to a group of industrial firms, many of which trade with each other. Linkages between firms and banks are cemented by each member of the group holding equity shares in the other members. Because of their equity holdings, banks have memberships on their keiretsu firms' supervisory boards (the boards of directors), and former bank executives are often placed in top managerial positions at these firms. Not surprisingly, banks favor firms of their keiretsu when making loans and hold a large fraction of these firms' debt.

Although nothing as formal or extensive as the keiretsu exists in Germany, German banks also hold shares in industrial firms and sit on their boards of directors.

The Japanese and German banking arrangements give banks tremendous advantages in collecting information and monitoring activities. Long-term customer relationships are strengthened because banks have ownership rights in firms to which they lend. For the reasons we discussed in the text, these stronger long-term relationships make it easier for banks to collect information and monitor firms, thus enabling banks to better reduce adverse selection and moral hazard problems. In addition, because the banks have a role in the management of firms, they have timely access to information and the ability to influence management to act in the banks' interest by not investing in projects deemed too risky.

You can see that Japanese and German banking arrangements give their banks a tremendous advantage that American banks do not have. Their financial systems might be better able to channel funds to firms with the most productive investment opportunities. Should similar banking arrangements be allowed in the United States? We will return to this question when we discuss financial regulation in Chapter 11.

commitment (for a specified future period of time) to provide a firm with loans up to a given amount at an interest rate that is tied to some market interest rate. The majority of commercial and industrial loans are made under the line of credit arrangement. The advantage to the firm is that it has a source of credit when it needs it. The advantage for the bank is that the line of credit promotes a long-term relationship, which facilitates information collection. In addition, provisions in the line of credit agreement require the firm to continually supply the bank with information about the firm's income, asset and liability position, business activities, and so on. A line of credit arrangement is a powerful method for reducing the bank's costs for screening and information collection.

Collateral and Compensating Balances

Collateral requirements for loans are important bank management tools. Collateral, which is property promised to the lender if the borrower defaults, lessens the consequences of adverse selection because it reduces the lender's losses in the case of a loan default. If a borrower defaults on a loan, the bank can sell the collateral and use the proceeds to make up for its losses on the loan. One particular form of collateral required when a bank makes commercial loans is called **compensating balances:** A firm receiving a loan must keep a required minimum amount of funds in a checking account at the bank. For example, a business getting a $10 million loan may be required to keep compensating balances of at least $1 million in its checking account at the bank. This $1 million in compensating balances then can be taken by the bank if the loan defaults to make up some of the losses on the loan.

Besides serving as collateral, compensating balances help increase the likelihood that a loan will be paid off. They do this by helping the bank monitor the borrower and consequently prevent moral hazard. Specifically, by requiring the borrower to use a checking account at the bank, the bank can observe the firm's check payment practices—which may yield a great deal of information about the borrower's financial condition. For example, a sustained drop in the amount of the borrower's checking account balance may signal that the borrower is having financial trouble. Or, account activity may suggest that the borrower is engaging in risky activities; perhaps a change in suppliers means that the borrower is pursuing new lines of business. Any significant change in the borrower's payment procedures is a signal to the bank that it should make inquiries. Compensating balances therefore make it easier for banks to monitor borrowers more effectively and are another important management tool.

Credit Rationing

Another way in which successful banks deal with adverse selection and moral hazard is by **credit rationing:** Lenders refuse to make loans even though borrowers are willing to pay the stated interest rate or even a higher rate.[5] Credit rationing takes two forms. The first occurs when a bank refuses to make a loan of *any amount* to a borrower, even when the borrower is willing to pay a higher interest rate. The second occurs when a bank is willing to make a loan but restricts the size of the loan to less than the borrower would like.

At first you might be puzzled by the first type of credit rationing. After all, even if the potential borrower is a credit risk, why doesn't the bank just give the loan but at a higher interest rate? The answer is that adverse selection prevents this solution. Individuals and firms with the riskiest investment projects are exactly those who are willing to pay the highest interest rates. If a borrower takes on a high-risk investment and succeeds, she would become an extremely rich woman. On the other hand, a bank wouldn't want to make such a loan because the investment *is* high risk and the likely outcome is that the borrower will *not* succeed and the bank will not be paid back. Charging a higher interest rate just makes adverse selection worse for the bank; that is, it increases the likelihood that the bank is lending to a bad credit risk. The bank therefore would rather not make any loans at a higher interest rate; instead, it would engage in the first type of credit rationing and would turn down loans.

To guard against moral hazard, banks engage in a second type of credit rationing: Banks grant loans to borrowers but not loans as large as they want. Such credit rationing is necessary because the moral hazard problem becomes more severe with larger loans since the benefits from moral hazard are much greater. If a bank gives you a $1,000 loan, for example, you are likely to take actions to enable you to pay it back since you don't want to hurt your credit rating for the future. On the other hand, if the bank lends you $10 million, you are more likely to fly off to Rio to celebrate. The larger your loan, the greater your incentives to engage in activities that make it less likely you will repay the loan. Since more borrowers repay their loans if the loan amounts are small, banks ration credit by providing borrowers with smaller loans than they prefer.

Bank Capital and Incentive Compatibility

Our discussion so far has shown that banks making loans can reduce the problems created by asymmetric information by engaging in information-producing activities such as screening and monitoring. There is a catch,

---

[5]Two important papers describing how asymmetric information can lead to credit rationing are Dwight Jaffee and Thomas Russell, "Imperfect Information, Uncertainty, and Credit Rationing," *Quarterly Journal of Economics* 90 (November 1976), pp. 651–666; and Joseph Stiglitz and Andrew Weiss, "Credit Rationing in Markets with Imperfect Information," *American Economic Review* 71 (June 1981), pp. 393–410.

however, involving moral hazard: Because all these activities are costly, banks could skip these activities and perhaps even run off with the depositors' money. How can depositors be sure that the bank *will* engage in the information-producing activities that enable them to receive the interest payments or services that the bank has promised?

The answer is provided by recognizing two facts: (1) deposits are just another form of debt and (2) net worth (equity capital) is a solution to the moral hazard problem in debt contracts. If a bank does not engage in information-producing activities, then it will make bad loans and will go broke. With a high enough amount of equity capital, the bank has a lot to lose if bankruptcy occurs. So the bank has the incentive to engage in the appropriate activities to ensure that it makes profits and pays off those that have supplied it with funds. The bank's equity capital makes the bank's relationship with its depositors incentive compatible; that is, the depositors and the bank have incentives to behave in a way that is desirable for both parties. The bank engages in information-producing activities as the depositors expect and want; as a result, depositors are willing to provide funds to the bank as the bank wants.

Diversification   Depositors, like any lenders, receive only the fixed payments due them from the bank; the bank keeps any surplus profits. Therefore depositors face the moral hazard problem that banks may take on too much risk. There is a way for a bank to assure depositors that it is not taking on too much risk and so continue to obtain their deposits. The bank can diversify its loan portfolio, thereby making clear that it is reducing its risk.[6] Diversification is an important principle of bank management because it too makes the bank's relationship with depositors incentive compatible. However, as we have seen before, there are also benefits to specialization in lending. Banks must balance the benefits and costs of pursuing diversification or specialization.

Government Regulation to Increase Incentive Compatibility   What if depositors are not sophisticated enough to recognize whether a bank has enough equity capital and is sufficiently diversified? Will depositors want the government to ensure that a bank is sufficiently diversified and has enough equity capital? Government regulation is one way of making a bank's relationship with depositors incentive compatible. Indeed, as we will see in the next chapter, bank equity capital requirements and restrictions to encourage diversification are features of government regulation of the banking system.

---

[6]See Douglas Diamond, "Financial Intermediation and Delegated Monitoring," *Review of Economic Studies* 51 (July 1984), pp. 393–414. Douglas Diamond and Phillip Dybvig, "Bank Runs, Deposit Insurance, and Liquidity," *Journal of Political Economy* 91 (June 1983), pp. 401–419, discuss other important features of the bank deposit contract and why these features may create the need for federal deposit insurance.

MANAGING INTEREST-RATE RISK

With the increased volatility of interest rates that occurred in the 1980s, banks became more concerned about their exposure to interest-rate risk, the riskiness of earnings and returns that is associated with changes in interest rates. To see what interest-rate risk is all about, let's again take a look at the First National Bank, which has the following balance sheet:

First National Bank			
Assets		Liabilities	
Rate-sensitive assets	$20 million	Rate-sensitive liabilities	$50 million
Variable-rate loans		Variable-rate CDs	
Short-term securities		Money market deposit accounts	
		Federal funds	
Fixed-rate assets	$80 million	Fixed-rate liabilities	$50 million
Reserves		Checkable deposits	
Long-term loans		Savings deposits	
Long-term securities		Long-term CDs	
		Equity capital	

A total of $20 million of its assets are rate-sensitive with interest rates that change frequently (at least once a year), and $80 million of its assets are fixed-rate with interest rates that remain unchanged for a long period (over a year). On the liabilities side, the First National Bank has $50 million of rate-sensitive liabilities and $50 million of fixed-rate liabilities. Suppose interest rates rise by 5 percentage points, say, on average from 10 to 15%. The income on the assets rises by $1 million (= 5% × $20 million of rate-sensitive assets), while the payments on the liabilities rise by $2.5 million (= 5% × $50 million of rate-sensitive liabilities). The First National Bank's profits now decline by $1.5 million (= $1 million − $2.5 million). On the other hand, if interest rates fall by 5 percentage points, similar reasoning tells us that the First National Bank profits rise by $1.5. This example illustrates the following point: *If a bank has more rate-sensitive liabilities than assets, a rise in interest rates will reduce bank profits, while a decline in interest rates will raise bank profits.*

Gap and Duration Analysis

The sensitivity of bank profits to changes in interest rates can be more directly measured using **gap analysis,** in which the amount of rate-sensitive liabilities is subtracted from rate-sensitive assets. In our example, this calculation (called the "gap") is −$30 million (= $20 million − $50 million). By multiplying the gap times the change in the interest rate, we can immediately obtain the effect on bank profits. For example, when interest rates rise by 5 percentage points, the change in profits is 5% × −$30 million, which equals −$1.5 million, as we saw.

The gap analysis conducted above is called "basic gap analysis," and it can be refined in two ways. Clearly, not all assets and liabilities in the fixed-rate category are of the same maturity. One refinement, the "maturity bucket approach," is to measure the gap for several maturity subintervals, called "maturity buckets," so that effects of interest-rate changes over a multiyear period can be calculated. The second refinement, called "standardized gap analysis," accounts for the differing degrees of rate sensitivity for different rate-sensitive assets and liabilities.

An alternative method for measuring interest-rate risk, called **duration analysis,** examines the sensitivity of the market value of the bank's total assets and liabilities to changes in interest rates. Duration analysis is based on Macaulay's concept of duration, which measures the average lifetime of a security's stream of payments.[7] Duration is a useful concept because it provides a good approximation of the sensitivity of a security's market value to a change in its interest rate:

Percent change in market value of security ≈
−(percentage point change in interest rate) ×
(duration in years)

where ≈ denotes "approximately equals."

Duration analysis involves comparing the average duration of the bank's assets to the average duration of its liabilities. Going back to our example of the First National Bank, suppose that with the balance sheet outlined above, the average duration of its assets is five years (that is, the average lifetime of the stream of payments is five years), while the average duration of its liabilities is three years. With a 5 percentage point increase in interest rates, the market value of the bank's assets falls by 25% (= −5% × 5 years) and the market value of the liabilities declines by 15% (= −5% × 3 years). The net result is that the net worth (the market value of the assets minus the liabilities) has declined by 10% of the total original asset value. (This can also be calculated more directly as −[percentage point change in the interest rate] × [duration of assets minus duration of liabilities], that is,

---

[7]Algebraically, Macaulay's duration, D, is defined as

$$D = \frac{\sum_{\tau=1}^{N} \tau \times CP_\tau/(1 + i)^\tau}{\sum_{\tau=1}^{N} CP_\tau/(1 + i)^\tau}$$

where τ = time until cash payment is made
CP_τ = cash payment (interest plus principal) at time τ
i = interest rate
N = time to maturity of the security

$-10\% = -5\% \times [5 - 3])$. Similarly, a 5 percentage point decline in interest rates increases the net worth of the First National Bank by 10% of the total asset value.

As our example makes clear, both duration and gap analysis indicate that the First National Bank will suffer from a rise in interest rates but will gain from a fall in interest rates. Duration and gap analysis are thus useful tools for telling a bank manager the bank's degree of exposure to interest-rate risk.

Strategies for Managing Interest-Rate Risk

Once Brenda the Bank Manager has done her duration and gap analysis for the First National Bank, she now needs to decide what alternative strategies she should pursue. If she firmly believes that interest rates will fall in the future, she may be willing to take no action because she knows that the bank has more rate-sensitive liabilities than rate-sensitive assets and so will benefit from the expected interest-rate decline. However, Brenda also realizes that the First National Bank is subject to substantial interest-rate risk because there is always a possibility that interest rates will rise rather than fall. Brenda might try to shorten the duration of the bank's assets to increase their rate sensitivity or, alternatively, lengthen the duration of the liabilities. By this adjustment of the bank's assets and liabilities, the bank will be less affected by interest-rate swings.

One problem with eliminating the First National Bank's interest-rate risk by altering the balance sheet is that doing so might be very costly in the short run. The bank may be locked into assets and liabilities of particular durations because of where its expertise lies. Financial instruments have been developed that help banks more easily manage their interest-rate risk. The "interest-rate swap," which first appeared in the Eurobond market in 1981, is an example of such a financial instrument. Interest-rate swaps enable a financial institution that has more rate-sensitive assets than rate-sensitive liabilities to "swap" payment streams with a financial institution that has more rate-sensitive liabilities than rate-sensitive assets, thereby reducing interest-rate risk for both parties. (See Box 9.3.) The beauty of this arrangement is that it does not require either financial institution to rearrange its balance sheet; thus interest-rate swaps are a relatively low-cost way of reducing interest-rate risk.

Banks also can use the financial futures market and the options market for debt instruments to reduce interest-rate risk by hedging. The workings of these markets are discussed in more detail in Chapter 13. Although financial futures markets and the options market for debt instruments have the advantage that they have lower transactions costs than the interest-rate swaps market, they do have an important disadvantage: Contracts in these markets are standardized and cannot be tailored to the precise needs of a

Using an Interest-Rate Swap to Eliminate Interest-Rate Risk

In order to eliminate its interest-rate risk and match up the rate sensitivity of its assets and liabilities, First National Bank would, in effect, like to convert $30 million of its fixed-rate assets into $30 million of rate-sensitive assets. Suppose that another financial intermediary, say, the Friendly Finance Company, has $30 million of fixed-rate liabilities and $30 million of rate-sensitive assets, so that it would like to eliminate its interest-rate risk by, in effect, converting its $30 million of rate-sensitive assets into fixed-rate assets. An intermediary, say, an investment bank, would get these two parties together for a fee and set up an agreement in which the First National Bank would pay the Friendly Fi-

nance Company the interest earned on the $30 million of fixed-rate assets, while, in return, the Friendly Finance Company would pay the First National Bank the interest earned on the $30 million of rate-sensitive assets. This interest-rate swap would now result in the complete elimination of interest-rate risk for both parties: The First National Bank would now have rate-sensitive income on $50 million of assets, which would exactly match the rate-sensitive payments on $50 million of its liabilities, and the Friendly Finance Company would have fixed-rate income on $30 million of assets, which would exactly match the fixed-rate payments on $30 million of liabilities.

bank. Thus interest-rate swaps, financial futures, and options for debt instruments are all used by banks to manage their interest-rate risk.

OFF-BALANCE-SHEET ACTIVITIES

Although asset and liability management has traditionally been the major concern of banks, in the more competitive environment of recent years banks have been aggressively seeking out profits by engaging in off-balance-sheet activities. **Off-balance-sheet activities** involve trading financial instruments and the generation of income from fees and loan sales, all of which affect bank profits but are not visible on bank balance sheets. We have already seen that banks' attempts to manage interest-rate risk have led to trading in financial futures, options for debt instruments, and interest-rate swaps. Banks engaged in international banking also conduct transactions in the foreign exchange market. All transactions in these markets are off-balance-sheet activities because they do not have a direct effect on the bank's balance sheet. Although bank trading in these markets is usually directed toward reducing risk or facilitating other bank business, banks sometimes do try to outguess the markets and engage in speculation. This speculation can be a very risky business and indeed has led to bank insolvencies—the most dramatic being the failure of the Franklin National Bank in 1974, which collapsed because of losses in the foreign exchange market.

A second type of off-balance-sheet activity that has grown in importance in recent years involves income generated by loan sales. A **loan sale,** which is also called a secondary loan participation, involves a contract that sells all or part of the cash stream from a specific loan and thereby removes the loan from the bank's balance sheet. Banks earn profits by selling loans for an amount slightly greater than the amount of the original loan. Buyers of the loan thus earn a slightly lower interest rate than the original interest rate on the loan, usually on the order of 0.15 percentage points.

A third type of off-balance-sheet activities involves the generation of income from fees that banks receive for providing specialized services to their customers, such as (1) making foreign exchange trades on a customer's behalf, (2) servicing a mortgage-backed security by collecting interest and principal payments and then paying them out, (3) guaranteeing debt securities such as bankers' acceptances (i.e., the bank promises to make interest and principal payments if the party issuing the security cannot), and (4) providing backup lines of credit. There are several types of backup lines of credit. The most traditional instrument is called a "standby letter of credit." Here, for a fee, the bank agrees that for a specified period of time it will provide a loan upon request by the customer up to a given dollar amount. Credit lines are also now available to bank depositors, who can write checks in excess of their deposit balances and, in effect, write themselves a loan. Other lines of credit for which banks get fees include letters of credit to back up issues of commercial paper and other securities and credit lines for underwriting Euronotes [called note-issuance facilities (NIFs) and revolving underwriting facilities (RUFs)].

Off-balance-sheet activities involving guarantees of securities and backup credit lines increase the risk a bank faces. Even though a guaranteed security does not appear on a bank balance sheet, it still exposes the bank to default risk: If the issuer of the security defaults, the bank is left holding the bag and must pay off the security's owner. Backup credit lines also expose the bank to risk because the bank may be forced to provide loans when it does not have sufficient liquidity or when the borrower is a very poor credit risk.

Because of the increased risk that banks are facing from their off-balance-sheet activities, many are carefully scrutinizing their risk-assessment procedures and are using the latest computer technology to overhaul them. As we will see in the next chapter, bank regulators have also become concerned about increased risk from banks' off-balance-sheet activities. Banking is no longer the staid profession it once was, prompting one banker to state, "Despite all the dark suits worn by its leaders, banking is a very dynamic industry."[8]

---

[8]As quoted in "Banking Takes a Beating," *Time Magazine* (December 3, 1984), p. 49.

SUMMARY

1. The balance sheet of commercial banks can be thought of as a list of the sources and uses of bank funds. The bank's liabilities are its sources of funds, which include checkable deposits, time deposits, discount loans from the Fed, borrowings from other banks and corporations, and bank capital. The bank's assets are its uses of funds, which include reserves, cash items in process of collection, deposits at other banks, securities, loans, and other assets (mostly physical capital).

2. Banks make profits through the process of asset transformation: They borrow short (issue deposits) and lend long (making loans). When a bank receives additional deposits, it gains an equal amount of reserves; when it loses deposits, it loses an equal amount of reserves.

3. Although more liquid assets tend to earn lower returns, banks still desire to hold them. Specifically, banks hold excess and secondary reserves because they provide insurance against the costs of a deposit outflow. Banks manage their assets to maximize profits by seeking the highest returns possible on loans and securities while, at the same time, trying to minimize risk and making adequate provisions for liquidity. Although liability management was once a staid affair, large (money center) banks now actively seek out sources of funds by issuing liabilities such as ne-

gotiable CDs or by actively borrowing from other banks and corporations.

4. Application of the concepts of adverse selection and moral hazard provides an explanation for many bank management principles involving loan activities: screening and monitoring, establishment of long-term customer relationships and lines of credit, collateral and compensating balances, and credit rationing.

5. With the increased volatility of interest rates that occurred in the 1980s, banks became more concerned about their exposure to interest-rate risk. Gap and duration analyses tell a bank if it has more rate-sensitive liabilities than assets (in which case a rise in interest rates will reduce bank profits, while a fall in interest rates will raise bank profits). Banks manage their interest-rate risk not only by modifying their balance sheets, but also by trading interest-rate swaps, financial futures, and options for financial instruments.

6. Off-balance-sheet activities consist of trading financial instruments and generating income from fees and loan sales, all of which affect bank profits but are not visible on bank balance sheets. Because these off-balance-sheet activities expose banks to increased risk, many banks are using the latest computer technology to update their risk assessment procedures.

KEY TERMS

balance sheet	excess reserves	discount rate	credit rationing
discount loans	secondary reserves	bank failure	gap analysis
reserves	T-account	insolvent	duration analysis
vault cash	deposit outflows	money center banks	off-balance-sheet activities
required reserves	liquidity management	line of credit	loan sale
required reserve ratio	interest-rate risk	compensating balances	

QUESTIONS AND PROBLEMS

1. Why might a bank be willing to borrow funds from other banks at a higher rate than it can borrow from the Fed?

* 2. Rank the following bank assets from most to least liquid:
   a) commercial loans

b) securities

c) reserves

d) physical capital

3. Using the T-accounts of the First National Bank and the Second National Bank, describe what happens when Jane Brown writes a $50 check on her account at the First National Bank to pay her friend Joe Green, who in turn deposits the check in his account at the Second National Bank.

* 4. What happens to reserves at the First National Bank if one person withdraws $1000 of cash and another person deposits $500 of cash? Use T-accounts to explain your answer.

5. The bank you own has the following balance sheet:

Assets		Liabilities	
Reserves	$ 75 million	Deposits	$500 million
Loans	$525 million	Bank capital	$100 million

If the bank suffers a deposit outflow of $50 million with a required reserve ratio on deposits of 10%, what actions must you take to keep your bank from failing?

* 6. If a deposit outflow of $50 million occurs, which balance sheet would a bank rather have initially: the balance sheet in the problem above or the following balance sheet? Why?

Assets		Liabilities	
Reserves	$100 million	Deposits	$500 million
Securities	$500 million	Bank capital	$100 million

7. Why has the development of overnight loan markets made it more likely that banks will hold fewer excess reserves?

* 8. If the bank you own has no excess reserves and a sound customer comes in asking for a loan, should you automatically turn him down, explaining that you don't have any excess reserves to loan out? Why or why not? What options are available for you to provide your customer with the funds he needs?

9. How will a bank alter its balance sheet if its managers expect the bank to have a deposit outflow in the near future?

*10. Banks almost always insist that firms it lends to keep compensating balances at the bank. Why?

11. Why is being nosy a desirable trait for a banker?

*12. True, false, or uncertain: "Since diversification is a desirable strategy for avoiding risk, it never makes sense for a bank to specialize in making specific types of loans."

13. Suppose you are the manager of a bank that has $15 million of fixed-rate assets, $30 million of rate-sensitive assets, $25 million of fixed-rate liabilities, and $20 million of rate-sensitive liabilities. Conduct a gap analysis for the bank and show what will happen to bank profits if interest rates rise by 5 percentage points. What actions could you take to reduce the bank's interest-rate risk?

*14. Suppose you are the manager of a bank whose $75 billion of assets have an average duration of four years, while its $75 billion of liabilities have an average duration of six years. Conduct a duration analysis for the bank and show what will happen to the net worth of the bank if interest rates rise by 2 percentage points. What actions could you take to reduce the bank's interest-rate risk?

15. Can gap and duration analyses ever disagree on whether a bank should lengthen the maturity of its liabilities relative to its assets in order to reduce interest-rate risk?

CHAPTER 10

The Banking Industry

PREVIEW   The operations of individual banks (how they acquire, use, and manage funds to make a profit) are roughly similar throughout the world. In all countries banks are financial intermediaries in the business of earning profits. When you consider the structure and operation of the banking industry as a whole, however, the United States is clearly in a class by itself. In most countries four or five large banks typically dominate the banking industry, but in the United States there are on the order of 12,000 commercial banks, 2500 savings and loan associations, 500 mutual savings banks, and over 15,000 credit unions.

Is more better? Does this diversity mean that the American banking system is more competitive and therefore more economically efficient and sound than banking systems in other countries? What in the American economic and political system explains this large number of banking institutions? In this chapter we try to answer these questions by examining the historical evolution, regulatory system, and overall structure of the banking industry. In addition to different types of banks there are five federal agencies plus numerous state banking commissions which regulate banking institutions. At any one time, several of these agencies, each with its own set of rules and regulations, may govern a given bank. Hence our banking system can be characterized as having numerous players—the banking institutions themselves and their many regulatory bodies. Since these players frequently have competing interests, conflicts that shape the structure of this dynamic industry arise frequently and stimulate change.

We start the chapter by examining the commercial banking industry in detail and then go on to look at the thrift industry, which includes the savings and loans, mutual savings banks, and credit unions. We spend more time on commercial banks because they are by far the largest depository institutions, accounting for over two-thirds of the deposits in the banking system. In addition to looking at our domestic banking system, we also examine the forces behind the growth in international banking to see how it has affected us in the United States.

DEVELOPMENT OF THE DUAL BANKING SYSTEM _____

As discussed in Chapter 3, political forces have pressured the government into becoming involved in regulating the banking system as follows: Government tries to (1) ensure the safety of deposits and the soundness of banks, (2) improve control of monetary policy, and (3) encourage home ownership. The primary motive for bank regulation is the desire for a sound banking system, so the government attempts to protect depositors who may not know whether their deposits are safe at a particular banking institution. Over the years this motive has been the driving force behind development of the current banking regulatory system.

Before 1863, all commercial banks in the United States were chartered by banking commissions of the states in which they operated. No national currency existed, and banks obtained funds primarily by issuing banknotes (currency issued by the banks which could be redeemed in gold). Because banking regulations were extremely lax in many states, banks regularly failed due to fraud or lack of sufficient bank capital; their banknotes became worthless.

To eliminate the abuses of the state-chartered banks (called **state banks**), the National Banking Act of 1863 (and subsequent amendments to it) created a new banking system of federally chartered banks (called **national banks**), supervised by the Office of the Comptroller of the Currency, a department of the U.S. Treasury. This legislation was originally intended to dry up sources of funds to state banks by imposing a prohibitive tax on their banknotes, while leaving the banknotes of the federally chartered banks untaxed. The state banks cleverly escaped extinction by acquiring funds through issuing deposits. As a result, today the United States has a **dual banking system** in which banks supervised by the federal government and by the states operate side by side.

The Federal Reserve System (the Fed) was created in 1913 to promote an even safer banking system. All national banks were required to become members of the Federal Reserve System and became subject to a new set of regulations issued by the Fed. State banks could choose (but were not required) to become members of the system, and most did not because of the high costs of membership stemming from the Fed's regulations.

During the Great Depression years from 1930 to 1933, massive bank failures (numbering 9000) wiped out the savings of many depositors at commercial banks. To prevent future depositor losses from such failures, in 1934 the Federal Deposit Insurance Corporation (FDIC), which provided federal deposit insurance, was established. Member banks of the Federal Reserve System were required to purchase FDIC insurance for their depositors, while non-Federal Reserve commercial banks could choose to buy this insurance (almost all of them did). The purchase of FDIC insurance made banks subject to another set of regulations imposed by the FDIC.

Multiple Regulatory Agencies

Commercial bank regulation in the United States has developed into a crazy quilt system of multiple regulatory agencies with overlapping jurisdictions. As of 1991, the Office of the Comptroller of the Currency has the primary supervisory responsibility for the 4000 national banks that own more than half of the assets in the commercial banking system. The Federal Reserve and the state banking authorities jointly have primary responsibility for the 1000 state banks that are members of the Federal Reserve System. The Fed also has the sole regulatory responsibility over companies that own one or more banks (called **bank holding companies**) and has a secondary responsibility for the national banks. The FDIC and the state banking authorities jointly supervise the 7000 state banks that have FDIC insurance but are not members of the Federal Reserve System. The state banking authorities have sole jurisdiction over the under 500 state banks without FDIC insurance. (Such banks hold less than 0.2% of the deposits in the commercial banking system.)

If you find the U.S. bank regulatory system confusing, imagine how confusing it is for the banks who have to deal with several regulatory agencies. In February 1991, the U.S. Treasury called for reform to rationalize this system by eliminating overlapping supervisory responsibilities of different agencies. Each bank would be regulated by only one regulatory agency and the number of bank regulatory agencies would be reduced to two: A new regulatory agency, the Federal Banking Agency, would regulate the national banks, and the Federal Reserve would regulate the state banks. It is highly likely that the bank regulatory system will be simplified in the near future, although it is not clear that the regulatory system will be restructured along the lines outlined by the Treasury.

CHARTERING AND EXAMINATION

The first contact a commercial bank has with regulatory agencies occurs when it obtains a charter either from the Comptroller of the Currency (in the case of a national bank) or from a state banking authority (in the case of a state bank). To obtain a charter, the group planning to organize the bank must submit an application that shows how they plan to operate the bank. In evaluating the application, the regulatory authority looks at whether the bank is likely to be sound by examining the quality of the bank's management, the likely earnings of the bank, and the amount of the bank's initial capital. Before 1980, the chartering agency typically explored the issue of whether the community needed a new bank. Often a new bank charter would not be granted if existing banks in a community would be severely hurt by its presence. Today this anticompetitive stance (justified by the desire to prevent bank failures of existing banks) is no longer as strong in the chartering agencies.

Once a bank has been chartered, it is required to file reports periodically (usually quarterly) which describe the bank's assets and liabilities, income and dividends, ownership, foreign exchange operations, and so on. The bank is also subject to periodic examination by the bank regulatory agencies to ascertain its financial condition. For example, when the safety of the banking system is threatened (as has occurred in recent years), the Office of the Comptroller of the Currency examines the large banks several times a year. The FDIC has a maximum period between bank examinations of thirty-six months but usually conducts examinations more often. The Federal Reserve conducts examinations every eighteen months. To avoid duplication of effort, the three federal agencies work together and usually accept each other's examinations. This means that, typically, national banks are examined by the Office of the Comptroller of the Currency, the state banks that are members of the Federal Reserve System are examined by the Fed, and non-member state banks are examined by the FDIC.

Bank examinations are conducted by bank examiners, who make unannounced visits to the bank (so that nothing can be "swept under the rug" in anticipation of their examination). The bank examiners study a bank's books to see whether it is complying with the rules and regulations that apply to its holdings of assets.

Suppose a bank is holding securities or loans that are too risky; the bank examiner can force the bank to get rid of them. If a bank examiner decides that a loan is unlikely to be repaid, she can force the bank to declare the loan worthless (called writing off a loan). If, after examining the bank, the examiner feels that it does not have sufficient capital or has been engaged in dishonest practices, the bank can be declared a "problem bank" and will be subject to more frequent bank examinations.

FEDERAL DEPOSIT INSURANCE AND THE FDIC

Sometimes a problem bank is unable to meet its obligations to its depositors and it fails. Before the FDIC was established on January 1, 1934, a bank failure meant that depositors would have to wait to get their deposited funds until the bank was liquidated (that is, its assets converted into cash). At that time, depositors would be paid only a fraction of the value of deposits. Bank failures were a serious problem even during the boom years of the 1920s, when the number of bank failures averaged around 600 per year. During the Great Depression years from 1930 to 1933, the number of bank failures averaged over 2000 per year, with over a third of the banks failing in those four years. To put these numbers into perspective, the number of banks failing from 1934 to 1981 averaged ten per year.

The reason for the sharp reduction in the number of bank failures is the creation of the FDIC, which initially insured deposits up to $2500 but now insures them up to $100,000. Since FDIC insurance protects depositors with under $100,000 from suffering any losses due to bank failure, depositors are less likely to withdraw their funds and cause a bank to fail.

Although the number of bank failures is greatly reduced, they are not a thing of the past. Over one-quarter of deposits in commercial banks are not insured by the FDIC because they are in excess of $100,000. While the first $100,000 of a $1 million negotiable CD is insured, the remaining $900,000 is not. Because those holding uninsured deposits will suffer huge losses if a bank fails, they will pull their funds out of a bank at the slightest hint of trouble. The resulting loss of deposits can cause the bank to fail.

Recently, the problem of bank failures has become more prominent in the news: Since 1981, the number of bank failures has climbed dramatically (to over 40 per year in 1982 and 1983 and over 70 in 1984), culminating in the largest collapse to date, that of Continental Illinois National Bank in 1984, then one of the ten largest banks in the United States. Unfortunately, the problem of bank failures has not gone away. Since 1985, bank failures have been running at a rate of over 100 per year, with a peak of 206 in 1984, the largest amount in over half a century.

There are two primary methods that the FDIC uses to handle a failed bank. In the first, called the "payoff method," the FDIC allows the bank to fail and pays off deposits up to $100,000 (with funds acquired from the insurance premiums paid by the banks who have bought FDIC insurance). Then after the bank is liquidated, the FDIC lines up with other creditors of the bank and gets paid its share of the proceeds from the liquidated assets. Typically, when the payoff method is used, those holding deposits in excess of the $100,000 limit receive back over ninety cents on a dollar of deposits, although the process can take several years to complete. The payoff method is the least-used method for guaranteeing deposits of a failed bank. It was used, however, when the Penn Square Bank of Oklahoma, a medium-sized bank, failed in July 1982 when many of its energy loans went sour.

In the second method, called the "purchase and assumption method," the FDIC reorganizes the bank, typically by finding a willing merger partner who assumes (takes over) *all* the failed bank's deposits so that *none* of the depositors loses a penny. The FDIC may help the merger partner by providing it with subsidized loans or by buying some of the failed bank's weaker loans. The net effect of the purchase and assumption method is that the FDIC has guaranteed *all* deposits, not just those under the $100,000 limit. The purchase and assumption method is the FDIC's most common procedure for dealing with a failed bank, particularly when the bank is large and the FDIC fears that depositor losses may spur business bankruptcies and other bank failures.

Is the FDIC's Bank Insurance Fund Large Enough?

The Bank Insurance Fund of under $10 billion (1990 figure) is raised by levying an annual insurance premium of 23 cents per $100 of deposits. (The Congress is currently considering proposals to substantially increase the amount of funds available to the FDIC.) In comparison to the total amount of insured deposits, $2 trillion, the under $10 billion of funds available to the FDIC is quite small. Clearly, if a large number of banks failed at the same time, the FDIC would not be able to pay off all the insured depositors. Should we all take our money out of the banks and hide it in our mattresses?

If the amount of insured deposits is more than 200 times larger than the FDIC's insurance fund, why is the public confident that deposits up to $100,000 are safe? The answer is that the public understands that the FDIC is implicitly backed by the Federal Reserve System and the U.S. Treasury, both of which have the resources to handle extensive bank failures. In the case of Continental Illinois, the Federal Reserve lent this troubled bank over $5 billion (not the first time the Fed has made such loans—see Chapter 19). Thus it is not the FDIC's funds but the government's commitment to prevent depositors' losses that is important to the public.

RESTRICTIONS ON ASSET HOLDINGS AND BANK CAPITAL REQUIREMENTS

There are two costs not borne by a bank when it fails and goes out of business. First, the FDIC (implicitly, the taxpayers) bears the cost of paying off insured depositors. Second, costs are imposed on other banks because the public may lose confidence in the banking system as a whole. Since a bank needn't take these two costs into account, the social costs of bank failure are greater than the bank's perceived (private) costs. As a result, banks may hold assets that have more risk than is socially optimal. Risky assets may provide the bank with higher earnings when they pay off; and if they do not pay off and the bank fails, the bank does not bear the full costs of the failure (which is shared by the FDIC and other banks). In order to prevent banks from holding assets that are too risky, regulatory agencies restrict their holdings of risky assets; for example, commercial banks are not allowed to hold common stocks. In addition (as we have already seen) if a bank examiner believes a bank's assets are too risky, she can request that the bank sell them.

Because the costs of bank failure are not fully borne by banks, banks may also not be willing to hold sufficient bank capital. To understand why, we first must understand why bank capital is important. As you may recall, bank capital is the amount by which a bank's assets exceed its liabilities. Bank capital is held by banks as a cushion against a temporary drop in the value of assets that might otherwise cause the bank to fail and out of business. For example, if a bank's capital is 10% of its assets, then even if the bank experiences defaults on its loans that lower the value of assets by 5%, the bank is still able to remain in business. A bank also holds bank capital to reassure loan customers and uninsured depositors that it is less likely to fail. The bank can thus obtain more funds from depositors and make more loans.[1]

---

[1] In Chapter 8 we described the reason for a bank's willingness to hold bank capital by saying that it makes the bank *incentive compatible*.

Box   1 0 . 1   **A Global Perspective**

The Basle Plan for Risk-Based Capital Requirements

The increased integration of financial markets across countries and the need to make the playing field equal for banks from different countries led to the Basle agreement in June 1988 to standardize bank capital requirements internationally. The stated purposes of the agreement were (1) to coordinate supervisory definitions of capital, risk assessments, and standards for capital adequacy across countries to promote world stability and (2) to link a bank's capital requirements systematically to the riskiness of its activities, including various off-balance-sheet forms of risk exposure.

The Basle plan works as follows. Assets and off-balance-sheet activities are allocated into four categories, each with a different weight to reflect the degree of credit risk. The lowest risk category carries a zero weight and includes items that have no default risk, such as cash and government securities. The next lowest risk category has a weight of 20% and includes assets with only low default risk, such as interbank deposits, fully backed municipal bonds, and securities issued by government agencies. The third category has a weight of 50%

and includes higher risk municipal bonds and residential mortgages. The last risk category has the maximum weight of 100% and includes all remaining securities and loans. Off-balance-sheet activities are treated in a similar manner by first assigning each activity a "credit equivalent" reflecting its credit risk. For example, a standby letter of credit backing a customer's commercial paper is assigned to the highest risk category and has a weight of 100%, because it exposes the bank to the same risk as a direct loan to this customer.

Once all the bank's assets and off-balance-sheet items have been assigned to each risk category, these assets and off-balance-sheet items, each weighted by the appropriate risk weight (0, 20, 50, or 100%), are added up to compute the total "risk-adjusted assets." The bank must then meet two capital requirements: It must have "core" capital (which corresponds to stockholder equity) of at least 4% of total risk-adjusted assets and have total capital (which includes equity plus loan loss reserves and other debt instruments) of 8% of total risk-adjusted assets.

A bank does not want to hold too much bank capital, however. For example, if a bank earns a net profit of $1 million on its total assets of $100 million and has bank capital equal to 10% of its assets ($10 million), then its stockholders will earn a return of 10% on the equity capital ($1 million/$10 million = .10 = 10%). On the other hand, with the same earnings, if bank capital is 5% of total assets ($5 million), then the return on equity will be 20% ($1 million/$5 million = .20 = 20%). The managers of a bank must weigh the costs of having a smaller cushion of bank capital against the higher returns on equity that are earned when bank capital is smaller.

Although a bank will want to hold some bank capital, it will not want to hold as much as it should because, as we have seen, it does not fully bear the costs when it fails. The desire of the regulatory agencies to prevent bank failures has thus led them to specify minimum requirements for bank capital. The minimum amount of bank capital is currently specified to be 3% of total bank assets for the strongest banks, but it rises as high as 6% for other banks. Up until recently, minimum bank capital in the United States has been specified only as a fixed percentage of total bank assets. But in the wake of the Continental Illinois and savings and loans bailouts, regulators in the United States and the rest of the world have become increasingly worried about banks' holdings of risky assets and about the increase in banks' off-balance-sheet activities, which also expose banks to risk. Under an agreement among banking officials from twelve industrial nations meeting under the auspices of the Bank for International Settlements in Basle, Switzerland, the Federal Reserve, the FDIC, and the Office of the Comptroller of the Currency have implemented an additional risk-based capital requirement (fully phased in, in December 1992). In this risk-based capital requirement, which the banks must meet as well as the fixed-percentage capital requirement, minimum capital standards are linked to off-balance-sheet activities such as interest-rate swaps and trading positions in futures and options. Box 10.1 outlines the structure of these capital requirements in more detail.

STRUCTURE OF THE COMMERCIAL BANKING INDUSTRY

There are around 12,000 commercial banks in the United States, far more than in any other country in the world (see Box 10.2). As Table 10.1 indicates, we have an extraordinary number of small banks. Nearly 30% of the

---

B o x   1 0 . 2   **Global Perspective**

A Comparison of U.S. and Foreign Banking Structure

The structure of the commercial banking industry in the United States is radically different from that in other industrialized countries. The United States is the only country without a true national banking system in which banks have branches throughout the country. In contrast to other countries, the United States has ended up with a crazy quilt pattern of state and federal regulations governing interstate banking that has blocked a national banking system. One result is that there are many more banks in the United States than in other industrialized countries. In contrast to the United States, which has on the order of 12,000 commercial banks, every other industrialized country has well less than 1000. Japan, for example, has around 150 commercial banks—just 1% of the number in the United States, even though its economy and

population is half that of the United States.

Another result of the restrictions on branching in the United States is that our banks are smaller than those in other countries. Only one U.S. bank, Citicorp, is ranked in the top ten of the world's largest banks, and the next largest bank in the United States, BankAmerica, doesn't even make it into the top twenty-five.

The uniqueness of banking structure in the United States will stand out in even sharper contrast to the rest of the world as Europe furthers its economic integration in 1992. Starting January 1, 1993, all banks licensed in European Economic Community (EEC) countries will be freely able to provide complete banking services in any other EEC country. The result will be a European-wide banking system, with even larger European banks.

Table 10.1   Size Distribution of Insured Commercial Banks, End of 1989

Asset Size	No. of Banks	% of Banks	% of Assets
Less than $25 million	3747	29.5	1.7
$25–50 million	3236	25.4	3.6
$50–100 million	2745	21.6	5.8
$100–500 million	2371	18.7	14.0
$500–1 billion	236	1.9	4.9
$1–10 billion	334	2.6	32.0
More than $10 billion	44	.3	38.0
TOTAL	12,713	100.0	100.0

Source: FDIC, *1989 Statistics on Banking.*

banks have less than $25 million in assets. Far more typical is the size distribution in Canada or the United Kingdom, where five or fewer banks dominate the industry. In contrast, the ten largest commercial banks in the United States (listed in Table 10.2) together hold less than 30% of the assets in their industry.

Most industries in the United States have far fewer firms than the commercial banking industry; typically, large firms tend to dominate these industries to a greater extent than in the commercial banking industry. (Consider, for example, the computer industry, which is dominated by IBM, or the automobile industry, which is dominated by General Motors.) Does the large number of banks in the commercial banking industry and the absence

Table 10.2   Ten Largest U.S. Banks, End of 1990

Bank	Assets (Billions of $)	% of All Commercial Bank Assets
1. Citicorp, New York	217	6.4
2. BankAmerica Corp., San Francisco	111	3.3
3. Chase Manhattan Corp., New York	98	2.9
4. J. P. Morgan & Co., New York	93	2.7
5. Security Pacific Corp., Los Angeles	85	2.5
6. Chemical Bank Corp., New York	73	2.2
7. NCNB Corp., Charlotte, N.C.	65	1.9
8. Bankers Trust Corp., New York	64	1.9
9. Manufacturers Hanover, New York	62	1.8
10. Wells Fargo & Co., San Francisco	56	1.7
TOTAL	924	27.3

Source: *American Banker*, February 21, 1991.

of a few dominant firms suggest that the commercial banking industry is more competitive than other industries?

Branching Regulations and the McFadden Act

The presence of so many commercial banks in the United States actually reflects regulations that restrict the ability of these financial institutions to open **branches** (additional offices that conduct banking operations). Each state has its own regulations on the type and number of branches that a bank can open. Regulations on the West and East Coasts, for example, tend to allow banks to open branches throughout their state, while in the middle part of the country, regulations on branching are more restrictive (see Figure 10.1). Some states, marked as "Unit Banking" states in Figure 10.1, do not allow commercial banks to open any branches, although limited banking

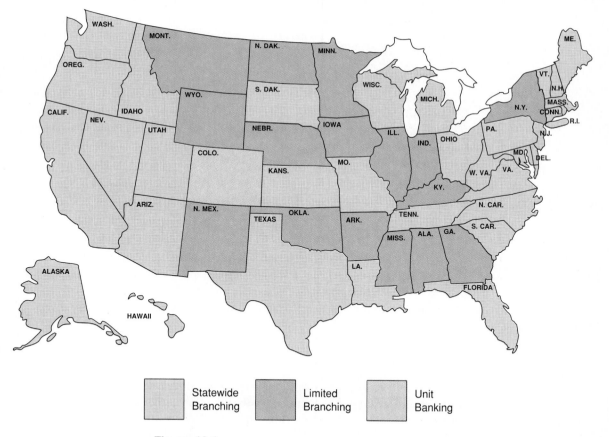

Statewide Branching

Limited Branching

Unit Banking

Figure 10.1
State Branching Regulations Source: Conference of State Bank Supervisors, December 1990.

facilities are often permitted. The McFadden Act of 1927, which was designed to put national banks and state banks on an equal footing, effectively prohibited banks from branching across state lines and forced all national banks to conform to the branching regulations in the state of their location.

The result of the McFadden Act and the state branching regulations is that many small banks stay in existence, since a large bank capable of driving them out of business is often restricted from opening a branch nearby. Advocates of restrictive state branching regulations say that these regulations foster competition by keeping so many banks in business. But the existence of large numbers of banks in the United States must be seen as an indication of *lack* of competition—*not* the presence of vigorous competition. Inefficient banks can remain in business because their customers cannot find a conveniently located branch of another bank where they can conduct their business.

The McFadden Act and state branching regulations must be seen as one of the strongest anticompetitive forces in the commercial banking industry. Since competition is beneficial to society, why have regulations restricting branching arisen in America? The simplest explanation is that the American public historically has been hostile to large banks. States with the most restrictive branching regulations are typically ones in which populist antibank sentiment was strongest in the nineteenth century. (These states usually had large farming populations whose relations with banks periodically became tempestuous when banks would foreclose on farmers who couldn't pay their debts.) The legacy of nineteenth-century politics is a banking system with restrictive branching regulations and hence an inordinate number of small banks.

Weakening of Branching Restrictions

An important feature of the banking industry is that competition can be repressed by regulation but not completely squashed. In Chapter 13 we will discuss how banks' search for profits has led to financial innovation that skirts restrictive regulations. In this chapter we will discuss two recent examples of competitive forces that have weakened the impact of restrictive branching regulations: the emergence of bank holding companies and the development of electronic banking facilities.

Bank Holding Companies   A holding company is a corporation that owns several different companies. This form of corporate ownership has important advantages for banks in that (1) it allows them to circumvent restrictive branching regulations, because the holding company can own a controlling interest in several banks even if branching is not permitted, (2) a bank holding company can engage in other activities related to banking, such as the provision of investment advice, data processing and transmission services, leasing, credit card services, servicing of loans in other states, and so on, and

(3) the holding company can issue commercial paper, allowing the bank to tap into nondeposit sources of funds.

Bank holding companies are restricted to owning businesses that are "closely related to banking." Permissible activities, which are specified by the Federal Reserve's Regulation Y, include the activities mentioned here as well as others—ranging from providing courier services to real estate appraisal. In the past, the Fed and congressional legislation have prohibited bank holding companies from engaging in activities such as real estate brokerage, underwriting securities, operating a travel agency, and general management consulting. However, in their continuing search for profits, bank holding companies have been seeking ways to get around these regulations and have been entering previously prohibited businesses. Indeed, the U.S. Treasury has proposed that banks in effect be allowed to enter the insurance, mutual fund, and securities business by affiliating with firms engaged in these activities under a holding company structure (see Chapter 11).

Significantly, more states are now allowing bank holding companies headquartered in other states to purchase banks in their state. In addition, since 1982, banks are permitted to purchase out-of-state banks that are failing, as Citicorp and Chase Manhattan have done. The result is that the McFadden Act's restrictions on branching no longer prevent these companies from providing banking services in other states. In addition, bank holding companies have opened limited-service banks that either don't make commercial loans or alternatively do not take in deposits. These so-called **nonbank banks** often are not subject to branching regulations and so allow bank holding companies effectively to branch across state lines. However, banking legislation passed in 1987 placed a moratorium on new nonbank banks. In response to the weakening of restrictions on branching across state lines, most states now allow some interstate branching.

In the past twenty-five years the growth of the bank holding companies has been dramatic. Currently, almost all large banks are owned by bank holding companies (such as Citibank, Chase Manhattan, Bank of America, First National Bank of Chicago, and Mellon Bank), and over 90% of all commercial bank deposits are held in banks owned by holding companies.

Electronic Banking Facilities   Through the wonders of modern computer technology bank customers are now able to receive banking services through computer terminals that are not located at a bank or one of its branches. The regulatory agencies and courts in most states have determined that if an electronic banking facility is owned by a bank, then it is considered to be a branch of that bank and is subject to a state's branching regulations. However, states typically have special provisions allowing for the wider establishment of electronic banking facilities than is permissible for what are known as "brick and mortar" branches (traditional branches).

A more far-reaching development is related to the use of shared electronic banking facilities, even if they span state lines. As long as a facility is not owned or rented by a bank but is paid for on a transaction fee basis, it is not considered a branch of a bank and, as such, is not subject to branching regulations. Because they enable banks to widen their markets, a number of these shared facilities have been established, some nationwide. As electronic banking becomes more prevalent in the future, the McFadden Act and state branching regulations will prove less of a barrier to competition in the banking industry. Indeed, the McFadden Act may soon be a dead letter: The U.S. Treasury has proposed that Congress abolish restrictions on branching across state lines be abolished entirely.

THRIFT INDUSTRY: REGULATION AND STRUCTURE

Not surprisingly, the regulation and structure of the thrift industry (savings and loan associations, mutual savings banks, and credit unions) parallels closely the regulation and structure of the commercial banking industry.

Savings and Loan Associations

Just as there is a dual banking system for commercial banks, savings and loan associations (S&Ls) can be chartered either by the federal government or by the states. Most S&Ls, whether state or federally chartered, are members of the Federal Home Loan Bank System (FHLBS). Established in 1932, the FHLBS was styled after the Federal Reserve System. It has twelve district Federal Home Loan Banks which are supervised by the Office of Thrift Supervision.

Federal deposit insurance (up to $100,000 of deposits) for S&Ls is provided by the Savings Association Insurance Fund, a subsidiary of the FDIC. The Office of Thrift Supervision regulates federally insured S&Ls by setting minimum capital requirements, requiring periodic reports, and examining the S&Ls. It is also the chartering agency for federally chartered S&Ls, and for these S&Ls it approves mergers and sets the rules for branching.

The branching regulations for S&Ls have been more liberal than for commercial banks: Almost all states permit branching, and since 1980, federally chartered S&Ls have been allowed to branch statewide in all states. Since 1981, mergers of financially troubled S&Ls have also been allowed across state lines, and nationwide branching of S&Ls may soon become common. A result of the less restrictive regulations on S&L branching is that the percentage of S&Ls with under $25 million in assets (10%) is less than the percentage of commercial banks with under $25 million in assets (30%).

The Federal Home Loan Bank System, like the Fed, makes loans to the members of the system (the FHLBS obtains funds for this purpose by issuing bonds). However, in contrast to the Fed's discount loans—which are expected to be repaid quickly—the loans from the FHLBS often need not be repaid for long periods of time. In addition, the rates charged to S&Ls for these loans are often below the rates that the S&Ls must pay when they borrow in the open market. In this way, the FHLBS loan program provides a subsidy to the savings and loan industry (and implicitly to the housing industry, since most of the S&Ls' loans are for residential mortgages).

Mutual Savings Banks

Of the 500 or so mutual savings banks, around half are chartered by the states. Although the mutual savings banks are primarily regulated by the states in which they are located, the majority have their deposits insured by the FDIC up to the limit of $100,000; these banks are also subject to many of the FDIC's regulations for state-chartered banks. As a rule, the mutual savings banks whose deposits are not insured by the FDIC have their deposits insured by state insurance funds.

The branching regulations for mutual savings banks are determined by the states in which they operate. Because these regulations are not too restrictive, there are few mutual savings banks with assets of less than $25 million.

Credit Unions

Credit unions are small cooperative lending institutions organized around a particular group (union members or employees of a particular firm). They can be chartered either by the states or the federal government, but over half are federally chartered. The National Credit Union Administration (NCUA) issues federal charters and regulates federally chartered credit unions by setting minimum capital requirements, requiring periodic reports, and examining the credit unions. Federal deposit insurance (up to the $100,000 limit) is provided to both federally chartered and state chartered credit unions by a subsidiary of the National Credit Union Administration, the National Credit Union Share Insurance Fund (NCUSIF). Since the majority of credit union lending is for consumer loans with fairly short terms to maturity, they have not suffered the recent financial difficulties of the S&Ls and mutual savings banks.

Because their members share a common bond, credit unions are typically quite small, with most holding less than $10 million of assets.[2] Often a credit union's shareholders are dispersed over many states, some even worldwide, so branching across state lines and into other countries is permitted for federally chartered credit unions. The Navy Federal Credit Union, for example, whose shareholders are members of the U.S. Navy and Marine Corps, has branches throughout the world.

---

[2]Because credit unions are tied to a particular industry or company, they are more likely to fail when, for example, large numbers of workers in that industry or company are laid off from their jobs and have trouble making their loan payments. Recent regulatory changes allow individual credit unions to cater to a more diverse group of people, and this may reduce credit union failures in the future.

INTERNATIONAL BANKING

In 1960, only eight U.S. banks operated branches in foreign countries, and their total assets were less than $4 billion. Currently over 100 American banks have branches abroad, with assets totaling over $500 billion. The spectacular growth in international banking can be explained by two factors.

First is the rapid growth in international trade and multinational (worldwide) corporations that has occurred since 1960. When American business firms operate abroad, they need banking services in foreign countries. Although these firms could use foreign banks, many of them prefer to do business with the U.S. banks with whom they have established long-term relationships and who understand American business customs and practices. As international trade has grown, international banking has grown with it.

Second, American banks have wanted to tap into the large pool of dollar-denominated deposits in foreign countries known as Eurodollars. To understand the structure of U.S. banking overseas, let us first look at the Eurodollar market, an important source of growth for international banking.

The Eurodollar Market

Eurodollars are created when deposits in accounts in the United States are transferred to a bank *outside* the country *and are kept in the form of dollars*. For example, if Rolls Royce Corporation deposits a $1 million check, written on an account at an American bank, in its bank in London—specifying that the deposit is payable in dollars—$1 million of Eurodollars are created. Over 90% of Eurodollar deposits are time deposits, with over half being certificates of deposit with maturities of thirty days or more. The total amount of Eurodollars outstanding exceeds $2 trillion, making the Eurodollar market one of the most important financial markets in the world economy (see Box 10.3).

Why would companies like Rolls Royce want to hold dollar deposits outside the United States? First, the dollar is the most widely used currency in international trade, so Rolls Royce might want to hold deposits in dollars to conduct its international transactions. Second, Eurodollars are "offshore" deposits; that is, they are held in countries that will not subject them to regulations such as reserve requirements or restrictions (called capital controls) on taking the deposits outside the country.[3]

---

[3]Although most "offshore" deposits are denominated in dollars, some are also denominated in other currencies. Collectively, these offshore deposits are referred to as Eurocurrencies. A German mark-denominated deposit held in London, for example, is called a Euromark, while a French franc-denominated deposit held in London is called a Eurofranc.

B o x   1 0 . 3   **A Global Perspective**

Birth of the Eurodollar Market

One of capitalism's great ironies is that the Eurodollar market, one of the most important financial markets used by capitalists, was fathered by the Soviet Union. In the early 1950s, during the height of the cold war, the Soviets had accumulated a substantial amount of dollar balances held by banks in the United States. Because the Russians feared that the U.S. government might freeze these assets in the United States, they wanted to move the deposits to Europe, where they would be safe from expropriation. (This fear was not unjustified: considering the U.S. freeze on Iranian assets in 1979.) However, they also wanted to keep the deposits in dollars to be used in their international transactions. The solution to the problem was to transfer the deposits to European banks but to keep the deposits denominated in dollars. When the Soviets did this, the Eurodollar was born.

The main center of the Eurodollar market is in London, a major international financial center for hundreds of years. Eurodollars are also held outside of Europe in locations that provide "offshore" status to these deposits—for example, Hong Kong, Singapore, and the Caribbean (the Bahamas and Cayman Islands).

The minimum-sized transaction in the Eurodollar market is typically $1 million, and approximately 75% of these deposits are held by banks. Plainly you and I are unlikely to come directly into contact with Eurodollars. The Eurodollar market is, however, an important source of funds to U.S. banks, whose borrowing of these deposits is over $90 billion. Rather than using an intermediary and borrowing all the deposits from foreign banks, American banks decided that they could earn higher profits by opening their own branches abroad to attract these deposits. Consequently, the Eurodollar market has been an important stimulus to U.S. banking overseas.

Structure of U.S. Banking Overseas

U.S. banks have most of their branches in Latin America, the Far East, the Caribbean, and London. The largest volume of assets is held by branches in London because it is a major international financial center and the central location for the Eurodollar market. Latin America and the Far East have many branches because of the importance of U.S. trade with these regions. The Caribbean (the Bahamas and Cayman Islands) has become an important location for international banking because it is a tax haven which has almost no taxation or restrictive regulations. In actuality, the branches in the Bahamas and the Cayman Islands are "shell operations" because they function primarily as bookkeeping operations and do not provide normal banking services.

B o x   1 0 . 4    **A Global Perspective**

The Third World Debt Crisis

An important aspect of international banking is the loans made to third world countries—particularly Argentina, Brazil, and Mexico. In the aftermath of the sharp rise in oil prices in 1973–1974, developing countries found their import bills rising dramatically due to increased costs for energy, while the OPEC countries found themselves with huge amounts of idle funds due to increased revenue from oil. U.S. banks were in the forefront of "recycling" these funds from the OPEC countries by accepting deposits from the OPEC countries and in turn lending out the proceeds to the developing countries. In contrast to earlier loans to developing countries, which were used for special development projects (for example, highway systems and dams), these new loans were often made to governments to pay for the higher level of imports.

This "recycling" of funds proceeded smoothly until the worldwide recession of 1980–1982, which led to a sharp fall in the exports of the third world countries; they had trouble meeting their debt (interest and principal) payments. When Mexico encountered difficulties with its debt payments in late 1982, the banks and international financial agencies (such as the International Monetary Fund) stepped in to help restructure the debt, that is, to change the terms of repayment and the interest rates. To date, this ongoing process with more than forty third world countries has so far been successful in preventing major defaults of third world debt.

The magnitude of the debt crisis is immense; in the past ten years, about forty developing countries with $300 billion of debt to commercial banks were involved in restructuring their debt.

U.S. banks hold more than $100 billion of third world debt, mostly of Latin American countries, particularly of Brazil and Mexico (over $20 billion each). The largest lenders to third world countries include the following money center banks: Citicorp, Manufacturers Hanover, BankAmerica, Chase Manhattan, Chemical, J.P. Morgan, Bankers Trust, and First Chicago. In 1982, when the first fears of third world default arose, there were worries that the U.S. banking system could be threatened with collapse, since many money center banks held amounts of third world debt well in excess of their bank capital. To date, however, the banking system has weathered the storm. Encouraged by regulators, money center banks have increased their primary capital from 4.2% of assets in 1981 to over 7% today. In addition, these banks have been continually setting aside income to increase their loan loss reserves, which are now in excess of 50% of their third world debt.

Although the third world debt crisis is still with us, fears of a financial collapse have subsided. However, banks who hoped to make substantial profits on their international banking business have come to regret this foray into international lending.

An alternative corporate structure for U.S. banks that operate overseas is the **Edge Act corporation,** which is a special subsidiary engaged primarily in international banking. This corporate structure, created by the Edge Act of 1919, allows American banks to compete more effectively against foreign banks by exempting the Edge Act corporation from certain U.S. banking regulations. Edge Act corporations, for example, are exempt from the prohibition on branching across state lines; they can have branches in different states to facilitate the financing of trade with different parts of the world— an office on the West Coast to handle the financing of trade with Japan, an office in Miami to handle the financing of trade with Latin America, and so forth.

U.S. banks (through their holding companies) can also own a controlling interest in foreign banks and in foreign companies that provide financial services, such as finance companies. The international activities of member banks of the Federal Reserve System, bank holding companies, and Edge Act corporations (which account for almost all international banking conducted by U.S. banks) are regulated by the Federal Reserve's Regulation K. As in the case of bank holding companies, these international activities must be "closely related to banking."

In late 1981, the Federal Reserve approved the creation of **international banking facilities (IBFs)** within the United States which can accept time deposits from foreigners but are not subject to either reserve requirements or any restrictions on interest payments. IBFs are also allowed to make loans to foreigners, but they are not allowed to make loans to domestic residents. States have encouraged the establishment of IBFs by exempting them from state and local taxes. In essence, IBFs are treated like foreign branches of U.S. banks and are not subject to domestic regulations and taxes. The purpose of establishing IBFs is to encourage American and foreign banks to do more banking business in the United States rather than abroad. From this point of view, IBFs have been a success: Within two years, their assets had climbed to nearly $200 billion and currently exceed this amount.

Foreign Banks in the United States

The growth in international trade not only has encouraged U.S. banks to open offices overseas, but also has encouraged foreign banks to establish offices in the United States. There are now around 500 offices of foreign banks operating in America, and they hold more than 20% of the total bank assets in the U.S.

Foreign banks engage in banking activities in the United States by operating (1) an agency office of the foreign bank, (2) a subsidiary U.S. bank, or (3) a branch of the foreign bank. An agency office can lend and transfer funds in the United States, but it cannot accept deposits from domestic residents. Agency offices have the advantage of not being subject to regulations that apply to full-service banking offices (such as requirements for FDIC insurance and restrictions on branching). A subsidiary U.S. bank is just like any other U.S. bank (it may even have an American-sounding name) and is subject to the same regulations, but it is owned by the foreign bank. A branch of a foreign bank bears the foreign bank's name and is usually a full-service office. Foreign banks also may form Edge Act corporations and IBFs.

Before 1978, foreign banks were not subject to many regulations that applied to domestic banks: They could open branches across state lines and were not subject to reserve requirements, for example. The passage of the International Banking Act of 1978, however, put foreign and domestic

B o x   1 0 . 5   **A Global Perspective**

Japanese Banks Are Coming on Strong

It's not just in industries like electronics and auto-mobiles that the Japanese are overtaking Americans; they are also overtaking the United States in the international banking industry.

As recently as 1984, U.S. banks were the dominant players in international banking, with a market share of over 25%. In the 1980s, however, the Japanese banks came on strong: By 1986 they surpassed the American competition—their market share increased to 32%, while the U.S. banks' share dropped to below 20%.

The Japanese have also been coming on strong in the United States. Currently, Japanese-owned banks have a market share of 25% of the banking business in California and 15% nationwide. Some bankers predict that the Japanese will capture 25% of the entire U.S. commercial loan market by the mid-1990s.

America is no longer number one in banking. In the early 1980s, Citicorp and BankAmerica were the two top-ranked banks in terms of asset size in the world. By 1990, seven of the ten largest banks in the world were Japanese, with Dai-Ichi Kangyo taking over the top-ranked spot. Citicorp is now the only U.S. bank remaining in the top ten.

banks on a more equal footing. Now foreign banks may open new full-service branches only in the state they designate their home state or in states that allow entry of out-of-state banks. Limited-service branches and agency offices in any other state are permitted, however, and foreign banks are allowed to retain any full-service branches opened before the International Banking Act of 1978.

The internationalization of banking, both by U.S. banks going abroad and by foreign banks entering the United States, has meant that financial markets throughout the world have become more integrated. As a result, there is a growing trend toward international coordination of bank regulation, one example of which is the 1988 Basle agreement to standardize minimum capital requirements in industrialized countries, which was mentioned earlier in the chapter. Another trend is the increasing dominance of Japanese banks in international banking and the decline in U.S. banks' market share (Box 10.5). The implications of this financial market integration for the operation of our economy are examined further in Chapters 21 and 22 when we discuss international finance in more detail.

SUMMARY

1. The United States has a dual banking system with commercial banks chartered by the states and the federal government. Multiple agencies regulate commercial banks: the Office of the Comptroller, the Federal Reserve, the FDIC, and the state banking authorities.

2. Chartering and examination of banks is carried out by the regulatory agencies mentioned above.

Their purpose is to keep the banking system financially sound.

3. Federal deposit insurance prevents bank failures by assuring depositors that their insured deposits are safe. The FDIC's role in bank failures has become more prominent with the increased number of failures.

4. Because private costs of bank failure are below social costs, banks may not hold enough capital and may hold assets that are too risky. To prevent this from happening, regulations specify minimum capital requirements and restrict banks from holding certain assets.

5. Restrictive state branching regulations and the McFadden Act, which prohibits branching across state lines, have led to a large number of small commercial banks. The large number of commercial banks in the United States reflects the *lack* of competition and not the presence of vigorous competition. Bank holding companies and electronic banking facilities are important forces that are weakening the anticompetitive effect of restrictive branching regulations.

6. The regulation and structure of the thrift industry (savings and loan associations, mutual savings banks, and credit unions) parallel closely the regulation and structure of the commercial banking industry. Savings and loans are primarily regulated by the Office of Thrift Supervision and deposit insurance is administered by the FDIC. Mutual savings banks are regulated by the states, and federal deposit insurance is provided by the FDIC. Credit unions are regulated by the National Credit Union Administration, and deposit insurance is provided by the National Credit Union Share Insurance Fund.

7. With the rapid growth of world trade since 1960, international banking has grown dramatically. U.S. banks engage in international banking activities by opening branches abroad, owning controlling interests in foreign banks, forming Edge Act corporations, and operating international banking facilities (IBFs) located in the United States. Foreign banks operate in the United States by owning a subsidiary American bank or by operating branches or agency offices in the United States.

KEY TERMS

state banks

national banks

dual banking system

bank holding companies

branches

nonbank banks

Edge Act corporation

international banking
 facilities (IBFs)

QUESTIONS AND PROBLEMS

* 1. Which regulatory agency has the primary responsibility for supervising the following categories of commercial banks?
   a) national banks
   b) bank holding companies
   c) non-Federal Reserve state banks
   d) Federal Reserve member state banks

2. Answer true, false, or uncertain: "Because banks can play one regulatory agency off against another, bank regulatory agencies have less control over banks. This lack of control is harmful to the health of the banking system."

* 3. How can the process of chartering banks lead to less competition in the banking industry? Are there any benefits from bank chartering?

4. If you have a $10,000 deposit in the First National Bank and it fails, do you care whether the FDIC uses the "payoff method" versus the "purchase and assumption method" to deal with the bank failure? How would your answer change if your deposit is $1 million?

* 5. If massive bank failures like those in 1930–1933 occurred, would the FDIC be able to pay off all insured depositors at failed banks? Does this af-

fect the ability of the FDIC to prevent bank failures?

6. Why is it necessary for regulators to restrict banks from holding certain assets?

* 7. Answer true, false, or uncertain: "Banks want to hold bank capital because it acts as a cushion against a temporary drop in the value of assets that might cause the bank to fail. Therefore, no regulations are needed to encourage banks to hold bank capital."

8. Answer true, false, or uncertain: "The commercial banking industry in Canada is less competitive than the commercial banking industry in the United States because in Canada only a few large banks dominate the industry, while in the United States there are around 12,000 commercial banks."

* 9. Why has new technology made it harder to enforce limitations on bank branching?

10. Why has there been such a dramatic increase in bank holding companies?

*11. Why is there a higher percentage of banks with under $25 million of assets among commercial banks than among savings and loans and mutual savings banks?

12. Unlike commercial banks, savings and loans, and mutual savings banks, credit unions do not have restrictions on locating branches in other states. Why then are credit unions typically smaller than the other depository institutions?

*13. What incentives have regulatory agencies created to encourage international banking? Why have they done this?

14. How could the approval of international banking facilities (IBFs) by the Fed in 1981 have reduced employment in the banking industry in Europe?

15. If the bank at which you keep your checking account is owned by Saudi Arabians, should you worry that your deposits are less safe than if the bank were owned by Americans?

CHAPTER 11

The Crisis in Banking Regulation

PREVIEW   The American banking industry is in a sorry state. In recent years the rate of commercial bank failures has been running at rates more than ten times that of the 1945–1981 period (see Figure 11.1). The FDIC's bank insurance fund spent more than it took in for the third straight year in 1990, an unprecedented set of deficits since the FDIC started operations in 1934. Indeed, the Bush administration projected that without an infusion of cash, the FDIC's bank insurance fund would run out of money by 1992.

Yet, if we find the state of the commercial banking industry troubling, it is nothing compared to the mess in the savings and loan industry. Losses in this industry were close to $20 billion in 1989, and legislation passed in that year to bail out the industry is costing taxpayers well in excess of $100 billion. Why is banking in the United States in such a mess? Who's to blame for the incredible losses in the savings and loan industry? Why did the crisis in banking occur in the 1980s?

In this chapter, we provide answers to these questions by developing an economic analysis of how banking regulation, and particularly federal deposit insurance, affects the behavior of banking institutions. This economic analysis will explain not only why the crisis in the banking industry has occurred, but also how the regulatory system might be reformed to prevent future disasters.

FEDERAL DEPOSIT INSURANCE, ADVERSE SELECTION, AND MORAL HAZARD

The most serious drawback of the banking regulatory system stems from **moral hazard,** which occurs when one party to a transaction has incentives to engage in activities detrimental to the other party. Moral hazard is an important feature of insurance arrangements in general because the existence of insurance provides increased incentives for taking risks that might result in an insurance payoff. For example, some drivers with automobile collision

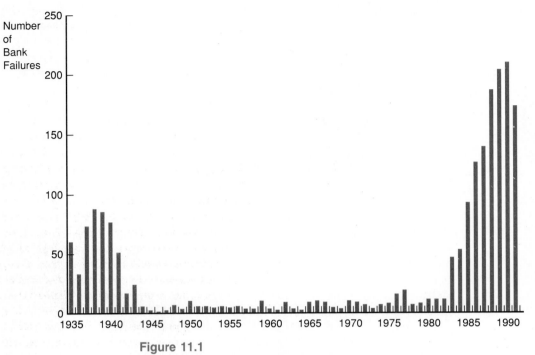

Figure 11.1
Bank Failures: 1934–1990 Source: Federal Deposit Insurance Corporation.

insurance that has a low deductible might be more likely to drive recklessly because if they get into a fender bender, the insurance company pays most of the costs for repairing the car.

Moral hazard is a prominent attribute in government arrangements to provide deposit insurance. Because insured depositors know that they will not suffer losses if a bank fails, they do not impose the discipline of the marketplace on banks by withdrawing deposits when they suspect that the bank is taking on too much risk. Consequently, banks with deposit insurance can (and do) take on greater risks than they otherwise would.

A further problem for deposit insurance arises because of **adverse selection,** which occurs when the people who are most likely to produce the adverse outcome insured against (e.g., bank failure) are those who most want to take advantage of the insurance. Bad drivers, for example, are more likely to take out automobile collision insurance with a low deductible than are good drivers. Since insured depositors have little reason to impose discipline on the bank, risk-prone entrepreneurs find the banking industry a particularly attractive one to enter—they know they will be able to engage in highly risky activities. Even worse, because insured depositors have so little reason to monitor the bank's activities, outright crooks also find banking an attractive industry for their activities, since it is easy for them to get away with fraud and the embezzlement of funds.

How Adverse Selection and Moral Hazard Explain Features of Banking Regulation

The concepts of adverse selection and moral hazard are especially useful in understanding why government has chosen the particular forms of banking regulation described in the previous chapter. As we have seen, adverse selection makes it more likely that criminals or entrepreneurs who have tendencies to engage in highly speculative activities will try to control a bank. Chartering of banks is one preventive method; through chartering, proposals for new banks are screened to prevent undesirable people from controlling them.

The moral hazard created by deposit insurance encourages too much risk taking on the part of banks, and bank regulations that restrict asset holdings and bank capital requirements are directed at preventing this moral hazard. Restrictions that prevent a bank from holding risky assets such as common stock are a direct means of making banks avoid too much risk. The requirement for a bank to have a large amount of equity capital decreases risk taking by changing the bank's incentives to take on risks: When a bank is forced to have a large amount of equity capital, the bank has more to lose if it fails and is thus more likely to pursue less risky activities.

Regular bank examinations, which allow regulators to monitor whether the bank is complying with capital requirements and restrictions on asset holdings, also function to limit moral hazard. With information about a bank's activities, regulators can enforce regulations and close a bank if necessary. Actions taken to reduce moral hazard by preventing banks from taking on too much risk further help to reduce the adverse selection problem because, with less of an opportunity for risk taking, risk-prone entrepreneurs will be less likely to be attracted to the banking industry.[1]

Even with all of these regulatory activities, moral hazard and adverse selection still bedevil the banking industry. Criminals and risk-prone entrepreneurs are often able to slip through the chartering process. Bankers have incentives to hide their risk-taking activities from the regulatory authorities, so regulators may find it difficult to keep banks away from taking too much risk. Thus, although deposit insurance has the virtue of protecting depositors from losses—indeed, deposits at commercial banks and thrifts have been almost totally safe in the United States since the establishment of fed-

---

[1]Note that the methods regulators use to cope with adverse selection and moral hazard have their counterparts in private financial markets (see Chapter 8). Chartering is similar to the screening process of potential borrowers; regulations restricting risky asset holdings are similar to restrictive covenants that prevent borrowing firms from engaging in risky investment activities; bank capital requirements act like restrictive covenants that require minimum amounts of net worth for borrowing firms; and regular bank examinations are similar to the monitoring of borrowers by lending institutions.

eral deposit insurance—there can be high costs to the taxpayer when increased risk taking leads to losses for the government deposit insurance agency.

The Too-Big-to-Fail Policy

The moral hazard created by deposit insurance and the desire to prevent bank failures have presented bank regulators with a particular quandary. Because a failure of a very large bank makes it more likely that a major financial disruption will occur, bank regulators are naturally reluctant to allow a big bank to fail and create losses for its depositors. Indeed, consider Continental Illinois, one of the ten largest banks in the United States when it became insolvent in May 1984. Not only did the FDIC guarantee depositors up to the $100,000 insurance limit, but it guaranteed *all* deposits, even those exceeding $100,000, and it even prevented losses for Continental Illinois bond holders. Shortly thereafter, the Comptroller of the Currency (the regulator of national banks) testified to Congress that the FDIC had a policy that the largest eleven banks were "too big to fail," that is, the FDIC would bail them out so that no depositor or creditor would suffer a loss. The FDIC would do this by using the "purchase and assumption method" (described in the previous chapter) in which it would find a willing merger partner to take over the insolvent bank (and its deposits) after the bank received a large infusion of capital from the FDIC. As Box 11.1 indicates, the too-big-to-fail policy applies to big banks that are not even among the eleven largest.

One problem with the too-big-to-fail policy is that it increases the incentives for moral hazard by big banks. If the FDIC were willing to close a bank using the alternative "payoff method," only paying depositors up to the $100,000 limit, then large depositors with more than $100,000 would suffer losses if the bank failed. Thus, they would have an incentive to monitor the bank and pull their money out when the bank was taking on too much risk. To prevent such a loss of deposits, the bank would be more likely to engage in less risky activities. On the other hand, once large depositors know that a bank is too big to fail, they have no incentive to monitor the bank and prevent it from risk taking by pulling out their deposits when it takes on too much risk: No matter what the bank does, large depositors will not suffer any losses. The result of the too-big-to-fail policy is that big banks take on even greater risks, thus making bank failures more likely.

Another serious problem with the too-big-to-fail policy is that it is basically unfair. Small banks are put at a competitive disadvantage because they will be allowed to fail, creating potential losses for their large depositors, while big banks have the advantage that their large depositors are immune from any losses. The unfairness of the too-big-to-fail doctrine came to a head with the different FDIC treatment of two insolvent banks in late 1990 and early 1991 (Box 11.1).

Box   1 1 . 1

A Tale of Two Bank Collapses—Bank of New England and Freedom National Bank

The FDIC's procedures for handling two bank collapses, those of the Bank of New England and Freedom National Bank, illustrate how the too-big-to-fail policy works.

The Bank of New England, based in Boston, was the thirty-third largest bank holding company in the United States, with over $20 billion of assets. In the 1980s, it was the region's most aggressive real estate lender; over 30% of its loan portfolio resided in commercial real estate. With the collapse of real estate prices in New England beginning in the late 1980s (commercial real estate values dropped over 25%), many of the bank's loans went sour. On Friday, January 4, 1991, the bank announced a projected $450 million fourth-quarter loss that exceeded the bank's capital of $255 million. Expecting the failure of the bank, in the next forty-eight hours depositors lined up at the bank and withdrew over $1 billion in funds, much of it from automatic teller machines.

The chairman of the FDIC, William Seidman, expressed his concern over the ramifications of the potential failure: "Given the condition of the financial system in New England, it would be unwise to send a signal that large depositors weren't going to be protected."* The FDIC followed its too-big-to-fail policy. Sunday night, January 6, the FDIC moved in to stop the run on the bank and agreed to guarantee all Bank of New England deposits, including those in excess of the $100,000 insurance limit. In order to keep the bank in operation until a buyer could be found and a "purchase and assumption method" could be used to make sure that no depositors would suffer any losses, the FDIC created what is called a "bridge bank." In this arrangement, the FDIC creates a new corporation to run the bank and immediately injects capital ($750 million in the case of the Bank of New England). The FDIC and the buyer of the bank then put additional capital into the bank over time and eventually the acquirer buys out the FDIC's share. The net result of these transactions is that the FDIC is expected to spend

$2.3 billion bailing out the Bank of New England, the third costliest bailout in the FDIC's history. However, when all is said and done and spent, none of the depositors will lose a penny.

The contrasting FDIC treatment of a small insolvent bank in Harlem several months earlier has raised serious questions of fairness. The Freedom National Bank was founded in 1964 by baseball-great Jackie Robinson and other minority investors. Despite its small size (under $100 million of deposits), it was one of the most prominent black-owned banks.

As a result of numerous speculative loans that went bad, the bank became insolvent in November 1990. Because of the bank's small size, the FDIC was not concerned that the failure of the bank would have serious repercussions for the rest of the banking system and so it decided to close the bank on November 9 using the "payoff method." The Freedom National Bank was liquidated and large depositors were paid only 50 cents on the dollar for deposits in excess of $100,000. It's not just fat cats that suffered losses when this bank failed: Charitable organizations like the United Negro College Fund, the National Urban League, and several churches were among the large depositors at the bank. William Seidman described the unfairness of the treatment of the Freedom National Bank in testimony to Congress: "My first testimony when I came to this job was that it's unfair to treat big banks in a way that covers all depositors but not small banks. I promised to do my best to change that. Five years later, I can report that my best wasn't good enough."†

---

*Quoted in John Meehan, "A Shock to the System: How Far Will Banking's Crisis of Confidence Spread," *Business Week* (January 21, 1991), p. 26.

†Quoted in Kenneth H. Bacon, "Failures of a Big Bank and a Little Bank Bring Fairness of Deposit-Security Policy into Question," *Wall Street Journal* (December 5, 1990), p. A18.

WHY DID THE CRISIS IN BANKING OCCUR IN THE 1980s?

Before the 1980s, federal deposit insurance seemed to work exceedingly well. In contrast to the pre-1934 period when bank failures were common and depositors frequently suffered losses, the period from 1934 to 1980 was one in which bank failures were a rarity, averaging fifteen a year for commercial banks and fewer than five a year for savings and loans. After 1981, this rosy picture changed dramatically. Failures in both commercial banks and savings and loans climbed to levels over ten times greater than in earlier years. Why did this happen? How did a deposit insurance system that seemed to be working well before the 1980s find itself in so much trouble during the 1980s?

Early Stages of the Crisis

The story starts with the burst of financial innovation in the 1970s and early 1980s (more on this in Chapter 13) which produced new financial instruments and markets that widened the scope for risk taking. New markets in financial futures, junk bonds, swaps, and so on, made it easier for banks to take on extra risk—making the moral hazard and adverse selection problems more severe. New legislation that deregulated the banking industry in 1980 and 1982 opened up even more avenues to savings and loans and mutual savings banks to take on more risk. These thrift institutions, which had been restricted almost entirely to making loans for home mortgages, now were allowed to have up to 40% of their assets in commercial real estate loans, up to 30% in consumer lending, and up to 10% in commercial loans and leases. In the wake of this legislation, savings and loans regulators allowed up to 10% of assets to be in junk bonds or in direct investments (common stocks, real estate, service corporations, and operating subsidiaries).

In addition, the 1980 legislation increased the mandated amount of federal deposit insurance from $40,000 per account to $100,000 and phased out Regulation Q deposit rate ceilings. Banks and S&Ls that wanted to pursue rapid growth and take on risky projects could now attract the necessary funds by issuing larger-denomination, insured certificates of deposits with interest rates much higher than those being offered by their competitors. Without deposit insurance, high interest rates would not have induced depositors to provide the high-rolling banks with funds because of the realistic expectation that they might not get the funds back. But, with deposit insurance, the government was guaranteeing that the deposits were safe, so depositors were more than happy to make deposits in banks with the highest interest rates.

A financial innovation that made it even easier for high-rolling banks to raise funds is called **brokered deposits,** which enable depositors to circumvent the $100,000 limit on deposit insurance. Brokered deposits work as follows: A large depositor with $10 million goes to a broker who breaks the $10 million into 100 packages of $100,000 each and then buys $100,000 CDs at 100 different banks. Since the amount of each CD is within the $100,000 limit for deposits at each bank, the large depositor has, in effect, obtained deposit insurance on all of his $10 million. The federal deposit insurance agencies did pass a regulation to ban brokered deposits in 1984, but a legal judgment in a federal court overturned the ban.

Financial innovation and deregulation in the permissive atmosphere of the Reagan years made the moral hazard problem more severe. In addition, the incentives for moral hazard were increased dramatically by a historical accident: the combination of the sharp increases in interest rates from late 1979 until 1981 and the severe recession in 1981–1982, both of which were engineered by the Federal Reserve to bring down inflation. The sharp rises in interest rates produced rapidly rising costs of funds for the savings and loans that were not matched by higher earnings on the S&Ls' principal asset, long-term residential mortgages (whose rates had been fixed at a time when interest rates were far lower). Then, the 1981–1982 recession and the collapse in the prices of energy and farm products hit the economies of certain parts of the country such as Texas very hard. As a result, there were defaults on many S&Ls' loans. Losses for savings and loan institutions mounted to $10 billion in 1981–1982, and by some estimates over half of the S&Ls in the United States had a negative net worth and were thus insolvent by the end of 1982.

Later Stages of the Crisis: Regulatory Forbearance

At this stage a logical step might have been for the savings and loans regulators (Federal Home Loan Bank Board and its deposit insurance subsidiary, the Federal Savings and Loan Insurance Fund [FSLIC], both now abolished) to close the insolvent S&Ls. Instead, these regulators pursued what is called **regulatory forbearance;** that is, they refrained from engaging in the regulatory right to put the insolvent S&Ls out of business. To sidestep their responsibility to close ailing S&Ls, they adopted irregular regulatory accounting principles that in effect substantially lowered capital requirements. For example, they allowed S&Ls to include in their capital calculations a high value for intangible capital, called "goodwill."

There were three main reasons why the Federal Home Loan Bank Board and FSLIC engaged in regulatory forbearance. First, the FSLIC did not have sufficient funds in its insurance fund to close the insolvent S&Ls and pay off their deposits. Second, the Federal Home Loan Bank Board was established to encourage the growth of the savings and loan industry and so the regulators were probably too close to those they were supposed to regulate. Third, since regulators do not like to admit that their agency is in trouble, the Federal Home Loan Bank Board and the FSLIC preferred to sweep their problems under the rug and hoped they would go away.

Regulatory forbearance increases moral hazard dramatically because an operating but insolvent S&L (nicknamed a "zombie S&L" by Edward Kane of Ohio State University because it is the "living dead") has almost nothing to lose by taking on great risk and "betting the bank": If it gets lucky and its risky investments pay off, then it gets out of insolvency. Unfortunately, if, as is likely, the risky investments don't pay off, the zombie S&L's losses will mount and the deposit insurance agency will be left holding the bag.

This strategy is similar to the "long-bomb" strategy in football. When a football team is almost hopelessly behind and time is running out, it often resorts to a high-risk play: the throwing of a long pass to try to score a touchdown. Of course, the long bomb is unlikely to be successful, but there is always a small chance that it will work. If it doesn't, the team has lost nothing since it would have lost the game anyway.

Given the sequence of events we have discussed here, it should be no surprise that savings and loans began to take huge risks: They built shopping centers in the desert, bought manufacturing plants to convert manure to methane, and purchased billions of dollars of high-risk, high-yield junk bonds. The savings and loan industry was no longer the staid industry that once operated on the so-called 3-6-3 Rule: You took in money at 3%, lent it at 6%, and played golf at 3 P.M. Although many savings and loans were making money, losses at other S&Ls were colossal.

Another outcome of regulatory forbearance was that with little to lose, zombie S&Ls attracted deposits away from healthy S&Ls by offering higher interest rates. Because there were so many zombie S&Ls in Texas pursuing this strategy, above-market interest rates on deposits at Texas S&Ls were said to have a "Texas premium." Potentially healthy S&Ls now found that to compete for deposits they had to pay higher interest rates, which made their operations less profitable and frequently pushed them into the zombie category. Similarly, zombie S&Ls in pursuit of asset growth made loans at below-market interest rates, thus lowering loan interest rates for healthy S&Ls and again made them less profitable. The zombie S&Ls had actually taken on attributes of vampires—their willingness to pay above-market rates for deposits and take below-market interest rates on loans was sucking the life-blood (profits) out of healthy S&Ls.

THE SAVINGS AND LOAN BAILOUT: THE FINANCIAL INSTITUTIONS REFORM, RECOVERY, AND ENFORCEMENT ACT (FIRREA) OF 1989

Toward the end of 1986, the growing losses in the savings and loan industry were bankrupting the insurance fund of the FSLIC. The Reagan administration sought $15 billion in funds for FSLIC, an amount that was completely inadequate since the funds needed to close down insolvent S&Ls were many times this amount. The legislation passed by Congress, the Competitive Equality Banking Act of 1987, did not even meet the administration's requests. It only provided $10.8 billion of funds to the FSLIC and, what was worse, included provisions that directed the Federal Home Loan Bank Board to continue to pursue regulatory forbearance (allow insolvent institutions to keep operating), particularly in economically depressed areas such as Texas.

The failure of Congress to deal with the savings and loan crisis was not going to make the problem go away and, consistent with our analysis, the situation deteriorated rapidly. Losses in the savings and loan industry climbed to over $10 billion in 1988 and reached almost $20 billion in 1989. The crisis was reaching epidemic proportions.

Immediately after taking office, the Bush administration proposed new legislation to provide adequate funding to close down the insolvent S&Ls. The resulting legislation, the Financial Institutions Reform, Recovery, and Enforcement Act (FIRREA) was signed into law on August 9, 1989. It was the most significant legislation to affect the thrift industry since the 1930s. FIRREA's major provisions are as follows: The regulatory apparatus was significantly restructured with the Federal Home Loan Bank Board and FSLIC, both of which failed in their regulatory tasks, being abolished. The regulatory role of the Federal Home Loan Bank Board was relegated to the Office of Thrift Supervision (OTS), a bureau within the U.S. Treasury Department, and its responsibilities are similar to those the Office of the Comptroller of the Currency has over the national banks. The regulatory responsibilities of the FSLIC were given to the FDIC and the FDIC became the sole administrator of the federal deposit insurance system with two separate insurance funds: the Bank Insurance Fund (BIF) and the Savings Association Insurance Fund (SAIF). Another new agency, the Resolution Trust Corporation (RTC), was established to manage and resolve insolvent thrifts placed in conservatorship or receivership. It was made responsible for selling more than $300 billion of real estate owned by failed institutions. The RTC is managed by the FDIC and is under the general supervision of the RTC Oversight Board (composed of the secretary of the Treasury, the chairman of the board of governors of the Federal Reserve, the secretary of Housing and Urban Development, and two other members).

Initially, the total cost of the bailout was estimated to be $159 billion over the ten-year period through 1999, but more recent estimates indicate that the cost will be far higher. Indeed, the General Accounting Office placed a cost for the bailout at over $500 billion over forty years. However, as pointed out in Box 4.1 in Chapter 4, this estimate is misleading because, for example, the value of a payment thirty years from now is worth much less in today's dollars. The present value of the bailout cost is on the order of $150 billion, with estimates ranging from $100 to $200 billion. The funding for the bailout comes partially from capital in the Federal Home Loan Banks (owned by the S&L industry) but mostly from the sale of government debt by both the Treasury and the Resolution Funding Corporation (RefCorp).

To replenish the reserves of the Savings Association Insurance Fund, insurance premiums for S&Ls were increased from 20.8 cents per $100 of deposits to 23 cents and can rise as high as 32.5 cents. Premiums for banks immediately rose from 8.3 cents to 15 cents per $100 of deposits, and were raised further to 23 cents in 1991.

FIRREA also imposed new restrictions on thrift activities that in essence re-regulated the S&L industry to the asset choices it had before 1982. S&Ls can no longer purchase junk bonds and must sell their holdings by 1994. Commercial real estate loans are restricted to four times capital rather than the previous limit of 40% of assets, and so this new restriction is a reduction for all institutions whose capital is less than 10% of assets. S&Ls must also hold at least 70%—up from 60%—of their assets in investments that are primarily housing related. Troubled thrifts are not allowed to accept brokered deposits. Among the most important provisions of FIRREA was the increase in the core capital requirement from 3 to 8% and the eventual adherence to the same risk-based capital standards imposed on commercial banks.

FIRREA also enhanced the enforcement powers of thrift regulators by making it easier for them to remove managers, issue cease and desist orders, and impose civil penalties. The Justice Department was also given $75 million per year for three years to uncover and prosecute fraud in the banking industry, and maximum fines rose substantially.

FIRREA was a serious attempt to deal with some of the problems created by the banking crisis since it provided substantial funds to close insolvent thrifts. It did little, however, to deal with the underlying adverse selection and moral hazard problems created by deposit insurance. Thus many economists fear that the crisis in banking we have been experiencing will continue in the future. All is not yet lost, though, because FIRREA mandated that the U.S. Treasury produce a comprehensive study and plan for reform of the federal deposit insurance system (discussed in the application at the end of this chapter) that may induce further reforms.

We will consider how the banking regulatory system might be reformed; but before we do, let us look at an economic analysis of the politics (referred to as the political economy) of the savings and loan mess. Such an analysis might influence what reforms you and I think are necessary for the banking regulatory system.

POLITICAL ECONOMY OF THE SAVINGS AND LOAN CRISIS

Although we now have a grasp of the regulatory and economic forces that created the S&L crisis, we still need to understand the political forces that produced the regulatory structure and activities that led to this crisis. The key to understanding the political economy of the S&L is to recognize that the relationship between voters-taxpayers and the regulators and politicians creates a particular type of moral hazard problem, the **principal-agent problem.** The principal-agent problem occurs when the agent has different incentives than the person he works for (the principal) and so the agent acts in his own interest rather than in the interest of his employer. Regulators and politicians are ultimately agents for voters-taxpayers (principals) because in the final analysis taxpayers bear the cost of any losses by the deposit insurance agency. The principal-agent problem occurs because the agent (a politician or regulator) does not have the same incentives to minimize costs to the economy as the principal (the taxpayer).

In order to act in the taxpayer's interest and lower costs to the deposit insurance agency, we have seen that regulators have several tasks. They must set tight restrictions on holding assets that are too risky, must impose high capital requirements, and must not engage in regulatory forbearance, which allows insolvent institutions to continue to operate. However, because of the principal-agent problem, regulators have incentives to do the opposite. Indeed, as our sad saga of the S&L debacle indicates, they have often loosened capital requirements and restrictions on risky asset holdings and pursued regulatory forbearance. One important incentive for regulators that explains this phenomenon is their desire to escape blame for poor performance by their agency. By loosening capital requirements and pursuing regulatory forbearance, regulators sweep the problem of an insolvent bank under the rug and hope that the situation will improve in the future. Such behavior on the part of regulators is described by Edward Kane of Ohio State University as "bureaucratic gambling."

Another important incentive for regulators is for them to protect their careers by acceding to pressures from the people who most influence their careers. These people are not the taxpayers but the politicians who try to keep regulators from imposing tough regulations on institutions that are major campaign contributors. Members of Congress have often lobbied regulators to ease up on a particular S&L that contributed large sums to their campaigns (see Box 11.2).

In addition, both Congress and the presidential administration promoted banking legislation in 1980 and 1982 that made it easier for savings and loans to engage in risk-taking activities. After the legislation passed, the need for monitoring the S&L industry increased because of the expansion of permissible activities. The S&L regulatory agencies needed more resources to carry out their monitoring activities properly, but Congress was unwilling to allocate the necessary funds because of lobbying by the S&L industry. As a result the S&L regulatory agencies became so short on personnel that they actually had to cut back on their on-site examinations when they were most needed. In the period from January 1984 until July 1986, for example, several hundred S&Ls were not even examined once. Even worse, spurred on by the intense lobbying efforts of the S&L industry, Congress refused to comply with the Reagan administration's request for $15 billion in funds for

B o x   1 1 . 2

A Case Study of What Went Wrong: Charles Keating and the Lincoln Savings & Loan Scandal

The scandal associated with Charles H. Keating, Jr. and the Lincoln Savings & Loan provides a graphic example of why the savings and loan crisis occurred. As Edwin Gray, a former chairman of the Federal Home Loan Bank Board, has stated, "This is a story of incredible corruption. I can't call it anything else."*

Charles Keating was allowed to acquire Lincoln Savings & Loan of Irvine, California, in early 1984, even though he had been accused of fraud by the SEC only four and a half years earlier. For Keating, whose construction firm, American Continental, planned to build huge real estate developments in Arizona, the S&L was a gold mine: With the lax regulatory atmosphere at the time, controlling the S&L gave his firm easy access to funds without having to be scrutinized by outside bankers. Within days of acquiring control, Keating got rid of Lincoln's conservative lending officers and internal auditors, even though he had promised regulators he would keep them. Once this was done, Lincoln plunged into high-risk investments such as currency futures, junk bonds, common stock, hotels, and vast tracts of desert land in Arizona.

Because of the shortage of savings and loan examiners that existed at the time, Lincoln was able to escape a serious examination until 1986, whereupon examiners from the Federal Home Loan Bank of San Francisco discovered that Lincoln had exceeded the 10% limit on equity investments by $600 million. Because of these activities and some evidence that Lincoln was deliberately trying to mislead the examiners, the examiners recommended federal seizure of the bank and all its assets. Keating was not about to take this lying down; he engaged hordes of lawyers—eventually seventy-seven law firms— and accused the bank examiners of bias. He also sued unsuccessfully to overturn the 10% equity limit. Keating is said to

have bragged that he spent $50 million fighting regulators.

Lawyers were not Keating's only tactic for keeping regulators off his back. After receiving $1.3 million of contributions to their campaigns from Keating, five senators—Dennis DeConcini and John McCain of Arizona, Alan Cranston of California, John Glenn of Ohio, and Donald Riegle of Michigan (now nicknamed the "Keating Five")—met with Edwin Gray, the chairman of the Federal Home Loan Board and later with four top regulators from San Francisco in April 1987. They complained that the regulators were being too tough on Lincoln and they urged the regulators to quit dragging out the investigation. After Edwin Gray was replaced by M. Danny Wall, Wall took the unprecedented step of removing the San Francisco examiners from the case in September 1987 and transferred the investigation to the bank board's headquarters in Washington. No examiners called on Lincoln for the next ten months, and as one of the San Francisco examiners described it, Lincoln dropped into a "regulatory black hole."

Lincoln Savings & Loan finally failed in early 1989, with estimated costs to taxpayers of $2.5 billion—possibly making it the most costly S&L failure to date. Charles Keating was indicted for abuses (such as having Lincoln pay him and his family $34 million), while M. Danny Wall was forced to resign as head of the Office of Thrift Supervision because of his involvement with the Keating scandal. As a result of their activities on behalf of Keating, the "Keating Five" senators were subjected to a congressional ethics investigation.

---

*Quoted in Tom Morganthau, Rich Thomas, and Eleanor Clift, "The S&L Scandal's Biggest Blowout," *Newsweek* (November 6, 1989), p. 35.

the FSLIC (a totally inadequate amount) so that it could close down insolvent S&Ls. Instead, Congress passed the Competitive Banking Equality Act of 1987 which provided only $10.8 billion. Congress also hampered the S&L regulators from doing their job properly by including provisions in the banking bill to encourage regulatory forbearance.

As these examples indicate, the structure of our political system has created a serious principal-agent problem; that is, politicians have strong incentives to act in their own interests rather than in the interests of taxpayers. Because of the high cost of running campaigns, American politicians have become dependent on raising substantial contributions. This situation may provide lobbyists and other campaign contributors with the opportunity to influence politicians to act against the public interest.

The unscrupulous behavior of some of our politicians has been highlighted by the savings and loan scandal. Jim Wright, a representative from Texas and the speaker of the House who delayed the banking legislation in 1987, was forced to resign in 1989, in part, because of allegations about his relationship with S&Ls. Congressman Tony Coelho of California, the House majority whip, resigned once it became known that Columbia Savings and Loan of Beverly Hills, California, supplied him with a loan to buy $100,000 of junk bonds. Senator Fernand St. Germain, one of the authors of the 1982 legislation that relaxed regulatory restrictions on the S&Ls, lost his bid for reelection after his constituents found out that he was using a credit card of the U.S. League of Savings Institutions for personal entertainment.

Although politicians have emphasized the amount of fraud involved in failed S&Ls so they won't be held responsible for the high costs of the savings and loan bailout, they all bear the ultimate responsibility for the high cost of the bailout. Some analysts estimate that if the Congress and the president had been willing to deal with the savings and loan crisis five years earlier, the cost to taxpayers would have been as much as $100 billion less. The savings and loan crisis illustrates the dangers of legislators depending heavily on campaign contributions from special interests. A parody of a famous line by Winston Churchill sums it all up: "Never has so much money gone to such key legislators who worked so hard for measures that cost taxpayers so dearly."[2]

HOW SHOULD THE BANKING REGULATORY SYSTEM BE REFORMED?

The central issue in preventing another savings and loan debacle is the reform of the banking regulatory system so that it reduces the adverse selection and moral hazard problems created by deposit insurance. Next we look

---

[2]Quoted in Steven Waldman and Rich Thomas, "How Did It Happen?" *Newsweek* (May 21, 1990), p. 28.

at nine proposed reforms and evaluate whether they are feasible and would improve the performance of the banking system.

Proposed Changes in the Deposit Insurance System

Eliminate Deposit Insurance Entirely   A simple solution to the adverse selection and moral hazard problems of deposit insurance would be to eliminate the insurance entirely. Then depositors would have the incentive to monitor banks and withdraw deposits when they thought a bank was taking on too much risk. Although elimination of deposit insurance removes many of the incentives for banks to engage in excessive risk taking, it creates another set of problems.

The basic problem with abolishing deposit insurance is that banks would be subject to runs, that is, to sudden withdrawals by nervous depositors. Such runs could by themselves lead to bank failures. Besides protecting individual depositors, the purpose of deposit insurance is to prevent a large number of bank failures, which would lead to an unstable banking system and an unstable economy as occurred periodically before the establishment of federal deposit insurance in 1934. From this perspective, federal deposit insurance has been a resounding success. Bank panics, in which there are simultaneous failures of many banks and consequent disruption of the financial system, have not occurred since federal deposit insurance was established.

The ability of deposit insurance to prevent bank panics makes many economists uncomfortable with the idea of abolishing it entirely. But perhaps, more importantly, deposit insurance is extremely popular with the American public. Americans remember or have heard about the hardships associated with bank panics before the establishment of federal deposit insurance and few would want to return to those days. Abolishing deposit insurance entirely does not seem to be a feasible political strategy.

Lower Limits on the Amount of Deposit Insurance   Other reform proposals suggest reducing the amount of deposit insurance below the current $100,000 limit, say to $50,000 or $20,000. With a smaller amount of deposit insurance, depositors with an amount in excess of the insurance limit would have the incentive to monitor the amount of risk a bank takes on. However, depositors with less than $100,000 in deposits are usually not the best equipped to effectively monitor a bank's activities. Because they are not necessarily well informed, these depositors are more likely to get nervous and cause a run on the bank. The outcome could be a less stable banking system.

On the other hand, depositors with extremely large amounts to deposit, say in the millions of dollars, should be sufficiently sophisticated to effectively monitor a bank's activities. To encourage them to monitor banks, another reform that has received wider support is to outlaw brokered deposits.

(Recall that such deposits allow depositors to get around the $100,000 deposit insurance.) One problem with this proposed reform is that enforcement might be difficult, because it would be hard to determine if a depositor has insured accounts at more than one bank.

Eliminate the Too-Big-To-Fail Policy If the FDIC allowed big banks to fail with the result that depositors would suffer losses when a big bank failed, then depositors at big banks would have greater incentives to monitor the banks and withdraw deposits when they felt the bank was taking on too much risk. So allowing big banks to fail would decrease their incentives to take on too much risk. It would also, however, create some of the same problems that would occur if deposit insurance were eliminated or limited in amount: The probability of bank panics would increase. If a big bank were allowed to fail, the repercussions in the financial system might be immense. Other banks with a correspondent relationship with the failed bank (that is, those that have deposits at the bank in exchange for a variety of services) would suffer large losses and might fail in turn, leading to a full-scale panic. In addition, the problem of liquidating the big bank's loan portfolio might create a major disruption in the financial market. Because of these fears, regulators have been unwilling to abandon the too-big-to-fail policy, even though they are aware of its unfairness and its costs, as the quote from William Seidman at the end of Box 11.1 indicates.

Institute Coinsurance Another proposed reform would institute a system of **coinsurance** in which only a percentage of a deposit, say 90%, would be covered by insurance. In this system, the insured depositor would suffer a percentage of the losses along with the deposit insurance agency. Because depositors would suffer losses if the bank goes broke, they will have an incentive to monitor the bank's activities. However, we again face the problem that most depositors are not well informed, so banks will be subject to runs and the banking system will be less stable.

Allow Deposit Insurance Only at "Narrow Banks" Another proposal suggests that deposit insurance only be allowed on deposits at "narrow banks"— those that restrict their assets to those that are virtually free of risk such as Treasury bills. The fact that insured depositors would not monitor these narrow banks would create almost no moral hazard since the assets of the narrow banks bear almost no risk anyway. Although this proposal would eliminate the adverse selection and moral hazard problems from deposit insurance, it would leave deposits at "wider banks," the ones that will make loans, uninsured. These wider banks would be subject to bank runs by nervous depositors and a less stable banking system might be the result.

Provide Deposit Insurance by Private Insurers Other proposals suggest that deposit insurance might be provided by private insurers, or that private insurance might be provided for deposit amounts that exceed the limits for federal deposit insurance. The advantage of private insurance is that the private insurer would have the incentive to carefully monitor the bank whose deposits it is insuring. The problem with this type of insurance is that private insurers can fail, leading to bank panics like the ones we have seen in Ohio, Maryland, and Rhode Island in recent years (see Box 16.2). Thus there still might be a need for a federal agency to guarantee that the private insurer won't fail. Without such a guarantee, fears about the health of the private insurer might lead depositors to withdraw their deposits and precipitate bank runs. Private insurance by itself would not prevent an unstable banking system.

Base Deposit Insurance Premiums on Risk   Some economists, as well as a former head of the FDIC, have suggested that deposit insurance be priced like automobile insurance: Accident-prone drivers pay higher insurance rates and so banks with riskier assets would be charged higher insurance premiums. Banks would have less incentive to take on higher risk because they would then have to pay higher deposit insurance premiums. Although some form of risk-based premiums makes sense, it might be hard for the deposit insurance agency to determine when a bank's loans are risky. The risk may not be apparent until it is too late and the bank is insolvent. Thus risk-based insurance premiums could not eliminate moral hazard entirely; other regulations to control risk taking would still be necessary.

Proposed Changes in Other Banking Regulations

Eliminate Branching Restrictions   Restrictions on branching, particularly interstate branching, have also contributed to the deposit insurance crisis. Because of these regulations, banks remain tied to economic conditions in their local area and are less able to diversify their loans. It is no coincidence that a higher proportion of bank failures has occurred in economically depressed states where farming and oil production are primary industries (such as Texas, Louisiana, Colorado, and Kansas). Although branching across state lines is becoming more common, a faster movement to a national banking system by eliminating branching restrictions altogether would decrease bank failures by promoting increased diversification.

Use Market-Value Accounting for Capital Requirements   We have seen that the requirement that a bank have high equity capital makes the bank less likely to fail. The requirement is also advantageous because the bank with high equity capital has more to lose if it takes on risky investments and so will have less incentive to hold risky assets. Unfortunately, minimum capital requirements, including new risk-based measures, are calculated on a historical-cost (book-value) basis in which the value of an asset is set at its initial purchase price. The problem with historical-cost accounting is that changes in the value of assets and liabilities because of changes in interest rates or default risk are not reflected in the calculation of the firm's equity capital. Yet changes in the market value of assets and liabilities and hence changes in market value of equity capital are what indicate if a firm is really insolvent. Furthermore, it is the market value of capital that determines the incentives for a bank to hold risky assets.

The deposit insurance reform that receives the widest support from economists is the use of market-value accounting to calculate capital requirements. All assets and liabilities could be marked to market values periodically, say every three months, to determine if a bank has sufficient market value of its capital to meet the minimum requirements. This market-value accounting information would let the deposit insurance agency know quickly when a bank was falling below its capital requirement. The bank could then be closed down before its net worth fell below zero, thus preventing a loss to the deposit insurance agency. The market-value-based capital requirement would also ensure that banks would not be operating with negative capital, thereby preventing the bet-the-bank strategy of taking on excessive risk.

Using market values to calculate equity capital would also have the advantage of making a bank insolvency more transparent. As we saw from our discussion of the political economy of the savings and loan fiasco, regulators and politicians are subject to a principal-agent problem because they often have incentives to hide insolvencies, even though taxpayers would be better off if they didn't. Market-value accounting would make hiding insolvencies more difficult, and so it would help taxpayers monitor regulators and politicians, who would have a harder time arguing for regulatory forbearance. Market-value accounting could therefore make regulators and politicians more accountable and give them better incentives to act in the interests of taxpayers.

Objections to market-value-based capital requirements center on the difficulty of making market-value estimates of capital that are accurate and straightforward to calculate. Historical-cost accounting has an important advantage in that accounting rules are easier to define and standardize when the value of an asset is just set at its purchase price. Market-value accounting, on the other hand, requires estimates and approximations that are harder to standardize. For example, it might be hard to assess the market value of your friend Joe's car loan, while it would be quite easy to value a government bond. In addition, conducting market-value accounting would prove costly to banks because estimation of market values requires the collection of more information about the characteristics of assets and liabilities.

Nevertheless, proponents of market-value accounting for capital requirements point out that although market-value accounting involves some estimates and approximations, it would still enable regulators to have a more accurate assessment of bank equity capital than does historical-cost accounting. They also point out that although opponents of market-value accounting claim that it would be too costly to collect the necessary information, market participants routinely evaluate the market value of bank assets when they purchase bank equity or debt. Furthermore, many banks already calculate market values of their assets in order to make business decisions. Some movement toward market-value accounting appears to be entirely feasible and could help decrease the likelihood of a future crisis in banking.

APPLICATION
EVALUATING THE TREASURY PLAN FOR REFORMING / / / / / / / / / / / / /
THE BANKING SYSTEM

In February 1991, the U.S. Treasury released its long-awaited plan for reform of the banking regulatory system (as required by the Financial Institutions Reform, Recovery, and Enforcement Act of 1989). The basic thrust of the plan is to limit deposit insurance coverage and strengthen the banks by giving them sweeping new powers to engage in a broad range of financial services activities. Based on the analysis in this chapter, we will now evaluate the most important provisions of the Treasury plan and ask whether it can cure the current crisis in banking.

Study Guide

First read the description of each set of provisions in the Treasury plan. Then, before you read the evaluation section, try to reason out how well the provisions will solve the current problems with banking regulation. This exercise will help you develop a deeper understanding of the material in this chapter.

Limits on Deposit Insurance

The Treasury plan would limit depositors to $200,000 of insurance per banking institution: $100,000 for a checking or savings account and $100,000 for a retirement account. Brokered deposits would no longer be covered by insurance and the FDIC would study whether further limits on deposit insurance would be feasible.

Evaluation   The first problem with the Treasury's proposed limits on deposit insurance is that they are easily circumvented; that is, depositors can open accounts in different banks. Thus these limits may not be very effective in shrinking the potential losses to the FDIC when there are bank failures and will not greatly increase the incentives of depositors to monitor the banks. Furthermore, as long as the FDIC continues to pursue a too-big-to-fail policy, deposit insurance limits at big banks will in effect be meaningless: Depositors know that no matter how large their accounts are at these banks, they will not be subject to any losses.

Nationwide Banking

The Treasury plan proposes the elimination of restrictions on nationwide banking. Full nationwide banking would be authorized for bank holding companies within three years. Banks would be permitted to open branches in other states, unless there are within-state restrictions disallowing branches. Many analysts consider this part of the Treasury plan most likely to be adopted soon.

Evaluation Nationwide branching would immediately produce cost savings for regional bank holding companies which could now consolidate banks in different states into a more efficient banking organization. Branching thus would likely increase bank profitability and improve the health of the banking industry. Treasury Secretary Brady has gone on record that nationwide branching could lead to increased efficiency that would save banks as much as $10 billion per year within five years—what he calls a "mind-boggling" figure.

Another advantage of nationwide branching is that it would enable banks to substantially increase diversification of their loan portfolios, since they would no longer be restricted to making loans in a narrow geographical area. Because a bank with increased diversification is less likely to fail, nationwide banking would eventually produce a banking system that is less prone to bank failures. In the short run, however, small banks might be hurt by the incursions into their local markets by large national banks. This could reduce some local banks' profitability and cause them to fail.

Securities, Mutual Fund, and Insurance Affiliates

Well-capitalized banks would be allowed to have securities, mutual fund, and insurance affiliates under a new financial-services holding company structure. These holding companies could be owned by commercial or financial corporations. In effect, the Treasury plan would allow banks to fully engage in the securities and insurance businesses. The plan also proposes separate capitalization of securities, mutual fund, and insurance affiliates and strict regulation of the financial-services holding company to prevent it from exposing the affiliated insured bank to greater risk.

Evaluation The advantage of allowing banks to enter the securities and insurance businesses is that it opens up potentially profitable activities to banks which could make them healthier. On the other hand, widening banks' activities to these areas might enable banks to take on greater risk. Indeed, widening the scope of activities was exactly what was done for the S&Ls in the banking legislation of 1980 and 1982, and the resulting increased risk taking was a major factor in the huge losses to the taxpayer that occurred thereafter. Allowing commercial corporations or securities firms to own financial-services holding companies, which in turn own banks, might lead to conflicts of interest in which banks provide loans to the owner-corporation which are too risky. Although, the Treasury plan does have provisions to prevent conflicts of interest, some analysts doubt whether the provisions would be sufficiently effective.

Bank Capital Provisions

The Treasury proposes that banking regulation be tied more directly to the amount of bank capital. Banks would be placed in five categories depending on the amount of their bank capital. The smaller the amount of bank capital, the stiffer regulation would be. Poorly capitalized banks would be formally required to cut dividends or sell assets at an earlier stage, thus making the costs of failure lower for the FDIC. Only well-capitalized banks would be allowed to become part of the financial-services holding companies. Well-capitalized banks would also have lower deposit insurance premiums than those that are poorly capitalized.

Evaluation The bank capital provisions of the Treasury plan are all directed at encouraging banks to hold more capital. Increased bank capital reduces moral hazard incentives for the bank because the bank now has more to lose if it fails and so is less likely to take on too much risk. In addition, encouraging banks to hold more capital reduces potential losses for the FDIC, because increased bank capital is a cushion that makes bank failure less likely. Tieing the size of deposit insurance premiums to the amount of bank capital is just a form of risk-based deposit insurance in which the safer banks have a lower cost of insurance.

Regulatory Consolidation

Commercial banks and savings and loans are currently regulated by four agencies with overlapping jurisdictions: the FDIC, the Federal Reserve, the Office of the Comptroller of the Currency, and the Office of Thrift Supervision. The Treasury plan proposes that the number of regulators be reduced to two: (1) a new regulatory agency, the Federal Banking Agency, which would regulate all nationally chartered banks and savings associations and (2) the Federal Reserve, which would regulate state-chartered banks. With this structure each banking institution would only be regulated by one regulator rather than several as is currently the case. The FDIC would no longer be in the business of regulation; it would act solely as an insurer, concentrating on dealing with insolvent institutions.

Evaluation   Regulatory consolidation in which each banking institution has only one regulator rather than many (the current system) eliminates duplication of effort, decreases confusion and uncertainty for banks about how they will be regulated, and keeps banks from playing one regulator off against the other, thereby reducing regulation. Some critics of the Treasury plan suggest that it doesn't go far enough because regulatory efficiency would be increased if there were only one regulator rather than two.

One problematic feature of the Treasury plan is that it takes the FDIC out of the regulation business. Because the FDIC most directly bears the cost of bank failures, it, among all the regulatory agencies, might be least subject to the principal-agent problem and have the greatest incentive to keep insured banks from taking on too much risk. Thus, taking regulation of banks away from the FDIC might lead to less rigorous regulation and more "bureaucratic gambling," which in turn might lead to more expensive bank bailouts in the future.

Overall Evaluation of the Plan

Although the Treasury plan includes provisions to decrease risk taking on the part of banks, many critics feel that it still leaves banks with far too great an incentive to engage in the moral hazard of risk taking. The limits on deposit insurance are unlikely to be effective at reducing risk-taking behavior by banks as long as the Treasury plan contains an important omission: It does not change the too-big-to-fail policy. Since a big bank knows that its depositors will not withdraw deposits when it engages in risky activities because the too-big-to-fail policy prevents depositors from suffering any losses, the bank has strong incentives to take on too much risk. Although the Treasury plan does create additional incentives for banks to increase their capital, the resulting increase in capital might not be enough to prevent large losses to the FDIC. This is especially true since the plan does not push for stringent market-value accounting procedures that would enable regulators to have a more accurate assessment of bank capital.

The failure of the Treasury plan to reform deposit insurance so that adverse selection and moral hazard problems are substantially reduced makes the other major features of the plan highly problematic. Without reforming deposit insurance so that risk-taking incentives are substantially reduced, allowing banks to engage in new lines of business such as securities underwriting and insurance might increase bank risk and be a prescription for disaster. The chairman of the House Banking Committee, Henry B. Gonzalez, has eloquently stated his objections to the Treasury plan along exactly these lines: "This is the same 'cart before the horse' mentality which plagued the deregulation of the savings and loan industry in the early 1980s. Let's set the speed limits and train the policemen before we open a new super-expressway for financial institutions."[3]

---

[3]Quoted in "Administration Presents Plan for Sweeping Overhaul of Banking System," *New York Times* (February 6, 1991), p. D6.

SUMMARY

1. Deposit insurance suffers from two serious problems: (1) adverse selection, in which risk-prone entrepreneurs or outright criminals are particularly anxious to control banks with insured deposits and (2) moral hazard, in which banks have incentives to take on too much risk.

2. Because of deregulation and a set of historical accidents, adverse selection and moral hazard problems increased in the 1980s and resulted in huge losses for the savings and loan industry and necessary bailout legislation in 1989.

3. The Financial Institutions Reform, Recovery, and Enforcement Act (FIRREA) of 1989 provided funds for the S&L bailout, created the Resolution Trust Corporation to manage the resolution of insolvent thrifts, eliminated the Federal Home Loan Bank Board and gave its regulatory role to the Office of Thrift Supervision, eliminated the FSLIC whose insurance role and regulatory responsibilities were taken over by the FDIC, imposed restrictions on thrift activities similar to those in effect before 1982, increased the capital requirements to those adhered to by commercial banks, and increased the enforcement powers of thrift regulators.

4. Regulators and politicians are subject to the principal-agent problem by which they may not have sufficient incentives to minimize the costs of deposit insurance to taxpayers. As a result, regulators and politicians relaxed capital standards, removed restrictions on holdings of risky assets, and engaged in regulatory forbearance, thereby increasing the costs of the S&L bailout.

5. Proposals for reforming the banking regulatory system include elimination of deposit insurance, lower limits on the amount of deposit insurance, elimination of the too-big-to-fail policy, coinsurance, "narrow bank" deposit insurance, private insurance, risk-based deposit insurance, elimination of branching restrictions, and market-value accounting for capital requirements.

KEY TERMS

moral hazard

adverse selection

brokered deposits

regulatory forbearance

principal-agent problem

coinsurance

QUESTIONS AND PROBLEMS

1. Give one example each of moral hazard and adverse selection in private insurance arrangements.

* 2. If casualty insurance companies provided fire insurance without any restrictions, what kind of adverse selection and moral hazard problems

might result?

3. What bank regulation is designed to reduce adverse selection problems for deposit insurance? Will it always work?

* 4. What bank regulations are designed to reduce moral hazard problems created by deposit insurance? Will they completely eliminate the moral hazard problem?

5. What are the costs and benefits of a too-big-to-fail policy?

* 6. Why did the S&L crisis not occur until the 1980s?

7. Why is regulatory forbearance a dangerous strategy for a deposit insurance agency?

* 8. The FIRREA legislation of 1989 is the most comprehensive banking legislation since the 1930s. Describe the major features of this legislation.

9. Will the FIRREA legislation of 1989 solve the current crisis in banking? Why or why not?

*10. Some advocates of campaign reform believe that government funding of political campaigns and restrictions on campaign spending might reduce the principal-agent problem in our political system. Do you agree? Explain.

11. How can the S&L crisis be blamed on the principal-agent problem?

*12. Do you think that eliminating or limiting the amount of deposit insurance would be a good idea? Explain.

13. Do you think that removing the impediments to a national banking system will be beneficial to the economy? Explain.

*14. How could higher deposit insurance premiums for banks with riskier assets benefit the economy?

15. How could market-value accounting for bank capital requirements benefit the economy? How difficult would it be to implement?

CHAPTER 12

Nonbank Financial Institutions

PREVIEW   Although banks may be the financial institution we deal with most often, they are not the only financial institutions we come in contact with. Suppose you purchase insurance from an insurance company, take out an installment loan on your new car from a finance company, or buy a share of common stock with the help of a broker. In each of these transactions you are dealing with a nonbank financial institution. In our economy, nonbank financial institutions play as important a role in channeling funds from lenders-savers to borrowers-spenders as do banks. Furthermore, the process of financial innovation has increased the importance of nonbank financial institutions. Through innovation, nonbank financial institutions now compete more directly with banks by providing banking-like services to their customers. This chapter examines in more detail how the major nonbank financial institutions operate and how they are regulated.

INSURANCE COMPANIES

Every day we face the possibility of the occurrence of certain catastrophic events that could lead to large financial losses. A spouse's earnings might disappear due to death or illness; a car accident might result in costly repair bills or payments to an injured party. Because financial losses from crises could be large relative to our financial resources, we protect ourselves against them by purchasing an insurance policy that will pay us a sum of money if catastrophic events occur. Life insurance companies specialize in selling policies that provide income if a person dies, is incapacitated by illness, or retires. Property and casualty companies specialize in policies that pay for losses incurred as a result of accidents, fire, or theft.

Principles of Insurance Management

Insurance companies, like banks, are in the financial intermediation business of transforming one type of asset into another for the public. Insurance companies use the premiums paid on policies to invest in assets such as bonds, stocks, mortgages and other loans; then, the earnings from these assets are used to pay out the claims on the policies. In effect, insurance companies transform assets such as bonds, stocks, and loans into insurance policies that provide a set of services (for example, claim adjustments, savings plans, friendly insurance agents). If the insurance company's production process of asset transformation efficiently provides its customers with adequate insurance services at low cost and if it can earn high returns on its investments, then it will make profits; if not, it will suffer losses.

In Chapter 9, the economic concepts of adverse selection and moral hazard allowed us to understand several principles of bank management; many of these also apply to the lending activities of insurance companies. Here again we use the adverse selection and moral hazard concepts to explain many management practices specific to the insurance industry.

In the case of an insurance policy, moral hazard occurs when the existence of insurance encourages the insured party to take risks that increase the likelihood of an insurance payoff. For example, a person covered by burglary insurance might not take as many precautions to prevent a burglary since the insurance company will reimburse him for most of the losses if he is robbed. Adverse selection occurs when those most likely to receive large insurance payoffs are the ones who want to purchase insurance the most. A person suffering from a terminal disease, for example, would want to take out the biggest life and medical insurance policies possible; thereby, the insurance company is exposed to potentially large losses. Both adverse selection and moral hazard can result in large losses to insurance companies since they lead to higher payouts on insurance claims. Minimizing adverse selection and moral hazard to reduce these payouts is therefore an extremely important goal for insurance companies, and this goal explains the set of insurance practices that follow.

Screening To reduce adverse selection, insurance companies try to screen out good insurance risks from poor ones. Effective information collection procedures therefore are an important principle of insurance management.

When you apply for auto insurance, the first thing your insurance agent does is ask you questions about your driving record (the number of speeding tickets and accidents), the type of car you are insuring, and even personal matters (age, marital status). If you are applying for life insurance, you go through a similar grilling, but you are asked even more personal questions about such things as your health, smoking habits, and drug and alcohol use. The life insurance company even invades your body by taking blood and urine samples. Just as a bank calculates a credit score to evaluate a potential borrower, the insurance company uses the information you provide to allocate you to a risk class—a statistical measure of how likely it is for you to have an insurance claim. Based on this information, the insurance company can decide whether to accept you for the insurance or to turn you down because you pose too high an insurance risk and thus would be an unprofitable customer for the insurance company.

Risk-Based Premiums Charging insurance premiums on the basis of how much risk a policyholder poses for the insurance company (called **risk-based premiums**) is a time-honored principle of insurance management. Adverse selection explains why this principle is so important to insurance company profitability.

To understand why an insurance company finds it necessary to have risk-based premiums, let's examine an example of risk-based insurance premiums that at first glance seems unfair. Harry and Sally, both college students with no accidents or speeding tickets, apply for auto insurance. Normally, Harry will be charged a much higher premium than Sally. Insurance companies do this because young males have a much higher rate of accidents on average than young females. Suppose, though, that one insurance company did not base its premiums on a risk classification but rather just charged a premium based on the average amount of risk for males and females. Then Sally would be charged too much and Harry too little. Sally could go to another insurance company and get a lower rate, while Harry would sign up for the insurance. Because Harry's premium isn't high enough to account for the accidents he is likely to have, on average the company would lose money on Harry. Only with a premium based on a risk classification, so that Harry is charged more, can the insurance company make a profit.[1]

Restrictive Provisions Restrictive provisions in policies are another insurance management tool for reducing moral hazard. Such provisions discourage policyholders from engaging in risky activities that make an insurance claim more likely. One type of restrictive provision keeps the policyholder from benefiting from behavior that makes a claim more likely. For example, life insurance companies have provisions in their policies that eliminate death benefits if the insured person commits suicide within the first two years that the policy is in effect. Restrictive provisions may also require certain behavior on the part of the insured that makes a claim less likely. A company renting motor scooters may be required to provide helmets for renters in order to be covered for any liability associated with the rental. The role of restrictive provisions is not unlike that of restrictive covenants on debt contracts described in Chapter 8: Both serve to reduce moral hazard by ruling out undesirable behavior.

Prevention of Fraud Insurance companies also face moral hazard because an insured person has an incentive to lie to the company and seek a claim

---

[1]You might recognize that the example here is just the "lemons problem" described in Chapter 8.

even if the claim is not valid. For example, a person who has not complied with the restrictive provisions of an insurance contract may still seek a claim. Even worse, a person may file claims for events that did not actually occur. Thus an important management principle for insurance companies is conducting investigations to prevent fraud so that only those with valid claims receive compensation.

Cancellation of Insurance   Being prepared to cancel policies is another insurance management tool. Insurance companies can discourage moral hazard if they threaten to cancel a policy when the insured person is engaging in activities that make a claim more likely. If your auto insurance company make it clear that any driver who gets too many speeding tickets will have his coverage canceled, you will be less likely to speed and have accidents.

Deductibles   A **deductible** is the fixed amount that is deducted from the insured's loss when a claim is paid off. A $250 deductible on an auto policy, for example, means that when you suffer a loss of $1000 because of an accident, the insurance company pays you only $750. Deductibles are an additional management tool that helps insurance companies reduce moral hazard. With a deductible, you experience a loss along with the insurance company when you make a claim. Because you also stand to lose when you have an accident, you have an incentive to drive more carefully. A deductible thus makes a policyholder act more in line with what is profitable for the insurance company; that is, moral hazard has been reduced. Since the moral hazard problem has been reduced, the insurance company can lower the premium by more than enough to compensate the policyholder for the existence of the deductible.

Coinsurance   When a policyholder shares a percentage of the losses along with the insurance company, their arrangement is called **coinsurance.** For example, some medical insurance plans provide coverage for 80% of medical bills and the insured person pays 20% after a certain deductible is met. Coinsurance works to reduce moral hazard in exactly the same way that a deductible does. Because the policyholder suffers a loss along with the insurance company, he has less incentive to take actions, like going to the doctor unnecessarily, that involve higher claims. Coinsurance is thus another useful management tool for insurance companies.

Limits on the Amount of Insurance   Another important principle of insurance management is that there should be limits on the amount of insurance provided, even though a customer is willing to pay for more coverage. The higher the insurance coverage, the more the insured person can gain from risky activities that make an insurance payoff more likely and hence the moral hazard greater. For example, if a person had a $10 million life insurance policy she might drive recklessly because she knows her family would benefit tremendously if she died. If she had a $10,000 policy, however, she might drive more carefully because she knows her family would not become rich after her death. Insurance companies must always make sure that their coverage is not so high that moral hazard leads to large losses.

All of the principles of insurance management—limiting the amount of insurance, coinsurance, deductibles, cancellation of insurance, prevention of fraud, and restrictive provisions—help insurance companies reduce adverse selection as well as moral hazard. As we have seen, these management tools make it harder for policyholders to benefit from engaging in activities that increase the amount and likelihood of claims. With smaller benefits available, the poor insurance risks (those who are more likely to engage in the activities in the first place) see less benefit from the insurance and are thus less likely to seek it out. For example, a person with a terminal illness is less likely to try to get life insurance if the amount of the policy is limited to a small amount. On the other hand, he will work very hard to get a policy if the amount is large. Insurance management tools that reduce moral hazard therefore reduce adverse selection as well and thereby help increase the profitability of insurance companies in two ways.

Summary Effective insurance management requires several practices: information collection and screening of potential policyholders, risk-based premiums, restrictive provisions, prevention of fraud, cancellation of insurance, deductibles, coinsurance, and limits on the amount of insurance. All of these practices serve as tools to reduce moral hazard and adverse selection.

Now that we have a general understanding of how insurance companies need to operate, we will look in more detail at the two different categories of companies: life insurance companies and property and casualty insurance companies.

Life Insurance Companies

The first life insurance company in the United States (Presbyterian Ministers' Fund in Philadelphia) was established in 1759 and is still in existence. There are currently about 2000 life insurance companies, which are organized in two forms: as stock companies or as mutuals. Stock companies are owned by stockholders, while mutuals are technically owned by the policyholders. Although over 90% of life insurance companies are organized as stock companies, the largest companies (including Prudential Insurance Company and Metropolitan Life) are organized as mutuals; indeed, over half the assets in the industry are owned by mutual companies.

Life insurance companies have never experienced widespread failures like commercial banks, so the federal government has not seen the need to regulate the industry; instead, regulation is left to the states in which the company operates. State regulation is directed at sales practices, the provision of adequate liquid assets to cover losses, and restrictions on the amount of risky assets (such as common stock) that the companies can hold. The regulatory authority is typically a state insurance commissioner.

Because death rates for the population as a whole are predictable with a high degree of certainty, life insurance companies can accurately predict what their payouts to policyholders will be in the future. Consequently, they hold long-term assets that are not particularly liquid—corporate bonds and commercial mortgages as well as some corporate stock.

There are two principal forms of life insurance policies: permanent life insurance (such as whole, universal and variable life) or temporary insurance (such as term). Permanent life insurance policies have a constant premium throughout the life of the policy. In the early years of the policy the size of this premium exceeds the amount needed to insure against death because the probability of death is low. Thus the policy builds up a cash value in its early years, but in later years the cash value declines because the constant premium falls below the amount needed to insure against death, whose probability is now higher. The policyholder can borrow against the cash value of the permanent life policy or can claim it by canceling the policy.

Term insurance, on the other hand, has a premium that is matched every year to the amount needed to insure against death during the period of the term (such as one year or five years). As a result, term policies have premiums that rise over time as the probability of death rises. Term policies have no cash value and thus, in contrast to permanent life policies, are pure insurance with no savings aspect.

Property and Casualty Insurance Companies

The property and casualty insurance companies number over 3000 in the United States, among which the two largest are State Farm Insurance and Allstate Insurance. Property and casualty companies are organized as both stock and mutual companies and are regulated by the states in which they operate in a similar fashion to life insurance companies. In recent years, property and casualty insurance companies have not fared well, and as a result insurance rates have skyrocketed. This "insurance crisis," which is discussed frequently in the media, is discussed in Box 12.1.

The investment policies of these companies are affected by two basic facts. First, because they are subject to federal income taxes, the largest share of their assets is held in tax-exempt municipal bonds. Second, because property losses are more uncertain than the death rate in a population, they are less able to predict how much they will have to pay policyholders than are life insurance companies. Therefore, property and casualty insurance companies hold more liquid assets than life insurance companies; municipal bonds and U.S. government securities amount to over half their assets and most of the remainder are held in corporate bonds and corporate stock.

Box 1 2 . 1

The Insurance Crisis

With the high interest rates in the 1970s, insurance companies had high investment income that enabled them to keep insurance rates low. In the mid-1980s, however, investment income fell with the decline in interest rates, while the growth in lawsuits involving property and casualty insurance and the explosion in amounts awarded in such cases produced substantial losses for companies. In order to return to profitability, insurance companies raised their rates dramatically—sometimes doubling or even tripling premiums—and even refused to provide coverage. This led to a backlash among the electorate; for example, some states like California have passed referendums to roll back insurance rates. Because of their decreased profit-

ability, insurance companies have campaigned actively for limits on insurance payouts, particularly for medical malpractice. In the search for profits, insurance companies are also branching out into uncharted territory by insuring the payment of interest on municipal and corporate bonds, as well as on mortgage-backed securities. A major concern has been that insurance companies may be taking on excessive risk in order to boost their profits. This concern is well founded because the number of insurance company insolvencies has climbed steadily from below five per year at the beginning of the 1980s to around 50 per year by 1990. Is there another S&L-type crisis in the making?

Property and casualty insurance companies will insure against losses from almost any type of event, including fire, theft, negligence, malpractice, earthquakes, automobile accidents, and so on. If a possible loss being insured is too large for any one firm, several firms will frequently join together to write a policy in order to share the risk. The most famous risk-sharing operation is Lloyd's of London, an association in which different insurance companies can insure a fraction of an insurance policy. Lloyd's of London has claimed that it will insure against any contingency—for a price.

PENSION FUNDS

In performing the financial intermediation function of asset transformation, pension funds provide the public with another kind of protection—income payments on retirement. Employers, unions, or private individuals can set up pension plans, which acquire funds through contributions paid in by the plan's participants. Although the purpose of all pension plans is the same, they can differ in a number of attributes.

First is the vesting of the plan, that is, the length of time that a person must be enrolled in the pension plan (by being a member of a union or an employee of a company) before being entitled to receive benefits. Typically, firms require that an employee work five years for the company before he or she is vested and can receive pension benefits; if the employee leaves the firm before the five years are up, either by quitting or being fired, all rights to benefits are lost.

A second characteristic is the method by which payments are made: If the benefits are determined by the contributions into the plan and their earnings, the pension is a defined contribution plan; if future income payments (benefits) are set in advance, the pension is a defined benefits plan. In the case of a defined benefits plan, a further attribute is related to how the plan is funded. Since this attribute is more complicated, we need to look at it in more detail.

A defined benefit plan is **fully funded** if the contributions into the plan and their earnings over the years are sufficient to pay out the defined benefits when they come due. If the contributions and earnings are not sufficient, then the plan is **underfunded.** If Jane Brown, for example, contributes $100 per year into her pension plan and the interest rate is 10%, after ten years the contributions and their earnings would be worth $1753.[2] If the defined benefit on her pension plan pays her $1753 or less after ten years, the plan is fully funded because her contributions and earnings will fully pay for this payment. On the other hand, if the defined benefit is $2000, the plan is underfunded because her contributions and earnings do not cover this amount.

Private Pension Plans

Private pension plans are administered either by a bank, a life insurance company, or a pension fund manager. In employer-sponsored pension plans, contributions are usually shared between the employer and the employee. An important tax incentive for these plans is that the employer's contributions are tax deductible. Because the benefits paid out of the pension fund each year are highly predictable, pension funds invest in long-term securities, with over half of their asset holdings in bonds and stocks.

Many companies' pension plans are underfunded because they plan to meet their pension obligations out of current earnings when the benefits come due. As long as companies have sufficient earnings, underfunding creates no problems, but this has not always been the case. Because of potential problems caused by corporate underfunding, mismanagement, fraudulent practices, and other abuses of private pension funds (Teamsters' pen-

---

[2]The $100 contributed in year one would become worth $100 \times (1 + .10)^{10} = 259.37 at the end of ten years; the $100 contributed in year two would become worth $100 \times (1 + .10)^9 =$ $235.79; \ldots$; and the $100 contributed in year ten would become worth $100 \times (1 + .10) =$ $110. Adding these together we get the total value of these contributions and their earnings at the end of ten years to be

$$\$259.37 + \$235.79 + \$214.36 + \$194.87 + \$177.16 + \$161.05 + \$146.41 +$$
$$\$133.10 + \$121 + \$110 = \$1753$$

sion funds are notorious), the Congress enacted the Employee Retirement Income Security Act (ERISA) in 1974. This act established minimum standards for reporting and disclosure of information, set rules for vesting and the degree of underfunding, and placed restrictions on investment practices.

ERISA also created the Pension Benefit Guarantee Corporation (called "Penny Benny"), which performs a role similar to that of the FDIC. It insures pension benefits up to a limit of $2250 per month per person if a company with an underfunded pension plan goes bankrupt or is not able to meet its pension obligations for other reasons. Penny Benny charges pension plans premiums to pay for this insurance, and it can also borrow funds up to $100 million from the U.S. Treasury. Unfortunately, Penny Benny, which insures the pensions of one of every three workers, is encountering severe financial difficulties that may require a federal bailout (Box 12.2).

Box 1 2 . 2

The Perils of Penny Benny: A Repeat of the S&L Bailout?

The current woes of "Penny Benny," the government pension insurance agency, unfortunately display many of the characteristics of the savings and loan crisis we discussed in the previous chapter. When an insured company with an underfunded pension plan files for bankruptcy, Penny Benny must pay the company's workers their retirement benefits. Again, we see the moral hazard principle at work: A company is more likely to risk underfunding its pension plan because if it goes bankrupt, Penny Benny will foot the pension bill. For example, the LTV Steel Company's bankruptcy in February 1987 resulted in Penny Benny paying out $400 million per year to LTV pensioners alone, even though Penny Benny was taking in only $280 million in premiums.

As we have seen, to keep the costs of government insurance programs from getting out of hand, the insurance agency must reduce moral hazard by monitoring the firms it is insuring to make sure they are not subjecting the agency to too much risk. In the case of Penny Benny, this means Penny Benny must audit pension plans to make sure they are not becoming too underfunded. The decrease in the amount of monitoring of S&Ls was one reason for the huge losses to their government insurance agency, the FSLIC; unfortunately, we see a similar pattern for Penny Benny. In the 1978 to 1988 period, the number of pension funds doubled to more than one million, and yet the number of federal audits of pension plans declined from more than 8000 to about 2000. As a result, less than 1% of private plans insured by Penny Benny are audited each year. Not surprisingly given the failure of Penny Benny to control moral hazard, its liabilities arising from its responsibility for troubled pension plans have grown at an alarming rate and are now estimated to exceed its assets by more than $15 billion. Taxpayers will surely be hit with another massive government bailout, whose size will keep on growing unless the government makes a concerted effort to reduce the underfunding of corporate pension plans.

Public Pension Plans

The most important public pension plan is Social Security (Old Age and Survivors Insurance Fund), which covers virtually all individuals employed in the private sector. Funds are obtained from workers through FICA (Federal Insurance Contribution Act) deductions from their paychecks and from employers through payroll taxes. Social Security benefits include retirement income, Medicare payments, and aid to the disabled.

When Social Security was established in 1935, the federal government intended to operate it like a private pension fund. However, unlike a private pension plan, paid-out benefits are not tied closely to a participant's past contributions, so typically they are paid out from current contributions. This "pay-as-you-go" system at one point led to a massive underfunding of the Social Security fund, estimated at over a trillion dollars.

The problems of the Social Security system could become worse in the future because today's aging American population will lead to a higher number of retired people relative to the working population. Congress has been grappling with the problems of the Social Security system for years, and progress has been made on reducing the underfunding by raising FICA contributions and limiting benefits.

State and local governments and the federal government, like private employers, have also set up pension plans for their employees. These plans are almost identical in operation to private pension plans and hold similar assets. Underfunding of the plans is also prevalent, and some investors in municipal bonds worry that it may lead to future difficulties in the ability of state and local governments to meet their debt obligations.

FINANCE COMPANIES

Finance companies acquire funds by issuing commercial paper or stocks and bonds and use the proceeds to make loans (often for small amounts) that are particularly suited to consumer and business needs. The financial intermediation process of finance companies can be described by saying that they borrow in large amounts but often lend in small amounts—a process quite different from that of commercial banks, which issue deposits in small amounts and then often make large loans.

A key feature of finance companies is that compared to commercial banks and thrift institutions they are virtually unregulated. States regulate the maximum amount they can loan to individual consumers and the terms of the debt contract, but there are no restrictions on branching, the assets they hold, and how they raise their funds. The lack of restrictions enables finance companies to better tailor their loans to customer needs than banking institutions.

There are three types of finance companies.

1. Sales finance companies make loans to consumers to purchase items from a particular retailer or manufacturer. Sears Roebuck Acceptance Corporation, for example, finances consumer purchases of all goods and services at Sears' stores, while General Motors Acceptance Corporation finances purchases of GM cars. Sales finance companies compete directly with banks for consumer loans and are used by consumers because loans can frequently be obtained faster and more conveniently at the location where an item is purchased.

2. Consumer finance companies make loans to consumers to buy particular items such as furniture or home appliances, for home improvements, or to help refinance small debts. Consumer finance companies are separate corporations (like Household Finance Corporation) or are owned by banks (Citicorp owns Person-to-Person Finance Company, which operates offices nationwide). Typically, these companies make loans to consumers who cannot obtain credit from other sources and charge higher interest rates.

3. Business finance companies provide specialized forms of credit to businesses by purchasing accounts receivable (bills owed to the firm) at a discount; this provision of credit is called factoring. For example, a dressmaking firm might have outstanding bills of $100,000 owed by the retail stores that have bought its dresses. If this firm needs cash to buy 100 new sewing machines, it can sell its accounts receivable for, say, $90,000 to a finance company, which is now entitled to collect the $100,000 owed to the firm. Besides factoring, business finance companies also specialize in leasing equipment (such as railroad cars, jet planes, and computers), which they purchase and then lease to businesses for a set number of years.

MUTUAL FUNDS

Mutual funds are financial intermediaries that pool the resources of many small investors by selling them shares and use the proceeds to buy securities. Through the asset-transformation process of issuing shares in small denominations and buying large blocks of securities, mutual funds can take advantage of volume discounts on brokerage commissions and purchase diversified holdings (portfolios) of securities. This allows the small investor to obtain the benefits of lower transactions costs in purchasing securities, as well as the reduction of risk by diversifying the portfolio of securities held. Originally, mutual funds invested solely in common stocks, but many now specialize in debt instruments. Funds that purchase common stocks may specialize even further and invest solely in foreign securities or in specialized industries, such as energy or high technology. Funds that purchase debt instruments also may specialize in corporate, U.S. government, tax-exempt municipal bonds or in long-term or short-term securities.[3]

Mutual funds are structured in two ways. The most common structure is an **open-end fund,** from which shares can be redeemed at any time at a price that is tied to the asset value of the fund. Mutual funds also can be structured as a **closed-end fund,** in which a fixed number of non-redeemable shares are sold at an initial offering and are then traded in the over-the-counter market like a common stock. The market price of these shares fluctuates with the value of the assets held by the fund. In contrast to the open-end fund, however, the price of the shares may be above or below the value of the assets held by the fund, depending on factors such as the liquidity of the shares or the quality of the management. The greater popularity of the open-end funds is explained by the greater liquidity of their redeemable shares relative to the nonredeemable shares of closed-end funds.

Originally, shares of most open-ended mutual funds were sold by salespeople (usually brokers) who were paid a commission. Since this commission is paid at the time of purchase and is immediately subtracted from the redemption value of the shares, these funds are called **load funds.** Most mutual funds currently are **no-load funds;** that is, they are sold directly to the public with no sales commissions. In both types of funds the managers earn their living from management fees paid by the shareholders. These fees amount to approximately 0.5% of the asset value of the fund per year.

Mutual funds are regulated by the Securities and Exchange Commission, which was given the ability to exercise almost complete control over investment companies in the Investment Company Act in 1940. Regulations require periodic disclosure of information on these funds to the public and restrictions on the methods of soliciting business.

Money Market Mutual Funds

An important addition to the family of mutual funds is the money market mutual fund. This type of mutual fund invests in short-term debt (money market) instruments of very high quality, such as Treasury bills, commercial paper, and bank certificates of deposit. There is some fluctuation in the market value of these securities, but because their maturity is typically less than six months, the change in the market value is sufficiently small that these funds allow their shares to be redeemed at a fixed value. (Changes in the market value of the securities are figured into the interest paid out by the fund.) Because these shares can be redeemed at a fixed value, the funds

---

[3]Tax-exempt bond funds did not appear until after 1976 when a change in the tax law allowed mutual funds to pass through to shareholders the tax exemption on the interest income from municipal bonds.

allow shareholders to redeem shares by writing checks above some minimum amount (usually $500) on the fund's account at a commercial bank. In this way, shares in money market mutual funds effectively function as checkable deposits that earn market interest rates on short-term debt securities.

In 1977, the assets in money market mutual funds were less than $4 billion; by 1980 they had climbed to over $50 billion and now are around $500 billion. Currently, money market mutual funds account for more than half the asset value of all mutual funds. You will see why these funds were the fastest-growing financial intermediary of the 1970s in Chapter 13, which describes the process of financial innovation.

GOVERNMENT FINANCIAL INTERMEDIATION

The government has become involved in financial intermediation in two basic ways: first, by setting up federal credit agencies that directly engage in financial intermediation and second, by supplying government guarantees for private loans.

Federal Credit Agencies

To promote residential housing, the government has created three government agencies that provide funds to the mortgage market by selling bonds and using the proceeds to buy mortgages: the Federal National Mortgage Association (FNMA, called "Fannie Mae"), the Government National Mortgage Association (GNMA, or "Ginnie Mae"), and the Federal Home Loan Mortgage Company (FHLMC, or "Freddie Mac"). Except for GNMA, which is a federal agency and is thus an entity of the U.S. government, the other agencies are federally sponsored agencies that function as private corporations with close ties to the government. As a result, the debt of sponsored agencies is not backed by the U.S. government, as is the case for Treasury bonds. As a practical matter however, it is unlikely that the federal government would allow a default on the debt of these sponsored agencies.

Agriculture is another area in which financial intermediation by government agencies plays an important role. The Farm Credit System (composed of Banks for Cooperatives, Federal Intermediate Credit Banks, and Federal Land Banks) issues securities and then uses the proceeds to make loans to farmers.

Students also benefit from government financial intermediation. The Student Loan Marketing Association (called "Sallie Mae") provides funds for higher education primarily by purchasing student loans granted by private financial institutions under the Guaranteed Student Loan Program.

In recent years, government financial intermediaries have been experiencing financial difficulties. The Farm Credit System is one example. The rising tide of farm bankruptcies meant losses in the billions of dollars for the

Farm Credit Banks and as a result they required a $4 billion government bailout in 1987. Because of high default rates on student loans, Sallie Mae has also experienced losses on some of its loan portfolio. There is growing concern in Washington about the health of the federal credit agencies. To head off government bailouts like that for the Farm Credit Banks, the Bush administration has pushed for new rules that require such agencies to increase their capital so they have a greater cushion to offset any potential losses.

Government Loan Guarantees: Another Crisis Waiting to Happen?

Another important government role in promoting financial intermediation has been the provision of government loan guarantees. A government loan guarantee acts just like insurance: It insures the lender, say a bank, from any loss if the borrower defaults. In the housing market, government loan guarantees are provided by the Federal Housing Administration (FHA) and the Veterans Administration. The Education Department guarantees student loans, and the Farmer's Home Administration guarantees loans to farmers.

Government loan guarantees have grown at a rapid rate in the past twenty years—increasing tenfold during this period. They have been particularly attractive to Congress because they subsidize activities that our politicians believe in, like going to college and home ownership, and yet do not involve any direct expenditures on the part of the government. An important economic principle that you hear all the time is, "You don't get something for nothing," and this is certainly true for the government. The problem with government loan guarantees is the same as that with government deposit insurance: Both are insurance schemes that lead to moral hazard problems which result in losses to the government. Since banks and other institutions making the loans don't suffer any losses if the loans default, they have little incentive to be careful about to whom they make their loans.

Losses to government agencies that provide the government loan guarantees from the resulting lax lending practices can be substantial. Notorious in this regard is the over 30% default rate on government-guaranteed loans for students in trade schools. The costs of loan guarantees to the government recently have been coming home to roost. In 1990 the General Accounting Office startled Congress by predicting that losses from government loan guarantees may end up exceeding $100 billion. Taxpayers may thus be hit with another costly bailout of the same magnitude as that required for the savings and loans industry.

SECURITIES MARKETS INSTITUTIONS

The smooth functioning of securities markets, in which bonds and stocks are traded, involves several financial institutions, including securities brokers and dealers, investment banks, and organized exchanges. None of these institutions was included in our list of financial intermediaries because they do not perform the intermediation function of acquiring funds by issuing liabilities and then, in turn, using the funds to acquire financial assets. Nonetheless, they are important in the process of channeling funds from savers to those with productive investment opportunities.

First, however, we must recall the distinction between primary and secondary securities markets discussed in Chapter 3. In a primary market, new issues of a security are sold by the corporation or government agency borrowing the funds to initial buyers. A secondary market then trades the securities that have been previously sold in the primary market (and so are secondhand). **Investment banks** are firms that assist in the initial sale of securities in the primary market, while securities brokers and dealers assist in the trading of securities in the secondary markets, some of which are organized into exchanges.

Investment Banks

When a corporation wishes to borrow (raise) funds, it normally hires the services of an investment bank to help sell its securities. (Despite its name, an investment bank is not a bank in the ordinary sense; that is, it is not a financial intermediary that takes in deposits and then lends them out.) Some of the well-known U.S. investment banking firms are Morgan Stanley, Merrill Lynch, Salomon Brothers, First Boston Corporation, and Goldman, Sachs.

Investment bankers assist in the sale of securities as follows: First, they advise the corporation on whether it should issue bonds or stock. If they suggest that the corporation issue bonds, investment bankers give advice on what the maturity and interest payments on the bonds should be. When the corporation decides which kind of financial instrument it will issue, it offers them to **underwriters**—investment banks that guarantee the corporation a price on the securities and then sell them to the public. If the size of the issue is small, only one investment bank underwrites the issue (usually the original investment banking firm hired to provide advice on the issue). If the issue is large, several investment banking firms form a syndicate to underwrite the issue jointly—thus limiting the risk that any one investment bank must take. The underwriters sell the securities to the general public by directly contacting potential buyers, such as banks and insurance companies, and by placing advertisements in newspapers like the *Wall Street Journal* (Figure 12.1). A particularly controversial investment banking activity in recent years has been the underwriting of "junk bonds" (Box 12.3).

The activities of investment banks and the operation of primary markets are heavily regulated by the Securities and Exchange Commission (SEC), which was created by the Securities and Exchange Acts of 1933 and 1934 to ensure that adequate information reaches prospective investors. Is-

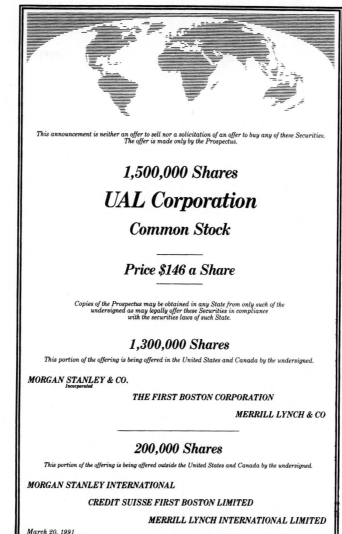

This announcement is neither an offer to sell nor a solicitation of an offer to buy any of these Securities.
The offer is made only by the Prospectus.

1,500,000 Shares

UAL Corporation

Common Stock

Price $146 a Share

Copies of the Prospectus may be obtained in any State from only such of the
undersigned as may legally offer these Securities in compliance
with the securities laws of such State.

1,300,000 Shares

This portion of the offering is being offered in the United States and Canada by the undersigned.

MORGAN STANLEY & CO.
Incorporated

THE FIRST BOSTON CORPORATION

MERRILL LYNCH & CO

200,000 Shares

This portion of the offering is being offered outside the United States and Canada by the undersigned.

MORGAN STANLEY INTERNATIONAL

CREDIT SUISSE FIRST BOSTON LIMITED

MERRILL LYNCH INTERNATIONAL LIMITED

March 20, 1991

FIGURE 12.1
An Advertisement for a New Security Issue
Three of the most important investment banks (listed toward the bottom of the advertisement) are involved in underwriting these securities for UAL Corporation, the parent corporation of United Airlines. As you can see from the bottom of the advertisement, a portion of the shares are being sold abroad, a demonstration of the continuing internationalization of financial markets.
Source: *Wall Street Journal* (Wednesday, March 20, 1991).

suers of new securities to the general public (for amounts greater than $1.5 million in a year with a maturity longer than 270 days) must file a registration statement with the SEC and must provide a prospectus to potential investors containing all relevant information on the securities. The issuer must then wait twenty days after the registration statement is filed with the SEC before it can sell any of the securities. If, after the twenty-day waiting period, the SEC does not object to the registration statement, the securities can finally be sold.

Box 1 2 . 3

Junk Bonds and the Rise and Fall of Michael Milken and Drexel Burnham

Before the 1980s, investment banks would only underwrite bonds of corporations with "investment grade" bond ratings of Baa or above. Some firms that had fallen on bad times, so-called fallen angels, had corporate bonds with ratings below Baa, and these bonds were pejoratively dubbed "junk bonds." In 1977, Michael Milken of Drexel Burnham, an investment banking firm, pioneered the concept of selling new public issues of junk bonds, not for fallen angels, but for companies that had not yet achieved investment-grade status. Junk bonds became an important factor in the corporate bond market, with the amount outstanding exceeding $200 billion by the late 1980s.

The junk bond underwriting of Drexel Burnham propelled it from a third-tier investment banking firm to the second largest in the industry (behind Goldman, Sachs), and it also made Michael Milken incredibly wealthy—in 1987 alone, his compensation from Drexel was $550 million. But the good times were not to last. Milken and Drexel's junk bond activities were highly controversial because they helped fuel the wave of takeovers and leveraged buyouts in the 1980s (discussed in an appendix to Chapter 8). In September 1988, the SEC

accused Milken and others at Drexel of insider trading and other violations of securities law; in March 1989 Milken was indicted on ninety-eight counts of racketeering and tax and securities fraud. In December 1988, Drexel pleaded guilty to six criminal charges in order to avoid racketeering charges and agreed to pay a $650 million fine. Milken pleaded guilty to six charges as well in April 1989 and was later sentenced to a ten-year prison sentence after paying a $600 million fine. With the collapse of junk bond prices in 1989 and early 1990, Drexel was finally put on the ropes. On February 13, 1990, Drexel Burnham filed for bankruptcy and closed down its operations. A Drexel employee commented as follows: "It feels like the [Humphrey Bogart movie] *Treasure of the Sierra Madre*. We went up in the mountains, worked like dogs, and mined a lot of gold. Then we lost it, and wound up no further ahead than when we started."*

---

*Quoted in David Hilder and Linda Sandler, "Rise and Fall: Wall Street Era Ends as Drexel Burnham Decides to Liquidate," *Wall Street Journal* (February 14, 1990), p. A6.

Securities Brokers and Dealers

Securities brokers and dealers conduct trading in secondary markets. Brokers are pure middlemen who act as agents for investors in the purchase or sale of securities. Their function is to match buyers with sellers, a function for which they are paid brokerage commissions. In contrast to brokers, dealers link buyers and sellers by standing ready to buy and sell securities at given prices. Therefore, dealers hold inventories of securities and make their living by selling these securities for a slightly higher price than they paid for them—that is, on the "spread" between the bid price and asked price. This is a high-risk business, since dealers hold securities that can rise or fall in price; in recent years, several firms specializing in bonds have collapsed. Brokers, on the other hand, are not as exposed to risk because they do not hold securities in conducting their business.

Many firms, called **brokerage firms,** engage in all three securities markets activities, acting as brokers, dealers, and investment bankers. The largest in the United States is Merrill Lynch (which is still small, however, by Japanese standards—see Box 12.4), while other well-known firms include Paine Webber, Dean Witter Reynolds, and Shearson Lehman Hutton. The SEC not only regulates the investment banking operation of the firms, but also restricts brokers and dealers from misrepresenting securities and from trading on insider information, nonpublic information known only to the management of a corporation.

The forces of competition led to an important development: Brokerage firms started to engage in activities traditionally carried out by commercial banks. In 1977, Merrill Lynch developed its cash management account (CMA), which provides a package of financial services that includes credit cards, immediate loans, check-writing privileges, automatic investment of proceeds from the sale of securities into a money market mutual fund, and unified record keeping. Cash management accounts were adopted by other brokerage firms and spread rapidly. The result is that the distinction between banking activities and the activities of nonbank financial institutions has become blurred. Walter Wriston, former head of Citicorp (the largest bank holding company in the country), has been quoted as saying, "The bank of the future already exists, and it's called Merrill Lynch."[4]

B o x   1 2 . 4 ## A Global Perspective

The International Role of Japanese Securities Firms

Japan not only has the largest banks in the world, but it has the largest securities firms as well. Nomura Securities is the world's largest securities firm with a market value of over $50 billion. Even the smallest of Japan's "Big Four" securities firms, Yamaichi Securities, is over five times larger than Merrill Lynch, the largest U.S. firm.

The role of Japanese securities firms in international finance was small until quite recently. In 1981, Japanese trading in foreign bonds was less than $10 billion, whereas it is on the order of $3 trillion today. In recent years, the Japanese have accounted for close to half the foreign purchases of U.S. Treasury bonds, and they control or partly own over one-quarter of the forty or so primary dealers in U.S. Treasury bonds. Japanese trading in U.S. stocks has also grown from under $5 billion per year in the early 1980s to over $100 billion. The growing importance of the Japanese role in international securities markets has been driven by two factors: (1) the elimination, starting in the early 1980s, of Japanese regulations that limited the ability of the Japanese to purchase foreign securities and (2) Japan's high savings rate, which has made Japan the world's largest creditor nation.

---

[4]Quoted in "Banking Takes a Beating," *Time Magazine* (December 3, 1984), p. 50.

Organized Exchanges

As discussed in Chapter 3, secondary markets can be organized either as over-the-counter markets, in which trades are conducted using dealers, or as organized exchanges, in which trades are conducted in one central location. The New York Stock Exchange (NYSE), trading thousands of securities, is the largest such organized exchange in the world, while the American Stock Exchange (AMEX) is a distant second. A number of smaller regional exchanges, which trade only a small number of securities (under 100), exist in places such as Boston and Los Angeles.

Organized stock exchanges actually function as a hybrid of an auction market (in which buyers and sellers trade with each other in a central location) and a dealer market (in which dealers make the market by buying and selling securities at given prices). Securities are traded on the floor of the exchange with the help of a special kind of dealer-broker called a **specialist.** A specialist matches buy and sell orders submitted at the same price and so performs a brokerage function. However, if buy and sell orders do not match up, the specialist buys stocks or sells from his inventories of securities—in this manner performing a dealer function. By assuming both these functions, the specialist maintains orderly trading of the set of securities for which he is responsible.

Organized exchanges in which securities are traded are also regulated by the SEC. Not only does the SEC have the authority to impose regulations that govern the behavior of brokers and dealers involved with exchanges, but it also has the authority to alter the rules set by exchanges. Early in 1975, for example, the SEC disallowed existing rules that set minimum brokerage commission rates. The result was a sharp drop in brokerage commission rates, especially for institutional investors (mutual funds and pension funds) who purchase large blocks of stock. The Securities Amendments Act of 1975 confirmed the SEC's action by making rules setting minimum brokerage commissions illegal.

Furthermore, the Securities Amendments Act directed the SEC to facilitate a national market system which consolidates trading of all securities listed on the national and regional exchanges as well as those traded in the over-the-counter market using the National Association of Securities Dealers' automated quotation system (NASDAQ). Computers and advanced telecommunications, which reduce the costs of linking up these markets, have encouraged the expansion of a national market system. We thus see that legislation and modern computer technology are leading the way to a more competitive securities industry.

The growing internationalization of capital markets also has encouraged another trend in securities trading. Increasingly, foreign companies are being listed on U.S. stock exchanges such as the NYSE. In addition, the markets are moving toward trading stocks internationally, twenty-four hours a day.

SEPARATION OF COMMERCIAL BANKING AND _____ THE SECURITIES INDUSTRY

Before 1933, investment banking and commercial banking often were conducted by the same financial institution. The combination of investment and commercial banking led to potential conflicts of interest, because investment bankers could sell otherwise unsellable securities to the trust funds that their own bank might be managing for a company's pension plan or for a private individual. Hence a bank's investment banking operation could earn profits at the expense of the trust funds. And if these unsellable securities were purchased by the bank itself, depositors might be subjected to a higher risk of the bank's failing.

After the bank failures of 1930–1933 and the public uproar over documented cases of abuses by bank trust departments, political pressure developed to eliminate conflicts of interest and to promote a banking system less prone to failure. In response to this pressure, Congress enacted the Banking Act of 1933, known as the Glass-Steagall Act. The act prohibited commercial banks from engaging in the underwriting and dealing of corporate securities (commercial banks *were* allowed to sell new issues of government securities) and limited banks to the purchase of debt securities approved by the bank regulatory agencies. Likewise it prohibited investment banks from engaging in commercial banking activities. In effect, the Glass-Steagall Act separated the activities of commercial banks from the securities industry.

Under the conditions of the Glass-Steagall Act, commercial banks had to sell off their investment banking operations. The First National Bank of Boston, for example, spun off its investment banking operations into the First Boston Corporation, now one of the largest investment banking firms in America. Investment banking firms typically discontinued their deposit business, although J.P. Morgan discontinued its investment banking business and reorganized as a commercial bank; however, some senior officers of J.P. Morgan went on to organize Morgan Stanley, one of the largest investment banking firms today.

The Case for Allowing Banks to Enter the Securities Business

Advocates of allowing banks to participate in securities market activities argue that it is unfair to keep commercial banks from pursuing these activities in competition with brokerage firms. Brokerage firms have been able to pursue traditional banking activities with the development of money market mutual funds and cash management accounts. Why shouldn't banks be allowed to compete with brokerage firms in those firms' traditional areas of business—the selling of corporate securities and the management of mutual funds?

Another argument in favor of allowing banks to enter the securities business is that the entry of banks will increase competition. Bank entry will mean that, in the case of a new issue of securities, there will be more bidders to underwrite the issue. As a result, the spread between the price guaranteed to the issuer of the security and the price paid for the security by the general public will fall. This reduction in the spread will mean that both borrowers and lenders in financial markets will be better off: Issuers of securities (borrowers) will receive a higher price for their securities and will thus bear a lower interest cost, while the purchasers of securities (lenders) will be able to buy the securities at a lower price, thereby giving them a higher interest rate. The fact that underwriting spreads for investment-grade bonds have dropped substantially since commercial banks have been allowed to underwrite these securities is powerful evidence in support of this view. If banks were also allowed to enter the brokerage business, increased competition in this industry would reduce brokerage commissions—another advantage to investors.

The Case Against Allowing Banks to Enter the Securities Business

Opponents of bank entry into the security business argue that banks have an unfair advantage in competing against brokerage firms. Deposits provide banks with an artificially low cost of funds because they are insured by the FDIC. Brokerage firms, on the other hand, have higher costs on the funds they acquire, which usually are obtained with loans from the banks.[5]

The securities business, particularly investment banking, involves more risk than traditional banking activities. An investment bank can suffer substantial losses if it is unable to sell securities it has underwritten for the price that it has agreed to pay the issuer. Thus, allowing commercial banks to engage in investment banking might produce more bank failures and a less stable financial system. This problem would be even more acute because of the existence of federal deposit insurance. As we saw in the previous chapter, allowing commercial banks to take advantage of additional risky activities increases the potential for moral hazard and adverse selection. So it is more likely that taxpayers would be subjected to a high-cost bailout of the commercial banking industry like the one we experienced in the savings and loan industry.

Another argument against allowing banks to enter the security business is that commercial banks face a potential conflict of interest if they engage in underwriting of securities. Congressional hearings prior to enactment of the

---

[5]Banks also have the tax advantage over brokerage firms that all interest costs are tax deductible even if acquired funds are used to purchase municipal bonds. Brokerage firms, on the other hand, are not allowed to deduct interest payments on funds used to acquire municipal bonds.

Glass-Steagall Act in 1933 turned up many abuses that were tied to commercial banking's activities in the investment banking area. Banks that were underwriting new issues of securities sold them to trust funds that they managed when they could not sell them to anyone else, and these trust funds often took substantial losses on the securities when sold later. Cases surfaced in which the bank itself would buy securities that it was underwriting when the securities could not be sold elsewhere. The resulting lower quality of the bank's assets could have contributed to a failure later on.

Proponents of allowing banks to enter the security business counter this argument by saying that the securities markets and commercial banking are very different industries today from what they were before 1933. Bank regulation and the SEC could probably prevent many of the abuses that occurred before the Glass-Steagall Act. Regulatory authorities now have much greater power than before 1933 to find and punish those who would abuse commercial banking's securities activities. Although proponents do not guarantee that no abuses would occur, they suggest that abuses would be infrequent enough so that any costs associated with them would be far smaller than the benefits of increased competition in the securities industry.

Where Is the Separation of Banking and the Securities Industry Heading?

The debate about whether banks should be involved in securities activities has not been resolved. However, the pursuit of profits has stimulated both banks and other financial institutions (e.g., Merrill Lynch with its CMA) to bypass the intent of the Glass-Steagall Act and encroach on each other's traditional territory. In addition, even primarily nonfinancial corporations are entering the banking and securities business. Sears, for example, has opened up "financial supermarkets" in its stores, where a customer can obtain insurance, purchase securities, make deposits into a money market mutual fund, and buy real estate.

Because commercial banks' market share in financial services had been falling, in January 1989 the Federal Reserve allowed bank holding companies to underwrite corporate debt securities and also to sell first-mortgage life insurance. The chairman of the Federal Reserve Board, Alan Greenspan, favors allowing banks to affiliate with securities firms, and in September 1990, the Federal Reserve took the historic step of allowing a commercial bank, J.P. Morgan, to underwrite stocks. The FDIC has also allowed banks to invest in real estate and to engage in some insurance activities, and the Treasury plan for reform of the banking system described in the previous chapter proposes that the Glass-Steagall Act be effectively abolished: well-capitalized banks would be allowed to affiliate with securities firms, mutual funds, and insurance companies.

The regulatory trend seems to be one of accepting what has already been occurring in the marketplace. An important factor is that foreign com-

B o x   1 2 . 5   **A Global Perspective**

Separation of the Banking and Securities Industry in Industrialized Countries

Major industrialized countries allow different relationships between the banking and securities industries. There are three basic frameworks for the separation of banking and the securities industry.

The first framework is "universal banking," which exists in Germany, the Netherlands, and Switzerland. It has effectively no separation at all between the banking and securities industry. In a universal banking system, commercial banks provide a full range of banking, securities, and insurance services, all within a single legal entity. Banks are allowed to own sizable equity shares in commercial firms, and often they do.

The British-style universal banking system, the second framework, is found in the United Kingdom as well as countries with close ties to it, such as Canada and Australia. The British-style universal bank engages in securities underwriting, but it differs from the German universal bank in three ways: (1) separate legal subsidiaries are more common,

(2) bank equity holdings of commercial firms are less common, and (3) combinations of banking and insurance firms are less common.

The third framework has a legal separation between banking and the securities industry as in the United States and Japan. A major difference between the U.S. and Japanese banking systems is that Japanese banks are allowed to hold substantial equity stakes in commercial firms, whereas American banks cannot. In addition, most American banks use a bank holding company structure, but bank holding companies are illegal in Japan. Although there is a legal separation between the banking and security industry through the Glass-Steagall Act in the United States and Section 65 of the Japanese Securities Act, in both countries commercial banks are engaging in more and more securities activities and are thus coming closer to a British-style universal bank.

mercial banks are often allowed to engage in the securities business, giving them a competitive edge over American banks (Box 12.5). Regulators may thus be reluctant to restrict commercial banks' securities activities if it puts American banks at a competitive disadvantage relative to foreign banks. The trend away from the separation of the banking and securities industry is therefore likely to continue, and the demise of the Glass-Steagall Act may not be far away.

SUMMARY

1. Insurance companies, which are regulated by the states, acquire funds by selling policies that pay out benefits if catastrophic events occur. Property and casualty insurance companies hold more liquid assets than life insurance companies because of greater uncertainty regarding the

benefits they will have to pay out. All insurance companies face moral hazard and adverse selection problems that explain the use of insurance management tools, such as information collection and screening of potential policyholders, risk-based premiums, restrictive provisions, prevention of fraud, cancellation of insurance, deductibles, coinsurance, and limits on the amount of insurance.

2. Pension plans provide income payments to people when they retire after contributing to the plans for many years. Many pension plans are underfunded, which means in future years they will have to pay out higher benefits than the value of their contributions and earnings. The problem of underfunding is especially acute for public pension plans such as Social Security. Because of abuses, Congress enacted the Employee Retirement Income Security Act (ERISA), which establishes minimum standards for reporting, vesting, and degree of underfunding of private pension plans. This act also created the Pension Benefit Guarantee Corporation, which insures pension benefits.

3. Finance companies raise funds by issuing commercial paper and stocks and bonds, then use the proceeds to make loans that are particularly suited to consumer and business needs. Virtually unregulated in comparison to commercial banks and thrift institutions, they have been able to enter new credit arrangements (such as equipment leasing) very quickly.

4. Mutual funds sell shares and use the proceeds to buy securities. Open-ended funds issue shares that can be redeemed at any time at a price tied to the asset value of the firm. Closed-end funds issue nonredeemable shares, which are traded like any common stock. They are less popular than open-ended funds because their shares are not as liquid. Money market mutual funds hold only short-term, high-quality securities, allowing shares to be redeemed at a fixed value using checks. Shares in these funds effectively function as checkable deposits that earn market interest rates. All mutual funds are regulated by the SEC.

5. Investment banks are firms that assist in the initial sale of securities in primary markets, while securities brokers and dealers assist in the trading of securities in the secondary markets, some of which are organized into exchanges. The SEC regulates the financial institutions in the securities markets and ensures that adequate information reaches prospective investors.

6. The Banking Act of 1933 (Glass-Steagall Act) separated commercial banking from the securities industry by prohibiting commercial banks from engaging in the sale or distribution of privately issued securities. But competitive forces have bypassed the intent of the Glass-Steagall Act and are causing a breakdown in the separation of the banking and securities industries.

KEY TERMS

risk-based premium

deductible

coinsurance

fully funded

underfunded

open-end fund

closed-end fund

load funds

no-load funds

investment banks

underwriters

brokerage firms

specialist

QUESTIONS AND PROBLEMS

* 1. If death rates were less predictable than they are, how would life insurance companies change the types of assets they hold?

2. Why do property and casualty insurance companies have large holdings of municipal bonds while life insurance companies do not?

* 3. Why are all defined contribution pension plans fully funded?

4. What explains the widespread use of deductibles in insurance policies?

* 5. Why might insurance companies restrict the amount of insurance a policyholder can buy?

6. Answer true, false, or uncertain: "In contrast to private pension plans, government pension plans are rarely underfunded."

* 7. If you needed to take out a loan, why might you

first go to your local bank rather than to a finance company?

8. Explain why shares in closed-end mutual funds typically sell for less than the market value of the stocks they hold.

* 9. Why might you buy a no-load mutual fund instead of a load fund?

10. Why can a money market mutual fund allow its shareholders to redeem shares at a fixed price while other mutual funds cannot?

*11. Why might government loan guarantees be a high-cost way for the government to subsidize certain activities?

12. If you like to take risks, would you rather be a dealer, a broker, or a specialist? Why?

*13. Is investment banking a good career for someone who is afraid of taking risks? Why or why not?

14. Suppose you establish a bank-managed trust fund for your child. Would you be for or against prohibiting banks from underwriting securities?

*15. Why have brokerage firms actively lobbied to uphold the provisions of the Glass-Steagall Act?

CHAPTER 13

Financial Innovation

PREVIEW   Twenty years ago many of the financial instruments that we now take for granted did not exist, for example, checking accounts that earn interest (such as NOW accounts). Today the number of financial instruments available to people with large, medium, or small amounts to invest has expanded rapidly and a number of new financial institutions (like money market mutual funds) have come into existence. What explains this revolutionary change in our financial system and the proliferation of new financial products available to consumers?

Like other industries, the financial industry is in business to earn profits by selling its products. If a soap company perceives that there is a need in the marketplace for a laundry detergent with fabric softener, it develops a product to fit the need. Similarly financial institutions develop products to satisfy their own needs as well as those of their customers. Innovations in this industry are stimulated by many of the same factors (changes in technology and market conditions) that stimulate innovation in other industries. Because financial institutions face more restrictive regulations than most firms in other industries, the nature of regulations and their changes are additional important factors in financial innovation.

In this chapter we use economic analysis to explain why various innovations have occurred. Then we try to predict the course of future financial innovation—an important task. Given its current rapid pace, the financial system we face in the future will surely be different from our own.

AN ECONOMIC ANALYSIS OF INNOVATION

Any analysis that explains innovation must address the incentives that cause innovations to appear. Economists contend that innovation is produced by the desire of individuals and businesses to maximize profits; in other words, innovation—which can be extremely beneficial to the economy—is driven by the desire to get (or stay) rich. This view leads to the following simple economic analysis: *A change in the economic environment will stimulate a search for innovations that are likely to be profitable.*

297

Starting in the 1960s, individuals and financial institutions operating in financial markets were confronted with drastic changes in the economic environment: Inflation and interest rates climbed sharply and became harder to predict, while computer technology advanced rapidly. Financial institutions found that many of the old ways of doing business were no longer profitable: The financial products they had been offering to the public were not selling. Many financial intermediaries found that they were no longer able to acquire funds with their traditional financial instruments, and without these funds they would soon be out of business. In order to survive in the new economic environment, financial institutions had to research and develop new products that would prove profitable. In their case, necessity was the mother of innovation.

Even in businesses (financial and otherwise) that were not threatened by the new economic environment, entrepreneurs recognized that changes in the financial environment could be exploited to make them rich. They began the search for new financial products that would be profitable. Their efforts produced many multimillionaires and led to the development of many of our present financial innovations.

Study Guide

To better understand why the financial innovations discussed in this chapter have appeared, keep in mind the simple idea that these innovations are the result of the search for profits.

FINANCIAL INNOVATION: CHANGING MARKET CONDITIONS

Now that we have an economic framework for understanding innovation, let's look at several examples of financial innovations that arose because of changes in market conditions. The most significant change in market conditions in recent years has been the dramatic increase in the volatility of interest rates. In the 1950s the interest rate on three-month Treasury bills fluctuated between 1% and 3.5%; in the 1970s it fluctuated between 4% and 11 1/2%. This volatility became even more pronounced in the 1980s, during which the three-month T-bill rate ranged from 5 to over 15%. We have seen in Table 4.2 of Chapter 4 that a rise in the interest rate from 10 to 20% would result in a capital loss of nearly 50% on a thirty-year bond and a negative return of over 40%. Large fluctuations in interest rates lead to substantial capital gains or losses and greater uncertainty about returns on investments. The risk that is related to the uncertainty about interest rate movements and returns is called **interest-rate risk,** and high volatility of interest rates, such as we saw in the 1970s and 1980s, leads to a higher level of interest-rate risk.

Since changes in the economic environment stimulate a search for profitable innovations, we would expect an increase in interest-rate risk to spur the creation of new financial instruments and markets that help lower the risk. Three examples of financial innovations in the 1970s confirm this prediction: (1) the development of adjustable-rate mortgages, (2) the creation of the futures market for financial instruments, and (3) the creation of an options market for debt instruments.

Adjustable-Rate Mortgages

Like other investors, financial institutions find that lending is more attractive if interest-rate risk is lower. They would not want to make a mortgage loan at a 10% interest rate and two months later find that they could obtain a 12% interest rate on that mortgage. To reduce interest-rate risk, in 1975 savings and loans in California began to issue adjustable-rate mortgages, mortgage loans on which the interest rate changes when a market interest rate (usually the Treasury bill rate) changes. Initially, an adjustable-rate mortgage might have a 10% interest rate. In six months this interest rate might increase or decrease by the amount of the increase or decrease in, say, the six-month Treasury bill rate, and the mortgage payment would change. Because adjustable-rate mortgages allow mortgage-issuing institutions to earn higher interest rates on mortgages when rates rise, profits are kept higher during these periods.

This attractive feature of adjustable-rate mortgages has encouraged mortgage-issuing institutions to issue adjustable-rate mortgages with lower initial interest rates than on conventional fixed-rate mortgages, making them popular with many households. However, because the mortgage payment can increase with variable-rate mortgages, many households continue to prefer fixed-rate mortgages. Hence both types of mortgages are widespread.

The Futures Market for Financial Instruments

A futures market conducts trades of **futures contracts,** in which the seller agrees to provide a certain standardized commodity to the buyer on a specified future date at an agreed-upon price.[1] Future markets for commodities such as wheat or pork bellies (the source of bacon) have been around for a long time, but futures contracts in which the standardized commodity is a

---

[1]An important feature of trading in futures contracts is that there is settlement of any gains or losses in the price of the contract after each day of trading: That is, if at the end of a trading day the price of the contract falls by $100, then the buyer must immediately pay $100 into the seller's account; if the price rises by $100, then the seller must immediately pay $100 to the buyer's account. On the specified day that the commodity is finally delivered, the purchaser of the contract pays the seller the difference between the agreed-upon purchase price and the funds he has already paid into the seller's account, for a total that equals the originally agreed-upon price.

particular type of financial instrument (a **financial futures contract**) did not appear until 1975. To understand why futures markets in financial instruments developed, we must first understand what a financial futures contract is and how it enables investors to **hedge** (protect themselves) against interest-rate risk.

For example, in December 1991 a financial futures contract for certificates of deposit (CDs) might specify that $1 million of CDs with a maturity of three months will be delivered by the seller of the contract to the buyer in June of 1992. On this date the buyer will have to purchase the $1 million of CDs with a discount yield which is stipulated by the contract price. The contract price for CDs (and also Treasury bills) is quoted as a price index which equals 100 minus the discount yield on the CD; a price of 90, for example, indicates a 10% discount yield on the CDs.

To see how the futures contract described here can help a buyer to hedge against interest-rate risk, suppose that in December 1991, Michelle the Money Manager expects that the money market mutual funds she manages will have an inflow of $1 million in June 1992. If Michelle purchases the CDs futures contract in December 1991 at 90, then, even if interest rates on CDs fall below 10% by June 1992, Michelle has *guaranteed* her mutual fund a 10% interest rate on the $1 million it will receive—she has been able to hedge against any interest-rate risk.[2]

Similarly, in December 1991, the First National Bank may make a commitment to loan $1 million to one of its customers in June 1992 at an interest rate of 10.5%. If interest rates on CDs rose in June 1992 to 11%, the bank would suffer a loss on the loan, because the interest cost of acquiring funds would be 11%, while the interest earned on the loan would be only 10.5%. The bank can protect itself from this interest-rate risk by being the one to sell Michelle the futures contract, which promises delivery of the CDs in June 1992 with a 10% interest rate. Now the bank knows that the CDs it will deliver to Michelle in June 1992 will have an interest cost of 10%—it has *locked in* a 10% interest rate on the cost of acquiring funds to make its loan. The financial futures contract has enabled the bank to hedge against any interest-rate risk and it definitely will make a profit on its loan.

So a financial futures market can enable both buyers and sellers of financial futures contracts to hedge against interest-rate risk. When interest-rate risk increased in the 1970s, the ability to hedge this risk became especially valuable, making it more likely that a large number of investors would be willing to trade in financial futures markets. Since large trading volume would result in higher profits for those who set up a financial futures market, our economic analysis of financial innovation predicts that such a market would develop. This prediction was realized in 1975 when the Chicago

---

[2]To simplify the discussion, the interest rates in our example are quoted on a discount yield basis.

Following the Financial News

Financial Futures

The prices for financial futures contracts are published daily. In the *Wall Street Journal,* these prices are found in the section, "Interest Rate Instruments," an excerpt of which is found below.

```
TREASURY BILLS (IMM) - $1 mil.; pts. of 100%
                              Discount   Open
       Open High Low Settle Chg Settle Chg Interest
June   94.26 94.28 94.23 94.27 + .01  5.73 - .01 32,241
Sept   93.99 94.00 93.95 93.99 + .02  6.01 - .02  6,817
Dec    93.53 93.53 93.50 93.50 - .01  6.50 + .01    659
  Est vol 4,393; vol Thur 5,812; open int 39,768, +641.
```

Source: *Wall Street Journal* (Monday, March 25, 1991).

The following information for each contract is included in the following columns. (The contract for delivery of T-bills in June 1991 is used as an example).

Open = opening price, which equals 100.00 minus the discount yield of the T-bills: 94.26 for the June contract.

High = highest traded price that day: 94.28 for the June contract.

Low = lowest traded price that day: 94.23 for the June contract.

Settle = settlement price, that is, the closing price that day: 94.27 for the June contract.

Chg = change in the closing (settlement) price from the previous trading day: +.01 change for the June contract.

Discount Settle = interest rate on a discount basis for delivered securities, calculated from settlement price: 5.73% on T-bills delivered in June.

Discount Chg = change in interest rate (discount basis) for delivered securities from previous trading day: −.01 for the June contract.

Open Interest = no. of contracts outstanding. 32,241 for the June contract.

Board of Trade (in which futures contracts for commodities such as wheat, corn, soybeans, and oats were already traded) created a futures market in Government National Mortgage Association (GNMA) securities.

The GNMA financial futures market was so successful that the Chicago Board of Trade (CBT) later opened futures markets in long-term U.S. Treasury bonds and notes, while the International Monetary Market (IMM), a subsidiary of the Chicago Mercantile Exchange (CME), organized a futures market in U.S. Treasury bills, bank CDs, and Eurodollars. The volume of trading in financial futures markets has grown to an extraordinary extent, and Treasury bonds and Eurodollars are now among the top ten of the 100 or so standardized commodities traded in both financial and nonfinancial futures markets.

The Options Market for Debt Instruments

Another financial instrument that enables investors to reduce interest-rate risk is options on debt instruments. An option contract provides the right to buy (a **call option**) or sell (a **put option**) a security at a specified price, called the exercise or strike price. A call option that expires in six months' time to buy $1 million face value of three-month Treasury bills at an exercise price of $975,000 is one example, while a six-month put option to sell a $100,000 face value Treasury bond at an exercise price of $102,000 is another.

An option contract is like a form of insurance against interest-rate risk. To understand this, let us consider the following two examples. Suppose Irving the Investor owns a $100,000 face value Treasury bond and buys a three-month put option for the bond, which gives him the right to sell it at an exercise price of $102,000 (which has a yield of 10%). Even if interest rates rise above 10% and the price of the bond falls below the exercise price of $102,000, Irving is protected from a loss because the option contract gives him the right to sell the bond for $102,000. Similarly, if Irving is thinking about buying the Treasury bond, he can ensure that at a minimum he will be able to obtain a 10% interest rate by buying a three-month call for the bond with an exercise price of $102,000. Now if interest rates fall below 10%, his option contract allows him to buy the bond for $102,000, providing him with a 10% interest rate.

Because options contracts provide a form of insurance, purchasers must pay a price for them called, naturally enough, a "premium." As you would expect, the increased volatility of interest rates in recent years has increased the demand for this type of insurance, making an option market in debt instruments potentially profitable. The Chicago Board Options Exchange (CBOE), in which options for stocks had been traded since 1973, initiated trading in options for debt instruments in 1981. Currently, the CBOE and other exchanges offer options not only for Treasury bonds and bills, but also for financial futures contracts.

Other Changes in Market Conditions: Discount Brokers and Stock Index Futures

Other changes in market conditions have been important to innovation in the financial marketplace. As mentioned in the previous chapter, before 1975 the stock exchanges had rules that fixed brokerage commission rates at a high level. Since brokerage firms were not allowed to compete on the basis of price, instead they competed on the quality of the services they provided. Brokerage firms supplied their customers with frequent reports on securities, had large research departments to provide financial analysis, and even had fancy offices in which their customers could watch price quotations.

In 1975, the SEC disallowed the rules that set the high brokerage commissions, and profits could now be made in the brokerage industry by competing on price. As our analysis of financial innovation predicts, a new type of brokerage emerged called a "discount broker." Like discount stores that have lower prices and provide fewer services, discount brokers have lower brokerage commissions but reduce the services they provide to their customers. For example, they lack large research departments to provide financial analysis and frequent reports for their customers. These discount brokers (the largest is Charles Schwab and Company) have carved out a substantial chunk of the brokerage business and have been an important factor in the drop in brokerage commission rates that has occurred since the 1975 regulatory change.

The sharp drop in brokerage commissions that occurred after 1975 was especially pronounced for traders of large blocks of stocks, pension funds, and mutual funds. The cheaper costs for these institutional investors meant that the traders could attract more customers, with the result that they became a more important force in the marketplace. In addition, many small investors recognized that mutual funds have a hard time beating the market, and index funds (mutual funds that focus on producing returns similar to those on broad market indexes) became increasingly popular. The increased importance of institutional investors along with the increased focus on tracking market indexes led to an increased demand for a more liquid market in a basket (group) of stocks that track the market.

Given this need in the marketplace, a natural extension to the already successful markets in financial futures occurred in 1982. The financial innovation was futures trading in stock price indexes at the Chicago Board of Trade (CBT), the Chicago Mercantile Exchange (CME), the Kansas City Board of Trade (KCBT), and the New York Futures Exchange (NYFE), a subsidiary of the New York Stock Exchange. The futures trading in stock price indexes is now quite controversial (Box 13.1) because critics assert that it has led to substantial increases in market volatility, especially in such episodes as the Black Monday Crash on October 19, 1987, or the 190-point decline in the Dow Jones Industrial Average on Friday, October 13, 1989 (most of which occurred in the last hour of trading).

FINANCIAL INNOVATION: ADVANCES IN TECHNOLOGY

The development of new technology can stimulate financial innovation by lowering the cost of providing new financial services and instruments and making it profitable to offer them to the public. When computer technology that substantially lowered the cost of processing financial transactions became available, financial institutions conceived new financial services and instruments dependent on this technology that might appeal to the public. Three such examples are bank credit cards, securitization, and the internationalization of financial markets, which is discussed in Box 13.2.

Bank Credit Cards

Credit cards have been around since well before World War II. Many individual stores (Sears, Macy's, Goldwater's) institutionalized charge accounts at their stores by providing customers with credit cards, which allowed them

B o x   1 3 . 1

Program Trading and Portfolio Insurance: Were They to Blame for the Stock Market Crash of 1987?

In the aftermath of the Black Monday Crash on October 19, 1987, in which the stock market declined by over 20% in one day, trading strategies involving stock price index futures markets have been accused (by the Brady Commission, for example) of being culprits in the market collapse. One such strategy called "program trading" involves computer-directed trading between the stock index futures and the stocks whose prices are reflected in the stock price index. Program trades are conducted to keep stock index futures and stock prices in line with each other (a process called arbitrage). For example, when the price of the stock index futures contract is far below the prices of the underlying stocks in the index, program trades buy index futures and sell the stocks. Critics of program trading assert that the sharp fall in stock index futures prices on Black Monday led to massive selling in the stock market in order to keep stock prices in line with the stock index futures prices.

Another trading strategy called "portfolio insurance" involves hedging against stock market declines by selling stock index futures. The idea behind such a strategy is that when stock prices fall, stock index futures prices fall with them, so that the investor can obtain capital gains on the futures which offset the losses on the stocks he or she is holding. Some experts blame portfolio insurance for amplifying the crash because they feel that an increased desire to hedge stocks led to massive selling of stock index futures; which precipitated large price declines in these contracts; which then led to massive selling of stocks by program traders to keep prices in line.

Because they view program trading and/or portfolio insurance as an important source of the October 1987 market collapse, critics of stock index futures have advocated restrictions on their trading. In response, certain brokerage firms as well as organized exchanges have placed limits on program trading. The New York Stock Exchange, for example, has curbed computerized program trading when the Dow Jones Industrial Average moves by more than 50 points within the day. However, some prominent financial economists (Nobel prizewinner Merton Miller of the University of Chicago, for example) do not accept the hypothesis that program trading and portfolio insurance helped promote the stock market crash. They believe that the prices of stock index futures primarily reflect the same economic forces that move stock prices—the changes in the market's underlying assessment of the value of stocks.

---

to make purchases at their stores without cash. Nationwide, credit cards were not established until after World War II, when Diners Club developed them to be used in restaurants all over the country (and abroad). Similar credit-card programs were started by American Express and Carte Blanche, but because of the high cost of operating these programs, cards were issued only to select persons and businesses who could afford expensive purchases.

A firm issuing credit cards earns income from loans it makes to credit-card holders and from payments made by stores on credit-card purchases (a percentage of the purchase price, say 5%). A credit-card program's costs arise from loan defaults, stolen cards, and the expense involved in processing credit-card transactions.

B o x   1 3 . 2   **A Global Perspective**

Internationalization of Financial Markets

Computers and advanced telecommunications are a driving factor behind the internationalization of financial markets. Technology to transmit share prices and information instantaneously around the world has led to dealers in New York or Tokyo not being constrained by the hours of organized exchanges; they can trade at any time of day or night. The low cost of international communications is making it easier to invest abroad, and we are rapidly moving to a world in which stocks and bonds will be traded internationally twenty-four hours a day.

The impact of advanced telecommunications on the internationalization of financial markets was most dramatically illustrated by the events during the Black Monday Crash of 1987. Just before the crash on October 19, 1987, there were substantial declines in foreign stock markets. As a result, there were huge sell orders at the U.S. markets' openings on October 19 and stock prices on the U.S. exchanges plummeted. Then the crash in U.S. stocks was transmitted to foreign markets which experienced declines of similar magnitude. For better or for worse, we now live in a world of highly integrated financial markets in which we all boom or bust together.

Bankers saw the success of Diners Club, American Express, and Carte Blanche and wanted to share in the profitable credit-card business. Several commercial banks attempted to expand the credit-card business to a wider market in the 1950s, but the cost of running these programs was so high that their early attempts to establish a credit-card business failed.

In the late 1960s, improved computer technology, which lowered the cost of providing credit-card services, made it more likely that bank credit-card programs would be profitable. The banks tried to enter this business again, and now their efforts led to the creation of two successful bank credit-card programs: BankAmericard (originally started by the Bank of America but now an independent organization called VISA) and MasterCard (Interbank Card Association). These programs have become phenomenally successful, with the number of bank credit cards around the 200 million mark. Consumers have benefited because credit cards are more widely accepted when paying for purchases than are checks (particularly abroad) and they allow consumers to take out loans more easily.

Securitization

Securitization is the process of transforming otherwise illiquid financial assets into marketable capital market instruments, and it too has been stimulated by advances in computer technology. With electronic record keeping, financial institutions find that they can cheaply bundle together a portfolio of loans (such as mortgages) with small denominations, collect the interest and principal payments, and then "pass them through" (pay them out) to a third party. The claims to these interest and principal payments can thus be sold to a third party as a security, and the financial institution makes a profit by servicing the securitized loans (collecting the interest and principal payments and paying them out) and charging a fee.

Securitization first started in 1970 when the GNMA (Government National Mortgage Association, "Ginnie Mae") developed the concept of a pass-through, mortgage-backed security when it began a program in which it guaranteed the timely payment of interest and principal on bundles of standardized mortgages. Under this program, private financial institutions such as savings and loans and commercial banks were now able to gather a group of GNMA-guaranteed mortgages into a bundle of, say, $1 million, and then sell this bundle as a security to a third party (usually a large institutional investor such as a pension fund). When individuals make their mortgage payments on the GNMA-guaranteed mortgage to the financial institution, the financial institution then passes the payments through to the owner of the security by sending a check for the total of all the payments. Because GNMA guarantees the payments, these pass-through securities have a very low default risk.

In the usual GNMA pass-through security, the buyer has direct ownership of the portfolio of mortgage loans. Other types of mortgage-backed securities do not provide ownership of the mortgage portfolio to the buyer, but instead are debt obligations of the mortgage lending institution for which the mortgage loans are the collateral. Mortgage-backed securities continue to be the most common form of securitization. Securitization of mortgages has expanded enormously; two-thirds of all residential mortgages are now securitized, and there are close to $1 trillion of securitized mortgages outstanding.

Securitization has not stopped with mortgages, however: Securitization of automobile loans, credit-card receivables, and commercial and computer leases began in the mid-1980s. Securitized automobile loans, called CARS or FASTBACs (see Box 13.3), with only $900 million issued in 1985 grew to a market of $10 billion in 1986. By 1989, securitized credit-card receivables had an amount outstanding in excess of $30 billion. Experts predict that nonmortgage securitization will be a market of over $100 billion within the next few years.

Computer technology also has enabled financial institutions to tailor securitization to produce securities that have payment streams considered especially desirable by the market. Collateralized mortgage obligations (CMOs), which are bonds that pass through the payments from a portfolio of mortgages, are a good example of such tailoring. Computerization enables a CMO to be split into four classes or "tranches." The first three classes receive interest payments according to the coupon rate on the CMO, with class 1 first receiving all principal payments and prepayments from the collateralized pool of mortgages. After the class 1 bonds are paid off, the principal payments and prepayments are used to sequentially retire the remaining classes

Box 13.3

What's in a Name?

As anyone in the advertising business knows, it's not enough to have a good product; a catchy name helps too. Even Wall Street now recognizes that a security's name can be a marketing tool. Merrill Lynch started the trend when it named its deep-discount bond TIGRs, for Treasury Investment Growth Receipts. Salomon Brothers soon followed with its CATS, for Certificates of Accrual on Treasury Securities. Securitization has spawned its own set of names too. Salomon Brothers named its security backed by automobile loans CARs (Certificates of Automobile Receivables), while Drexel Burnham called its version FASTBACs (First Automotive Short-Term Bonds and Certificates). Securitized credit-card receivables have been named, naturally enough, CARDS, for Certificates for Amortizing Revolving Debts. Who knows what nifty names they'll think up next?

of bonds. The fourth class, called the "accrual" or "Z" bond, receives interest and principal payments only after the other three classes are paid off. The CMO has the advantage of containing bonds of both short maturity (class 1) and long maturity (class 3 or Z), thus increasing its potential market.

Although securitization could not take place without modern computer technology (think of the cost of trying to collect payments and paying them out by hand), technology is not the only factor encouraging it; the government has played an important role too. Securitization first started with GNMA guarantees of mortgage payments and even today involves mostly assets directly or indirectly guaranteed by the government. Tax rules also have stimulated new securitized instruments. A change of IRS regulations made possible real estate mortgage investment conduits (REMICs), which are essentially CMOs with a more favorable tax treatment.

FINANCIAL INNOVATION: AVOIDING EXISTING REGULATIONS

Thus far we've seen that financial innovation can arise from the desire to reduce risk and to exploit new technology in order to make profits. Similarly, regulation can lead to financial innovation by creating incentives for business firms to skirt regulations that restrict their ability to earn profits. Edward Kane describes this process of avoiding regulations as "loophole mining."[3] The economic analysis of innovation suggests that when regulatory constraints are so burdensome that large profits can be made by avoiding them, loophole mining and innovation are more likely to occur.

---

[3]Edward J. Kane, "Accelerating Inflation, Technological Innovation, and the Decreasing Effectiveness of Bank Regulation," *Journal of Finance*, vol. 36 (May 1981), pp. 355–367.

As we have seen in earlier chapters, the banking industry is one of the most heavily regulated industries in America. As such, it is an industry in which loophole mining is especially likely to occur. The rise in inflation and interest rates from the late 1960s to 1980 made the regulatory constraints imposed on this industry even more burdensome. Under these circumstances, we would expect the pace of financial innovations in banking to be rapid, and, indeed, it has been.

Regulations Behind Financial Innovation

Two sets of regulations have seriously restricted the ability of banks to make profits: (1) reserve requirements which force banks to keep a certain fraction of their deposits as reserves and (2) restrictions on the interest rates that can be paid on deposits. For the following reasons, these regulations have been among the major forces behind financial innovation in recent years.

Reserve Requirements   The key to understanding why reserve requirements affect financial innovation is to recognize that they act, in effect, as a tax on deposits. Since the Fed does not pay interest on reserves, the opportunity cost of holding them is the interest that a bank could earn by lending the reserves out. For each dollar of deposits, reserve requirements therefore impose a cost on the bank equal to the interest rate that could be earned if the reserves could be lent out (i), times the fraction of deposits required as reserves (r_D). The cost of $i \times r_D$ imposed on the bank is just like a tax on bank deposits of $i \times (r_D)$.

It is a great tradition to avoid taxes if possible, and banks do not act differently. Just as taxpayers look for loopholes to lower their tax bills, banks seek to increase their profits by loophole mining and by producing new financial innovations that allow them to escape the "tax" on deposits imposed by reserve requirements.

Restrictions on the Interest Rates Paid on Deposits   Until 1980, banking legislation prohibited banks (except in a few states) from paying interest on checking account deposits and, through Regulation Q, the Fed set maximum limits on the interest rate that could be paid on time deposits. The desire to avoid these restrictions on interest rates paid on deposits (called **deposit rate ceilings**) also produced financial innovations.

If market interest rates rose above the maximum rates that banks paid on time deposits under Regulation Q, depositors withdrew funds from banks to put them into higher-yielding securities. This loss of deposits from the banking system restricted the amount of funds that banks could lend (called **disintermediation**) and thus limited bank profits. Banks had an incentive to get around deposit rate ceilings because, by so doing, they could acquire funds to make loans and earn higher profits.

We can now look at how the desire to avoid restrictions on interest payments and the "tax" from reserve requirements led to several financial innovations.

Eurodollars and Bank Commercial Paper

In the late 1960s, inflation was accelerating and (from our analysis of the Fisher effect in Chapter 6) interest rates began to rise. The "tax" on deposits from reserve requirements, $i \times r_D$, also began to rise, and the incentives to avoid this "tax" increased. In addition, higher interest rates meant that market interest rates exceeded the maximum rate payable on time deposits under Regulation Q, and as market interest rates climbed to then record highs in 1969, investors reduced their time deposits to invest in higher-yielding securities. By the late 1960s, commercial banks had a strong incentive to search for new funds that would (1) not be subject to reserve requirements and so would not be subject to the tax of $i \times r_D$ and (2) not be subject to the interest rate ceiling set by Regulation Q.

As the economic analysis of innovation predicts, the banks began to mine loopholes and discovered two sources of funds that avoided reserve requirements *and* deposit rate ceilings: Eurodollars and bank commercial paper. Because Eurodollars (deposits abroad that are denominated in dollars) were borrowed from banks outside the United States, they were not subject to reserve requirements or to Regulation Q. Similarly, commercial paper issued by a bank's parent holding company was not treated as deposits and so was also free of these regulations. Not surprisingly, the markets for Eurodollars and bank commercial paper began to expand rapidly in the late 1960s.

NOW Accounts, ATS Accounts, and Overnight RPs

The rise in interest rates in the late 1960s, which made the avoidance of restrictions on deposit rates profitable, also stimulated the development of new types of checking accounts. Because of Regulation Q ceilings, savings and loans and mutual savings banks were especially hard hit by the rise in interest rates in the late 1960s. They lost large amounts of funds to financial instruments that paid higher interest rates, and they needed to find new sources of funds to continue to make profitable loans.

In 1970, as a result of diligent loophole mining, a mutual savings bank in Massachusetts struck gold by discovering a loophole in the prohibition of interest payments on checking accounts. In effect, by calling a check a negotiable order of withdrawal (NOW), accounts on which these NOWs could be written were not legally checking accounts. Thus NOW accounts were not subject to regulations on checking accounts and could pay interest. In May 1972, after two years of litigation, mutual savings banks in Massachusetts were allowed to issue NOW accounts that paid interest. Subsequently, in September 1972, the courts approved NOW accounts in New Hampshire.

NOW accounts were immediately successful in New Hampshire and Massachusetts, and they enabled savings and loans and mutual savings banks in those states to earn higher profits because they were able to attract more funds which could be loaned out. Since commercial banks did not want competition from other financial intermediaries for checking account deposits (at the time only commercial banks were legally allowed to issue checking accounts), they mounted a campaign to prevent the spread of these accounts to other states. The result was congressional legislation enacted in January 1974 that limited NOW accounts to New England. Legislation in 1980 finally authorized NOW accounts nationwide for savings and loans, mutual savings banks, and commercial banks, while similar accounts at credit unions (**share draft accounts**) were authorized for credit unions.

Another innovation that enables banks to effectively pay interest on checking accounts is the ATS (automatic transfer from savings) account. In this case a checking account automatically has balances above a certain amount transferred into a savings account that pays interest. When a check is written on the ATS account, the necessary funds to cover the check are automatically transferred from the savings account into the checking account. Thus balances earning interest in a savings account are effectively part of the depositor's checking account because they are available for writing checks. Legally, however, it is the savings account and not the checking account that pays interest to the depositor.

Commercial banks provide a variant of the ATS account to their corporate depositors, which involves the use of a "sweep account" to engage in overnight repurchase agreements (RPs). In this type of arrangement any balances above a certain amount in a corporation's checking account at the end of a business day are "swept out of the account" and are invested in overnight RPs that pay the corporation interest. (As you may recall from Chapter 3, the RP is an agreement in which a corporation purchases Treasury bills which the bank agrees to repurchase the next day at a slightly higher price.) Again, although the checking account does not legally pay interest, in effect the corporation is receiving interest on balances that are available for writing checks.

The financial innovations of ATS accounts and overnight RP arrangements were stimulated not only by deposit rate ceilings, but also by new technology. Without low-cost computers to process inexpensively the additional transactions required by these accounts, neither of these innovations would be profitable and therefore would not have been developed. Technological factors often combine with other incentives, such as the desire to get around restrictions on deposit rates, to produce financial innovation.

Money Market Mutual Funds

The desire to avoid deposit rate ceilings and the "tax" on deposits imposed by reserve requirements led to the development of money market mutual funds. Money market mutual funds issue shares that are redeemable at a fixed price (usually $1) by writing checks. For example, if you buy 5000 shares ($5000), the money market fund uses these funds to invest in short-term money market securities (Treasury bills, certificates of deposit, commercial paper) which provide you with interest payments. In addition, you are able to write checks up to the $5000 held as shares in the money market fund. Although money market fund shares effectively function as checking account deposits that earn interest, they are not legally deposits and so are not subject to reserve requirements or prohibitions on interest payments. For this reason they can pay higher interest rates than deposits at banks.

The first money market mutual fund was created by two Wall Street mavericks, Bruce Bent and Henry Brown, in 1971. However, the low market interest rates from 1971 to 1977 (which were just slightly above Regulation Q ceilings of 5¼ to 5½%) kept them from being particularly advantageous relative to bank deposits. In early 1978, the situation changed rapidly as market interest rates began to climb over 10%, well above the 5½% maximum interest rates payable on savings accounts and time deposits under Regulation Q. In 1977, money market mutual funds had assets under $4 billion; in 1978, their assets climbed to close to $10 billion; in 1979, to over $40 billion; and in 1982, to $230 billion. Currently, their assets are around $500 billion. To say the least, money market mutual funds have been a successful financial innovation, which is exactly what we would have predicted for the late 1970s and early 1980s when interest rates soared relative to Regulation Q ceilings.

FINANCIAL INNOVATION: RESPONSE OF REGULATION

Just as financial institutions change in response to regulation, the regulatory authorities change their regulations in response to financial innovation. This process can be thought of as a cat-and-mouse game between the financial institutions and the regulators in which they adapt continually to each other.

Two major objectives of the regulatory authorities have governed their response to financial innovation in the past twenty-five years: (1) the encouragement of home ownership, as reflected in attempts by the regulatory authorities to ensure flows of funds into mortgage-issuing institutions; and (2) the encouragement of stability in the financial system, as reflected in attempts to prevent bank failures.

Changing Banking Regulation in the 1960s and 1970s

We have seen that once market interest rates began to rise above the Regulation Q ceilings on deposit rates in the mid-1960s, funds began to leave depository institutions, particularly the savings and loans and mutual savings banks. Because savings and loans and mutual savings banks were the most important issuers of residential mortgages, their loss of deposits meant that there were fewer funds available to issue residential mortgages. Therefore, to encourage the flow of funds into these mortgage-issuing institutions, the Fed adjusted its Regulation Q ceilings to allow savings and loans and mutual savings banks to pay slightly higher interest rates (by one-quarter of one percent) on their time deposits than commercial banks could pay on theirs. In addition, to put everyone on a more equal footing, deposit rate ceilings were extended to previously unregulated institutions such as credit unions.

Regulators also pursued a second strategy to discourage financial market instruments that would compete with deposits. They convinced the U.S. Treasury in 1970 to raise the minimum denomination on Treasury bills to $10,000, so that small savers would be forced to put their savings into savings and loans and mutual savings banks. In addition they encouraged bank holding companies and corporations not to issue small-denomination debt. This strategy discriminated against small savers (typically with low incomes) who were prevented from earning market interest rates. Large savers (typically with high incomes), on the other hand, had sufficient resources to buy large-denomination securities and earn market interest rates. This strategy of discrimination against lower-income people is both peculiar and somewhat paradoxical; most of us do not advocate an anti-Robin-Hood policy of taking from the poor to give to the rich.

Although deposit rate ceilings worked in the short run to provide funds to the mortgage-issuing institutions, financial innovation worked to undo these regulations. By the late 1970s the success of money market mutual funds and overnight repurchase agreements was causing mortgage-issuing institutions to lose so many deposits that their financial health was severely threatened. One temporary solution was to allow these institutions to issue money market certificates (MMCs), which paid market interest rates. An interesting feature of this regulatory change is that it continued to discriminate against the small saver because these certificates were issued in denominations of $10,000. The large-denomination MMCs kept small savers from shifting their deposits into these certificates. This enabled the mortgage-issuing institutions to hold on to their low-cost deposits and thus have an overall lower cost of funds.

By 1980, after all of these regulatory changes to help the savings and loans and mutual savings banks, the continuing rise in interest rates left them in even deeper financial trouble, and commercial banks were threatened as well. A major financial reform was needed and it came in the form of congressional legislation—the Depository Institutions Deregulation and Monetary Control Act of 1980.

Depository Institutions Deregulation and Monetary Control Act of 1980

As often happens with major legislation, an attempt is made to please as many opposing parties as possible to enhance the chances of passage. An important intent of the Depository Institutions Deregulation and Monetary Control Act (DIDMCA) was to help the mortgage-issuing institutions (savings and loan associations and mutual savings banks). These institutions were allowed to compete more effectively against commercial banks by allowing them wider latitude in the loans they could make. Savings and loans, for example, whose loans had effectively been restricted to mortgages, were now allowed to invest up to 20% of their assets in consumer loans, commercial paper, and corporate bonds. Mutual savings banks were allowed to make commercial loans up to 5% of their assets and were allowed to open checking accounts in connection with these loans. In addition, savings and loans were allowed to expand into new lines of business such as trust services and credit cards.

DIDMCA also approved NOW and ATS accounts nationwide at all depository institutions, thereby allowing all of these institutions to compete more effectively against money market mutual funds. It also mandated a phaseout of Regulation Q, completed by 1986, and set up a Depository Institutions Deregulation Committee (made up of representatives from the Fed, the Treasury, the FDIC, the Federal Home Loan Bank Board, and the National Credit Union Administration) to supervise the phaseout. The provisions of DIDMCA not only had advantages for the mortgage-issuing institutions, but they also benefited commercial banks and credit unions, thus garnering their support for this legislation. These provisions were popular with the public since they allowed depositors to earn higher interest payments on their deposits.

Other provisions of DIDMCA involved the elimination of usury ceilings (maximum interest rates) on mortgage loans and the elimination of the usury ceiling for three years on certain business and agricultural loans in excess of $25,000.[4] Finally, DIDMCA imposed uniform reserve requirements on all depository institutions and allowed all of these institutions access to Federal Reserve facilities, such as the discount window and Fed check-clearing services. This final set of provisions put all of these institutions on an equal footing and made them more subject to control by the Fed. The Fed argued strenuously for provisions of this type to stem the loss of members from the Federal Reserve System and to improve monetary control.

Impact of DIDMCA The expansion of NOW and ATS account deposits after they were authorized by DIDMCA starting in 1981 was dramatic, with the amount of these deposits increasing from $27 billion to $101 billion from 1980 to 1982. However, since the Regulation Q deposit rate ceilings were being phased out gradually and market interest rates climbed to record lev-

---

[4]Both of these provisions, however, allowed the states to reimpose usury ceilings if they acted by April 1, 1983.

els in 1981–1982, money market funds continued to grow rapidly (averaging $76 billion in 1980 and $230 billion in 1982). As a result, savings and loans and mutual savings banks were losing deposits at the same time that the cost of their acquired funds climbed higher. As we saw in Chapter 11, the result was an unprecedented (for the period after World War II) number of failures of these institutions. Thus further reform legislation was needed to help these institutions.

Depository Institutions (Garn-St Germain) Act of 1982

In October 1982, the Depository Institutions (Garn-St Germain) Act was passed to deal with the immediate emergency stemming from the unprecedented number of failures of savings and loans and mutual savings banks (over 250 in 1982). To compete more effectively with money market funds, depository institutions were allowed to offer money market deposit accounts (MMDAs), which provide services comparable to money market mutual funds and are not subject to Regulation Q ceilings or reserve requirements. Since depository institutions are able to pay high interest rates on these accounts, they became immensely popular: By the end of 1983, MMDA deposits had grown to almost $400 billion and now are around $500 billion.

The Garn-St Germain Act had additional provisions to help savings and loans and mutual savings banks. By 1984 federally chartered savings and loans and mutual savings banks were allowed to invest up to 10% of their assets in commercial loans, and the maximum amount of consumer lending was raised to 30% of their assets. Because the provisions put these institutions on a more equal footing with commercial banks, the Garn-St Germain Act required that from 1984 on, Regulation Q ceilings should be applied equally to all depository institutions until they expired in 1986.

A final set of provisions was designed to assist the FDIC and FSLIC in dealing with the emergency situation due to bank failures. For example, the FDIC and FSLIC were given emergency powers to merge troubled institutions across state lines or to merge thrift institutions (mutual savings banks and savings and loans) into commercial banks.

Impact of the Garn-St Germain Act   The net effect of the Garn-St Germain Act, combined with the earlier DIDMCA legislation of 1980, was to make the banking system as a whole more competitive: All depository institutions are treated more equally and the distinctions between the different depository institutions have become blurred. Although the deregulation in DIDMCA and the Garn-St Germain Act produced the benefit of a more competitive banking system, it also led to increased risk taking on the part of savings and loans, which resulted in disastrous consequences as we have seen in Chapter 11. The subsequent bailout of the savings and loan industry in the Financial

Institutions Reform, Recovery, and Enforcement Act (FIRREA) of 1989 has been described in that earlier chapter. An additional important feature of FIRREA is that it has increased the regulation of the savings and loan industry. It substantially raises capital requirements for S&Ls, restricts their investment activities, and places the responsibility for monitoring the industry with a much tougher regulator, the FDIC.

The trend to *re*regulation has also arisen for the commercial banking industry. Capital requirements have been increased for commercial banks, and a new risk-based capital requirement is being put into place. In our dynamic world of financial markets driven by financial innovation, there are growing opportunities for risk taking. This is likely to mean increased regulation by our bank regulatory agencies in order to minimize the adverse selection and moral hazard problems created by deposit insurance.

APPLICATION
FUTURE EVOLUTION OF THE FINANCIAL SYSTEM / / / / / / / / / / / / / / / / /

While the evolution of our financial system is well explained by our analysis of financial innovation, useful economic analysis must also help us predict the future. This is crucial because, unfortunately, economists do not have access to crystal balls. Now we will use the economic analysis of financial innovation to explain what may happen to the financial system in years to come.

Study Guide
In the examples that follow, try to use the analysis outlined earlier in the chapter to predict what *you* think will happen to the financial system before reading the explanation in the text. This will reinforce earlier material and at the same time give you some feel for how economic analysis is applied to the real world.

What If Interest-Rate Risk Falls in the Future?

The 1970s and 1980s witnessed an unprecedented rise in interest-rate risk. Since "what comes up must come down," it is possible that interest-rate risk will decline in the future. What effect would a decline have on the financial system?

With lower interest-rate risk, investors would have less need to protect themselves against interest-rate risk. As a result less hedging would occur in financial futures markets and so less trading of financial futures contracts would take place. In addition, there would be less demand for the insurance against interest-rate risk provided by options for debt instruments. The growth in both these markets experienced in the late 1970s and 1980s would slow and the markets might even shrink. If volume of trading declined sufficiently, some financial futures and options markets could disappear.[5]

What If Inflation Declines in the Future?

There have been many periods in U.S. history in which the inflation rate has declined. If inflation should drop to a level that is permanently lower than it is now, how will the financial system respond?

A decline in inflation would, through the Fisher effect we described in Chapter 6, lower interest rates. The fall in interest rates would then lower the "tax" on deposits imposed by reserve requirements, $i \times r_D$. Since there would be less incentive for banks to avoid this "tax," they might borrow less from the bank commercial paper or Eurodollar markets, which currently have no reserve requirements, and would look for deposit business instead. Another factor that would increase the quantity of deposits is that the lower "tax" on deposits would allow banks to pay a higher interest rate on them and so make them more competitive with money market funds. Depositors would now find deposits more attractive relative to money market funds so that deposits would rise further and money market funds would decline.

The examples here indicate that our economic analysis of financial innovation can help us predict how the financial system may respond to possible changes. Additional examples of the usefulness of this analysis appear in the problems at the end of the chapter. However, the analysis cannot precisely predict every financial innovation of the future, since the actual form an innovation takes reflects the mysterious process of human ingenuity. Technological change also plays an important role in financial innovation and predicting technological change is notoriously difficult. Who could have imagined thirty years ago that computers that once filled large rooms would be outperformed by personal computers that fit on a desktop?

The fact that economic analysis does not tell us everything we want to know about the phenomenon of financial innovation does not reduce its value. Economic analysis is a useful tool—but it has limitations—and a large part of the art of using economics to understand what is happening around us is recognizing the purposes for which it will be useful.

---

[5]There would also be a slowing in the growth of adjustable-rate mortgages and interest-rate swaps discussed in Chapter 9, which are also used to protect financial institutions from financial risk.

SUMMARY

1. The economic analysis of innovation suggests that a change in the economic environment will stimulate the search for innovations that are likely to be profitable.

2. Changes in market conditions that stimulated the search for profits have resulted in financial innovations such as adjustable-rate mortgages, financial futures, options for debt instruments, discount brokers, and stock index futures.

3. The development of new technology also stimulates financial innovation because it can lower the cost of providing new financial services and instruments and thus make them profitable. Three examples of how technology has worked to produce financial innovation are bank credit cards, securitization, and the internationalization of financial markets.

4. Regulation leads to financial innovation by encouraging loophole mining. Starting in the late 1960s, for example, higher interest rates (resulting from higher inflation) combined with deposit rate ceilings and the "tax" on deposits to limit bank profits. The desire to avoid these regulations encouraged financial innovations, including increased use of Eurodollars and bank commercial paper, NOW accounts, ATS accounts, overnight RPs, and money market mutual funds.

5. Just as financial institutions change in response to regulation, regulatory authorities change their regulations in response to financial innovations. In the 1960s and 1970s the regulatory authorities' objective of ensuring flows of funds into mortgage-issuing institutions led them to encourage discrimination against the small saver and to plug loopholes in Regulation Q. Although this strategy worked well in the short run, it led eventually to severe financial difficulties for depository institutions. In order to encourage a more stable financial system, major reform legislation was passed in 1980 and 1982, which allowed nationwide NOW accounts, money market deposit accounts (MMDAs), uniform reserve requirements for all depository institutions, and the phaseout of deposit rate ceilings.

KEY TERMS

interest-rate risk	put option
futures contract	securitization
financial futures contract	deposit rate ceilings
hedge	disintermediation
call option	share draft accounts

QUESTIONS AND PROBLEMS

* 1. "Rather than view greed as a vice, we should view it as a positive element in our society that improves our well-being." Discuss this statement in the context of financial innovation.

2. What explains the appearance of futures markets for financial instruments and options markets for debt instruments in the 1970s and early 1980s?

* 3. If you plan to take out a three-month loan nine months from now, how can you use the financial futures market to reduce your interest-rate risk?

4. Your rich uncle has just died and left you $1 million, but you will not receive your inheritance for six months. If interest rates are currently high, how can you use the financial futures market to make sure that you will earn a high interest rate

on the $1 million when you get it? How can you use the options market?

* 5. If high-speed computers had been developed ten years earlier, would the first attempts by banks to mass-merchandise credit cards have met with failure? Why or why not?

6. Why did banks devote more resources to loop-hole mining in the late 1960s and 1970s than they did in the 1950s?

* 7. Answer true, false, or uncertain: "An important source of growth in the Eurodollar market has been government regulations."

8. Why was it more likely that NOW accounts would be developed by a savings and loan or a mutual savings bank rather than a commercial bank?

* 9. How successful has banking regulation been in achieving its goal of encouraging home ownership? Explain.

10. How has banking legislation in the 1980s helped the small saver?

Using Economic Analysis to Predict the Future

*11. If the Federal Reserve begins to pay interest on reserves in order to improve monetary control, what effect would this have on the financial system?

12. If the stock exchanges were again allowed to set minimum brokerage commissions, what would happen to the employment of financial analysts?

*13. If inflation becomes more variable in the future, would you expect to see a rise or a fall in the volume of trading in financial futures markets? in options markets for debt instruments?

14. If reserve requirements were eliminated in the future, as some economists advocate, what effects would this have on money market mutual funds?

*15. Predict what would happen to the financial system if Regulation Q ceilings were reimposed.

PART IV

The Money
Supply Process

CHAPTER 14

Multiple Deposit Creation: Introducing the Money Supply Process

PREVIEW   On the evening news you have just heard that last week the money supply rose by $5 billion. The news immediately sets off a chain reaction. Interest rates may rise because people expect that the increase in the money supply will lead to inflation; the stock market may boom because financial markets expect a stronger economy in the future; and firms may decide to invest more while consumers decide to spend more. Politicians will also react to the news: Some will berate the Fed for promoting inflation by letting the money supply expand *too much,* and others will berate the Fed for *not* expanding the money supply *enough* in order to eliminate unemployment.

   Movements in the money supply affect the health of the economy, thereby affecting us all, so you need to understand how the money supply is determined. Who controls it? What causes it to change? How might its control be improved? In this and subsequent chapters we answer these questions by providing a detailed description of the money supply process, that is, the mechanism that determines the level of the money supply.

   Because deposits at banks are by far the largest component of the money supply, understanding how these deposits are created is the first step to understanding the money supply process. This chapter provides an overview of how the banking system creates deposits. In addition, it outlines the basic building blocks needed in later chapters for you to understand in greater depth how the money supply is determined.

FOUR PLAYERS IN THE MONEY SUPPLY PROCESS

The "cast of characters" in the money supply story is as follows:

1. The **central bank:** the government agency that oversees the banking system and is responsible for the conduct of monetary policy. In the United States, it is the Federal Reserve System.

2. Banks (depository institutions): the financial intermediaries that accept deposits from individuals and institutions and make loans—commercial banks, savings and loan associations, mutual savings banks, and credit unions.

3. Depositors: individuals and institutions that hold deposits in banks.

4. Borrowers from banks: individuals and institutions that borrow from the depository institutions, or institutions that issue bonds that are purchased by the depository institutions.

Of the four "players," the central bank, the Federal Reserve System, is the most important. We first must understand its function in order to explore the money supply process.[1]

OVERVIEW OF THE FEDERAL RESERVE SYSTEM

The **Federal Reserve System,** commonly called the Fed or the Federal Reserve, is the central bank of the United States. It consists of twelve Federal Reserve banks in major cities (for example, New York, Chicago, Boston, Dallas, Atlanta, and San Francisco) and the Board of Governors of the Federal Reserve System, located in Washington, D.C.

The Federal Reserve System performs several essential functions:

1. It conducts monetary policy by affecting the behavior of banks, thereby affecting the money supply.

2. It clears checks, that is, transfers funds between banks to settle claims that arise as a result of the depositing of checks in one bank that have been written on an account at another bank.

3. It performs a regulatory function by setting rules for how banks can operate.

The operation of the Fed and its conduct of monetary policy involve actions that affect its balance sheet (holdings of assets and liabilities). Here we discuss a simplified balance sheet, which includes just four items that are essential to our analysis of the money supply process. (Chapter 18 contains the complete balance sheet.)

Federal Reserve System (the Fed)	
Assets	Liabilities
Government securities	Currency in circulation
Discount loans	Reserves

---

[1] A more detailed discussion of the Fed's structure and operation is in Chapters 17–20.

Liabilities

The two liabilities in the balance sheet, currency in circulation and reserves, are often referred to as the monetary liabilities of the Fed. They are an important part of the money supply story because increases in either or both will lead to an increase in the money supply (everything else being constant). The sum of the Fed's monetary liabilities (currency in circulation and reserves) and the U.S. Treasury's monetary liabilities (Treasury currency in circulation, primarily coins) is called the **monetary base.** When discussing the monetary base, we will focus only on the monetary liabilities of the Fed, since the monetary liabilities of the Treasury amount to less than 10% of the base.[2]

1. Currency in Circulation. The Fed issues currency (those green pieces of paper in your wallet that say Federal Reserve Note at the top). Currency in circulation is the amount of currency circulating in the hands of the public (outside of banks)—an important component of the money supply. (Currency held by depository institutions is also a liability of the Fed but is included as part of reserves.)

Federal Reserve notes are IOUs from the Fed to the bearer and are also liabilities, but unlike most, they promise to pay back the bearer solely with Federal Reserve notes; that is, they pay off IOUs with other IOUs. Accordingly, if you bring a $100 bill to the Federal Reserve and demand payment, you will receive two $50s, five $20s, ten $10s, or one hundred $1 bills.

People are more willing to accept IOUs from the Fed than from you or me because Federal Reserve notes are a recognized medium of exchange; that is, they are accepted as a means of payment and so function as money. Unfortunately neither you nor I can convince people that our IOUs are worth anything more than the paper they are written on.[3]

2. Reserves. All banks have an account at the Fed in which they hold deposits. **Reserves** include deposits at the Fed plus currency that is physi-

---

[2]It is also safe to ignore the Treasury's monetary liabilities when discussing the monetary base since the Treasury cannot actively supply its monetary liabilities to the economy because of legal restrictions (see Chapter 18).

[3]The currency item in the balance sheet above refers only to currency *in circulation,* that is, the amount circulating in the hands of the public. The fact that currency has been printed by the U.S. Bureau of Printing and Engraving does not make it a liability of the Fed. For example, consider the importance of having $1 million of your own IOUs printed up. You give out $100 worth to other people and keep the other $999,900 in your pocket. The $999,900 of IOUs does not make you richer or poorer and does not affect your indebtedness. You only care about the $100 of liabilities from the $100 of circulated IOUs. The same reasoning applies for the Fed in regard to its Federal Reserve Notes.

For similar reasons, the currency component of the money supply, no matter how it is defined, includes only the currency in circulation. It does not include any additional currency that is not yet in the hands of the public. The fact that currency has been printed but is not circulating means that it is not anyone's asset or liability and thus cannot affect anyone's behavior. Therefore, it makes sense not to include it in the money supply.

cally held by banks (called vault cash because it is stored in bank vaults). Reserves are assets for the banks but liabilities of the Fed because the banks can demand payment on them at any time and the Fed is obliged to satisfy its obligation by paying Federal Reserve Notes. As you will see, an increase in reserves leads to an increase in the level of deposits and hence in the money supply.

Total reserves can be divided into two categories: reserves that the Fed requires banks to hold **(required reserves)** and any additional reserves the banks choose to hold **(excess reserves).** For example, the Fed might require that for every dollar of deposits at a depository institution, a certain fraction (say 10 cents) must be held as reserves. This fraction (10%) is called the **required reserve ratio.** Currently, the Fed pays no interest on reserves.

Assets

The two assets in the Fed's balance sheet are important for two reasons. First, changes in the asset items lead to changes in reserves and consequently to changes in the money supply. Second, because these assets (government securities and discount loans) earn interest while the liabilities (currency in circulation and reserves) do not, the Fed makes billions of dollars every year—its assets earn income and its liabilities cost nothing. Although it returns most of its earnings to the federal government, the Fed does spend some of it on "worthy causes," such as supporting the research of economists.

1. Government Securities. This category of assets includes the Fed's holdings of securities issued by the U.S. Treasury. As you will see, the Fed provides reserves to the banking system by purchasing securities, thereby increasing its holdings of these assets. An increase in government securities held by the Fed leads to an increase in the money supply.

2. Discount Loans. The Fed can provide reserves to the banking system by making discount loans to banks. An increase in discount loans can also be the source of an increase in the money supply. The interest rate charged banks for these loans is called the **discount rate.**

MULTIPLE DEPOSIT CREATION: A SIMPLE MODEL

With our understanding of the basic functions of the Federal Reserve and how banks operate (Chapter 9), we now have the tools necessary to explain how deposits are created. When the Fed supplies the banking system with $1 of additional reserves, deposits increase by a multiple of this amount—a process called **multiple deposit creation.** Let us begin with the Fed and see how its actions lead to an increase in reserves.

How the Fed Provides Reserves to the Banking System

There are two ways in which the Fed can provide additional reserves to the banking system:

1. It can make loans to the banks.
2. It can purchase government bonds.

Loans to Banks Suppose the Fed makes a $100 discount loan to the First National Bank. Once the Fed makes the loan, it immediately credits the proceeds from the loan to the account of the First National Bank at the Fed. The bank's reserves rise by $100, while its borrowings from the Fed have increased by $100:

First National Bank			
Assets		Liabilities	
Reserves	+ $100	Discount loan from the Fed	+ $100

The same items appear in the Fed's T-account but in the opposite columns, because for the Fed, reserves are a liability (payable on demand) and the discount loan is an asset (earns income for the Fed):

The Fed			
Assets		Liabilities	
Discount loan to First National Bank	+ $100	Reserves	+ $100

You can see that the Fed can provide reserves to the banking system by loaning them to the banks.

Purchase of Government Bonds The Fed's buying (or selling) of bonds in the open market is called an **open market operation.** Suppose the Fed buys $100 worth of bonds from the First National Bank and pays for them with a check written on the New York Federal Reserve Bank. The First National Bank then deposits the check with the Fed and it is credited to the First National Bank's reserves account. The net result of the open market operation on the First National Bank's balance sheet is that it reduces its holdings of securities by $100 while it has gained $100 in reserves:

First National Bank		
Assets		Liabilities
Securities	− $100	
Reserves	+ $100	

The Fed finds that its liabilities have increased by $100 because reserves have increased by this amount, yet it now finds itself holding an extra $100 of bonds, which appear in its assets column as an increase of $100 in government securities. Its T-account is

The Fed			
Assets		Liabilities	
Government securities	+ $100	Reserves	+ $100

You can see that the Fed can exercise control over the size of reserves by varying its holdings of government securities via open market operations.[4]

With this information in mind, we now examine how an increase in reserves can create deposits.

Deposit Creation: The Single Bank

After the Fed has bought the $100 bond from the First National Bank, the bank finds that it has an increase in reserves of $100. To analyze what the bank will do with these additional reserves, assume that the bank does not want to hold excess reserves because it earns no interest on them. We begin the analysis with the following T-account:

First National Bank		
Assets		Liabilities
Securities	− $100	
Reserves	+ $100	

Because the bank has no increase in its checkable deposits, required reserves remain the same and the bank finds that its additional $100 of reserves means that its excess reserves have increased by $100. Let's say the bank decides to make a loan equal in amount to the $100 increase in excess re-

---

[4]The next chapter details further how the Fed uses open market operations to affect reserves. For example, we show that an open market operation has the same effect on reserves if bonds are purchased from the nonbank public rather than from banks.

serves. When the bank makes the loan, it sets up a checking account for the borrower and puts the proceeds of the loan into this account. In this way the bank alters its balance sheet by increasing its liabilities with $100 of checkable deposits and at the same time increasing its assets with the $100 loan. The resulting T-account follows:

First National Bank			
Assets		Liabilities	
Securities	− $100	Checkable deposits	+ $100
Reserves	+ $100		
Loans	+ $100		

The bank has created checkable deposits by its act of lending. Since checkable deposits are part of the money supply, the bank's act of lending has in fact created money.

With its current balance sheet position, the First National Bank still has excess reserves that it could lend out. However, these reserves will not stay at the bank for very long. The borrower took out a loan, not to leave $100 idle at the First National Bank, but to purchase goods and services from other individuals and corporations. When the borrower makes these purchases by writing checks, they will be deposited at other banks and the $100 of reserves will leave the First National Bank. *A bank cannot safely loan out a greater amount than the excess reserves it has before it makes the loan.*

The final T-account of the First National Bank is

First National Bank			
Assets		Liabilities	
Securities	− $100		
Loans	+ $100		

The increase in reserves of $100 has been converted into additional loans of $100 at the First National Bank, plus an additional $100 of deposits that have made their way to other banks. (All the checks written on account at the First National Bank are deposited in banks rather than converted into cash, because we are assuming the public does not want to hold any additional currency.) Now let's see what happens to these deposits at the other banks.

Deposit Creation: The Banking System

To simplify the analysis, let us assume that the $100 of deposits created by First National Bank's loan is deposited at Bank A and that this bank and all other banks hold no excess reserves. Bank A's T-account becomes

Bank A			
Assets		Liabilities	
Reserves	+ $100	Checkable deposits	+ $100

If the required reserve ratio is 10%, this bank will now find itself with a $10 increase in required reserves, leaving it $90 of excess reserves. Because Bank A (like the First National Bank) does not want to hold on to excess reserves, it will loan out the entire amount. Its loans and checkable deposits will then increase by $90, but when the borrower spends the $90 of checkable deposits they and the reserves at Bank A will fall back down by this same amount. The net result is that Bank A's T-account will look as follows:

Bank A			
Assets		Liabilities	
Reserves	+ $10	Checkable deposits	+ $100
Loans	+ $90		

If the money spent by the borrower to whom Bank A lent the $90 is deposited in another bank, such as Bank B, then the T-account for Bank B will be

Bank B			
Assets		Liabilities	
Reserves	+ $90	Checkable deposits	+ $90

The checkable deposits in the banking system have increased by another $90, for a total increase of $190 ($100 at Bank A plus $90 at Bank B). The distinction between Bank A and Bank B actually is not needed to obtain the same result on the overall expansion of deposits. If the borrower from Bank A writes his checks to someone who deposits them back at Bank A, the same change in deposits would occur. The T-accounts for Bank B would just apply to Bank A, and its checkable deposits would increase by the total amount of $190.

Bank B will want to modify its balance sheet further. It must keep 10% of $90 ($9) as required reserves and has 90% of $90 ($81) in excess reserves to lend out. Bank B will make an $81 loan to a borrower, who spends the proceeds from the loan. Bank B's T-account will be

Bank B			
Assets		Liabilities	
Reserves	+ $ 9	Checkable deposits	+ $90
Loans	+ $81		

The $81 spent by the borrower from Bank B will be deposited in another bank (Bank C). Consequently, from the initial $100 increase of reserves in the banking system, the total increase of checkable deposits in the system so far is $271, which equals $100 + $90 + $81.

Following the same reasoning, if all banks loan out all their excess reserves, further increments in checkable deposits will continue (at Banks C, D, E, and so on), as depicted in Table 14.1.

Therefore, the total increase in deposits from the initial $100 increase in reserves will be $1000: the increase is tenfold, the reciprocal of the reserve requirement.

If the bank(s) chooses to invest its excess reserves in securities, the result is the same. If Bank A had taken its excess reserves and purchased securities instead of making loans, its T-account would have looked like this:

Bank A			
Assets		Liabilities	
Reserves	+ $10	Checkable deposits	+ $100
Securities	+ $90		

Table 14.1   Creation of Deposits (assuming 10% reserve requirement and a $100 increase in reserves)

Bank	Change in Deposits	Change in Loans	Change in Reserves
A	+$ 100.00	+$ 90.00	+$ 10.00
B	+$ 90.00	+$ 81.00	+$ 9.00
C	+$ 81.00	+$ 72.90	+$ 8.10
D	+$ 72.90	+$ 65.61	+$ 7.29
E	+$ 65.61	+$ 59.05	+$ 6.56
F	+$ 59.05	+$ 53.14	+$ 5.91
.	.	.	.
.	.	.	.
.	.	.	.
Total for All Banks	+$1000.00	+$900.00	+$100.00

When the bank buys $90 of securities, it writes a $90 check to the seller of the securities, who in turn deposits the $90 at a bank such as Bank B. Bank B's checkable deposits rise by $90, and the deposit expansion process is the same as before. ***Whether a bank chooses to use its excess reserves to make loans or to purchase securities, the effect on deposit expansion is the same.***

You can now see the difference in deposit creation for the single bank versus the banking system as a whole. Because a single bank can create deposits equal only to the amount of its excess reserves, it cannot by itself generate multiple deposit expansion. A single bank cannot loan out more than its excess reserves because the bank will lose these reserves as the deposits created by the loan find their way to other banks. The banking system as a whole, however, can generate a multiple expansion of deposits, because when a bank loses its excess reserves, these reserves do not leave the banking system even though they are lost to an individual bank. So as each bank makes a loan and creates deposits, the reserves find their way to another bank, which uses them to make additional loans and create additional deposits. As you have seen, this process continues until the initial increase in reserves results in a multiple increase in deposits.

The multiple increase in deposits generated from an increase in the banking system's reserves is called the **simple deposit multiplier.**[5] In our example with a 10% required reserve ratio, the simple deposit multiplier is 10. More generally, the simple deposit multiplier equals the reciprocal of the required reserve ratio, expressed as a fraction (10 = 1/.10), so that the formula for the multiple expansion of deposits can be written as[6]

$$\Delta D = \frac{1}{r_D} \times \Delta R \qquad (14.1)$$

where ΔD = the change in total checkable deposits in the banking system
r_D = the required reserve ratio (.10 in the example)
ΔR = the change in reserves for the banking system ($100 in the example)

---

[5]This multiplier should not be confused with the Keynesian multiplier, which is derived with a similar step-by-step analysis. That multiplier relates an increase in income to an increase in investment, while the simple deposit multiplier relates an increase in deposits to an increase in reserves.

[6]A formal derivation of this formula follows. Using the reasoning in the text above, the change in checkable deposits is $100 (= $\Delta R \times 1$) plus $90 [= $\Delta R \times (1 - r_D)$] plus $81 [= $\Delta R \times (1 - r_D)^2$] and so on, which can be rewritten as

$$\Delta D = \Delta R \times [1 + (1 - r_D) + (1 - r_D)^2 + (1 - r_D)^3 + \cdots]$$

Using the formula for the sum of an infinite series found in Footnote 5 in Chapter 4, this can be rewritten as

$$\Delta D = \Delta R \times \frac{1}{1 - (1 - r_D)} = \Delta R \times \frac{1}{r_D}.$$

Multiple Deposit Contraction

The multiple deposit creation process also should work in reverse; that is, when the Fed withdraws reserves from the banking system, there should be a multiple contraction of deposits. To prove this, let us trace the effect of a reduction of reserves in the banking system when again we assume that banks do not hold on to any excess reserves.

Study Guide

Test your understanding of multiple deposit creation by writing down the appropriate T-account for each step in the process of multiple deposit contraction before you look at the T-accounts in the text.

Let's start our analysis with a $100 reduction in the reserves of the First National Bank (by the Fed's sale of a $100 bond to the bank). The First National Bank finds it has lost $100 of reserves, and because it has not been holding any excess reserves, its holdings of reserves are $100 short of the required amount. It can obtain the reserves needed by selling $100 of securities or by demanding repayment of $100 of loans. When it sells the securities, it will receive $100 of checks written on an account with another bank that will be deposited at the Fed, thus raising its reserves by the same amount. Similarly, the repayment of the loan will also be made with checks written on an account with another bank. In both cases the reserves at the First National Bank will be increased by $100, but the bank on which the checks are drawn (such as Bank A) will lose $100 of checkable deposits and $100 of reserves. Bank A's T-account will then be

Bank A			
Assets		Liabilities	
Reserves	− $100	Checkable deposits	− $100

Bank A will now find it cannot meet its reserve requirements—it will be $90 short. Its reserves have fallen by $100, but its required reserves have also fallen by $10 (10% of the $100 decline in checkable deposits). To meet this reserve shortfall, Bank A will reduce its holdings of loans or securities by $90, transforming its T-account to

Bank A			
Assets		Liabilities	
Reserves	− $10	Checkable deposits	− $100
Loans and securities	− $90		

If the checks that Bank A receives as a result of reducing its loans or securities were written on accounts at Bank B, then Bank B finds itself with the following T-account:

Bank B			
Assets		Liabilities	
Reserves	− $90	Checkable deposits	− $90

Bank B now has a reserve shortfall of $81 ($90 − 10% × $90), and so it reduces its loans and securities by this amount, lowering another bank's checkable deposits by $81. This process keeps on going, with the level of checkable deposits in the banking system changing by

$$-\$100 - \$90 - \$81 - \$72.90 - \$65.61 - \$59.05 - \cdots = -\$1000$$

You can see that the process of multiple deposit contraction is symmetrical to the process of multiple deposit creation.

Deriving the Formula for Multiple Deposit Creation

The formula for the multiple creation of deposits can also be derived directly—by using algebra. We obtain the same answer for the relationship between a change in deposits and a change in reserves, but more quickly.

Our assumption that banks do not hold on to any excess reserves means that the total amount of required reserves for the banking system (RR) will equal the total reserves in the banking system (R):

$$RR = R$$

The total amount of required reserves equals the required reserve ratio (r_D) times the total amount of checkable deposits (D):

$$RR = r_D \times D$$

Substituting $r_D \times D$ for RR in the first equation,

$$r_D \times D = R$$

and dividing both sides of the preceding equation by r_D gives us

$$D = \frac{1}{r_D} \times R$$

Taking the change in both sides of this equation and using the Δ sign to denote a change,

$$\Delta D = \frac{1}{r_D} \times \Delta R$$

which is the same formula for deposit creation found in Equation (14.1).

This derivation provides us with another way of looking at the multiple creation of deposits because it forces us to look directly at the banking system as a whole rather than one bank at a time. For the banking system as a whole, deposit creation (or contraction) will stop only when all excess reserves in the banking system are gone; that is, the banking system will be in equilibrium when the total amount of required reserves equals the total amount of reserves, as seen in the equation $RR = R$. When $r_D \times D$ is substituted for RR, the resulting equation ($R = r_D \times D$) tells us how high checkable deposits will have to be in order for required reserves to equal total reserves. Accordingly, a given level of reserves in the banking system determines the level of checkable deposits when the banking system is in equilibrium; or, put another way, the given level of reserves supports a given level of checkable deposits.

In our example, the required reserve ratio is 10%. If reserves increase by $100, checkable deposits must rise to $1000 in order for total required reserves also to increase by $100. If the increase in checkable deposits is less than this, say, $900, then the increase in required reserves of $90 remains below the $100 increase in reserves, so that there are still excess reserves somewhere in the banking system. The banks with the excess reserves will lend them out, creating new deposits, and this process will continue until all reserves in the system are used up. This occurs when checkable deposits have risen to $1000.

We can also see this by looking at the T-account of the banking system as a whole (including the First National Bank) that results from this process:

Banking System			
Assets		Liabilities	
Securities	− $ 100	Checkable deposits	+ $1000
Reserves	+ $ 100		
Loans	+ $1000		

The procedure of eliminating excess reserves by loaning them out means that the banking system (First National Bank, Banks A, B, C, D, etc.) continues to make loans up to the $1000 amount until deposits have reached the $1000 level. In this way, $100 of reserves supports $1000 (10 times the quantity) of deposits.

CRITIQUE OF THE SIMPLE MODEL

Our model of multiple deposit creation seems to indicate that the Federal Reserve is able to exercise complete control over the level of checkable deposits by setting the required reserve ratio and the level of reserves. The actual creation of deposits is much less mechanical than the simple model indicates. If proceeds from Bank A's $90 loan are not deposited but are kept in cash, nothing is deposited in Bank B and the deposit creation process stops dead in its tracks. The total increase in checkable deposits is only $100—considerably less than the $1000 we found in the previous section. So if some proceeds from loans are used to raise the holdings of currency, checkable deposits will not increase by as much as our streamlined model of multiple deposit creation tells us.

Another situation ignored in our model is when banks do not fully lend out or buy securities with their excess reserves. If Bank A decides to hold on to all $90 of its excess reserves, no deposits would be made in Bank B, and this also would stop the deposit creation process. The total increase in deposits would again be only $100 and not the $1000 increase in our example. Hence, if banks choose to hold all or some of their excess reserves, the full expansion of deposits predicted by the simple model of multiple deposit creation does not occur.

The preceding examples rightly indicate that the Fed is not the only player whose behavior influences the level of deposits and therefore the money supply. Banks' decisions regarding the amount of excess reserves they wish to hold and depositors' decisions regarding how much currency to hold can cause the money supply to change. In later chapters we stress the behavior and interactions of the four players in constructing a more realistic model of the money supply process.

SUMMARY

1. There are four players in the money supply process: (a) the central bank, (b) banks (depository institutions), (c) depositors, and (d) borrowers from banks.

2. The central bank in the United States is the Federal Reserve System, also called the Fed. It conducts monetary policy, clears checks, and performs a regulatory function. The Fed has monetary liabilities (currency in circulation and reserves), which make up the bulk of the monetary base; it has assets of government securities and the discount loans it grants to banks.

3. The Fed provides reserves to the banking system by purchasing bonds or by making loans to the banks. A single bank can make loans up to the amount of its excess reserves, thereby creating an equal amount of deposits. The banking system can create a multiple expansion of deposits, because as each bank makes a loan and creates deposits, the reserves find their way to another bank, which uses them to make loans and create additional deposits. In the simple model of multiple deposit creation in which banks do not hold on to excess reserves, the multiple increase in checkable deposits (simple deposit multiplier) equals the reciprocal of the required reserve ratio.

4. The simple model of multiple deposit creation has serious deficiencies. Decisions by depositors to increase their holdings of currency or of banks to hold excess reserves will, for example, result in a smaller expansion of deposits than the simple model predicts. All four players—the Fed, banks, depositors, and borrowers from banks—are important in the determination of the money supply.

KEY TERMS

central bank

Federal Reserve System

monetary base

reserves

required reserves

excess reserves

required reserve ratio

discount rate

multiple deposit creation

open market operation

simple deposit multiplier

QUESTIONS AND PROBLEMS

* 1. Answer true, false, or uncertain: "When a bank takes some of its cash and deposits it at the Fed, its reserves increase."

2. Show what happens to the T-accounts of the Fed and the First National Bank when the Fed sells $1000 of securities to the First National Bank. What happens to reserves at the First National Bank?

* 3. If the Fed loans the First National Bank $1 million and the First National Bank uses the proceeds to buy $1 million of bonds from the Fed, what happens to reserves at the First National Bank? Explain your answer using T-accounts for the Fed and the First National Bank.

4. The First National Bank receives an extra $100 of reserves, but decides not to loan any of these reserves out. How much deposit creation takes place for the entire banking system?

Unless otherwise noted, the following assumptions are made in all the remaining problems: The required ratio on checkable deposits is 10%, banks do not hold on to excess reserves, and the public's holdings of currency do not change.

* 5. Using T-accounts, show what happens to checkable deposits in the banking system when the Fed loans an additional $1 million to the First National Bank.

6. Using T-accounts, show what happens to checkable deposits in the banking system when the Fed sells $2 million of bonds to the First National Bank.

* 7. Suppose the Fed buys $1 million of bonds from the First National Bank. If the First National Bank and all other banks use the resulting increase in reserves to purchase securities only and not to make loans, what will happen to checkable deposits?

8. If the Fed buys $1 million of bonds from the First National Bank, but an additional 10% of any deposit is held as excess reserves, what is the total increase in checkable deposits? (*Hint:* Use T-accounts to show what happens at each step of the multiple expansion process.)

* 9. If a bank depositor withdraws $1000 of currency from his account, what happens to reserves and checkable deposits?

10. If reserves in the banking system increase by $1 billion as a result of discount loans of $1 billion and checkable deposits increase by $9 billion, why isn't the banking system in equilibrium? What will continue to happen in the banking system until equilibrium is reached? Show the T-account for the banking system in equilibrium.

*11. If the Fed reduces reserves by selling $5 million worth of bonds to the banks, what will the T-account of the banking system look like when the banking system is in equilibrium? What has happened to the level of checkable deposits?

12. If the required reserve ratio on checkable deposits increases to 20%, how much multiple deposit creation will take place when reserves are increased by $100?

CHAPTER 15

Determinants of the Money Supply

PREVIEW   In Chapter 14 we developed a simple model of multiple deposit creation which showed us how the Fed can control the level of checkable deposits by setting the required reserve ratio and the level of reserves. Unfortunately for the Fed, life isn't that simple; control of the money supply is a complicated task. Our critique of this model indicated that decisions by depositors about their holdings of currency and by banks about their holdings of excess reserves also affect the money supply. To deal with these criticisms, in this chapter we develop a money supply model in which depositors and banks assume their important roles. The resulting framework provides an in-depth description of the money supply process to help you understand the complexity of the Fed's role.

To simplify the analysis, we separate the development of our model into several steps. First we will see that the Fed can exert more precise control over the monetary base (currency in circulation plus total reserves in the banking system) than it can over total reserves alone. So our model links changes in the money supply to changes in the monetary base. This link is achieved by deriving a **money multiplier** (a ratio that relates the change in the money supply to a given change in the monetary base). Finally we will examine the determinants of the money multiplier.

Study Guide

One reason for breaking the money supply model into its component parts is to help you answer questions using intuitive step-by-step logic rather than memorizing how changes in the behavior of the Fed, depositors, or banks will affect the money supply.

In deriving a model of the money supply process, we will focus here on a simple definition of money (currency plus checkable deposits) which corresponds to the $M1$ definition. Although other broader definitions of money are frequently used in policy-making, particularly $M2$, we conduct the analysis with a $M1$ definition because it is less complicated and yet provides us with a basic understanding of the money supply process. Furthermore, all analyses and results using the $M1$ definition apply equally well to the $M2$ definition. A somewhat more complicated money supply model for the $M2$ definition is developed in the appendix at the end of this chapter.

CONTROL OF THE MONETARY BASE

The monetary base (also referred to as **high-powered money**) equals currency in circulation (C) plus the total reserves in the banking system (R).[1] The monetary base (MB) is expressed as

$$MB = C + R$$

Chapter 14 depicted how the Fed provides additional reserves to the banking system by purchasing government bonds or making loans to the banks. We will see shortly that, in actuality, while these actions are sure to increase the monetary base, their effect on reserves is more uncertain. This is why models describing the determination of the money supply and the Fed's role in this process normally focus on the monetary base rather than reserves.

Federal Reserve Open Market Operations

One way the Fed causes changes in the monetary base is to purchase or sell government bonds through an open market operation. A purchase of bonds by the Fed is called an **open market purchase,** while a sale of bonds by the Fed is called an **open market sale.**

Open Market Purchase from a Bank   As described in Chapter 14, the Fed purchases $100 of bonds from a bank and pays for them with a $100 check. The bank either will deposit the check in its account with the Fed or cash it in for currency, which will be counted as vault cash. Either action means the bank will find itself with $100 more reserves and a reduction in its holdings of securities of $100. The T-account for the banking system then is

Banking System		
Assets		Liabilities
Securities	− $100	
Reserves	+ $100	

---

[1] Currency in circulation includes both Federal Reserve currency (Federal Reserve notes) and Treasury currency (primarily coins).

The Fed meanwhile finds that its liabilities have increased by the additional $100 of reserves, while its assets have increased by the $100 of additional securities that it now holds. Its T-account is

The Fed				
Assets			**Liabilities**	
Securities	+ $100		Reserves	+ $100

The net result of this open market purchase is that reserves have increased by $100, the amount of the open market purchase. Because there has been no change of currency in circulation, the monetary base has also risen by $100.

Open Market Purchase from the Nonbank Public   Two cases need to be examined. First, let's assume that the person or corporation that sells the $100 of bonds to the Fed deposits the Fed's check in its local bank. The nonbank public's T-account after this transaction is

Nonbank Public			
Assets		**Liabilities**	
Securities	− $100		
Checkable deposits	+ $100		

After the bank receives the check, it credits the depositor's account with the $100 and then deposits the check in its account at the Fed, thereby adding to its reserves. The banking system's T-account becomes

Banking System			
Assets		**Liabilities**	
Reserves	+ $100	Checkable deposits	+ $100

The effect on the Fed's balance sheet is that it has gained $100 of securities in its assets column, while it has an increase of $100 of reserves in its liabilities column:

Fed buys securities

The Fed				
Assets			**Liabilities**	
Securities	+ $100		Reserves	+ $100

As you can see in the T-account above, when the Fed's check is deposited in a bank, the net result of the Fed's open market purchase from the nonbank public is identical to the open market purchase from a bank: Reserves increase by the $100 amount of the open market purchase and the monetary base increases by the same $100 amount.

If, on the other hand, the person (or corporation) selling the bonds to the Fed cashes the Fed's check either at a local bank or at a Federal Reserve Bank for currency, then the effect on reserves is different.[2] This person will receive currency of $100 while reducing his holdings of securities by $100. His T-account will be

Nonbank Public		
Assets		Liabilities
Securities	− $100	
Currency	+ $100	

The Fed now finds that it has exchanged $100 of currency for $100 of securities, so that its T-account is

The Fed		
Assets		Liabilities
Securities	+ $100	Currency in circulation + $100

The net effect of the open market purchase in this case is that reserves are unchanged, while currency in circulation increases by the $100 of the open market purchase. Thus the monetary base (currency in circulation plus reserves) increases by the $100 amount of the open market purchase, while reserves do not. This contrasts with the case in which the seller of the bonds deposits the Fed's check in a bank; in this case, reserves increase by $100, as does the monetary base.

The analysis reveals that *the effect of an open market purchase on reserves differs depending on whether the seller of the bonds keeps the proceeds from the sale in currency or in deposits.* If the proceeds are kept in currency, the open market purchase has no effect on reserves; if the proceeds are kept as deposits, reserves increase by the amount of the open market purchase.

---

[2] If the person cashes in his check at his local bank, then its balance sheet will be unaffected because the $100 of vault cash that it pays out will be exactly matched by the deposit of the $100 check at the Fed. Thus its reserves will remain the same and there will be no effect on its T-account. This is why a T-account for the banking system does not appear here.

The effect of an open market purchase on the monetary base, however, is always the same, whether the proceeds from the sale are kept in deposits or currency. The impact of an open market purchase on reserves is much more uncertain than its impact on the monetary base.

Open Market Sale   If the Fed sells $100 of bonds to a bank or the nonbank public, the monetary base will decline by $100. For example, if the Fed sells the bonds to an individual who pays for them with currency, then the buyer exchanges $100 of currency for $100 of bonds and the resulting T-account is

Nonbank Public		
Assets		Liabilities
Securities	+ $100	
Currency	− $100	

The Fed, on the other hand, has reduced its holdings of securities by $100 and has also lowered its monetary liability by accepting the currency as payment for its bonds, thereby reducing the amount of currency in circulation by $100:

The Fed		
Assets		Liabilities
Securities	− $100	Currency in circulation − $100

The effect of the open market sale of $100 of bonds is to reduce the monetary base by an equal amount, although reserves remain unchanged. Manipulations of T-accounts in cases in which the buyer of the bonds is a bank, or the buyer pays for the bonds with a check written on a checkable deposit account at his local bank, leads to the same $100 reduction in the monetary base, although the reduction occurs because the level of reserves has fallen by $100.

Study Guide

The best way to learn how open market operations affect the monetary base is to use T-accounts. Using T-accounts, try to verify that an open market sale of $100 of bonds to a bank, or to a person who pays for it with a check written on his bank account, leads to a $100 reduction in the monetary base.

The following conclusion can now be drawn from our analysis of open market purchases and sales: *The effect of open market operations on reserves is much more uncertain than the effect on the monetary base.* Therefore, the Fed can more effectively control the monetary base with open market operations than it can control reserves.

Shifts from Deposits into Currency

Even if the Fed does not conduct open market operations, a shift from deposits to currency will affect the reserves in the banking system. However, such a shift will have no effect on the monetary base, another reason why the Fed has more control over the monetary base than over reserves.

Let's suppose that Jane Brown (who opened a $100 checking account at the First National Bank in Chapter 9) decides that tellers are so abusive in all banks that she closes her account by withdrawing the $100 balance in cash and vows never to deposit it in a bank again. The effect on the T-account of the nonbank public is

Nonbank Public		
Assets		Liabilities
Checkable deposits	− $100	
Currency	+ $100	

The banking system loses $100 of deposits and hence $100 of reserves:

Banking System		
Assets		Liabilities
Reserves	− $100	Checkable deposits − $100

For the Fed, Jane Brown's action means that there is $100 of additional currency circulating in the hands of the public, while reserves in the banking system have fallen by $100. The Fed's T-account is

The Fed		
Assets		Liabilities
		Currency in circulation + $100
		Reserves − $100

The net effect on the monetary liabilities of the Fed is a wash; the monetary base is unaffected by Jane Brown's disgust at the banking system. On the other hand, reserves *are* affected. Random fluctuations of reserves can occur as a result of the random shifts into currency and out of deposits, and vice versa. The same is not true for the monetary base, making it a more stable variable.

Discount Loans

In this chapter so far we have seen changes in the monetary base solely as a result of open market operations. However, when the Fed makes a discount loan to a bank, this also affects the monetary base. In Chapter 14, when the Fed made a $100 discount loan to the First National Bank, the bank was credited with $100 of reserves from the proceeds of the loan. The effects on the balance sheet of the banking system and the Fed were as follows:

Banking System		The Fed	
Assets	Liabilities	Assets	Liabilities
Reserves + $100	Discount + $100 loans	Discount + $100 loans	Reserves + $100

The monetary liabilities of the Fed have now increased by $100 and the monetary base, too, has increased by this amount. On the other hand, if a bank pays off a loan from the Fed, thereby reducing its borrowings from the Fed by $100, the T-accounts of the banking system and the Fed are as follows:

Banking System		The Fed	
Assets	Liabilities	Assets	Liabilities
Reserves − $100	Discount − $100 loans	Discount − $100 loans	Reserves − $100

The net effect on the monetary liabilities of the Fed, and hence on the monetary base, is then a reduction of $100. We see that the monetary base changes one-for-one with the change in the borrowings from the Fed.

Overview of the Fed's Ability to Control the Monetary Base

The general conclusion from the preceding analysis is that the Fed can control the monetary base better than it can control reserves. However, while the amount of open market purchases or sales is completely controlled by the Fed's placement of orders with dealers in bond markets, it lacks complete control over the monetary base because it cannot unilaterally determine, and therefore perfectly predict, the amount of borrowing by banks from the Fed. The Federal Reserve sets the discount rate (interest rate on discount loans) and then banks make a decision about whether to borrow. The amount of discount loans, although influenced by the Fed's setting of the discount rate, is not completely controlled by the Fed; banks' decisions play a role too.[3]

Therefore, we might want to split the monetary base into two components: one that the Fed can control completely, and the other that is less tightly controlled. The less tightly controlled component is the amount of the base that is created by discount loans from the Fed. The remainder of the base (called the **nonborrowed monetary base**) is under the Fed's control because it results primarily from open market operations.[4] The nonborrowed monetary base is formally defined as the monetary base minus discount loans from the Fed:

$$MB_n = MB - DL$$

where MB_n = nonborrowed monetary base
  MB = monetary base
  DL = discount loans from the Fed

The reason for distinguishing the nonborrowed monetary (MB_n) from the monetary base (MB) is that the nonborrowed monetary base, which is tied to open market operations, is directly under control of the Fed, while the monetary base, which is also influenced by discount loans from the Fed, is not.

THE MONEY SUPPLY MODEL AND THE MONEY MULTIPLIER

Because the Fed can control the monetary base better than it can control reserves, it makes sense to link the money supply (M) to the monetary base (MB) through a relationship such as the following:

$$M = m \times MB \qquad (15.1)$$

The variable m is the money multiplier, which tells us how much the money supply changes for a given change in the monetary base (MB). This multiplier tells us what multiple of the monetary base is transformed into the money supply. Because the money multiplier is found to be larger than one, the alternative name for the monetary base, "high-powered money," is logi-

---

[3] The Fed, like any banker, can also decide whether or not to make such a loan, thus giving it further control over the amount of borrowings from the Fed. The key point, however, is not altered by this fact. Decisions of the banks as well as the Fed are important to the level of discount loans from the Fed.

[4] Actually, there are other items in the Fed's balance sheet (discussed in Chapter 18) that affect the magnitude of the nonborrowed monetary base. Since their effects on the nonborrowed base relative to open market operations are both small and predictable, these other items do not present the Fed with difficulties in controlling the nonborrowed base.

cal; a dollar change in the monetary base leads to more than a dollar change in the money supply.

The money multiplier reflects the effect on the money supply of other factors besides the monetary base, and the following model will explain the factors that determine the size of the money multiplier. Depositors' decisions about their holdings of currency and checkable deposits are one set of factors affecting the money multiplier. Another involves the reserve requirements imposed by the Fed on the banking system. Banks' decisions about excess reserves also affect the money multiplier.

Deriving the Money Multiplier

In our model of multiple deposit creation in Chapter 14, we ignored the effects on deposit creation of changes in the public's holdings of currency and holdings of excess reserves. Now we incorporate these changes into our model of the money supply process by assuming that the level of currency (C) and excess reserves (ER) grow proportionally with checkable deposits (D); in other words, we assume that the ratio of these items to checkable deposits are constants:

$$\{C/D\} = \text{currency-checkable deposits ratio}$$
$$\{ER/D\} = \text{excess reserves ratio}$$

where {. . .} indicates that we are treating the ratio as a constant.

We will now derive a formula that describes how the depositor and excess reserves ratios defined above and the required reserve ratio set by the Fed affect the multiplier (m). We begin our derivation of the model of the money supply with the equation

$$R = RR + ER$$

which states that the total amount of reserves in the banking system (R) equals the sum of required reserves (RR) and excess reserves (ER). (Note that this equation corresponds to the equilibrium condition $R = RR$ in the previous chapter where excess reserves were assumed to be zero.)

The total amount of required reserves equals the required reserve ratio (r_D) times the amount of checkable deposits (D):

$$RR = r_D \times D$$

Substituting $r_D \times D$ for RR in the first equation yields an equation that links reserves in the banking system to the amount of checkable deposits and excess reserves they can support.

$$R = (r_D \times D) + ER$$

A key point here is that the Fed sets the required reserve ratio, r_D, to be less than one. Thus a dollar of reserves can support more than a dollar of deposits, and the multiple expansion of deposits can occur.

Let's see how this works in practice. If excess reserves are held at zero ($ER = 0$), the required reserve ratio is set at $r_D = .10$, and the level of checkable deposits in the banking system is $800 billion, then the amount of reserves needed to support these deposits is $80 billion (=$.10 \times \$800b$). The $80 billion of reserves can support ten times this amount in checkable deposits, just as in the previous chapter, because multiple deposit creation will occur.

Because the monetary base (MB) equals currency plus reserves ($R + C$), we can generate an equation that links the amount of monetary base to the levels of checkable deposits and currency by adding currency to both sides of the equation above:

$$MB = R + C = (r_D \times D) + ER + C$$

Another way of thinking about this equation is to recognize that it tells us the amount of the monetary base that is needed to support the existing amounts of checkable deposits, currency, and excess reserves.

An important feature of the preceding equation is that an additional dollar of MB that arises from an additional dollar of currency does not support any additional deposits. This occurs because such an increase leads to an identical increase in the right-hand side of the equation with no change occurring in D. The currency component of MB does not lead to multiple deposit creation as does the reserves component. Put another way, an increase in the monetary base that goes into currency is *not* multiplied, while an increase that goes into supporting deposits *is* multiplied.

Another important feature of this equation is that an additional dollar of MB that goes into excess reserves, ER, does not support any additional deposits or currency. The reason for this is that when a bank decides to hold excess reserves, it does not lend them out and so they create no deposits. Therefore if the Fed injects reserves into the banking system and they are held as excess reserves, there will be no effect on deposits or currency and hence no effect on the money supply. In other words, you can think of excess reserves as an idle component of reserves that are not being used to support any deposits (although they are important for bank liquidity management, as we saw in Chapter 9). This means that for a given level of reserves, a higher amount of excess reserves implies that the banking system in effect has fewer reserves to support deposits.

In order to derive the money multiplier formula in terms of the depositor ratio, $\{C/D\}$, and the excess reserves ratio, $\{ER/D\}$, we rewrite the above equation, specifying C as $\{C/D\} \times D$, and ER as $\{ER/D\} \times D$:

$$MB = r_D \times D + \{ER/D\} \times D + \{C/D\} \times D$$

or

$$= \quad [r_D + \{ER/D\} + \{C/D\}] \times D$$

We next divide both sides of the equation by the term inside the brackets to get an expression linking checkable deposits (D) to the monetary base (MB); we have

$$D = \frac{1}{[r_D + \{ER/D\} + \{C/D\}]} \times MB \tag{15.2}$$

Using the definition of the money supply as currency plus checkable deposits ($M = D + C$) and again specifying C as $\{C/D\} \times D$:

$$M = D + \{C/D\} \times D = [1 + \{C/D\}] \times D$$

Substituting in the preceding equation the expression for D from Equation (15.2), we have

$$M = \frac{1 + \{C/D\}}{[r_D + \{ER/D\} + \{C/D\}]} \times MB \tag{15.3}$$

Finally, we have achieved our objective of deriving an expression in the form of our earlier Equation (15.1). As you can see, the ratio that multiplies MB is the money multiplier that tells us how much the money supply changes in response to a given change in the monetary base (high-powered money). The money multiplier m is thus equal to

$$m = \frac{1 + \{C/D\}}{[r_D + \{ER/D\} + \{C/D\}]} \tag{15.4}$$

and it is a function of the depositor ratio, $\{C/D\}$ and the required reserve ratio set by the Fed, r_D, and the excess reserve ratio, $\{ER/D\}$.

Although the algebraic derivation we have just completed shows you how the money multiplier is constructed, you need to understand the basic intuition behind it in order to be able to understand and apply the money multiplier concept without having to memorize it.

Intuition Behind the Money Multiplier

To "get a feel" for what the money multiplier means, let us again construct a numerical example with realistic numbers for the following variables:

r_D = required reserve ratio = .10
C = currency in circulation = $400 billion
D = checkable deposits = $800 billion
ER = excess reserves = $.8 billion
M = money supply (M1) = $C + D$ = $1200 billion

From these numbers we can calculate the values for the currency-checkable deposits and time deposit-checkable deposits ratios to be,

$\{C/D\}$ = currency-checkable deposits ratio = $400b/$800b = .5
$\{ER/D\}$ = excess reserves ratio = $.8/$800b = .001

The resulting value of the money multiplier is

$$m = \frac{1 + .50}{[.10 + .001 + .50]} = \frac{1.500}{.601} = 2.50$$

The money multiplier of 2.50 tells us that given the required reserve ratio of 10% on checkable deposits and the behavior of depositors as represented by $\{C/D\} = .50$ and banks as represented by $\{ER/D\} = .001$, a \$1 increase in the monetary base leads to a \$2.50 increase in the money supply ($M1$).

An important characteristic of the money multiplier is that it is less than the simple deposit multiplier of 10 found in Chapter 14. The key to understanding this result and our money supply model is to realize that ***although there is multiple expansion of deposits, there is no such expansion for currency.*** Thus if some portion of the increase in high-powered money finds its way into currency, then this portion does not undergo multiple deposit expansion. In our analysis in Chapter 14, we did not allow for this possibility and so the increase in reserves led to the maximum amount of multiple deposit creation. However, in our current model of the money multiplier, the level of currency *does* increase when the base (MB) and checkable deposits (D) increase, because $\{C/D\}$ is greater than zero. As previously stated, any increase in MB that goes into an increase in currency is not multiplied, so only part of the increase in MB is available to support checkable deposits that undergo multiple expansion. The overall level of multiple deposit expansion must be lower so that the increase in M, given an increase in MB, is smaller than the simple model in Chapter 14 indicates.[5]

Factors That Determine the Money Multiplier

To develop our intuition of the money multiplier even further, let us look at how the money multiplier changes in response to changes in the variables in our money multiplier model: $\{C/D\}$, r_D, and $\{ER/D\}$. The "game" we are playing is a familiar one in economics: We ask what happens when one of these variables changes, leaving all other variables the same (i.e., *ceteris paribus*).

---

[5] Another reason the money multiplier is smaller is that $\{ER/D\}$ is a constant fraction greater than zero, indicating that an increase in MB and D leads to higher excess reserves. The resulting higher amount of excess reserves means that the amount of reserves used to support checkable deposits will not increase as much as it otherwise would. Hence, the increase in checkable deposits and the money supply will be lower, and the money multiplier will be smaller. However, because $\{ER/D\}$ is currently so tiny, around .001, the impact of this ratio on the money multiplier is now quite small. However, there have been other periods in our history when the $\{ER/D\}$ ratio has been much larger and so has had a more important role in lowering the money multiplier.

Changes in the Required Reserve Ratio (r_D)   If the required reserve ratio on checkable deposits increases while all the other variables stay the same, the same level of reserves cannot support as large an amount of checkable deposits; more reserves are needed because required reserves for these checkable deposits have risen. The resulting deficiency in reserves then means that banks must contract their loans, causing a decline in deposits and hence in the money supply. The reduced money supply relative to the level of MB, which has remained unchanged, indicates that the money multiplier has declined as well. Another way to see this is to realize that when r_D is higher, less multiple expansion of checkable deposits occurs. With less multiple deposit expansion, the money multiplier must fall.[6]

We can verify that the preceding analysis is correct by seeing what happens to the value of the money multiplier in our numerical example when r_D increases from 10 to 15%. The money multiplier becomes

$$m = \frac{1 + .50}{[.15 + .001 + .50]} = \frac{1.500}{.651} = 2.30$$

which, as we would expect, is less than 2.50.

The analysis just conducted can also be applied to the case in which the required reserve ratio falls. In this case there will be more multiple expansion for checkable deposits because the same level of reserves can now support more checkable deposits, and the money multiplier will rise. For example, if r_D falls from 10 to 5%, plugging this value into our money multiplier formula (leaving all the other variables unchanged) yields a money multiplier of

$$m = \frac{1 + .50}{[.05 + .001 + .50]} = \frac{1.500}{.551} = 2.72$$

which is above the initial value of 2.50.

We can now state the following result: ***The money multiplier and the money supply are negatively related to the required reserve ratio, r_D.***[7]

---

[6] This result can be demonstrated algebraically as follows: When r_D rises, the denominator of the money multiplier rises and the money multiplier therefore must fall.

[7] Before December 1990, the Federal Reserve required reserves on time deposits as well as on checkable deposits. A modification of the analysis to reflect the situation before 1990 is straightforward. If we assume that time deposits (T) grow proportionally with checkable deposits so that (T/D) is a constant, then we just need to recognize that in the formulas above the required reserve ratio, r_D, should be replaced by $[r_D + r_T\{T/D\}]$, where r_T is the required reserve ratio for time deposits. The intuition behind this replacement is that for every dollar of checkable deposits there are $\{T/D\}$ dollars of time deposits which have required reserves of $r_T\{T/D\}$. Thus the total amount of required reserves that banks must have per dollar of checkable deposits is the Fed's requirement of r_D plus the additional amount arising from time deposits, $r_T\{T/D\}$. Note that either a rise in the required reserve ratio for time deposits, r_T, or a rise in the time deposits-checkable deposits ratio, $\{T/D\}$, in effect raises the amount of required reserves per dollar of checkable deposits and thus lowers the money multiplier and the money supply.

Changes in the Currency-Checkable Deposits Ratio {C/D}   Next, what happens to the money multiplier when depositor behavior causes {C/D} to increase with all other variables unchanged? An increase in {C/D} means that depositors are converting some of their checkable deposits into currency. As shown before, checkable deposits undergo multiple expansion while currency does not. Hence when checkable deposits are being converted into currency, there is a switch from one component of the money supply that undergoes multiple expansion to one that does not. The overall level of multiple expansion declines and so must the multiplier.[8]

This reasoning is confirmed by our numerical example where {C/D} rises from .50 to .75. The money multiplier then falls from 2.50 to

$$m = \frac{1 + .75}{[.10 + .001 + .75]} = \frac{1.750}{.851} = 2.06$$

We have now demonstrated another result: ***The money multiplier and the money supply are negatively related to the currency-checkable deposits ratio {C/D}.***

Changes in the Excess Reserves Ratio {ER/D}   When banks increase their holdings of excess reserves relative to checkable deposits, the banking system in effect has fewer reserves to support checkable deposits. This means that given the same level of *MB*, banks will contract their loans, causing a decline in the level of checkable deposits and a decline in the money supply; so the money multiplier will fall.[9]

This reasoning is supported in our numerical example when {ER/D} rises from .001 to .005. The money multiplier declines from 2.50 to

$$m = \frac{1 + .50}{[.10 + .005 + .50]} = \frac{1.500}{.605} = 2.48$$

Note that although the excess reserves-checkable deposit ratio has risen fivefold, there has only been a small decline in the money multiplier. This decline is so small because in recent years the {ER/D} ratio has been extremely small, so that changes in it have only a small impact on the money multiplier. However, there have been other periods in our history, particularly during the Great Depression, when this ratio was far higher so that its movements had a substantial effect on the money supply and the money multiplier. Thus our final result is still an important one. ***The money multiplier and the***

---

[8] As long as r_D + {ER/D} is less than 1 (as is the case using the realistic numbers above), an increase in {C/D} raises the denominator of the money multiplier proportionally by more than it raises the numerator. The increase in {C/D} causes the multiplier to fall.

[9] This result can be demonstrated algebraically as follows: When {ER/D} rises, the denominator of the money multiplier rises and so the money multiplier must fall.

money supply are negatively related to the excess reserves-checkable deposits ratio {ER/D}.

Additional Factors That Determine the Money Supply

To complete the money supply model, we just need to remember that the monetary base is made up of two components: (1) the nonborrowed monetary base (MB_n), which is directly controlled by the Fed through open market operations and (2) discount loans (DL), in which banks' decisions play a role along with the Fed's setting of the discount rate. Using the fact that $MB = MB_n + DL$, we can rewrite the money supply model as:

$$M = m \times [MB_n + DL] \tag{15.5}$$

where the money multiplier m is defined as in Equation (15.4). Thus, in addition to the effects of the required reserve ratio, currency-checkable deposits ratio, and excess reserves ratio on the money supply, the expanded model stipulates that the money supply is also affected by changes in MB_n and DL. Because the money multiplier is positive, Equation (15.5) immediately tells us that the money supply is positively related to both the nonborrowed monetary base and discount loans. However, it is still worth developing the intuition for these results.

Changes in the Nonborrowed Monetary Base (MB_n)   As shown at the beginning of this chapter, the Fed's open market purchases increase the nonborrowed monetary base, while their open market sales decrease it. Holding all other variables constant, an increase in MB_n arising from an open market purchase increases the amount of the monetary base that is available to support currency and deposits, so that the money supply will increase. Similarly, an open market sale that decreases MB_n will shrink the amount of the monetary base available to support currency and deposits, thereby causing the money supply to decrease.

We have the following result: ***The money supply is positively related to the nonborrowed monetary base, MB_n.***

Changes in Discount Loans from the Fed (DL)   With the nonborrowed monetary base (MB_n) unchanged, more discount loans from the Fed provide additional reserves (hence higher MB) to the banking system that are used to support more currency and deposits. As a result the increase in DL will lead to a rise in the money supply. If banks reduce the level of their discount loans, with all other variables held constant, the amount of MB available to support currency and deposits will decline, causing the money supply to decline.

Our final result is: ***The money supply is positively related to the level of discount loans from the Fed, DL.***

An Overview

We now have a model of the money supply process in which three of the "players"—the Federal Reserve System, the depositors, and the banks—directly influence the money supply. The Federal Reserve is an important player because it controls both the nonborrowed monetary base, MB_n, through open market operations and the required reserve ratio, r_D. Depositors matter because they decide on the $\{C/D\}$ ratio. The banks are important through their decisions about the excess reserves ratio, $\{ER/D\}$, and their borrowing of discount loans, DL, from the Fed. As we will see in the following chapter, the fourth "player" (borrowers from banks) enters indirectly by affecting bank decisions about $\{ER/D\}$ and DL.

As a study aid, Table 15.1 summarizes the response of the money supply ($M1$) to changes in all these variables. An upward arrow ($\uparrow$) indicates an increase while a downward arrow ($\downarrow$) indicates a decrease.

Study Guide

To improve your understanding of the money supply process, slowly work through the logic behind the results in Table 15.1 rather than just memorizing the results. Then see if you can construct your own table in which all the variables decrease rather than increase.

APPLICATION
EXPLAINING MOVEMENTS IN THE MONEY SUPPLY, / / / / / / / / / / / / / / / / 1980–1990

To complete your understanding of the money supply process, you must understand what motivates depositors' and bankers' decisions. But before examining bank and depositor behavior in Chapter 16, you should see

Table 15.1   **Summary: Response of the Money Supply to Changes in MB_n, DL, r_D, $\{ER/D\}$, and $\{C/D\}$**

Change in Variable		Money Supply Response
MB_n	$\uparrow$	$\uparrow$
DL	$\uparrow$	$\uparrow$
r_D	$\uparrow$	$\downarrow$
ER/D	$\uparrow$	$\downarrow$
$\{C/D\}$	$\uparrow$	$\downarrow$

Note: Only increases ($\uparrow$) in the variables are shown; the effects of decreases in the variables on the money supply would be the opposite of those indicated in the second column.

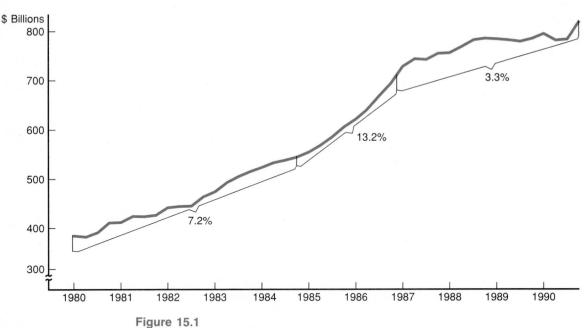

Figure 15.1
Money Supply (*M*1): 1980–1990 Sources: Federal Reserve *Bulletin* and Citibase databank.

whether the model of the money supply process developed here helps you understand recent movements of the money supply. We look at money supply movements from 1980 to 1990, a particularly interesting period because the growth rate of the money supply displayed unusually high variability.

Figure 15.1 shows the movements of the money supply (*M*1) from 1980 to 1990, with the percentage next to each bracket representing the growth rate (at an annual rate) for the bracketed period: From January 1980 to October 1984, for example, the money supply grew at a 7.2% annual rate. The variability of money growth in the 1980–1990 period is quite apparent, swinging from 7.2% to 13.2%, and then back down to 3.3%. What explains these sharp swings in the growth rate of the money supply?

Our money supply model, as represented by Equation (15.5), suggests that the movements in the money supply that we see in Figure 15.1 are explained by either changes in $MB_n + DL$ (the nonborrowed monetary base plus discount loans) or by changes in m (the money multiplier). Figure 15.2 plots these variables and shows their growth rates for the same bracketed periods as in Figure 15.1. Notice that the money multiplier m fluctuates within a fairly narrow band between 2.7 and 3.0.

Over the whole period, the average growth rate of the money supply (7.0%) is fairly well explained by the average growth rate of the nonborrowed monetary base MB_n (7.2%). In addition we see that the term DL is rarely an important source of fluctuations in the money supply since $MB_n + DL$ is closely tied to MB_n, except for the unusual period in 1984

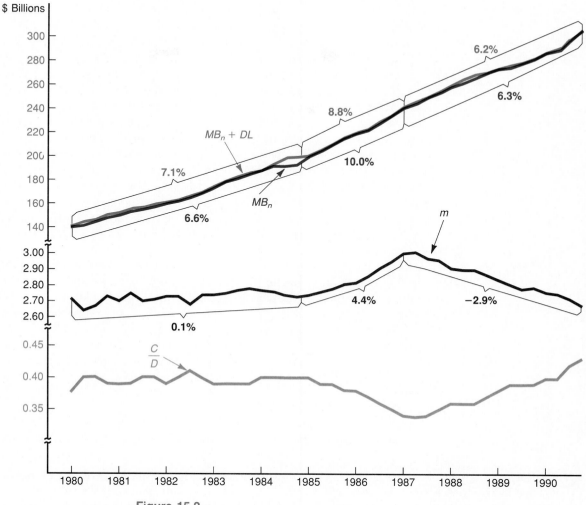

Figure 15.2
Determinants of the Money Supply: 1980–1990 Sources: Federal Reserve *Bulletin* and
Citibase databank.

when discount loans increased dramatically (the Fed extended $5 billion of
loans to the financially troubled Continental Illinois Bank).

The conclusion drawn from this analysis follows: ***Over long periods, the
primary determinant of movements in the money supply is the nonborrowed
monetary base (MB$_n$), which is controlled by Federal Reserve open market
operations.***

For shorter time periods, the link between the growth rates of the nonborrowed monetary base and the money supply is not always close, primarily
because the money multiplier (m) has substantial short-run swings that have
a major impact on the growth rate of the money supply. The currency-

checkable deposits ratio $\{C/D\}$, which is also plotted in Figure 15.2, explains most of these movements in the money multiplier.

From January 1980 until October 1984 $\{C/D\}$ is relatively constant. Not surprisingly, there is almost no trend in the money multiplier, m, so that the growth rate of the money supply and the nonborrowed monetary base have similar magnitudes. The upward movement in the money multiplier from October 1984 to December 1986 is explained by the downward trend in the currency-checkable deposits ratio. The decline in $\{C/D\}$ meant that there was a shift from one component of the money supply with less multiple expansion (currency) to another (checkable deposits) with more, so that the money multiplier rose. In the period from December 1986 to December 1990, $\{C/D\}$ underwent a substantial rise. The rise should have led to a fall in the money multiplier because there was a shift from checkable deposits with more multiple expansion to currency which had less. As our money supply model predicts, the money multiplier did indeed fall in this period and there was a sharp deceleration in money growth.

Although our examination of the 1980 to 1990 period indicates that factors such as changes in the $\{C/D\}$ ratio can have a major impact on the money supply over short subperiods, we must not forget that over the entire period the growth rate of the money supply is closely linked to the growth rate of the nonborrowed monetary base, MB_n. Indeed, empirical evidence suggests that over three-quarters of the fluctuations in the money supply can be attributed to Federal Reserve open market operations, which determine MB_n.

SUMMARY

1. This chapter develops a model that describes how the money supply is determined. First, we see how the monetary base is determined and why it is easier to control than reserves in the banking system. Second, we link the monetary base to the money supply using the concept of the money multiplier, which tells us how much the money supply changes when there is a change in the monetary base.

2. An open market purchase increases the monetary base and an open market sale decreases it. The monetary base also changes one-for-one with changes in discount loans from the Fed. The monetary base can be broken up into two components: The first, the nonborrowed monetary base, is directly under the control of the Fed

because it is the result of open market operations; the second, which results from discount loans, is not as closely controlled by the Fed because banks' decisions play an important role in determining this component.

3. The money supply is negatively related to the required reserve ratio, r_D, the currency-checkable deposits ratio, $\{C/D\}$, and the excess reserves ratio, $\{ER/D\}$. It is positively related to the level of discount loans from the Fed, DL, and the nonborrowed base, MB_n, which is determined by Fed open market operations. The money supply model therefore allows for the behavior of all four players in the money supply process: the Fed through its setting of the required reserve ratios and open market operations; the deposi-

tors through their decisions about the currency-checkable deposits ratio; the banks through their decisions about the excess reserves ratio and discount loans from the Fed; and the borrowers from banks indirectly through their effect on bank decisions regarding the excess reserves ratio and borrowings from the Fed.

KEY TERMS

money multiplier

high-powered money

open market purchase

open market sale

nonborrowed monetary base

QUESTIONS AND PROBLEMS

1. If the Fed sells $2 million of bonds to the First National Bank, what happens to reserves and the monetary base? Explain your answer with T-accounts.

* 2. If the Fed sells $2 million of bonds to Irving the Investor, who pays for the bonds with a briefcase filled with currency, what happens to reserves and the monetary base? Explain your answer with T-accounts.

3. If the Fed lends five banks an additional $100 million but depositors withdraw $50 million and hold it as currency, what happens to reserves and the monetary base? Explain your answer with T-accounts.

* 4. Answer true, false, or uncertain: "The money multiplier is necessarily greater than one." Explain.

5. Answer true, false, or uncertain: "If reserve requirements on checkable deposits were set at zero, the amount of multiple deposit expansion would go on indefinitely." Explain.

* 6. During the Great Depression years 1930–1933, the {C/D} ratio rose dramatically. What do you think happened to the money supply and why?

7. During the Great Depression, the {ER/D} ratio rose dramatically. What do you think happened to the money supply and why?

* 8. Traveler's checks have no reserve requirements and are included in the M1 measure of the money supply. When people travel during the summer and convert some of their checking accounts into traveler's checks, what happens to the money supply? Why?

9. If Jane Brown closes her account at the First National Bank and uses the money instead to open up a money market mutual fund account, what happens to M1 and M2? Why?

*10. Some economists have suggested that reserve requirements on checkable deposits and time deposits should be set equal because this would improve control of M2. Does this argument make sense? (*Hint:* Think about what happens when checkable deposits are converted into time deposits or vice versa.)

Using Economic Analysis to Predict the Future

11. Predict what will happen to the money supply if the Fed increases r_D.

*12. The Fed buys $100 million of bonds from the public and also lowers r_D. What will happen to the money supply?

13. Predict what will happen to the money supply if there is a sharp rise in the currency-checkable deposits ratio.

*14. If the Fed sells $1 million of bonds and banks reduce their discount loans by $1 million, predict what happens to the money supply.

15. If banks borrow an additional $1 million from the Fed and also reduce {ER/D}, what will happen to the money supply?

The *M2* Money Multiplier

The derivation of a money multiplier for the *M2* definition of money requires only slight modifications to the analysis in the chapter. The definition of *M2* is

$$M2 = D + C + T + MMF$$

where C = currency in circulation
D = checkable deposits
T = time deposits
MMF = primarily money market mutual fund shares and money market deposit accounts, plus overnight repurchase agreements and overnight Eurodollars

We again assume that all the variables above rise proportionally with checkable deposits, so that the ratios $\{C/D\}$, $\{T/D\}$, and $\{MMF/D\}$ are treated as constants. Replacing C by $\{C/D\} \times D$, T by $\{T/D\} \times D$, and MMF by $\{MMF/D\} \times D$ in the definition of *M2* above:

$$M2 = D + (\{C/D\} \times D) + (\{T/D\} \times D) + (\{MMF/D\} \times D)$$
$$= [1 + \{C/D\} + \{T/D\} + \{MMF/D\}] \times D$$

Substituting in the expression for D from Equation (15.2) in the chapter, we have[1]

$$M2 = \frac{1 + \{C/D\} + \{T/D\} + \{MMF/D\}}{[r_D + \{ER/D\} + \{C/D\}]} \times MB \qquad \text{(A15.1)}$$

To see what this formula implies about the *M2* money multiplier, we continue with the same numerical example in the chapter, with the additional information that $T = \$2400$ billion and $MMF = \$400$ billion so that $\{T/D\} =$

---

[1] From the derivation here it is clear that the quantity of checkable deposits, D, is unaffected by the depositor ratios $\{T/D\}$ and $\{MMF/D\}$ even though time deposits and money market mutual fund shares are included in *M2*. This is just a consequence of the absence of reserve requirements on time deposits and money market mutual fund shares so that T and MMF do not appear in any of the equations in the derivation of D earlier in the chapter.

3.00 and $\{MMF/D\} = .50$. The resulting value of the multiplier for $M2$ ($m2$) is

$$m2 = \frac{1 + .50 + 3.00 + .50}{[.10 + .001 + .50]} = \frac{5.000}{.601} = 8.32$$

An important feature of the $M2$ multiplier is that it is substantially above the $M1$ multiplier of 2.50 that we found in the chapter. The crucial concept in understanding this difference is that a lower required reserve ratio for a deposit or a money market mutual fund share means that it undergoes more multiple expansion, because fewer reserves are needed to support the same amount of them. Time deposits and MMFs have a lower required reserve ratio than checkable deposits—zero—and they will therefore have more multiple expansion than will checkable deposits. Thus the overall multiple expansion for the sum of these deposits will be greater than for checkable deposits alone, and so the $M2$ money multiplier will be greater than the $M1$ money multiplier.

RESPONSE OF THE $M2$ MONEY MULTIPLIER TO CHANGES IN DEPOSITOR AND REQUIRED RESERVE RATIOS

Response to Changes in r_D, $\{C/D\}$, and $\{ER/D\}$ The economic reasoning analyzing the effect of changes in the required reserve ratio and the currency-checkable deposits ratio on the $M2$ money multiplier is identical to that used for the $M1$ multiplier in the chapter. An increase in the required reserve ratio, r_D, will decrease the amount of multiple deposit expansion, thus lowering the $M2$ money multiplier. An increase in $\{C/D\}$ means that depositors have shifted out of checkable deposits into currency, and since currency has no multiple deposit expansion, the overall level of multiple deposit expansion for $M2$ must also fall, lowering the $M2$ multiplier. An increase in the excess reserves ratio, $\{ER/D\}$, means that banks use fewer reserves to support deposits, so deposits and the $M2$ money multiplier fall.

We thus have the same results we found for the $M1$ multiplier: *The $M2$ money multiplier and M2 money supply are negatively related to the required reserve ratio, r_D, the currency-checkable deposits ratio, $\{C/D\}$, and the excess reserves ratio, $\{ER/D\}$.*

Response to Changes in $\{T/D\}$ and $\{MMF/D\}$ An increase in either $\{T/D\}$ or $\{MMF/D\}$ leads to an increase in the $M2$ multiplier because the required reserve ratios on time deposits and money market mutual fund shares are zero and hence are lower than the required reserve ratio on checkable deposits.

Both time deposits and money market mutual fund shares undergo more multiple expansion than checkable deposits. Thus a shift out of checkable deposits into time deposits or money market mutual funds, increasing $\{T/D\}$ or $\{MMF/D\}$, implies that the overall level of multiple expansion will increase, raising the $M2$ money multiplier.

A decline in $\{T/D\}$ or $\{MMF/D\}$ will result in less overall multiple expansion and the $M2$ money multiplier will decrease, resulting in the following: *The $M2$ money multiplier and $M2$ money supply are positively related to both the time deposit-checkable deposits ratio, $\{T/D\}$, and the money market fund-checkable deposits ratio, $\{MMF/D\}$.*

The response of the $M2$ multiplier to all the depositor and required reserve ratios is summarized in Table 15A.1.

Table 15A.1 **Summary: Response of the $M2$ Money Multiplier to Changes in r_D, $\{C/D\}$, $\{ER/D\}$, $\{T/D\}$, and $\{MMF/D\}$**

Change in Variable		$M2$ Multiplier Response
r_D	↑	↓
$\{C/D\}$	↑	↓
$\{ER/D\}$	↑	↓
$\{T/D\}$	↑	↑
$\{MMF/D\}$	↑	↑

Note: Only increases (↑) in the variables are shown; the effects of decreases in the variables on the money multiplier would be the opposite of those indicated in the second column.

CHAPTER 16

Explaining Depositor and Bank Behavior: The Complete Money Supply Model

PREVIEW   In the previous two chapters we developed, step by step, the building blocks necessary to understand the money supply process. We saw first how deposits are created, and then we developed a money multiplier in which depositor and bank behavior plays an important role in the deposit creation process. Although we now understand *what* effect depositor and bank behavior has on the money supply, we do not yet know *why* depositors or banks choose to behave one way or another. This chapter completes the development of the money supply model by explaining depositor and bank behavior.

    Although fairly simple in structure, the complete model is the basis of much of the money supply analysis performed by practicing economists in the private sector and the government. The model is used, for example, at the Federal Reserve Board for forecasting and policy analysis. In this and the following chapters, we will use the model to understand the difficulties that the Federal Reserve faces in conducting monetary policy. The model will provide you with answers to some of the questions that policymakers in the United States must answer when formulating their economic policies: How do money market conditions affect the money supply? How can the Federal Reserve control the money supply? What factors make the control of the money supply a difficult problem for the Fed? How do bank panics occur, and what is their effect on the money supply? How do expectations about the future affect the money supply?

BEHAVIOR OF THE CURRENCY-CHECKABLE DEPOSITS RATIO $\{C/D\}$

The general outline of the movements of the currency-checkable deposits ratio, $\{C/D\}$, since 1892 is shown in Figure 16.1. As you can see, several episodes stand out:

359

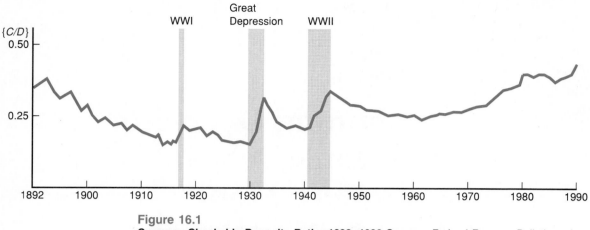

Figure 16.1
Currency-Checkable Deposits Ratio: 1892–1990 Sources: Federal Reserve *Bulletin* and *Banking and Monetary Statistics*.

1. The declining trend in the ratio from 1892 until 1917 when the United States entered World War I

2. The sharp increase in the ratio during World War I and the decline thereafter

3. The steepest increase in the ratio that we see in the figure, which occurs during the Great Depression years from 1930 to 1933

4. The increase in the ratio during World War II

5. The reversal in the early 1960s of the downward trend in the ratio and the rise thereafter

To be worthwhile, our analysis of {C/D} must be able to explain these movements. These movements, however, will help us develop the analysis because they provide clues to the factors that influence {C/D}.

A natural way to approach the analysis of the relative amount of assets (currency and checkable deposits) people want to hold, hence the currency-checkable deposits ratio, is to use the theory of asset demand developed in Chapter 5. Recall the theory states that four categories of factors influence the demand for an asset such as currency or checkable deposits: (1) the total resources available to individuals, that is, wealth; (2) the expected return on one asset relative to the expected return on alternative assets; (3) the degree of uncertainty or risk associated with the return from this asset relative to alternative assets; and (4) the liquidity of one asset relative to alternative assets. Because risk and liquidity factors have not changed independently of wealth and expected returns and lead to similar conclusions on the historical movements of {C/D}, we will focus only on how factors affecting wealth and expected returns influence {C/D}.

Effect of Changes in Wealth

What is the relative response of currency to checkable deposits when an individual's resources change? Currency is used extensively by people with low incomes and wealth, which means the demand for currency grows proportionally less with accumulation of wealth. In contrast, checkable deposits are held by people with greater wealth and checkable deposits are less of a necessity. Put another way, as wealth grows, the holdings of checkable deposits relative to the holdings of currency increase; and the amount of currency relative to checkable deposits should fall, causing the currency-checkable deposits ratio, $\{C/D\}$, to decline. A decrease in income will lead to an increase in the amount of currency relative to checkable relative to checkable deposits, causing $\{C/D\}$ to increase. ***The currency-checkable deposits ratio is negatively related to income or wealth.***

Effect of Changes in Expected Returns

The second set of factors influencing the decision to hold currency versus checkable deposits involves the expected returns on checkable deposits relative to currency as well as other assets. Three primary factors influence expected returns and hence the currency-checkable deposits ratio:[1] (1) interest rates on checkable deposits, (2) bank panics, and (3) illegal activity.

Interest Rates on Checkable Deposits   By its very nature, currency cannot pay interest. On the other hand, banks can and do pay interest on checkable deposits. One measure of the expected return on checkable deposits relative to currency is its interest rate. As the interest rate increases, the theory of asset demand tells us that people will want to hold less currency relative to checkable deposits, and $\{C/D\}$ will fall. Conversely, a decline in this interest rate will cause $\{C/D\}$ to rise. ***The currency-checkable deposits ratio is negatively related to the interest rate paid on checkable deposits.***

Between 1933 and 1980, regulations prevented banks from paying interest on most checkable deposits,[2] while before 1933, these interest rates were low and did not undergo substantial fluctuations. However, since 1980 banks have been allowed to pay any interest rate they choose on checkable deposits, suggesting that fluctuations in these rates can now be an important factor influencing $\{C/D\}$ movements.

---

[1]Changes in interest rates on other alternative assets (e.g., U.S. Treasury bills) could have a differential effect on the demand for currency versus checkable deposits, resulting in some effect on $\{C/D\}$. However, the evidence for this effect is weak.

[2]Although banks could not pay interest on checkable deposits, they provided services to their checking account customers that can be thought of as implicit interest payments. Because these services changed only slowly over time, these implicit interest payments were not a major factor causing the demand for checkable deposits to fluctuate.

Bank Panics Our discussion of interest rate effects suggests that they did not have a substantial impact on {C/D} before 1980. You might conclude that expected returns have had little importance in determining this ratio for most of its history. Figure 16.1 provides us with an important clue—that we are overlooking an important factor when measuring expected returns solely by the interest rates on assets. The steepest rise in {C/D} occurred during the Great Depression years 1930–1933 when the banking system nearly collapsed. Legend has it that during this period, people stuffed their mattresses with cash rather than keep it in banks because they had lost confidence in them as a safe haven for their hard-earned savings. Can the theory of asset demand explain this phenomenon?

A bank failure occurs when the bank is no longer able to pay back its depositors. Before creation of the FDIC in 1933, if you had an account at a bank that failed, you would suffer a substantial loss—you could not withdraw your savings and might receive only a small fraction of the value of your deposits sometime in the future. The simultaneous failure of many banks is called a **bank panic** and the Great Depression years 1930–1933 witnessed the worst set of bank panics in U.S. history. From the end of 1930 to the bank holiday in March of 1933, more than one-third of the banks in the United States failed.

Bank panics can have a devastating effect on the expected returns to holding deposits. When a bank is likely to fail during a bank panic, depositors know that if they have deposits in this bank, they are likely to suffer substantial losses and the expected return on deposits can be quite negative. The theory of asset demand predicts that depositors will shift their holdings from checkable deposits to currency by withdrawing currency from their bank accounts, and {C/D} will rise. This is exactly what we see in Figure 16.1 during the bank panics of the Great Depression period 1930–1933 and to a lesser extent in 1893 and 1907 (years when smaller-scale bank panics occurred). The conclusion is that ***bank panics lead to a sharp increase in the currency-checkable deposits ratio.*** Bank panics have been an important source of fluctuations in the currency-checkable deposits ratio in the past and could be important in the future.

Illegal Activity Expected returns on checkable deposits relative to currency also can be affected by the amount of illegal activities conducted in the economy. U.S. law allows government prosecutors access to bank records when conducting a criminal investigation. If engaged in some illegal activity, you would not conduct your transactions with checks because they are traceable and therefore a potentially powerful piece of evidence against you. Currency, on the other hand, is much harder to trace. The expected return on currency relative to checkable deposits is higher when you are engaged in illegal transactions. Hence when illegal activity in a society increases, there is an increase in the use of currency relative to checkable deposits and {C/D} rises. *There is a positive association between illegal activity and the currency-checkable deposits ratio.*[3]

Looking at Figure 16.1, what types of increases in illegal activity would lead to an increase in {*C/D*}? Beginning in the 1960s, {*C/D*} began to climb—just when the illegal drug trade began to undergo phenomenal growth. Since illegal drug transactions are always carried out with currency, it is likely that the rise in drug trade is related to the rise in {*C/D*}. Supporting evidence is the current huge flow of currency into the south Florida region, the major center for illegal drug importing in the United States.[4] Other illegal activities—prostitution, black markets, gambling, loan sharking, fencing of stolen goods, the employment of illegal aliens—also could be the source of a higher currency-checkable deposits ratio.

Another interesting set of movements in {*C/D*} are the two increases during both world wars, which are associated with large increases in income taxes. Income taxes were raised substantially in 1917 to help finance America's entry into World War I. Although income tax rates were reduced after the war, they were again raised substantially during World War II to finance that conflict—never to return to prewar levels.

Increases in {*C/D*} when income tax rates rise can be explained as follows: Higher tax rates promote the evasion of taxes. When income tax rates rise, the incentive is high to evade taxes by conducting transactions in cash. If you receive a cash payment for some service (say, as a cab driver, waiter, or doctor), it is less likely that the Internal Revenue Service can prove that you are understating your income. If you are paid with a check or credit card, be cautious (and honest) and declare the income. The conclusion: *Higher tax rates will lead to a rise in {C/D}.*

Not only does the income tax evasion explain the rise in {*C/D*} during the two world wars, but is also helps explain the rise in the 1960s and 1970s. This may seem surprising, because the income tax rate schedule was not raised during this period. However, the burden of income taxes was increasing because the American income tax system is progressive (as income increases, the tax rate rises). A rising price level in the 1960s and 1970s raised nominal income and pushed more individuals into higher tax brackets (a phenome-

---

[3]One exception to this is an increase in street crime. Checkable deposits have the advantage over currency that if you are mugged, the loss from carrying checks is likely to be far less than the loss from carrying currency. Thus if muggings are on the rise, the expected return on currency will fall relative to the expected return on checkable deposits and you would hold less currency relative to checkable deposits. The resulting negative association of the illegal activity of street crime and {*C/D*} is ignored in the text because it is not an important source of fluctuations in {*C/D*}.

[4]The Drug Enforcement Agency has estimated that the retail value of the illegal drug trade exceeds $100 billion, making it one of the largest businesses in the United States. Evidence that the drug trade has affected {*C/D*} is found in Ralph C. Kimball, "Trends in the Use of Currency," *New England Economic Review* (September/October 1981), pp. 43–53.

non called "bracket creep"). This meant that the effective tax rate increased even though the tax schedule was unchanged. As a result, incentives increased to evade paying taxes by not declaring income, and people would avoid the use of checkable deposits. In other words, the expected return on checkable deposits fell and so $\{C/D\}$ rose.

Increased tax evasion and other illegal activities not only mean an increase in the currency-checkable deposits ratio, but also that more income will go unreported to the government. The result is an understatement of statistics on economic activity such as gross national product (GNP), which measures total production of goods and services in the economy.

This unreported economic activity has been labeled the **underground economy** (or subterranean economy). Evidence of its scope is the fact that the amount of currency per every man, woman, and child in the United States (as measured by currency in circulation in 1990 divided by the population) is almost $1,000. Very few people hold this amount of currency; the likelihood is that much is used to conduct transactions in the underground economy. Calculations of the size of the underground economy indicate it may exceed 10% of total economic activity (see Box 16.1). If this is true, and unreported income could be taxed, America would solve its budget deficit problems overnight!

APPLICATION
EXPLAINING THE HISTORICAL RECORD OF $\{C/D\}$ / / / / / / / / / / / / / / / / /

The interaction of historical data with the theory of asset demand has helped us to identify the factors that influence the currency-checkable deposits ratio. We have seen that the theory of asset demand developed in Chapter 5 can be stretched to give us a fairly deep understanding of how these different factors influence $\{C/D\}$.

To put our analysis in perspective, let us proceed to explain the major movements of $\{C/D\}$ in Figure 16.1 by time periods.

Study Guide
An excellent way to test your understanding of the factors influencing $\{C/D\}$ is to explain the movements in Figure 16.1 before referring to this section of the text. This exercise will provide you with practice using the ideas developed in the previous section and should help make the abstract analysis clearer.

1892–1917 The general decline in $\{C/D\}$ reflected in this period is explained by the increase in wealth. Because checkable deposits have a higher wealth elasticity than currency, the general trend of rising wealth over this

B o x   1 6 . 1

Size of the Underground Economy

As its name implies, the underground economy is very difficult to study and measure. One clue to its size is found in the currency-checkable deposits ratio. In a paper written in 1977, Peter Guttman outlined a procedure for measuring the underground economy by examining $\{C/D\}$.* He assumed that the rise in $\{C/D\}$ since the 1937–1941 period can be attributed solely to the growth of the underground economy and calculated its size to exceed 10% of GNP. This procedure has been criticized primarily on the grounds that $\{C/D\}$ should not have remained unchanged from the 1937–1941 value even if no underground economy developed.[†] In a related paper by Edgar Feige, however, the estimates for the fraction of economic activity occurring in the underground economy are even larger than Guttman's. Indeed, Feige states that his "estimate implies that a covert unrecorded economic sector the size of the entire economy of Canada exists *within* the overall U.S. economy."[‡] More recent estimates of the size of the underground economy are in the range of 5 to 15% of GNP.[§]

The existence of a sizable underground economy in the United States has enormous implications for the measurement of economic statistics.

The official statistics on how rapidly the economy is growing could be very misleading if the underground economy is growing at a different rate from the rest of the economy. The official unemployment rate may be substantially overstated since those employed in illegal activities could be reported as unemployed. The poverty statistics also might be overstated if some of the individuals earning substantial sums in the underground economy have reported incomes that are very low. If more precise measures of the underground economy demonstrated without doubt that this sector is sizable, policymakers might have quite a different view of how to conduct economic policy.

------

*Peter Guttman, "The Subterranean Economy," *Financial Analysts Journal* (November–December 1977).

[†]See the March–April 1978 volume of the *Financial Analysts Journal*.

[‡]Edgar Feige, "How Big Is the Irregular Economy?" *Challenge* (November–December 1979), pp. 5–13.

[§]See Joel F. Houston, "The Underground Economy: A Troubling Issue for Policymakers," in Federal Reserve Bank of Philadelphia *Business Review* (September/October 1987), pp. 3-12.

span implies that the holdings of currency will grow more slowly than the holdings of checkable deposits, thus lowering $\{C/D\}$.

The upward blips in the ratio seen in 1893 and 1907 were due to bank panics, which temporarily reduced the expected return on checkable deposits and increased the risk—these factors led to a temporary increase in the holdings of currency relative to checkable deposits, temporarily increasing $\{C/D\}$.

1917-1919   The upward surge in $\{C/D\}$ when America entered World War I is explained by the use of the income tax to help finance the war. The resulting attempts at tax evasion encouraged people to avoid the use of checks, which would make their income visible to the IRS or, put another way, the increased desire to avoid taxes lowered the expected return of checkable deposits, resulting in a lower demand for them. The resulting increase in the use of currency relative to checkable deposits raised {C/D}.

1919-1921   When income taxes were reduced after the war, the demand for currency relative to checkable deposits began to fall back toward its old level, and the rise in {C/D} that occurred during the war was reversed. However, a severe recession in 1920–1921 led to a decline in wealth along with an increased number of bank failures, both of which might have caused a rise in {C/D} at that time. The decline in wealth led to a decline in the demand for both currency and checkable deposits, but the higher wealth elasticity of checkable deposits meant that they declined more than currency, raising the currency-checkable deposits ratio. The increased number of bank failures also made checkable deposits less desirable because it lowered their expected return, also leading to a rise in {C/D}.

1921–1929   During the prosperous period of the Roaring Twenties we would expect to see the downward trend in {C/D} reasserting itself. The rise in wealth would lead to a fall in {C/D} because the holdings of currency would grow slower than the holdings of checkable deposits.

1929–1933   The decline in income during the Great Depression was one factor in the rise in {C/D}, but far more important were the bank panics which began in late 1930 and ended in March 1933. The sharp rise in {C/D} from 1930 to 1933 as a result was a major factor in the financial and economic collapse. These panics (the most severe in all of U.S. history) lowered the expected return of deposits, thereby raising the demand for currency relative to checkable deposits.

1933–1941   With the end of the bank panics and some restoration of the confidence in banks (helped by establishment of the FDIC), {C/D} fell. This decline was further strengthened by a rise in wealth. {C/D}, however, did not return to pre-Depression levels primarily because a loss of confidence in the U.S. banking system lingered in the minds of the public. As a result, expected returns on deposits did not return to their pre-Depression levels, leaving a high level of {C/D}.

1941–1945   When income tax rates were raised to unprecedented levels to finance combat in World War II, {C/D} underwent a substantial rise. The incentive to evade taxes was especially strong; hence the expected return on checkable deposits fell. Price controls imposed during the war also may have contributed to the rise in {C/D} because they stimulated illegal black market activity, whose transactions could be hidden using currency.

1945–Early 1960s   After the war, income tax rates were reduced slightly, but not to anywhere near their prewar levels. Income taxes remained at permanently higher levels because of the revenue needed to support an expanded role for the U.S. military as the "world's policemen" and enlarged social programs such as welfare, unemployment insurance, housing and urban development, and social security. Although some decline in {C/D} occurred after the war due to a reduction in tax rates, permanently higher income tax rates left strong incentives for tax evasion, and {C/D} remained high. The steady rise in wealth after the war promoted a return to a declining trend in {C/D}, but its effect was not sufficiently strong to reduce the ratio below prewar levels.

Early 1960s–1980 The declining trend beginning at the end of World War II began to reverse in the early 1960s for a number of reasons. Most important was the growth of the underground economy, both because of the spectacular rise in illegal drug trade and because of the increased desirability of evading taxes due to "bracket creep," which raised the effective tax rates. The increase in illegal activity lowered the expected return on checkable deposits, leading to an increased use of currency in relation to checkable deposits, thereby raising {C/D}.

1980–1990 A halt in the upward trend in {C/D} can be attributed to two factors. First, deregulation of the banking system allowed banks to pay interest on checkable deposits, which raised their expected return relative to currency. The resulting reduced demand for currency helped to lower {C/D}. Second, the Reagan tax cuts might also have lowered the incentive to evade taxes, thus contributing to a lower {C/D}.

APPLICATION
PREDICTING THE FUTURE OF {C/D}/ /

A good economic model not only explains the past but also helps predict the response of economic variables to new events. The analysis of factors that influence the currency-checkable deposits ratio outlined here has this capability. Let us consider two possible changes in the economic environment of the future and ask what our analysis would predict will happen to the currency-checkable deposits ratio as a result. These predictions could be of interest to policymakers, who would want to know how the money supply might be affected in each of these cases.

Study Guide

Try to provide the reasoning for the predictions here without having to refer to the text. This will give you excellent practice with the economic analysis of {C/D} we have developed in this chapter. You can get additional practice by answering problems at the end of the chapter, which also ask you to predict the future movements in {C/D}.

A Rise in Income Tax Rates to Balance the Budget Much talk is circulating about balancing the budget by further increasing taxes. What would happen to the currency-checkable deposits ratio if income tax rates were raised?

Higher tax rates would increase the incentives to evade taxes. The expected return on checkable deposits would then effectively have declined. The use of currency would increase relative to checkable deposits (if other factors are held constant), and we would predict a rise in $\{C/D\}$.

Abolishment of Interest Payments on Checking Accounts There have always been swings back and forth from deregulation to increased regulation. What if the present tide of deregulation is reversed and regulations were imposed that returned us to the situation of a decade or so ago, in which banks were not allowed to pay interest on checkable deposits? What would happen to the currency-checkable deposits ratio in this case?

This policy would mean that the expected return on checkable deposits would fall below its current levels, and the expected return on checkable deposits relative to currency also would fall. The resulting decreased attractiveness of checkable deposits relative to currency would mean the holdings of currency relative to checkable deposits would increase, raising $\{C/D\}$.

The usefulness of the preceding analysis is not restricted to the predictions of the response of $\{C/D\}$ to the events discussed here. With this framework, many other possible changes in our economic environment that would have an impact on $\{C/D\}$ can be analyzed (a few are discussed in the problems at the end of the chapter).

EXPLAINING BANK BEHAVIOR

In Chapter 15 we saw that when banks decrease the excess reserves ratio, $\{ER/D\}$, or increase the amount of discount loans they borrow from the Fed, the money supply increases. Here we outline a model of bank behavior that explains the determinants of $\{ER/D\}$ and discount loans from the Fed.

Determinants of the Excess Reserves Ratio, $\{ER/D\}$

To understand the factors that determine the level of $\{ER/D\}$ in the banking system, you must look at the costs and benefits to banks of holding excess reserves. When the costs of holding excess reserves rise, we would expect the level of excess reserves and hence $\{ER/D\}$ to fall; when the benefits of holding excess reserves rise, we would expect the level of excess reserves and $\{ER/D\}$ to rise. You will see that there are two main factors that affect these costs and benefits and hence affect the excess reserves ratio: market interest rates and expected deposit outflows.

Market Interest Rates   As you may recall from our analysis of bank management in Chapter 9, the cost to a bank of holding excess reserves is its opportunity cost: the interest that could have been earned on loans or securities if they had been held instead of excess reserves. For the sake of simplicity, we will assume that loans and securities earn the same interest rate of i, which we will call the market interest rate. If i increases, the opportunity cost of holding excess reserves rises and the desired ratio of excess reserves to deposits will fall. A decrease in i, on the other hand, will reduce the opportunity cost of excess reserves and $\{ER/D\}$ will rise. ***The banking system's excess reserves ratio, $\{ER/D\}$, is negatively related to the market interest rate i.***

Another way of understanding the negative effect of market interest rates on $\{ER/D\}$ is to again use the theory of asset demand, which states that if the expected returns on alternative assets rise relative to the expected returns on an asset, the demand for it will decrease. As the market interest rate increases, the expected return on loans and securities rises relative to the zero return on excess reserves, and the excess reserves ratio falls.

Figure 16.2 shows us that (as the theory of asset demand predicts) there is a negative relationship between the excess reserves ratio and a representative market interest rate, the federal funds rate. In the period shown, there

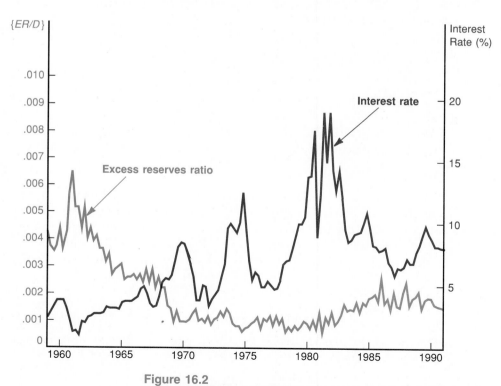

Figure 16.2
The Excess Reserves Ratio, $\{ER/D\}$, and the Interest Rate (Federal Funds Rate)
Sources: Federal Reserve *Bulletin* and Citibase databank.

has been a declining trend in $\{ER/D\}$ and an upward trend in the federal funds rate. In addition, there is a tendency for the level of $\{ER/D\}$ to hit its peaks when the federal funds rate is falling to its depths, and vice versa. The empirical evidence supports our analysis that the excess reserves ratio is negatively related to market interest rates.

Expected Deposit Outflows Our previous analysis of bank management showed us that the primary benefit to a bank of holding excess reserves is that they provide insurance against losses due to deposit outflows; that is, they enable the bank experiencing deposit outflows to escape the costs from (1) calling in loans, (2) selling securities, (3) borrowing from the Fed or other corporations, or (4) bank failure. If banks fear that deposit outflows are more likely (that is, expected deposit outflows increase), they will want more insurance against this possibility and will increase the excess reserves ratio. Another way to put it is: If expected deposit outflows rise, the expected benefits, and hence the expected return to holding excess reserves, increase. As the theory of asset demand predicts, excess reserves will then rise. A decline in expected deposit outflows, on the other hand, will reduce the insurance benefit of excess reserves, and their level should fall. We have the following result: ***The excess reserves ratio, $\{ER/D\}$, is positively related to expected deposit outflows.***

Determinants of Discount Loan Borrowing

Our analysis of what determines discount loan borrowing from the Federal Reserve again relies on identifying the costs and benefits of borrowing from the Fed. Two primary factors affect these costs and benefits and subsequently the volume of discount loans: market interest rates and the discount rate.

Market Interest Rates and the Discount Rate The principal benefit of borrowing from the Fed is straightforward. With additional borrowed reserves, a bank can acquire loans and securities, which earn the market interest rate, i. The primary cost of borrowing, on the other hand, is the discount rate (i_d), the interest rate the Fed charges on its loans to banks.[5] The greater the

---

[5] The "cost" of the Fed's disapproval of borrowing and potential termination of future discount privileges (discussed in Chapter 9) is ignored here because it is hard to quantify. Changes in the discount rate, i_d, can also have an effect on the excess reserves ratio, $\{ER/D\}$. The costs to a bank of experiencing a deposit outflow rises when i_d rises, since it is now more costly to borrow from the Fed when an outflow occurs. Thus a rise in i_d increases the benefits to holding excess reserves and $\{ER/D\}$ rises. This effect of the discount rate on the excess reserves ratio has not been emphasized in the text because it is believed to be small.

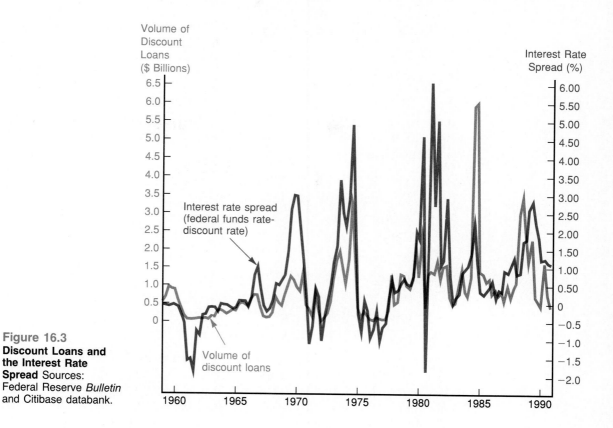

Figure 16.3
Discount Loans and the Interest Rate Spread Sources: Federal Reserve *Bulletin* and Citibase databank.

difference between the benefits (earnings) obtained from the use of borrowed funds (i) and the cost of borrowing (i_d), the more a bank will borrow from the Fed. Thus discount loan borrowing is positively related to $i - i_d$. This relationship in turn implies that ***the amount of discount loans (DL) is positively related to the market interest rate, i, and negatively related to the discount rate, i_d.***

Again, empirical evidence strongly confirms this economic analysis. Figure 16.3 shows a strong positive relationship between the volume of discount loans and the difference between a representative market interest rate (the federal funds rate) and the discount rate.

THE COMPLETE MONEY SUPPLY MODEL

Using the analysis of depositor and bank behavior, we can now summarize the complete money supply $(M1)$ model, which has the following form:

$$M = m \times [MB_n + DL] \tag{16.1}$$

where M = money supply (currency plus checkable deposits)

$$m = \text{money multiplier} = \frac{1 + \{C/D\}}{[r_D + \{ER/D\} + \{C/D\}]}$$

MB_n = nonborrowed monetary base

DL = discount loans from the Fed

Our money supply analysis has focused on the following nine variables which influence the money supply by affecting the money multiplier or the monetary base:

1. r_D = required reserve ratio
2. MB_n = nonborrowed monetary base
3. i_d = discount rate
4. Wealth
5. Illegal activity
6. Interest rates on checkable deposits
7. Bank panics
8. Expected deposit outflows
9. i = representative market interest rate

The required reserve ratio (r_D), wealth, illegal activity, interest rate on checkable deposits, bank panics, expected deposit outflows, and market interest rate (i) variables influence the money supply by affecting the money multiplier (m); while the nonborrowed monetary base (MB_n) and discount rate (i_d) variables influence the money supply by affecting the monetary base (MB).

Determinants of the Money Supply

To see how the money supply model works, let's analyze what effect changes in each of these variables has on the money supply, holding all the others constant.

Study Guide

The analysis in this and the previous chapters should enable you to reason out the effects of changes in these nine variables on the money supply. It is important not to simply memorize these effects, but to use intuitive reasoning to work out the response of the money supply to a change in each variable.

Required Reserve Ratio on Checkable Deposits (r_D) If r_D increases, the required reserves on checkable deposits increase, and so the same level of reserves cannot support as large an amount of checkable deposits. Because of the resulting deficiency in reserves, banks must contract their loans, causing a decline in deposits and in the money supply. A more insightful explanation is that a rise in r_D lowers the amount of multiple deposit expansion, lowering the money supply. If r_D decreases, more multiple expansion occurs and the money supply will increase. ***The money supply, then, is negatively related to r_D, the required reserve ratio on checkable deposits.***

Nonborrowed Monetary Base (MB_n) An increase in MB_n (as a result of an open market purchase) increases the amount of the monetary base available to support currency and checkable deposits, raising the money supply. A decline in MB_n (as a result of an open market sale) reduces the monetary base, lowering the money supply. ***The money supply is positively related to MB_n, the nonborrowed monetary base.***

Discount Rate (i_d) If the discount rate i_d rises, the cost of borrowing from the Fed increases, and the amount of discount loans decreases; less monetary base will be available to support currency and checkable deposits, lowering the money supply. If i_d falls, then discount loans from the Fed and the monetary base increase, and the money supply increases. ***Consequently, the money supply is negatively related to i_d, the discount rate.***

Wealth An increase in wealth increases the demand for checkable deposits more than the demand for currency, so the currency-checkable deposits ratio, {C/D} falls. Because of the shift from currency, which does not undergo multiple expansion, to checkable deposits, which do, the overall level of multiple expansion rises and the money supply rises. If wealth falls, {C/D} rises, the overall level of multiple expansion falls, and the money supply falls. ***The money supply is positively related to wealth.***

Illegal Activity Because checkable deposits make illegal activity easier to detect, if illegal activity climbs—say because higher tax rates lead to increased tax evasion or because of an increase in the drug trade—then there is a shift into currency, which does not undergo multiple expansion, from checkable deposits, which do. The resulting rise in {C/D} and the fall in multiple deposit expansion causes the money supply to fall. A decline in illegal activity causes {C/D} to fall, multiple expansion to rise, and the money supply to rise. ***The money supply is negatively related to illegal activity.***

Interest Rates on Checkable Deposits If the interest rates on checkable deposits rise, then there is a shift from currency to checkable deposits because the relative expected return on currency has fallen. The resulting decline in {C/D} and rise in multiple expansion leads to an increase in the money supply. Alternatively, if the interest rate on checkable deposits falls, {C/D} rises, multiple expansion falls, and the money supply falls. ***The money supply is positively related to the interest rate on checkable deposits.***

Bank Panics   When a bank panic occurs, depositors shift into currency from checkable deposits because they are more likely to suffer losses on their deposits; thus the relative expected return on currency increases. The resulting rise in {C/D} reduces multiple expansion and lowers the money supply. When the bank panic subsides, depositors shift back into checkable deposits, {C/D} falls, multiple expansion increases, and the money supply rises. ***The money supply falls during a bank panic and rises when the bank panic subsides.***

Expected Deposit Outflows   If expected deposit outflows rise because banks fear that deposit withdrawals are more likely, they will want to have more insurance against this possibility by holding more excess reserves. The resulting increase in the excess reserves ratio, {ER/D}, means that the banking system uses fewer reserves to support checkable deposits, and the level of checkable deposits and the money supply falls. On the other hand, if expected deposit outflows fall, {ER/D} falls and the money supply rises. ***Therefore, the money supply is negatively related to expected deposit outflows.***

Market Interest Rates (i)   If the interest rate on loans and securities, represented by the market interest rate i, rises, the opportunity cost of holding excess reserves increases and {ER/D} falls. As a result, more reserves will be available to support checkable deposits and the money supply rises. In addition, the rise in i will increase the benefits of borrowing from the Fed because banks can earn higher profits by taking out discount loans and using the proceeds to acquire loans and securities. The rise in i then leads to an increase in discount loans, a higher level of the monetary base, and hence a higher money supply. Since both effects of an increase in i on the money supply are in the same direction, we see that an increase in i raises the money supply. If i decreases, the excess reserves ratio rises and the volume of discount loans falls, both of which lower the money supply. ***Consequently, the money supply is positively related to i, the market interest rate.***[6]

As a study aid, Table 16.1 charts the money supply ($M1$) response to all nine variables discussed and gives a brief synopsis of the reasoning behind the result. The variables are grouped by the "player" or "players" who either influence the variable or are most influenced by it. The Federal Reserve, for example, influences the money supply by controlling the first three variables—r_D, MB_n, and i_d—also known as the tools of the Fed (these will be discussed extensively in subsequent chapters).

Depositors influence the money supply through their decisions about the currency-checkable deposits ratio {C/D}, which is affected by wealth, illegal activity, the interest rate on checkable deposits, and bank panics. Banks

---

[6] There are other possible effects of i on the money supply through the {C/D} ratio, but they are small enough to be ignored here.

Table 16.1   **Summary: Money Supply Response in the Complete Model**

Players	Change in Variable		M Response	Reason
Federal Reserve System	r_D	↑	↓	Less multiple deposit expansion
	MB_n	↑	↑	More MB to support currency and checkable deposits
	i_d	↑	↓	DL ↓ so less MB to support D and C
Depositors	Wealth	↑	↑	{C/D} ↓ so more overall multiple expansion
	Illegal activity	↑	↓	{C/D} ↑ so less overall multiple expansion
Depositors and banks	Interest rates on checkable deposits	↑	↑	{C/D} ↓ so more overall multiple expansion
	Bank panics	↑	↓	{C/D} ↑ so less overall multiple expansion
	Expected deposit outflows	↑	↓	{ER/D} ↑ so less reserves to support D
Borrowers from banks and other three players	i	↑	↑	{ER/D} ↓ so more reserves to support D; DL ↑ so more MB to support D and C

Note: Only increases (↑) in the variables are shown. The effect of decreases on the money supply would be the opposite of those indicated in the third column.

influence the money supply by their decisions about {ER/D}, which are affected by their expectations about deposit outflows and by their decisions about the interest rate on checkable deposits, which affects {C/D}. Since depositors' behavior also influences bankers' expectations about deposit outflows and bankers' decisions affect the probability that bank panics will occur, both these variables also reflect the role of both depositors and bankers in the money supply process.

Market interest rates, as represented by i, affect the money supply through the excess reserves ratio, {ER/D}. As Chapter 6 has shown, the demand for loans by borrowers influences market interest rates, as does the supply of money. Therefore all four players are important in the determination of i.

The most important of these variables to money supply movements is the nonborrowed monetary base (MB_n). Over three-quarters of the fluctuations in the money supply can be attributed to Federal Reserve open market operations, which determine MB_n. The other tools of the Fed, the required reserve ratio and the discount rate (r_D and i_d), have normally not been as important a source of money supply fluctuations, nor have the other six variables. However, as you will see in the next section, during periods such as the Great Depression, bank panics and expected deposit outflows have been the most important variables affecting the money supply.

We have now completed our study of the money supply model. In Chapter 14 you learned that the money supply resulted from the interaction of four players: (1) the Fed, (2) depositors, (3) banks, and (4) borrowers from banks. The complete money supply model summarized in Table 16.1 shows you how these players interact and what the outcomes of their actions are.

ANATOMY OF A BANK PANIC

The money supply model we have developed is a powerful tool; we will use it in later chapters to examine many issues that arise about how monetary policy operates and how it might be improved. To apply the model, let's use it to analyze a particularly interesting economic phenomenon—a bank panic in which a large number of banks fail at one time. Bank panics have had major historical impact; they have been blamed for some of our most severe economic contractions, including the Great Depression. The danger of bank panics has appeared in the news lately because of the recent bank panics in Ohio, Maryland, and Rhode Island (Box 16.2) and the collapse of several of our largest banking institutions—Continental Illinois, First Republic Bank of Texas, and Bank of New England. Although rare, the possibility of bank panics affects the way we conduct monetary policy because their prevention requires an active role on the part of the Federal Reserve.

Since most bank panics involve only a few banks at first, it is helpful to begin with a look at why an individual bank fails during such a crisis.

The Individual Bank

In an economy without federal deposit insurance, a bank failure means that depositors will not recover the full value of their deposits. If depositors suspect for any reason (unfounded or not) that a bank might fail, they will immediately withdraw their deposits. The bank loses reserves and is even more vulnerable to future deposit outflows. Other depositors who see this happening will begin to question the bank's health and withdraw their funds too. The more depositors withdraw funds, the fewer reserves the bank will have and the more likely it is to fail. The likelier it is to fail, the more likely depositors will show up to withdraw their deposits. This snowballing process, called a "run on the bank," usually terminates with a failure of the bank unless something can be done to restore the public's confidence.

Recent Bank Panics in Ohio, Maryland, and Rhode Island

Until the 1980s, most people believed that bank panics were a thing of the past, last occurring during the Great Depression. Events in Ohio, Maryland, and Rhode Island in recent years, however, have demonstrated that bank panics are still a danger to the health of the financial system.

In all three states, deposits were not covered by federal deposit insurance; instead, they were guaranteed by a private state insurance fund: in Ohio by the Ohio Deposit Guarantee Fund, in Maryland by the Maryland Savings-Share Insurance Corporation, and in Rhode Island by the Rhode Island Share & Deposit Indemnity Corporation. When the reserves held in these insurance funds were exceeded by losses at failed insured institutions, depositors feared that they would suffer losses on their deposits at other banking institutions. As our analysis in the chapter predicts, bank panics reminiscent of those in the 1930s then ensued when runs on these other institutions began to occur.

The first bank panic since the Great Depression occurred in Ohio after the Ohio Deposit Guarantee Fund was depleted by losses from the failure of the Home State Savings Bank of Cincinnati in March 1985 because of bad loans to a securities firm that was engaged in fraudulent activities. The governor of Ohio declared a bank holiday, temporarily closing seventy savings institutions, but these banks were later reopened with the help of the Federal Reserve and the Federal Home Loan Bank Board after they were able to obtain federal deposit insurance.

Soon afterwards in May 1985, the failure of two insured Maryland S&Ls bankrupted the Maryland Savings-Share Insurance Corporation. A panic at 100 Maryland S&Ls was finally stopped by the governor's temporary decree establishing a $1000 per month withdrawal limit and by the replacement of private deposit insurance by a newly created, state-backed deposit insurance fund.

The most damaging bank panic occurred in Rhode Island in January 1991. After a failure of a bank in Providence, Rhode Island, due to embezzlement, the governor was forced to declare a bank holiday on New Year's Day, closing forty-five small banks and credit unions. The result was the freezing of $1.3 billion in 359,000 accounts, in a state with only one million people. The governor's bailout proposal gave to each depositor at failed institutions up to only $12,500 in cash and, for the remainder of their deposits up to the $100,000 insured limit, non-interest-bearing state scrip (small-denomination paper IOUs) which would be paid back over several years. (Scrip like this was last issued during the bank panics of the 1930s.) Any deposit amount over $100,000 at a failed bank was unlikely to be paid back. The economic hardship imposed on Rhode Island has been severe. As one depositor who found his life savings of $60,000 frozen in a North Kingstown, Rhode Island, credit union said one month after the panic, "This place is going to become a ghost town if something doesn't happen fast."*

---

*Quoted in John R. Wilke, "Fear Strikes Old Stone Depositors in Rhode Island, Prompting Many to Demand Cash Immediately," *Wall Street Journal* (January 28, 1991), p. A2.

During the bank panics, anxious depositors lined up at savings institutions to withdraw their deposits.

Photo by Gerry Wolter/*The Cincinnati Enquirer*

Fear of a bank's failing can feed on itself and force even a healthy bank to fail. Although it may be in the best interest of the individual depositor to withdraw his or her funds, it is not necessarily in the best interests of the bank's depositors as a whole. Depositors' attempts to withdraw their funds lead to what they fear most—closing of the bank and the reality of not being able to recover their deposits.

The Banking System

A failure of one bank could cause depositors at another bank to suspect that their bank also could be the victim of a run and fail, setting in motion the whole process of a run on this second bank. The failure of this bank can trigger runs on other banks, and the whole process can multiply until there is a full-fledged bank panic in which a large number of banks fail.

Oddly enough, the desire of banks to protect themselves can increase the panic. If a bank is experiencing a run or fears it will happen in the near future, it needs to acquire excess reserves to avoid the costs associated with expected deposit outflows. To increase excess reserves in a banking panic (known as the "scramble for liquidity"), the bank sells securities and calls in loans, keeping the proceeds as excess reserves for protection. The scramble for liquidity results in deposit outflows from other banks and multiple deposit contraction, with the net result that other banks are more likely to fail. As with depositors, the desire of individual banks to protect themselves, even though in their best personal interest, may be damaging to the banking system as a whole.

Bank runs and a banking panic can be stopped by restoring depositors' as well as bankers' confidence in the health of the banks. It is not surprising that Franklin Delano Roosevelt's statement, "The only thing we have to fear is fear itself," was made after the United States had already experienced the most severe bank panics in its history.

To eliminate the climate of fear, banks sometimes have banded together in an attempt to prevent bank failures by lending the troubled bank enough reserves to survive the run. Why would a group of banks want to save a competitor who potentially takes away some of their business? Because it is in their self-interest to prevent a bank panic.

Another way to prevent a panic is for the central bank to supply substantial reserves to the banking system when bank failures occur so that other banks have enough reserves to handle the potential deposit outflows. It can do this either by increasing the nonborrowed monetary base (MB_n) or by freely lending to banks in this time of crisis. If the central bank's policy of preventing a panic becomes known, depositors no longer will feel the need to withdraw their deposits and bankers will not feel the need to call in loans and build up their excess reserves. The knowledge alone that the central bank will attempt to prevent a panic is often enough to stop a bank panic in its tracks.

As you will see in Chapter 17, the central bank in the United States, the Federal Reserve System, was created in response to the banking panic of 1907. Its intended role was to be the **lender of last resort** in a banking crisis; that is, the Fed was supposed to provide reserves to banks when no one else would, in order to prevent bank failures. Unfortunately, the Fed did not fulfill its role during the Great Depression (see Box 16.3), a failure that had dire consequences for the U.S. economy.

A final and most important way to prevent bank panics is in the creation of federal insurance for bank deposits. If depositors know that they will recover the full value of their deposits if their bank fails, suspicion of a bank failure will no longer cause them to make a run on the bank. As a result of the bank panics during the Great Depression, the Federal Deposit Insurance Corporation (FDIC) was put into operation on January 1, 1934. Since its birth, federal deposit insurance has been successful in sharply reducing the number of bank failures in the United States, although as we have seen in Chapter 11 it has created other problems.

Study Guide
To test your knowledge of the money supply model, see if you can analyze (without referring to the text) the effects of a bank panic on the money supply as a result of depositor and bank behavior.

Bank Panics and the Money Supply

We can now apply the preceding model to see what will be the effect of a bank panic on the money supply.

When a bank panic occurs, depositors will try to avoid the losses due to bank failures by turning their deposits into currency, and $\{C/D\}$ will rise. As the money supply model predicts, the overall level of multiple expansion will then decline, and the money supply will fall. In addition, deposit outflows will be expected to be higher and banks will want to hold more insurance in the form of excess reserves. The resulting scramble for liquidity, which raises the level of the excess reserves ratio, $\{ER/D\}$, will reduce the amount of reserves available to support checkable deposits, and this will also cause the money supply to fall. So a bank panic will have very negative effects on the money supply.

The following application examines the worst episode of bank panics in the United States, which started in late 1930 and ended with the bank holiday of March 1933. Not surprisingly, the largest decline of the money supply ever recorded in U.S. history occurs in this same period.

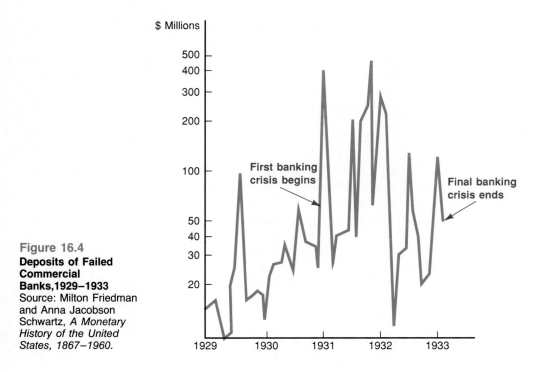

Figure 16.4
Deposits of Failed Commercial Banks,1929–1933
Source: Milton Friedman and Anna Jacobson Schwartz, *A Monetary History of the United States, 1867–1960.*

APPLICATION
THE GREAT DEPRESSION BANK PANICS: 1930–1933 / / / / / / / / / / / / / / / / /

We have used our model of the money supply process to understand the dynamics of a bank panic. To put this model to the test, we look here at a particular historical period—the Great Depression. Figure 16.4 traces the banking crisis in this period by showing the volume of deposits at failed commercial banks from 1929 to 1933. In their classic book, *A Monetary History of the United States, 1867–1960,* Milton Friedman and Anna Schwartz describe the onset of the first banking crisis in late 1930 as follows:[7]

> Before October 1930, deposits of suspended [failed] commercial banks had been somewhat higher than during most of 1929 but not out of line with experience during the preceding decade. In November 1930, they were more than double the highest value recorded since the start of monthly data in 1921. A crop of bank failures, particularly in Missouri, Indiana, Illinois, Iowa, Arkansas, and North Carolina, led to widespread attempts to convert

---

[7]Milton Friedman and Anna Jacobson Schwartz, *A Monetary History of the United States, 1867–1960* (Princeton: Princeton University Press, 1963), pp. 308–311.

checkable and time deposits into currency, and also, to a much lesser extent, into postal savings deposits. A contagion of fear spread among depositors, starting from the agricultural areas, which had experienced the heaviest impact of bank failures in the twenties. But failure of 256 banks with $180 million of deposits in November 1930 was followed by the failure of 532 with over $370 million of deposits in December (all figures seasonally unadjusted), the most dramatic being the failure on December 11 of the Bank of the United States with over $200 million of deposits. That failure was of especial importance. The Bank of United States was the largest commercial bank, as measured by volume of deposits, ever to have failed up to that time in U.S. history. Moreover, though an ordinary commercial bank, its name had led many at home and abroad to regard it somehow as an official bank, hence its failure constituted more of a blow to confidence than would have been administered by the fall of a bank with a less distinctive name.

The first banking panic, from October 1930 until January 1931, is clearly visible in Figure 16.4 at the end of 1930, when there is a rise in the amount of deposits at failed banks. According to the money supply model, {C/D} should have risen sharply with the onset of the first banking crisis, and the banks should have tried to protect themselves by substantially increasing

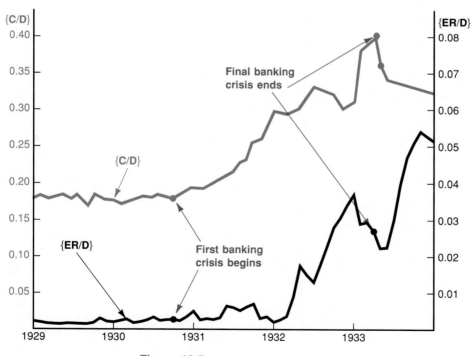

Figure 16.5

The Excess Reserves and Currency-Checkable Deposits Ratio: 1929–1933 Sources: Federal Reserve *Bulletin*, and Milton Friedman and Anna Jacobson Schwartz, *A Monetary History of the United States, 1867–1960.*

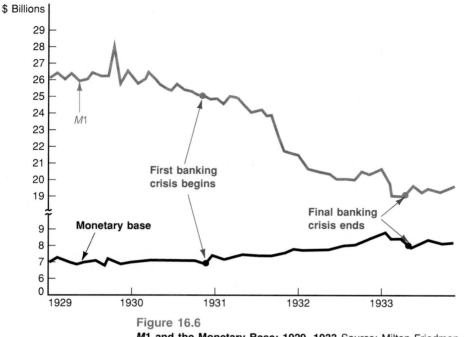

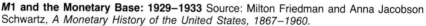

Figure 16.6

*M*1 **and the Monetary Base: 1929–1933** Source: Milton Friedman and Anna Jacobson Schwartz, *A Monetary History of the United States, 1867–1960.*

their excess reserves ratio, {*ER/D*}. Both these predictions are borne out by the data in Figure 16.5. {*C/D*} began to climb during the first banking panic (October 1930–January 1931). Even more striking is the behavior of {*ER/D*}, which more than doubled from November 1930 to January 1931. The money supply model also predicts that when {*ER/D*} and {*C/D*} increase, the money supply will fall—a prediction borne out by the evidence in Figure 16.6. The money supply declined sharply in December 1930 and January 1931 during the first banking panic.

Banking crises continued to occur from 1931 to 1933, and the normal pattern predicted by our model continued: {*C/D*} continued to rise, as did {*ER/D*}. By the end of the banking crises in March 1933, the money supply (*M*1) had declined by over 25%—by far, the largest decline in all of American history—and it may be no coincidence that it coincided with the worst economic contraction (see Chapter 8). Even more remarkable is that this decline occurred despite a 20% rise in the level of the monetary base—which illustrates how important the changes in {*C/D*} and {*ER/D*} during bank panics can be in the determination of the money supply. It also illustrates that the Fed's job of conducting monetary policy can be complicated by depositor and bank behavior (see Box 16.3).

B o x   1 6 . 3

Why Did the Fed Let the Bank Panics of 1930–1933 Happen?

The Federal Reserve System was totally passive during the banking panics of the Great Depression period and did not perform its intended role of "lender of last resort" to prevent them. In retrospect the Fed's behavior seems quite extraordinary, but it should be remembered that hindsight is always better than foresight.

The primary reason for the Fed's inaction was that Federal Reserve officials did not understand the negative impact bank failures could have on the money supply and economic activity. Friedman and Schwartz state that the Federal Reserve officials "tended to regard bank failures as regrettable consequences of bank management or bad banking practices, or as inevitable reactions to prior speculative excesses, or as a consequence but hardly a cause of the financial and economic collapse in process." In addition, bank failures in the early stages of the bank panics "were concentrated among smaller banks and, since the most influential figures in the system were big-city bankers who deplored the existence of smaller banks, their dis-

appearance may have been viewed with complacency."*

Friedman and Schwartz also point out that political in-fighting may have played an important role in the passivity of the Fed during this period. The Federal Reserve Bank of New York, which until 1928 was the dominant force in the Federal Reserve System, strongly advocated an active program of open market purchases to provide reserves to the banking system during the bank panics. However, other powerful figures in the Federal Reserve System opposed the New York Bank's position, and the New York Bank was outvoted. (Friedman and Schwartz's discussion of the politics of the Federal Reserve System during this period makes for fascinating reading, and you might enjoy their highly readable book.)

---

*Milton Friedman and Anna Jacobson Schwartz, *A Monetary History of the United States, 1867–1960* (Princeton: Princeton University Press, 1963), p. 358.

SUMMARY

1. The interaction between the theory of asset demand and empirical data provides a framework that allows us to identify four primary factors that influence the currency-checkable deposits ratio: (a) wealth, (b) interest rates on checkable deposits, (c) bank panics, and (d) illegal activity. The currency-checkable deposits ratio is positively related to bank panics and illegal activity, while it is negatively related to wealth and interest rates on checkable deposits.

2. The desired level of the excess reserves ratio is negatively related to interest rates and positively related to expected deposit outflows. Discount

loan borrowing from the Fed is positively related to market interest rates and is negatively related to the discount rate.

3. The complete money supply model focuses on the effects of nine factors. The results are summarized in Table 16.1, which shows how the money supply is affected by changes in these factors.

4. The phenomenon of a bank panic illustrates many of the principles of money supply analysis. Fearing bank failures, depositors turn their deposits into currency, causing a sharp rise in $\{C/D\}$ and contraction in the money supply. Banks, try-

ing to protect themselves against the resulting deposit outflows, increase their excess reserves ratio, {ER/D}, resulting in a further decline in the money supply. This is exactly what transpired in the Great Depression period, in which the money supply declined by 25% (even though the monetary base rose by 20%).

KEY TERMS

bank panic

underground economy

lender of last resort

QUESTIONS AND PROBLEMS

1. If the currency-checkable deposits ratio rises from its current level, what might this imply about the growth of the underground economy?

* 2. Why might the procyclical behavior of interest rates (they rise during business cycle expansions and fall during recessions) lead to procyclical movements in the money supply?

3. Answer true, false, or uncertain: "Self-preservation can be self-destructive during a banking panic." Explain.

Using Economic Analysis to Predict the Future

* 4. In contrast to procedures in the United States, Swiss government investigations are not allowed to access bank records of individuals or corporations. If the United States decided to adopt this attribute of the Swiss system, what do you predict would happen to the currency-checkable deposits ratio?

5. Predict what would happen to the currency-checkable deposits ratio if cigarette smoking were made illegal.

* 6. With all other factors held constant, predict what will happen to the currency-checkable deposits ratio over the next twenty years if wealth continues to rise.

7. If the government reinstituted regulations to prevent the payment of interest on checkable deposits, what would happen to the currency-checkable deposits ratio?

* 8. The Fed has been discussing the possibility of paying interest on excess reserves. If this occurred, what would happen to the level of {ER/D}?

9. If the FDIC were abolished, what would happen to the money supply as a result of bank behavior? depositor behavior?

*10. What do you predict would happen to the money supply if expected inflation suddenly increases?

11. If the economy starts to boom and loan demand picks up, what do you predict will happen to the money supply?

*12. Milton Friedman once suggested that Federal Reserve discount lending should be abolished. Predict what would happen to the money supply if Friedman's suggestion is put into practice.

13. If the Fed paid a market interest rate on reserves and also set its discount rate equal to this same rate, what do you predict would happen to the money supply if interest rates were to rise?

*14. If Congress reduced the penalties for check forgery, what would happen to the money supply?

15. Predict what would happen to the money supply if the Fed makes open market purchases of bonds at the same time that market interest rates are rising.

PART V

The Federal Reserve System and the Conduct of Monetary Policy

CHAPTER 17

The Structure of the Federal Reserve System

PREVIEW   Our money supply analysis in previous chapters attests to the critical role in the money supply process played by the Federal Reserve System—the U.S. government authority in charge of the country's monetary policy. Indeed, over three-quarters of the fluctuations in the money supply can be attributed to changes in the monetary base (currency in circulation plus reserves) that can be controlled by the Fed; the Fed clearly is the "lead player," and others are "supporting characters." But who controls the Fed and determines its actions? What motivates its behavior? Who holds the reins of power?

In this chapter we look at the formal institutional structure of the Fed and the more relevant informal structure that determines where the true power within the Federal Reserve System lies. By understanding who makes the decisions, we will have a better idea of how they are made. Consequently, the actual conduct of monetary policy described in the subsequent two chapters will be more comprehensible.

ORIGINS OF THE FEDERAL RESERVE SYSTEM

Of all the central banks throughout the world, the Federal Reserve System probably has the most unusual structure. To understand why this structure arose, we must regress to a time before 1913, when the Federal Reserve System was created.

Before the twentieth century, a major characteristic of American politics was the fear of centralized power, as can be seen in the checks and balances of the Constitution and the preservation of states' rights. This fear of centralized power was one source of the hostility of Americans until 1913 to the establishment of a central bank. Another was the traditional American distrust of moneyed interests, the most prominent symbol of which was the central bank. The open hostility of the American public to the existence of a central bank resulted in the demise of the first two experiments in central banking, whose function was to police the banking system: the First Bank of the United States (disbanded in 1811) and the Second Bank of the United States (abolished in 1836 by President Andrew Jackson).

The termination of the Second Bank of the United States in 1836 created a severe problem for American financial markets, because there was no lender of last resort who could provide reserves to the banking system to avert a banking panic. In the nineteenth and early twentieth centuries, nationwide bank panics had become a regular occurrence—happening in 1819, 1837, 1857, 1873, 1884, 1893, and 1907. The 1907 panic resulted in such widespread bank failures and substantial losses to depositors that the American public was finally convinced that a central bank was needed to prevent future panics.

The hostility of the American public to banks and centralized authority created great opposition to the establishment of a single central bank like the Bank of England. Fear was rampant that the moneyed interests on Wall Street (including the largest corporations and banks) would be able to use such an institution to exercise control over the economy and that federal control of the central bank might result in too much intervention in the affairs of private banks. Serious disagreements existed over whether the central bank should be a private bank or a government institution. Because of the heated debates on these issues, a compromise was struck. In the great American tradition, Congress wrote an elaborate system of checks and balances into the Federal Reserve Act of 1913, which created the Federal Reserve System with its twelve regional Federal Reserve banks.

FORMAL STRUCTURE OF THE FEDERAL RESERVE SYSTEM

The formal structure of the Federal Reserve System was intended by designers of the Federal Reserve Act to diffuse power along regional lines, between the private sector and the government, and among bankers, businesspeople, and the public. This initial diffusion of power has resulted in the evolution of the Federal Reserve System to include the following entities: the **Federal Reserve Banks,** the **Board of Governors of the Federal Reserve System,** the **Federal Open Market Committee (FOMC),** the Federal Advisory Council, and around 5000 member commercial banks. Figure 17.1 outlines the relationships of these entities to each other and to the three policy tools of the Fed (open market operations, the discount rate, and reserve requirements).

Federal Reserve Banks

Each of the twelve Federal Reserve districts has one main Federal Reserve Bank, some of which have several additional branches in other cities in the district. The locations of these districts, the Federal Reserve Banks, and their branches are shown in Figure 17.2. The three largest Federal Reserve Banks

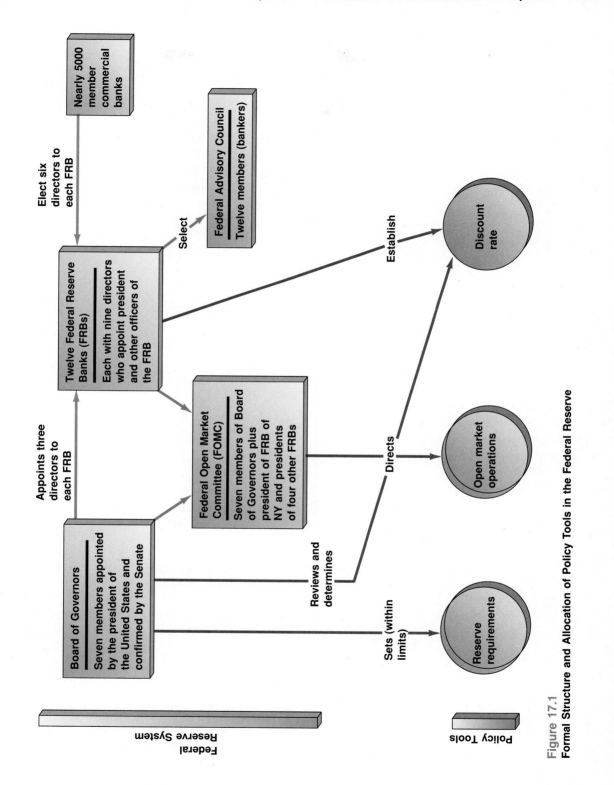

Figure 17.1
Formal Structure and Allocation of Policy Tools in the Federal Reserve

● Board of Governors of the Federal
Reserve System

① Federal Reserve Districts

● Federal Reserve Bank cities

▬ Boundaries of Federal Reserve districts
(Alaska and Hawaii are in District 12)

• Federal Reserve branch cities

— Boundaries of Federal Reserve branch
territories

Figure 17.2
Federal Reserve System Source: Federal Reserve *Bulletin*.

in terms of assets are those of New York, Chicago, and San Francisco—combined they hold over 50% of the assets (discount loans, securities, etc.) in the Federal Reserve System. The New York Bank, with over 30% of the assets, is the most important of the Federal Reserve Banks because its district contains many of the largest commercial banks in the United States and because it is in direct contact with the major financial markets, which operate out of New York City.

Each of the Federal Reserve Banks is a quasi-public incorporated institution owned by the private commercial banks in the district who are members of the Federal Reserve System. These member banks have purchased stock in their district Federal Reserve Bank (a requirement of membership), and the dividends paid by that stock are limited to 6% annually. The member banks elect six directors for each district Federal Reserve Bank; three more are appointed by the Board of Governors of the Federal Reserve System. Together, these nine directors appoint the president of the bank (subject to the approval of the Board of Governors).

The directors of a district bank are classified into three categories (A, B, and C): the three A directors (elected by the member banks) are professional bankers, and the three B directors (also elected by the member banks) are prominent businesspeople in the areas of industry, commerce, and agriculture. The three C directors who are appointed by the Board of Governors to represent the public interest are not allowed to be officers, employees, or stockholders of banks. This design of choosing directors was intended by the Federal Reserve Act to ensure that the directors of each Federal Reserve Bank would reflect all constituencies of the American public.

The twelve Federal Reserve Banks (1) clear checks, (2) issue new currency, (3) withdraw damaged currency from circulation, (4) evaluate some merger applications, (5) administer and make discount loans to banks in their districts, (6) act as liaisons between the business community and the Federal Reserve System, (7) examine state member banks, (8) collect data on local business conditions, and (9) with their large staffs of professional economists, research topics related to the conduct of monetary policy and publish reviews (a good source of supplemental material for money and banking students) that present the staffs' views.

The twelve Federal Reserve Banks are involved in monetary policy in several ways: (1) they "establish" the discount rate (although the discount rate in each district is reviewed and determined by the Board of Governors), (2) they decide which banks, member and nonmember alike, can obtain discount loans from the Federal Reserve Bank, (3) they each select one commercial banker to serve on the Federal Advisory Council, which consults with the Board of Governors and makes recommendations on the conduct of monetary policy, and (4) five bank presidents each have a vote in the Federal Open Market Committee (FOMC), which directs open market operations (the purchase and sale of government securities that affect the monetary base). The president of the New York Fed always has a vote in the FOMC, making it the most important of the banks, while the other four votes allocated to the district banks rotate among the remaining eleven presidents.

Member Banks

All national banks (those commercial banks chartered by the Office of the Comptroller of the Currency) are required to be members of the Federal Reserve System. Commercial banks chartered by the states are not required to be members, but they can choose to do so. Currently, around 40% of the commercial banks in the United States are members of the Federal Reserve System, having declined from a peak figure of 49% in 1947.

Before 1980, only member banks were required to keep reserves as deposits at the Federal Reserve Banks; nonmember banks were subject to reserve requirements determined by their states, which typically allowed them to hold much of their reserves in interest-bearing securities. Because no interest is paid on reserves deposited at the Federal Reserve Banks, it was quite costly to be a member of the system, and as interest rates rose, the relative cost of membership rose and more and more banks left the system.

This decline in Fed membership was a major concern of the Board of Governors (one reason was that it lessened the Fed's control over the money supply, making it more difficult for the Fed to conduct monetary policy). The chairman of the Board of Governors repeatedly called for new legislation that required all commercial banks to be members of the Federal Reserve System. One result of the Fed's pressure on Congress was a provision in the Depository Institutions Deregulation and Monetary Control Act of 1980: All banks would become subject (by 1987) to the same requirements to keep deposits at the Fed, so member and nonmember banks would be on an equal footing in terms of their reserve requirements. In addition, all banks have been given access to the Federal Reserve facilities such as the discount window and Fed check clearing on an equal basis. These provisions have ended the decline in Fed membership and have reduced the distinction between member and nonmember banks.

Board of Governors of the Federal Reserve System

At the head of the Federal Reserve System is the seven-member Board of Governors headquartered in Washington, D.C. Each governor is appointed by the president of the United States and confirmed by the Senate. To limit a particular president's control over the Fed and insulate the Fed from other political pressures, the governors serve one nonrenewable fourteen-year term, with one governor's term expiring every other January.[1] The governors (many are professional economists) are required to come from different Federal Reserve districts in order to prevent one region of the country's interests from being overrepresented. The chairman of the Board of Governors is chosen from among the seven governors and serves a four-year term. Traditionally, once a new chairman is chosen, the old chairman resigns from the Board of Governors, even if there are many years left to his or her term as a governor.

---

[1] Although technically a governor's term is nonrenewable, a governor can resign just before his or her term expires and then be reappointed by the president. This explains how one governor served for twenty-eight years. Since William McChesney Martin, the chairman from 1951–1970, retired from the Board in 1970, the practice of extending a governor's term past fourteen years is no longer common.

The Board of Governors is actively involved with decisions concerning the conduct of monetary policy. All seven governors are members of the Federal Open Market Committee and vote on the conduct of open market operations. Since there are only twelve voting members in this committee (seven governors and five presidents of the district banks), the Board has the majority of the votes. The Board also sets (within limits imposed by legislation) reserve requirements and effectively controls the discount rate by the "review and determination" process, whereby it approves or disapproves the discount rate "established" by the Federal Reserve Banks. The chairman of the Board advises the president of the United States on economic policy, testifies in Congress, and speaks for the Federal Reserve System to the media. The chairman and other governors also may represent the United States in negotiations with foreign governments on economic matters. The Board has a staff of professional economists (larger than those of individual Federal Reserve Banks), which provides economic analysis that the board uses in making its decisions.

Through legislation, the Board of Governors has often been given duties not directly related to the conduct of monetary policy. In the past, for example, the Board set the maximum interest rates payable on certain types of time deposits under Regulation Q. (Since Regulation Q was eliminated in 1986, the Board no longer has this authority.) Under the Credit Control Act of 1969 (which expired in 1982), the Board had the ability to regulate and control credit once the president of the United States approved. The Board of Governors also sets margin requirements, the fraction of the purchase price of the securities that has to be paid for with cash rather than borrowed funds. It also sets the salary of the president and all officers of each Federal Reserve Bank and reviews each bank's budget. Finally, the Board has substantial bank regulatory functions: It approves bank mergers and specifies the permissible activities of bank holding companies.

Federal Open Market Committee (FOMC)

The FOMC usually meets eight times a year (about every six weeks) and makes decisions regarding the conduct of open market operations, which influence the monetary base. The committee consists of the seven members of the Board of Governors, the president of the Federal Reserve Bank of New York, and presidents of four other Federal Reserve Banks. The chairman of the Board of Governors also presides as the chairman of the FOMC. Even though only presidents of five of the Federal Reserve Banks are voting members of the FOMC, the other seven presidents of the district banks attend the FOMC meetings and participate in its discussions. Hence they have some input into the committee's decisions.

Since open market operations are the most important policy tool that the Fed has for controlling the money supply, the FOMC is necessarily the

Box 17.1 **A Global Perspective**

Europe 1992: Will There Be a New European Central Bank—the EuroFed?

As part of the Europe 1992 initiative to promote economic integration of the twelve European Community (EC) countries, the European Economic Community (EEC) has unveiled a plan for setting up an EC central bank by January 1, 1993. The future European central bank would be patterned after the Federal Reserve System in which central banks for each country would have a role similar to regional Federal Reserve Banks. The European central bank, which has been appropriately called the "EuroFed," would have price stability as its central objective and would be independent from the EC and national governments. It would conduct monetary policy and intervene in foreign exchange markets just as the Federal Reserve does.

Despite the EEC plan, the creation of the EuroFed is by no means certain. Because the establishment of the EuroFed would mean some loss of national sovereignty and power, it has produced concern in individual countries. The United Kingdom government, for example, has raised objections to the EuroFed plan, particularly about the intent of having a single currency based on the ECU (European currency unit) as part of the EuroFed operations.

focal point for policy-making in the Federal Reserve System. Although reserve requirements and the discount rate are not actually set by the FOMC, decisions in regard to these policy tools are effectively made here. The FOMC does not actually carry out security purchases or sales. Rather it issues a directive to the trading desk at the Federal Reserve Bank of New York, where the manager for domestic open market operations supervises a roomful of people who execute the purchases and sales of the government or agency securities.[2] The manager communicates daily with the FOMC members and their staffs concerning the activities of the trading desk.

The formal structure that we have just reviewed may be the model for a European central bank, as described in Box 17.1.

INFORMAL STRUCTURE OF THE FEDERAL RESERVE SYSTEM

The Federal Reserve Act and other legislation give us some idea of the formal structure of the Federal Reserve System and who makes decisions at the

---

[2]The decisions contained in the directive are often not unanimous, and the dissenting views are made public. However, except in rare cases, the chairman's vote is always on the winning side.

Fed. However, what is written in black and white is not necessarily a reflection of the reality of power and the decision-making structure.

As envisioned in 1913, the Federal Reserve System was to be a highly decentralized system designed to function as twelve separate, cooperating central banks. The original plan did not include the Fed's being responsible for the health of the economy through its control of the money supply and its ability to affect interest rates. Over time it has acquired the responsibility for promoting a stable economy, and this responsibility has caused the Federal Reserve System to slowly evolve into a more unified central bank.

The designers of the Federal Reserve Act of 1913 intended the Fed to have only one basic tool of monetary policy, the control of discount loans to member banks. The use of open market operations as a tool for monetary control was not yet well understood, and reserve requirements were fixed by the Federal Reserve Act. The discount tool was to be controlled by the joint decision of the Federal Reserve Banks and the Federal Reserve Board (which later became the Board of Governors), so that both would share equally in the determination of monetary policy. However, the Board's ability to "review and determine" the discount rate effectively allowed it to dominate the district banks in setting this policy tool.

The banking legislation during the Great Depression years centralized power within the newly created Board of Governors by giving it effective control over the remaining two tools of monetary policy—open market operations and changes in reserve requirements. The Banking Act of 1933 granted the FOMC authority to determine open market operations, and the Banking Act of 1935 gave the Board the majority of votes in the FOMC. The Banking Act of 1935 also gave the Board authority to change reserve requirements.

Over time, then, the Board of Governors has acquired the reins of control over the tools for conducting monetary policy. In recent years, the power of the Board has become even greater. It frequently suggests a choice (often a professional economist) for president of a Federal Reserve Bank to the directors of the bank, who normally follow the Board's suggestions. Since the Board sets the salary of the bank's president and reviews the budget of each Federal Reserve Bank, it has further influence over the district banks' activities.

If the Board of Governors has so much power, what power do the Federal Advisory Council and the "owners" of the Federal Reserve Banks—the member banks—actually have within the Federal Reserve system? The answer is "almost none." Although member banks own stock in the Federal Reserve Banks, they covet none of the usual benefits of ownership. First, they have no claim on the earnings of the Fed and get paid only a 6% annual dividend, regardless of how much the Fed earns. Second, they have no say over how their "property" is used by the Federal Reserve System, in contrast to stockholders of private corporations. Third, there is usually only a single candidate for each of the six A and B directorships "elected" by the member banks, and this candidate is frequently suggested by the president of the Federal Reserve Bank (who, in turn, is usually suggested by the Board of Governors, although on paper the directors of the bank elect the president). The net result is that member banks are essentially frozen out of the political process at the Fed and have no effective power. Fourth, the Federal Advisory Council has little impact on Federal Reserve policy-making and serves mostly a ceremonial function.

A fair characterization of the Federal Reserve System as it has evolved is that it functions as a central bank, headquartered in Washington, D.C., with branches in twelve cities. Since all aspects of the Federal Reserve System are essentially controlled by the Board of Governors, who controls the Board? Although the chairman of the Board of Governors does not have legal authority to exercise control over this body, the chairman effectively does so through the ability to set the agenda of the Board and FOMC meetings, act as spokesperson for the Fed, and negotiate with Congress and the president of the United States. The chairman also influences the Board through the force of stature and personality. Chairmen of the Board of Governors (such as Marriner S. Eccles, William McChesney Martin, Jr., Arthur Burns, Paul A. Volcker, and Alan Greenspan) have typically had strong personalities and have wielded great power.

The chairman also exercises power by supervising the board's staff of professional economists and advisors. Since the staff gathers information for the Board and conducts the analyses the Board uses in its decisions, it also has some influence over monetary policy. In addition, several recent appointments to the Board itself have come from within the ranks of its professional staff, making the chairman's influence even more far-reaching and long-lasting than a four-year term.

The informal power structure of the Fed, in which power is centralized in the chairman of the Board of Governors, is summarized in Figure 17.3.

WHAT MOTIVATES THE FED?

When we look, in the next three chapters, at how the Federal Reserve conducts monetary policy, we will want to know why the Fed decides to take certain policy actions but not others. To understand its actions, we must understand the incentives that motivate the Fed's behavior. How free is the Fed from presidential and congressional pressures? Do economic, bureaucratic, or political considerations guide it? Is the Fed truly independent of outside pressures?

How Independent Is the Fed?

The Federal Reserve appears to be remarkably free of the political pressures that influence other government agencies. Not only are the members of the

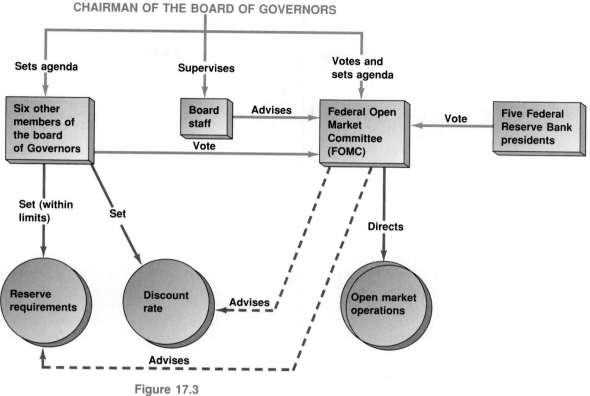

Figure 17.3
Informal Power Structure of the Federal Reserve System

Board of Governors appointed for a fourteen-year term (and so cannot be ousted from their offices), but the term is technically not renewable, eliminating some of the incentive for the governors to curry favor with the president and Congress.

Probably even more important to its independence from the whims of Congress is the Fed's independent and substantial source of revenue from its holdings of securities and, to a lesser extent, from its loans to banks. In recent years, for example, the Fed has had net earnings after expenses of over $15 billion dollars per year—not a bad living if you can find it! Since it returns the bulk of these earnings to the Treasury, it does not get rich from its activities, but this income gives the Fed an important advantage over other government agencies: It is not subject to the appropriations process usually controlled by Congress. Indeed, the Fed can (and has) refused an audit by the General Accounting Office, the auditing agency of the federal government. Because the power to control the purse strings is usually synonymous with the power to control, this feature of the Federal Reserve System contributes to its independence more than any other factor.

Yet the Federal Reserve is still subject to the influence of Congress, because the legislation that structures it is written by Congress and is subject to change at any time. When legislators are upset with the Fed's conduct of monetary policy, they frequently threaten to take control over the Fed's finances and force it to submit a budget request like other government agencies. (Often during the year, you will spot newspaper articles describing a call by a member of Congress for tighter supervision of the Fed.) This is a powerful club to wave, and it certainly has some clout in keeping the Fed from straying too far from congressional wishes.

Congress has also passed legislation to make the Federal Reserve more accountable for its actions. In 1975, Congress passed House Concurrent Resolution 133, which requires the Fed to announce its objectives for the growth rates of the monetary aggregates. In the Full Employment and Balanced Growth Act of 1978 (the Humphrey-Hawkins bill) the Fed is required to explain how these objectives are consistent with the economic plans of the president of the United States.

The president can also influence the Federal Reserve. Because congressional legislation can affect the Fed directly or affect its ability to conduct monetary policy, the president can be a powerful ally through his influence on Congress. Second, although ostensibly a president might be able to appoint only one or two members to the Board of Governors during each presidential term, in actual practice the president appoints members far more often. One reason is that most governors do not serve out their full fourteen-year terms. (One explanation is that governors' salaries are substantially below what they can earn in the private sector, thus providing governors with an incentive to take a private-sector job before their term expires.) In addition, the president is able to appoint a new chairman of the Board of Governors every four years, and traditionally a chairman who is not reappointed resigns from the Board so that a new member of the Board can be appointed.

The power that the president enjoys through his appointments to the Board of Governors is limited, however. Because the term of the chairman is not necessarily concurrent with the presidential term, a president frequently finds himself with a chairman of the Board of Governors who was appointed by a previous administration. Paul Volcker, for example, was appointed as chairman in 1979 by then-President Jimmy Carter, and his term did not expire until 1983—three years into President Reagan's term. Reagan was put under tremendous pressure to reappoint Volcker when his term expired. He then *did* reappoint Volcker, even though Volcker was first appointed by a Democrat (Jimmy Carter).[3]

---

[3]Similarly, William McChesney Martin, the chairman from 1951 to 1970, was appointed by President Truman, but was reappointed by Presidents Eisenhower, Kennedy, and Nixon.

You can see that the Federal Reserve has extraordinary independence for a government agency, but nonetheless is not free of political pressures. Indeed, to understand the Fed's behavior, we must recognize that politics plays a very important role.

Explaining the Fed's Behavior

One view of governmental bureaucratic behavior is that bureaucracies serve the public interest. Yet some economists have developed a theory of bureaucratic behavior that suggests other factors that influence how bureaucracies operate. The *theory of bureaucratic behavior* suggests that the objective of a bureaucracy is to maximize its own welfare, just as a consumer's behavior is motivated by the maximization of his or her welfare and a business firm's behavior is motivated by the maximization of profits. The welfare of a bureaucracy is related to its power and prestige. Thus this theory suggests that an important factor that affects the Fed's behavior is its attempt to increase its power and prestige.

What predictions does this view of the Fed's behavior suggest? One is that the Federal Reserve will fight vigorously to preserve its autonomy, a prediction verified time and time again as the Fed has continually counterattacked congressional attempts to control its budget. In fact, it is quite extraordinary how effectively the Fed has been able to mobilize a lobby of bankers and businesspeople to preserve its independence when threatened.

Another prediction is that the Federal Reserve will try to avoid conflict with powerful groups that may threaten to curtail its power and reduce its autonomy. The Fed's behavior may take several forms. To avoid a conflict with the President and Congress over increases in interest rates, the Fed often tries to prevent the increases. The desire to avoid conflict with the Congress and the President also may explain why the Fed (particularly the chairman of the Board of Governors) has become so expert at avoiding blame for its past mistakes and also may explain why Fed officials have devised clever stratagems to obscure what they have been doing in the past and what they plan to do in the future (see Box 17.2).

The desire of the Fed to hold as much power as possible also explains why it vigorously pursued a campaign to gain control over more banks. The campaign culminated in legislation that expanded jurisdiction of the Fed's reserve requirements to *all* banks by 1987 (not just the member commercial banks).

The theory of bureaucratic behavior seems applicable to the Federal Reserve's behavior, but we must recognize that this view of the Fed as being solely concerned with its own self-interest is too extreme. Maximizing one's welfare does not rule out altruism. (You might give generously to the Salvation Army because it makes you feel good about yourself, but in the process you *are* helping a worthy cause.) The Fed surely is concerned that it conduct

B o x   1 7 . 2

Games the Fed Plays

As the theory of bureaucratic behavior predicts, the Fed may play games to obscure its actions in order to avoid congressional interference in its activities. In 1975, Congress passed House Concurrent Resolution 133, which instructed the Fed to report quarterly to the banking committees of the House and the Senate its target ranges for the growth in the monetary aggregates over the next twelve months and to report how successful it had been in achieving its previous targets. One game that the Fed played was to report on several monetary aggregates (such as $M1$, $M2$, and $M3$) rather than on one: Then when the Fed testified to Congress on its success in achieving its past targets, it would focus on the *particular* monetary aggregate whose growth rate was closest to the target range.

In addition to this clever tactic, the Fed devised a procedure for setting its target for monetary aggregates (called "base drift") that made it more likely that it would hit its targets, thereby avoiding a conflict with Congress. Every quarter the Fed would revise the target values for monetary aggregates by applying target growth rates to the amount at which the aggregate had *ended up* (a new base). When the Fed overshot its targets, as fre-

quently occurred after 1975, it revised future target values upward, making it less likely that the monetary aggregates would exceed target ranges in the future. Similarly, if the Fed undershot its targets, it revised future target values downward, making it less likely that the monetary aggregates would fall below the target ranges in the future. Subsequent legislation now restricts the Fed from changing the base for its target ranges to once a year, reducing the extent of base drift.

Another indication that the Fed actively wants to obscure its actions is its desire for secrecy, as reflected in the active defense of its continual delay in releasing FOMC directives to Congress or to the public. A former Fed official has stated that, "a lot of staffers would concede that (secrecy) is designed to shield the Fed from political oversight."*

_____

*This quotation is from "Monetary Zeal: How Federal Reserve Under Volcker Finally Slowed Down Inflation," *Wall Street Journal* (Friday, December 7, 1984), p. 23. Note that the official also stated that this was not a bad thing because "most politicians have a shorter time horizon than is optimal for monetary policy."

monetary policy on behalf of the public interest. However, much uncertainty and disagreement exist over what monetary policy should be.[4] When it is unclear what is in the public interest, other motives may influence the Fed's behavior. In these situations, the theory of bureaucratic behavior may be a useful guide to predicting what motivates the Fed.

_____

[4]One example of the uncertainty over how best to conduct monetary policy was discussed in Chapter 2. We saw that economists are not sure how to measure money. Thus, even if economists agreed that controlling the quantity of money is the appropriate way to conduct monetary policy (a controversial position as we will see in later chapters), the Fed cannot be sure of which monetary aggregate it should control.

SHOULD THE FED BE INDEPENDENT? _____

As we have seen, the Federal Reserve is probably the most independent government agency in the United States. Every few years the question arises in Congress of whether the independence of the Fed should be curtailed. Politicians who strongly oppose a Fed policy often want to bring it under their supervision in order to change the policy more to their liking. Should the Fed be independent, or would we be better off with a central bank under the control of the president or Congress?

The Case for Independence

The strongest argument for an independent Federal Reserve rests on the view that subjecting the Fed to more political pressures would impart an inflationary bias to monetary policy. In the view of many, politicians in a democratic society are shortsighted because they are driven by the need to win their next election. With this primary goal, they are unlikely to focus on long-run objectives, such as promoting a stable price level. Instead, they will seek short-run solutions to problems, like high unemployment and high interest rates—even if the short-run solutions have undesirable long-run consequences. For example, we saw in Chapter 6 that high money growth might lead initially to a drop in interest rates, but might cause an increase in interest rates later as inflation heats up. Would a Federal Reserve under the control of Congress or the president be more likely to pursue a policy of excessive money growth when interest rates are high, even though it would eventually lead to inflation and even higher interest rates in the future? The advocates of an independent Federal Reserve say "yes." They believe a politically insulated Fed is more likely to be concerned with long-run objectives and thus be a defender of a sound dollar and a stable price level. Evidence supporting this view is found in Box 17.3.

A variant of the preceding argument is that the political process in America leads to the so-called political business cycle, in which just before an election expansionary policies are pursued to lower unemployment and interest rates. After the election the bad effects of these policies—high inflation and high interest rates—come home to roost, requiring contractionary policies that politicians hope the public will forget before the next election. There is some evidence that such a political business cycle exists in the United States, and a Federal Reserve under the control of Congress or the president might make the cycle even more pronounced than it already is.

Putting the Fed under the control of the president (making it more subject to influence by the Treasury) is also considered dangerous because the Fed can be used to facilitate Treasury financing of large budget deficits

Box 1 7 . 3   **A Global Perspective**

A Comparison of Central Bank Independence and Macroeconomic Performance in Seventeen Countries

Advocates of an independent central bank believe that macroeconomic performance will be improved by making the central bank more independent. Recent research seems to support this conjecture:* When central banks are ranked from 1 (least independent) to 4 (most independent), the inflation performance is found to be the best for countries with the most independent central bank. As you can see in the bar graph, Germany and Switzerland, with the two most independent central banks, are also the countries with the lowest inflation rates in the 1973–1988 period. On the other hand, the countries with the highest inflation—Spain, New Zealand, Australia, and Italy—are also the countries

with the least independent central banks. Although a more independent central bank appears to lead to a lower inflation rate, this is not achieved at the expense of poorer real economic performance. Countries with independent central banks are not more likely to have high unemployment or greater output fluctuations than are countries with less independent central banks.

_____

*Alberto Alesina and Lawrence H. Summers, "Central Bank Independence and Macroeconomic Performance: Some Comparative Evidence," Harvard University, mimeo, 1990.

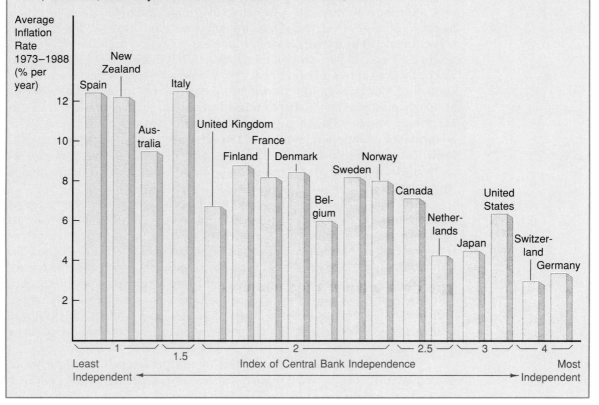

by its purchases of Treasury bonds.[5] As we saw in Chapter 15, the Fed's purchase of Treasury bonds leads to an expansion in the monetary base and hence in the money supply. Treasury pressure on the Fed to "help them out" might lead to a more inflationary bias in the economy. An independent Fed is better able to resist this pressure from the Treasury.

Another argument for Fed independence is that control of monetary policy is too important to leave to politicians, a group that has repeatedly demonstrated their lack of expertise at making hard decisions on issues of great economic importance, such as reducing the budget deficit or reforming the banking system.[6] Indeed, some politicians may prefer to have an independent Fed, which can be used as a public "whipping boy" to take some of the heat off their shoulders. It is possible that a politician who, in private, opposes an inflationary monetary policy will be forced to support such a policy in public for fear of not being reelected to office. An independent Fed can pursue policies that are politically unpopular yet in the public interest.

The Case Against Independence

Proponents of a Fed under the control of the president or the Congress argue that it is undemocratic to have monetary policy (which affects almost everyone in the economy) controlled by an elite group responsible to no one. The current lack of accountability of the Federal Reserve has serious consequences: If the Fed performs badly, there is no provision for replacing members (as there is with politicians). True, the Fed needs to pursue long-run objectives, but elected officials of Congress vote on long-run issues also (foreign policy, for example). If we push the argument further that policy is always performed better by elite groups like the Fed, then we end up with such conclusions as: the Joint Chiefs of Staff should determine military budgets or the IRS should set tax policies with no oversight from the president or Congress. Would you advocate this degree of independence for the Joint Chiefs and the IRS?

The public holds the president and the Congress responsible for the economic well-being of the country, yet they lack control over the government agency that may well be the most important factor in determining the

---

[5]The Federal Reserve Act prohibited the Fed from buying Treasury bonds directly from the Treasury (except to roll over maturing securities); instead the Fed buys Treasury bonds from the open market. One possible reason for this prohibition is consistent with the argument above: The Fed would find it harder to facilitate Treasury financing of large budget deficits.

[6]Another way to state this argument is in terms of the principal-agent problem discussed in Chapters 8 and 11. Both the Federal Reserve and politicians are agents of the public (the principal), and as we have seen both politicians and the Fed have incentives to act in their own interest rather than in the interest of the public. The argument supporting Federal Reserve independence is that the principal-agent problem is worse for politicians than for the Fed because politicians have less incentives to act in the public interest.

health of the economy. In addition, in order to obtain a cohesive economic program to promote economic stability, monetary policy must be coordinated with fiscal policy (management of government spending and taxation). Only by placing monetary policy under the control of the politicians who also control fiscal policy can these two policies be prevented from working at cross-purposes.

Another argument against Federal Reserve independence is that an independent Fed has not always used its freedom successfully. As shown in Chapter 16, the Fed failed miserably in its stated role as a lender of last resort during the Great Depression, and its independence certainly didn't prevent it from pursuing an overly expansionary monetary policy in the 1960s and 1970s which contributed to the rapid inflation in this period.

Our earlier discussion also suggests that the Federal Reserve is not immune from political pressures.[7] Its independence may encourage it to pursue a course of narrow self-interest rather than the public interest.

No widespread consensus exists currently on whether Federal Reserve independence is a good thing. As you might expect, those who like the Fed's policies support its independence, while those who dislike its policies advocate a less independent Fed.

SUMMARY

1. The Federal Reserve System was created in 1913 to lessen the occurrence of bank panics. Because of the hostility to central banks and the centralization of power, the Federal Reserve System was created with many checks and balances to diffuse power.

2. The formal structure of the Federal Reserve System consists of twelve regional Federal Reserve Banks, around 5000 member commercial banks, the Board of Governors of the Federal Reserve System, the Federal Open Market Committee, and the Federal Advisory Council.

3. Although on paper the Federal Reserve System appears to be decentralized, in practice it has come to function as a unified central bank controlled by the Board of Governors and especially the chairman of the Board of Governors.

4. The Federal Reserve is more independent than most agencies of the U.S. government, but it is still subject to political pressures because the legislation that structures the Fed is written by Congress and can be changed at any time. The theory of bureaucratic behavior indicates that one factor driving the Fed's behavior is its attempt to increase its power and prestige. This view explains many of the Fed's actions, although it may also try to act in the public interest.

5. The case for an independent Federal Reserve rests on the view that curtailing the Fed's independence and subjecting it to more political

---

[7]For evidence on this issue, see Robert E. Weintraub, "Congressional Supervision of Monetary Policy," *Journal of Monetary Economics* 4 (April 1978): 341–362. Some economists even suggest that lessening the independence of the Fed might even reduce the incentive for politically motivated monetary policy. See Milton Friedman, "Monetary Policy: Theory and Practice," *Journal of Money, Credit and Banking* 14 (February 1982): 98–118.

pressures would impart an inflationary bias to monetary policy. An independent Fed can afford to take the long view and not respond to short-run problems that will result in expansionary monetary policy and a political business cycle. The case against an independent Fed holds that it is undemocratic to have monetary policy (so important to the public) controlled by an elite that is not accountable to the public. An independent Fed also makes the coordination of monetary and fiscal policy difficult, and in any case it is by no means clear that the Fed has used its independence wisely: The Fed may be no less shortsighted than politicians and may still pursue its own narrow self-interest.

KEY TERMS

Federal Reserve Banks

Board of Governors of the
 Federal Reserve System

Federal Open Market
 Committee (FOMC)

QUESTIONS AND PROBLEMS

* 1. Why was the Federal Reserve System set up with twelve regional Federal Reserve Banks rather than one central bank, as in other countries?

  2. What political realities might explain why the Federal Reserve Act of 1913 placed two Federal Reserve Banks in Missouri?

* 3. "The Federal Reserve System resembles the U.S. Constitution in that it was designed with many checks and balances." Discuss.

  4. In what ways can the regional Federal Reserve Banks influence the conduct of monetary policy?

* 5. Which entities in the Federal Reserve System control the discount rate? reserve requirements? open market operations?

  6. Do you think that the fourteen-year, nonrenewable terms of the governors effectively insulate the Board of Governors from political pressure?

* 7. Over time, which entities have gained power in the Federal Reserve System and which have lost power? Why do you think this has happened?

  8. The Fed is the most independent of all government agencies. What is the main difference between it and other government agencies that explains its greater independence?

* 9. What is the primary tool that Congress uses to exercise some control over the Fed?

  10. In the 1960s and 1970s the Federal Reserve System lost members at a rapid rate. How can the theory of bureaucratic behavior explain the Fed's campaign for legislation to require all commercial banks to become members? Was the Fed successful in this campaign?

*11. Answer true, false, or uncertain: "The theory of bureaucratic behavior indicates that the Fed never operates in the public interest."

  12. Why might eliminating the Fed's independence lead to a more pronounced political business cycle?

*13. Answer true, false, or uncertain: "The independence of the Fed leaves it completely unaccountable for its actions."

  14. Answer true, false, or uncertain: "The independence of the Fed has meant that it takes the long view and not the short view."

CHAPTER 18

Understanding Movements in the Monetary Base

PREVIEW Now that you have examined the structure of the Federal Reserve System, in this and the succeeding two chapters you are ready to look at how the Fed actually conducts monetary policy. Our analysis of the money supply process demonstrated that movements in the monetary base (also called high-powered money) are the main driving force behind changes in the money supply and that the Fed influences the monetary base through the policy tools of open market operations (the purchase and sale of government securities) or changes in the discount rate. Although these two policy tools are the primary determinants of the monetary base, other factors also affect it. In this chapter we examine these other factors, because the Fed must take account of them if it is to exercise accurate control over the money supply.

THE FED'S BALANCE SHEET AND THE MONETARY BASE

We first examine the balance sheet of the Federal Reserve System, since it can be used to identify factors that affect the monetary base.

Assets

1. Securities. These include the Fed's holdings of securities, which consist primarily of Treasury securities, but also in the past have included bankers' acceptances. The total amount of securities is controlled by open market operations (the Fed's purchase and sale of these securities). As shown in Table 18.1, it is the most important category of assets in the Fed's balance sheet.

2. Discount Loans. These are loans the Fed makes to banks, and the amount is affected by the Fed's setting of the interest rate on these loans (the discount rate).

Table 18.1 Consolidated Balance Sheet of the Federal Reserve System (end of 1990, billions of dollars)

Assets		Liabilities	
Securities: U.S. government and agency, and bankers acceptances	252.1	Federal Reserve notes outstanding	267.7
Discount loans	0.2	Bank deposits	38.7
Gold and SDR certificate accounts	21.1	U.S. Treasury deposits	9.0
Coin	0.5	Foreign and other deposits	0.6
Cash items in process of collection	6.1	Deferred availability cash items	3.5
Other Federal Reserve assets	47.6	Other Federal Reserve liabilities and capital accounts	8.1
TOTAL	327.6	TOTAL	327.6

Source: Federal Reserve *Bulletin*.

3. Gold and SDR Certificate Accounts. Special Drawing Rights (SDRs) are issued to governments by the International Monetary Fund (IMF) to settle international debts and have replaced gold in international financial transactions. When the Treasury acquires gold or SDRs, it issues certificates to the Fed, which are a claim on the gold or SDRs, and in turn is credited with deposit balances at the Fed. The gold and SDR accounts are made up of these certificates issued by the Treasury.

4. Coin. This is the smallest item in the balance sheet, and it includes Treasury currency (mostly coins) held by the Fed.

5. Cash Items in Process of Collection. These arise from the Fed's check-clearing process described in Chapter 9. When a check is given to the Fed for clearing, the Fed will present it to the bank on which it is written and will collect funds by deducting the amount of the check from the bank's deposits (reserves) at the Fed. Before these funds are collected, the check is a cash item in the process of collection and is a Fed asset.

6. Other Federal Reserve Assets. These include deposits and bonds denominated in foreign currencies as well as physical goods such as computers, office equipment, or buildings owned by the Federal Reserve.

Liabilities

1. Federal Reserve Notes Outstanding. These are the Federal Reserve notes (currency) issued by the Fed.

2. Bank Deposits. These include the deposits that banks have made at the Fed. These deposits plus vault cash at the banks equal reserves.

3. U.S. Treasury Deposits. These are deposits that the Treasury keeps at the Fed, which it uses to write all its checks.

4. Foreign and Other Deposits. These include the deposits at the Fed owned by foreign governments, foreign central banks, international agencies (such as the World Bank and the United Nations), and U.S. government agencies (such as the FDIC and Federal Home Loan Banks).

5. Deferred Availability Cash Items. Like cash items in the process of collection, these also arise from the Fed's check-clearing process. When a check is given to the Fed for clearing, it does not immediately credit the bank who gave it the check. Instead, it promises to credit the bank within a certain prearranged time limit, which never exceeds two days. These promises are the deferred availability items and are a liability of the Fed.

6. Other Federal Reserve Liabilities and Capital Account. This item includes all the remaining Federal Reserve liabilities not included elsewhere in the balance sheet. Stock in the Federal Reserve System purchased by member banks, for example, is included in this category.

The Monetary Base

As you may recall, the monetary base (*MB*) is made up of the monetary liabilities [currency in circulation (*C*) plus reserves (*R*)], which equal Federal Reserve notes outstanding, plus bank deposits at the Fed, plus Treasury currency that is not held at the Fed (Treasury currency outstanding minus the "Coin" asset in the Fed's balance sheet):[1]

$$MB = C + R = (F.R.\ notes) + (bank\ deposits) +$$
$$(Treasury\ currency\ outstanding) - (coin)$$

The items on the right-hand side of this equation indicate how the base is used and are called the **uses of the base.** Unfortunately, this equation does not tell us the factors that determine the base (the **sources of the base**), but the Federal Reserve balance sheet in Table 18.1 comes to the rescue, because like all balance sheets, it has the property that the total assets on the left-hand side must equal the total liabilities on the right-hand side. Since the *F.R. notes* and *bank deposits* items in the uses of the base are Federal Reserve liabilities, the assets = liabilities property of the Fed balance sheet enables us to solve for *F.R. notes* and *bank deposits* in terms of the Fed balance sheet items that are included in the sources of the base: Specifically, *F.R. notes* and *bank deposits* equal the sum of all the Fed assets minus all the other Fed liabilities.

$$(F.R.\ notes) + (bank\ deposits) = (securities) + (discount\ loans) +$$
$$(gold\ and\ SDRs) + (coin) + (cash\ items\ in\ process\ of\ collection) +$$
$$(other\ F.R.\ assets) - (Treasury\ deposits) - (foreign\ and\ other\ deposits) -$$
$$(deferred\ availability\ cash\ items) - (other\ F.R.\ liabilities)$$

---

[1] In the member bank reserves data that the Fed publishes every week, Treasury currency outstanding is actually defined to include Treasury currency that is held at the Treasury (called "Treasury cash holdings"). What we have defined as "Treasury currency outstanding" is actually equal to the Fed's definition of "Treasury currency outstanding" minus "Treasury cash holdings."

Table 18.2 **Summary: Factors Affecting the Monetary Base (end of 1990, billions of dollars)**

Factor		Change in Factor	Change in Monetary Base
Factors That Increase the Monetary Base			
1. Securities: U.S. government and agency and bankers acceptances	252.1	↑	↑
2. Discount loans	0.2	↑	↑
3. Gold and SDR certificate accounts	21.1	↑	↑
4. Float	2.6	↑	↑
5. Other Federal Reserve assets	47.6	↑	↑
6. Treasury currency outstanding	20.4	↑	↑
SUBTOTAL 1	322.9		
Factors That Decrease the Monetary Base			
7. Treasury deposits at the Fed	9.0	↑	↓
8. Foreign and other deposits at the Fed	0.6	↑	↓
9. Other Federal Reserve liabilities and capital accounts	8.1	↑	↓
SUBTOTAL 2	17.7		
Monetary Base Equals Subtotal 1 − Subtotal 2 =	305.2		

Source: Federal Reserve *Bulletin.*

The two balance sheet items related to check clearing can be collected into one term called **float,** defined as *cash items in process of collection* minus *deferred availability cash items.* Then, substituting all the right-hand-side items in the equation above for *(F.R. notes) + (bank deposits)* in the uses of the base equation, we obtain the following expression describing the sources of the monetary base:

$$MB = (securities) + (discount\ loans) + (gold\ and\ SDRs) + (float) +$$
$$(other\ F.R.\ assets) + (Treasury\ currency\ outstanding) - (Treasury\ deposits)$$
$$- (foreign\ and\ other\ deposits) - (other\ F.R.\ liabilities) \qquad (18.1)$$

"Playing accountant" has led us to a very useful equation, which immediately identifies the nine factors affecting the monetary base listed in Table 18.2. As Equation (18.1) and Table 18.2 depict, increases in the first six factors add to the monetary base, while increases in the last three subtract from the monetary base.[2]

---

[2] Some bank deposits at the Fed are not included in reserves and, hence, in the monetary base because they are service-related deposits. These balances are included in an entry, service-related balances and adjustment, which should be subtracted from the right-hand side of the expression describing the sources of the base in order to obtain the correct measure of the monetary base. The service-related balances and adjustment entry ($2.3 billion at the end of 1990) is ignored in the expression in the text.

Now that we have identified these nine factors and their effect on the monetary base, let's look more carefully at *why* they affect the monetary base. To do this, we will go on playing accountant and make use of T-accounts.

Study Guide

It is not hard to understand how each of the following factors affects the monetary base if you work through the effects of a particular transaction on the T-account of each individual or institution in the transaction. Having done this, you will know what has happened to reserves or to currency and can then see what has happened to the monetary base. To test your understanding, work through what happens to the T-accounts when the factor falls rather than rises.

FACTORS THAT AFFECT THE MONETARY BASE

As we examine the effect of changes in each factor on the monetary base, we assume that there are no changes elsewhere in the Fed's balance sheet. Let us look first at the factors whose increase adds to the monetary base.

Factors That Add to the Monetary Base

Securities and Discount Loans   Since we have already described in detail how changes in discount loans and the Fed's holding of securities via open market operations affect the monetary base in Chapters 14 and 15, we only restate our conclusions here. ***An increase in the Fed's holding of securities or in discount loans leads to an equal increase in the monetary base*** (as shown in Table 18.2).

Gold and SDR Accounts and Other Federal Reserve Assets   A Fed purchase of gold, SDRs, a deposit denominated in a foreign currency or any other asset is just an open market purchase of these assets. Thus the effect on the monetary base is the same as an open market purchase of bonds (as Box 18.1 demonstrates). ***An increase in gold and SDR accounts or in other Federal Reserve assets leads to an equal increase in the monetary base.***

Float   As shown in Chapter 9, the Federal Reserve's check-clearing process involves a deposit of a check received by a bank into its Fed account, a credit of the amount of its check to its reserves, and an equal debit to the reserves of the bank on which the check is drawn. We might assume that these transactions all occurred simultaneously and immediately, but in reality, the Fed frequently credits the amount of a check to a bank that has deposited it (increases the bank's reserves) before it debits (decreases the reserves of) the

B o x   1 8 . 1   **A Global Perspective**

Foreign Exchange Rate Intervention and the Monetary Base

It is common to read in the newspaper about a Federal Reserve intervention in the foreign exchange market to buy or sell dollars. Can this also be a factor that affects the monetary base? The answer is "yes," because a Federal Reserve intervention in the foreign exchange market involves a purchase or sale of assets denominated in a foreign currency, which is included in the *other Federal Reserve assets* category in the Fed's balance sheet.

Suppose the Fed purchases $10 million of deposits denominated in French francs in exchange for $10 million of dollar deposits at the Fed (called a sale of dollars for francs). As discussed in the text,

a Federal Reserve purchase of any asset, whether it be a U.S. government bond or a deposit denominated in a foreign currency, is just an open market purchase and so leads to an equal rise in the monetary base. Hence the purchase of the $10 million in franc deposits leads to a $10 million increase in *other Federal Reserve assets* and a $10 million increase in the monetary base. Similarly, a sale of foreign currency deposits leads to a decline in *other Federal Reserve assets* and a decline in the monetary base. Federal Reserve interventions in the foreign exchange market can thus be an important influence on the monetary base, a topic that we discuss further in Chapter 21.

bank on which the check is drawn.[3] The resulting net increase in the total amount of reserves in the banking system is called *float,* and it equals the difference between the asset, *cash items in process of collection* (checks on which the Fed has not yet collected payment) and the liability, *deferred availability cash items* (checks that have not yet been credited to the bank depositing them).

Float occurs because sometimes the Fed cannot present checks for payment as fast as it credits the bank depositing the check; float fluctuates when weather conditions and other factors cause delays in presenting checks for payment. If, for example, a severe snowstorm hits New York City, the Fed will not be able to move some checks that it wants to present for payment, and float will rise sharply. When the weather clears, the checks will be presented for payment and float will fall back down again.[4]

To better understand the concept, let's return to our example (Chapter 9) in which Jane Brown takes a $100 check written on an account at the Second National Bank in Los Angeles and deposits it in her account at the First National Bank in New York City. The First National Bank takes the

---

[3] Many people take advantage of the fact that it takes time for a check they have written to be debited from their account (they write a check on Friday for money they don't have, thinking it won't clear till Tuesday after they have gone to the bank and deposited the necessary money). This is called taking advantage of the float.

[4] Note that although float is usually positive, there are some instances in which it turns negative. This occurs if the Fed has been able to present checks for payment faster than it has credited the banks depositing the checks.

check to the Fed for clearing, with the following effect on the Fed balance sheet:

Federal Reserve			
Assets		Liabilities	
Cash items in process of collection	+ $100	Deferred availability cash items	+ $100

The $100 of *deferred availability cash items* is the liability incurred by the Fed when it accepts the checks from the First National Bank, because it promises to credit the First National Bank with $100 of deposits within a certain prearranged time limit (never exceeding two days). The $100 of *cash items in the process of collection* is a Fed asset, because the Fed will deduct this amount from the Second National Bank's deposits when it presents the check to Second National Bank for payment.

At this point reserves have not changed anywhere in the banking system, and since *cash items in process of collection* equals *deferred availability cash items*, their difference—equal to float—is also unchanged. Because of possible delays due to bad weather conditions, the Fed may not be able to move the check to Los Angeles before the prearranged time limit is up. However, it still dutifully does as it promised and credits the First National Bank with $100 of deposits (reserves) and cancels out its liability of $100 of *deferred availability cash items*. The Fed's T-account now becomes

Federal Reserve			
Assets		Liabilities	
Cash items in process of collection	+ $100	Reserves (of First National Bank)	+ $100

Float, the difference between *cash items in process of collection* ($100) and *deferred availability cash items* ($0), is now + $100, and reserves in the banking system have also increased by this same amount. What has happened is that the Fed has not yet been able to collect what is owed by the Second National Bank but has credited the First National Bank anyway. The result is that, in effect, the Fed has extended First National Bank an interest-free loan equal to the amount of the float, thus raising reserves and hence the monetary base.

This "loan" will be only temporary, however, because when the Fed finally gets the check to Los Angeles and presents it to the Second National Bank, it deducts $100 from the Second National Bank's deposits (reserves)

and cancels out the $100 of *cash items in process of collection*. The Fed's T-account ends up as follows:

	Federal Reserve	
Assets	Liabilities	
	Reserves (of First National Bank)	+ $100
	Reserves (of Second National Bank)	− $100

The end result of the check-clearing process is that total reserves in the banking system have not changed, even though reserves have moved from one bank to another. In the process of clearing the Second National Bank's check, however, reserves and the monetary base have been *temporarily increased*. If you multiply these temporary increases in the monetary base by the *millions* of checks cleared per day, it can lead to sizable week-to-week fluctuations in the monetary base. Yet since most fluctuations in float are temporary, they are not a major source of fluctuations in the monetary base over longer periods of time (such as a month or three months).

Our conclusion from the manipulations of these T-accounts is consistent with Table 18.2: *An increase in float leads to an equal increase in the monetary base.*

Treasury Currency Outstanding   Although this term is not on the Federal Reserve's balance sheet, it still has an effect on the monetary base. An increase in Treasury currency outside the Treasury finds its way either into bank vaults (where it counts as reserves) or into the hands of the public (where it counts as currency in circulation). Thus, as Table 18.2 indicates, *the monetary base rises when there is an increase in Treasury currency outstanding.*[5]

---

[5] Although an increase in Treasury currency outstanding will increase the monetary base *if all other balance sheet items are held constant*, most increases in Treasury currency are accompanied by offsetting changes in other balance sheet items so that the monetary base remains unchanged. If, for example, the public uses more coins because of the video game craze, the Treasury has more coins minted, which it sends to the Fed, and in exchange, the Fed credits the dollar amount of the coins to Treasury deposits at the Fed. When these coins are distributed to the public, Treasury currency outstanding has increased, but Treasury deposits have increased by an equal amount. The net result, then, is that the monetary base will remain unchanged (the increase from higher Treasury currency outstanding is exactly offset by the decrease from higher Treasury deposits). We thus see that a change in the public's preference for Treasury currency (mostly coins) relative to Federal Reserve notes (paper currency) will have no effect on the monetary base.

Factors That Subtract from the Monetary Base

Treasury Deposits at the Fed   The funds the Treasury gets from tax payments and proceeds from the sale of government bonds are initially held in accounts at commercial banks called *tax and loan accounts* and are then deposited in accounts at the Fed used by the Treasury to write all its checks. Suppose the Treasury intends to pay for a $100 million B2 stealth bomber, and it transfers $100 million from its tax and loan accounts to its account at the Fed, resulting in the following T-account:

U.S. Treasury		
Assets		Liabilities
Deposits in commercial banks	− $100m	
Deposits at Fed	+ $100m	

The commercial banks now find that they have lost $100 million in deposits and hence $100 million in reserves, so their T-account is

Commercial Banks			
Assets		Liabilities	
Reserves	− $100m	U.S. Treasury deposits	− $100m

At the Fed, reserves decrease by $100 million while Treasury deposits have increased by $100 million:

Federal Reserve			
Assets		Liabilities	
		Reserves	− $100m
		U.S. Treasury deposits	+ $100m

Consequently, ***an increase in U.S. Treasury deposits reduces reserves and the monetary base*** (as shown in Table 18.2).

When the Treasury pays for the stealth bomber, the preceding process is reversed. U.S. Treasury deposits at the Fed fall by $100 million, and the defense contractor deposits the check received from the Treasury in its bank, whose reserves rise by $100 million. The T-account for the Federal Reserve is

Federal Reserve		
Assets	Liabilities	
	Reserves	+ $100m
	U.S. Treasury deposits	− $100m

We again see that the monetary base moves in an opposite direction to Treasury deposits with the Federal Reserve.

Because Treasury purchases and receipts change dramatically during the course of a year, Treasury deposits with the Fed have large fluctuations and consequently can be an important source of weekly fluctuations in the monetary base. Fluctuations are fairly predictable though, because the Treasury usually knows in advance when it plans to move funds from its tax and loan accounts into its accounts at the Fed. In addition, because most of the fluctuations in Treasury deposits are temporary, they are not a major source of fluctuations in the monetary base over longer periods of time (such as three months or a year).

Foreign and Other Deposits at the Fed   When these deposits rise, either because funds from accounts at commercial banks are transferred into accounts at the Fed or because checks written on U.S. banks are being deposited, the T-accounts are identical to that described for Treasury deposits with the Fed. Therefore, ***an increase in foreign and other deposits leads to a decline in the monetary base.***

Other Liabilities and Capital Accounts   Suppose a bank has just joined the Federal Reserve System and buys the required amount of stock in the Fed, raising the capital accounts at the Fed. Its deposits at the Fed will be reduced by the dollar value of the stock, and reserves in the banking system will decline by this amount. Therefore, ***an increase in other liabilities and capital leads to a decline in the monetary base.***

Summary   Our analysis of the Fed's balance sheet identifies nine factors that affect the monetary base. Increases in six factors increase the monetary base (the Fed's holdings of securities, discount loans, gold and SDR accounts, float, other Federal Reserve assets, and Treasury currency outstanding), and increases in three factors reduce the monetary base (Treasury deposits with the Fed, foreign and other deposits with the Fed, and other Federal Reserve liabilities and capital accounts).

The factor that most affects the monetary base is the Fed's holdings of securities, which are completely controlled by the Fed through its open market operations. Factors not controlled by the Fed (for example, float and Treasury deposits at the Fed) undergo substantial short-run variations and can be important sources of fluctuations in the monetary base over time periods as short as a week. However, these fluctuations are usually quite predictable and so can be offset through open market operations. *Although float and Treasury deposits at the Fed undergo substantial short-run fluctuation, which complicates control of the monetary base, they do not prevent the Fed from accurately controlling it.*

THE BUDGET DEFICIT AND THE MONETARY BASE

Although you now understand what factors directly affect the monetary base, another important factor indirectly affects it: government budget deficits. To see why budget deficits can matter to the monetary base, you need to look at how spending by the government is financed.

The Government Budget Constraint

Because the government (like us) has to pay its bills, it has a budget constraint. There are two ways we can pay for our spending: We can raise revenue (by working) or borrow. The government also enjoys these two options: It can raise revenue by levying taxes or it can go into debt by issuing government bonds. Unlike us, it has a third option: The government can create money and use it to pay for the goods and services it buys.

Methods of financing government spending are described by an expression called the **government budget constraint,** which states the following: The government budget deficit (*DEFICIT*), which equals the excess of government spending (*G*) over tax revenue (*T*), must equal the sum of the change in the monetary base (ΔMB) and the change in government bonds held by the public ($\Delta BONDS$). Algebraically, this expression can be written as

$$DEFICIT = G - T = \Delta MB + \Delta BONDS \qquad (18.2)$$

To see what the government budget constraint means in practice, let's look at the case in which the only government purchase is a $100 million stealth bomber. If the government convinces the electorate that such a plane is worth paying for, it will probably be able to raise the $100 million of taxes to pay for it and the budget deficit will equal zero. The government budget constraint then tells us that no issue of money or bonds is needed to pay for the bomber because the budget is balanced. If taxpayers balk at paying for military weapons and refuse to pay taxes for the bomber, the budget constraint indicates that the government must pay for it by selling $100 million of new bonds to the public or by printing $100 million of currency to pay for the bomber. In either case, the budget constraint is satisfied; the $100 million deficit is balanced by the change in the stock of government bonds held by the public ($\Delta BONDS$ = $100 million) or by the change in the monetary

Following the Financial News

Reserves Data and Sources of Change in the Monetary Base

Data for bank reserves and the sources of changes in the monetary base (which are the same as the sources of changes in reserves) are published every Friday or Monday. In the *Wall Street Journal* they are found in the "Federal Reserve Data" column, an example of which is included here.

"Member Bank Reserves Changes" shows the sources of changes in bank reserves (the sources of changes in the monetary base described in the chapter). Float, for example, averaged $612 million for the week ending March 6, 1991, and changed +$449 million from the week ending February 27, 1991, and +$159 million from the week ending March 7, 1990 (one year earlier).

"Reserves Aggregates" provides data on different measures of reserves and the monetary base. The monetary base, for example, averaged $317,496 million for the two weeks ended March 6, 1991, and $318,359 million for the two weeks ended February 20.

FEDERAL RESERVE DATA

MEMBER BANK RESERVE CHANGES

Changes in weekly averages of reserves and related items during the week and year ended March 6, 1991 were as follows (in millions of dollars)

	Mar. 6, 1991	Chg fm Feb. 27, 1991	wk end Mar. 7, 1990
Reserve bank credit:			
U.S. Gov't securities:			
Bought outright	238,066 +	2,283 +	17,600
Held under repurch agreemt	2,886 +	2,716 +	2,272
Federal agency issues:			
Bought outright	6,342	.... −	183
Held under repurch agreemt	345 −	330 +	281
Acceptances			
Borrowings from Fed:			
Adjustment credit	405 +	140 +	349
Seasonal borrowings	38 −	5 −	21
Extended credit	40 −	20 −	1,904
► Float	612 +	449 +	159 ◄
Other Federal Reserve Assets	38,165 −	744 −	303
Total Reserve Bank Credit	286,899 −	942 +	18,251

Gold Stock	11,058	.... −	1
SDR certificates	10,018	.... +	1,500
Treasury currency			
outstanding	20,494 +	10 +	721
Total	328,470 −	932 +	20,471
Currency in circulation	285,528 +	993 +	29,875
Treasury cash holdings	606 +	36 +	92
Treasury dpts with F.R. Bnks	9,192 −	4,153 +	2,999
Foreign dpts with F.R. Bnks	232 −	3 +	21
Other dpts with F.R. Bnks	215 +	27 −	108
Service related balances, adj	2,855 +	4 +	334
Other F.R. liabilities			
& capital	8,047 −	970 −	713
Total	306,674 −	4,066 +	32,500

RESERVE AGGREGATES
(daily average in millions)

	Two weeks ended:	
	Mar. 6	Feb. 20
Total Reserves (sa)	60,662	61,489
Nonborrowed Reserves (sa)	60,236	61,310
Required Reserves (sa)	59,475	59,725
Excess Reserves (nsa)	1,187	1,764
Borrowings from Fed (nsa)-a	376	152
Free Reserves (nsa)	811	1,612
► Monetary Base (sa)	317,496	318,359 ◄

a-Excluding extended credit. nsa-Not seasonally adjusted. sa-Seasonally adjusted.

Source: *Wall Street Journal* (Friday, March 8, 1991).

base (ΔMB = $100 million). A combination of all three methods of financing can be used to pay for spending. The $100 million stealth bomber, for example, could be financed by raising $50 million in taxes, printing $25 million of currency, and selling $25 million of bonds.

Financing Government Spending

Now that you recognize the three methods for financing government spending, you need to know the effect of each method on the monetary base, holding everything else constant. Therefore, we will use T-accounts to examine the mechanics of using each method to pay for the government purchase of the stealth bomber.

Tax Financing Suppose that when the government levies $100 million of taxes to pay for the bomber, the public sends the Treasury $100 million of checks. After the Treasury receives its tax payment checks from the public, it deposits them into its *tax and loan* accounts and then transfers them to its account with the Fed. The result is that $100 million of deposits have left the banking system, reducing reserves by $100 million, and the Treasury finds itself with $100 million of deposits with the Fed. The T-accounts of the nonbank public, the Treasury, the banking system, and the Fed follow:

Nonbank Public			U.S. Treasury	
Assets	Liabilities		Assets	Liabilities
Deposits at banks − $100m	Taxes due − $100m		Deposits at Fed + $100m Taxes due − $100m	

Banking System			Federal Reserve	
Assets	Liabilities		Assets	Liabilities
Reserves − $100m	Deposits − $100m			Reserves − $100m Treasury deposits + $100m

When the Treasury pays for the stealth bomber, it writes a check for $100 million and gives it to the public (defense contractors), who then deposits it in banks. The overall balance sheet changes of the four groups is then

Nonbank Public			U.S. Treasury	
Assets	Liabilities		Assets	Liabilities
Deposits at banks 0 Bomber − $100m	Taxes due − $100m		Deposits at Fed 0 Taxes due − $100m Bomber + $100m	

Banking System				Federal Reserve		
Assets		Liabilities			Assets	Liabilities
Reserves	0	Deposits	0			Reserves 0
						Treasury
						deposits 0

Since the net effect of these transactions is that the monetary base is unaffected, we can conclude that *financing government spending with taxes has no effect on the monetary base.*

Suppose (somewhat less realistically) that, when the government levies $100 million of taxes to pay for the bomber, the public sends the Treasury $100 million of currency rather than checks. Then the T-accounts for the Treasury and public will be as follows:

U.S. Treasury			Nonbank Public		
Assets		Liabilities	Assets		Liabilities
Currency			Currency		Taxes
+ $100m			− $100m		due − $100m
Taxes					
due − $100m					

The currency in the hands of the public (and hence in circulation) declines by $100 million and the Treasury uses the $100 million to pay for the bomber. The public receives back the $100 million of currency and, in exchange, gives the government the bomber it ordered. The overall balance sheet changes of the Treasury and the public are as follows:

U.S. Treasury			Nonbank Public		
Assets		Liabilities	Assets		Liabilities
Currency	0		Currency	0	Taxes
Taxes			Bomber		due − $100m
due − $100m			− $100m		
Bomber					
+ $100m					

The net effect on the monetary base is the same as when checks are used to pay taxes—there is none.

Because results are the same and are easier to follow when transactions are carried out with currency, we will examine only currency transactions in our analysis of debt financing which follows.

Debt Financing (ΔBONDS)   Now suppose that the government finances its purchase of the bomber by selling $100 million of bonds to the public, which, in turn, pays for them with $100 million of currency. The T-accounts of the Treasury and the public are as follows:

U.S. Treasury		Nonbank Public	
Assets	Liabilities	Assets	Liabilities
Currency + $100m	Securities + $100m	Currency − $100m	
		Securities + $100m	

The currency in circulation declines by $100 million and the Treasury uses the currency to pay for the bomber. The public receives back the $100 million of currency and gives the government the bomber. The overall balance sheet changes of the Treasury and public then are as follows:

U.S. Treasury		Nonbank Public	
Assets	Liabilities	Assets	Liabilities
Currency 0	Securities	Currency 0	
Bomber	+ $100m	Securities	
+ $100m		+ $100m	
		Bomber	
		− $100m	

Since the net effect of these transactions is that the items in the monetary base are unaffected, we can conclude that ***the financing of government spending by issuing debt has no effect on the monetary base.***

Financing with Money Creation (ΔMB)   Finally, we look at the case in which the government finances the purchase of the stealth bomber by creating money. In many countries this is a straightforward operation because the treasury has the legal right to issue currency with which it can pay for government spending. Thus, as the budget constraint indicates, this method of financing government spending leads to an increase in the monetary base (high-powered money). In the United States, this process is somewhat more complicated, because the Treasury does not have the legal right to issue currency to pay for goods and services, but can only issue securities.[6] Financing government spending with money creation thus takes on a more circuitous route in which the Treasury sells bonds to the public which are then purchased by the Federal Reserve.

This method of financing government spending proceeds in two steps. First, the Treasury purchases the bomber and finances it by selling $100 million of bonds to the public. As we have just seen, this results in a T-account in which the monetary base remains unchanged. Second, the Fed buys these same bonds from the public through an open market purchase, which (as you saw earlier in the chapter) raises the monetary base by $100 million. The outcome is that the monetary base has increased by $100 million, yielding this conclusion: ***The finance of government spending through a Treasury sale of bonds which are then purchased by the Fed increases the monetary base.***

This last method of financing government spending is frequently called **printing money** because high-powered money (the monetary base) is created in the process.[7] It is also referred to as **monetizing the debt,** because as the two-step process described indicates, government debt issued to finance government spending has been removed from the hands of the public and has been replaced by high-powered money.

Summary What does the preceding discussion tell us about the different methods of financing the government budget deficit? When government spending is fully financed by taxes, resulting in a balanced budget, there is no effect on the monetary base. When government spending is greater than tax revenues, the resulting budget deficit can be financed by selling government bonds to the public, and/or by creating money, which (in the United States) involves the purchase of government bonds by the Federal Reserve. The first method, debt financing, has no effect on the monetary base, while the second method, money creation, leads to an expansion of the monetary base (high-powered money).

DOES THE BUDGET DEFICIT INFLUENCE THE _____ MONETARY BASE?

In some countries the government can simply decide to print money in order to finance the deficit by having its treasury issue currency to pay for

---

[6] The Treasury does have the legal right to mint coins, but it cannot issue them to pay for goods and services. Instead, it is restricted to passively supplying coins to the public in exchange for deposits or Federal Reserve notes.

[7] Use of the word *printing* in this phrase is somewhat misleading. What is essential to this method of financing government spending is not the actual printing of money, but rather the issuing of monetary liabilities to the public after they have been printed.

goods and services. This option is not open to the U.S. Treasury; a government budget deficit can only lead to an expansion of the monetary base if the Fed allows this to happen by willingly purchasing bonds issued by the Treasury to finance the deficit. Since the decision to create money to finance a deficit is not automatic but, rather, is up to the Fed, a natural question arises: Which method of financing is most used and why? Why do we read so much about "the deficit"?

Whether the budget deficit influences the monetary base or not depends critically on how the Federal Reserve chooses to conduct monetary policy. If the Fed pursues a policy goal of preventing high interest rates (a likely possibility, as you will see in Chapter 20), many economists contend that a budget deficit will lead to the printing of money. Their reasoning, using the supply and demand analysis of the bond market we learned in Chapter 6, follows: When the Treasury issues bonds to the public, the supply of bonds rises (from B_1^s to B_2^s in Figure 18.1), causing interest rates to rise from i_1 to i_2) and bond prices to fall. If the Fed considers the rise in interest rates undesirable, it will buy bonds to prop up bond prices and reduce interest rates. The net result is that the government budget deficit has led to Federal Reserve open market purchases, which raise the monetary base (that is, create high-powered money).

Economists such as Robert Barro of Harvard University, however, do not agree that budget deficits influence the monetary base in the manner described above. Their analysis (which Barro named "Ricardian Equivalence" after the nineteenth-century British economist David Ricardo) con-

Figure 18.1
Interest Rates and the Government Budget Deficit When the Treasury issues bonds to finance the budget deficit, the supply curve for bonds shifts out from B_1^s to B_2^s. Many economists take the position that the equilibrium moves to point 2 because the bond demand curve remains unchanged, with the result that the interest rate rises from i_1 to i_2. Adherents of "Ricardian Equivalence," however, suggest that the demand curve for bonds also increases to B_R^d, moving the equilibrium to point 2′ where the interest rate is unchanged at i_1.

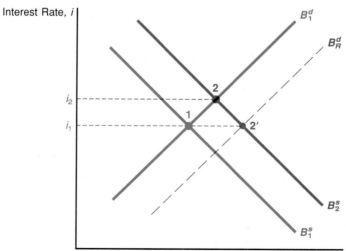

tends that when the government runs deficits and issues bonds, the public recognizes that it will be subject to higher taxes in the future in order to pay off these bonds. The public thus saves more in anticipation of these future taxes, with the net result that the public demand for bonds increases to match the increased supply. The demand curve for bonds shifts out to B_R^d in Figure 18.1, leaving the interest rate unchanged at i_1. There is now no need for the Fed to purchase bonds to keep the interest rate from rising.

The effect of budget deficits on interest rates and monetary policy is quite controversial and we will return to the issue of budget deficits and their effect on the monetary base and the money supply when we look at the more general issue of budget deficits and inflation in Chapter 28. For now, the important point to remember is that budget deficits *may* lead to money creation.

SUMMARY

1. Nine factors affect the monetary base: the Fed's holdings of securities, discount loans, gold and SDR accounts, float, other Federal Reserve assets, Treasury currency outstanding, Treasury deposits at the Fed, foreign and other deposits at the Fed, and other Federal Reserve liabilities and capital accounts. Increases in the first six add to the monetary base, while increases in the last three subtract from the monetary base.

2. The most important of these factors is the Fed's holdings of securities, which it controls completely through its open market operations. Treasury deposits at the Fed and float (factors that cannot be controlled by the Fed) can undergo substantial short-run variations and can be important sources of fluctuations in the monetary base in time periods as short as a week. However, because changes in these factors are predictable, they can be offset by open market operations, so they do not prevent the Fed from accurately controlling the monetary base.

3. A budget deficit can be financed by debt financing, that is, selling government debt to the public, and by money creation (printing money), which, in the United States, involves selling government securities to the Federal Reserve. Debt financing has no effect on the monetary base, while money creation leads to an expansion of the monetary base.

4. Budget deficits do not have to influence the monetary base, since the decision to finance a deficit by money creation is up to the Fed. However, budget deficits *can* lead to money creation if the Fed pursues a policy goal of preventing high interest rates. When the Treasury sells bonds to the public to finance a deficit, bond prices might fall and interest rates rise. To prevent the rise in interest rates, the Fed would buy bonds to prop up bond prices, and the open market purchases would raise the monetary base (high-powered money).

KEY TERMS

uses of the base

sources of the base

float

government budget
  constraint

printing money

monetizing the debt

QUESTIONS AND PROBLEMS

Answer the questions using T-accounts when possible.

1. During its financial difficulties in 1984, Continental Illinois borrowed several billion dollars from the Federal Reserve. What effect did this have on the monetary base?

* 2. What happens to the monetary base if the Fed sells $200 billion of bonds to commercial banks? to private investors?

3. If Fed discounting is abolished as Milton Friedman suggests (Chapter 19), what will happen to the monetary base?

4. Because the price of gold soars from $400 to $800 an ounce, the U.S. government decides to sell one million ounces of gold in the open market. What will happen to the monetary base?

* 5. If an earthquake hits California, what effect will this have on float and the monetary base?

6. If the Fed puts in a new electronic mail system that allows it to present checks for payment on average a day faster than at present, what will happen to float and the monetary base?

* 7. The Board of Governors decides that its building in Washington, D.C. is shabby and needs to be thoroughly rebuilt. When they spend $100 million to rebuild it, what effect will this have on the monetary base?

8. If the Treasury gets ready to buy a $100 million bomber by adding to its deposits at the Fed but then decides at the last minute not to buy it, what will happen to the monetary base?

* 9. If the Treasury is better able to predict when it needs to make payments out of its Fed account and so only makes deposits at the Fed at the same time it writes checks to pay for goods and services, what will happen to the average level of Treasury deposits at the Fed and the monetary base?

10. If people make $1 million of UNICEF donations to the United Nations and it deposits the donations in its account at the Fed, what will happen to the monetary base?

*11. What will happen to the monetary base when the Treasury finances a $200 billion deficit by selling bonds to the public? to commercial banks? to the Fed?

12. Answer true, false, or uncertain: "An increase in the budget deficit will not necessarily lead to a higher level of the monetary base in the future."

*13. If the deficit falls from $200 billion to $100 billion, will the monetary base rise by more or less than it otherwise would? Explain how the Fed's desire to prevent higher interest rates affects your answer.

CHAPTER 19

The Tools of Monetary Policy

PREVIEW   In the chapters describing the money supply process and the structure of the Federal Reserve System, we mentioned three policy tools that the Fed can use to manipulate the money supply: open market operations, which affect the monetary base; changes in the discount rate, which affect the monetary base by influencing the quantity of discount loans; and changes in reserve requirements, which affect the money multiplier. Because the Fed's use of these policy tools has such impact on economic activity, it is important to understand how the Fed wields them in practice and how relatively useful each tool is. We will also seek an answer to the following question: What modifications in the use of these policy tools can lead to improved control over the money supply?

OPEN MARKET OPERATIONS

Open market operations are the most important monetary policy tool because they are the most important determinant of changes in the monetary base, the main source of fluctuations in the money supply. Open market purchases expand the monetary base, thereby raising the money supply, while open market sales shrink the monetary base, lowering the money supply. (The details and T-accounts of this mechanism are found in Chapter 15.) Now that you have an understanding of the factors that influence the monetary base, we can examine how the Federal Reserve conducts open market operations with the object of controlling the money supply.

There are two types of open market operations: **Dynamic open market operations** are intended to change the level of reserves and the monetary base, and **defensive open market operations** are intended to offset movements in other factors that affect the monetary base, such as changes in Treasury deposits with the Fed or float. The Fed conducts open market operations in U.S. Treasury and government agency securities, especially

U.S. Treasury bills.[1] The Fed conducts most of its open market operations in Treasury securities because the market for these securities is the most liquid and has the largest trading volume. It has the capacity to absorb the Fed's substantial volume of transactions without experiencing excessive price fluctuations which would disrupt the market.

As we saw in Chapter 17, the decision-making authority for open market operations is the Federal Open Market Committee (FOMC). The actual execution of these operations, however, is conducted by the Trading Desk at the Federal Reserve Bank of New York. The best way to see how these transactions are executed is to look at a typical day at the Trading Desk, located in a room on the eighth floor of the Federal Reserve Bank of New York.

A Day at the Trading Desk

The manager for domestic operations supervises the traders who execute the purchases and sales of securities. He starts his work day by reading a report that estimates the total amount of reserves in the banking system as of the night before. This information on reserves helps him decide how large a change in reserves is needed to obtain a desired level of the money supply. He also examines the current federal funds rate, which tells him something about the amount of reserves in the banking system. If the banking system has a large amount of reserves, many banks will have excess reserves to lend to other banks and the federal funds rate will probably fall. If the level of reserves is low, few banks will have excess reserves to lend and the Fed funds rate will probably rise.

At 9:00 AM the manager has discussions with several government securities dealers (who operate out of private firms or commercial banks) to get a feel for what may happen to prices of these securities in the course of the day. After the meeting with the dealers, at around 10:00 AM, the manager receives a report from his research staff with a detailed forecast of what will be happening to some of the short-term factors affecting the monetary base (discussed in Chapter 18). If, for example, float is predicted to decrease because good weather throughout the country is speeding up check delivery, the manager knows he will need to conduct a defensive open market operation (a purchase of securities) to offset the expected decline in the monetary base from the decreased float. However, if Treasury deposits and/or foreign deposits at the Fed are predicted to fall, a defensive open market sale would be needed to offset the expected increase in the monetary base. The report also predicts the change in the public's holding of currency. If currency holdings are expected to rise, then, as we have seen in our money

---

[1] The Fed does not conduct open market operations in privately issued securities in order to avoid conflicts of interest. (For example, think of the conflict of interest if the Federal Reserve purchased bonds issued by a company owned by the chairman's brother-in-law.)

supply model of Part IV, an open market purchase is needed to raise the monetary base to prevent the money supply from falling.

At 10:15 AM the manager or a member of his staff telephones the U.S. Treasury to compare his staff's forecasts on such items as Treasury deposits with the Treasury's forecasts. Since the Treasury may have additional information on the changes in its own deposits, its forecasts help the manager to refine his staff's forecasts. The call to the Treasury is also used to procure other pieces of helpful information which provide some clues as to what will be happening in the bond market: for example, the timing of future Treasury sales of securities.

After collecting all these data, the manager looks at the directive he has received from the FOMC, which tells him the growth rate of several monetary aggregates (expressed as a range, say, 4 to 6% at an annual rate) and the range on the federal funds (say, 10 to 14%) that the FOMC would like to achieve. He then figures out the dynamic open market operations that are needed to satisfy the FOMC directive. By combining the necessary defensive open market operations with the desired dynamic open market operations, the manager puts together the "game plan" for open market operations that day.

The whole process is completed at 11:15 AM, at which time the manager makes his daily conference calls to several members of the FOMC and outlines his strategy. After the plan is approved, normally a little after 11:30 AM, he has the traders in the trading room call the primary dealers (numbering around forty) who trade government securities, and request selling price quotations (if open market purchases are planned). For instance, if the manager wants to purchase $250 million of Treasury bills in order to increase the monetary base, the traders list on a large board the quantity of bills at the selling prices that dealers are asking, with the offers ranked top to bottom—from the lowest to the highest price. Since the Fed wants to get the best prices possible, it goes down the list and purchases the bills until the desired amount of $250 million has been bought.

Collecting quotes and executing trades, which takes about 45 minutes, is completed around 12:15 PM. The trading room then quiets down, but the traders continue to monitor conditions in the money market and in bank reserves in the rare instance the manager decides that additional trades are necessary.

Sometimes the open market operations are conducted by straightforward purchases or sales of securities. But ordinarily the Trading Desk engages in repurchase agreements or reverse repurchase agreements. In a **repurchase agreement** (often called a **repo**), the Fed purchases securities with an agreement that the seller will repurchase them in a short period of time, usually less than a week. A repo is actually a temporary open market purchase and is an especially desirable way of conducting a defensive open market purchase that will be reversed shortly. When the Fed wants to conduct a temporary open market sale, it engages in a **matched sale-purchase**

transaction (sometimes called a **reverse repo**) in which the Fed sells securities and the buyer agrees to sell them back to the Fed in the near future.

Advantages of Open Market Operations

Open market operations have several advantages over the other tools of monetary policy.

1. Open market operations occur at the initiative of the Fed, which has complete control over the volume of open market operations. This control is not found, for example, in discount operations in which the Fed can encourage or discourage banks to take out discount loans but cannot directly control the volume of discounting.

2. Open market operations are flexible and precise; they can be used to any degree. No matter how small a change in reserves or the monetary base is desired, open market operations can achieve it with a small purchase or sale of securities. Conversely, if the desired change in reserves or the base is very large, the open market operations tool is strong enough to do the job through a very large purchase or sale of securities.

3. Open market operations are easily reversed. When a mistake is made in conducting an open market operation, the Fed can immediately reverse its use of this tool. If the Fed decides that the money supply is growing too fast because it has made too many open market purchases, it can immediately make a correction by conducting open market sales.

4. Open market operations can be implemented quickly; they involve no administrative delays. When the Fed decides that it wants to change the monetary base or reserves, it just places an order with a securities dealer and the trade is executed immediately.

DISCOUNT POLICY

Discount policy, which primarily involves changes in the discount rate, affects the money supply by affecting the volume of discount loans and the monetary base. A rise in discount loans adds to the monetary base and expands the money supply, while a fall in discount loans reduces the monetary base and shrinks the money supply. The Federal Reserve facility at which discount loans are made to banks is called the **discount window.** As with open market operations, it is easiest to understand how the Fed affects the volume of discount loans by looking at how the discount window operates.

Operation of the Discount Window

The Fed can affect the volume of discount loans in two ways: by affecting the *price* of the loans (the discount rate) or by affecting the *quantity* of the loans through its administration of the discount window.[2]

The mechanism through which the Fed's discount rate affects the volume of discount loans is straightforward: A higher discount rate raises the cost of borrowing from the Fed, so banks will take out fewer discount loans; a lower discount rate makes discount loans more attractive to banks and the loan volume will increase.

To examine how the Fed affects the quantity of discount loans through its administration of the discount window, we have to examine more closely the way these loans are made.

The Fed's discount loans to the banks are of three types: adjustment credit, seasonal credit, and extended credit. *Adjustment credit loans*, the most common category, are intended to be used by banks to help them with short-term liquidity problems that may result from a temporary deposit outflow. Adjustment credit, which can be obtained with a phone call, is expected to be repaid fairly quickly—by the end of the next business day for the larger banks. *Seasonal credit* is given to meet the seasonal needs of a limited number of banks in vacation and agricultural areas that have a seasonal pattern. *Extended credit,* given to banks that have experienced severe liquidity problems because of deposit outflows, is not expected to be repaid quickly. Banks obtaining this type of credit have to submit a proposal outlining the need for extended credit and a plan for restoring the liquidity of the bank. The most important example of extended credit to a bank was the Fed's loans to Continental Illinois in 1984, which exceeded $5 billion.

The Fed administers the discount window in several ways to prevent its credit funds from being misused and to limit this borrowing. In recent years, as depicted in Figure 19.1, the discount rate has frequently been below market interest rates, so there is a great incentive for banks to take out low interest discount loans from the Fed and use the proceeds to make loans or purchase securities with higher interest rates. (Figure 16.3 in Chapter 16 shows that the volume of discount loans rises abruptly when the discount rate falls below market interest rates.) Banks are not supposed to make a profit from discount loans and the Fed tries to prevent it by setting rules for individual banks that limit how often they can take out discount loans. If a bank comes to the discount window too frequently, the Fed will deny it loans in the future. Their stance is that coming to the discount window is a privilege, not a right.

A bank faces three costs when it borrows from the discount window: (1) the interest cost represented by the discount rate; (2) the cost of complying with Fed investigations of the soundness of the bank when it borrows at the discount window; and (3) the cost of being more likely to be turned down for

---

[2]Each Federal Reserve Bank administers its own discount window facility. In our discussion here of discount policy, when we discuss the Fed's administration of the discount window, we are actually referring to the district banks' administration of their discount window facilities.

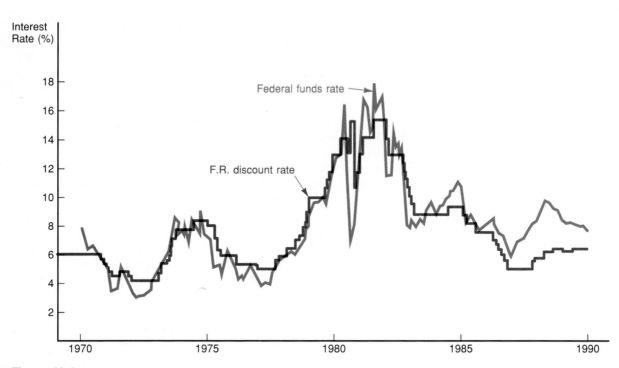

Federal funds rate

F.R. discount rate

Figure 19.1
**Market Interest Rates
and the Discount Rate:
1970–1990** Source:
Federal Reserve
Bulletin, various issues.

a discount loan in the future because of too frequent trips to the discount window. The Fed's setting of rules for use of the discount window is frequently referred to as "moral suasion," although this tool of monetary policy has little to do with morality.

Lender of Last Resort Function

In addition to its use as a tool to influence the monetary base and the money supply, discounting is important in preventing financial panics. When the Federal Reserve System was created, its most important role was intended to be as a lender of last resort; it was to provide reserves to the banking system when bank failures threatened to get out of control, thereby preventing bank and financial panics. Discounting is a particularly effective way to provide reserves to the banking system during a banking crisis because reserves are immediately channeled to the banks that need them most.

Using the discount tool to avoid financial panics by performing the role of lender of last resort is an extremely important requirement of successful monetary policy-making. As we demonstrated with our money supply analysis in Chapter 16, the banking panics in the 1930–1933 period were the cause of the sharpest decline in the money supply in U.S. history, which many economists see as the driving force behind the collapse of the economy during the Great Depression. Financial panics also can severely damage the economy because they interfere with the ability of these markets to move funds to those with productive investment opportunities (Chapter 8).

Unfortunately, the discount tool has not always been used by the Fed to prevent financial panics, as our discussion of massive bank failures during the Great Depression in Chapter 16 indicated. The Fed learned its lesson the hard way from its mistakes of that period and has performed admirably in its role of lender of last resort in the post-World War II period. Two examples of the use of the Fed's discount weapon to avoid bank panics are the provisions of huge loans to Franklin National Bank in 1974 and, more recently, to Continental Illinois (Box 19.1).

At first glance it might appear as though the presence of the FDIC, which insures depositors from losses due to a bank's failure up to a limit of $100,000, would make the lender of last resort function of the Fed superfluous. (The FDIC is described in detail in Chapter 10.) There are two reasons why this is not the case. First, it is important to recognize that the FDIC's insurance fund that guarantees deposits under $100,000 amounts to less than 1% of the amount of these deposits outstanding. If a large number of bank failures occurred, the FDIC would *not* be able to cover all the deposi-

B o x   1 9 . 1

Discounting to Troubled Banks: Franklin National Bank and Continental Illinois

In May 1974 the public learned that Franklin National Bank, the twentieth largest bank in the United States with deposits close to $3 billion, had suffered large losses in foreign exchange trading and had made many bad loans. Large depositors, whose deposits exceeded the $100,000 limit insured by the FDIC, began to withdraw their deposits and the failure of the bank was imminent. Because the immediate failure of Franklin National would have had repercussions on other vulnerable banks, possibly leading to more bank failures, the Fed announced that discount loans would be made available to Franklin National so that depositors, including the largest, would not suffer any losses. By the time that Franklin National was merged into the European-American Bank in October 1974, the Fed had lent Franklin National the sum of $1.75 billion, nearly 5% of the total amount of reserves in the banking system. The quick Fed action was completely successful in preventing any other bank failures, and a possible banking panic was avoided.

A more recent episode in 1984 involved Continental Illinois National Bank and the Fed in a similar action. Continental Illinois had made many bad loans (primarily to businesses in the energy industry and to foreign countries) and rumors of financial trouble in early May 1984 caused large depositors to withdraw over $10 billion of deposits from the bank. The FDIC arranged a rescue effort in July 1984, which culminated in a $4.5 billion commitment of funds to save the bank; still, the Fed had to lend Continental Illinois over $5 billion—making its $1.75 billion loan to Franklin National look like small potatoes! The Fed's action prevented further bank failures and, again, a possible banking panic was successfully avoided.

tors' losses. Indeed, the large number of bank failures in recent years, described in Chapter 11, has led to large losses and a shrinkage in the FDIC's insurance fund, which has reduced the FDIC's ability to cover depositors' losses. This fact has not weakened the confidence of small depositors in the banking system because the Fed has been ready to stand behind the FDIC and to provide whatever reserves the banking system needs to prevent bank panics. Second, over $500 billion of large-denomination deposits in the banking system are not guaranteed by the FDIC because they exceed the $100,000 limit. A loss of confidence in the banking system could still lead to runs on banks from the large-denomination depositors and bank panics could still occur despite the existence of the FDIC. The importance of the Federal Reserve's role as lender of last resort is, if anything, more important today because we have experienced a growing number of bank failures in the 1980s and 1990s.

Not only can the Fed be a lender of last resort to banks, it can also play the same role for the financial system as a whole. The Fed's discount policy can be used to prevent financial panics that are not triggered by bank failures. The Black Monday stock market crash of 1987 provides a clear-cut example of how the Fed can prevent a financial panic by using the discount window to keep markets operating (Box 19.2).

Although the Fed's role as a lender of last resort has the benefit of preventing bank and financial panics, it does have a cost. If a bank expects that the Fed will provide it with discount loans when it gets into trouble, as occurred with Continental Illinois, then it will be willing to take on more risk knowing that the Fed will come to the rescue. The Fed's lender of last resort role has thus created a moral hazard problem similar to the one created by deposit insurance we discussed in Chapter 11: Banks take on more risk, thus exposing the deposit insurance agency, and hence the taxpayers, to greater losses. The moral hazard problem is most severe for large banks who may believe that the Fed and the FDIC view them as "too big to fail"; that is, they will always receive Fed loans when they are in trouble since their failure would be more likely to precipitate a bank panic.

Similarly, Federal Reserve actions to prevent a financial panic, as occurred after the October 1987 stock market crash, may encourage financial institutions besides banks to take on greater risk. They, too, expect the Fed to ensure they could get loans if a financial panic seemed imminent. When the Fed considers using the discount weapon to prevent panics, it therefore needs to consider the trade-off between the moral hazard cost of its role as lender of last resort against the benefit of preventing financial panics. This trade-off explains why the Fed must be careful not to perform its role as a lender of last resort too frequently.

Announcement Effect

Discount policy serves another function for the Federal Reserve; it can be used to signal the Fed's intentions about future monetary policy. Hence, if

Box   1 9 . 2

Discounting to Prevent a Financial Panic: The Black Monday Stock Market Crash of 1987

Although October 19, 1987, dubbed Black Monday, will go down in the history books as the largest one-day decline in stock prices to date, it was on Tuesday, October 20, 1987, that financial markets almost stopped functioning. Felix Rohatyn, one of the most prominent men on Wall Street, has stated, "Tuesday was the most dangerous day we had in 50 years."* Much of the credit for prevention of a market meltdown after Black Monday must be given to the Federal Reserve System and the chairman of the Board of Governors, Alan Greenspan.

The stress of keeping markets functioning during the sharp decline in stock prices on Monday, October 19, meant that many brokerage houses and specialists (dealers-brokers who maintain orderly trading on the stock exchanges) were severely in need of additional funds to finance their activities. However, understandably enough, New York banks, as well as foreign and regional U.S. banks, growing very nervous about the financial health of securities firms, began to cut back credit to the securities industry at a time when it was most needed. Panic was in the air. One chairman of a large specialist firm commented that on Monday, "From 2 p.m. on, there was total despair. The entire investment community fled the market. We were left alone on the field." It was time for the Fed, like the cavalry, to come to the rescue.

Upon learning of the plight of the securities industry, Greenspan and E. Gerald Corrigan, president of the New York Federal Reserve Bank and the Fed official most closely in touch with Wall Street, became fearful of a spreading collapse of securities firms. To prevent this from occurring, Greenspan announced before the market opened on Tuesday, October 20, the Federal Reserve System's "readiness to serve as a source of liquidity to support the economic and financial system." In addition to this extraordinary announcement, the Fed made it clear that it would provide discount loans to any bank that would make loans to the security industry. As one New York banker said, the Fed's message was, "We're here. Whatever you need, we'll give you."

The outcome of the Fed's timely action was that a financial panic was averted. The markets kept functioning on Tuesday and a market rally ensued that day with the Dow Jones Industrial Average climbing over 100 points.

—————

*Quoted in "Terrible Tuesday: How the Stock Market Almost Disintegrated a Day After the Crash," *Wall Street Journal* (Friday, November 20, 1987). This article provides a fascinating and more detailed view of the events described in this box and is the source of the other quotations here.

the Fed decides to slow down expansion in the economy by letting interest rates rise, it can signal its intent to do so by raising the discount rate. This signal may help slow down the economic expansion because the public will expect monetary policy to be less expansionary in the future.

The problem with the announcement effect is that it is subject to misinterpretation. In Chapter 16 we saw that if market interest rates are rising relative to the discount rate, the volume of discount loans will rise. In such a situation the Fed may have no intention of changing its policy to be less expansionary; but in order to keep the amount of discounting from getting excessive, it may raise the discount rate to keep it more in line with market interest rates. When the discount rate rises, the market may interpret this as a signal that the Fed is moving to a contractionary policy when this is not the case. The announcement effect may be a hindrance rather than a help. A more sensible approach probably is for the Fed to communicate directly with the public by announcing its intentions outright and then carrying them out. Fed announcements would be believed and the market would respond accordingly.

Advantages and Disadvantages of Discount Policy

The most important advantage of discount policy is that the Fed can use it to perform its role of lender of last resort. Experiences with Continental Illinois, the Franklin National Bank, and the Black Monday Crash indicate that this role has become more important in the past twenty years. Yet two significant disadvantages of discount policy cause many economists to suggest that it should not be used as a tool of monetary control. First is the confusion about the Federal Reserve's intentions which may be created by the announcement of discount rate changes. Second, when the Fed sets the discount rate at a particular level, large fluctuations will occur in the spread between market interest rates and the discount rate ($i - i_d$) as market interest rates change. As we have seen in Chapter 16 (see Figure 16.3), these fluctuations lead to large unintended fluctuations in the volume of discount loans and hence in the money supply. Discount policy can make it harder to control the money supply.

The use of discount policy to control the money supply seems to have little to recommend it. Not only does it suffer from the two disadvantages described, it is not as effective as open market operations in controlling the money supply for two additional reasons. Open market operations are completely at the discretion of the Fed while the volume of discount loans is not—the Fed can change the discount rate but can't make banks borrow (you can lead a horse to water . . .). Additionally, open market operations are more easily reversed than are changes in discount policy. The disadvantages of discount policy as a tool of monetary control have prompted economists to suggest several proposed reforms of discount policy.

Proposed Reforms of Discount Policy

Should Discounting Be Abolished?   Milton Friedman once proposed that the Fed should terminate its discount facilities in order to establish better monetary control.[3] Friedman has contended that the presence of the FDIC eliminates the possibility of bank panics, therefore the use of discounting is

---

[3]Milton Friedman, *A Program for Monetary Stability* (New York: Fordham University Press, 1960).

no longer as necessary. Abolishing discounting would eliminate fluctuations in the monetary base due to changes in the volume of discount loans and so would reduce unintended fluctuations in the money supply.

The critics of Friedman's proposal emphasize that the FDIC is effective at preventing bank panics only because the Fed stands behind it and plays the role of lender of last resort. Furthermore, as we have seen in the case of the Black Monday Crash, the Federal Reserve's discount facilities can be used to avert a financial panic unrelated to bank failures. Because of the increased number of bank failures in recent years, the need for the Fed's use of the discount facility to preserve the health of the financial system has become more apparent. Hence most economists do not support Friedman's proposal.

Should the Discount Rate Be Tied to a Market Rate of Interest? An alternative proposal, much less radical than abolishing discounting, is that the discount rate should be tied to a market rate of interest, such as the three-month U.S. Treasury bill rate or the federal funds rate. One version of this proposal, called the *penalty discount rate concept,* involves setting the discount rate at a fixed amount above the market interest rate—say, at 3 percentage points above the three-month bill rate—and allowing banks to borrow all they want at that rate.

The advantages of tying the discount rate to a market rate of interest are many. First, the Fed could continue to use discounting to perform its role of lender of last resort. Second, most fluctuations in the spread between market interest rates and the discount rate $(i - i_d)$ would be eliminated, removing a major source of fluctuations in the volume of discount loans. Third, if the penalty discount rate concept were used, the administration of the discount window would be greatly simplified because banks would no longer be borrowing from the discount window to make a profit. Fourth, since discount rate changes would be automatic, there would be no false signals about the Federal Reserve's intentions, and the announcement effect would disappear.

Tying the discount rate to a market rate of interest is supported by many professional economists. In fact, if we look at Figure 19.1, we can see that the Fed already pursues a discount policy that is not too far removed from this proposal. It does not let the discount rate move too far away from market rates of interest because it does not want to let the volume of discount loans get out of hand.[4]

---

[4]One reason why it may keep the discount rate fixed when market interest rates change is that the Fed thinks this will reduce fluctuations in market interest rates. Such a policy will cause discount loans and hence reserves to rise when market interest rates rise, possibly countering some of the rise in market interest rates. Another possible reason is provided by the theory of bureaucratic behavior discussed in Chapter 17. By tying the discount rate to a market interest rate, the Fed will have given up one of its policy tools. It may oppose this reform, perceiving it as a reduction of its power.

RESERVE REQUIREMENTS _____

As you saw in Chapter 15, changes in reserve requirements affect the money supply by causing the money supply multiplier to change. A rise in reserve requirements reduces the amount of deposits that can be supported by a given level of the monetary base and will lead to a contraction of the money supply. A decline in reserve requirements, on the other hand, leads to an expansion of the money supply because more multiple deposit creation can take place. The Fed has had the authority to vary reserve requirements since the 1930s, and this is a powerful way of affecting the money supply. Indeed, changes in reserve requirements have such large effects on the money supply that the Fed rarely resorts to using this tool to control it.

The Depository Institutions Deregulation and Monetary Control Act of 1980 provides a simpler scheme for setting reserve requirements. All depository institutions including commercial banks, savings and loan associations, mutual savings banks, and credit unions are now subject to the same reserve requirements as follows: Required reserves on all checkable deposits—including non-interest-bearing checking accounts, NOW accounts, super-NOW accounts, and ATS (automatic transfer savings) accounts—are equal to (1) 3% of the bank's first $42 million of checkable deposits[5] and (2) 12% of the checkable deposits over $42 million, and the percentage set initially at 12% can be varied between 8% and 14% at the Fed's discretion. In extraordinary circumstances the percentage can be raised as high as 18%.

Advantages and Disadvantages of Reserve Requirement Changes

The main advantage of using reserve requirements to control the money supply is that they affect all banks equally and have a powerful effect on the money supply. The fact that changing reserve requirements is a powerful tool, however, is probably more of a curse than a blessing, because small changes in the money supply will be hard to engineer by varying reserve requirements. With checkable deposits currently hovering near the $600 billion level, a one-half percentage point increase in the reserve requirement on these deposits would reduce excess reserves by $3 billion. Since this decline in excess reserves would result in multiple deposit contraction, the decline in the money supply would be even greater. It is true that small changes in the money supply could be obtained by extremely small changes in reserve requirements (say, by .001 percentage points), but because it is so expensive to administer changes in reserve requirements, such a strategy is

_____

[5]The $42 million figure is as of the end of 1990. Each year, the figure is adjusted upwards by 80% of the percentage increase in checkable deposits in the United States.

not practical. Using reserve requirements to engineer fine-tuning adjustments to the money supply is like trying to use a jackhammer to cut a diamond.

Another disadvantage of using reserve requirements to control the money supply is that raising the requirements can cause immediate liquidity problems for a bank with low excess reserves. When the Fed has raised these requirements in the past, it has usually softened the blow by conducting open market purchases or by making the discount window more available, thus providing reserves to banks that needed them. Continually fluctuating reserve requirements would also create more uncertainty for banks and make their liquidity management more difficult.

The policy tool of changing reserve requirements does not have much to recommend it, and it is rarely used.

Proposed Reforms of Reserve Requirements

Two extreme proposals have been suggested to reform reserve requirements. One is to abolish reserve requirements entirely, and the other is to set required reserves at 100% of deposits.

Should Reserve Requirements Be Abolished? Because the Fed currently pays no interest on reserves, reserve requirements act as a tax on bank deposits; banks cannot earn as much on these deposits because they cannot fully lend them out and so they will pay lower interest rates on them. Some economists consider this undesirable and have suggested that reserve requirements be abolished.[6] If you had only studied the simple deposit multiplier (Chapter 14), you might think that abolishing reserve requirements would result in an infinite money supply. However, as our more sophisticated money supply model (Chapters 15 and 16) indicates, this reasoning would be incorrect. Banks would still want to hold reserves to protect themselves against deposit outflows and there would still be a demand for currency. Both these factors would limit the size of the money supply.

The case for keeping reserve requirements must rest on the proposition that having reserve requirements results in a more stable money multiplier and hence a more controllable money supply. Since the evidence for or against this view is limited, the desirability, or lack of it, for this proposed reform is an open question.

Should Reserve Requirements Be Raised to 100%? At the same time that Milton Friedman suggested abolishing discounting he also suggested that

---

[6]Many economists believe the Fed should pay market interest rates on reserves, another suggestion for dealing with this problem.

required reserves be set equal to 100% of deposits.[7] With 100% reserve requirements, the money supply could be strictly controlled by the Fed because it would be equal to the monetary base. The advantage of this proposal is clear, yet several major disadvantages surface. Banks would no longer be able to make loans because, with 100% reserve requirements, no excess reserves would be available. Loans would have to be made by other financial intermediaries. Not only would this restructuring of the banking system be extremely costly, but the financial intermediaries not subject to reserve requirements might develop ways of making their liabilities function more like checkable deposits in order to attract funds.[8] The outcome might be that the Fed would enjoy complete control of the *official* money supply, but the *economically relevant* money supply might be even less under the Fed's control because it is affected by the activities of the nonbank financial intermediaries. In addition, the Fed's control over the financial system could be weakened further because all the loan activity would be in the hands of financial institutions not subject to the Fed's reserve requirements.

SUMMARY

1. The number of open market operations conducted in any given day by the Trading Desk at the Federal Reserve Bank of New York is determined by the number of dynamic open market operations intended to change the monetary base, and by the number of defensive open market operations used to offset other factors that affect the monetary base. Open market operations are the primary tool used by the Fed to control the money supply because they occur at the initiative of the Fed, are flexible, are easily reversed, and can be implemented quickly.

2. The volume of discount loans is determined by the discount rate and the discouragement of borrowing by moral suasion. Besides its effect on the monetary base and the money supply, discounting allows the Fed to perform its role as a lender of last resort. However, discount policy does make control of the money supply more difficult because it results in unintended fluctuations in the volume of discount loans and, hence, in the money supply. Many economists support tying the discount rate to a market interest rate which would lessen these unintended fluctuations in the volume of discount loans.

3. Changing reserve requirements is too blunt a tool to use for controlling the money supply and it is rarely used.

---

[7]Again, in his *A Program for Monetary Stability,* op. cit. This proposal was outlined earlier by Henry Simons in his *Economic Policy for a Free Society* (Chicago: University of Chicago Press, 1948).

[8]We would expect this to happen because it would resemble the process of financial innovation discussed in Chapter 13.

KEY TERMS

dynamic open market
    operations

matched sale-purchase
    transaction

defensive open market
    operations

discount window

repurchase agreement

QUESTIONS AND PROBLEMS

* 1. If the manager of domestic operations hears that a snowstorm is about to strike New York, making it difficult to present checks for payment there, what defensive open market operations will she undertake?

2. During Christmas time, when the public's holdings of currency increase, what defensive open market operations typically occur? Why?

* 3. If the Treasury has just paid for a bomber and as a result its deposits at the Fed fall, what defensive open market operations will the manager of domestic operations undertake?

4. If float decreases below its normal level, why might the manager of domestic operations consider it more desirable to use repurchase agreements to affect the monetary base rather than an outright purchase of bonds?

* 5. The bulk of open market operations are currently repurchase agreements. What does this tell us about the likely volume of defensive open market operations relative to dynamic open market operations?

6. Answer true, false, or uncertain: "The only way that the Fed can affect the level of discount loans is by adjusting the discount rate."

* 7. If the Fed did not administer the discount window to limit borrowing, what do you predict would happen to the money supply if the discount rate were several percentage points below the interest rate on loans?

8. Answer true, false, or uncertain: "If the discount rate were always kept above the interest rate on

loans, the Fed would rarely have to administer the discount window to limit borrowing."

* 9. "Discounting is no longer needed because the presence of the FDIC eliminates the possibility of bank panics." Discuss.

10. The benefits of using Fed discount operations to prevent bank panics are straightforward. What are the costs?

*11. You often read in the newspaper that the Fed has just lowered the discount rate. Does this signal that the Fed is moving to a more expansionary monetary policy? Why or why not?

12. How can the procyclical movement of interest rates lead to a procyclical movement in the money supply as a result of Fed discounting? Why might this movement of the money supply be undesirable?

*13. Which proposal would lead to tighter control of the money supply: abolishing discounting or tying the discount rate to a market rate of interest? Which of the two proposals would you prefer and why?

14. "Since raising reserve requirements to 100% makes complete control of the money supply possible, Congress should authorize the Fed to raise reserve requirements to this level." Discuss.

*15. Compare the use of (1) open market operations, (2) discounting, and (3) changes in reserve requirements to control the money supply, on the following criteria: flexibility, reversibility, effectiveness, and speed of implementation.

CHAPTER 20

The Conduct of Monetary Policy: Targets and Goals

PREVIEW   In previous chapters you have seen how the Fed can use its tools to affect the money supply. Although we have hinted that the conduct (planning and implementation) of monetary policy is an inexact procedure, an examination of the Fed's conduct of monetary policy gives rise to an important question: Given the tools at its disposal, how well can the Fed *actually* control the money supply?

To explore this subject, we look at the goals the Fed establishes for its monetary policy and its strategies for attaining them. After examining the goals and strategies, we can evaluate the Fed's conduct of monetary policy in the past, with the hope that it will give us some clues to where monetary policy may head in the future.

GOALS OF MONETARY POLICY

Six basic goals are continually mentioned by Federal Reserve personnel when they discuss the objectives of monetary policy: (1) high employment, (2) economic growth, (3) price stability, (4) interest rate stability, (5) stability in financial markets, and (6) stability in the foreign exchange markets.

High Employment

The Employment Act of 1946 and the Full Employment and Balanced Growth Act of 1978 (more commonly called the Humphrey-Hawkins Act) commit the U.S. government to promoting high employment consistent with a stable price level. High employment is a worthy goal for two main reasons: (1) the alternative situation, high unemployment, causes much human misery, with families suffering financial distress, loss of personal self-respect, and increase in crime (though this last conclusion is highly controversial), and (2) when unemployment is high, the economy not only has idle workers but also idle resources (closed factories and unused equipment) resulting in a loss of output (lower GNP).

Although it is clear that high employment is desirable, how high should it be? At what point can we say that the economy is at full employment? At first it might seem that full employment is the point at which no worker is out of a job, that is, when unemployment is zero. But this definition ignores the fact that some unemployment, called frictional unemployment, is beneficial to the economy. For example, when a worker decides to look for a better job, he or she might be unemployed for a period of time during job search. Workers often voluntarily decide to leave work temporarily to pursue other activities (raising a family, travel, returning to school) and when they decide to reenter the job market, it again takes some time for them to find the right job. The benefit of having some unemployment is similar to the benefit of having a nonzero vacancy rate in the market for rental apartments. As many of you who have looked for an apartment have discovered, when the vacancy rate in the rental market is too low, you will have a difficult time finding the right apartment.

The goal for high employment should, therefore, not seek an unemployment level of zero, but rather, a level above zero consistent with full employment at which the demand for labor equals the supply of labor. Economists call this level of unemployment the **natural rate of unemployment.**

Although this definition sounds neat and authoritative, it isn't, since it leaves a troublesome question unanswered: What unemployment rate is consistent with full employment? In some cases it is clear that the unemployment rate is too high: The over 20% unemployment rate during the Great Depression is, for example, clearly far too high. In the early 1960s, on the other hand, economists thought that a reasonable goal was 4%, a level that was probably too low because it led to accelerating inflation. Current estimates of the natural rate of unemployment place it around 6%, but even this estimate is subject to uncertainty and disagreement. In addition, it is possible that appropriate government policy, such as the provision of better information about job vacancies or job training programs, might decrease the natural rate of unemployment.

Economic Growth

The goal of steady economic growth is closely related to the high employment goal because businesses are more likely to invest in capital equipment to increase productivity and economic growth when unemployment is low. Conversely, if unemployment is high and factories are idle, it does not pay for a firm to invest in additional plants and equipment. Although the two goals are closely related, policies can be specifically aimed at encouraging economic growth by directly encouraging firms to invest or encouraging people to save which provides more funds for firms to invest. In fact, this was the stated purpose of Ronald Reagan's supply-side economics policies, which were intended to spur economic growth by providing tax incentives for business firms to invest in plants and equipment and for the average taxpayer to save more.

Price Stability

Over the past two decades, the American public and professional economists have become more aware of the social and economic costs of inflation. They have become more concerned with a stable price level as a goal of economic policy. Price stability is desirable because a rising price level (inflation) creates uncertainty in the economy. For example, the information contained in the prices of goods and services is harder to interpret when the overall level of prices is changing, and then decision making by consumers, businesses, and government can become very difficult. The most extreme example of unstable prices is hyperinflation, such as Germany experienced in 1921–1923. In the last two years of hyperinflation, Germany's economic activity (as measured by GNP) underwent a sharp slowdown because of the costs imposed by the rising price level.

Inflation also makes it difficult to plan for the future. It is more difficult to decide how much funds should be put aside to provide for your children's college education in an inflationary environment. Further, inflation may strain a country's social fabric: conflict may result because each group in the society may compete with other groups to make sure that its wages keep up with the rising level of prices.

Interest Rate Stability

Interest rate stability is desirable because fluctuations in interest rates can create uncertainty in the economy and make it harder to plan for the future. Fluctuations in interest rates which affect consumers' willingness to buy houses, for example, may not only make consumers' decisions about when to purchase a house more difficult, but may make it more difficult for construction firms to plan how many houses they should build. The Fed may also want to reduce upward movements in interest rates for the reasons we discussed in Chapter 17: Upward movements in interest rates create great hostility toward the Fed and lead to demands that the Fed's power be curtailed.

Stability of Financial Markets

An explicit reason for the creation of the Federal Reserve System was that it could promote a more stable financial system. One way the Fed promotes stability is helping prevent financial panics (particularly bank panics) through its role as lender of last resort. Throughout the text, we have seen that the Fed has performed this role many times in the past twenty years.

The stability of financial markets is also promoted by interest rate stability since fluctuations in interest rates create great uncertainty for financial institutions. An increase in interest rates produces large capital losses on long-term bonds and mortgages, losses that can cause the failure of financial institutions holding them. In recent years, more pronounced interest rate fluctuations have been a particularly severe problem for savings and loan associations and mutual savings banks, many of whom as we have seen have gotten into serious financial trouble.

Stability in Foreign Exchange Markets

With the increasing importance of international trade to the U.S. economy, the value of the dollar relative to other currencies has become a major consideration for the Fed. As we will see in Chapters 21 and 22, a rise in the value of the dollar makes American industry less competitive with that abroad, while declines in the value of the dollar stimulate inflation in the United States. In addition, preventing large changes in the value of the dollar makes it easier for firms and individuals purchasing or selling goods abroad to plan ahead. Stabilizing extreme movements in the value of the dollar in foreign exchange markets is thus viewed as a worthy goal of monetary policy.

Conflict Among Goals

Although many of the goals mentioned are consistent with each other—high employment with economic growth or interest rate stability with financial market stability—this is not always the case. The goal of price stability often conflicts with the goals of interest rate stability and high employment in the short run. When, for example, the economy is expanding and unemployment is falling, both inflation and interest rates may start to rise. If the Fed tries to prevent a rise in interest rates by buying bonds, bidding up their price and thus causing interest rates to fall, the resulting open market purchases will cause the monetary base and the money supply to rise, stimulating inflation. On the other hand, if the Fed slows down money supply growth to prevent the inflation, in the short run both interest rates and unemployment may rise. The conflict among goals may thus present the Fed with some hard decisions. We will return to the issue of how the Fed should choose between conflicting goals in later chapters where we will examine how monetary policy affects the economy.

THE FED'S STRATEGY: USE OF MONETARY TARGETS _____

The Fed is faced with the problem that it wishes to achieve certain goals such as price stability with high employment, but it does not directly influence the goals. It has a set of tools to employ (open market operations, changes in the discount rate, and changes in reserve requirements) that can affect the goals indirectly after a period of time (typically more than a year). If the Fed waits to see what the outcome of the price level and employment will be one year later, it will be too late to make any corrections to its policy—mistakes will be irreversible.

The Fed thus pursues a different strategy for conducting monetary policy by aiming at variables that lie between its tools and the achievement of its goals. The Fed's game plan (outlined in Figure 20.1) is as follows: After deciding on its goals for employment and the price level, it chooses a set of variables to "aim for" called **intermediate targets,** such as the monetary aggregates ($M1$, $M2$, or $M3$) or interest rates (short- or long-term), which have a direct affect on employment and the price level. However, even these intermediate targets are not directly affected by the Fed's policy tools. Therefore, it chooses another set of variables to aim for called **operating targets,** such as reserve aggregates (reserves, nonborrowed reserves, monetary base, or nonborrowed base) or interest rates (federal funds rate or Treasury bill rate), which are more responsive to its policy tools. (Recall that nonborrowed reserves are total reserves minus borrowed reserves [the amount of discount loans], the nonborrowed base is the monetary base minus borrowed reserves, and the federal funds rate is the interest rate on funds loaned overnight between banks.)[1]

The Fed pursues this strategy because it is easier to hit a goal by aiming at targets than by aiming at the goal directly. Specifically, by using intermediate and operating targets it can more quickly judge whether its policies are on the right track, rather than waiting until it sees the final outcome of its policies on employment and the price level.[2] By analogy, NASA employs the strategy of using targets when it is trying to send a spaceship to the moon. It will check to see whether the spaceship is positioned correctly as it leaves the atmosphere (we can think of this as NASA's "operating target"). If the spaceship is off course at this stage, NASA engineers will adjust its thrust (a policy tool) to get it back on target. NASA may check the position of the spaceship again when it is halfway to the moon (NASA's "intermediate target") and can make a midcourse correction if necessary.

The Fed's strategy works in a similar way. Suppose that the Fed's employment and price level goals are consistent with a growth rate of nominal GNP of 5%. If the Fed feels that the 5% growth rate of nominal GNP will be

---

[1]There is some ambiguity as to whether to call a particular variable an operating target or an intermediate target. Some economists view the monetary base and the Treasury bill rate as being possible intermediate targets, even though they may function as operating targets as well. In addition, if the Fed wants to pursue a goal of interest rate stability, then an interest rate can be both a goal variable as well as a target variable.

[2]This reasoning for the use of monetary targets is not without criticism because information on employment and the price level can be useful in evaluating policy. See Benjamin M. Friedman, "The Inefficiency of Short-Run Monetary Targets for Monetary Policy," *Brookings Papers on Economic Activity* 2 (1977): 292–346.

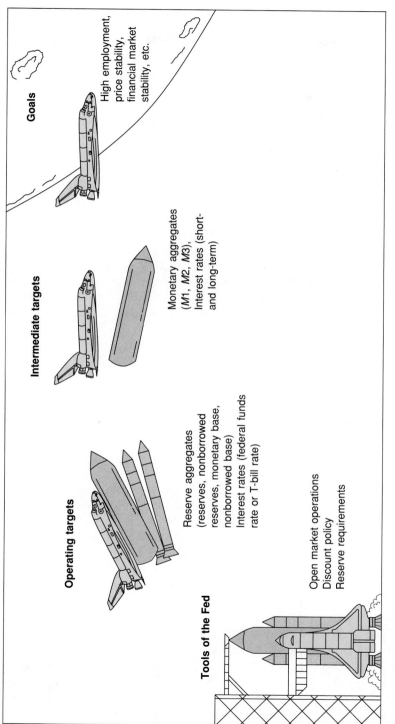

Goals

High employment, price stability, financial market stability, etc.

Intermediate targets

Monetary aggregates (*M1*, *M2*, *M3*), Interest rates (short- and long-term)

Operating targets

Reserve aggregates (reserves, nonborrowed reserves, monetary base, nonborrowed base) Interest rates (federal funds rate or T-bill rate)

Tools of the Fed

Open market operations
Discount policy
Reserve requirements

Figure 20.1   Strategy of the Fed

achieved by a 4% growth rate of $M2$ (its intermediate target), which, in turn, will be achieved by a growth rate of the monetary base of $3\frac{1}{2}$% (its operating target), then it will carry out open market operations (its tool) to achieve the $3\frac{1}{2}$% growth rate of the monetary base. Within days after implementing this policy, the Fed may find that the monetary base is growing too slowly, say, at a 2% rate; then it can correct this too slow growth by increasing the amount of its open market purchases. Somewhat later, the Fed will begin to see how its policy is affecting the growth rate of the money supply. If $M2$ is growing too fast, say, at a 7% rate, the Fed may decide to reduce its open market purchases or make open market sales to reduce the $M2$ growth rate.

One way of thinking about the Fed's strategy (illustrated in Figure 20.1) is that it is using its operating and intermediate targets to direct monetary policy (the spaceship) toward the achievement of its goals. After the initial setting of the policy tools (the liftoff), an operating target such as the monetary base, which the Fed can control fairly directly, is used to reset the tools so that monetary policy is channeled toward achieving the intermediate target of a certain rate of money supply growth. Midcourse corrections in the policy tools can be made again when the Fed sees what is happening to its intermediate target, thus directing monetary policy so that it will achieve its goals of high employment and price stability (the spaceship reaches the moon).

CHOOSING THE TARGETS

As we see in Figure 20.1, there are two different types of target variables: (1) interest rates and (2) aggregates (monetary aggregates and reserve aggregates). In the example above, the Fed chose a 4% growth rate of $M2$ to achieve a 5% rate of growth of nominal GNP. It could have chosen to lower the interest rate on the three-month Treasury bills, say, to 8%, to achieve the same goal. Can the Fed choose to pursue both of these targets at the same time? The answer is "no." The application of the supply and demand analysis of the money market that we covered in Chapter 6 explains why the Fed must choose between one or the other.

Let's first see why a monetary aggregate target involves losing control of the interest rate. Figure 20.2 contains a supply and demand diagram for the money market. Although the Fed expects the demand curve for money to be at M^{d^*}, it fluctuates between $M^{d'}$ and $M^{d''}$ because of unexpected increases or decreases in output or changes in the price level. The money demand curve might also shift unexpectedly because the public's preferences about holding bonds versus money may change. If the Fed's monetary aggregate target of a 4% growth rate in $M2$ results in a money supply of M^*, then it expects that the interest rate will be at i^*. However, as the figure indicates, the fluctuations in the money demand curve between $M^{d'}$ and $M^{d''}$ will result in the interest rate fluctuating between i' and i''. Pursuing a monetary aggregate target implies that interest rates will fluctuate.

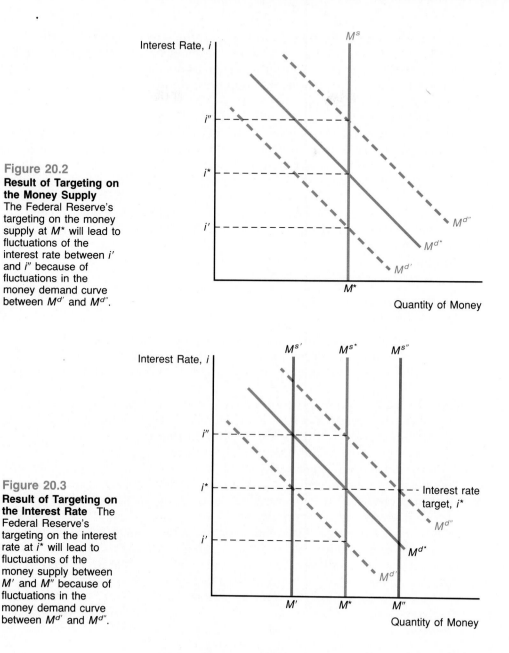

Figure 20.2
Result of Targeting on the Money Supply
The Federal Reserve's targeting on the money supply at *M** will lead to fluctuations of the interest rate between *i'* and *i"* because of fluctuations in the money demand curve between $M^{d'}$ and $M^{d"}$.

Figure 20.3
Result of Targeting on the Interest Rate   The Federal Reserve's targeting on the interest rate at *i** will lead to fluctuations of the money supply between *M'* and *M"* because of fluctuations in the money demand curve between $M^{d'}$ and $M^{d"}$.

Figure 20.3 contains a supply and demand diagram which shows the consequences of an interest rate target set at *i**. Again, the Fed expects the money demand curve to be at M^{d*}, but it fluctuates between $M^{d'}$ and $M^{d"}$ due to unexpected changes in output, the price level, or in the public's preferences toward holding money. If the demand curve falls to $M^{d'}$, then the interest rate will begin to fall below *i** and the price of bonds will rise. With an interest rate target, the Fed will prevent the interest rate from falling by selling bonds to drive their price back down and the interest rate back up to its former level. The Fed will make open market sales until the money supply declines to $M^{s'}$, at which point the equilibrium interest rate is again i^*. On the other hand, if the demand curve rises to $M^{d''}$ and drives up the interest rate, the Fed would keep the interest rates from rising by buying bonds to keep their prices from falling. The Fed will make open market purchases until the money supply rises to $M^{s''}$ and the equilibrium interest rate is at i^*. The Fed's adherence to the interest rate target thus leads to a fluctuating money supply as well as fluctuations in reserve aggregates such as the monetary base.

The conclusion from the supply and demand analysis is that interest rate and monetary aggregate targets are incompatible: The Fed can hit one or the other but cannot hit both. Since a choice between them has to be made, we need to examine what criteria should be used to decide on the target variable.

Criteria for Choosing Intermediate Targets

The rationale behind the Fed's strategy of using targets suggests three criteria for choosing an intermediate target: It must be measurable, it must be controllable by the Fed, and it must have a predictable effect on the goal.

Measurability Quick and accurate measurement of an intermediate target variable is necessary because the intermediate target will be useful only if it signals when policy is "off track" more rapidly than the goal. What good does it do for the Fed to plan to hit a 4% growth rate of $M2$ if it has no way of quickly and accurately measuring $M2$? Data on the monetary aggregates are obtained after a two-week delay, and interest rate data are available almost immediately. Data on a goal variable like GNP, on the other hand, are compiled quarterly and are made available with a month's delay. In addition, the GNP data are less accurate than data on the monetary aggregates or interest rates. On these grounds alone, focusing on interest rates and monetary aggregates as intermediate targets rather than on a goal like GNP can provide clearer signals about the status of the Fed's policy.

At first glance, interest rates seem to be more measurable than monetary aggregates and hence more useful as intermediate targets. Not only are the data on interest rates available more quickly than on monetary aggregates, but they are also measured more precisely and are rarely revised, in contrast to the monetary aggregates which are subject to a fair amount of revision (as you saw in Chapter 2). However, as we learned in Chapter 4, the interest rate that is quickly and accurately measured, the nominal interest rate, is typically a very poor measure of the real cost of borrowing which more certainly tells us about what will happen to GNP. This real cost of borrowing is more accurately measured by the real interest rate—the interest rate adjusted for expected inflation ($i_r = i - \pi^e$). Unfortunately, the real interest rate is extremely hard to measure because we have no direct way to measure *expected* inflation. Since both interest rate and monetary aggregates have measurability problems, it is not clear whether one should be preferred to the other as an intermediate target.

Controllability   The Fed must be able to exercise effective control over a variable if it is to function as a useful target. If the Fed cannot control an intermediate target, then knowing that it is "off track" does the Fed little good because it has no way of getting it back "on track." Some economists have suggested that nominal GNP should be used as an intermediate target, but since the Fed has little direct control over nominal GNP, it will not provide much guidance to the Fed on how the Fed should set its policy tools. The Fed does, however, have a good deal of control over the monetary aggregates and interest rates.

Our discussion of the money supply process and the Fed's policy tools indicates that the Fed does have the ability to exercise a powerful effect on the money supply, although its control is not perfect. We have also seen that open market operations can be used to set interest rates by directly affecting the price of bonds. Because the Fed can set interest rates directly while it cannot completely control the money supply, it might appear that interest rates dominate the monetary aggregates on the controllability criterion. The Fed, however, cannot set *real* interest rates because it does not have control over expectations of inflation. Thus again, a clear-cut case cannot be made that interest rates are preferred to monetary aggregates as an intermediate target or vice versa.

Ability to Predictably Affect Goals   The most important characteristic a variable must have to be useful as an intermediate target is that it must have a *predictable* impact on a goal. If the Fed can accurately and quickly measure the price of tea in China and can completely control its price, what good will it do? The Fed cannot use the price of tea in China to affect unemployment or the price level in the United States. Because the ability to affect goals is so critical to the usefulness of an intermediate target variable, the linkage of the money supply and interest rates with the goals—output, employment, and the price level—is a matter of much debate in the economics profession. The evidence seems to favor a closer (more predictable) link of these goals with the money supply than with interest rates, thus lending some support to the use of monetary aggregates as intermediate targets. We will discuss the evidence on this issue extensively in Chapter 27.

Criteria for Choosing Operating Targets

The choice of an operating target can be based on the same criteria used to evaluate intermediate targets. Both the federal funds rate and reserve aggregates are measured accurately and are available daily with almost no delay; both are easily controllable using the policy tools that we discussed in the previous chapter. When we look at the third criterion, however, we can think of the intermediate target as the goal for the operating target. An operating target that has a more predictable impact on the most desirable intermediate target is preferred. If the desired intermediate target is an interest rate, then the preferred operating target will be an interest rate variable like the federal funds rate because interest rates are closely tied to each other (as you saw in Chapter 7). On the other hand, if the desired intermediate target is a monetary aggregate, our money supply model of Part IV shows that a reserve aggregate operating target such as the monetary base will be preferred. Since there does not seem to be much reason to choose an interest rate over a reserve aggregate on the basis of measurability or controllability, the choice of which operating target is best rests on the choice of the intermediate target (the goal of the operating target).

THE FED'S POLICY PROCEDURES: A HISTORICAL PERSPECTIVE

The well-known adage, "The road to hell is paved with good intentions," applies as much to the Federal Reserve as it does to us. Understanding the Fed's goals and the strategies it can use to pursue its goals cannot tell us *how* monetary policy is actually conducted. To understand the practical results of the theoretical underpinnings, we have to look at the Fed's past policy procedures: its choice of goals, policy tools, operating targets, and intermediate targets. This historical perspective will not only show us how our central bank carries out its duties, but it will help us interpret the Fed's activities and see where monetary policy may be heading in the future.

Study Guide

The following discussion of the Fed's policy procedures and their effect on the money supply provides a review of the money supply process and how the Fed's policy tools work. If you have trouble understanding how the particular policies described affect the money supply, it might be helpful to review the material in Part IV.

The Early Years: Discount Policy as the Primary Tool

When the Fed was created, changing the discount rate was the primary tool of monetary policy—the Fed had not yet discovered that open market operations were a more powerful tool for influencing the money supply, and the

Federal Reserve Act made no provisions for changes in reserve requirements. The guiding principle for the conduct of monetary policy was that as
long as loans were being made for "productive" purposes, that is, to support
the production of goods and services, then providing reserves to the banking
system to make these loans would not be inflationary.[3] This theory, which is
now thoroughly discredited, became known as the **real bills doctrine.** In
practice, it meant that the Fed would make loans to member commercial
banks when they showed up at the discount window with "eligible paper,"
that is, loans to facilitate the production and sale of goods and services. (Note
that since the 1920s, the Fed does not conduct discount operations in this
way.) The Fed's act of making the loans to the member banks was initially
called rediscounting because the original bank loans to businesses were
made by discounting (loaning less than) the face value of the loan and the
Fed would be discounting them again. (Over time when the Fed's emphasis
on eligible paper diminished, the Fed's loans to banks became known as
discounts and the interest rate on these loans the discount rate, which is the
terminology we use today.)

By the end of World War I, the Fed's policy of rediscounting eligible
paper and keeping interest rates at low levels to help the Treasury finance
the war had led to a raging inflation; in 1919 and 1920, the inflation rate
averaged 14%. The Fed decided that it could no longer follow the passive
policy prescribed by the real bills doctrine because it was inconsistent with
the goal of price stability, and for the first time since the Fed's creation, it
accepted the responsibility of playing an active role in influencing the economy. In January 1920, the Fed raised the discount rate from 4¾ to 6%, the
largest jump in its history, and eventually raised it further to 7% in June
1920 where it remained until May 1921. The result of this policy was a sharp
decline in the money supply and an especially sharp recession in 1920–1921.
Although the blame for this severe recession can clearly be laid at the Fed's
doorstep, in one sense the Fed's policy was very successful: After an initial
decline in the price level, the inflation rate went to zero, paving the way for
the prosperous Roaring Twenties.

Discovery of Open Market Operations

In the early 1920s, a particularly important event occurred—the Fed acci-
dentally discovered open market operations. When the Fed was created, its
revenue came exclusively from the interest it received on the discount loans
that it made to member banks. After the 1920–1921 recession, the volume of
discount loans shrank dramatically and the Fed was hard pressed for in-

---

[3]Another guiding principle was the maintenance of the gold standard, which we will discuss in
Chapter 22.

come. It solved this problem by purchasing income-earning securities. When this was done, the Fed found that reserves in the banking system grew and there was a multiple expansion of bank loans and deposits. This result is obvious to us now (we have studied the multiple deposit creation process in Chapter 14), but to the Fed at that time it was a revelation. A new monetary policy tool was born, and by the end of the 1920s, it was the most important weapon in the Fed's arsenal.

The Great Depression

The stock market boom in 1928 and 1929 created a dilemma for the Fed. It wanted to slow down the boom by raising the discount rate, but it was reluctant to do so because that would have meant raising interest rates to businesses and individuals who had "legitimate" needs for credit. (The Fed did not yet have the authority to set margin requirements as it does today.) Finally, in August 1929, the Fed raised the discount rate, but by then it was too late; the speculative excesses of the market boom had already occurred and the Fed's action only hastened the stock market crash and helped the economy into recession. In Chapter 16 we discussed the Fed's many policy blunders from 1930 to 1933, when its failure to perform its role of lender of last resort allowed over a third of the commercial banks in the United States to fail. The resulting unprecedented decline in the money supply during this period is thought by many economists to have been the major contributing factor to the severity of the depression, which has never been equaled before or since.

Reserve Requirements as a Policy Tool

The Thomas Amendment to the Agricultural Adjustment Act of 1933 provided the Board of Governors with the emergency power to alter reserve requirements with the approval of the president of the United States. In the Banking Act of 1935, this emergency power was expanded to allow the Fed to alter reserve requirements unilaterally without the president's approval.

The first use of reserve requirements as a tool of monetary control proved that the Federal Reserve was capable of adding to the blunders that it had made during the banking panics of the early 1930s. By the end of 1935, banks had increased their holdings of excess reserves to unprecedented levels, a sensible strategy considering their discovery during the 1930–1933 period that the Fed would not always perform its intended role as lender of last resort. Bankers now understood that they would have to protect themselves against a bank run by holding substantial amounts of excess reserves. The Fed viewed these excess reserves as a nuisance that made it harder to exercise monetary control. Specifically, the Fed worried that these excess reserves might be loaned out and would produce "an uncontrollable expansion of credit in the future."[4]

To improve monetary control, the Fed raised reserve requirements in three steps: August 1936, January 1937, and May 1937. The result of this action was, as we would expect from our money supply model, a slowdown of money growth toward the end of 1936 and an actual decline in 1937. The recession of 1937–1938, which commenced in May 1937, was a severe one and was especially upsetting to the American public because even at its outset unemployment was intolerably high. So not only does it appear that the Fed was at fault for the severity of the Great Depression contraction in 1929–1933, but to add insult to injury, it appears that it was also responsible for the aborting of the subsequent recovery. The Fed's disastrous experience with varying its reserve requirements made it far more cautious in the use of this policy tool in the future.

War Finance and the Pegging of Interest Rates: 1942–1951

With the entrance of the United States into World War II in late 1941, government spending skyrocketed, and to finance it, the Treasury issued huge amounts of bonds. The Fed agreed to help the Treasury finance the war cheaply by pegging interest rates at the low levels that had prevailed before the war: $3/8$ of 1% on Treasury bills and $2\frac{1}{2}$% on long-term Treasury bonds. Whenever interest rates would rise above these levels and the price of bonds would begin to fall, the Fed would make open market purchases, thereby bidding up bond prices and driving interest rates down again. The Fed had thus in effect relinquished its control of monetary policy to meet the financing needs of the government. The result was a substantial monetization of the debt and a rapid growth in the monetary base and the money supply.

When the war ended, the Fed continued to peg interest rates, and because there was little pressure on them to rise, this policy did not result in an explosive growth in the money supply. When the Korean war occurred in 1950, however, interest rates began to climb and the Fed found that it was again forced to expand the monetary base at a rapid rate. Because inflation began to heat up with the consumer price index rising by 8% between 1950 and 1951, the Fed decided that it was time to reassert its control over monetary policy by abandoning the interest rate peg. A debate, often quite bitter, ensued between the Fed and the Treasury, which wanted to keep its interest costs down and so favored a continued pegging of interest rates at low levels. In March 1951, the Fed and Treasury came to an agreement known as the

---

[4]Friedman and Schwartz, *A Monetary History of the United States, 1867–1960,* op. cit., p. 524.

"Accord," in which pegging was abandoned but the Fed promised that it would not allow interest rates to rise precipitously. After Eisenhower's election as president in 1952, the Fed was given complete freedom to pursue its monetary policy objectives.

Targeting Money Market Conditions: The 1950s and 1960s

With its freedom restored, the Federal Reserve, then under the chairmanship of William McChesney Martin, took the view that monetary policy should be grounded in intuitive judgment based on a "feel" for the money market. The policy procedure that resulted can be described as one in which the Fed targeted on money market conditions, a vague collection of variables that were supposed to describe supply and demand conditions in the money market. Included among these variables were short-term interest rates and **free reserves** (FR), excess reserves in the banking system (ER) minus the volume of discount loans (DL):

$$FR = ER - DL$$

The Fed considered free reserves to be a particularly good indicator of money market conditions because it thought that free reserves represented the amount of slack in the banking system. The Fed viewed banks as having a first priority in using their excess reserves to repay their discount loans, so only the excess reserves not borrowed from the Fed represented the "free" reserves which could be used to make loans and create deposits. The Fed interpreted an increase in free reserves as an easing of money market conditions and used open market sales to withdraw reserves from the banking system. A fall in free reserves meant a tightening of money market conditions and the Fed made open market purchases.

An important characteristic of this policy procedure is that it led to more rapid growth in the money supply when the economy was expanding and a slowing of money growth when the economy was in recession. The so-called procyclical monetary policy (that is, a positive association of money supply growth with the business cycle) is explained by the following step-by-step reasoning. As we learned in Chapter 6, a rise in national income ($Y \uparrow$) leads to a rise in market interest rates ($i \uparrow$), thus raising the opportunity cost of holding excess reserves and causing excess reserves to decline ($ER \downarrow$). The rise in interest rates also increases the incentives to borrow from the discount window because bank loans become more profitable and so the volume of discount loans will rise ($DL \uparrow$). The decline in excess reserves and rise in the volume of discount loans then imply that free reserves will fall ($FR \downarrow = ER \downarrow - DL \uparrow$). When the Fed reacts to the decline in free reserves by making open market purchases, it raises the monetary base ($MB \uparrow$) and therefore the money supply ($M \uparrow$). The reasoning outlined can be summarized as follows:

$$Y \uparrow \rightarrow i \uparrow \rightarrow ER \downarrow, DL \uparrow \rightarrow FR \downarrow \rightarrow MB \uparrow \rightarrow M \uparrow$$

A business cycle contraction causes the opposite chain of events, so that the fall in income leads to a fall in the money supply ($Y \downarrow \rightarrow M \downarrow$). Thus the Fed's use of a free reserves target results in a positive association of money supply movements with national income, hence a procyclical monetary policy.

During this period, many economists, especially Karl Brunner and Allan Meltzer, criticized the Fed's use of free reserves as a target variable because of the procyclical monetary policy that it created. When the money supply grows more rapidly during a business cycle expansion, it can add to inflationary pressures; when it grows more slowly during a recession, it is likely to make the economic contraction worse. Indeed, a stated objective of the Fed during this period was that monetary policy should "lean against the wind": In other words, monetary policy should be anticyclical—contractionary when there is a business cycle expansion and expansionary when there is a business cycle contraction.

The Fed's other primary operating target, short-term interest rates, performed no better as a target variable than free reserves and also led to procyclical monetary policy. If the Fed saw interest rates rising as a result of a rise in income, it would purchase bonds to bid their price up and lower interest rates to their target level. The resulting increase in the monetary base caused the money supply to rise and the business cycle expansion to be accompanied by a faster rate of money growth. In summary,

$$Y \uparrow \rightarrow i \uparrow \rightarrow MB \uparrow \rightarrow M \uparrow$$

In a recession, the opposite sequence of events would occur and the decline in income would be accompanied by a slower rate of growth of the money supply ($Y \downarrow \rightarrow M \downarrow$).

By the late 1960s, the rising chorus of criticism of procyclical monetary policy finally led the Fed to abandon its focus on money market conditions.

Targeting Monetary Aggregates? The 1970s

In 1970, Arthur Burns was appointed chairman of the Board of Governors, and soon thereafter the Fed stated that it was committing itself to the use of monetary aggregates as intermediate targets. Did monetary policy cease to be procyclical? A glance at Figure 1.3 in Chapter 1 indicates that monetary policy was as procyclical in the 1970s as in the 1950s and 1960s. What went wrong? Why did the conduct of monetary policy not improve? The answers to these questions lie in the Fed's operating procedures during the period, which suggest that its commitment to targeting monetary aggregates was not very strong.

Every six weeks the FOMC would set target ranges for the growth rate of various monetary aggregates and would determine what federal funds rate (the interest rate on funds loaned overnight between banks) it thought consistent with these aims. The target ranges for the growth in monetary aggregates were fairly broad—a typical range for $M1$ growth might be 3 to 6% and for $M2$, 4 to 7%—while the range for the federal funds rate was a narrow band, say, from 7½ to 8¼%. The Trading Desk at the New York Fed was then instructed to meet both sets of targets, but as we saw earlier, interest rate targets and monetary aggregate targets might not be compatible. If the two targets were incompatible, say, the federal funds rate began to climb higher than the top of its target band when $M1$ was growing too rapidly, the Trading Desk was instructed to give precedence to the federal funds rate target. In the situation we have just described, this would mean that although $M1$ growth was too high, the Trading Desk would make open market purchases to keep the federal funds rate within its target range.

The Fed was actually using the federal funds rate as its operating target. During the six-week period between FOMC meetings, an unexpected rise in income (which would cause the federal funds rate to hit the top of its target band) would then induce open market purchases and a too rapid growth of the money supply. When the FOMC met again, it would try to bring money supply growth back "on track" by raising the target range on the federal funds rate. However, if income continued to rise unexpectedly, then money growth would overshoot again. This is exactly what occurred from June 1972 to June 1973, when the economy boomed unexpectedly: $M1$ growth greatly exceeded its target, increasing at approximately an 8% rate, while the federal funds rate climbed from 4½ to 8½%. The economy soon became overheated and inflationary pressures began to mount.

The opposite chain of events occurred at the end of 1974 when the economic contraction was far more severe than anyone had predicted. The federal funds rate fell precipitously from over 12 to 5% and persistently bumped against the bottom end of its target range. The Trading Desk conducted open market sales to keep the federal funds rate from falling, and money growth dropped precipitously, actually turning negative by the beginning of 1975. Clearly, this sharp drop in money growth when the United States was experiencing its worst economic contraction of the postwar era was a serious mistake.

Using the federal funds rate as an operating target promoted a procyclical monetary policy despite the Fed's lip service to monetary aggregate targets. If the Federal Reserve really intended to pursue monetary aggregate targets, it seems peculiar that it would have chosen an interest rate for an operating target rather than a reserve aggregate. (However, as Box 20.1 makes clear, more effective monetary control can be achieved even when an interest rate is used as an operating target.) The explanation for why the Fed chose an interest rate as an operating target is that it was still very concerned

Box   2 0 . 1   **A Global Perspective**

A Comparison of Japanese and U.S. Monetary Policy Procedures

Since 1975 the Bank of Japan, the Japanese central bank, has conducted monetary policy with operating procedures that are similar in many ways to those that the Federal Reserve has used in the United States. Like the Fed in the 1970–1979 period, the Bank of Japan has stated monetary aggregate targets and uses the interest rate in the Japanese interbank market (which has a function similar to that of the federal funds market in the United States) as its daily operating target. Although the Bank of Japan's open market operations play an important role in setting the interbank interest rate, greater use is made of discounting in Japan than in the United States: In Japan the level of discount borrowing frequently exceeds the level of required reserves, whereas the level of discount borrowing in the United States is typically less than 5% of the amount of required reserves. Unlike the Fed, the Bank of Japan has complete control over the level of discounting because it decides how much each bank will borrow on any given day.

Although the Bank of Japan uses an interest rate as its operating target just as the Fed has done, surprisingly its monetary policy performance has been much better than the Fed's. There has been a gradual slowdown in Japanese money growth since 1975, and Japanese money growth has been much less variable than that of the United States. The outcome has been a more rapid slowing of inflation and an average inflation rate that is lower in Japan. These excellent results on inflation have been achieved with lower variability in real output in Japan than in the United States. The success of Japanese monetary policy using an interest rate as an operating target, in contrast to the lack of success in the 1970–1979 period in the United States when the Fed used a similar operating procedure, suggests that using an interest rate as an operating target is not necessarily a barrier to successful monetary policy. More important might be a strong commitment to a low inflation rate, something that was true for the Bank of Japan after 1975, but was less true for the Federal Reserve in the 1970–1979 period.

---

with achieving interest rate stability and was reluctant to relinquish control over interest rate movements. The incompatibility of the Fed's policy procedure with its stated intent of targeting on the monetary aggregates had become very clear by October 1979, when the Fed's policy procedures underwent drastic revision.

The New Fed Operating Procedures: October 1979–October 1982

In October 1979, soon after Paul Volcker became chairman of the Board of Governors (in August 1979), the Fed finally deemphasized the federal funds rate as an operating target by widening its target range more than fivefold: A typical range might be from 10 to 15%. The primary operating target became nonborrowed reserves which the Fed would set after estimating the volume of discount loans the banks would borrow. Figure 20.4 shows us what happened to the federal funds rate and the growth rate of $M1$ money supply both before and after October 1979. Not surprisingly, the federal funds rate underwent much greater fluctuations after it was deemphasized

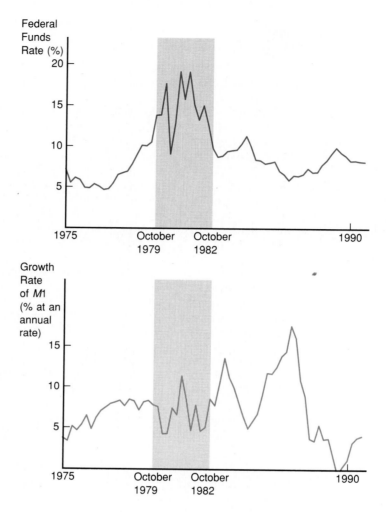

Figure 20.4
**Federal Funds Rate
and the Growth Rate
of the Money Supply:
Before and After
October 1979** Sources:
Federal Reserve
Bulletin, various issues;
Board of Governors of
the Federal Reserve
System, "Money Stock
Revisions," February
1991, mimeo.

as an operating target. What is surprising, however, is that the deemphasis of
the federal funds target did not result in improved monetary control: After
October 1979, the fluctuations in the rate of money supply growth *increased*
rather than decreased as would have been expected. In addition, the Fed
missed its $M1$ growth target ranges in all three years of the 1979–1982 period.[5] What went wrong?

------

[5]The $M1$ target ranges and actual growth rates for 1980 through 1982 are as follows:

Year	Range	Actual
1980	4.5–7.0	7.5
1981	6.0–8.5	5.1
1982	2.5–5.5	8.8

Source: Board of Governors of the Federal Reserve System. *Monetary Policy Objectives, 1981–
1983.*

There are several possible answers to this question. The first is that the economy was exposed to several shocks during this period that made monetary control more difficult: the acceleration of financial innovation and deregulation, which added new categories of deposits such as NOW accounts to the measures of monetary aggregates; the imposition of credit controls from March to July 1980, which restricted the growth of consumer and business loans; and the back-to-back recessions of 1980 and 1981–1982.[6]

A more persuasive explanation for poor monetary control, however, is that controlling the money supply was never really the intent of Volcker's policy shift. Despite Volcker's statements about the need to target monetary aggregates, he was not committed to these targets. Rather, he was far more concerned with using interest rate movements to wring inflation out of the economy. Volcker's primary reason for changing the Fed's operating procedure was to free his hand to manipulate interest rates in order to fight inflation. It was necessary to abandon interest rate targets if Volcker were to be able to raise interest rates sharply when a slowdown in the economy was required to dampen inflation. This view of Volcker's strategy suggests that the Fed's announced attachment to monetary aggregate targets may have been a smokescreen to keep the Fed from being blamed for the high interest rates that would result from the new policy.

The interest rate movements in Figure 20.4 support this interpretation of Fed strategy. After the October 1979 announcement, short-term interest rates were driven up by nearly 5%, until in March 1980 they exceeded 15%. With the imposition of credit control in March 1980 and the rapid decline in real GNP in the second quarter of 1980, the Fed eased up on its policy and allowed interest rates to decline sharply. With the recovery starting in July 1980, inflation remained persistent, still exceeding a 10% rate. Since the inflation fight was not yet won, the Fed tightened the screws again, sending short-term rates above the 15% level for a second time. Finally, the 1981–1982 recession with its large decline in output and high unemployment began to bring inflation down. With the inflationary psychology apparently broken, interest rates were allowed to fall.

The Fed's anti-inflation strategy during the October 1979–October 1982 period was neither intended nor likely to produce smooth growth in the monetary aggregates. Indeed, the large fluctuations in interest rates and the business cycle, along with financial innovation, helped generate volatile money growth.

---

[6]Another explanation focuses on the technical difficulties of monetary control when using a nonborrowed reserves operating target under a system of lagged reserve requirements, in which required reserves for a given week are calculated on the basis of the level of deposits two weeks earlier. See David Lindsey, "Nonborrowed Reserve Targeting and Monetary Control," in Laurence Meyer, ed., *Improving Money Stock Control* (Boston: Kluwer-Nijhoff, 1983), pp. 3–41.

Deemphasis of Monetary Aggregates: October 1982 and Beyond

In October 1982, with inflation in check, the Fed returned, in effect, to a policy of smoothing interest rates. It did this by placing less emphasis on monetary aggregate targets and shifting to borrowed reserves (discount loan borrowings) as an operating target. To see how a borrowed reserves target produces interest rate smoothing, let's consider what happens when the economy expands $(Y\uparrow)$ so that interest rates are driven up. The rise in interest rates $(i\uparrow)$ increases the incentives for banks to borrow more from the Fed, so borrowed reserves rise $(DL\uparrow)$. In order to prevent the resulting rise in borrowed reserves from exceeding the target level, the Fed must lower interest rates by bidding up the price of bonds with open market purchases. The outcome of targeting on borrowed reserves, then, is that the Fed prevents a rise in interest rates. In doing so, however, the Fed's open market purchases increase the monetary base $(MB\uparrow)$ and lead to a rise in the money supply $(M\uparrow)$, which produces a positive association of money and national income $(Y\uparrow\ M\uparrow)$. Schematically,

$$Y\uparrow\ \rightarrow i\uparrow\ \rightarrow DL\uparrow\ \rightarrow MB\uparrow\ \rightarrow M\uparrow$$

A recession causes the opposite chain of events, so that the borrowed reserves target prevents interest rates from falling and results in a fall in the monetary base, leading to a fall in the money supply $(Y\downarrow M\downarrow)$.

The deemphasis of monetary aggregates and the change to a borrowed reserves target is visible in Figure 20.4, where we see much smaller fluctuations in the federal funds rate after October 1982, but continue to have large fluctuations in money supply growth. Finally, in February 1987, the Fed announced that it would no longer even set $M1$ targets. The abandonment of $M1$ targets has been defended on two grounds. The first is that the rapid pace of financial innovation and deregulation has made the definition and measurement of money very difficult. The second is that there has been a breakdown in the stable relationship between $M1$ and economic activity (discussed in Chapter 23). These two arguments suggest that a monetary aggregate such as $M1$ may no longer be a reliable guide for monetary policy and the Fed now focuses more on $M2$.

The Fed's continuing deemphasis of monetary aggregates suggests that the Fed has returned to interest-smoothing operating procedures that, as we have seen, are likely to produce procyclical money supply growth in the future.

International Considerations: 1985 and Beyond

The increasing importance of international trade to the American economy has brought international considerations to the forefront of Federal reserve policy-making in recent years. By 1985, the strength of the dollar helped lead to a deterioration in American competitiveness with foreign businesses. In public pronouncements, Volcker and other Fed officials made it clear that the dollar was at too high a value and needed to come down. Since, as we will see in the next chapter, expansionary monetary policy is one way to lower the value of the dollar, it is no surprise that the Fed engineered an acceleration in the growth rates of the monetary aggregates in 1985 and 1986 and that the value of the dollar declined. By 1987, policymakers at the Fed agreed that the dollar had fallen sufficiently and sure enough, monetary growth in the United States slowed. These monetary policy actions by the Fed were encouraged by the process of **international policy coordination** (agreements among countries to enact policies cooperatively) that led to the Plaza Agreement in 1985 and the Louvre Accord in 1987 (Box 20.2). International considerations are likely to be a major factor in the conduct of American monetary policy in the future.

Box 20.2 **A Global Perspective**

International Policy Coordination: The Plaza Agreement and the Louvre Accord

By 1985 the decrease in the competitiveness of American corporations as a result of the strong dollar was raising strong sentiment in Congress for restricting imports. This protectionist threat to the international trading system stimulated finance ministers and the heads of central banks from the Group of Five (G-5) industrial countries—the United States, the United Kingdom, France, West Germany, and Japan—to reach an agreement at New York's Plaza Hotel in September 1985 to bring down the value of the dollar. From September 1985 until the beginning of 1987, the value of the dollar did indeed undergo a substantial decline, falling by 35% on average relative to foreign currencies. At this point, there was growing controversy over the decline in the dollar, and another meeting of the economic policymakers from the G-5 countries plus Canada took place in February 1987 at the Louvre Museum in Paris. There the policymakers agreed that exchange rates should be stabilized around the levels currently prevailing. Although the value of the dollar did continue to fluctuate relative to foreign currencies after the Louvre Accord, its downward trend had been checked as intended.

Because exchange rate movements were pretty much in line with the Plaza Agreement and the Louvre Accord, these attempts at international policy coordination have been seen as a success. However, other aspects of the agreements were not adhered to by the different countries. For example, West German and Japanese policymakers agreed that their countries should pursue more expansionary policies by increasing government spending and cutting taxes, while the United States agreed to try to bring down its budget deficit. The United States has not been particularly successful in lowering its deficit, and the Germans have been reluctant to pursue expansionary policies because of their concerns about inflation.

HOW WELL CAN THE FED CONTROL THE MONEY SUPPLY?

Our examination of the historical record of the Fed's conduct of monetary policy comes sadly to the conclusion that the Fed has not been able to exercise effective control over the money supply. Does this mean that the Fed cannot control the money supply? Some economists, particularly those at the Fed, contend that the Fed's failure to control the money supply in the past implies that this objective is unachievable. Our analysis of the money supply process in the last six chapters gives some credence to this position because we have seen that several factors outside of the Fed's control affect both the monetary base and money multiplier. Empirical evidence, however, supports a strong link between open market operations and the money supply, suggesting that over longer time periods—six months to a year—the money supply can be controlled quite accurately.

Many economists contend that the Fed's failure to control the money supply in the past has occurred because, despite Fed statements to the contrary, the Fed really did *not want* to control it. Specifically, the Fed was not willing to commit itself to policy procedures that would ensure better control.[7] They suggest that the Fed could obtain far better results if it were willing to do two things: (1) tie the discount rate to a market interest rate to decrease unwanted fluctuations in the volume of discount loans and (2) focus less on stabilizing interest rates and more on control of the monetary base and the money supply. There is some evidence that policy procedures utilizing these suggestions could result in greatly improved control of the money supply over even shorter time periods (such as three months).[8]

SUMMARY

1. There are six basic goals of monetary policy: high employment, economic growth, price stability, interest rate stability, stability of financial markets, and stability in foreign exchange markets.

2. By using intermediate and operating targets the Fed can more quickly judge whether its policies are on the right track and make midcourse corrections, rather than waiting a longer time until

it sees the final outcome of its policies on such goals as employment and the price level. The Fed's policy tools directly affect its operating targets which, in turn, affect the intermediate targets, which, in turn affect the goals.

3. Because interest rate and monetary aggregate targets are incompatible, the Fed must choose between them using three criteria: measurability, controllability, and the ability to predictably

---

[7]One possible reason is that such policy procedures would make the Fed more accountable for its actions, something that the theory of bureaucratic behavior suggests the Fed may want to avoid.

[8]See, for example, James Johannes and Robert Rasche, "Predicting the Money Multiplier," *Journal of Monetary Economics* 5 (July 1979): 301–325.

affect goal variables. Unfortunately, these criteria do not establish an overwhelming case for one set of targets over another.

4. Our examination of the historical record of the Fed's conduct of monetary policy suggests that the Fed has not been able to exercise effective control over the money supply.

5. Some economists contend that the historical record indicates that the Fed cannot control the money supply, while other economists contend the Fed could obtain better control over the money supply if it wants to. Empirical evidence supports a strong link between open market operations and the money supply, suggesting that over longer time periods, such as six months to a year, the money supply can be controlled quite effectively.

KEY TERMS

natural rate of
  unemployment

intermediate targets

operating targets

real bills doctrine

free reserves

international policy
  coordination

QUESTIONS AND PROBLEMS

* 1. "Unemployment is a bad thing and the government should make every effort to eliminate it." Do you agree? Explain.

2. Classify the following as either operating targets or intermediate targets and explain the reasons for your classifications.
   a) The three-month Treasury bill rate
   b) The monetary base
   c) $M2$

* 3. Answer true, false, or uncertain: "If the demand for money did not fluctuate, then the Fed could pursue both a money supply target and an interest rate target at the same time."

4. If the Fed has an interest rate target, why will an increase in money demand lead to a rise in the money supply?

* 5. What procedures can the Fed use to control the three-month Treasury bill rate? Why does control of this interest rate imply that the Fed will lose control of the money supply?

6. Compare the monetary base to $M1$ on the grounds of controllability and measurability. Which do you prefer as an intermediate target? Why?

* 7. "Interest rates are more accurately and quickly measured than the money supply. Thus an interest rate is preferred over the money supply as an intermediate target." Do you agree? Explain.

8. Explain why the rise in the discount rate in 1920 led to a sharp decline in the money supply.

* 9. How did the Fed's failure to perform its role as a lender of last resort contribute to the decline of the money supply in the 1930–1933 period?

10. Excess reserves are frequently called idle reserves, suggesting that they are not useful. Does the episode of the rise in reserve requirements in 1936–1937 indicate that this view is correct?

*11. "When the economy enters a recession, both a free reserve target or an interest rate target will lead to a slower rate of growth of the money supply." Explain why this statement is true. What does it say about the use of free reserves or interest rates as targets?

12. "The failure of the Fed to control the money supply in the 1970s and 1980s suggests that the Fed is not able to control the money supply." Do you agree? Why or why not?

*13. Which is more likely to produce smaller fluctuations in the federal funds rate, a nonborrowed reserves target or a borrowed reserves target? Why?

14. How can bank behavior and the Fed's behavior cause money supply growth to be procyclical (rising in booms and falling in recessions)?

*15. Why might the Fed say that it wants to control the money supply, but, in reality, is not serious about doing so?

PART VI

International Finance

CHAPTER 21

The Foreign Exchange Market

PREVIEW
In recent years, fewer Americans have traveled abroad than in the early- to mid-1980s. The decrease in foreign travel did not occur because Americans suddenly lost their taste for foreign adventure. The decrease occurred because American dollars had become worth less in terms of foreign currencies which made it more expensive to travel abroad.

The price of one currency in terms of another is called the **exchange rate.** It affects the economy and our daily lives because when the U.S. dollar becomes less valuable relative to foreign currencies, foreign goods and travel become more expensive. When the U.S. dollar rises in value, foreign goods and travel become cheaper. We begin our study of international finance by examining the **foreign exchange market,** in which exchange rates are determined.

In the 1980s, exchange rates were highly volatile. As shown in Figure 21.1, from the beginning of 1980 to early 1985, the dollar strengthened and its value relative to many other currencies climbed sharply—100% against the British pound, 90% against the West German mark, and 75% against the Swiss franc. From early 1985 to the end of 1990, the dollar weakened and fell in value relative to other currencies—50% against the Japanese yen, 55% against the West German mark, and 55% against the Swiss franc. What factors explain the former strength and later weakness of the dollar that has caused foreign goods to be more expensive since 1985 and has made overseas travel less of a bargain? Why are exchange rates so volatile from day to day?

In order to answer these questions, we develop a modern view of exchange rate determination that explains recent behavior in the foreign exchange market. Also in this and the next chapter we examine how international financial transactions are executed and what their effects are on the U.S. economy in general and on the conduct of monetary policy in particular.

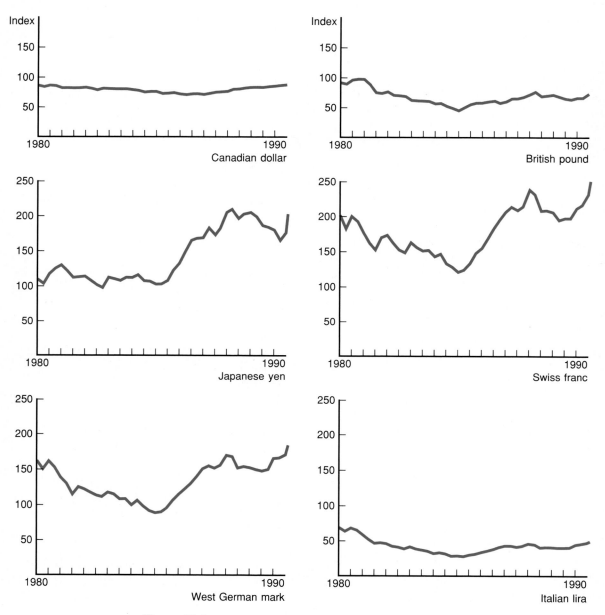

Figure 21.1
Exchange Rates: 1980–1990 Dollar prices of selected foreign currencies—monthly averages (index: March 1973 = 100). Note that a decline in these plots means a strengthening of the dollar, and an increase indicates a weakening of the dollar. Sources: *International Financial Statistics* and Citibase databank.

THE FOREIGN EXCHANGE MARKET

Most countries of the world have their own currencies: The United States has its dollar; France, its franc; Brazil, its cruziero; and India, its rupee. Trade between countries involves the exchange of different currencies (or more usually bank deposits denominated in different currencies) for one another. When an American firm buys foreign goods, services, or financial assets, for example, U.S. dollars (typically bank deposits denominated in U.S. dollars) must be exchanged for foreign currency (bank deposits denominated in the foreign currency).

The trading of currency and bank deposits denominated in particular currencies takes place in the foreign exchange market. The volume of these transactions in the United States alone averages over $100 billion daily. Transactions conducted in the foreign exchange market determine the rates at which currencies are exchanged for one another, which, in turn, determine the cost of purchasing foreign goods and financial assets.

What Are Foreign Exchange Rates?

There are two kinds of exchange rate transactions. The predominant set, called **spot transactions,** involve the immediate (although it takes two days for the exchange to take place) exchange of bank deposits. **Forward transactions** involve the exchange of bank deposits at some specified future date.

The Following the Financial News box that follows contains exchange rates as of Thursday, April 4, 1991. The first entry for the French franc lists the exchange rate for the spot transaction (called the **spot exchange rate**) on Thursday and is quoted in two ways: $.17748 per franc or 5.6345 francs per dollar. Americans generally regard the exchange rate with France as $.17748 per franc, while the French think of it as 5.6345 francs per dollar. The three entries immediately below the spot exchange rates list the rates for forward transactions (the **forward exchange rates**) that will take place 30, 90, and 180 days in the future.

When a currency increases in value, it has **appreciated;** when a currency falls in value and is worth fewer U.S. dollars, it has **depreciated.** At the beginning of 1980, for example, the French franc was valued at 25 cents, and on April 4, 1991, it was valued at 17.7 cents. The franc *depreciated* by 30%. Conversely, we could say that the U.S. dollar *appreciated* by 40%.

Why Are Exchange Rates Important?

Exchange rates are important because they affect the relative price of domestic and foreign goods. The dollar price of French goods to an American is determined by the interaction of two factors: (1) the price of French goods in francs and (2) the franc/dollar exchange rate.

Following the Financial News

Foreign Exchange Rates

Foreign Exchange Rates are published daily and appear in the "Currency Trading" column of the *Wall Street Journal*. The entries in an example of this column below are explained in the text.

CURRENCY TRADING

EXCHANGE RATES

Thursday, April 4, 1991

The New York foreign exchange selling rates below apply to trading among banks in amounts of $1 million and more, as quoted at 3 p.m. Eastern time by Bankers Trust Co.and other sources. Retail transactions provide fewer units of foreign currency per dollar.

Country	U.S. $ equiv. Thurs.	U.S. $ equiv. Wed.	Currency per U.S. $ Thurs.	Currency per U.S. $ Wed.
Argentina (Austral) ...	.0001031	.0001031	9700.26	9700.26
Australia (Dollar)	.7855	.7807	1.2731	1.2809
Austria (Schilling)	.08540	.08500	11.71	11.76
Bahrain (Dinar)	2.6532	2.6532	.3769	.3769
Belgium (Franc)				
Commercial rate	.02920	.02905	34.25	34.42
Brazil (Cruzeiro)	.00402	.00421	249.00	237.65
Britain (Pound)	1.7910	1.7725	.5583	.5642
30-Day Forward	1.7810	1.7629	.5615	.5672
90-Day Forward	1.7652	1.7469	.5665	.5724
180-Day Forward	1.7472	1.7276	.5723	.5788
Canada (Dollar)	.8657	.8651	1.1552	1.1560
30-Day Forward	.8632	.8627	1.1585	1.1591
90-Day Forward	.8586	.8580	1.1647	1.1655
180-Day Forward	.8527	.8522	1.1728	1.1735
Chile (Peso)	.002917	.002997	342.84	333.66
China (Renmimbi)	.191663	.191663	5.2175	5.2175
Colombia (Peso)	.001706	.001747	586.00	572.33
Denmark (Krone)	.1566	.1557	6.3877	6.4242
Ecuador (Sucre)				
Floating rate	.000966	.000966	1035.00	1035.00
Finland (Markka)	.25566	.25310	3.9207	3.9510
► France (Franc)	.17748	.17606	5.6345	5.6800
30-Day Forward	.17701	.17558	5.6495	5.6954
90-Day Forward	.17612	.17469	5.6780	5.7245
180-Day Forward	.17489	.17344	5.7180	5.7657
Germany (Mark)	.6011	.5972	1.6635	1.6745
30-Day Forward	.5996	.5957	1.6678	1.6786
90-Day Forward	.5966	.5927	1.6763	1.6872
180-Day Forward	.5923	.5884	1.6883	1.6995
Greece (Drachma)	.005546	.005504	180.30	181.70
Hong Kong (Dollar) ...	.12825	.12826	7.7970	7.7965
India (Rupee)	.05112	.05112	19.56	19.56
Indonesia (Rupiah)	.0005255	.0005255	1903.02	1903.02
Ireland (Punt)	1.6665	1.5965	.6001	.6264
Israel (Shekel)	.4494	.4571	2.2251	2.1878
Italy (Lira)	.0008081	.0008031	1237.50	1245.25
Japan (Yen)	.007375	.007281	135.60	137.35
30-Day Forward	.007363	.007270	135.82	137.55
90-Day Forward	.007348	.007255	136.10	137.84
180-Day Forward	.007332	.007241	136.38	138.11
Jordan (Dinar)	1.5029	1.5029	.6654	.6654
Kuwait (Dinar)	z	z	z	z
Lebanon (Pound)	.001060	.001060	943.00	943.00
Malaysia (Ringgit)	.3639	.3642	2.7480	2.7455
Malta (Lira)	3.0303	3.0303	.3300	.3300
Mexico (Peso)				
Floating rate	.0003351	.0003351	2984.01	2984.01
Netherland (Guilder) .	.5333	.5306	1.8750	1.8845
New Zealand (Dollar)	.5935	.5930	1.6849	1.6863
Norway (Krone)	.1543	.1534	6.4795	6.5197
Pakistan (Rupee)	.0439	.0439	22.78	22.78
Peru (New Sol)	1.7809	1.8457	.56	.54
Philippines (Peso)	.03676	.03676	27.20	27.20
Portugal (Escudo)	.006826	.006836	146.50	146.28
Saudi Arabia (Riyal) ..	.26752	.26752	3.7381	3.7381
Singapore (Dollar)	.5650	.5659	1.7700	1.7670
South Africa (Rand)				
Commercial rate	.3694	.3709	2.7073	2.6958
Financial rate	.3003	.2996	3.3300	3.3380
South Korea (Won)	.0013779	.0013779	725.75	725.75
Spain (Peseta)	.009723	.009653	102.85	103.60
Sweden (Krona)	.1662	.1650	6.0155	6.0615
Switzerland (Franc) ..	.7145	.7050	1.3995	1.4185
30-Day Forward	.7130	.7035	1.4025	1.4215
90-Day Forward	.7102	.7009	1.4080	1.4267
180-Day Forward	.7077	.6982	1.4131	1.4323
Taiwan (Dollar)	.036470	.037120	27.42	26.94
Thailand (Baht)	.03906	.03906	25.60	25.60
Turkey (Lira)	.0002701	.0002715	3703.02	3683.01
United Arab (Dirham) .	.2723	.2723	3.6725	3.6725
Uruguay (New Peso)				
Financial	.000563	.000563	1775.00	1775.00
Venezuela (Bolivar)				
Floating rate	.01835	.01880	54.50	53.19
SDR	1.35766	1.35966	.73656	.73548
ECU	1.22380	1.22961	....	....

Special Drawing Rights (SDR) are based on exchange rates for the U.S., German, British, French and Japanese currencies. Source: International Monetary Fund.

European Currency Unit (ECU) is based on a basket of community currencies. Source: European Community Commission.

z-Not quoted.

Source: *Wall Street Journal* (April 5, 1991).

Suppose, for example, that Wanda the Winetaster, an American, decides to buy a bottle of 1961 (a very good year) Chateau Lafite Rothschild to complete her wine cellar. If the price of the wine in France is 2000 francs and the exchange rate is $.17748 to the franc, the wine will cost Wanda $355 (= 2000 francs × .17748). Now suppose Wanda delays her purchase by two months, at which time the French franc exchange rate has appreciated to $.20 per franc. If the domestic price of the bottle of Lafite Rothschild remains at 2000 francs, its dollar cost will have risen from $355 to $400.

The same currency appreciation, however, makes the price of foreign goods in that country less expensive. At an exchange rate of $.17748 per franc, an Apple computer priced at $2000 costs Claude the Computer Programmer 11,269 francs; if the exchange rate appreciates to $0.20 per franc, the computer will cost only 10,000 francs.

A depreciation of the franc will lower the cost of French goods in America, but will raise the cost of American goods in France. If the franc drops in value to $0.10, then Wanda's bottle of Lafite Rothschild will cost her only $200 instead of $355, while the Apple computer will cost Claude 20,000 francs rather than 11,269.

Such reasoning leads to the conclusion: ***When a country's currency appreciates (rises in value relative to other currencies), the country's goods abroad become more expensive and foreign goods in that country become cheaper (holding domestic prices constant in the two countries). Conversely, when a country's currency depreciates, its goods abroad become cheaper while foreign goods in that country become more expensive.***

An appreciation of a currency can make it harder for domestic manufacturers to sell their goods abroad and can increase the competition at home from foreign goods because they cost less. From 1980 to early 1985, the appreciating dollar hurt American industries. For instance, the American steel industry was hurt not just because sales abroad of the more expensive American steel declined, but also because sales of relatively cheap foreign steel in the United States increased. Although appreciation of the U.S. dollar hurt some domestic businesses, American consumers benefited because foreign goods were less expensive. Japanese video cassette recorders and cameras and the cost of vacationing in Europe fell in price as a result of the strong dollar.

How Is Foreign Exchange Traded?

You cannot go to a centralized location to watch exchange rates being determined; currencies are not traded on exchanges such as the New York Stock Exchange. Instead, the foreign exchange market is organized as an over-the-counter market in which several hundred dealers (mostly banks) stand ready to buy and sell deposits denominated in foreign currencies. Because these dealers are in constant telephone and computer contact, the market is very competitive; in effect, it functions no differently from a centralized market.

An important point to note is that while banks, companies, and governments talk about buying and selling currencies in foreign exchange markets, they do not take a fistful of dollar bills and sell them for British pound notes. Rather, most trades involve the buying and selling of bank deposits denominated in different currencies. So when we say that a bank is buying dollars in the foreign exchange market, what we actually mean is that the bank is buying deposits *denominated in dollars*.

Trades in the foreign exchange market consist of transactions in excess of $1 million. The market that determines the exchange rates in the Following the Financial News box is not where one would buy foreign currency for a trip abroad. Instead, we buy foreign currency in the retail market from dealers such as American Express or from banks. Because retail prices are higher than wholesale, when we buy foreign exchange, we obtain fewer units of foreign currency per dollar than exchange rates in the box indicate.

EXCHANGE RATES IN THE LONG RUN

Like the price of any good or asset in a free market, exchange rates are determined by the interaction of supply and demand. To simplify our analysis of exchange rates in a free market, we will divide it into two parts. First, we will examine how exchange rates are determined in the long run; then we will use our knowledge of the long-run determinants of the exchange rate to help us understand how they are determined in the short run.

The Law of One Price

The starting point for understanding how exchange rates are determined is a simple idea called the **law of one price,** which states: If two countries produce an identical good, the price of the good should be the same throughout the world no matter which country produces it. Suppose American steel costs $100 per ton and Japanese steel costs 10,000 yen per ton and the steel is identical. The law of one price suggests that the exchange rate between the yen and the dollar must be 100 yen per dollar ($0.01 per yen) in order for one ton of American steel to sell for 10,000 yen in Japan (the price of Japanese steel) and one ton of Japanese steel to sell for $100 in the United States. If the exchange rate were 200 yen/$, then Japanese steel would sell for $50 per ton in the United States or $50 less than the American steel, while American steel would sell for 20,000 yen per ton in Japan (10,000 yen more than Japanese steel). Because American steel would be more expensive than Japanese steel in both countries and it is identical to Japanese steel, the demand for American steel would go to zero. Given a fixed dollar price for the American steel, the resulting excess supply of American steel will be eliminated only if the exchange rate falls to 100 yen/$, making the price of American equal to Japanese steel in both countries.

The Theory of Purchasing Power Parity

One of the most prominent theories of how exchange rates are determined is the **theory of purchasing power parity (PPP).** It states that exchange rates between any two currencies will adjust to reflect changes in the price levels of the two countries. The theory of PPP is simply an application of the law of one price to countries' price levels rather than to individual prices. Suppose the yen price of Japanese steel rises 10% (to 11,000 yen) relative to the dollar price of American steel (unchanged at $100). In order for the law of one price to hold, the exchange rate must rise to 110 yen/$, a 10% appreciation of the dollar. Applying the law of one price to the price levels in the two countries produces the theory of purchasing power parity, which maintains that if the Japanese *price level* rises 10% relative to the U.S. *price level*, the dollar will appreciate by 10%.

As our U.S./Japanese example demonstrates, the theory of PPP suggests that if one country's price level rises relative to another's, its currency should depreciate (the other country's currency should appreciate). As you can see in Figure 21.2, this prediction is borne out in the long run. From 1973 to early 1990, the British price level rose 75% relative to the U.S. price level, and as the theory of PPP predicts, the dollar appreciated, although by 40%, an amount smaller than the 75% increase predicted by PPP.

On the other hand, as the same figure indicates, PPP theory often has little predictive power in the short run. From early 1985 to the end of 1987, for example, the British price level rose relative to that of the United States. Instead of appreciating, as PPP theory predicts, the U.S. dollar actually depreciated by 40%. Thus though PPP theory provides *some* guidance to the long-run movement of exchange rates, it is not perfect and in the short run is a particularly poor predictor. What explains PPP theory's failure to always predict well?

Why the Theory of Purchasing Power Parity Cannot Fully Explain Exchange Rates   The PPP conclusion that exchange rates are determined solely by

Figure 21.2
Purchasing Power Parity: United States/ United Kingdom. 1973– 1990 (Index: March 1973 = 100) Source: *International Financial Statistics.*

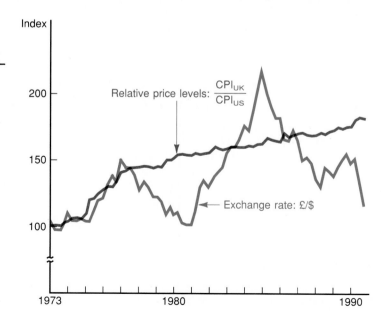

changes in relative price levels rests on the assumption that all goods are identical in both countries. When this assumption is true, the law of one price states that the relative prices of all these goods (that is, the relative price level between the two countries) will determine the exchange rate. The assumption that goods are identical may not be too unreasonable for American and Japanese steel, but is it a reasonable assumption for American and Japanese cars? Is a Toyota the equivalent of a Chevrolet?

Since Toyotas and Chevys are obviously not identical, their prices do not have to be equal. Toyotas can be more expensive relative to Chevys and both Americans and Japanese will still purchase Toyotas. Because the law of one price does not hold for all goods, a rise in the price of Toyotas relative to Chevys will not necessarily mean that the yen must depreciate by the amount of the relative price increase of Toyotas over Chevys.

PPP theory furthermore does not take into account that many goods and services (whose prices are included in a measure of a country's price level) are not traded across borders. Housing, land, and services such as restaurant meals, haircuts, and golf lessons are not traded goods. Thus, even though the prices of these items might rise and lead to a higher price level relative to another country's, there would be little direct effect on the exchange rate.

Factors That Affect Exchange Rates in the Long Run

Our analysis indicates that relative price levels as well as additional factors affect the exchange rate. In the long run there are four major ones: (1) relative price levels, (2) tariffs and quotas, (3) preferences for domestic versus foreign goods, and (4) productivity. We will examine how each of these factors affects the exchange rate while holding the others constant.

The basic reasoning proceeds along the following lines: Anything that increases the demand for domestic goods relative to foreign goods tends to appreciate the domestic currency because domestic goods will continue to sell well even when the value of the domestic currency is higher. Similarly, anything that increases the demand for foreign goods relative to domestic goods tends to depreciate the domestic currency because domestic goods will only continue to sell well if the value of the domestic currency is lower.

Relative Price Levels In line with PPP theory, when prices of American goods rise (holding prices of foreign goods constant), the demand for American goods falls and the dollar tends to depreciate so that American goods can still sell well. On the other hand, if prices of Japanese goods rise so that the relative prices of American goods fall, the demand for American goods increases and the dollar tends to appreciate because American goods will continue to sell well even with a higher value of the domestic currency. ***In the long run, a rise in a country's price level (relative to the foreign price level)*** *causes its currency to depreciate, while a fall in the country's relative price level causes its currency to appreciate.*

Tariffs and Quotas   Barriers to free trade such as **tariffs** (taxes on imported goods) and **quotas** (restrictions on the quantity of foreign goods that can be imported) can affect the exchange rate. Suppose that the United States imposes a tariff or a quota on Japanese steel. These trade barriers increase the demand for American steel, and the dollar tends to appreciate because American steel will still sell well even with a higher value of the dollar. *Tariffs and quotas cause a country's currency to appreciate in the long run.*

Preferences for Domestic versus Foreign Goods   If the Japanese develop an appetite for American goods, say, for Florida oranges and American movies, then the increased demand for American goods (exports) tends to appreciate the dollar because the American goods will continue to sell well even with a higher value of the dollar. Likewise, if Americans decide that they prefer Japanese cars to American cars, the increased demand for Japanese goods (imports) tends to depreciate the dollar. *Increased demand for a country's exports causes its currency to appreciate in the long run, while increased demand for imports causes its currency to depreciate.*

Productivity   If one country becomes more productive than other countries, businesses in that country can lower the prices of domestic goods relative to foreign goods and still earn a profit. As a result, the demand for domestic goods rises and the domestic currency tends to appreciate because domestic goods will continue to sell well with a higher value of the currency. If its productivity lags behind other countries, on the other hand, its goods become relatively more expensive and the currency tends to depreciate. *In the long run, as a country becomes more productive relative to other countries, its currency appreciates.*[1]

Study Guide

The trick to figuring out what long-run effect a factor has on the exchange rate is to remember the following: *If a factor increases the demand for domestic goods relative to foreign goods, the domestic currency will appreciate, while if a factor decreases the relative demand for domestic goods, the*

---

[1] A country might be so small that a change in productivity or the preferences for domestic versus foreign goods would have no effect on prices of these goods relative to foreign goods. In this case changes in productivity or changes in preferences for domestic versus foreign goods affect the country's income but will not necessarily affect the value of the currency. In our analysis, we are assuming that these factors can affect relative prices and consequently the exchange rate.

Table 21.1 **Summary: Factors That Affect Exchange Rates in the Long Run**

Factor		Response of the Exchange Rate $(E)^b$	
Domestic price level[a]	↑	E	↓
Tariffs and quotas[a]	↑	E	↑
Import demand	↑	E	↓
Export demand	↑	E	↑
Productivity[a]	↑	E	↑

Note: Only increases (↑) in the factors are shown; the effects of decreases in the variables on the exchange rate are the opposite of those indicated in the second column.
[a] relative to foreign countries
[b] E is defined so that E ↑ means that the currency has appreciated. For the United States, this means that E represents units of foreign currency per dollar.

domestic currency will depreciate. See how this works by explaining what happens to the exchange rate when any of the factors in Table 21.1 declines rather than increases.

Our long-run theory of exchange rate behavior is summarized in Table 21.1. We use the convention that the exchange rate (E) is quoted so that an appreciation of the currency corresponds to a rise in the exchange rate. In the case of the United States, this means that we are quoting the exchange rate as units of foreign currency per dollar (say yen/\$).[2]

DETERMINATION OF THE EXCHANGE RATE IN THE SHORT RUN

We have developed a theory of the long-run behavior of exchange rates. However, if we are to understand why exchange rates exhibit such large changes (sometimes several percent) from day to day, we must develop a theory of how current exchange rates (spot exchange rates) are determined in the short run.

The key to understanding the short-run behavior of exchange rates is to recognize that an exchange rate is the price of domestic bank deposits (those denominated in the domestic currency) in terms of foreign bank deposits

---

[2] In their professional writings, many economists quote exchange rates as units of domestic currency per foreign currency so that an appreciation of the domestic currency is labeled as a fall in the exchange rate. The opposite convention is used in the text here because it is more intuitive to think of an appreciation of the domestic currency as a rise in the exchange rate.

(those denominated in the foreign currency). Because the exchange rate is the price of one asset in terms of another, the natural way to investigate the short-run determination of exchange rates is through an asset market approach that relies heavily on the theory of asset demand developed in Chapter 5. As you will see, however, the long-run determinants of the exchange rate we have just outlined also play an important role in the short-run asset market approach.[3]

Earlier approaches to exchange rate determination emphasized the role of import and export demand. The more modern asset market approach used here does not emphasize the flows of purchases of exports and imports over short periods, because these transactions are quite small relative to the amount of domestic and foreign bank deposits at any given time. For example, foreign exchange transactions in the United States each year are well over twenty-five times greater than the amount of U.S. exports and imports. Thus, over short periods such as a year, decisions to hold domestic versus foreign assets play a much greater role in exchange rate determination than does the demand for exports and imports.

Comparing Expected Returns of Domestic and Foreign Deposits

In this analysis we treat the United States as the home country; so domestic bank deposits are denominated in dollars. For simplicity we will use francs to mean the foreign country's currency, so that foreign bank deposits are denominated in francs. The theory of asset demand suggests that the most important factor affecting the demand for domestic (dollar) deposits and foreign (franc) deposits is the expected return on these assets relative to one another. When Americans or foreigners expect the return on dollar deposits to be high relative to the return on foreign deposits, there is a higher demand for dollar deposits and a correspondingly lower demand for franc deposits. To understand how the demands for dollar and foreign deposits change, we need to compare the expected returns on dollar deposits and foreign deposits.

To illustrate further, suppose that dollar deposits have an interest rate (expected return payable in dollars) of $i^\$$, while foreign bank deposits have an interest rate (expected return payable in the foreign currency, francs) of i^F. To compare the expected returns of dollar deposits and foreign deposits, investors must convert the returns into the currency unit they use.

First let us examine how Francois the Foreigner compares the returns on dollar and foreign deposits denominated in his currency, the franc.

---

[3] For a further description of the modern asset market approach to exchange rate determination that we use here, see Paul Krugman and Maurice Obstfeld, *International Economics* (New York: HarperCollins, 1991).

When he considers the expected return of dollar deposits in terms of foreign currency he recognizes that it does not equal $i^\$$: Instead, the expected return must be adjusted for any expected appreciation or depreciation of the dollar. If the dollar were expected to appreciate by 7%, for example, then the expected return on dollar deposits in terms of francs is 7% higher because the dollar has become worth 7% more in terms of francs. Thus if the interest rate on dollar deposits is 10%, with an expected appreciation of the dollar of 7%, the expected return on the dollar deposit in terms of francs is 17% (the 10% interest rate plus the 7% expected appreciation of the dollar). On the other hand, if the dollar were expected to depreciate by 7% over the year, the expected return on dollar deposits in terms of the foreign currency would be only 3%—the 10% interest rate minus the 7% expected depreciation of the dollar.

Writing the currency exchange rate (the spot exchange rate) as E_t and the expected exchange rate for the next period as E^e_{t+1}, we can write the expected rate of appreciation of the dollar as $(E^e_{t+1} - E_t)/E_t$. Our reasoning indicates that the expected return on the dollar deposit ($RET^\$$) in terms of foreign currency can be written as the sum of the interest rate on dollar deposits plus the expected appreciation of the dollar:[4]

$$RET^\$ \text{ in terms of francs} = i^\$ + (E^e_{t+1} - E_t)/E_t$$

On the other hand, Francois' expected return on the foreign franc deposit (RET^F) in terms of francs is just i^F. Thus in terms of francs, the relative expected return for dollar deposits (that is, the difference between the expected return for dollar deposits and foreign deposits) is calculated by subtracting i^F from the above expression to yield

$$\text{relative } RET^\$ = i^\$ - i^F + (E^e_{t+1} - E_t)/E_t \tag{21.1}$$

As the relative expected return on dollar deposits increases, foreigners will want to hold more dollar deposits and fewer foreign deposits.

Next let us look at the decision to hold dollar deposits versus franc deposits from Al the American's point of view. Following the same reasoning we used to evaluate the decision for Francois, we know that the expected

---

[4] This expression is actually an approximation of the expected return in terms of francs, which can be more precisely calculated by thinking how a foreigner invests in the dollar deposit. Suppose that Francois decides to put one franc into dollar deposits. First he buys $1/E_t$ of U.S. dollar deposits (recall that E_t, the exchange rate between dollar and franc deposits, is quoted in francs/\$) and at the end of the period is paid $(1 + i^\$) \times 1/E_t$ in dollars. To convert this amount into the number of francs he expects to receive at the end of the period, he multiplies this quantity by E^e_{t+1}. Francois' expected return on his initial investment of one franc can thus be written down as $(1 + i^\$) \times E^e_{t+1}/E_t$ minus his initial investment of one franc:

$$(1 + i^\$) \times E^e_{t+1}/E_t - 1$$

which can be rewritten as

$$i^\$ \times (E^e_{t+1}/E_t) + (E^e_{t+1} - E_t)/E_t$$

which is approximately equal to the expression in the text, since E^e_{t+1}/E_t is typically close to one.

return on foreign deposits (RET^F) in terms of dollars is the interest rate on foreign deposits (i^F) plus the expected appreciation of the foreign currency [equal to minus the expected appreciation of the dollar, $-(E^e_{t+1} - E_t)/E_t$], that is,

$$RET^F \text{ in terms of dollars} = i^F - (E^e_{t+1} - E_t)/E_t$$

If the interest rate on franc deposits is 5%, for example, and the dollar is expected to appreciate by 4%, then the expected return on a franc deposit in terms of dollars is 1%. Al earns the 5% interest rate, but he expects to lose 4% because he expects the franc to be worth 4% less in terms of dollars as a result of the dollar appreciation.

Al's expected return on the dollar deposit ($RET^\$$) in terms of dollars is just $i^\$$. Hence in terms of dollars, the relative expected return for dollar deposits is calculated by subtracting the above expression from $i^\$$ to obtain

$$\text{relative } RET^\$ = i^\$ - [i^F - (E^e_{t+1} - E_t/E_t)] = $$
$$i^\$ - i^F + (E^e_{t+1} - E_t)/E_t$$

This equation is the same as the one describing Francois' relative expected return on dollar deposits (calculated in terms of francs). The key point here is that the relative expected return of dollar deposits is the same whether it is calculated by Francois in terms of francs or by Al in terms of dollars. Thus, as the relative expected return on dollar deposits increases, both foreigners and domestic residents respond in exactly the same way—both will want to hold more dollar deposits and fewer foreign deposits.

The Interest Parity Condition

We currently live in a world in which there is **capital mobility,** that is, foreigners can easily purchase American assets such as dollar deposits and Americans can easily purchase foreign assets such as franc deposits. Because foreign bank deposits and American bank deposits have similar risk and liquidity and because there are few impediments to capital mobility, it is reasonable to assume that the deposits are perfect substitutes (that is, equally desirable). When capital is mobile and when bank deposits are perfect substitutes, if the expected return on dollar deposits is above that for foreign deposits, then both foreigners and Americans will only want to hold dollar deposits and will be unwilling to hold foreign deposits. On the other hand, if the expected return on foreign deposits is higher than on dollar deposits, both foreigners and Americans will not want to hold any dollar deposits and will only want to hold foreign deposits. In order for existing supplies of both dollar deposits and foreign deposits to be held, it therefore must be true that there is no difference in their expected returns; that is, the relative expected return in expression (21.1) must equal zero. This condition can be rewritten from (21.1) as:

$$i^\$ = i^F - (E^e_{t+1} - E_t)/E_t \tag{21.2}$$

This equation is called the **interest parity condition** and it states that the domestic interest rate equals the foreign interest rate minus the expected appreciation of the domestic currency. Equivalently, this condition can be stated in a more intuitive way: The domestic interest rate equals the foreign interest rate plus the expected appreciation of the foreign currency. If the domestic interest rate is above the foreign interest rate, this means that there is a positive expected appreciation of the foreign currency which compensates for the lower foreign interest rate. A domestic interest rate of 15% versus a foreign interest rate of 10% means that the expected appreciation of the foreign currency must be 5% (or equivalently, that the expected depreciation of the dollar must be 5%).

There are several ways to look at the interest parity condition. First, we should recognize that interest parity just means that the expected returns are the same for dollar deposits and foreign franc deposits. To see this, note that the left side of the interest parity condition (21.2) is the expected return on dollar deposits, while the right side is the expected return on franc deposits, both calculated in terms of a single currency, the U.S. dollar. Given our assumption that domestic and foreign bank deposits are perfect substitutes (equally desirable), the interest parity condition is an equilibrium condition for the foreign exchange market. (Later in the chapter we will show how our analysis can be modified if domestic and foreign bank deposits are not perfect substitutes.) Only when the exchange rate is such that expected returns on domestic and foreign deposits are equal—that is, interest parity holds—will the outstanding domestic and foreign deposits be willingly held.

Equilibrium in the Foreign Exchange Market

To see how the interest parity equilibrium condition works in determining the exchange rate, our first step is to examine how the expected returns on franc and dollar deposits change as the current exchange rate changes.

Expected Return on the Franc Deposit   As we demonstrated earlier, the expected return in terms of dollars on the foreign deposit, RET^F, is the foreign interest rate minus the expected appreciation of the domestic currency: $i^F - (E^e_{t+1} - E_t)/E_t$. Suppose that the foreign interest rate, i^F, is 10% and the expected exchange rate next period, E^e_{t+1}, is 10 francs/\$. When the current exchange rate E_t is at 9.5 francs/\$, the expected appreciation of the dollar is $(10.0 - 9.5)/9.5 = 0.052 = 5.2\%$, so that the expected return in terms of dollars for the franc deposit, RET^F, is 4.8% (= the 10% foreign interest rate minus the 5.2% dollar appreciation). This expected return when $E_t = 9.5$ francs/\$ is plotted as point A in Figure 21.3. At a higher current exchange rate of $E_t = 10$ francs/\$, the expected appreciation of the dollar is zero since E^e_{t+1} also equals 10 francs/\$. Hence RET^F, the expected dollar return of the franc deposit, is now just $i^F = 10\%$. This expected return

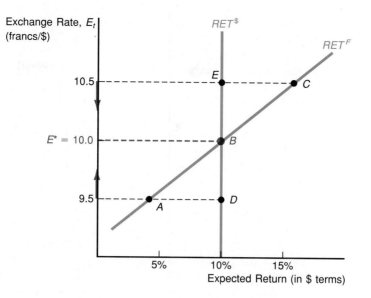

Figure 21.3
Equilibrium in the Foreign Exchange Market   Equilibrium in the foreign exchange market occurs at the intersection of the expected return on franc deposits schedule (RET^F) and the expected return on dollar deposits schedule ($RET^\$$) at point B. The equilibrium exchange rate is $E^* = 10$ francs/$.

of franc deposits when $E_t = 10$ francs/$ is plotted as point B. At an even higher exchange rate of $E_t = 10.5$ francs/$, the expected appreciation of the dollar is now -4.8% [$= (10.0 - 10.5)/10.5 = -.048$]; so the expected dollar return of the foreign deposit, RET^F, has now risen to 14.8% [$= 10\% - (-4.8\%)$]. This combination of this exchange rate and expected return for franc deposits is plotted as point C.

The curve connecting these points is the expected return on franc deposits schedule in Figure 21.3, marked as RET^F, and as you can see it is upward sloping; that is, as the exchange rate E_t rises, the expected return on franc deposits rises. The intuition for this upward slope is that, because the expected exchange rate next period is held constant, as the current exchange rate rises, there is less expected appreciation of the dollar. Thus a higher current exchange rate means a greater expected appreciation of the foreign currency in the future, which increases the expected return on foreign deposits in terms of dollars.

Expected Return on Dollar Deposits   The expected return on dollar deposits in terms of dollars, $RET^\$$, is always the interest rate on dollar deposits, $i^\$$, no matter what the exchange rate is. Suppose that the interest rate on dollar deposits is 10%. The expected return on dollar deposits whether at an exchange rate of 9.5, 10.0, or 10.5 francs/$ is always 10% (points D, B, and E). The line connecting these points is the expected return on dollar deposits schedule, marked as $RET^\$$ in Figure 21.3.

Equilibrium   The intersection of the expected return on dollar deposits ($RET^\$$) and the expected return on franc deposits (RET^F) schedules is where equilibrium occurs in the foreign exchange market. At the equilibrium point B where the exchange rate, E^*, is 10 francs/\$, the interest parity condition is satisfied because the expected returns on dollar and franc deposits are equal.

To see that the exchange rate will actually head toward the equilibrium exchange rate, E^*, let's see what happens if the exchange rate is at 10.5 francs/\$, a value above the equilibrium exchange rate. As we can see in Figure 21.3, the expected return on franc deposits at point C is greater than the expected return on dollar deposits at point E. Since dollar and franc deposits are equally desirable, people will not want to hold any dollar deposits, and holders of dollar deposits will try to sell them for franc deposits in the foreign exchange market (which is referred to as selling dollars and buying francs). However, because the expected return on these dollar deposits is below that on franc deposits, no one holding francs will be willing to exchange them for dollar deposits. The resulting excess supply of dollar deposits means that the price of the dollar deposits relative to franc deposits must fall; that is, the exchange rate falls as is illustrated by the downward arrow drawn in the figure at the exchange rate of 10.5 francs/\$. The decline in the exchange rate will continue until point B is reached at the equilibrium exchange rate of 10 francs/\$ where the expected return on dollar and franc deposits is now equalized.

Now let us look at what happens when the exchange rate is at 9.5 francs/\$, a value below the equilibrium level. Here the expected return on dollar deposits is greater than that on franc deposits. No one will want to hold franc deposits and so they will try to sell them to buy dollar deposits (sell francs and buy dollars), thus driving up the exchange rate as illustrated by the upward arrow. As the exchange rate rises, there is a smaller expected appreciation of the dollar and so a higher expected appreciation of the franc, thereby increasing the expected return on franc deposits. Finally, when the exchange rate has risen to $E^* = 10$ francs/\$, the expected return on franc deposits has risen enough so that it again equals the expected return on dollar deposits.

EXPLAINING CHANGES IN EXCHANGE RATES

In order to explain how an exchange rate changes over time, we have to understand the factors that shift the expected return schedules for domestic (dollar) deposits and foreign (franc) deposits.

Shifts in the Expected Return Schedule for Foreign Deposits

As we have seen, the expected return on foreign (franc) deposits depends on the foreign interest rate, i^F, and on minus the expected appreciation of the dollar, $-(E_{t+1}^e - E_t)/E_t$. Since a change in the current exchange rate, E_t, results in a *movement along* the expected return schedule for franc deposits, factors that *shift* this schedule must work through the foreign interest rate, i^F, and the expected future exchange rate, E_{t+1}^e. We will examine the effect of changes in these factors on the expected return schedule for franc deposits (RET^F), holding everything else constant.

Study Guide

To grasp how the expected return schedule for franc deposits shifts, just think of yourself as an investor who is considering putting funds into foreign deposits. When a variable changes (i^F, for example), decide whether at a given level of the current exchange rate, holding all other variables constant, you would earn a higher or lower expected return on franc deposits.

Changes in the Foreign Interest Rate (i^F)   If the interest rate on foreign deposits (i^F) increases, holding everything else constant, the expected return on these deposits must also increase. Hence at a given exchange rate, the increase in i^F leads to a rightward shift in the expected returns schedule for franc deposits from RET_1^F to RET_2^F in Figure 21.4. As you can see in the figure, the outcome is a depreciation of the dollar from E_1 to E_2. An alternative way to see this is to recognize that the increase in the expected return on franc deposits at the original equilibrium exchange rate resulting from the rise in i^F means that people will want to buy francs and sell dollars so the value of the dollar must fall. Our analysis thus generates the following con-

Figure 21.4
Shifts in the Expected Return on Foreign Deposits Schedule (RET^F) An increase in the expected return on foreign deposits, which occurs when either the foreign interest rate rises or the expected future exchange rate falls, shifts the expected return on foreign deposits schedule from RET_1^F to RET_2^F and the exchange rate falls from E_1 to E_2.

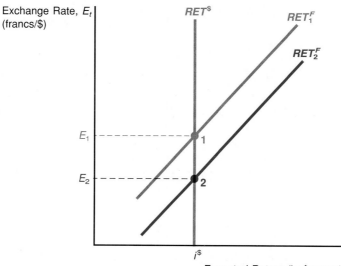

clusion: ***An increase in the foreign interest rate, i^F, shifts the RET^F schedule to the right and causes the domestic currency to depreciate ($E \downarrow$).***

On the other hand, if i^F falls, the expected return on franc deposits falls, the RET^F schedule shifts in to the left, and the exchange rate rises. This yields the conclusion: ***A decrease in i^F shifts the RET^F schedule to the left and causes the domestic currency to appreciate ($E \uparrow$).***

Changes in the Expected Future Exchange Rate (E^e_{t+1})   Any factor that causes the expected future exchange rate to fall decreases the expected appreciation of the dollar and hence raises the expected appreciation of the franc. The result is a higher expected return on franc deposits, which shifts the expected return on franc deposits schedule to the right and leads to a decline in the exchange rate as in Figure 21.4. On the other hand, a rise in E^e_{t+1} raises the expected appreciation of the dollar, lowers the expected return on foreign deposits, shifts the RET^F schedule to the left, and raises the exchange rate. To summarize: ***A rise in the expected future exchange rate shifts the expected return on foreign deposits schedule to the left and causes an appreciation of the domestic currency; a fall in the expected future exchange rate shifts the RET^F schedule to the right and causes a depreciation of the domestic currency.***

Our analysis of the long-run determinants of the exchange rate indicates the factors that influence the expected future exchange rate: the relative price level, relative tariffs and quotas, import demand, export demand, and relative productivity (refer back to Table 21.1). The theory of purchasing power parity suggests that if a higher American price level relative to the foreign price level is expected to persist, the dollar will depreciate in the long run. A higher expected relative American price level should thus have a tendency to raise the expected return on franc deposits, shift the RET^F schedule to the right, and lower the current exchange rate.

Similarly, the four other long-run determinants of the exchange rate we discussed can also influence the expected return on franc deposits and the current exchange rate. Briefly, the following changes will increase the expected return on franc deposits, shift the RET^F schedule to the right, and cause a depreciation of the domestic currency, the dollar: (1) expectations of a rise in the American price level relative to the foreign price level, (2) expectations of lower American tariffs and quotas relative to foreign tariffs and quotas, (3) expectations of higher American import demand, (4) expectations of lower foreign demand for American exports, and (5) expectations of lower American productivity relative to foreign productivity.

Shifts in the Expected Return Schedule for Domestic Deposits

Since the expected return on domestic (dollar) deposits is just the interest rate on these deposits, $i^\$$, this interest rate is the only factor that shifts the expected return on the dollar deposits schedule.

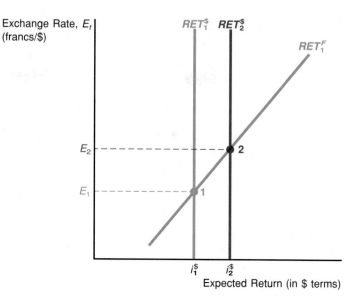

Figure 21.5
Shifts in the Expected Return on Domestic Deposits Schedule (RET$^\$$) An increase in the expected return on dollar deposits ($i^\$$) shifts the expected return on domestic (dollar) deposits from $RET_1^\$$ to $RET_2^\$$ and the exchange rate from E_1 to E_2.

Changes in the Domestic Interest Rate ($i^\$$) A rise in $i^\$$ raises the expected return on dollar deposits, shifts the $RET^\$$ schedule to the right, and leads to a rise in the exchange rate, as is shown in Figure 21.5. Another way of seeing this is to recognize that a rise in $i^\$$, which raises the expected return on dollar deposits, creates an excess demand for dollar deposits at the original equilibrium exchange rate, and the resulting purchases of dollar deposits causes an appreciation of the dollar. *A rise in the domestic interest rate ($i^\$$) shifts the expected return on domestic deposits to the right and causes an appreciation of the domestic (dollar) currency: a fall in $i^\$$ shifts the $RET^\$$ schedule to the left and causes a depreciation of the dollar.*

Study Guide

As a study aid, the factors that shift the RET^F and $RET^\$$ schedules and lead to changes in the current exchange rate, E_t, are listed in Table 21.2. The table shows what happens to the exchange rate when there is an increase in each of these variables, holding everything else constant. To give yourself practice, see if you can work out what will happen to the RET^F and $RET^\$$ schedules and to the exchange rate if each of these factors falls rather than rises. Check your answers by seeing if you get the opposite change in the exchange rate to those found in Table 21.2.

Two Important Examples of Changes in the Equilibrium Exchange Rate

Our analysis has shown us the factors that affect the value of the equilibrium exchange rate. Now we use this analysis to take a close look at the response of the exchange rate to changes in interest rates and money growth.

Table 21.2 **Summary: Factors That Shift the RET^F and $RET^\$$ Schedules and Affect the Exchange Rate**

Factor		Response of Exchange Rate, E_t
Domestic interest rate ($i^\$$)	↑	↑
Foreign interest rate (i^F)	↑	↓
Expected domestic price level[a]	↑	↓
Expected tariffs and quotas[a]	↑	↑
Expected import demand	↑	↓
Expected export demand	↑	↑
Expected productivity[a]	↑	↑

Note: Only increases (↑) in the factors are shown; the effects of decreases in the variables on the exchange rate are the opposite of those indicated in the second column.
[a] Relative to foreign countries.

Changes in Interest Rates Changes in domestic interest rates ($i^\$$) are often cited as a major factor affecting exchange rates. For example, we see headlines in the financial press like the following: "Dollar Recovers as Interest Rates Edge Upward." But is the view presented in this headline always correct?

Not necessarily, because to analyze the effects of interest rate changes, we must carefully distinguish the sources of the changes. The Fisher equation (Chapter 4) states that a (nominal) interest rate equals the *real* interest rate plus expected inflation ($i = i_r + \pi^e$). The Fisher equation indicates that an interest rate (i) can change for two reasons: (1) the real interest rate (i_r) changes, or (2) the expected inflation rate (π^e) changes. The effect on the exchange rate is quite different depending on which of these two factors is the source of the change in the nominal interest rate.

Suppose that the domestic real interest rate increases so that the nominal interest rate ($i^\$$) rises while expected inflation remains unchanged. In this case, it is reasonable to assume that the expected appreciation of the dollar will be unchanged because expected inflation is unchanged, and so the expected return on foreign deposits will remain unchanged for any given exchange rate. The result is that the RET^F schedule stays put and the $RET^\$$ schedule shifts out to the right, so that we have the situation already depicted in Figure 21.5, which analyzes an increase in $i^\$$, holding everything else constant. Our model of the foreign exchange market produces the following result: **When domestic real interest rates rise, the domestic currency appreciates.**

When the nominal interest rate rises because of an increase in expected inflation, we get a different result from the one found in Figure 21.5. The rise in domestic expected inflation leads to a decline in the expected appreciation of the dollar (a higher appreciation of the franc), which is typically

Figure 21.6
Effect of a Rise in the Domestic Nominal Interest Rate as a Result of an Increase in Expected Inflation
Because a rise in domestic expected inflation leads to a decline in expected dollar depreciation that is larger than the resulting increase in the domestic interest rate, the expected return on foreign deposits rises by more than the expected return on domestic (dollar) deposits. RET^F shifts out more than $RET^\$$ so the equilibrium exchange rate falls from E_1 to E_2.

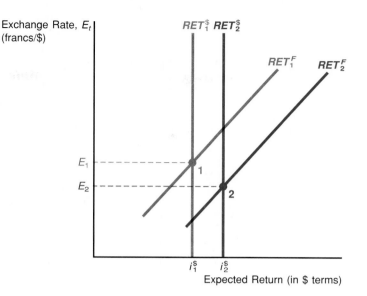

thought to be larger than the increase in the domestic interest rate $(i^\$)$.[5] As a result, at any given exchange rate, the expected return on foreign deposits rises more than the expected return on dollar deposits. Thus, as we see in Figure 21.6, the RET^F schedule shifts out more than the $RET^\$$ schedule and the exchange rate falls. Our analysis leads to this conclusion: ***A higher domestic interest rate due to a higher domestic expected inflation rate is associated with a depreciation of the domestic currency.***

Since this conclusion is completely different from that reached when the rise in the domestic interest rate is associated with a higher real interest rate, we must always distinguish between real and nominal when analyzing the effects of interest rates on exchange rates.

Changes in the Money Supply   Suppose the Fed decides to increase the level of the money supply in order to reduce unemployment, which it believes to be excessive. The higher money supply will lead to a higher American price level in the long run (as we will see in Chapters 23 and 26) and hence to a

---

[5] This conclusion is a standard one in asset market models of exchange rate determination [see Rudiger Dornbusch, "Expectations and Exchange Rate Dynamics," *Journal of Political Economy* 84 (December 1976), pp. 1061–1076]. It is also consistent with empirical evidence that suggests that nominal interest rates do not rise one-for-one with increases in expected inflation. See Frederic S. Mishkin, "The Real Interest Rate: An Empirical Investigation," in Karl Brunner and Allan H. Meltzer, eds., *The Costs and Consequences of Inflation, Carnegie-Rochester Conference Series on Public Policy* 15 (Autumn 1981), 151–200; and Lawrence Summers, "The Nonadjustment of Nominal Interest Rates: A Study of the Fisher Effect," in James Tobin, ed., *Macroeconomics, Prices and Quantities* (Washington, D.C.: Brookings Institution, 1983), 201–240.

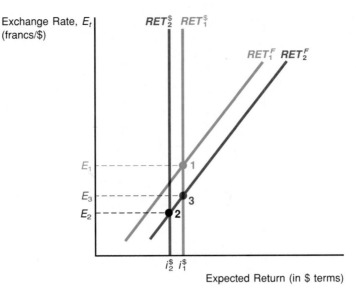

Figure 21.7
Effect of a Rise in the Money Supply A rise in the money supply leads to a higher domestic price level in the long run, which leads to a lower expected future exchange rate. The resulting decline in the expected appreciation of the dollar raises the expected return on foreign deposits, shifting the RET^F schedule out from RET_1^F to RET_2^F. In the short run, the domestic interest rate $i^\$$ falls, shifting $RET^\$$ from $RET_1^\$$ to $RET_2^\$$. The short-run outcome is that the exchange rate falls from E_1 to E_2. In the long run, however, the interest rate returns to $i_1^\$$ and $RET^\$$ returns to $RET_1^\$$. The exchange rate thus rises from E_2 to E_3 in the long run.

lower expected future exchange rate. The resulting decline in the expected appreciation of the dollar increases the expected return of foreign deposits at any given current exchange rate and so shifts the RET^F schedule out from RET_1^F to RET_2^F in Figure 21.7. In addition, the higher money supply will lead to a higher real money supply, M/P, because the price level does not immediately increase in the short run. As suggested in Chapter 6, the resulting rise in the real money supply causes the domestic interest rate to fall from $i_1^\$$ to $i_2^\$$, which lowers the expected return on domestic (dollar) deposits, shifting the $RET^\$$ schedule in from $RET_1^\$$ to $RET_2^\$$. As we can see in Figure 21.7, the result is a decline in the exchange rate from E_1 to E_2. The conclusion is: *A higher domestic money supply causes the domestic currency to depreciate.*

Exchange Rate Overshooting

Our analysis of the effect of a money supply increase on the exchange rate is not yet over—we still need to look at what happens to the exchange rate in the long run. A basic proposition in monetary theory, called **monetary neutrality,** states the following: In the long run, a one-time percentage rise in the money supply is matched by the same one-time percentage rise in the price level, leaving unchanged the real money supply and all other economic variables such as interest rates. An intuitive way to understand this proposition is to think of what would happen if our government announced overnight that an old dollar would now be worth 100 new dollars. The money supply in new dollars would be 100 times its old value and the price level would also be 100 times higher, but nothing in the economy would really have changed; interest rates and the real money supply would remain the same. Monetary neutrality tells us that in the long run the rise in the money supply would not lead to a change in the domestic interest rate and so it would return to $i_1^\$$ in the long run, and the expected return on domestic deposits schedule would return to $RET_1^\$$. As we can see in Figure 21.7, this means that the exchange rate would rise from E_2 to E_3 in the long run.

The phenomenon we have described here in which the exchange rate falls by more in the short run than it does in the long run when the money supply increases is called **exchange rate overshooting.** It is important because, as we will see in the following application, it can help explain why exchange rates exhibit so much volatility.

Another way of thinking about why exchange rate overshooting occurs is to recognize that when the domestic interest rate falls in the short run, equilibrium in the foreign exchange market means that the expected return on foreign deposits must be lower. With the foreign interest rate given, this lower expected return on foreign deposits means that there must be an expected appreciation of the dollar (depreciation of the franc) in order for the expected return on foreign deposits to decline when the domestic interest rate falls. This can only occur if the current exchange rate falls below its long-run value.

APPLICATION
WHY ARE EXCHANGE RATES SO VOLATILE? /

The high volatility of foreign exchange rates surprises many people. Twenty years ago economists generally believed that allowing exchange rates to be determined in the free market would not lead to large fluctuations in their values. Recent experience has proved them wrong. If we refer back to Figure 21.1, we see that exchange rates over the 1973 to 1990 period have been very volatile.

The asset market approach to exchange rate determination that we outlined here gives a straightforward explanation of volatile exchange rates. Because expected appreciation of the domestic currency affects the expected return on foreign deposits, expectations about the price level, inflation, tariffs and quotas, productivity, import demand, export demand, and the money supply play an important role in determining the exchange rate. When expectations about any of these variables change, our model indicates that there will be an immediate effect on the expected return of foreign deposits and therefore on the exchange rate. Since expectations on all these variables change with just about every bit of news that appears, it is not surprising that the exchange rate is volatile. In addition, we have seen that our exchange rate analysis produces exchange rate overshooting when the money supply increases. Exchange rate overshooting produces an additional reason for the high volatility of exchange rates.

Because earlier models of exchange rate behavior focused on goods markets rather than asset markets, they did not emphasize changing expectations as a source of exchange rate movements, and so these earlier models could not predict substantial fluctuations in exchange rates. The failure of earlier models to explain volatility is one reason why they are no longer so popular. The more modern approach developed here emphasizes that the foreign exchange market is like any other asset market in which expectations of the future matter. The foreign exchange market, like other asset markets such as the stock market, displays substantial price volatility, and foreign exchange rates are notoriously hard to forecast[6] (Box 21.1).

APPLICATION
THE DOLLAR AND INTEREST RATES: 1973–1990 /

In the chapter preview, we mentioned that the dollar was weak in the late 1970s, rose substantially from 1980 to 1985, and fell back down again in the late 1980s. We can use our analysis of the foreign exchange market to understand exchange rate movements and help explain the dollar's rise and fall in the 1980s.

Some important information for tracing the dollar's changing value is presented in Figure 21.8. It plots measures of real and nominal interest rates and the value of the dollar in terms of a basket of foreign currencies (called an **effective exchange rate index**). We can see that the value of the dollar and the measure of real interest rates rise and fall together. In the late 1970s

---

[6] The efficient markets analysis of stock prices as developed in Chapter 29 applies equally well to foreign exchange rates, because exchange rates like stock prices should reflect all available information. Efficient markets theory, for example, implies that stock prices should generally follow a random walk. A similar conclusion follows for exchange rates and the reasoning is as follows: If people could predict that a currency would appreciate by 1% in the coming week, they could earn over a 50% return by buying this currency. Since this is likely to be far above the equilibrium return for holding a currency, people would immediately buy the currency and bid up its current price, thereby reducing the expected return. The process would only stop when the predictable change in the exchange rate dropped to near zero so that the optimal forecast of the return no longer differed from the equilibrium return. Likewise, if people could predict that the currency would depreciate by 1% in the coming week, they would sell it until the predictable change in the exchange rate was again near zero. Efficient markets theory therefore implies that future changes in exchange rates should, for all practical purposes, be unpredictable; in other words, exchange rates should approximately follow random walks. Similar reasoning to that found in Chapter 29 also indicates that exchange rates should respond only to new information (surprises).

Box   2 1 . 1   A Global Perspective

Forecasting Exchange Rates

Forecasting foreign exchange rates is a lucrative activity for economists. Speculators and businesses (particularly multinational corporations) are especially interested in what will happen to exchange rates in the future. Businesses need accurate predictions of exchange rates because changes in the rates can affect the demand for their products. A rise in the value of the dollar, for example, can make American products more expensive abroad and foreign products cheaper in the United States, thereby lowering the demand for American goods. Multinational corporations that are contemplating investing abroad also are concerned with exchange rate movements. If a foreign country's currency appreciates, the cost of building a new plant there will be higher—and may no longer be profitable.

In predicting exchange rate movements, forecasters look at the factors mentioned in this chapter. If, for example, they expect domestic real interest rates to rise, they will predict in line with our analysis that the domestic currency will appreciate; if, on the other hand, they expect domestic inflation to increase, they will predict that the domestic currency will depreciate. Exchange rate forecasters are no more or less accurate than other economic forecasters and they often make large errors. Reports on foreign exchange rate forecasts and how well forecasters are doing appear from time to time in the *Wall Street Journal* and in the trade magazine *Euromoney*.

Figure 21.8
Value of the Dollar and Interest Rates: 1973–1990 Sources: *International Financial Statistics* and Figure 4.3 in Chapter 4 of this text.

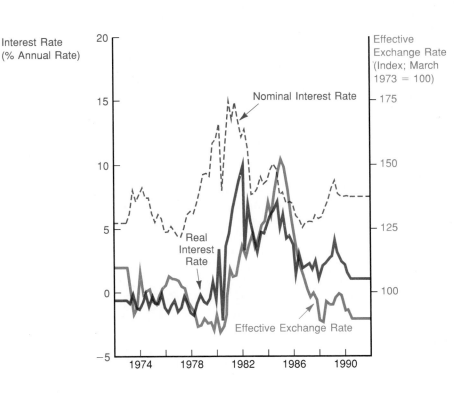

real interest rates were at low levels and so was the value of the dollar. Beginning in 1980, however, real interest rates in the United States began to climb sharply and at the same time so did the dollar. After 1984, the real interest rate declined substantially, as did the dollar.

Our model of exchange rate determination does help to explain the rise and fall in the dollar in the 1980s. As Figure 21.5 indicates, a rise in the U.S. real interest rate raises the expected return on dollar deposits while leaving the expected return on foreign deposits unchanged. The resulting increased demand for dollar deposits then leads to purchases of dollar deposits (and sales of foreign deposits) which raise the exchange rate. This is exactly what occurred in the 1980–1984 period. The subsequent fall in U.S. real interest rates then lowered the expected return on dollar deposits relative to foreign deposits and the resulting sales of dollar deposits (and purchases of foreign deposits) lowered the exchange rate.

The plot of nominal interest rates in Figure 21.8 also demonstrates that the correspondence between *nominal* interest rates and exchange rate movements is not nearly as close as that between *real* interest rates and exchange rate movements. This is also exactly what our analysis predicts. The rise in nominal interest rates in the late 1970s is not reflected in a corresponding rise in the value of the dollar; indeed, the dollar actually falls in the late 1970s. Figure 21.8 explains why the rise in nominal rates in the late 1970s did not produce a rise in the dollar. As a comparison of the real and nominal interest rates in the late 1970s indicates, the rise in nominal interest rates reflected an increase in expected inflation and not an increase in real interest rates. As our analysis in Figure 21.6 demonstrated, the rise in nominal interest rates stemming from a rise in expected inflation should lead to a decline in the dollar, and this is exactly what transpired.

If there is a moral to the story it is that a failure to distinguish between real and nominal interest rates can lead to very poor predictions of exchange rate movements: The weakness of the dollar in the late 1970s and the strength of the dollar in the early 1980s can be explained by movements in *real* interest rates, but not *nominal* interest rates.

INTERVENTION IN THE FOREIGN EXCHANGE MARKET

In an idealized world, the foreign exchange market would respond to all market pressures and would function as a completely free market. However, the foreign exchange market, like many others, is not free of government intervention, since central banks can and do intervene regularly. Our current international financial arrangement, called a **managed float regime** (or a **dirty float**), is one in which exchange rates fluctuate from day to day, but central banks attempt to influence their countries' exchange rates by buying and selling currencies. The exchange rate analysis we have developed can be used to explain the impact this central bank intervention has on the foreign exchange market.

Foreign Exchange Intervention and the Money Supply

The first step in understanding how central bank intervention in the foreign exchange market affects exchange rates is to see the impact on the monetary base from a central bank sale in the foreign exchange market of some of its holdings of assets denominated in a foreign currency (called **international reserves**). Suppose the Fed decides to sell $10 billion of its foreign assets in exchange for $10 billion of currency. The Fed's purchase of dollars has two effects. First, it reduces the Fed's holding of international reserves by $10 billion. Second, because its purchase of currency removes it from the hands of the public, currency in circulation falls by $10 billion. We can see this in the following T-account for the Federal Reserve:

Federal Reserve		
Assets		Liabilities
Foreign assets (international reserves)	−$10 billion	Currency in circulation −$10 billion

Because the monetary base is made up of currency in circulation plus reserves, this decline in currency implies that the monetary base has fallen by $10 billion.

If instead of paying for the foreign assets sold by the Fed with currency, the persons buying the foreign assets pay for them by checks written from accounts at domestic banks, then the Fed deducts the $10 billion from the deposit accounts these banks have at the Fed. The result is that deposits at the Fed (reserves) decline by $10 billion as is shown in the following T-account:

Federal Reserve		
Assets		Liabilities
Foreign assets (international reserves)	−$10 billion	Deposits at Fed (reserves) −$10 billion

In this case, the outcome of the Fed sale of foreign assets and the purchase of dollar deposits is a $10 billion decline in reserves and a $10 billion decline in the monetary base since reserves are also a component of the monetary base.

We now see that the outcome for the monetary base is exactly the same when a central bank sells foreign assets to purchase domestic bank deposits or domestic currency. This is why when we say that a central bank has purchased its domestic currency, we do not have to distinguish whether it actually purchased currency rather than bank deposits denominated in the domestic currency. We have thus reached an important conclusion: *A central bank purchase of domestic currency and corresponding sale of foreign as-*

sets in the foreign exchange market leads to an equal decline in its international reserves and the monetary base.

We could have reached the same conclusion by a more direct route. A central bank sale of a foreign asset is no different than an open market sale of a government bond. We learned in our chapters on the money supply process that an open market sale leads to an equal decline in the monetary base; therefore, a sale of foreign assets also leads to an equal decline in the monetary base. By similar reasoning, a central bank purchase of foreign assets paid for by selling the domestic currency, like an open market purchase, leads to an equal rise in the monetary base. Thus we have the following conclusion: *A central bank sale of domestic currency to purchase foreign assets in the foreign exchange market results in an equal rise in its international reserves and the monetary base.*

The intervention we have just described in which a central bank allows the purchase or sale of domestic currency to have an affect on the monetary base is called an **unsterilized foreign exchange intervention.** But what if the central bank does not want the purchase or sale of the domestic currency to affect the monetary base? All it has to do is to counter the effect of the foreign exchange intervention by conducting an offsetting open market operation in the government bond market. For example, in the case of a $10 billion purchase of dollars by the Fed and hence a corresponding $10 billion sale of foreign assets, which we have seen would decrease the monetary base by $10 billion, the Fed can conduct an open market purchase of $10 billion of government bonds which would increase the monetary base by $10 billion. The resulting T-account for the foreign exchange intervention and the offsetting open market operation thus leaves the monetary base unchanged:

Federal Reserve			
Assets		Liabilities	
Foreign assets (international reserves)	−$10 billion	Monetary base (reserves)	+$0 billion
Government bonds	+$10 billion		

The foreign exchange intervention with an offsetting open market operation that leaves the monetary base unchanged is called a **sterilized foreign exchange intervention.**

Now that we understand that there are two types of foreign exchange interventions, unsterilized and sterilized, let's look at how each of these interventions affects the exchange rate.

Unsterilized Intervention

Your intuition might lead you to suspect that if a central bank wants to lower the value of the domestic currency, it should sell the currency in the foreign exchange market and purchase foreign assets. Indeed, this intuition is correct for the case of an unsterilized intervention.

Recall that with an unsterilized intervention, if the Federal Reserve decides to sell dollars in order to buy foreign assets in the foreign exchange market, this works just like an open market purchase of bonds to increase the monetary base. Hence the sale of dollars leads to an increase in the money supply, and we thus find ourselves analyzing exactly the situation already described in Figure 21.7. The higher money supply leads to a higher U.S. price level in the long run and so to a lower expected future exchange rate. The resulting decline in the expected appreciation of the dollar increases the expected return for foreign deposits and shifts out the RET^F schedule. In addition, the increase in the money supply will lead to a higher real money supply in the short run, which causes the interest rate on dollar deposits to fall. The resulting lower expected return on dollar deposits means an inward shift in the $RET^\$$ schedule. The fall in the expected return of dollar deposits and the increase in the expected return on foreign deposits means that foreign assets have a higher expected return than dollar deposits at the old equilibrium exchange rate. Hence, people will try to sell their dollar deposits and the exchange rate will fall. Indeed, as we saw in Figure 21.7, the increase in the money supply will lead to exchange rate overshooting in which the exchange rate falls by more in the short run than it does in the long run.

Our analysis leads us to the following conclusion about unsterilized interventions in the foreign exchange market: *An unsterilized intervention in which the domestic currency is sold to purchase foreign assets leads to (1) a gain in international reserves, (2) an increase in the money supply, and (3) a depreciation in the domestic currency.*

The reverse result is found for an unsterilized intervention in which the domestic currency is purchased by selling foreign assets. The purchase of domestic currency by selling foreign assets (reducing international reserves), works like an open market sale to reduce the monetary base and the money supply. The decrease in the money supply raises the interest rate on dollar deposits and shifts $RET^\$$ out, while it causes RET^F to shift in because it leads to a higher expected appreciation of the dollar and hence a lower expected return on foreign deposits. The increase in the expected return on dollar deposits relative to foreign deposits will mean that people will want to buy more dollar deposits and the exchange rate will rise. *An unsterilized intervention in which domestic currency is purchased by selling foreign assets leads to (1) a fall in international reserves, (2) a fall in the money supply, and (3) an appreciation of the domestic currency.*

Sterilized Intervention

The key point to remember about a sterilized intervention is that the central bank engages in offsetting open market operations so there is no impact on the monetary base and the money supply. In the context of the model of exchange rate determination we have developed here, it is straightforward to show that a sterilized intervention has *no effect on the exchange rate*. Remember that in our model foreign and domestic deposits are perfect substitutes, so that equilibrium in the foreign exchange market occurs when the expected returns on foreign and domestic deposits are equal. A sterilized intervention leaves the money supply unchanged and so has no way of directly affecting interest rates or the expected future exchange rate.[7] Since the expected returns on dollar and foreign deposits are unaffected, the expected return schedules will remain at $RET_1^\$$ and RET_1^F in Figure 21.7 and the exchange rate will remain unchanged at E_1.

At first it might seem puzzling that a central bank purchase or sale of domestic currency that is sterilized does not lead to a change in the exchange rate. A central bank purchase of domestic currency cannot raise the exchange rate because any resulting rise in the exchange rate would mean that the expected return on foreign deposits would be greater than the expected return on domestic deposits. Given our assumption that foreign and domestic deposits are perfect substitutes (equally desirable), this would mean that no one would want to hold domestic deposits. So the exchange rate would have to fall back to its previous level where the expected returns on domestic and foreign deposits were equal.

Sterilized Intervention When Foreign and Domestic Deposits Are Not Perfect Substitutes So far in our analysis we have assumed that foreign and domestic deposits are perfect substitutes. Now we look at what might happen if foreign and domestic deposits are *not* perfect substitutes. Perhaps they have different risk and liquidity characteristics or governments have erected barriers (called **capital controls**) that prevent domestic residents from investing abroad or foreign residents from investing domestically. In such cases the expected returns on domestic and foreign deposits do not have to be equal; they can differ by a risk premium that reflects the difference between the riskiness or liquidity of domestic deposits and foreign deposits or the effects of capital controls. In this situation, the equilibrium interest parity condition in the foreign exchange market becomes:

$$i^\$ = i^F - (E_{t+1}^e - E_t)/E_t + \delta$$

---

[7] However, it is possible that a sterilized intervention could provide a signal about what central banks would want to happen to the future exchange rate and so might provide a signal about the course of future monetary policy. In this way, a sterilized intervention could lead to shifts in the RET^F schedule, but in reality it is the future change in monetary policy not the sterilized intervention that is the ultimate source of exchange rate effects. For a discussion of the signaling effect in recent years, see Maurice Obstfeld, "The Effectiveness of Foreign-Exchange Intervention: Recent Experience, 1985–1988," in William H. Branson, Jacob A. Frenkel, and Morris Goldstein, eds., *International Policy Coordination and Exchange Rate Fluctuations* (Chicago: University of Chicago Press, 1990), pp. 197–237.

Figure 21.9

Response to a Sterilized Intervention If Domestic and Foreign Deposits Are Not Perfect Substitutes
A sterilized sale of dollars leaves the expected returns on domestic and foreign deposits unchanged at $RET^\$_1$ and RET^F_1; however, it does increase the risk premium from δ_1 to δ_2. The $RET^F + \delta$ schedule thus shifts from $RET^F_1 + \delta_1$ out to $RET^F_1 + \delta_2$, leading to a decline in the exchange rate from E_1 to E_2.

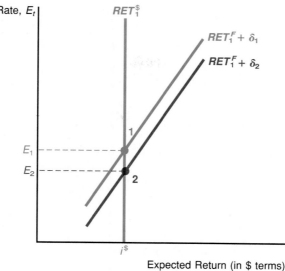

or equivalently,

$$RET^\$ = RET^F + \delta \tag{21.3}$$

where δ is the risk premium. Equilibrium in the foreign exchange market is now described as in Figure 21.9, in which the RET^F schedule is replaced by $RET^F + \delta$.

If foreign and domestic deposits are not perfect substitutes, an increase in the amount of domestic deposits held by the public could mean that holders of domestic deposits are now subjected to more exchange rate risk. This is so because they are less well diversified than if they held deposits denominated in many different currencies. In order to be compensated for higher risk when they hold more domestic deposits and so be willing to hold them, investors would thus have to be paid a higher expected return. A higher supply of domestic deposits is thus likely to lead to an increase in the risk premium from δ_1 to δ_2. Even though the expected returns on foreign and domestic deposits remain unchanged, the sterilized sale of dollars thus leads to a shift of the $RET^F + \delta$ schedule in Figure 21.9 from $RET^F_1 + \delta_1$ out to $RET^F_1 + \delta_2$ and hence to a decline in the exchange rate from E_1 to E_2. We thus obtain the usual result: A sale of the domestic currency leads to a depreciation of the domestic currency.

We have demonstrated that if domestic and foreign deposits are not perfect substitutes, a sterilized intervention can affect the exchange rate. Does the empirical evidence suggest that sterilized intervention affects the exchange rate in line with the analysis in Figure 21.9? The answer seems to be "no." Most studies by both academic and government economists find little evidence to support the position that sterilized intervention has a significant impact on foreign exchange rates.[8] The available evidence seems to suggest that for foreign exchange intervention to work, it must not be sterilized.

SUMMARY

1. Foreign exchange rates (the price of one country's currency in terms of another's) are important because they affect the cost of goods sold abroad and the cost of foreign goods bought domestically.

2. The theory of purchasing parity suggests that long-run changes in the exchange rate between two countries are determined by changes in the relative price levels of the two countries. Other factors that affect exchange rates in the long run are tariffs and quotas, import demand, export demand, and productivity.

3. Exchange rates are determined in the short run by the interest parity condition which states that the expected return on domestic deposits is equal to the expected return on foreign deposits.

4. Any factor that changes the expected returns on domestic and foreign deposits will lead to changes in the exchange rate. These factors include changes in the interest rates on domestic and foreign deposits as well as changes in any of the factors that affect the long-run exchange rate and hence the expected future exchange rate. Changes in the money supply lead to exchange rate overshooting in which the exchange rate changes by more in the short run than it does in the long run.

5. The asset market approach to exchange rate determination can explain both the volatility of exchange rates and the rise of the dollar in the 1980–1984 period and its subsequent fall.

6. An unsterilized central bank intervention in which the domestic currency is sold to purchase foreign assets leads to (1) a gain in international reserves, (2) an increase in the money supply, and (3) a depreciation of the domestic currency. Available evidence suggests, on the other hand, that sterilized central bank interventions have little effect on the exchange rate.

KEY TERMS

exchange rate

foreign exchange market

spot transactions

forward transactions

spot exchange rate

forward exchange rate

appreciate

depreciate

law of one price

theory of purchasing power parity (PPP)

tariffs

quotas

capital mobility

interest parity condition

monetary neutrality

exchange rate overshooting

effective exchange rate index

managed float regime (dirty float)

international reserves

unsterilized foreign exchange intervention

sterilized foreign exchange intervention

capital controls

---

[8] See Maurice Obstfeld, "Can We Sterilize? Theory and Evidence," *American Economic Review* 72 (May 1982), pp. 45–50; Kenneth Rogoff, "On the Effects of Sterilized Intervention: An Analysis of Weekly Data," *Journal of Monetary Economics* 14 (September 1984), pp. 133–150; and Dale W. Henderson and Stephanie Sampson, "Intervention in Foreign Exchange Markets: A Summary of Ten Staff Studies," *Federal Reserve Bulletin* 69 (November 1983), pp. 830–836. The lack of evidence for effects from sterilized intervention appears even though there is strong evidence that domestic and foreign deposits are not perfect substitutes. For example, see Robert J. Hodrick and Sanjay Srivastava, "An Investigation of Risk and Return in Forward Foreign Exchange," *Journal of International Money and Finance* 3 (April 1984), pp. 5–29.

QUESTIONS AND PROBLEMS

1. When the French franc appreciates are you more likely to drink California or French wine?

* 2. Answer true, false, or uncertain: "A country is always worse off when its currency is weak (falls in value)."

3. Check in a newspaper the exchange rates for the foreign currencies listed in the Following the Financial News box. Which of these currencies have appreciated and which have depreciated since April 4, 1991?

* 4. If the French price level rises by 5% relative to the United States, what does the theory of purchasing power parity predict will happen to the value of the French franc in terms of dollars?

5. If the demand for a country's exports falls at the same time that tariffs on imports are raised, will the exchange rate tend to appreciate or depreciate in the long run?

* 6. In the middle to late 1970s, the yen appreciated relative to the dollar even though Japan's inflation rate was higher than America's. How can this be explained by an improvement in the productivity of Japanese industry relative to American industry?

Using Economic Analysis to Predict the Future

In the remaining problems, answer the questions by drawing the appropriate exchange market diagrams.

7. The president of the United States announces that he will reduce inflation with a new anti-inflation program. If the public believes him, predict what will happen to the U.S. exchange rate.

* 8. If the British central bank prints money to reduce unemployment, what will happen to the value of the pound in the short and the long run?

9. If the French government unexpectedly announces that it will be imposing higher tariffs and quotas on foreign goods one year from now, what will happen to the value of the franc today?

*10. If nominal interest rates in America rise but real interest rates fall, predict what will happen to the U.S. exchange rate.

11. If American auto companies make a breakthrough in automobile technology and are able to produce a car that gets 60 miles to the gallon, what will happen to the U.S. exchange rate?

*12. If Americans go on a spending spree and buy twice as much French perfume, Japanese TVs, English sweaters, Swiss watches, and Italian wine, what will happen to the value of the U.S. dollar?

13. If expected inflation drops in Europe so that interest rates fall here, predict what will happen to the U.S. exchange rate.

*14. If the Federal Reserve buys dollars in the foreign exchange market but conducts an offsetting open market operation to sterilize the intervention, what will be the impact on international reserves, the money supply, and the exchange rate?

15. If the Federal Reserve buys dollars in the foreign exchange market but does not sterilize the intervention, what will be the impact on international reserves, the money supply, and the exchange rate?

CHAPTER 22

The International Finance System and Monetary Policy

PREVIEW   The growing interdependence between the U.S. economy and the economies of the rest of the world has meant that a country's monetary policy can no longer be conducted without taking international considerations into account. Now that you understand how the foreign exchange market works, we can examine how monetary policy is affected by the structure of the international financial system and by international financial transactions. We will also examine the evolution of the international financial system during the past fifty years and where it may be heading in the future.

BALANCE OF PAYMENTS

Since international financial transactions have considerable effect on monetary policy, it is worth knowing how these transactions are measured. The **balance of payments** is a bookkeeping system for recording all payments that have a direct bearing on the movement of funds between a nation (private sector and government) and foreign countries.

The balance of payments account you see in the Following the Financial News box that follows uses a standard double-entry bookkeeping accounting procedure much like that which you or I might use to keep a record of all our payments and receipts. All payments from foreigners to Americans are entered in the "Receipts" column with a plus (+) sign to reflect that they are credits; that is, they result in a flow of funds to Americans. Receipts include foreign purchases for American products such as computers and wheat (exports), payments from foreign tourists (services), income earned from American investment abroad (investment income), foreign gifts and pensions paid to Americans (unilateral transfers), and foreign payments for American assets (capital inflows).

Following the Financial News

The Balance of Payments

Newspapers periodically report information on the balance of payments. Balance of trade figures (merchandise exports minus imports) are reported monthly in the last week of the month. The complete set of items in the balance of payments is published on a quarterly basis with the previous quarter's figures published between the eighteenth and twentieth day of the last month of the following quarter. An example of the balance of payments accounts for the United States appears below.

U.S. Balance of Payments in 1990 (billions of dollars)

	Receipts (+)	Payments (−)	Balance
Current Account			
(1) Merchandise exports	+389		
(2) Merchandise imports		−498	
Trade balance			−109
(3) Net investment income	+8		
(4) Net services	+23		
(5) Net unilateral transfers		−21	
Current account balance			−99
[(1) + (2) + (3) + (4) + (5)]			
Capital Account			
(6) Capital outflows		−59	
(7) Capital inflows	+56		
(8) Statistical discrepancy	+73		
Official reserve transactions balance			−29
[(1) + (2) + (3) + (4) + (5) + (6) + (7) + (8)]			
Method of Financing			
(9) Increase in U.S. official reserve assets (−)		−2	
(10) Increase in foreign official assets (+)	+31		
Total financing of surplus			+29
Sum of (1) through (10)			0

Source: *Survey of Current Business.*

All payments to foreigners are entered in the "Payments" column with a minus (−) sign to reflect that they are debits because they result in flows of funds to other countries. Payments include American purchases of foreign products such as French wine and Japanese cars (imports), American travel abroad (services), income earned by foreigners from investments in the United States (investment income), foreign aid, gifts and pensions paid to foreigners (unilateral transfers), and American payments for foreign assets (capital outflows).

Current Account

The **current account** shows international transactions that involve currently produced goods and services. The difference between merchandise exports (line 1) and imports (line 2) is called the **trade balance.** When merchandise imports are greater than exports (here by $109 billion), we have a trade balance deficit; if exports are greater than imports, we have trade balance surplus.

The next three items in the current account are the net payments or receipts that arise from investment income, the purchase and sale of services, and unilateral transfers (gifts, pensions, and foreign aid). In 1990, for example, net investment income was a positive $8 billion (in line 3) for the United States because Americans received more investment income than they paid out. Americans bought less services from foreigners than foreigners bought from Americans so that net services generated $23 billion in receipts (line 4). Since Americans made more unilateral transfers to foreign countries (especially foreign aid) than foreigners made to the United States, there is a $21 billion payment in line (5).

The sum of the items in lines (1) through (5) is the current account balance, which in 1990 showed a deficit of $99 billion. The current account balance is an important balance of payments concept for several reasons. As we can see from the balance of payments account, any surplus or deficit in the current account must be balanced either by capital account transactions (lending or borrowing abroad) or by changes in government reserve asset items:

$$\text{Current account} + \text{capital account} =$$
$$\text{change in government reserve assets}$$

The current account balance tells us whether the United States (private sector and government combined) is increasing or decreasing its claims on foreign wealth. A surplus indicates that America is increasing its claims on foreign wealth, while a deficit, as in 1990, indicates that this country is reducing its claims on foreign wealth.[1]

Economists closely follow the current account balance because they believe it can provide information on the future movement of exchange rates. The current account balance provides some indication of what is happening to the demand for imports and exports which, as we saw in Chapter 21, can affect the exchange rate. In addition, the current account balance provides information about what will be happening to U.S. claims on foreign wealth in the long run. Since a movement of foreign wealth to American residents can affect the demand for dollar assets, changes in U.S. claims on foreign wealth, reflected in the current account balance, can affect the exchange rate over time.[2]

Capital Account

The **capital account** describes the flow of capital between the United States and other countries. Capital outflows are American purchases of foreign assets (a payments item) and capital inflows are foreign purchases of American assets (a receipts item). The capital outflows (line 6) are more than the capital inflows (line 7), resulting in a net flow of $3 billion in funds from American individuals and corporations in exchange for claims against foreigners.

The statistical discrepancy (line 8) represents errors in measuring transactions because of unrecorded transactions involving smuggling and other capital flows. Statistical discrepancy, which keeps the balance of payments account in balance, is a whopping +$73 billion, which suggests that some of the other items in the balance of payments may not be measured very accurately. Many experts believe that statistical discrepancy is primarily the result of large hidden capital flows into the United States and so the item has been placed in the capital account part of the balance of payments.

Official Reserve Transactions Balance

The sum of lines (1) through (8), called the **official reserve transactions balance,** equals the current account balance plus the items in the capital

---

[1]The current account balance can also be viewed as showing how much total saving exceeds investment by both private sector and government in the United States. We can see this by noting that total U.S. saving equals the increase in total wealth held by the U.S. private sector and government. Total investment equals the increase in the U.S. capital stock (wealth physically in the United States). The difference between them is the increase in U.S. claims on foreign wealth.

[2]If American residents have a greater preference for dollar assets than do foreigners, a movement of foreign wealth to American residents when there is a balance of payments surplus will increase the demand for dollar assets over time and will cause the dollar to appreciate.

account. When we refer to surplus or deficit in the balance of payments, we actually mean a surplus or deficit in the official reserve transactions balance. Because the balance of payments account must balance, the official reserve transactions balance tells us the net amount of international reserves that must move between central banks in order to finance international transactions. One reason we are particularly interested in the movements of international reserves is that, as we saw in the previous chapter, these movements have an important impact on the money supply.

Methods of Financing the Balance of Payments

Because most countries do not have their currencies held as international reserves by other countries, they must finance an excess of payments over receipts (a deficit in the balance of payments) by providing international reserves to foreign governments and central banks. A balance of payments deficit is associated with a loss of international reserves. Likewise, a balance of payments surplus is associated with a gain.

In contrast to other countries' currencies, the U.S. dollar and dollar-denominated assets are the major component of international reserves held by other countries. Thus a U.S. balance of payments deficit can be financed by a decrease in U.S. international reserves and/or an increase in foreign central banks' holdings of international reserves (dollar assets). A U.S. balance of payments surplus, on the other hand, can be financed either by an increase in U.S. international reserves or a decrease in foreign central banks' international reserves.

For the United States in 1990, the official reserve transactions deficit of $29 billion was financed by a $2 billion increase in U.S. international reserves (in the payments column of line 9)[3] and a $31 billion increase of foreign holdings of dollars (in the receipts column of line 10). On net, the United States indebtedness to foreign governments (central banks) increased by $29 billion (the $31 billion foreign increase in holdings of U.S. dollars minus the $2 billion increase in U.S. holdings of international reserves). This $29 billion increase in net U.S. government indebtedness just matches the $29 billion official reserve transactions deficit so that the sum of lines (1) through (10) is zero, and the account balances.

---

[3]At first it may appear strange that when the United States gains $2 billion of international reserves, it is entered in the balance of payments as a payment with a negative sign. Recall, however, that when a central bank gains international reserves it has bought foreign assets. Thus a decrease in international reserves is just like an outflow of capital in the capital account and appears as a payment with a negative sign.

EVOLUTION OF THE INTERNATIONAL FINANCIAL SYSTEM

Before examining the impact of international financial transactions on monetary policy, you need to understand the past and current structure of the international financial system.

The Gold Standard

Before World War I, the world economy operated under a **gold standard,** under which the currency of most countries was convertible directly into gold. American dollar bills, for example, could be turned in to the U.S. Treasury and exchanged for approximately ¹⁄₂₀ of an ounce of gold. Likewise, the British Treasury would exchange ¼ of an ounce of gold for one pound sterling. Because an American could convert twenty dollars into one ounce of gold, which could be used to buy four British pounds, the exchange rate between the British pound and the dollar was effectively fixed roughly at $5.00 to the pound. Tying currencies to gold resulted in an international financial system with fixed exchange rates between countries. The fixed exchange rates under the gold standard had the important advantage of encouraging world trade by eliminating the uncertainty that occurs when exchange rates fluctuate.

To see how the gold standard operated in practice, let us see what occurs if, under a gold standard, the British pound begins to appreciate above the $5 par value. If an American importer of £100 of English tweed tries to pay for the tweed with dollars, it costs her more than the $500 it cost before. Nevertheless, the importer has another option involving the purchase of gold that can reduce the cost of the tweed. Instead of using dollars to pay for the tweed, the American importer can exchange the $500 for gold, ship the gold to Britain, and convert it into £100. The shipment of gold to Britain is cheaper as long as the British pound is above the $5 par value (plus a small amount to pay for the cost of shipping the gold).

The appreciation of the pound leads to a British gain of international reserves (gold) and an equal U.S. loss. Because a change in a country's holdings of international reserves (gold) leads to an equal change in its monetary base, the movement of gold from the United States to Britain causes the British monetary base to rise and the American monetary base to fall. The resulting rise in the British money supply raises the British price level while the fall in the U.S. money supply lowers the U.S. price level. The resulting increase in the British price level relative to the United States then causes the pound to depreciate. This process will continue until the value of the pound falls back down to its $5 par value.

A depreciation of the pound below the $5 par value, on the contrary, stimulates gold shipments from Britain to the United States. These shipments raise the American money supply and lower the British money supply, causing the pound to appreciate back toward the $5 par value. We thus see that under a gold standard, a rise or fall of the exchange rate sets forces in motion that return it to the par value.

As long as countries abided by the "rules of the game" under the gold standard and kept their currencies backed by and convertible into gold, exchange rates remained fixed. However, as in our example, adherence to the gold standard meant that a country no longer had control over its monetary policy because its money supply was, for the most part, determined by gold flows between countries. Additionally, monetary policy throughout the world was greatly influenced by the production of gold and gold discoveries. When gold production was low in the 1870s and 1880s, the money supply throughout the world grew slowly and did not keep pace with the growth of the world economy. The result was deflation, that is, falling price levels. The gold discoveries in Alaska and South Africa in the 1890s then greatly expanded gold production, which, in turn, caused money supplies to increase rapidly and price levels to rise (inflation) up until World War I.

The Bretton Woods System and the IMF

With the coming of World War I, which led to massive trade disruptions, countries could no longer convert their currencies into gold. The gold standard collapsed. Despite attempts to revive it in the interwar period, the worldwide depression, beginning in 1929, led to its permanent demise. As the allied victory in World War II loomed certain in 1944, the Allies met in Bretton Woods, New Hampshire, to develop a new international monetary system to promote world trade and prosperity. The agreement worked out among the allies was one in which central banks bought and sold their own currencies to keep their exchange rates fixed at a certain level (called a **fixed exchange rate regime**). The agreement lasted from 1945 to 1971 and has become known as the **Bretton Woods system.**

The Bretton Woods agreement created the **International Monetary Fund (IMF),** which had 30 original member countries in 1945 and currently has over 150. The IMF was given the task of promoting the growth of world trade by setting rules for the maintenance of fixed exchange rates and by making loans to countries that were experiencing balance of payments difficulties.[4] As part of its role of monitoring the compliance of member countries with its rules, the IMF also took on the job of collecting and standardizing international economic data.

The Bretton Woods agreement also set up the **World Bank** (International Bank for Reconstruction and Development), which currently pro-

---

[4]Rules for the conduct of trade between countries (the setting of tariffs and quotas) were given to the General Agreement on Tariffs and Trade (GATT), an organization which operates out of Geneva. For a discussion of how this agency operates, see John Williamson, *The Open Economy and the World Economy* (New York: Basic Books, 1983).

vides long-term loans to assist developing countries to build dams, roads, and other physical capital that would contribute to their economic development. The funds for these loans are obtained primarily by the issue of World Bank bonds, which are sold in the capital markets of the developed countries.[5]

Because the United States emerged from World War II as the world's largest economic power with over half of the world's manufacturing capacity and the greater part of the world's gold, the Bretton Woods system of fixed exchange rates was based on the convertibility of U.S. dollars into gold (for foreign governments and central banks only) at $35 to the ounce. The fixed exchange rates were to be maintained by intervention in the foreign exchange market by central banks in countries besides the United States who bought and sold dollar assets which they held as international reserves. The U.S. dollar, which was used by other countries to denominate the assets that they held as international reserves, was called a **reserve currency.** Thus an important feature of the Bretton Woods system was the establishment of the United States as the reserve-currency country.

How a Fixed Exchange Rate Regime Works   The most important feature of the Bretton Woods system was that it set up a fixed exchange rate regime. Figure 22.1 shows how a fixed exchange rate regime works in practice using the model of exchange rate determination we learned in the previous chapter. Panel (a) describes a situation in which the domestic currency is initially overvalued: The expected return on foreign deposits schedule (RET_1^F) intersects the expected return on domestic deposits schedule (RET_1^D) at an exchange rate E_1, which is lower than the par (fixed) value of the exchange rate, E_{par}. To keep the exchange rate at E_{par}, the central bank must intervene in the foreign exchange market to purchase the domestic currency by selling foreign assets, and, like an open market sale, this action means that the monetary base and the money supply decline. Since the exchange rate will continue to be fixed at E_{par}, the expected future exchange rate remains unchanged and so the expected return on foreign deposits schedule remains at RET_1^F). However, the purchase of domestic currency which leads to a fall in the money supply also causes the interest rate on domestic deposits (i^D) to rise. This increase in turn shifts the expected return on domestic deposits RET^D out to the right. The central bank will continue purchasing domestic currency and selling foreign assets until the RET^D curve reaches RET_2^D and the equilibrium exchange rate is at E_{par} at point 2 in panel (a).

---

[5]In 1960, the World Bank established an affiliate, the International Development Association (IDA), which provides particularly attractive loans to third-world countries (with fifty-year maturities and zero interest rates, for example). Funds for these loans are obtained by direct contributions of member countries.

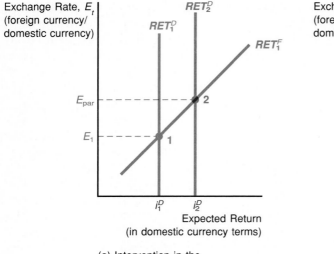
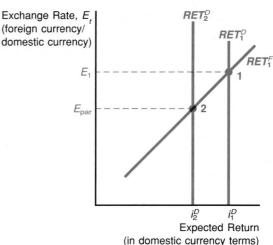

(a) Intervention in the
   case of an overvalued
   exchange rate

(b) Intervention in the
   case of an undervalued
   exchange rate

Figure 22.1

Intervention in the Foreign Exchange Market Under a Fixed Exchange Rate Regime
In panel (a) the exchange rate at E_{par} is overvalued. To keep the exchange rate at E_{par}
(point 2), the central bank must purchase the domestic currency to shift the expected return
on domestic deposits schedule to RET_2^D. In panel (b) the exchange rate at E_{par} is
undervalued so that a central bank sale of domestic currency is needed to shift RET^D to
RET_2^D to keep the exchange rate at E_{par} (point 2).

We have thus come to the conclusion that *when the domestic currency is
overvalued, the central bank must purchase the domestic currency to keep
the exchange rate fixed, but as a result it loses international reserves.*

Panel (b) in Figure 22.1 shows how a central bank intervention keeps the
exchange rate fixed at E_{par} when the exchange rate is initially undervalued,
that is, when RET_1^F and the initial RET_1^D intersect at an exchange rate E_1
which is above E_{par}. Here the central bank must sell the domestic currency
and purchase foreign assets, and this works like an open market purchase to
raise the money supply and to lower the interest rate on domestic deposits,
i^D. The central bank keeps selling the domestic currency and lowers i^D until
RET^D shifts all the way in to RET_2^D where the equilibrium exchange rate is at
E_{par} (point 2 in panel (b)). Our analysis thus leads us to the following result:
*When the domestic currency is undervalued, the central bank must sell the
domestic currency to keep the exchange rate fixed, but as a result it gains
international reserves.*

As we have seen, if a country has an overvalued exchange rate, its central bank's attempts to keep its currency from depreciating will result in a loss
of international reserves. If the country's central bank eventually runs out of
international reserves, it cannot keep its currency from depreciating and a

devaluation must occur in which the par exchange rate is reset at a lower level.

If, on the other hand, a country has an undervalued exchange rate, then its central bank's intervention to keep the currency from appreciating leads to a gain of international reserves. Because, as we will see shortly, the central bank might not want to acquire these international reserves, it might want to reset the par value of its exchange rate at a higher level (a **revaluation**).

Note that if domestic and foreign deposits are perfect substitutes, as is assumed in the model of exchange rate determination used here, a sterilized exchange rate intervention will not be able to keep the exchange rate at E_{par} because, as we have seen in the previous chapter, neither the RET^F or RET^D schedule will shift. For example, if the exchange rate is overvalued, a sterilized purchase of the domestic currency will still leave the expected return on domestic deposits below the expected return on foreign deposits at the par exchange rate - thus the pressure for a depreciation of the domestic currency is not removed. If the central bank keeps on purchasing its domestic currency but continues to sterilize, it will just keep on losing international reserves until it finally runs out of them and is forced to let the value of the currency seek a lower level. If domestic and foreign deposits are not perfect substitutes, then, as was demonstrated in Figure 21.9 in the previous chapter, there is the possibility that sterilized interventions can be used to fix the exchange rate. However, as was also pointed out earlier, the available evidence does not suggest that sterilized interventions can work to keep the exchange rate fixed.

The Bretton Woods System of Fixed Exchange Rates   Under the Bretton Woods system, exchange rates were supposed to change only when a country was experiencing a "fundamental disequilibrium," that is, large persistent deficits or surpluses in its balance of payments. To maintain fixed exchange rates when countries had balance of payments deficits and were losing international reserves, the IMF would loan deficit countries international reserves contributed by other members. As a result of its power to dictate loan terms to borrowing countries, the IMF could encourage deficit countries to pursue contractionary monetary policies that would strengthen their currency or eliminate their balance of payment deficits. If the IMF loans were not sufficient to prevent depreciation of a currency, the country was allowed to devalue its currency by setting a new, lower exchange rate.

A notable weakness of the Bretton Woods system was that although deficit countries losing international reserves could be pressured into devaluing their exchange rate or pursuing contractionary policies, the IMF had no way to force surplus countries to either revalue their exchange rates upwards or pursue more expansionary policies. Particularly troublesome in this regard was the fact that the reserve-currency country, the United States, could not devalue its currency under the Bretton Woods system even if the dollar was overvalued. When the United States attempted to reduce domestic unemployment in the 1960s by pursuing an inflationary monetary policy (see Chapter 28), a "fundamental disequilibrium" of an overvalued dollar developed. Because surplus countries were not willing to revalue their exchange rates upwards, adjustment in the Bretton Woods system did not take place and the system collapsed in 1971.

APPLICATION
TWO INTERNATIONAL FINANCIAL CRISES: /
THE BRITISH DEVALUATION OF 1967
AND THE COLLAPSE OF THE
BRETTON WOODS SYSTEM IN 1971

Among its shortcomings, the Bretton Woods system promoted destabilizing international financial crises in which there would be a "speculative attack" on a currency, that is, massive sales of a weak currency (or purchases of a strong currency) that would hasten a change in the exchange rate. Two major examples of international financial crises that occurred under the Bretton Woods system were the devaluation of the British pound in November 1967 and the events leading up to the collapse of the Bretton Woods system in May 1971. We will study how speculative attacks occurred in these two crises by using our model of exchange rate determination.

Figure 22.2 indicates that before the speculative attack on the pound, the intersection of the RET_1^D and RET_1^F schedules was below the par exchange rate of \$2.80 per pound. (In this example the domestic currency is

Figure 22.2
Foreign Exchange Market for British Pounds in 1967 The realization by speculators that Britain would soon devalue the pound increased the expected return on foreign (dollar) deposits and shifted RET^F out to RET_2^F. The result was the need for a much greater purchase of pounds by the British central bank to raise the interest rate to i_3^D to keep the exchange rate at \$2.80 per pound.

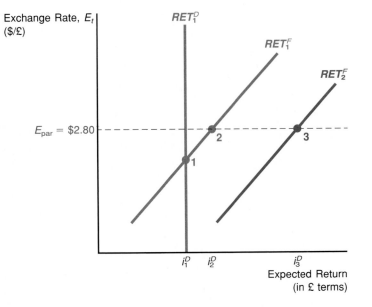

the pound so RET^D is the expected return on pound deposits, while the foreign currency is the dollar so RET^F is the expected return on dollar deposits.) The pound was overvalued and the British central bank (the Bank of England) needed to purchase pounds and sell foreign (dollar) assets so that the money supply would fall and the interest rate on pound deposits would rise to i_2^D, leaving the exchange rate at the par value of $2.80 per pound. (The shift of the RET^D schedule to intersect at point 2 is not shown in the figure to reduce clutter.) The purchase of these pounds resulted in a loss of international reserves that was reflected in persistent deficits in British balance of payments.

By November 17, 1967, the British loss of several billion dollars of reserves was so great that speculators began to suspect that, despite IMF loans, the British would soon devalue. As soon as speculators became convinced that a devaluation was imminent, and thus that the value of foreign (dollar) deposits would rise relative to pound deposits, the expected return on foreign deposits climbed sharply, shifting the expected return on foreign deposits schedule out to RET_2^F in Figure 22.2. The huge increase in the expected return on foreign deposits relative to pound deposits caused a massive sell-off of pounds by speculators. Intervention by the British central bank to prop up the exchange rate became much greater and required a rise in the interest rate on British deposits to i_3^D. Attempts by the Bank of England to meet the speculative attack by purchasing pounds resulted in a colossal loss of international reserves on their part. In fact, on *one day alone*, November 17, the Bank of England was forced to purchase over *$1 billion* of British pounds to keep the exchange rate from falling. The Bank of England now recognized that it could not successfully defend the pound, and the next day it capitulated and devalued the pound by 14%.

Speculators who sold $1 billion worth of pounds to the Bank of England for 1 billion U.S. dollars on November 17 made a fortune. The 14% devaluation on November 18 meant that the dollars they had bought with their pounds rose 14% in value relative to pounds, giving them a profit of $140 million (14% of $1 billion). Not bad for a day's work! The Bank of England, of course, lost $140 million. Defending a currency from a speculative attack is an expensive proposition.

Other financial crises plagued the Bretton Woods system after the British devaluation (the French crisis of 1968, French devaluation in August 1969, the West German float and revaluation in September–October 1969). The system was finally toppled by the international financial crisis that started in early 1971. In 1970 the U.S. balance of payments deficit began to grow rapidly, reaching nearly $10 billion for the year. In the first quarter of 1971 it grew even larger, exceeding $5 billion. These U.S. balance of payments deficits meant that there were matching surpluses in other countries, of which the most important was West Germany.

Figure 22.3 depicts the situation in the foreign exchange market for West German marks. The overvaluation of the U.S. dollar meant that the

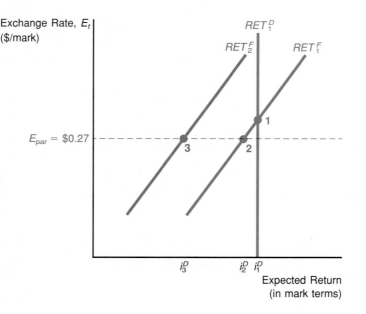

Exchange Rate, E_t
($/mark)

RET_1^D

RET_2^F RET_1^F

$E_{par} = \$0.27$

1

3   2

i_3^D i_2^D i_1^D

Expected Return
(in mark terms)

Figure 22.3
Foreign Exchange Market for German Marks in 1971   The realization by speculators that Germany would soon have to revalue the mark lowered the expected return on foreign (dollar) deposits and shifted RET^F to RET_2^F. The result was the need for a much greater purchase of dollars by the German central bank to lower the interest rate to i_3^D to keep the exchange rate at \$0.27 per mark.

German mark was undervalued at the par exchange rate of approximately \$0.27 to the mark (as shown by the initial schedules RET_1^D and RET_1^F intersecting at point 1). The West German central bank (the Bundesbank) was selling marks and buying dollars in order to shift the RET^D schedule in to the left and as a result was gaining international reserves. From January to March 1971, the Bundesbank bought \$2 billion of U.S. dollars in fulfilling its obligation to keep the exchange rate fixed at \$0.27 per mark. It thus gained \$2 billion of international reserves. In April the West Germans acquired another \$3 billion of international reserves as a result of defending the exchange rate.

The huge purchase of international reserves meant that the German monetary base began to surge upwards, leading to an extremely rapid growth of the German money supply. Because the Bundesbank did not want this process to continue, at some point in the near future it would be forced to revalue the mark upward. Once participants in the foreign exchange market recognized that the upward revaluation of the mark was likely, and thus that foreign (dollar) deposits would likely fall in value relative to the mark, the expected return on foreign dollar deposits decreased sharply, shifting the RET^F schedule in to RET_2^F.

As our analysis predicts, the German central bank now would have to intervene massively to sell marks and buy dollars to keep the exchange rate fixed. On May 4, the Bundesbank bought \$1 billion to defend the dollar and preserve the German exchange rate, as it was obligated to do under the Bretton Woods system. When the foreign exchange market opened on May 5, the game was over. In the *first hour* of trading the Bundesbank was forced to buy *1 billion dollars* to keep the exchange rate fixed. The German central bank then announced that it was halting its foreign exchange operations and the mark (along with several other currencies tied to it) was allowed to float.[6]

In August, President Nixon announced the end of the Bretton Woods system. He suspended the convertibility of dollars into gold as part of his "new economic policy" (which also included domestic wage and price controls). Attempts to patch up the Bretton Woods system of fixed exchange rates with the Smithsonian agreement in December 1971 proved to be unsuccessful, and by 1973, America and its trading partners agreed to allow exchange rates to float.

The Current Managed Float System

Although exchange rates are currently allowed to change daily in response to market forces, central banks have not been willing to give up their option of intervening in the foreign exchange market. Preventing large changes in exchange rates makes it easier for firms and individuals purchasing or selling goods abroad to plan into the future. Furthermore, countries with surpluses in their balance of payments frequently do not want to see their currencies appreciate because it makes their goods more expensive abroad and foreign goods cheaper in their country. Since an appreciation might hurt sales for domestic businesses and increase unemployment, surplus countries often have sold their currencies in the foreign exchange market and acquired international reserves.

Countries with balance of payments deficits do not want to see their currency lose value because it makes foreign goods more expensive for domestic consumers and can stimulate inflation. To keep its value high, deficit countries have often bought their own currency in the foreign exchange market and lost international reserves.

The current international financial system is a hybrid of a fixed exchange and a flexible exchange rate system. These rates fluctuate in response to, but are not determined solely by market forces. Furthermore, many countries continue to keep the value of their currencies fixed against other currencies. Some countries keep their currencies pegged to the dollar, while a group of European countries have formed the European Monetary System (EMS), in which the values of their currencies against each other are not allowed to fluctuate outside a range called the "snake" ($\pm 2.25\%$ for most

---

[6]Not only can it be costly for a central bank to keep its currency from depreciating, as in the British foreign exchange crisis of 1967, but it is also costly to keep its currency from appreciating, as the Germans found in 1971. After the Bundesbank halted its foreign exchange operations, the mark appreciated by 3.7%. The $1 billion bought in one hour on May 5 by the Bundesbank immediately thereafter became worth 3.7% less in terms of German marks. It was, to say the least, an expensive hour for the German central bank.

of them, Spain being an exception). In addition, the EMS countries have developed a new monetary unit, the European Currency Unit (ECU), which they hope will eventually supplant the U.S. dollar in international financial transactions.

The IMF continues to function as a data collector and international lender but does not attempt to encourage fixed exchange rates. The IMF's role of international lender has also become important recently because of the third world debt crisis (discussed in Chapter 10). The IMF has been directly involved in helping those developing countries that have been experiencing difficulties in repaying their loans to come to terms with lenders in the West.

Another important feature of the current system is the continuing deemphasis of gold in international financial transactions. Not only has the United States suspended convertibility of dollars into gold for foreign central banks, but since 1970 the IMF has been issuing a paper substitute for gold, **Special Drawing Rights (SDRs).** Like gold in the Bretton Woods system, SDRs function as international reserves. Unlike gold, whose quantity is determined by gold discoveries and the cost of production, SDRs can be created by the IMF whenever it decides there is an additional need for international reserves to promote world trade and economic growth.

The use of gold in international transactions was further deemphasized by the IMF's elimination of the official gold price in 1975 and by the sale of gold by the U.S. Treasury and the IMF to private interests in order to "demonetize" it. Currently, the price of gold is determined in a free market. Investors who want to speculate in it are able to purchase and sell at will, as do jewelers and dentists who use gold in their businesses.

INTERNATIONAL CONSIDERATIONS AND MONETARY POLICY

Our analysis in this chapter so far has suggested several ways monetary policy can be affected by international considerations. These considerations can have significant implications for the way monetary policy is conducted.

Direct Effects of the Foreign Exchange Market on the Money Supply

When central banks intervene in the foreign exchange market, they acquire or lose international reserves and their monetary base is affected. When a central bank intervenes in the foreign exchange market, it gives up some control of its money supply. For example, in the early 1970s, the German central bank was faced with a dilemma. In attempting to keep the German mark from appreciating too much against the U.S. dollar, the Germans acquired huge quantities of international reserves, leading to a rapid rate of money growth which the German central bank considered to be inflationary.

The German central bank could have tried to eliminate the growth of the money supply by stopping its intervention in the foreign exchange market and reasserting control over its own money supply. Such strategy has a major drawback when the central bank is under pressure not to allow its currency to appreciate: The lower price of imports and higher price of exports as a result of an appreciation in its currency will hurt domestic producers and create unemployment.

Because the U.S. dollar has been treated as a reserve currency, the U.S. monetary base and money supply have been less affected by developments in the foreign exchange market. As long as foreign central banks, rather than the Fed, intervene to keep the value of the dollar from changing, American holdings of international reserves are unaffected. The ability to conduct monetary policy is typically easier when a country's currency is a reserve currency.[7]

Balance of Payments Considerations

Under the Bretton Woods system, balance of payments considerations were more important than they are under the current managed float system. When a nonreserve-currency country is running balance of payments deficits, it necessarily loses international reserves. To keep from running out of these reserves, under the Bretton Woods system it had to implement contractionary monetary policy to strengthen its currency. Exactly that occurred in Britain before the devaluation in 1967. When policy became expansionary, the balance of payments deteriorated and the British were forced to "slam on the brakes" by implementing contractionary policy. Once the balance of payments improved, policy became more expansionary until the deteriorating balance of payments again forced the British to pursue contractionary policy. Such on-again off-again actions became known as a "stop-go" policy and the domestic instability it created was criticized severely.

Since the United States is a major reserve-currency country, it can run large balance of payments deficits without losing huge amounts of international reserves. It does not mean, however, that the Federal Reserve is never influenced by developments in the U.S. balance of payments. Current account deficits in the United States suggest that American businesses may be losing some of their ability to compete because the value of the dollar is too high. In addition, large U.S. balance of payments deficits lead to balance of payments surpluses in other countries, which can lead to large increases in their holdings of international reserves (which was especially true under the Bretton Woods system). Because such increases put a strain on the international financial system and may stimulate world inflation, the Fed worries

---

[7]Yet the central bank of a reserve-currency country faces the disadvantage that it needs to worry about a shift away from the use of its currency as international reserves.

about U.S. balance of payments and current account deficits. Sometimes it tries to shrink them through more contractionary monetary policy.

Exchange Rate Considerations

Unlike balance of payments considerations, which have become less important under the current managed float system, exchange rate considerations now have a more important role to play in the conduct of monetary policy. If a central bank does not want to see its currency fall in value, it may pursue a more contractionary monetary policy of reducing the money supply to raise the domestic interest rate, thereby strengthening its currency. Similarly, if a country experiences an appreciation in its currency, domestic industry may suffer from increased foreign competition and may pressure the central bank to pursue a higher rate of money growth in order to lower the exchange rate.

The pressure to manipulate their exchange rates seems to be greater for central banks in countries other than the United States, but even the Federal Reserve is not completely immune. The growing tide of protectionism stemming from the inability of American firms to compete with foreign firms because of the strengthening dollar from 1980 to early 1985 stimulated congressional critics of the Fed to call for more expansionary monetary policy to lower the value of the dollar. As we saw in Chapter 20, the Fed then did let money growth surge to very high levels. A policy to bring the dollar down was confirmed in the so-called Plaza Agreement of September 1985, in which the finance ministers from the five most important industrial nations in the free world (United States, Japan, West Germany, United Kingdom, and France) agreed to intervene in foreign exchange markets to achieve a desired decline in the dollar. The dollar continued to fall rapidly after the Plaza Agreement, and the Fed played an important role in this decline by continuing to expand the money supply at a rapid rate.

SHOULD THE WORLD RETURN TO THE GOLD STANDARD?

Although monetary policy is currently affected by international considerations, some critics of the current international monetary system suggest that international considerations should play an even more decisive role in the conduct of monetary policy. They advocate a return to the gold standard in which all currencies are convertible into gold. They view the current managed float system as being inherently inflationary because monetary authorities are given too much leeway to pursue expansionary policies. If national currencies were again tied to gold, monetary discipline would be imposed on central banks as a result of the outflow of gold when the country is experiencing inflation and is running a balance of payments deficit. Furthermore, a country whose monetary policies are too contractionary would find gold flowing in, thus making for a more stable economy. The fixed-exchange-rate gold standard system also has the advantage of promoting world trade by decreasing the uncertainty that occurs as a result of fluctuating exchange rates.

The advocates of returning to the gold standard succeeded in getting President Reagan to appoint a U.S. Gold Commission in 1981 to study a possible return to the gold standard. Although the commission's report issued in 1982 agreed with the advocates of a gold standard that there is a strong need for monetary discipline, they did not advocate a return to gold. There are several reasons why they and other economists have rejected the gold standard.

First, the price of gold has undergone large swings in recent years, ranging from $300 to nearly $900 per ounce. Pegging the dollar to gold might produce a dollar whose value fluctuates wildly relative to the value of goods and services so that the price level would undergo wide fluctuations. It would probably not produce the price stability that the advocates of the gold standard seek.

Second, the period during which the gold standard operated most effectively, in the late nineteenth and early twentieth centuries, was not a period of stable prices and high employment. Although the world economy was much less prone to sustained inflation than it is today, there were larger swings in the business cycle and the price level from year to year. Indeed, uncertainty about prices appears to have been even greater under the gold standard than it is today.

Presently, critics of the gold standard seem to have the upper hand and a return to it is unlikely. Nonetheless, the search goes on for an international monetary system that will promote a more stable world economy, lower inflation, and enhance international trade.

SUMMARY

1. The balance of payments is a bookkeeping system for recording all payments between a country and foreign states that have a direct bearing on the movement of funds between them. The official reserve transactions balance is the sum of the current account balance plus the items in the capital account. It indicates the amount of international reserves that must move between countries to finance international transactions.

2. Before World War I, the gold standard was predominant. Currencies were convertible into gold, thus fixing exchange rates between countries. After World War II, the Bretton Woods system and the IMF were established to promote a fixed exchange rate system in which the U.S. dollar was convertible into gold. The Bretton Woods system finally collapsed in 1971 and the international financial system consequently evolved into the managed float regime that we observe today. Exchange rates fluctuate from day to day yet central banks intervene in the foreign exchange market.

3. Three international considerations affect the conduct of monetary policy: direct effects of the

foreign exchange market on the money supply, balance of payments considerations, and exchange rate considerations. Because the United States has been a reserve-currency country in the post–World War II period, U.S. monetary policy has been less affected by developments in the foreign exchange market and its balance of payments than is true for other countries. However, in recent years, exchange rate considerations have been playing a more prominent role in in-fluencing U.S. monetary policy.

4. Some critics of the current international finan-cial system, who contend that it is inherently in-flationary, advocate a return to the gold stan-dard. Although many economists agree with these proponents that there is a greater need for monetary discipline, they do not believe that a gold standard will promote a more stable world economy including a more stable price level.

KEY TERMS

balance of payments

current account

trade balance

capital account

official reserve trans-
  actions balance

gold standard

fixed exchange rate
  regime

Bretton Woods system

International Monetary
  Fund (IMF)

World Bank

reserve currency

devaluation

revaluation

Special Drawing Rights
  (SDRs)

QUESTIONS AND PROBLEMS

1. For each of the following, show in which part of the balance of payments account it appears (cur-rent account, capital account, or method of fi-nancing) and whether it is a receipt or a pay-ment.
   a) An Englishperson's purchase of a share of Johnson and Johnson stock
   b) An American's purchase of an airline ticket from Air France
   c) The Swiss government's purchase of U.S. Treasury bills
   d) A Japanese's purchase of California oranges
   e) $50 million of foreign aid to Honduras
   f) A loan by an American bank to Mexico
   g) An American bank's borrowing of Eurodol-lars

* 2. Why does a balance of payments deficit for the United States have a different effect on its inter-national reserves than a balance of payments deficit for the Netherlands?

3. Under a gold standard, if Britain became more productive relative to the United States, what would happen to the money supplies in the two countries? Why would the changes in the money supply help preserve a fixed exchange rate be-tween the United States and Britain?

* 4. What is the exchange rate between dollars and francs if one dollar is convertible into $\frac{1}{20}$ of an ounce of gold and one franc is convertible into $\frac{1}{40}$ of an ounce of gold?

5. If a country's par exchange rate was underval-ued during the Bretton Woods fixed exchange rate regime, what kind of intervention would that country's central bank be forced to under-take and what effect would it have on its interna-tional reserves and the money supply?

* 6. Why were speculative attacks on a currency more prevalent under the Bretton Woods system than under the current managed float system?

7. Why would an announcement from the IMF that it would make unlimited loans to a country that is suffering from a speculative attack on its cur-rency immediately end the attack? Explain your answer with a diagrammatic analysis of the for-eign exchange market.

* 8. How can a country's large balance of payments surplus contribute to its country's inflation rate?

9. Answer true, false, or uncertain: "If a country

wants to keep its exchange rate from changing, it must give up some control over its money supply."

*10. Why can balance of payments deficits force some countries to implement contractionary monetary policy?

11. Answer true, false, or uncertain: "Balance of payments deficits always cause a country to lose international reserves."

*12. How can persistent U.S. balance of payments deficits help stimulate world inflation?

13. Answer true, false, or uncertain: "Inflation is not possible under a gold standard."

*14. Why is it that in a pure flexible exchange rate system there are no direct effects of the foreign exchange market on the money supply? Does this mean that there is no effect of the foreign exchange market on monetary policy?

15. Answer true, false, or uncertain: "The abandonment of fixed exchange rates after 1973 has meant that countries have pursued more independent monetary policies."

PART VII

Monetary Theory

CHAPTER 23

The Demand for Money

PREVIEW   In earlier chapters you spent much time and effort learning about what the money supply is, how the money supply is determined, and the role of the Federal Reserve System in this process. Now you are ready to explore the role of the money supply in determining the price level and total production of goods and services (aggregate output) in the economy. The study of the effect of money on the economy is called **monetary theory,** and we examine this branch of economics here and in the following chapters.

When economists mention supply, the word *demand* is sure to follow, and the discussion of money is no exception. The supply of money is an essential building block to our understanding of how monetary policy affects the economy, because it suggests the factors that influence the quantity of money in the economy. Not surprisingly, another essential part of monetary theory is the demand for money.

This chapter describes how the theories of the demand for money have evolved over time. We begin with the classical theories refined at the start of the century by economists such as Irving Fisher, Alfred Marshall, and A. C. Pigou; then we move to the Keynesian theories of the demand for money; and we end with Milton Friedman's modern quantity theory.

A central question in monetary theory is whether or to what extent the quantity of money demanded is affected by changes in interest rates. Since this issue is crucial to how we view money's effects on aggregate economic activity, we focus on the role of interest rates in the demand for money.[1]

THE QUANTITY THEORY OF MONEY

Developed by the classical economists in the nineteenth and early twentieth centuries, the quantity theory of money is a theory of how the nominal value of aggregate income is determined. Because it also tells us how much money

---

[1]We will also see in Chapter 25 that the responsiveness of the quantity of money demanded to changes in interest rates has important implications for the relative effectiveness of monetary policy and fiscal policy in influencing aggregate economic activity.

is held for a given amount of aggregate income, it is also a theory of the demand for money. The most important feature of this theory is that it suggests that interest rates have no effect on the demand for money.

Velocity of Money and the Equation of Exchange

The clearest exposition of the classical quantity theory approach is found in the work of the American economist Irving Fisher, in his influential book, *The Purchasing Power of Money*, published in 1911.[2] Fisher wanted to examine the link between the total quantity of money, M (the money supply), and the total amount of spending on final goods and services produced in the economy, PY, where P is the price level and Y is aggregate output. (Total spending, PY, is also thought of equivalently as aggregate nominal income for the economy or as nominal GNP.) The concept that provides the link between M and PY is called the **velocity of money** (or more simply **velocity**— the rate of turnover of money, that is, the average number of times per year that a dollar is spent in buying the total amount of goods and services produced in the economy. Velocity (V) is defined more precisely as total spending, PY, divided by the quantity of money, M:

$$V = \frac{PY}{M} \tag{23.1}$$

If, for example, nominal GNP (PY) in a year is \$5 trillion and the quantity of money is \$1 trillion, then velocity is 5, meaning that the average dollar bill is spent five times in purchasing final goods and services in the economy.

By multiplying both sides of this definition by M, we obtain the **equation of exchange,** which relates nominal income to the quantity of money and velocity:

$$MV = PY \tag{23.2}$$

The equation of exchange thus states that the quantity of money multiplied by the number of times this money is spent in a given year must equal nominal income (the total nominal amount spent on goods and services in that year).[3]

---

[2]Irving Fisher, *The Purchasing Power of Money* (New York: Macmillan, 1911).

[3]Irving Fisher actually first formulated the equation of exchange in terms of the nominal value of transactions in the economy (PT):

$$MV_T = PT$$

where P is the average price per transaction, T is the number of transactions conducted in a year, and V_T, defined as PT/M, is known as the transactions velocity of money. Since T, the nominal value of transactions, is difficult to measure, the quantity theory has been formulated in terms of Y, aggregate output, as follows: T is assumed to be proportional to Y so that $T = vY$, where v is the constant of proportionality. Substituting vY for T in Fisher's equation of exchange above yields $MV_T = vPY$, which can be written as Equation (23.2) in the text in which $V = V_T/v$.

As it stands, Equation (23.2) is nothing more than an identity—a relationship that is true by definition. It does not tell us, for instance, that when the money supply (*M*) changes, nominal income (*PY*) changes in the same direction; a rise in *M*, for example, could be offset by a fall in *V* that leaves *MV* (and therefore *PY*) unchanged. To convert the equation of exchange (an *identity*) into a *theory* of how nominal income is determined requires an understanding of the factors that determine velocity.

Irving Fisher reasoned that velocity is determined by the institutions in an economy that affect the way individuals conduct transactions. If people use charge accounts and credit cards to conduct their transactions and consequently use money less often when making purchases, less money is required to conduct the transactions generated by nominal income (*M* ↓ relative to *PY*), and velocity (*PY/M*) will increase. On the other hand, if it is more convenient for purchases to be paid for with cash or checks (both of which are money), more money is used to conduct the transactions generated by the same level of nominal income, and velocity will fall. Fisher took the view that the institutional and technological features of the economy would affect velocity only slowly over time, so velocity would normally be reasonably constant in the short run.

The Quantity Theory of Money

Fisher's view that velocity is fairly constant in the short run transforms the equation of exchange into the **quantity theory of money,** which states that nominal income is determined solely by movements in the quantity of money: When the quantity of money (*M*) doubles, *MV* doubles and so must *PY*, the value of nominal income. To see how this works, let's assume that velocity is 5 and initially nominal income (GNP) is $5 trillion and the money supply is $1 trillion. If the money supply doubles to $2 trillion, then the quantity theory of money tells us that nominal income will double to $10 trillion (= 5 × $2 trillion).

Because the classical economists (including Irving Fisher) thought that wages and prices were completely flexible, they believed that the level of aggregate output produced in the economy (*Y*) during normal times would remain at the full employment level, so *Y* in the equation of exchange could also be treated as reasonably constant in the short run. The quantity theory of money then implies that if *M* doubles, since *V* and *Y* are constant, *P* also must double. In our preceding example, if aggregate output is $5 trillion, the velocity of 5 and a money supply of $1 trillion indicates that the price level equals 1, since 1 × $5 trillion equals the nominal income of $5 trillion. When the money supply doubles to $2 trillion, the price level must also double to 2, since 2 × $5 trillion equals the nominal income of $10 trillion.

For the classical economists, the quantity theory of money provided an explanation of movements in the price level: *Movements in the price level result solely from changes in the quantity of money.*

The Quantity Theory of Money Demand

Because the quantity theory of money tells us how much money is held for a given amount of aggregate income, it is in fact a theory of the demand for money. We can see this by dividing both sides of the equation of exchange by V, thus rewriting it as

$$M = \frac{1}{V} \times PY$$

When the money market is in equilibrium, the quantity of money that people hold (M) equals the quantity of money demanded (M^d), and we can replace M in the above equation by M^d. Defining $k = (1/V)$, which is a constant because V is a constant, we can rewrite the above equation as

$$M^d = k \times PY \tag{23.3}$$

Equation (23.3) tells us that because k is a constant (since V is a constant), the level of transactions generated by a fixed level of nominal income (PY) determines the quantity of money (M^d) that people demand. Therefore, *Fisher's quantity theory of money suggests that the demand for money is purely a function of income, and interest rates have no effect on the demand for money.*

Fisher came to this conclusion because he believed that people hold money only to conduct transactions and have no freedom of action in terms of the amount they want to hold. The demand for money is determined by (1) the level of transactions generated by the level of nominal income (PY) and (2) the institutions in the economy that affect the way people conduct transactions which determine velocity and hence k.

THE CAMBRIDGE APPROACH TO MONEY DEMAND _____

While Irving Fisher was developing his quantity theory approach to the demand for money, a group of classical economists in Cambridge, England, which included Alfred Marshall and A. C. Pigou, were studying the same topic. Although their analysis led them to an equation that is identical to Fisher's money demand equation ($M^d = k \times PY$), their approach differs significantly. Instead of studying the demand for money by looking solely at the level of transactions and the institutions that affect the way that people conduct transactions as the key determinants, the Cambridge economists asked how much money individuals would want to hold, given a set of circumstances. In the Cambridge model, then, individuals are allowed some flexibility in their decision to hold money and are not completely bound by institutional constraints such as whether they can use credit cards to make purchases. Accordingly, the Cambridge approach did not rule out effects of interest rates on the demand for money.

The classical Cambridge economists recognized that money has two properties that motivate people to want to hold it:

1. Money functions as a medium of exchange that people can use to carry out transactions. The Cambridge economists agreed with Fisher that the demand for money would be *related to* (but not determined solely by) the level of transactions and that there would be a transactions component of money demand proportional to nominal income.

2. Money functions as a store of wealth. This property of money led the Cambridge economists to suggest that the level of people's wealth also affects the demand for money. As an individual's wealth grows, he or she needs to store it by holding a larger quantity of assets—one of which is money. Because the Cambridge economists believed that wealth in nominal terms is proportional to nominal income, they also believed that the wealth component of money demand is proportional to nominal income.

The Cambridge economists concluded that the demand for money would be proportional to nominal income and expressed the demand for money function as

$$M^d = k \times PY$$

where k is the constant of proportionality. Since this equation looks just like Fisher's money demand equation (23.3), it seems that the Cambridge group agreed with Fisher that interest rates play no role in the demand for money in the short run. However, this would be a misleading characterization of the Cambridge approach.

Although the Cambridge economists often treated k as a constant and agreed with Fisher that nominal income is determined by the quantity of money, their approach allowed individuals to choose how much money they wished to hold. It allowed for the possibility that k could fluctuate in the short run, because the decisions about using money to store wealth would depend on the yields and expected returns of other assets that also function as stores of wealth. If these characteristics of other assets changed, then k might change as well. Although this seems a minor distinction between the Fisher and Cambridge approaches, you will see that when John Maynard Keynes (a later Cambridge economist) extended the Cambridge approach, he arrived at a very different view from the quantity theorists on the importance of interest rates to the demand for money.

Summary Both Irving Fisher and the Cambridge economists developed a classical approach to the demand for money in which the demand for money is proportional to income. However, their two approaches differ in that Fisher's emphasized technological factors and ruled out any possible effect of interest rates on the demand for money in the short run, while the Cambridge approach emphasized individual choice and did not rule out effects of interest rates.

IS VELOCITY A CONSTANT?

The classical economists' conclusion that nominal income is determined by movements in the money supply rested on their belief that velocity (PY/M) could be treated as reasonably constant.[4] Is it reasonable to assume that velocity is constant? To answer this, let's look at Figure 23.1, which shows the value of velocity from 1915 to 1990 (nominal income is represented by nominal GNP and the money supply by $M1$ and $M2$), and Table 23.1, which shows the year-to-year changes in velocity from 1915 to 1990.

What we see in Figure 23.1 and Table 23.1 is that even in the short run, velocity fluctuates too much to be viewed as a constant. Prior to 1950, velocity exhibited large swings up and down. This may reflect the substantial instability of the economy in this period, which included two world wars and the Great Depression. (Velocity actually falls, or at least has a decline in its rate of growth, in years when recessions are taking place.) After 1950, velocity appears to have more moderate fluctuations, yet there are large differences in the growth rate of velocity from year to year. The percentage change in $M1$ velocity $(GNP/M1)$ from 1981 to 1982, for example, was -4.7%, while from 1980 to 1981 velocity grew at a rate of 4.9%. This difference of 9.6% means that nominal GNP was 9.6% lower than it otherwise would have been if

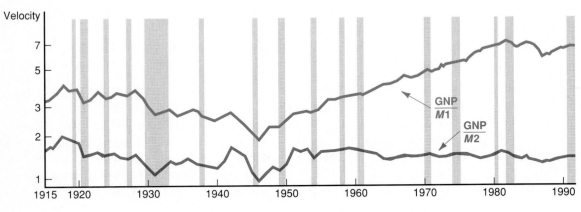

Figure 23.1
Velocity of Money (Annually, 1915–1946; Seasonally Adjusted, Quarterly, 1947–1990)
Shaded areas indicate periods of recessions. Source: *Economic Report of the President.*

---

[4]Actually, the classical conclusion still holds if velocity grows at some uniform rate over time that reflects changes in transactions technology. Thus the concept of a constant velocity should more accurately be thought of here as a lack of upward and downward fluctuations in velocity.

Table 23.1   Change in Velocity from Year to Year: 1915–1990

Year	% Change in M1 Velocity	% Change in M2 Velocity	Year	% Change in M1 Velocity	% Change in M2 Velocity
1915–16	−0.5	1.9	1953–54	−2.5	−3.6
1916–17	9.0	9.3	1954–55	6.7	6.5
1917–18	10.4	12.5	1955–56	4.2	3.2
1918–19	−6.1	−5.0	1956–57	6.1	2.9
1919–20	−2.5	5.7	1957–58	−2.4	−5.0
1920–21	−13.4	−17.7	1958–59	6.8	6.9
1921–22	3.7	−4.9	1959–60	3.3	−0.9
1922–23	7.1	10.6	1960–61	0.3	−3.5
1923–24	−7.2	−7.7	1961–62	5.7	−0.4
1924–25	3.5	2.1	1962–63	1.9	−2.6
1925–26	7.0	4.2	1963–64	2.3	−0.9
1926–27	−5.8	−6.4	1964–65	3.6	0.3
1927–28	1.2	−1.3	1965–66	6.8	4.9
1928–29	7.4	7.9	1966–67	−0.8	−3.2
1929–30	−5.8	−8.7	1967–68	1.5	1.2
1930–31	−5.8	−1.1	1968–69	4.6	3.7
1931–32	−18.1	−16.0	1969–70	0.1	−1.1
1932–33	−0.8	5.9	1970–71	1.9	−4.3
1933–34	0.0	2.9	1971–72	0.7	−2.7
1934–35	−5.0	−3.6	1972–73	6.2	4.8
1935–36	−0.6	2.6	1973–74	3.8	2.7
1936–37	15.0	12.0	1974–75	0.7	−3.6
1937–38	−12.9	−9.6	1975–76	7.5	−1.9
1938–39	−5.9	−5.0	1976–77	3.4	1.0
1939–40	−6.1	−1.4	1977–78	4.4	4.7
1940–41	8.9	12.5	1978–79	4.1	3.4
1941–42	16.5	3.0	1979–80	2.2	0.0
1942–43	−11.0	−3.5	1980–81	4.9	1.5
1943–44	−9.2	−5.5	1981–82	−4.7	−4.8
1944–45	−6.9	−12.5	1982–83	−2.1	−3.9
1945–46	−11.5	−6.7	1983–84	4.3	2.1
1946–47	8.2	6.3	1984–85	−5.3	−1.8
1947–48	11.4	12.0	1985–86	−9.7	−3.7
1948–49	0.6	−0.3	1986–87	3.1	3.1
1949–50	7.6	6.8	1987–88	2.9	2.3
1950–51	9.6	9.8	1988–89	5.7	1.8
1951–52	1.5	9.8	1989–90	1.2	1.8
1952–53	4.6	2.9			

Source: *Economic Report of the President*

velocity had kept growing at the same rate as in 1980–1981.[5] The drop is enough to account for the severe recession that took place in 1981–1982. After 1982, $M1$ velocity appears to have become even more volatile, a fact that has puzzled researchers when they examined the empirical evidence on the demand for money. (See the appendix to this chapter.) $M2$ velocity, on the other hand, has remained more stable than $M1$ velocity after 1982, with the result that the Federal Reserve dropped its $M1$ targets in 1987 and in recent years has focused more on $M2$ targets (and related inflation indicators, see Box 23.1).

Until the Great Depression, economists did not recognize that velocity sharply declines during severe economic contractions. Why did the classical economists not recognize this fact when it is easy to see in the pre-Depression period in Figure 23.1? Unfortunately, accurate data on GNP and the money supply did not exist before World War II. (Only after the war did the government step in and start to collect these data.) The economists had no way of knowing that their view of velocity as a constant was demonstrably false. The decline in velocity during the Great Depression years was so great, however, that even the crude data available to economists at that time suggested that velocity was not constant. This explains why, after the Great Depression, John Maynard Keynes and other economists began to search for other factors influencing the demand for money that might help explain the large fluctuations in velocity.

Let's now examine the theories of money demand that arose from this search for a better explanation of the behavior of velocity.

KEYNES' LIQUIDITY PREFERENCE THEORY

In his famous book, *The General Theory of Employment, Interest and Money* (1936), John Maynard Keynes abandoned the classical view that velocity was a constant and developed a theory of money demand that emphasized the importance of interest rates. Keynes, who was at Cambridge when he wrote *The General Theory*, naturally enough followed the approach developed by his Cambridge predecessors. His theory of the demand for money, which he called **liquidity preference theory,** also asked the question, Why do individuals hold money? But Keynes was far more precise than his predecessors on what influences the decisions of individuals. He postulated that there are three motives behind the demand for money: (1) the transactions motive, (2) the precautionary motive, and (3) the speculative motive.

---

[5]We reach a similar conclusion if we use $M2$ velocity. The percentage change in $M2$ velocity (GNP/$M2$) from 1981 to 1982 was −4.8%, while from 1980 to 1981 it was 1.5%. This difference of 6.3% means that nominal GNP was 6.3% lower than it would have been otherwise if $M2$ velocity had kept growing at the same rate as in 1980–1981.

B o x   2 3 . 1

*P**, the Federal Reserve's New Inflation Indicator

The relative stability of *M2* velocity has prompted development of the so-called *P** concept by the Federal Reserve as a guide for monetary policy.* *P** is defined as follows:

$$P^* = \frac{M2 \times V2^*}{Y^*}$$

where, *V2** = long-run average *M2* velocity, and *Y** = potential (full employment) real GNP. If *M2* velocity does indeed settle down to *V2** in the long run, then given the amount of *M2* relative to potential GNP, the price level, *P*, should also settle down to *P**. Hence, when *P** exceeds *P*, so the theory goes, the price level must rise faster and future inflation will rise above the current inflation rate, indicating a need for tighter monetary policy. On the other hand, when *P** lies below *P*, future inflation will begin to fall.

To see how the *P** indicator would work in practice, let's look at a numerical example. *V2** is calculated as the average value of *M2* velocity since the 1950s and is approximately equal to 1.65, while potential GNP is easily calculated since the proponents of the *P** concept assume that potential GNP grows at a steady rate of 2.5% per year. Suppose that potential GNP (in 1982 dollars) is $5 trillion and *M2* is $4 trillion. Then *P** is calculated as:

$$P^* = \frac{4 \times 1.65}{5} = \frac{6.6}{5} = 1.32$$

If the price level were only 1.25, that is, 25% higher than in 1982, then *P** would be greater than *P*, and inflation is predicted to rise above current levels. On the other hand, if the price level were at 1.4, *P** would be below P, and inflation is predicted to fall.

A key assumption for the usefulness of the *P** concept is that *M2* velocity quickly returns to its long-run level *V2** as is suggested by the quantity theory of money. If this quantity theory assumption is invalid, then *P** might prove to be an unreliable indicator of the path of future inflation. Not surprisingly, some economists are critical of the usefulness of the *P** concept as a guide for monetary policy.[†]

---

*Jeffrey Hallman Hall, Richard Porter, and David Small, "*M2* Per Unit of Potential GNP as an Anchor for the Price Level," Board of Governors of the Federal Reserve System, *Staff Papers,* no. 117 (April 1989).

[†]See Lawrence Christiano, "P*: Not the Inflation Forecaster's Holy Grail," Federal Reserve Bank of Minneapolis *Quarterly Review* 13 (1989), pp. 3–18; and R. A. Pecchenino and Robert H. Rasche, "P* Type Models: Evaluation and Forecasts," National Bureau of Economic Research Working Paper no. 3406 (August 1990).

Transactions Motive

In both the Fisher and Cambridge classical approaches, individuals are assumed to hold money because it is a medium of exchange that can be used to carry out current everyday transactions. Following the classical tradition, Keynes emphasized that this component of the demand for money is primarily determined by the level of people's transactions. Since he believed that these transactions were proportional to income, like the classical economists, he took the transactions component of the demand for money to be proportional to income.

Precautionary Motive

Keynes went beyond the classical analysis by recognizing that, besides holding money to carry out current transactions, people hold additional money as a cushion against an unexpected need. Suppose you've been thinking about buying a fancy stereo; you walk by a store that is having a 50% off sale on the one you want. If you are holding money as a precaution against this occurring, you can purchase the stereo right away. On the other hand, if you are not holding precautionary money balances, you cannot take advantage of the sale. Precautionary money balances also come in handy if you are hit with an unexpected bill, say for a major car repair or hospitalization.

Keynes believed that the amount of precautionary money balances people want to hold is determined primarily by the level of transactions they expect to make in the future and that these transactions are proportional to income. Therefore he postulated that the demand for precautionary money balances is proportional to income.

Speculative Motive

If Keynes had ended his theory with the transactions and precautionary motives, income would be the only important determinant of the demand for money, and he would not have added much to the Cambridge approach. Keynes, however, agreed with the classical Cambridge economists that money is a store of wealth and called this motive for holding money the speculative motive. Since he also agreed with the classical Cambridge economists that wealth is tied closely to income, the speculative component of money demand would be related to income. However, Keynes looked more carefully at the factors that influence the decisions regarding how much money to hold as a store of wealth. Unlike the classical Cambridge economists, who were willing to treat the wealth component of money demand as proportional to income, Keynes believed that interest rates, too, have an important role to play.

Keynes divided the assets that can be used to store wealth into two categories: money and bonds. He then asked the following question: Why would individuals decide to hold their wealth in the form of money rather than bonds?

Thinking back to the discussion of the theory of asset demand (Chapter 5), you would want to hold money if its expected return was greater than the expected return from holding bonds. Keynes assumed that the expected return on money was zero, since in his time (unlike today) most checkable deposits did not have interest payments. For bonds, there are two components of the *expected* return: the interest payment and the *expected* rate of capital gains.

You learned in Chapter 4 that when interest rates rise, the price of a bond falls. If you expect interest rates to rise, you expect the price of the bond to fall and therefore suffer a negative capital gain—that is, a capital loss. If you expect the rise in interest rates to be substantial enough, the capital loss might outweigh the interest payment and your *expected* return on the bond would be negative. In this case, you would want to store your wealth as money because its expected return is higher; that is, its zero return exceeds the negative return on the bond.

Keynes assumed that individuals believe interest rates gravitate to some normal value (an assumption less plausible in today's world). If interest rates are below this normal value, individuals expect the interest rate on bonds to rise in the future and so expect to suffer capital losses on them. As a result, individuals will be more likely to hold their wealth as money rather than bonds, and the demand for money will be high.

What would you expect to happen to the demand for money when interest rates are above the normal value? In general, people will expect interest rates to fall, bond prices to rise, and capital gains to be realized. At higher interest rates they are more likely to expect the return from holding a bond to be positive, thus exceeding the expected return from holding money. They will be more likely to hold bonds than money and the demand for money will be quite low. From Keynes' reasoning, we can conclude that as interest rates rise, the demand for money falls, and therefore, *money demand is negatively related to the level of interest rates.*

Putting the Three Motives Together

In putting the three motives for holding money balances together into a demand for money equation, Keynes was careful to distinguish between *nominal* quantities and *real* quantities. Money is valued in terms of what it can buy. If, for example, all prices in the economy double (the price level doubles), then the same nominal quantity of money will be able to buy only one-half as many goods. Keynes thus reasoned that people want to hold a certain amount of **real money balances** (the quantity of money in real terms)—an amount that his three motives indicated would be related to *real* income (Y) and to interest rates (i).[6] Keynes wrote down the following demand for money equation, known as the liquidity preference function, which says that the demand for real money balances (M^d/P) is a function of (related to) i and Y:

$$\frac{M^d}{P} = f(\underset{-}{i}, \ \underset{+}{Y}) \tag{23.4}$$

---

[6]The classical economists' money demand equation can also be written in terms of real money balances by dividing both sides of Equation (23.3) by the price level, P, to obtain

$$\frac{M^d}{P} = k \times Y$$

The − below i in the liquidity preference function means that the demand for real money balances is negatively related to the interest rate (i), while the + below Y means that the demand for real money balances and real income (Y) are positively related: This is exactly the same money demand function that we discussed in Chapter 6.

Keynes' conclusion that the demand for money is not only related to income but also to interest rates is a major departure from Fisher's view of money demand in which interest rates can have no effect on the demand for money—but it is less of a departure from the Cambridge approach, which did not rule out possible effects of interest rates. However, the classical Cambridge economists did not explore the explicit effects of interest rates on the demand for money.

By deriving the liquidity preference function for velocity (PY/M), we can see that Keynes' theory of the demand for money implies that velocity is not constant but instead fluctuates with movements in interest rates. The liquidity preference equation can be rewritten as

$$\frac{P}{M^d} = \frac{1}{f(i,Y)}$$

By multiplying both sides of this equation by Y and recognizing that M^d can be replaced by M because they must be equal in money market equilibrium, we solve for velocity:

$$V = \frac{PY}{M} = \frac{Y}{f(i,Y)} \tag{23.5}$$

We know that the demand for money is negatively related to interest rates; when i goes up, $f(i,Y)$ declines and therefore velocity rises. In other words, a rise in interest rates encourages people to hold fewer real money balances for a given level of income; therefore the rate of turnover of money (velocity) must be higher. This reasoning indicates that because interest rates have substantial fluctuations, the liquidity preference theory of the demand for money indicates that velocity has substantial fluctuations as well.

An interesting feature of Equation (23.5) is that it explains some of the velocity movements in Figure 23.1, in which we noticed that when recessions occur, velocity falls or its rate of growth declines. What fact regarding the cyclical behavior of interest rates that we discussed in Chapter 6 might help us explain this phenomenon? You might recall that interest rates are procyclical—rising in expansions and falling in recessions. The liquidity preference theory indicates that a rise in interest rates will cause velocity to rise also. Thus the procyclical movements of interest rates should induce procyclical movements in velocity, and this is exactly what we see in Figure 23.1 and Table 23.1.

Keynes' model of the speculative demand for money provides another reason why velocity might have substantial fluctuations. What would happen to the demand for money if the view of the "normal" level of interest rates changes? For example, what if people expect the future normal interest rate to be higher than the current normal interest rate? Because interest rates are then expected to be higher in the future, more people will expect the prices of bonds to fall and will expect capital losses. Thus the expected returns from holding bonds will decline, and money will become more attractive relative to bonds. The result: The demand for money will increase. This means that $f(i,Y)$ will increase and so velocity will fall. Velocity will change as expectations about future normal levels of interest rates change, and unstable expectations about future movements in normal interest rates can lead to instability of velocity. This is one more reason why Keynes rejected the view that velocity could be treated as a constant.

Study Guide

Keynes' explanation of how interest rates affect the demand for money will be easier to understand if you think of yourself as an investor who is trying to decide whether to invest in bonds or, alternatively, hold money. Ask yourself what you would do if you expected the normal interest rate to be lower in the future than it is currently. Would you rather be holding bonds or money?

Summary   Keynes' liquidity preference theory is an extension of the classical Cambridge approach but is far more precise about the reasons why people hold money. Specifically, Keynes postulated three motives for holding money: (1) the transactions motive, (2) the precautionary motive, and (3) the speculative motive. Although Keynes viewed the transactions and precautionary components of the demand for money to be proportional to income, he reasoned that the speculative motive would be negatively related to the level of interest rates.

Keynes' model of the demand for money has the important implication that velocity is not constant but instead is positively related to interest rates, which fluctuate substantially. His theory also rejected the constancy of velocity because changes in people's expectations about the normal level of interest rates would cause a shift in the demand for money that would cause velocity to shift as well. Thus Keynes' liquidity preference theory casts doubt on the classical quantity theory that nominal income is determined primarily by movements in the quantity of money.

ADDITIONAL DEVELOPMENTS IN THE KEYNESIAN APPROACH

After World War II, economists began to take the Keynesian approach to the demand for money even further by developing more precise theories to explain the three Keynesian motives for holding money. Because interest rates were viewed as a crucial element in monetary theory, a key focus of this research was to better understand the role of interest rates in the demand for money.

Transactions Demand

William J. Baumol and James Tobin independently developed similar demand for money models, which demonstrated that even money balances held for transactions purposes are sensitive to the level of interest rates.[7] In developing their models, they considered a hypothetical individual who receives a payment once a period and spends it over the course of this period. In their model, money, which earns zero interest, is held only because it can be used to carry out transactions.

To refine this analysis, let's say that Grant Smith receives $1000 at the beginning of the month and spends it on transactions that occur at a constant rate during the course of the month. If Grant keeps the $1000 in cash in order to carry out his transactions, then his money balances follow the saw-toothed pattern displayed in Figure 23.2. At the beginning of the month he has $1000, and by the end of the month he has no cash left because he has

Figure 23.2
Cash Balances for an Individual Who Keeps All the Monthly Payment in Cash The $1000 payment at the beginning of each month is held entirely as cash and is spent at a constant rate until it is exhausted by the end of the month. At this point, a new $1000 payment is received and the whole process begins again.

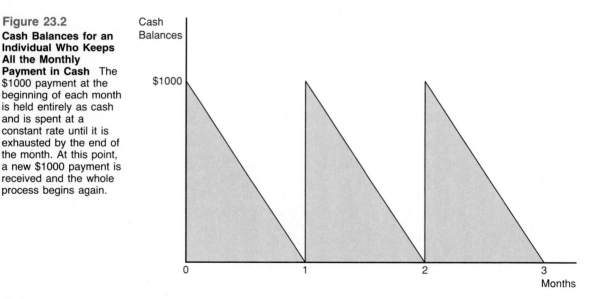

[7]William J. Baumol, "The Transactions Demand for Cash: An Inventory Theoretic Approach," *Quarterly Journal of Economics* 66 (November 1952), pp. 545–556; James Tobin, "The Interest-Elasticity of the Transactions Demand for Cash," *Review of Economics and Statistics* 38 (August 1956), pp. 241–247.

spent it all. Over the course of the month his holdings of money will on average be $500 (his holdings at the beginning of the month, $1000, plus his holdings at the end of the month, $0, divided by 2).

At the beginning of the next month, Grant receives another $1000 payment, which he puts into cash, and the same decline in money balances begins again. This process repeats monthly, and his average money balance during the course of the year is $500. Since his yearly nominal income is $12,000 and his holdings of money average out to $500, the velocity of money $(V = PY/M)$ is $12,000/$500 = 24.

Suppose that as a result of taking a money and banking course, Grant realizes that he can improve his situation by not always holding cash. In January, then, he decides to hold part of his $1000 in cash and puts part of it into an income-earning security such as bonds. At the beginning of each month Grant keeps $500 in cash and uses the other $500 to buy a Treasury bond. As you can see in Figure 23.3, he starts out each month with $500 of cash and $500 of bonds, and by the middle of the month, his cash balances are run down to zero. Because bonds cannot be used directly to carry out transactions, Grant must sell them and turn them into cash so he can carry out the rest of the month's transactions. At the middle of the month, then, Grant's bond holdings drop to zero and his cash balances rise back up to $500. By the end of the month, the cash is gone. When he again receives his next $1000 monthly payment, he again divides it into $500 of cash and $500 of bonds, and the process continues. The net result of this process is that the average cash balance held during the month is $500/2 = $250—just half of what it was before. Velocity has doubled to $12,000/$250 = 48.

Figure 23.3
Cash and Bond Balances for an Individual Who Keeps Only Half the Monthly Payment in Cash Half of a monthly $1000 payment is put into bonds and half into cash. At the middle of the month, cash balances are zero and bonds must be sold to bring balances up to $500. By the end of the month, cash balances dwindle to zero.

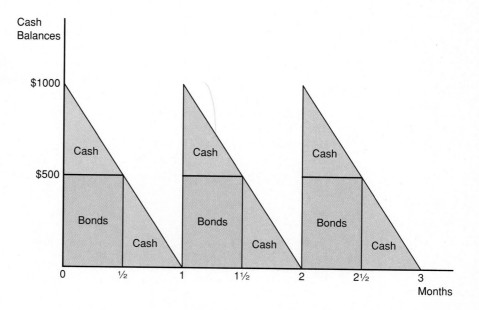

What has Grant Smith gained from his new strategy? He has earned interest on $500 of bonds that he held for half the month. If the interest rate is 1% per month, he has earned an additional $2.50 (= ½ × 1% × $500) per month.

Sounds like a pretty good deal, doesn't it? In fact, if he had kept $333.33 in cash at the beginning of the month, he would have been able to hold $666.67 in bonds for the first third of the month. Then he could have sold $333.33 of bonds and held on to $333.34 of bonds for the next third of the month. Finally, two-thirds of the way through the month, he would have had to sell the remaining bonds to raise cash. The net result of this is that Grant would have earned $3.33 per month [= (⅓ × 1% × $666.67) + (⅓ × 1% × $333.34)]. This is an even better deal. His average cash holdings in this case would be $333.33/2 = $166.67. Clearly, the lower his average holdings of cash balances, the more interest he will earn.

As you might expect, there is a catch to all this. In buying bonds, Grant incurs transactions costs of two types. First, he must pay a straight brokerage fee for the buying and selling of the bonds. These fees increase when average cash balances are lower because Grant will be buying and selling bonds more often. Second, by holding less cash, he will have to make more trips to the bank to get the cash, once he has sold some of his bonds. Since "time is money," this must also be counted as part of the transactions costs.

Grant is faced with a trade-off. If he holds very little cash, he can earn a lot of interest on bonds, but he will incur greater transactions costs. If the interest rate is high, the benefits of holding bonds will be high relative to the transactions costs and he will hold more bonds and less cash. On the other hand, if interest rates are low, the transactions costs from holding a lot of bonds may outweigh the interest payments and Grant would then be better off holding more cash and fewer bonds.

The conclusion of the Baumol-Tobin analysis may be stated thus: As interest rates increase, the amount of cash held for transactions purposes will decline, which, in turn, means that velocity will increase as interest rates increase.[8] ***Put another way, the transactions component of the demand for money is negatively related to the level of interest rates.***

The basic idea in the Baumol-Tobin analysis is that there is an opportunity cost of holding money—the interest that can be earned on other assets. On the other hand, there is a benefit to holding money—the avoidance of transactions costs. When interest rates increase, people will try to economize on their holdings of money for transactions purposes because the opportunity cost of holding money has increased. By using simple models, Baumol

---

[8]Similar reasoning leads to the conclusion that as brokerage fees increase, the demand for transactions money balances increases as well. When these fees rise, the benefits from holding transactions money balances increase because, by holding these balances, an individual will not have to sell bonds as often, thereby avoiding these higher brokerage costs. The greater benefits to holding money balances relative to the opportunity cost of interest foregone, then, lead to a higher demand for transactions balances.

and Tobin revealed something we might otherwise not have seen: that the transactions demand for money, and not just the speculative demand for money, will be sensitive to interest rates. The Baumol-Tobin analysis presents a nice demonstration of the value of economic modeling.

Study Guide

The idea that as interest rates increase, the opportunity cost of money increases so that the demand for money falls can be stated equivalently with the terminology of expected returns used earlier. As interest rates increase, the expected return on the other asset, bonds, increases so that the relative expected return on money falls, thus lowering the demand for money. These two explanations are in fact identical because as we saw in Chapter 6, changes in the opportunity cost of an asset are just a description of what is happening to the relative expected return. The opportunity cost terminology was used by Baumol and Tobin in their work on the transactions demand for money, and that is why we used this terminology in the text. To make sure you understand the equivalence of the two terminologies, try to translate the reasoning in the precautionary demand section from an opportunity cost terminology to an expected returns terminology.

Precautionary Demand

Models that explore the precautionary motive of the demand for money have been developed along lines similar to the Baumol-Tobin framework, so we will not go into great detail about them here. We have already discussed the benefits of holding precautionary money balances, but weighed against these benefits must be the opportunity cost of the interest foregone by holding money. We therefore have a trade-off similar to the one for transactions balances. As interest rates rise, the opportunity cost of holding precautionary balances rises and so the holdings of these money balances fall. We then have a result similar to the one found for the Baumol-Tobin analysis.[9] *The precautionary demand for money is negatively related to interest rates.*

Speculative Demand

Keynes' analysis of the speculative demand for money was open to several serious criticisms. It indicates that an individual holds only money as a store of wealth when the expected return on bonds is less than the expected return

---

[9]These models of the precautionary demand for money also reveal that as uncertainty about the level of future transactions grows, the precautionary demand for money will increase. This is so because greater uncertainty means that individuals are more likely to incur transactions costs if they are not holding precautionary balances. The benefit of holding such balances then increases relative to the opportunity cost of foregone interest and so the demand for them then rises.

on money, and holds only bonds when the expected return on bonds is greater than the expected return on money. Solely in the rare instance when people have expected returns on bonds and money that are exactly equal would they hold both. Keynes' analysis therefore implies that practically no one holds a diversified portfolio of bonds and money as a store of wealth—that is, holds money and bonds at the same time. Since diversification is apparently a sensible strategy for choosing which assets to hold (recall Chapter 5), the fact that it rarely occurs in Keynes' analysis is a serious shortcoming of his theory of the speculative demand for money.

Tobin developed a model of the speculative demand for money that attempted to avoid this criticism of Keynes' analysis.[10] His basic idea was that not only do people care about the expected return on one asset versus another when they decide what to hold in their portfolio, but they also care about the riskiness of the returns from each asset. Specifically, Tobin assumed that most people are risk-averse—that is, they do not like risk. An important characteristic of money is that its expected return is certain; Tobin assumed it to be zero. Bonds, on the other hand, can have substantial fluctuations in price, and their returns can be quite risky and even quite negative. Hence, even if the expected returns on bonds exceed the expected return on money, people still might want to hold money as a store of wealth, because it has less risk associated with its return than do bonds.

The Tobin analysis also shows that people can reduce the total amount of risk in a portfolio by diversifying, that is, by holding both bonds and money. The model suggests that individuals will hold bonds and money simultaneously as stores of wealth. Since this is probably a more realistic description of people's behavior than that of Keynes, Tobin's rationale for the speculative demand for money seems to rest on more solid ground.

Tobin's attempt to improve on Keynes' rationale for the speculative demand for money was only partially successful, however. It is still not clear that the speculative demand even exists. What if there are assets that have no risk—like money—but earn a higher return? Will there be any speculative demand for money? No, because an individual will always be better off holding such an asset rather than money. His or her resulting portfolio will enjoy a higher expected return, yet has no higher risk. Do such assets exist in the American economy? The answer is "yes." U.S. Treasury bills, money market mutual fund shares, and other assets that have no default risk provide certain returns that are greater than those available on money. Therefore, why would anyone want to hold money balances as a store of wealth? (Remember, however, we have seen that people would want to hold money for transactions and precautionary reasons.)

Although Tobin's analysis did not explain why money is held as a store of wealth, it was an important development in our understanding of how

---

[10]James Tobin, "Liquidity Preference as Behavior Towards Risk," *Review of Economic Studies* 25 (February 1958), pp. 65–86.

people should choose among assets. Indeed, his analysis was an important step in the development of the academic field of finance, which examines asset pricing and portfolio choice (the decision to buy one asset over another).

Summary   More recent developments in the Keynesian approach have attempted to give a more precise explanation for the transactions, precautionary, and speculative demand for money. The attempt to improve the rationale of Keynes for the speculative demand for money has been only partially successful; it is still not clear that this demand even exists. However, the models of the transactions and precautionary demand for money indicate that these components of money demand are negatively related to interest rates. Thus Keynes' proposition that the demand for money is sensitive to interest rates—suggesting that velocity is not constant so that nominal income might be affected by other factors than the quantity of money—is still supported by this more recent analysis.

FRIEDMAN'S MODERN QUANTITY THEORY OF MONEY

In 1956, Milton Friedman developed a theory of the demand for money in his famous article, "The Quantity Theory of Money, A Restatement."[11] Although Friedman frequently refers to Irving Fisher and the quantity theory, his analysis of the demand for money is actually closer to that of Keynes and the Cambridge approach than it is to that of Fisher.

Like those before him, Friedman pursued the question of why people choose to hold money. Instead of analyzing the specific motives for holding money, as did Keynes, Friedman simply stated that the demand for money must be influenced by the same factors that influence the demand for any asset. Friedman then applied the theory of asset demand to money.

The theory of asset demand (Chapter 5) indicates that the demand for money should be a function of the resources available to individuals (that is, their wealth) and the expected returns on other assets relative to the expected return on money. Like Keynes, Friedman recognized that people want to hold a certain amount of real money balances (the quantity of money in real terms). From this reasoning, Friedman expressed his formulation of the demand for money as follows:[12]

---

[11]Milton Friedman, "The Quantity Theory of Money: A Restatement," in Milton Friedman, ed., *Studies in the Quantity Theory of Money* (Chicago: University of Chicago Press, 1956).

[12]Friedman also added to his formulation a term *h* which represented the ratio of human to nonhuman wealth. He reasoned that if a person had more of his permanent income coming from labor income and thus from his human capital, he would be less liquid than if he were receiving his income from financial assets. In this case, the person might want to hold more money because it is a more liquid asset than the alternatives. This *h* term plays no essential role in Friedman's theory and has no important implications for monetary theory. This is why we ignore it in the money demand function.

$$\frac{M^d}{P} = f(\underset{+}{Y_p}, \underset{-}{r_b - r_m}, \underset{-}{r_e - r_m}, \underset{-}{\pi^e - r_m}) \tag{23.6}$$

in which the signs underneath the equation indicate whether the demand for money is positively (+) or negatively (−) related to the terms immediately above them, and

M^d/P = the demand for real money balances

Y_p = Friedman's measure of wealth known as *permanent income* (technically, the present discounted value of all expected future income, but more easily described as expected average long-run income)

r_m = the expected return on money

r_b = the expected return on bonds

r_e = the expected return on equity (common stocks)

π^e = the expected inflation rate

Let us look in more detail at the variables in Friedman's money demand function and what they imply for the demand for money.

Since the demand for an asset is positively related to wealth, money demand is positively related to Friedman's wealth concept, permanent income (indicated by the + underneath it). Unlike our usual concept of income, permanent income (which can be thought of as expected average long-run income) has much smaller short-run fluctuations, because many movements of income are transitory (short-lived). For example, in a business cycle expansion income increases rapidly, but because some of this increase is temporary, average long-run income does not change very much. Thus in a boom permanent income rises much less than does income. During a recession much of the income decline is transitory, and average long-run income (hence permanent income) falls less than does income. One implication of Friedman's use of the concept of permanent income as a determinant of the demand for money is that the demand for money will not fluctuate much with business cycle movements.

An individual can hold wealth in several forms besides money; Friedman categorized them into three types of assets: bonds, equity (common stocks), and goods. The incentives for holding these assets rather than money are represented by the expected return on each of these assets relative to the expected return on money, the last three terms in the money demand function. The minus sign underneath each indicates that, as each term rises, the demand for money will fall.

The expected return on money (r_m), which appears in all three terms, is influenced by two factors:

1. The services provided by banks on deposits included in the money supply, such as provision of receipts in the form of canceled checks or the automatic paying of bills, and so forth. When these services are increased, the expected return from holding money rises.

2. The interest payments on money balances. NOW accounts and other deposits that are included in the money supply currently pay interest. As these interest payments rise, the expected return on money rises.

The terms $r_b - r_m$ and $r_e - r_m$ represent the expected returns on bonds and equity relative to money; as they rise, the relative expected return of money falls and the demand for money falls. The final term $(\pi^e - r_m)$ represents the expected return on goods relative to money. The expected return from holding goods is the expected rate of capital gains that occurs when their prices rise and thus is equal to the expected inflation rate (π^e). If the expected inflation rate is 10%, for example, then goods prices are expected to rise at a 10% rate and their expected return is 10%. When $\pi^e - r_m$ rises, the expected return on goods relative to money rises and the demand for money falls.

Distinguishing Between the Friedman and Keynesian Theories

There are several differences between Friedman's theory of the demand for money and the Keynesian theories. One is that by including many assets as alternatives to money, Friedman recognized that more than one interest rate is important to the operation of the aggregate economy. Keynes, on the other hand, lumped financial assets other than money into one big category—bonds—because he felt that their returns move sufficiently together. If this is so, the expected return on bonds will be a good indicator of the expected returns on other financial assets and there will be no need to include them separately in the money demand function.

Also in contrast to Keynes, Friedman viewed money and goods as substitutes; that is, people choose between them when deciding how much money to hold. This is why Friedman included the expected return on goods relative to money as a term in his money demand function. The assumption that money and goods are substitutes indicates that changes in the quantity of money may have a direct effect on aggregate spending.

In addition, Friedman stressed two issues in discussing his demand for money function that distinguish it from Keynes' liquidity preference theory. First, Friedman did not take the expected return on money to be a constant, as did Keynes. When interest rates rise in the economy, banks make more profits on their loans, and they want to attract more deposits to increase the volume of their now more profitable loans. If there are no restrictions on interest payments on deposits, banks attract deposits by paying higher interest rates on them. Because the industry is competitive, the expected return on money held as bank deposits then rises with the higher interest rates on bonds and loans. The banks compete to get deposits until there are no excess profits, and in doing so they close the gap between interest earned on loans versus interest paid on deposits. The net result of this competition in the banking industry is that $r_b - r_m$ stays relatively constant when the interest rate i rises.[13]

What if there are restrictions on the amount of interest that can be paid by banks on their deposits? Will the expected return on money be a constant? As interest rates rise, will $r_b - r_m$ rise as well? Friedman thought not. He argued that although banks might be restricted from making pecuniary payments on their deposits, they can still compete with each other on the quality dimension. They can, for example, provide more services to a depositor by providing more tellers, paying bills for the depositor automatically, providing more cash machines at more accessible locations, and so on. The result of these improvements in money services is that the expected return from holding deposits will rise. Hence, despite the restrictions on pecuniary interest payments, we still might find that a rise in market interest rates will raise the expected return on money sufficiently so that $r_b - r_m$ will remain relatively constant.[14] *Unlike Keynes' theory, which indicates that interest rates are an important determinant of the demand for money, Friedman's theory suggests that changes in interest rates should have little effect on the demand for money.*

Therefore, Friedman's money demand function is essentially one in which permanent income is the primary determinant of money demand, and his money demand equation can be approximated by

$$\frac{M^d}{P} = f(Y_p) \tag{23.7}$$

In Friedman's view, the demand for money is insensitive to interest rates—not because he viewed the demand for money as insensitive to changes in the incentives for holding other assets relative to money, but rather because changes in interest rates should have little effect on these incentive terms in the money demand function. The incentive terms remain relatively constant, because any rise in the expected returns on other assets as a result of the rise in interest rates would be matched by a rise in the expected return on money.

The second issue Friedman stressed is the stability of the demand for money function. In contrast to Keynes, Friedman suggested that random fluctuations in the demand for money are small and that the demand for

---

[13]Friedman does suggest that there is some increase in $r_b - r_m$ when i rises because part of the money supply (especially currency) is held in forms that cannot pay interest either in a pecuniary or nonpecuniary form. See, for example, Milton Friedman, "Why a Surge of Inflation Is Likely Next Year," *Wall Street Journal* (Thursday, September 1, 1983).

[14]Competing on the quality of services is characteristic of many industries that are restricted from competing with prices. For example, in the 1960s and early 1970s when airfares were set at too high a level by the Civil Aeronautics Board, airlines were not allowed to lower their fares to attract customers. Instead, they improved the quality of their service by providing free wine, fancier food, piano bars, movies, and wider seats.

money can be predicted accurately by the money demand function. When combined with his view that the demand for money is insensitive to changes in interest rates, this means that velocity is highly predictable. We can see this by writing down the velocity that is implied by the money demand Equation (23.7):

$$V = \frac{Y}{f(Y_p)} \tag{23.8}$$

Since the relationship between Y and Y_p is usually quite predictable, a stable money demand function (that is, a money demand function that does not undergo pronounced shifts so that it predicts the demand for money accurately) implies that velocity is predictable as well. If we can predict what velocity will be next period, then a change in the quantity of money will produce a predictable change in aggregate spending. Even though velocity is no longer assumed to be constant, the money supply continues to be the primary determinant of nominal income as in the quantity theory of money. Therefore, Friedman's theory of money demand is indeed a restatement of the quantity theory, because it leads to the same conclusion about the importance of money to aggregate spending.

You might recall that we said that the Keynesian liquidity preference function (in which interest rates *are* an important determinant of the demand for money) is able to explain the procyclical movements of velocity that we find in the data. Can Friedman's money demand formulation explain this procyclical velocity phenomenon as well?

The key clue to answering this question is the presence of permanent income rather than measured income in the money demand function. What happens to permanent income in a business cycle expansion? Because much of the increase in income will be transitory, permanent income rises much less than income. Friedman's money demand function then indicates that the demand for money rises only a small amount relative to the rise in measured income, and as Equation (23.8) indicates, velocity rises. Similarly, in a recession, the demand for money falls less than income because the decline in permanent income is small relative to income, and velocity falls. In this way we have the procyclical movement in velocity.

Summary   Friedman's theory of the demand for money used a similar approach to that of Keynes and the earlier Cambridge economists, but did not go into detail about the motives for holding money. Instead, Friedman made use of the theory of asset demand to indicate that the demand for money will be a function of permanent income and the expected returns on alternative assets relative to the expected return on money. There are two major differences between Friedman's theory and Keynes'. Friedman believed that changes in interest rates have little effect on the expected returns of other assets relative to money. Thus, in contrast to Keynes, he viewed the demand for money as insensitive to interest rates. In addition, he differed from

Keynes in stressing that the money demand function does not undergo substantial shifts and so is stable. These two differences also indicate that velocity is predictable, yielding a quantity theory conclusion that money is the primary determinant of aggregate spending.

SUMMARY

1. Irving Fisher developed a transactions-based theory of the demand for money in which the demand for real balances is proportional to real income and is insensitive to interest rate movements. An implication of his theory is that velocity, the rate of turnover of money, is constant. This generates the quantity theory of money, which implies that aggregate spending is determined solely by movements in the quantity of money.

2. The classical Cambridge approach tried to answer the question of how much money individuals want to hold. This approach also viewed the demand for real balances as proportional to real income, but it differs from Fisher's analysis in that it does not rule out interest rate effects on the demand for money.

3. The classical view that velocity can be effectively treated as a constant is not supported by the data. The nonconstancy of velocity became especially clear to the economics profession after the sharp drop in velocity during the years of the Great Depression.

4. Keynes extended the Cambridge approach by suggesting three motives for holding money: the transactions motive, the precautionary motive, and the speculative motive. His resulting liquidity preference theory views the transactions and precautionary components of money demand as proportional to income. However, the speculative component of money demand is viewed as sensitive to interest rates as well as to expectations about the future movements of interest rates. This theory, then, implies that velocity is very unstable and cannot be treated as a constant.

5. Additional developments in the Keynesian approach provided a better rationale for the three Keynesian motives for holding money. Interest rates were found to be important to the transactions and precautionary components of money demand as well as to the speculative component.

6. Milton Friedman's theory of money demand used a similar approach to that of Keynes and the classical Cambridge economists. Treating money as any other asset, Friedman made use of the theory of asset demand to derive a demand for money that is a function of the expected returns on other assets relative to the expected return on money and permanent income. In contrast to Keynes, Friedman believed the demand for money is stable and insensitive to interest rate movements. His belief that velocity is predictable (although not constant), in turn leads to the quantity theory conclusion that money is the primary determinant of aggregate spending.

KEY TERMS

monetary theory

velocity (of money)

equation of exchange

quantity theory of money

liquidity preference theory

real money balances

QUESTIONS AND PROBLEMS

* 1. The money supply has been growing at 10% per year and nominal GNP has been growing at 20% per year. The data are as follows (in billions of dollars):

	1992	1993	1994
M	$ 100	$ 110	$ 121
PY	$1000	$1200	$1440

Calculate the velocity in each year. At what rate is velocity growing?

2. Calculate what happens to nominal GNP if velocity remains constant at 5 and the money supply increases from $200 billion to $300 billion.

* 3. What happens to nominal GNP if the money supply grows by 20% but velocity declines by 30%?

4. If credit cards were made illegal by congressional legislation, what would happen to velocity? Explain your answer.

* 5. If velocity and aggregate output are reasonably constant (as the classical economists believed), what happens to the price level when the money supply increases from $1 trillion to $4 trillion?

6. If velocity and aggregate output remain constant at 5 and 1000, respectively, what happens to the price level if the money supply declines from $400 billion to $300 billion?

* 7. Answer true, false, or uncertain: "Since both Fisher and the classical Cambridge economists ended with the same equation for the demand for money, $M^d = k \times PY$, their theories are equivalent."

8. Using data from the *Economic Report of the President,* calculate velocity for the M2 definition of the money supply in the past five years. Does velocity appear to be constant?

* 9. In Keynes' analysis of the speculative demand for money, what will happen to money demand if suddenly people decide that the "normal" level of the interest rate has declined? Why?

10. Why is Keynes' analysis of the speculative demand for money important to his view that velocity will undergo substantial fluctuations and thus cannot be treated as constant?

*11. If interest rates on bonds go to zero, what does the Baumol-Tobin analysis suggest Grant Smith's average holdings of money balances should be?

12. If brokerage fees go to zero, what does the Baumol-Tobin analysis suggest Grant Smith's average holdings of money should be?

*13. Answer true, false, or uncertain: "In Tobin's analysis of the speculative demand for money, people will hold both money and bonds, even if bonds are expected to earn a positive return."

14. Both Keynes' and Friedman's theories of the demand for money suggest that as the relative expected return of money falls, the demand for it will fall. Why does Friedman think that money demand is unaffected by changes in interest rates, while Keynes thought that money demand is affected by changes in interest rates?

*15. Why does Friedman's view of the demand for money suggest that velocity is predictable, whereas Keynes' view suggests the opposite?

Empirical Evidence on the Demand for Money

As we have seen, the alternative theories of the demand for money can have very different implications for our view of the role of money in the economy. Which of these theories is an accurate description of the real world is an important question, and it is the reason why evidence on the demand for money has been at the center of many debates on the effects of monetary policy on aggregate economic activity. Here we examine the empirical evidence on the two primary issues that distinguish the different theories of money demand and that affect their conclusions about whether the quantity of money is the primary determinant of aggregate spending: (1) Is the demand for money sensitive to changes in interest rates? and (2) Is the demand for money function stable over time?

Interest Rates and Money Demand

In Chapter 23 we saw that if interest rates do not affect the demand for money, then velocity is more likely to be a constant—or at least predictable—so that the quantity theory view that aggregate spending is determined by the quantity of money is more likely to be true. On the other hand, the more sensitive is the demand for money to interest rates, the more unpredictable velocity will be and the link between the money supply and aggregate spending will be less clear. Indeed, there is an extreme case of ultrasensitivity of the demand for money to interest rates, called the "liquidity trap," in which monetary policy has no effect on aggregate spending.

James Tobin conducted one of the earliest studies on the link between interest rates and money demand using U.S. data.[1] Tobin separated out transactions balances from other money balances, which he called "idle balances," by assuming that transactions balances were proportional to income only, while idle balances were related to interest rates only. He then looked at whether his measure of idle balances was inversely related to interest rates in the period 1922–1941 by plotting the average level of idle balances in each

---

[1] James Tobin, "Liquidity Preference and Monetary Policy," *Review of Economics and Statistics* 29 (May 1947), pp. 124–131.

year against the average interest rate on commercial paper in that year. When he found a clear-cut inverse relationship between interest rates and idle balances, Tobin concluded that the demand for money is sensitive to interest rates.[2]

Additional empirical evidence on the demand for money strongly confirms Tobin's finding.[3] Does this sensitivity ever become so high that we approach the case of the liquidity trap in which monetary policy is ineffective? The answer is almost certainly "no." Keynes suggested in *The General Theory* that a liquidity trap might occur when interest rates are extremely low. (However, he did state that he had never yet seen an occurrence of a liquidity trap.)

Typical of the evidence demonstrating that the liquidity trap has never occurred is that of David Laidler, Karl Brunner, and Allan Meltzer, who looked at whether the interest sensitivity of money demand increased in periods when interest rates were very low.[4] Laidler and Meltzer looked at this question by seeing if the interest sensitivity of money demand differed across periods, especially in periods such as the 1930s when interest rates were particularly low.[5] They found that there was no tendency for the interest sensitivity to increase as interest rates fell—in fact, the interest sensitivity did not change from period to period. Brunner and Meltzer explored this question by recognizing that a higher interest sensitivity in the 1930s as a result of a liquidity trap implies that a money demand function estimated for this period should not predict well in other more normal periods. What

---

[2]A problem with Tobin's procedure is that idle balances are not really distinguishable from transactions balances. As the Baumol-Tobin model of transactions demand for money makes clear, transactions balances will be related to both income and interest rates just like idle balances.

[3]See David E. W. Laidler, *The Demand for Money: Theories and Evidence,* 3rd ed. (New York: Harper and Row, 1985). There is only one major study that finds that the demand for money is insensitive to interest rates: Milton Friedman, "The Demand for Money—Some Theoretical and Empirical Results," *Journal of Political Economy* 67 (June 1959), pp. 327–351. He concluded that the demand for money is not sensitive to interest rate movements, but as later work by David Laidler (using the same data as Friedman) demonstrated, Friedman used a faulty statistical procedure that biased his results: David Laidler, "The Rate of Interest and the Demand for Money—Some Empirical Evidence," *Journal of Political Economy* 74 (December 1966), pp. 545–555. When a correct statistical procedure was employed by Laidler, he found the usual result that the demand for money is sensitive to interest rates. In later work, Friedman has also concluded that the demand for money is sensitive to interest.

[4]David Laidler, "Some Evidence on the Demand for Money," *Journal of Political Economy* 74 (February 1966), pp. 55–68; Allan H. Meltzer, "The Demand for Money: The Evidence from the Time Series," *Journal of Political Economy* 71 (June 1963), pp. 219–246; Karl Brunner and Allan H. Meltzer, "Predicting Velocity: Implications for Theory and Policy," *Journal of Finance* 18 (May 1963), pp. 319–354.

[5]Interest sensitivity is measured by the interest elasticity of money demand which is defined as

$$\frac{\text{Percentage change in the demand for money}}{\text{Percentage change in the interest rate}}$$

Brunner and Meltzer found was that a money demand function, estimated mostly with data from the 1930s, accurately predicted the demand for money in the 1950s. This result provided little evidence in favor of the existence of a liquidity trap during the Great Depression period.

The evidence on the interest sensitivity of the demand for money found by different researchers is remarkably consistent. Neither extreme case is supported by the data: The demand for money is sensitive to interest rates, but there is little evidence that a liquidity trap has ever existed.

Stability of Money Demand

If the money demand function is unstable and undergoes substantial unpredictable shifts, as Keynes thought, then velocity is unpredictable and the quantity of money may not be tightly linked to aggregate spending, as in the modern quantity theory. The stability of the money demand function is also crucial to whether the Federal Reserve should target on interest rates or the money supply (see Chapter 25). Thus it is important to look at the question of whether the money demand function is stable or not, because it has important implications for how monetary policy should be conducted.

As our discussion of the Brunner and Meltzer article indicates, evidence on the stability of the demand for money function is related to the evidence on the existence of a liquidity trap. Brunner and Meltzer's finding that a money demand function estimated using data mostly from the 1930s predicted the demand for money well in the postwar period not only suggests that a liquidity trap did not exist in the 1930s, but also indicates that the money demand function has been stable over long periods of time. The evidence that the interest sensitivity of the demand for money did not change from period to period also suggests that the money demand function is stable, since a changing interest sensitivity would mean that the demand for money function estimated in one period would not be able to predict well in another period.

By the early 1970s, the evidence using quarterly data from the postwar period strongly supported the stability of the money demand function when $M1$ was used as the definition of the money supply. For example, a well-known study by Stephen Goldfeld published in 1973 found not only that the interest sensitivity of $M1$ money demand did not undergo changes in the postwar period, but also the $M1$ money demand function predicted extremely well throughout the postwar period.[6] As a result of this evidence, the $M1$ money demand function became the conventional money demand function used by economists.

---

[6]Stephen M. Goldfeld, "The Demand for Money Revisited," *Brookings Papers on Economic Activity* 3 (1973), pp. 577–638.

i ∂ md highly elastic.

The Case of the Missing Money The stability of the demand for money, then, was a well-established fact when starting in 1974 the conventional $M1$ money demand function began to severely overpredict the demand for money. Stephen Goldfeld labeled this phenomenon of instability in the demand for money function, "The Case of the Missing Money."[7] It has presented a serious challenge to the usefulness of the money demand function as a tool for understanding how monetary policy affects aggregate economic activity. In addition, it has important implications for how monetary policy should be conducted. As a result, the instability of the $M1$ money demand function stimulated an intense search for a solution to the mystery of the missing money so that a stable money demand function could be resurrected.

The search for a stable money demand function took two directions. The first direction focused on whether an incorrect definition of money could be the reason why the demand for money function has become so unstable. Because of inflation, high nominal interest rates, and advances in computer technology, the payments mechanism and cash management techniques have undergone rapid changes since 1974. In addition, many new financial instruments have emerged and grown in importance. This led some researchers to suspect that the rapid pace of financial innovation since 1974 means that the conventional definitions of the money supply no longer apply. They searched for a stable money demand function by actually searching directly for the missing money; that is, they looked for financial instruments that have been incorrectly left out of the definition of money.

Overnight Repurchase Agreements (RPs) are one example. These are one-day loans with little default risk, because they are structured to provide Treasury bills as collateral. (Chapter 3 gives a more detailed discussion of the structure of this type of loan.) Corporations with demand deposit accounts at commercial banks frequently loan out substantial amounts of their account balances overnight with these RPs, lowering the measures of the money supply. However, the amounts loaned out are very close substitutes for money, since the corporation can quickly make a decision to decrease these loans if it needs more money in its demand deposit account to pay its bills. Gillian Garcia and Simon Pak, for example, found that including overnight RPs in measures of the money supply substantially reduced the degree to which money demand functions overpredicted the money supply.[8] More recent evidence using data from the 1979–1981 period casts some doubt on

---

[7]Stephen Goldfeld, "The Case of the Missing Money," *Brookings Papers on Economic Activity* 3 (1976), pp. 683–730.

[8]Gillian Garcia and Simon Pak, "Some Clues in the Case of the Missing Money," *American Economic Review* 69 (May 1979), pp. 330–334.

whether including overnight RPs and other highly liquid assets in measures of the money supply produces money demand functions that are stable.[9]

The second direction of search for a stable money demand function was to look for new variables to include in the money demand function that will make it stable. Michael Hamburger, for example, found that including the average dividend-price ratio on common stocks (average dividends divided by the average price) as a measure of their interest rate resulted in a money demand function that is stable.[10] Other researchers, such as H. Heller and Moshin Khan, added the entire term structure of interest rates to their money demand function and found that this produces a stable money demand function.[11]

These attempts to produce a stable money demand function have been criticized on the grounds that these additional variables do not accurately measure the opportunity cost of holding money, and so the theoretical justification for including them in the money demand function is weak.[12] Also, later research questions whether these alterations to the money demand function really do lead to continuing stability in the future.[13]

Velocity Slowdown in the 1980s The woes of conventional money demand functions increased in the 1980s. We have seen that they overpredicted money demand in the middle and late 1970s; that is, they underpredicted velocity (PY/M), which rose faster than expected. The tables turned beginning in 1982; as can be seen in Figure 23.1, economists were now faced with a surprising slowdown in $M1$ velocity, which conventional money demand

---

[9]See the survey in John P. Judd and John L. Scadding, "The Search for a Stable Money Demand Function," *Journal of Economic Literature* 20 (September 1982), pp. 993–1023.

[10]Michael Hamburger, "Behavior of the Money Stock: Is There a Puzzle?" *Journal of Monetary Economics* 3 (July 1977), pp. 265–288. The stability of his money demand function also depends on his assumption that the income elasticity of the demand for money is unity. This assumption has been strongly criticized by many critics including R. W. Hafer and Scott E. Hein, "Evidence on the Temporal Stability of the Demand for Money Relationship in the United States," *Federal Reserve Bank of St. Louis Review* (December 1979), pp. 3–14, who find that this assumption is strongly rejected by the data.

[11]H. Heller and Moshin S. Khan, "The Demand for Money and the Term Structure of Interest Rates," *Journal of Political Economy* 87 (February 1979), pp. 109–129.

[12]Frederic S. Mishkin, "Discussion of Asset Substitutibility and the Impact of Federal Deficits," in Laurence H. Meyer, ed., *The Economic Consequences of Government Deficits* (Boston: Kluwer-Nijhoff, 1983), pp. 117–120, and "Discussion of Recent Velocity Behavior, The Demand for Money and Monetary Policy," in *Monetary Targeting and Velocity* (Federal Reserve Bank of San Francisco, 1983), pp. 129–132.

[13]This research is discussed in Judd and Scadding, "The Search for a Stable Money Demand Function," op. cit.

functions also could not predict. Although researchers have tried to explain this velocity slowdown, they have not been entirely successful.[14]

M2 to the Rescue?   As we saw in Figure 23.1 in the chapter, $M2$ velocity remained far more stable than $M1$ velocity in the 1980s. The relative stability of $M2$ velocity suggests that money demand functions in which the money supply is defined as $M2$ might perform substantially better than those in which the money supply is defined as $M1$. Researchers at the Federal Reserve do find that $M2$ money demand functions performed well in recent years, with $M2$ velocity moving quite closely with the opportunity cost of holding $M2$ (market interest rates minus an average of the interest paid on deposits and financial instruments that make up $M2$).[15] However, because of the difficulties in finding $M1$ money demand functions that remain stable after they have been estimated, there is concern that estimated $M2$ money demand functions may also become unstable in the future.

Conclusion   The main conclusion from the research on the money demand function seems to be that the most likely cause of its instability is the rapid pace of financial innovation occurring after 1973. The evidence is still somewhat tentative, however, and a truly stable and satisfactory money demand function has not yet been found. And so the search for a stable money demand function goes on.

The recent instability of the money demand function calls into question whether our theories and empirical analyses are adequate.[16] It also has important implications for the way monetary policy should be conducted, because it casts doubt on the usefulness of the money demand function as a tool to provide guidance to policymakers. In particular, because the money demand function has become unstable, velocity is now harder to predict, and setting rigid money supply targets in order to control aggregate spending in the economy may not be an effective way to conduct monetary policy.

---

[14]See, for example, Robert H. Rasche, "$M1$—Velocity and Money-Demand Functions: Do Stable Relationships Exist?" in Karl Brunner and Allan H. Meltzer, eds., *Empirical Studies of Velocity, Real Exchange Rates, Unemployment and Productivity, Carnegie-Rochester Conference Series on Public Policy* (Autumn 1987), pp. 9–88.

[15]See David H. Small and Richard D. Porter, "Understanding the Behavior of $M2$ and $V2$," *Federal Reserve Bulletin* 75 (April 1989), pp. 244–254.

[16]Thomas F. Cooley and Stephen F. LeRoy, "Identification and Estimation of Money Demand," *American Economic Review* 71 (December 1981), pp. 825–844, is especially critical of the empirical research on the demand for money.

CHAPTER 24

The Keynesian Framework and the *ISLM* Model

PREVIEW In the media you often see forecasts of GNP and interest rates by economists and government agencies. At times these forecasts seem to come from a crystal ball, but economists actually make their predictions using a variety of economic models. One model widely used by economic forecasters is the *ISLM* model, which was developed by Sir John Hicks in 1937 and is based on the analysis in John Maynard Keynes' influential book, *The General Theory of Employment, Interest and Money,* published in 1936.[1] The *ISLM* model explains how interest rates and total output produced in the economy (aggregate output or, equivalently, aggregate income) are determined, given a fixed price level.

   The *ISLM* model is valuable not only because it can be used in economic forecasting, but also because it provides a deeper understanding of how government policy can affect aggregate economic activity. In Chapter 25 we will use it to evaluate the effects of monetary and fiscal policy on the economy and to learn some lessons about how monetary policy might best be conducted.

   In this chapter we begin by developing the simplest framework for determining aggregate output, in which all economic "actors" (consumers, business firms, etc.) except the government play a role. Government fiscal policy (spending and taxes) is then added to the framework to see how it can affect the determination of aggregate output. Finally, we secure a complete picture of the *ISLM* model by adding monetary policy variables: the money supply and the interest rate.

---

[1]John Hicks, "Mr. Keynes and the Classics: A Suggested Interpretation," *Econometrica* (April 1937).

554

DETERMINATION OF AGGREGATE OUTPUT

Keynes was especially interested in explaining movements of aggregate output because he wanted to explain why the Great Depression had occurred and how government policy could be used to increase employment in a similar economic situation. Keynes' analysis started with the recognition that the total quantity demanded of an economy's output was the sum of four types of spending: (1) **consumer expenditure (C),** the total demand for consumer goods and services (hamburgers, stereos, rock concerts, etc.); (2) **planned investment spending (I),** the total planned spending by business firms on new physical capital (machines, computers, factories, raw materials, apartment buildings, etc.) plus planned spending on new residential homes; (3) **government spending (G),** the spending by all levels of government on goods and services (typewriters, aircraft carriers, government workers, red tape, etc.); (4) **net exports (NX),** the net foreign spending on domestic goods and services, equal to exports minus imports.[2] The total quantity demanded of an economy's output, called **aggregate demand (Y^{ad}),** can be written as

$$Y^{ad} = C + I + G + NX \tag{24.1}$$

Using the commonsense concept from supply and demand analysis, Keynes recognized that equilibrium would occur in the economy when total quantity of output supplied (aggregate output produced, Y) equals quantity of output demanded (Y^{ad}), that is, when

$$Y = Y^{ad} \tag{24.2}$$

When this equilibrium condition is satisfied, producers are able to sell all of their output and have no reason to change their production. Keynes' analysis involves explaining why aggregate output is at a certain level by understanding what factors affect each component of aggregate demand and how the sum of these components could add up to an output smaller than the economy is capable of producing, resulting in less than full employment.

Keynes was especially concerned with explaining the low level of output and employment during the Great Depression. Because inflation was not a serious problem during this period, he assumed that output could change without causing change in prices. ***Keynes' analysis assumes that the price level is fixed;*** that is, dollar amounts for such variables as consumer expendi-

---

[2]Imports are subtracted from exports in arriving at the net exports component of the total quantity demanded of an economy's output because imports are already counted in $C, I,$ and G (consumer expenditure, planned investment spending, and government spending), but do not add to the demand for that economy's output.

ture, investment, aggregate output, and so on do not have to be adjusted for changes in the price level to tell us how much the real quantities of these variables change. Because the price level is assumed to be fixed, when we talk in this chapter about changes in nominal quantities, we are talking about changes in real quantities as well.

Our discussion of Keynes' analysis begins with a simple framework of aggregate output determination in which the role of government, net exports, and the possible effects of money and interest rates are ignored. Because we are assuming that government spending and net exports are zero ($G = 0$ and $NX = 0$), we need only examine consumer expenditure and investment spending to explain how aggregate output is determined. This simple framework is unrealistic because both government and monetary policy are left out of the picture, and it makes other simplifying assumptions, such as a fixed price level. Still, the model is worth studying because it provides a simplified view that helps us understand the key factors that explain how the economy works. It also clearly illustrates the Keynesian idea that the economy can come to rest at a level of aggregate output below the full employment level. Once you understand this simple framework, we can proceed to more complex, realistic models.

Consumer Expenditure and the Consumption Function

Suppose you ask yourself what determines how much you spend on consumer goods and services. Your likely response is that your income is the most important factor, because as your income rises, you would be willing to spend more. Keynes reasoned similarly that consumer expenditure is related to **disposable income,** the total income available for spending, equal to aggregate income minus taxes ($Y - T$). He called this relationship between disposable income (DI) and consumer expenditure (C) the **consumption function** and expressed it as

$$C = a + mpc \times DI \tag{24.3}$$

The term mpc, called the **marginal propensity to consume,** is the slope of the consumption function line ($\Delta C/\Delta DI$) and reflects the change in consumer expenditure that results from an additional dollar of disposable income. Keynes assumed that the mpc was a constant between the values of 0 and 1. If, for example, a \$1.00 increase of disposable income leads to an increase in consumer expenditure of \$0.50, then $mpc = .5$.

The term a stands for **autonomous consumer expenditure,** the amount of consumer expenditure that is independent of disposable income. It tells us how much consumers will spend when disposable income is 0 (they still

Table 24.1   **Example of a Consumption Function** [schedule of consumer expenditure (C) when *mpc* = .5 and a = 200, (billions of dollars)]

Point in Figure 24.1	DI (disposable income) (1)	ΔDI (2)	ΔC .5 × ΔDI (3)	C (4)
E	0	—	—	200 (= a)
F	400	400	200	400
G	800	400	200	600
H	1200	400	200	800

must have food, clothing, and shelter). If *a* is $200 billion, when disposable income is 0, consumer expenditure will equal $200 billion.[3]

A numerical example of a consumption function using the values of *mpc* = .5 and *a* = 200 will clarify the preceding concept. The $200 billion of consumer expenditure at a disposable income of 0 is listed in the first row of Table 24.1 and is plotted as point E in Figure 24.1. (Remember that through-

Figure 24.1
Example of a Consumption Function
The consumption function plotted here is from Table 24.1 and has *mpc* = .5 and *a* = 200.

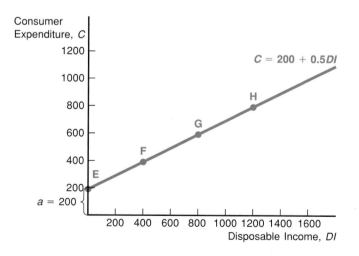

out this chapter dollar amounts for all variables in the figures correspond to real quantities because Keynes assumed that the price level is fixed.) Because *mpc* = .5, when disposable income increases by $400 billion, the change in consumer expenditure [ΔC in column (3) of Table 24.1] is $200 billion (.5 × $400b). Thus when disposable income is $400 billion, consumer expenditure is $400 billion (initial value of $200 billion when income is zero plus the $200 billion change in consumer expenditure). This combination of consumer expenditure and disposable income is listed in the second row of Table 24.1 and is plotted as point F in Figure 24.1. Similarly, at point G, where disposable income has increased by another $400 billion to $800 billion, consumer expenditure will rise by another $200 billion to $600 billion. By the same reasoning, at point H, at which disposable income is $1200 billion, consumer expenditure will be $800 billion. The line connecting these points in Figure 24.1 graphs the consumption function.

Study Guide

The consumption function is an intuitive concept that you can readily understand if you think about how your own spending behavior changes as you receive more disposable income. One way to make yourself more comfortable with this concept is to estimate your marginal propensity to consume (for example, it might be .8) and your level of consumer expenditure when your disposable income is zero (it might be $2000) and then construct a consumption function similar to that in Table 24.1.

Investment Spending

It is important to understand that there are two types of investment. The first type, **fixed investment,** is the spending by business firms on equipment (machines, computers, airplanes) and structures (factories, office buildings, shopping centers) and planned spending on residential houses. The second type, **inventory investment,** is spending by business firms on additional holdings of raw materials, parts, and finished goods, calculated as the change in holdings of these items in a given time period, say a year. (Box 24.1 explains how economists' use of the word *investment* differs from everyday usage of the term.)

Suppose Texas Instruments, a company that produces personal computers, has 100,000 computers sitting in its warehouses on December 31, 1991, ready to be shipped to dealers. If each computer has a wholesale price of $1000, then Texas Instruments has an inventory worth $100 million. If by December 31, 1992, its inventory of personal computers has risen to $150 million, then its inventory investment in 1992 is $50 million, the *change* in the level of its inventory over the course of the year ($150 million minus $100 million). Suppose, on the other hand, there is a drop in the level of inventories; inventory investment will then be negative.

Usage of the Word *Investment*

The usage of the word *investment* by economists is somewhat different from the more common every-day usage. When people say that they are making an investment, they are normally referring to purchase of a common stock or a bond. This usage differs from that of the economist in the phrase *investment spending* because these purchases do not involve an increase in demand for newly produced goods and services. When economists speak of investment spending, they are referring to the purchase of a *new* physical asset such as a *new* machine or a *new* house—purchases that do add to aggregate demand.

Texas Instruments may also have additional inventory investment if the level of raw materials and parts that it is holding to produce these computers increases over the course of the year. If on December 31, 1991, it holds $20 million of computer chips used to produce its computers and on December 31, 1992, it holds $30 million, then it has another $10 million of inventory investment in 1992.

An important feature of inventory investment is that—in contrast to fixed investment, which is always planned—some inventory investment can be unplanned. Suppose the reason Texas Instruments finds itself with an additional $50 million of computers on December 31, 1992, is because $50 million less of its computers were sold in 1989 than expected. This $50 million of inventory investment in 1992 is then unplanned. In this situation, Texas Instruments is producing more computers than it can sell and will cut production. Indeed, this is exactly what happened to Texas Instruments in 1983 when a huge unplanned inventory of TI-99 home computers accumulated and the company decided to abandon production of these machines.

Planned investment spending, a component of aggregate demand (Y^{ad}), is equal to planned fixed investment plus the amount of inventory investment *planned* by business firms. Keynes mentioned two factors that influence planned investment spending: interest rates and businesses' expectations about the future. How these factors affect investment spending will be discussed later in the chapter. For now, planned investment spending will be treated as a known value. At this stage we want to see how aggregate output is determined for a given level of planned investment spending; once we understand this, we can examine how interest rates and business expectations influence aggregate output by affecting planned investment spending.

Equilibrium

We have now assembled the building blocks (consumer expenditure and planned investment spending) that will enable you to understand how ag-

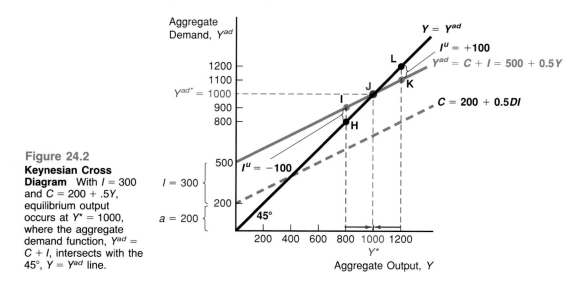

Figure 24.2
Keynesian Cross Diagram   With $I = 300$ and $C = 200 + .5Y$, equilibrium output occurs at $Y^* = 1000$, where the aggregate demand function, $Y^{ad} = C + I$, intersects with the 45°, $Y = Y^{ad}$ line.

gregate output is determined when we ignore the government. Although unrealistic, this stripped-down analysis clarifies the basic principles of output determination. In the next section government enters the picture and makes our model more realistic.

The Keynesian Cross Diagram   The diagram in Figure 24.2, called the Keynesian cross diagram, displays how aggregate output is determined. The vertical axis measures aggregate demand and the horizontal axis measures the level of aggregate output. The 45° line shows all the points at which aggregate output (Y) equals aggregate demand (Y^{ad}); that is, it shows all the points at which the equilibrium condition $Y = Y^{ad}$ is satisfied. Since government spending is zero ($G = 0$), aggregate demand is

$$Y^{ad} = C + I$$

Because there is no government sector to collect them, there are no taxes in our simplified economy; disposable income then equals aggregate output ($DI = Y$) (remember that aggregate income and aggregate output are equivalent, see the appendix to Chapter 1). Thus the consumption function with $a = 200$ and $mpc = .5$ plotted in Figure 24.1 can be written as $C = 200 + .5Y$ and is plotted in Figure 24.2. Given that planned investment spending is $300 billion, aggregate demand can then be expressed as

$$Y^{ad} = C + I$$
$$= 200 + .5Y + 300$$
$$= 500 + .5Y$$

The preceding equation, plotted in Figure 24.2, represents the quantity of aggregate demand at any given level of aggregate output and is called the **aggregate demand function.**

This aggregate demand function, $Y^{ad} = C + I$, is the vertical sum of the consumption function line ($C = 200 + .5Y$) and planned investment spending ($I = 300$). The point at which the aggregate demand function crosses the $45°$, $Y = Y^{ad}$ line indicates the equilibrium level of aggregate demand and aggregate output. In Figure 24.2, equilibrium occurs at point J, with both aggregate output (Y^*) and aggregate demand (Y^{ad*}) at $1000 billion.

As you learned in Chapter 6, the concept of equilibrium is only useful if there is a tendency for the economy to settle there. To see whether the economy heads toward the equilibrium output level of $1000 billion, let's first look at what happens if the amount of output produced in the economy is $1200 billion and is therefore above the equilibrium level. At this level of output, aggregate demand is $1100 billion (point K), $100 billion less than the $1200 billion of output (point L on the $45°$ line). Since output exceeds aggregate demand by $100 billion, business firms are saddled with $100 billion of unsold inventory. To keep from accumulating unsold goods, business firms will cut production, as Texas Instruments did when it could not sell its TI-99 home computers. As long as it is above the equilibrium level, output will exceed aggregate demand and firms will cut production, sending aggregate output toward the equilibrium level.

Another way to observe a tendency of the economy to head toward equilibrium at point J is from the viewpoint of inventory investment. When firms do not sell all output produced, they add unsold output to their holdings of inventory, and inventory investment increases. At an output level of $1200 billion, for instance, the $100 billion of unsold goods leads to $100 billion of unplanned inventory investment, which business firms do not want. Companies will decrease production to reduce inventory to the desired level, and aggregate output will fall (indicated by the arrow). This viewpoint means that unplanned inventory investment for the entire economy (I^u) equals the excess of output over aggregate demand. In our example, at an output level of $1200 billion, $I^u = 100$ billion. If I^u is positive, firms will cut production and output will fall. Output will stop falling only when it has returned to its equilibrium level at point J where $I^u = 0$.

What happens if aggregate output is below the equilibrium level of output? Let's say output is $800 billion. At this level of output, aggregate demand at point I is $900 billion, $100 billion higher than output (point H on the $45°$ line). At this level firms are selling $100 billion more goods than they are producing, so inventory falls below the desired level. The negative unplanned inventory investment ($I^u = -100$ billion) will induce firms to increase their production in order to raise inventory to desired levels. As a result, output rises toward the equilibrium level, shown by the arrow in Figure 24.2. As long as output is below the equilibrium level, unplanned inventory investment will remain negative, firms will continue to raise production, and output will continue to rise. We again see the tendency for the economy to settle at point J, where aggregate demand equals output ($Y = Y^{ad}$) and unplanned inventory investment is zero ($I^u = 0$).

The Expenditure Multiplier

Now that you understand that equilibrium aggregate output is determined by the position of the aggregate demand function, we can examine how different factors shift the function and consequently change aggregate output. You will find that (1) a rise in planned investment spending or (2) a rise in autonomous consumer expenditure shifts up the aggregate demand function and leads to an increase in aggregate output.

Output Response to a Change in Planned Investment Spending Suppose a new electric motor is invented that makes all factory machines three times more efficient. Because business firms are suddenly more optimistic about the profitability of investing in new machines that use this new motor, planned investment spending increases by $100 billion from an initial level of $I_1 = \$300$ billion to $I_2 = \$400$ billion. What effect does this have on output?

The effects of this increase in planned investment spending are analyzed in Figure 24.3 using a Keynesian cross diagram. Initially, when planned investment spending (I_1) is $300 billion, the aggregate demand function is Y_1^{ad} and equilibrium occurs at point 1, where output is $1000 billion. The $100 billion increase in planned investment spending adds directly to aggregate demand and shifts up the aggregate demand function to Y_2^{ad}. Aggregate demand now equals output at the intersection of Y_2^{ad} with the $45°$, $Y = Y^{ad}$ line (point 2). As a result of the $100 billion increase in planned investment spending, equilibrium output rises by $200 billion to $1200 billion ($Y_2$). For every dollar increase in planned investment spending, aggregate output has increased twofold.

The ratio of the change in aggregate output to a change in planned investment spending ($\Delta Y/\Delta I$) is called the **expenditure multiplier.** (This

Figure 24.3
Response of Aggregate Output to a Change in Planned Investment A $100 billion increase in planned investment spending from $I_1 = 300$ to $I_2 = 400$ shifts up the aggregate demand function from Y_1^{ad} to Y_2^{ad}. The equilibrium moves from point 1 to point 2 and equilibrium output rises from $Y_1 = 1000$ to $Y_2 = 1200$.

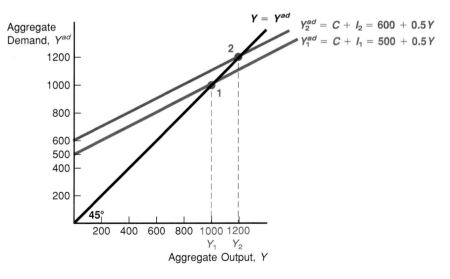

$$Y = Y^{ad}$$
$$Y_2^{ad} = C + I_2 = 600 + 0.5Y$$
$$Y_1^{ad} = C + I_1 = 500 + 0.5Y$$

multiplier should *not* be confused with the money supply multiplier developed in Chapter 15, which measures the ratio of the change in the money supply from a change in the monetary base.) In Figure 24.3, the expenditure multiplier is 2.

Why does a change in planned investment spending lead to an even larger change in aggregate output so that the expenditure multiplier is greater than one? The expenditure multiplier is greater than one because an increase in planned investment spending, which raises output, also leads to an additional increase in consumer expenditure ($mpc \times \Delta Y$). The increase in consumer expenditure in turn raises aggregate demand and output further, resulting in a multiple change of output from a given change in planned investment spending. This conclusion can be derived algebraically by solving for the unknown value of Y in terms of a, mpc, and I, resulting in[4]

$$Y = (a + I) \times \frac{1}{1 - mpc} \tag{24.4}$$

Since I is multiplied by the term ($1/(1 - mpc)$), this equation tells us that a \$1 change in I leads to a $\$1/(1 - mpc)$ change in aggregate output; thus $1/(1 - mpc)$ is the expenditure multiplier. When $mpc = .5$, the change in output for a \$1 change in I is \$2 [$= 1/(1 - .5)$]; if $mpc = .8$, the change in output for a \$1 change in I is \$5. The larger is the marginal propensity to consume, the higher is the expenditure multiplier.

Response to Changes in Autonomous Spending Since a is also multiplied by the term $1/(1 - mpc)$ in Equation (24.4), a \$1 change in autonomous consumer expenditure (a) also changes aggregate output by $1/(1 - mpc)$, the amount of the expenditure multiplier. Therefore, we see that the expenditure multiplier applies equally well to changes in autonomous consumer expenditure. In fact, Equation (24.4) can be rewritten as

$$Y = A \times \frac{1}{1 - mpc} \tag{24.5}$$

in which A = autonomous spending = $a + I$.

---

[4]Substituting the consumption function, $C = a + mpc \times Y$, into the aggregate demand function, $Y^{ad} = C + I$, yields

$$Y^{ad} = a + mpc \times Y + I$$

In equilibrium, where aggregate output equals aggregate demand,

$$Y = Y^{ad} = a + mpc \times Y + I$$

Subtracting the term $mpc \times Y$ from both sides of this equation in order to collect the terms involving Y on the left side, we have

$$Y - mpc \times Y = Y \times (1 - mpc) = a + I$$

Dividing both sides by $(1 - mpc)$ to solve for Y leads to Equation (24.4) in the text.

This rewritten equation tells us that any change in autonomous spending, whether from a change in a, a change in I, or a change in both, will lead to a multiple change in Y. If both a and I decrease by $100 billion each and $mpc = .5$, the expenditure multiplier is 2 [= 1/(1 − .5)] and aggregate output (Y) will fall by 2 × $200 billion = $400 billion. A rise in I by $100 billion that is offset by a $100 billion decline in a will, on the other hand, leave autonomous spending (A), and hence Y, unchanged. The expenditure multiplier 1/(1 − mpc) can therefore be defined more generally as the ratio of change in aggregate output to a change in autonomous spending ($\Delta Y / \Delta A$).

Another way to reach this conclusion—any change in autonomous spending will lead to a multiple change in aggregate output—is to recognize that the shift in the aggregate demand function in Figure 24.3 did not have to come from an increase in I; it could also have come from an increase in a, which directly raises consumer expenditure and therefore aggregate demand. Alternatively, it could have come from an increase in both a and I. Changes in the attitudes of consumers and business firms about the future, which cause changes in their spending, will result in multiple changes in aggregate output.

Keynes believed that changes in autonomous spending are dominated by unstable fluctuations in planned investment spending, which is influenced by emotional waves of optimism and pessimism—factors he referred to as **"animal spirits."** His view was colored by the collapse in investment spending during the Great Depression, which he saw as the primary reason for the economic contraction. We will examine the consequences of this fall in investment spending in the following application.

APPLICATION
THE COLLAPSE OF INVESTMENT SPENDING AND/ / / / / / / / / / / / / / / / /
THE GREAT DEPRESSION

From 1929 to 1933, the U.S. economy experienced the largest percentage decline in investment spending ever recorded. In 1982 dollars, investment spending fell from $139.2 billion to $22.7 billion—a decline of over 80%. What does the Keynesian analysis developed so far suggest should have happened to aggregate output in this period?

Figure 24.4 demonstrates how the $116.5 billion drop in planned investment spending would shift the aggregate demand function down from Y_1^{ad} to Y_2^{ad}, moving the economy from point 1 to point 2. Aggregate output would then fall sharply; real GNP actually fell by $211.1 billion (a multiple of the $116.5 billion drop in investment spending), from $709.6 billion to $498.5 billion (1982 dollars). Since the economy was at full employment in 1929, the fall in output resulted in massive unemployment, with over 25% of the labor force unemployed in 1933.

After witnessing the events in the Great Depression, Keynes took the view that an economy would continually suffer major output fluctuations

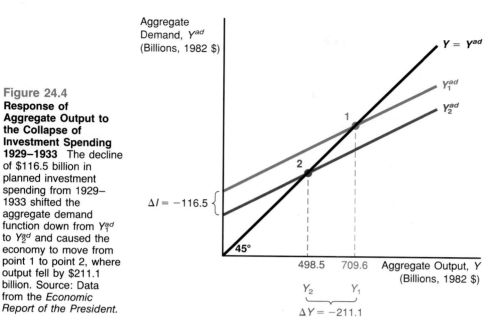

Figure 24.4
Response of Aggregate Output to the Collapse of Investment Spending 1929–1933 The decline of $116.5 billion in planned investment spending from 1929–1933 shifted the aggregate demand function down from Y_1^{ad} to Y_2^{ad} and caused the economy to move from point 1 to point 2, where output fell by $211.1 billion. Source: Data from the *Economic Report of the President.*

because of the volatility of autonomous spending, particularly planned investment spending. He was especially worried about sharp declines in autonomous spending, which would inevitably lead to large declines in output and an equilibrium with high unemployment. If autonomous spending fell sharply, as it did during the Great Depression, how could an economy be restored to higher levels of output and more reasonable levels of unemployment? Not by an increase in autonomous spending, since the business outlook was so grim. Keynes' answer to this question involved looking at the role of government in determining aggregate output.

Government's Role

Keynes realized that government spending and taxation could also affect the position of the aggregate demand function and hence be manipulated to restore the economy to full employment. As shown in the aggregate demand equation $Y^{ad} = C + I + G + NX$, government spending (G) adds directly to aggregate demand. Taxes, however, do not affect aggregate demand directly, as does government spending. Instead, taxes lower the amount of income that consumers have available for spending and affect aggregate demand by affecting consumer expenditure; that is, when there are taxes, disposable income (DI) does not equal aggregate output; it equals aggregate output (Y) minus taxes (T), $DI = Y - T$. The consumption function $C = a + mpc \times DI$ can be rewritten as follows:

$$C = a + mpc \times (Y - T) = a + mpc \times Y - mpc \times T \qquad (24.6)$$

This consumption function looks similar to the one used in the absence of taxes ($C = a + mpc \times Y$), but it has an additional term ($- mpc \times T$) on the right side. This term indicates that if taxes increase by \$100, consumer expenditure declines by mpc times this amount; if $mpc = .5$, consumer expenditure declines by \$50. This occurs because consumers view \$100 of taxes as equivalent to a \$100 reduction in income and reduce their expenditure by the marginal propensity to consume times this amount.

To see how inclusion of government spending and taxes modifies our analysis, first we will observe the effect of a positive level of government spending on aggregate output in the Keynesian cross diagram of Figure 24.5. Let's say that in the absence of government spending or taxes, the economy is at point 1, where the aggregate demand function, $Y_1^{ad} = C + I = 500 + .5Y$, crosses the 45°, $Y = Y_1^{ad}$ line. Here equilibrium output is at \$1000 billion. Suppose, however, that the economy reaches full employment at an aggregate output level of \$1800 billion. How can government spending be used to restore the economy to full employment at \$1800 billion of aggregate output?

If government spending is set at \$400 billion, the aggregate demand function shifts up to $Y_2^{ad} = C + I + G = 900 + .5Y$. The economy moves to point 2 and aggregate output rises by \$800 billion to \$1800 billion. Figure 24.5 indicates that aggregate output is positively related to government spending and that change in government spending leads to a multiple change in aggregate output, equal to the expenditure multiplier, $2 = 1/(1 - mpc) = 1/(1 - .5)$. Therefore, declines in planned investment spending that produce high unemployment (as occurred during the Great Depression) can be offset by raising government spending.

What happens if the government decides that it must collect taxes of \$400 billion to balance the budget? Before taxes are raised, the economy is in equilibrium at the same point 2 found in Figure 24.5 Our discussion of the consumption function (which allows for taxes) indicates that taxes (T) reduce consumer expenditure by $mpc \times T$ because there is \$$T$ less income now available for spending. In our example, $mpc = .5$, so consumer expenditure and the aggregate demand function shift down by \$200 billion ($= .5 \times 400$); at the new equilibrium, point 3, the level of output has declined by twice this amount (the expenditure multiplier) to \$1400 billion.

Although you can see that aggregate output is negatively related to the level of taxes, it is important to recognize that the change in aggregate output from the \$400 billion increase in taxes ($\Delta Y = -\$400$ billion) is smaller than the change in aggregate output from the \$400 billion increase in government spending ($\Delta Y = \$800$ billion). If both taxes and government spending are raised equally by \$400 billion, as occurs in going from point 1 to point 3 in Figure 24.5, then aggregate output will rise.

The Keynesian framework indicates that the government can play an important role in determining aggregate output by changing the level of government spending or taxes. If the economy enters into a deep recession,

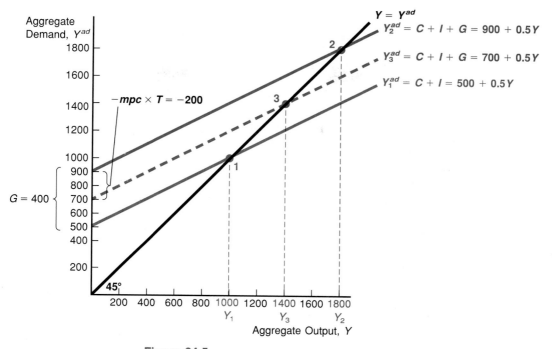

Figure 24.5

Response of Aggregate Output to Government Spending and Taxes With no government spending or taxes, the aggregate demand function is Y_1^{ad} and equilibrium output is $Y_1 = 1000$. With government spending of \$400 billion, the aggregate demand function shifts up to Y_2^{ad} and aggregate output rises by \$800 billion to $Y_2 = \$1800$ billion. Taxes of \$400 billion lower consumer expenditure and the aggregate demand function by \$200 billion from Y_2^{ad} to Y_3^{ad}, and aggregate output falls by \$400 billion to $Y_3 = 1400$ billion.

in which output drops severely and unemployment climbs, the analysis we have just developed provides a prescription for restoring the economy to health. The government might raise aggregate output by increasing government spending, or it could lower taxes and reverse the process described in Figure 24.5 (that is, a tax cut makes more income available for spending at any level of output, shifting up the aggregate demand function and causing the equilibrium level of output to rise).

Role of International Trade

International trade also plays a role in determining aggregate output because net exports (exports minus imports) is a component of aggregate demand. To analyze the effect of net exports in the Keynesian cross diagram of Figure 24.6, suppose that initially net exports are equal to zero ($NX_1 = 0$) so that the economy is at point 1, where the aggregate demand function, $Y_1^{ad} = C + I + G + NX_1 = 500 + .5Y$, crosses the $45°$, $Y = Y_1^{ad}$. Equilibrium output

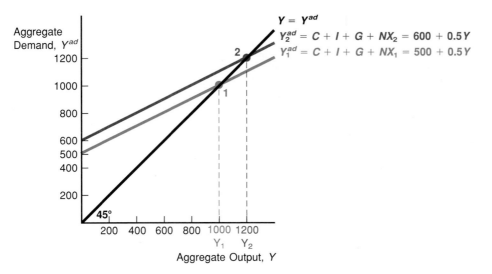

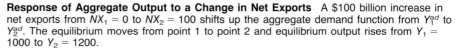

Figure 24.6

Response of Aggregate Output to a Change in Net Exports A $100 billion increase in net exports from $NX_1 = 0$ to $NX_2 = 100$ shifts up the aggregate demand function from Y_1^{ad} to Y_2^{ad}. The equilibrium moves from point 1 to point 2 and equilibrium output rises from $Y_1 = 1000$ to $Y_2 = 1200$.

is again at $1000 billion. Now foreigners suddenly get an urge to buy more American products so that net exports rise to $100 billion ($NX_2 = 100$). The $100 billion increase in net exports adds directly to aggregate demand and shifts up the aggregate demand function to $Y_2^{ad} = C + I + G + NX_2 = 600 + .5Y$. The economy moves to point 2 and aggregate output rises by $200 billion to $1200 billion ($Y_2$). Figure 24.6 indicates that just as we found for planned investment spending and government spending, a rise in net exports leads to a multiple rise in aggregate output, equal to the expenditure multiplier, $2 = 1/(1 - mpc) = 1/(1 - .5)$. Therefore, changes in net exports can be another important factor affecting fluctuations in aggregate output.

Summary of the Determinants of Aggregate Output

Our analysis of the Keynesian framework so far has identified five autonomous factors (factors independent of income) that shift the aggregate demand function and hence the level of aggregate output:

1. Changes in autonomous consumer expenditure (a)
2. Changes in planned investment spending (I)
3. Changes in government spending (G)
4. Changes in taxes (T)
5. Changes in net exports (NX)

Table 24.2   Summary: Response of Aggregate Output to Autonomous Changes in *a*, *I*, *G*, *T*, and *NX*

Change in Variable	Aggregate Output Response
a ↑	*Y* ↑
I ↑	*Y* ↑
G ↑	*Y* ↑
T ↑	*Y* ↓
NX ↑	*Y* ↑

Note: Only increases (↑) in the variables are shown; the effects of decreases in the variables on aggregate output would be the opposite of those indicated in the second column.

The effects of changes in each of these variables on aggregate output are summarized next and in Table 24.2.

Changes in Autonomous Consumer Spending (a)   A rise in autonomous consumer expenditure, *a* (let us say because consumers become more optimistic about the economy when the stock market booms), directly raises consumer expenditure and shifts up the aggregate demand function, resulting in an increase in aggregate output. A decrease in *a* causes consumer expenditure to fall, leading ultimately to a decline in aggregate output. Therefore, ***aggregate output is positively related to autonomous consumer expenditure, a.***

Changes in Planned Investment Spending (I)   A rise in planned investment spending adds directly to aggregate demand, thus raising the aggregate demand function and aggregate output. A fall in planned investment spending lowers aggregate demand and causes aggregate output to fall. Therefore, ***aggregate output is positively related to planned investment spending, I.***

Changes in Government Spending (G)   A rise in government spending also adds directly to aggregate demand and raises the aggregate demand function, raising aggregate output. A fall directly reduces aggregate demand, lowers the aggregate demand function, and causes aggregate output to fall. Therefore, ***aggregate output is positively related to government spending, G.***

Changes in Taxes (T)   A rise in taxes does not affect aggregate demand directly, but instead lowers the amount of income available for spending, reducing consumer expenditure. The decline in consumer expenditure then leads to a fall in the aggregate demand function, resulting in a decline in aggregate output. A lowering of taxes, on the other hand, makes more income available for spending, raises consumer expenditure, and leads to higher aggregate output. Therefore, ***aggregate output is negatively related to the level of taxes, T.***

Changes in Net Exports (NX) A rise in net exports adds directly to aggregate demand and raises the aggregate demand function, raising aggregate output. A fall directly reduces aggregate demand, lowers the aggregate demand function, and causes aggregate output to fall. Therefore, ***aggregate output is positively related to net exports, NX.***

The Expenditure Multiplier and Size of the Effects from the Five Factors
The aggregate demand function in the Keynesian cross diagrams shifts vertically by the full amount of the change in a, I, G, or NX, resulting in a multiple effect on aggregate output through the effects of the expenditure multiplier, $1/(1 - mpc)$. A change in taxes has a smaller effect on aggregate output because consumer expenditure changes by only mpc times the change in taxes ($-mpc \times \Delta T$), which in the case of $mpc = .5$ means that aggregate demand shifts vertically by only half of the change in taxes.

If there is a change in one of these autonomous factors that is offset by a change in another (say, I rises by \$100 billion, but a, G, or NX falls by \$100 billion, or T rises by \$200 billion when $mpc = .5$), then the aggregate demand function will remain in the same position and aggregate output will remain unchanged.[5]

---

[5]These results can be derived algebraically as follows. Substituting in the consumption function allowing for taxes (Equation 24.6) into the aggregate demand function (Equation 24.1), we have

$$Y^{ad} = a - mpc \times T + mpc \times Y + I + G + NX$$

If we assume that taxes (T) are unrelated to income, we can define autonomous spending in the aggregate demand function to be

$$A = a - mpc \times T + I + G + NX$$

and the expenditure equation can be rewritten as

$$Y^{ad} = A - mpc \times Y$$

In equilibrium, aggregate demand equals aggregate output so that

$$Y = A + mpc \times Y$$

which can be solved for Y. The resulting equation,

$$Y = \frac{A}{1 - mpc}$$

is the same equation that links autonomous spending and aggregate output in the text (Equation 24.5), but it now allows for additional components of autonomous spending in A. We see that any increase in autonomous expenditure leads to a multiple increase in output. Thus any component of autonomous spending that enters A with a positive sign (a, I, G, and NX) will have a positive relationship with output, while any component with a negative sign ($-mpc \times T$) will have a negative relationship with output. This algebraic analysis also show us that any rise in a component of A that is offset by a movement in another component of A, leaving A unchanged, will also leave output unchanged.

Study Guide

To test your understanding of the Keynesian analysis of how aggregate output changes in response to changes in the factors described, see if you can use Keynesian cross diagrams to illustrate what happens to aggregate output when each variable decreases rather than increases. Also, be sure to do the problems at the end of the chapter that ask you to predict what will happen to aggregate output when certain economic variables change.

THE *ISLM* MODEL

So far our analysis has excluded monetary policy. We now include money and interest rates in the Keynesian framework in order to develop the more intricate *ISLM* model of how aggregate output is determined, in which monetary policy plays an important role. Why another complex model? The *ISLM* model is more versatile and allows us to understand economic phenomena that cannot be analyzed with the simpler Keynesian cross framework used earlier. With the *ISLM* model you will understand how monetary policy affects economic activity and interacts with fiscal policy (changes in government spending and taxes) to produce a certain level of aggregate output; how the level of interest rates is affected by changes in investment spending as well as by changes in monetary and fiscal policy; how best to conduct monetary policy; and finally, how it generates the aggregate demand curve, an essential building block for the aggregate supply and demand analysis used in Chapter 26 and later chapters.

Like our simplified Keynesian model, the full Keynesian *ISLM* model examines an equilibrium in which aggregate output produced equals aggregate demand, and since it assumes a fixed price level, real and nominal quantities are the same. The first step in constructing the *ISLM* model is to examine the effect of interest rates on planned investment spending and hence on aggregate demand. Next, we use the Keynesian cross diagram learned earlier to see how the interest rate affects the equilibrium level of aggregate output. The resulting relationship between equilibrium aggregate output and the interest rate is known as the **IS curve.**

Just as a demand curve alone cannot tell us the quantity of goods sold in a market, the *IS* curve by itself cannot tell us what the level of aggregate output will be because the interest rate is still unknown. We need another relationship, called the **LM curve,** which describes the combinations of interest rates and aggregate output for which the quantity of money demanded equals the quantity of money supplied. When the *IS* and *LM* curves are combined in the same diagram, the intersection of the two curves determines the equilibrium level of aggregate output as well as the interest rate.

Finally, we will have obtained a more complete analysis of the determination of aggregate output in which monetary policy plays an important role.

Equilibrium in the Goods Market: The *IS* Curve

In Keynesian analysis, the primary way that interest rates affect the level of aggregate output is through their effects on planned investment spending and net exports. After explaining why interest rates affect planned investment spending and net exports, we will use Keynesian cross diagrams to learn how interest rates affect equilibrium aggregate output.[6]

Interest Rates and Planned Investment Spending Business firms make investments in physical capital (machines, factories, and raw materials) as long as they expect to earn more from the physical capital than the interest cost of a loan to finance the investment. When the interest rate is high, few investments in physical capital will earn more than the cost of borrowed funds, so planned investment spending is low. When the interest rate is low, many investments in physical capital normally will earn more than the interest cost of borrowed funds. Therefore, when interest rates are lower, business firms are more likely to undertake an investment in physical capital and planned investment spending will be higher.

Even if a company has surplus funds and does not need to borrow in order to undertake an investment in physical capital, its planned investment spending will still be affected by the interest rate. Instead of investing in physical capital, it could purchase a security, like a bond. If the interest rate on this security is high, the opportunity cost (foregone interest earnings) of an investment is high and planned investment spending will be low because the firm would probably prefer to purchase the security rather than invest in physical capital. As the interest rate and the opportunity cost of investment falls, planned investment spending will increase, because investments in physical capital are more likely to earn greater income for the firm than the security.

The relationship between the amount of planned investment spending and any given level of the interest rate is illustrated by the investment schedule in panel (a) of Figure 24.7. The downward slope of the schedule reflects the negative relationship between planned investment spending and the interest rate. For a low level of interest rate, i_1 the level of planned investment spending, I_1, is high; for a high level of the interest rate, i_3, planned investment spending is low, I_3.

---

[6]More modern Keynesian approaches suggest that consumer expenditure, particularly for consumer durables (cars, furniture, appliances, etc.), is influenced by the interest rate. This interest sensitivity of consumer expenditure can be allowed for in the model here by defining planned investment spending more generally to include the interest-sensitive component of consumer expenditure.

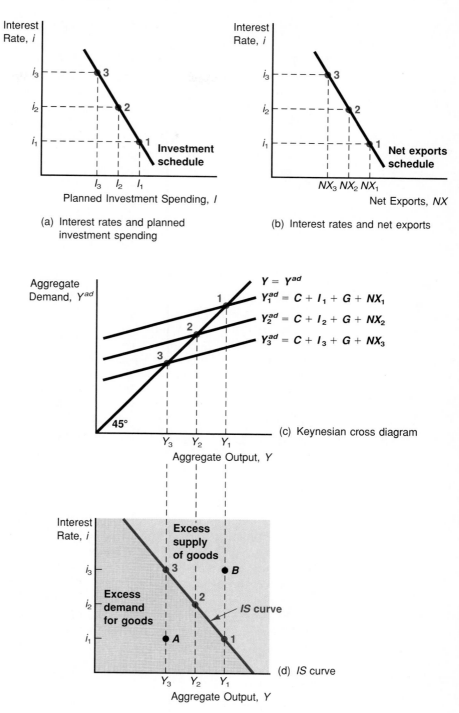

Figure 24.7
Deriving the *IS* Curve
The investment schedule in panel (a) shows that as the interest rate rises from i_1 to i_2 to i_3, planned investment spending falls from I_1 to I_2 to I_3, while panel (b) shows that net exports also fall from NX_1 to NX_2 to NX_3. Panel (c) then indicates the levels of equilibrium output Y_1, Y_2, and Y_3 that correspond to those three levels of planned investment and net exports. Finally, panel (d) plots the level of equilibrium output corresponding to each of the three interest rates; the line that connects these points is the *IS* curve.

Interest Rates and Net Exports   As Chapter 21 discussed in more detail, when interest rates rise in the United States (with the price level fixed), U.S. dollar bank deposits become more attractive relative to deposits denominated in foreign currencies, thereby causing a rise in the value of dollar deposits relative to other currency deposits, that is, a rise in the exchange rate. The higher value of the dollar resulting from the rise in interest rates makes domestic goods more expensive than foreign goods, thereby causing a fall in net exports. Therefore, as the interest rate rises, the value of the dollar rises, domestic goods become more expensive, and net exports fall. The resulting negative relationship between interest rates and net exports is shown in panel (b) of Figure 24.7. With a low level of the interest rate, i_1, the exchange rate is low and net exports, NX_1, is high; with a high level of the interest rate, i_3, the exchange rate is high and net exports, NX_3, is low.

Deriving the IS Curve   We can now use what we have learned about the relationship of interest rates with planned investment spending and net exports in panels (a) and (b) to examine the relationship between interest rates and the equilibrium level of aggregate output (holding government spending and autonomous consumer expenditure constant). The three levels of planned investment spending and net exports in panels (a) and (b) are represented in the three aggregate demand functions in the Keynesian cross diagram of panel (c). The lower interest rate, i_1, has the highest level of both planned investment spending, I_1, and net exports, NX_1, and thus the highest aggregate demand function, Y_1^{ad}. Point 1 in panel (d) shows the resulting equilibrium level of output Y_1, which corresponds to interest rate i_1. As the interest rate rises to i_2, both planned investment spending and net exports fall to I_2 and NX_2, so equilibrium output falls to Y_2. Point 2 in panel (d) shows the lower level of output, Y_2, which corresponds to interest rate i_2. Finally, the highest interest rate of i_3 leads to the lowest level of planned investment spending and net exports, and hence the lowest level of equilibrium output, which is plotted as point 3.

The line connecting the three points in panel (d), the *IS* curve,[7] shows the combinations of interest rates and equilibrium aggregate output, for which aggregate output produced equals aggregate demand. The negative slope indicates that higher interest rates result in lower planned investment spending and net exports, and hence lower equilibrium output.

What the IS Curve Tells Us   The *IS* curve traces out the points for which total quantity of goods produced equals total quantity of goods demanded. The *IS* curve describes points for which the goods market is in equilibrium.

---

[7]The *IS* curve received its name from Sir John Hicks, op. cit., who gave it the initials *IS* because in the simplest Keynesian framework with no government sector, equilibrium in the Keynesian cross diagram occurs when investment spending (*I*) equals saving (*S*).

For each given level of the interest rate, the *IS* curve tells us what aggregate output must equal in order for there to be equilibrium in the goods market. As the interest rate rises, planned investment spending and net exports fall, which in turn lowers aggregate demand; aggregate output must be lower in order for it to equal aggregate demand and satisfy goods market equilibrium.

The *IS* curve is a useful concept because output tends to move toward points on the curve that satisfy goods market equilibrium. If the economy is located in the area to the right of the *IS* curve, it has an excess supply of goods. At point B, for example, aggregate output, Y_1, is greater than the equilibrium level of output, Y_3, on the *IS* curve. This excess supply of goods results in unplanned inventory accumulation which causes output to fall toward the *IS* curve. The decline stops only when output is again at its equilibrium level on the *IS* curve.

If the economy is located in the area to the left of the *IS* curve, it has an excess demand for goods. At point A, aggregate output, Y_3, is below the equilibrium level of output, Y_1, on the *IS* curve. The excess demand for goods results in an unplanned decrease in inventory which causes output to rise toward the *IS* curve, stopping only when aggregate output is again at its equilibrium level on the *IS* curve.

Significantly, the equilibrium in the goods market does not produce a unique equilibrium level of aggregate output. Although we now know where aggregate output will head for a given level of the interest rate, we cannot determine aggregate output because we do not know what the interest rate is. To complete our analysis of aggregate output determination, we need to introduce another market that produces an additional relationship that links aggregate output and interest rates. The money market fulfills this function with the *LM* curve. When the *LM* curve is combined with the *IS* curve, a unique equilibrium that determines both aggregate output and the interest rate is obtained.

Equilibrium in the Money Market: The *LM* Curve

Just as the *IS* curve is derived from the equilibrium condition in the goods market (aggregate output equals aggregate demand), the *LM* curve is derived from the equilibrium condition in the money market, which requires that the quantity of money demanded equal the quantity of money supplied. The main building block in Keynes' analysis of the money market is the demand for money he called *liquidity preference*. We will review his theory of the demand for money (discussed in Chapters 6 and 23) briefly here.

Keynes' liquidity preference theory states that the demand for money in real terms (M^d/P) depends on income (aggregate output, Y) and interest rates (i). The demand for money is positively related to income for two reasons. First, a rise in income raises the level of transactions in the economy, which, in turn, raises the demand for money since it is used to carry out these transactions. Second, a rise in income increases the demand for money because it increases the wealth of individuals who want to hold more assets, one of which is money. The opportunity cost of holding money is the interest sacrificed by not holding other assets (such as bonds) instead. As interest rates rise, the opportunity cost of holding money rises and the demand for money falls. According to the liquidity preference theory, the demand for money is positively related to aggregate output and negatively related to interest rates.

Deriving the LM Curve In Keynes' analysis, the level of interest rates is determined by money market equilibrium, in which the quantity of money demanded equals the quantity of money supplied. Figure 24.8 depicts what happens to equilibrium in the money market as the level of output changes. Since the *LM* curve is derived holding the money supply at a fixed level, it is fixed at the level of $\overline{M}$ in panel (a). Each level of aggregate output has its own money demand curve because as aggregate output changes, the level of transactions in the economy changes, which in turn changes the demand for money.

When aggregate output is Y_1, the money demand curve is $M^d(Y_1)$: It slopes downward because a lower interest rate means that the opportunity cost of holding money is lower so that the quantity of money demanded is higher. Equilibrium in the money market occurs at point 1, at which the interest rate is i_1. When aggregate output is at a higher level, Y_2, the money demand curve shifts out to $M^d(Y_2)$ because the higher level of output means that at any given interest rate the quantity of money demanded is higher.

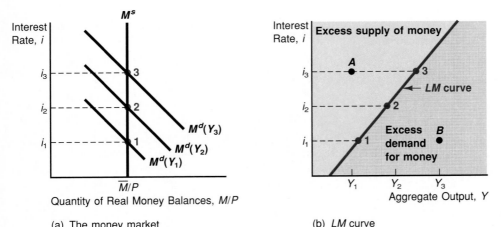

(a) The money market

(b) *LM* curve

Figure 24.8
Deriving the *LM* Curve Panel (a) shows the equilibrium levels of the interest rate in the money market that arise when aggregate output is at Y_1, Y_2, and Y_3. Panel (b) plots the three levels of the equilibrium interest rate, i_1, i_2, and i_3, corresponding to these three levels of output; the line that connects these points is the *LM* curve.

Equilibrium in the money market now occurs at point 2, at which the interest rate is at the higher level of i_2. Similarly, a still higher level of aggregate output, Y_3, results in an even higher level of the equilibrium interest rate, i_3.

Panel (b) plots the equilibrium interest rates that correspond to the different output levels, with points 1, 2, and 3 corresponding to the equilibrium points 1, 2, and 3 in panel (a). The line connecting these points is the *LM* curve, which shows the combinations of interest rates and output for which the money market is in equilibrium.[8] The positive slope arises because higher output raises the demand for money and thus raises the equilibrium interest rate.

What the LM Curve Tells Us   The *LM* curve traces out the points that satisfy the money market equilibrium condition that the quantity of money demanded equals the quantity of money supplied. For each given level of aggregate output, the *LM* curve tells us what the interest rate must equal for there to be equilibrium in the money market. As aggregate output rises, the demand for money increases and the interest rate rises, so that money demanded equals money supplied and the money market is in equilibrium.

Just as the economy tends to the equilibrium points represented by the *IS* curve, it also moves toward the equilibrium points on the *LM* curve. If the economy is located in the area to the left of the *LM* curve, there is an excess supply of money. At point A, for example, the interest rate is above the equilibrium level and people are holding more money than they want to. To eliminate their excess money balances, they will purchase bonds, which causes the price of the bonds to rise and their interest rate to fall. (The inverse relationship between the price of a bond and its interest rate is discussed in Chapter 4.) As long as an excess supply of money exists, the interest rate will fall until it comes to rest on the *LM* curve.

If the economy is located in the area to the right of the *LM* curve, there is an excess demand for money. At point B, for example, the interest rate is below the equilibrium level and people want to hold more money than they currently do. To acquire this money, they will sell bonds and drive down bond prices, and the interest rate will rise. This process will stop only when the interest rate rises to an equilibrium point on the *LM* curve.

THE *ISLM* APPROACH TO AGGREGATE OUTPUT AND INTEREST RATES

Now that we have derived the *IS* and *LM* curves, we can put these into the same diagram (Figure 24.9) to produce a model that enables us to determine both aggregate output and the interest rate. The only point at which the

---

[8]Hicks gave this curve the *LM* initials to indicate that it represents the combinations of interest rates and output for which money demand (which Keynes denoted as L to represent liquidity preference) equals money supply (M).

Figure 24.9
***ISLM* Diagram: Simultaneous Determination of Output and the Interest Rate** Only at point E, when the interest rate is *i** and output is *Y**, is there equilibrium simultaneously in both the goods market (as measured by the *IS* curve) and the money market (as measured by the *LM* curve). At other points such as A, B, C, or D, one of the two markets is not in equilibrium and there will be a tendency to head toward the equilibrium, point E.

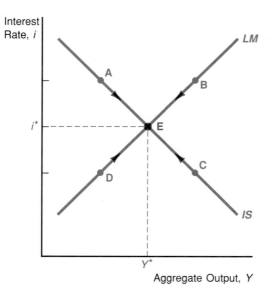

goods and money markets are in simultaneous equilibrium is at the intersection of the *IS* and *LM* curves, point E. At this point, aggregate output equals aggregate demand (*IS*) and the quantity of money demanded equals the quantity of money supplied (*LM*). At any other point in the diagram, at least one of these equilibrium conditions is not satisfied and market forces move the economy toward the "general" equilibrium, point E.

To learn how this works, let's consider what happens if the economy is at point A, which is on the *IS* curve but not on the *LM* curve. Even though at point A the goods market is in equilibrium so that aggregate output equals aggregate demand, the interest rate is above its equilibrium level, so the demand for money is less than the supply. Because people have more money than they want to hold, they will try to get rid of it by buying bonds. The resulting rise in bond prices causes a fall in interest rates, which in turn causes both planned investment spending and net exports to rise, and thus aggregate output rises. The economy then moves down along the *IS* curve and the process continues until the interest rate falls to *i** and aggregate output rises to *Y**, that is, until the economy is at equilibrium point E.

If the economy is on the *LM* curve but off the *IS* curve at point B, it will also head toward the equilibrium at E. At point B, even though money demand equals money supply, output is higher than the equilibrium level and exceeds aggregate demand. Business firms are thus unable to sell all their output and unplanned inventory accumulates, prompting them to cut production and lower output. The decline in output means that the demand for money will fall, lowering interest rates. The economy then moves down along the *LM* curve until it reaches equilibrium point E.

Study Guide

To test your understanding of why the economy heads toward equilibrium point E at the intersection of the *IS* and *LM* curves, see if you can provide the reasoning behind the movement to point E from points such as C and D in the figure.

We have finally developed a model, the *ISLM* model, which tells us how both interest rates and aggregate output are determined when the price level is fixed. Although we have demonstrated that the economy will head to an aggregate output level of Y^*, there is no reason to assume that at this level of aggregate output the economy is at full employment. If the unemployment rate is too high, government policymakers might want to increase aggregate output to reduce it. The *ISLM* apparatus indicates that they can do this by manipulating monetary and fiscal policy. *ISLM* analysis of how monetary and fiscal policy can affect economic activity will be discussed in Chapter 25.

SUMMARY

1. In the simple Keynesian framework in which the price level is fixed, output is determined by the equilibrium condition in the goods market that aggregate output equals aggregate demand. Aggregate demand equals the sum of consumer expenditure, planned investment spending, government spending and net exports. Consumer expenditure is described by the consumption function, which indicates that consumer expenditure will rise as disposable income increases. Keynes' analysis shows that aggregate output is positively related to autonomous consumer expenditure, planned investment spending, government spending, and net exports; while it is negatively related to the level of taxes. A change in any of these factors leads, through the expenditure multiplier, to a multiple change in aggregate output.

2. The *ISLM* model determines aggregate output and the interest rate for a fixed price level using the *IS* and *LM* curves. The *IS* curve traces out the combinations of the interest rate and aggregate output for which the goods market is in equilibrium, and the *LM* curve traces out the combinations for which the money market is in equilibrium. The *IS* curve slopes downward because higher interest rates lower planned investment spending and so lower equilibrium output. The *LM* curve slopes upward because higher aggregate output raises the demand for money and so raises the equilibrium interest rate.

3. The simultaneous determination of output and interest rates occurs at the intersection of the *IS* and *LM* curves, where both the goods and money markets are in equilibrium. At any other level of interest rates and output, at least one of the markets will be out of equilibrium and forces will move the economy toward the "general" equilibrium point at the intersection of the *IS* and *LM* curves.

KEY TERMS

consumer expenditure

planned investment
  spending

government spending

net exports

aggregate demand

disposable income

consumption function

marginal propensity to
  consume

autonomous consumer
  expenditure

fixed investment

inventory investment

aggregate demand
  function

expenditure multiplier

"animal spirits"

IS curve

LM curve

QUESTIONS AND PROBLEMS

1. Calculate the values of the consumption function at each level of disposable income in Table
   24.1 if $a = 100$ and $mpc = .9$.

* 2. Why do companies cut production when they
   find that their unplanned inventory investment
   is greater than zero? If they didn't cut production, what effect would this have on their profits?
   Why?

3. Plot the consumption function $C = 100 + .75 \times
   Y$ on graph paper.
   a) Assuming no government sector, if planned
      investment spending is 200, what is the equi-
      librium level of aggregate output? Show this
      equilibrium level on the graph you have
      drawn.
   b) If businesses become more pessimistic about
      the profitability of investment and planned
      investment spending falls by 100, what hap-
      pens to the equilibrium level of output?

* 4. If the consumption function is $C = 100 + .8 \times Y$
   and planned investment spending is 200, what is
   the equilibrium level of output? If planned investment falls by 100, how much does the level of
   output fall?

5. Why are the multipliers in problems 3 and 4 different? Explain intuitively why one is higher
   than the other.

* 6. If business firms suddenly become more optimistic about the profitability of investment so
   that planned investment spending rises by $100
   billion, while consumers become more pessimis-

tic so that autonomous consumer spending falls
by $100 billion, what happens to aggregate out-
put?

7. Answer true, false, or uncertain: "A rise in
   planned investment spending by $100 billion at
   the same time that autonomous consumer expenditure falls by $50 billion has the same effect
   on aggregate output as a rise in autonomous consumer expenditure alone by $50 billion."

* 8. If the consumption function is $C = 100 + .75 \times
   Y$, $I = 200$, and government spending is 200,
   what will be the equilibrium level of output?
   Demonstrate your answer with a Keynesian cross
   diagram. What happens to aggregate output if
   government spending rises by 100?

9. If the marginal propensity to consume is .5, how
   much would government spending have to rise
   in order to raise output by $1000 billion?

*10. Suppose government policymakers decide that
   they will change taxes to raise aggregate output
   by $400 billion and $mpc = .5$. How much will
   taxes need to be changed?

11. What happens to aggregate output if both taxes
   and government spending are lowered by $300
   billion and $mpc = .5$? Explain.

*12. Will aggregate output rise or fall if an increase in
   autonomous consumer expenditure is matched
   by an equal increase in taxes?

13. If a change in the interest rate has no effect on
   planned investment spending, trace out what
   happens to the equilibrium level of aggregate

output as interest rates fall. What does this imply about the slope of the *IS* curve?

*14. Using a supply and demand diagram for the money market, show what happens to the equilibrium level of the interest rate as aggregate output falls. What does this imply about the slope of the *LM* curve?

15. Answer true, false, or uncertain: "If the point describing the combination of the interest rate and aggregate output is not on either the *IS* or *LM* curves, then the economy will have no tendency to head toward the intersection of the *IS* and *LM* curves."

CHAPTER 25

Monetary and Fiscal Policy in the *ISLM* Model

PREVIEW Since World War II, government policymakers have tried to promote high employment without creating inflation. If the economy experiences a recession as occurred at the time of Iraq's invasion of Kuwait in 1990, policymakers have two principal sets of tools by which to affect aggregate economic activity: monetary policy—the control of interest rates or the money supply; and fiscal policy—the control of government spending and taxes.

The *ISLM* model can help policymakers predict what will happen to aggregate output and interest rates if they decide to increase the money supply or increase government spending. In this way, *ISLM* analysis enables us to answer some important questions about the usefulness and effectiveness of monetary and fiscal policy on economic activity.

But which is better? When is monetary policy most effective relative to fiscal policy for controlling the level of aggregate output, and when is it least effective? Will fiscal policy be more effective if it is conducted by changing government spending rather than changing taxes? Should the monetary authorities conduct monetary policy by manipulating the money supply or interest rates?

In the present chapter we use the *ISLM* model to help answer these questions and to learn how the model generates the aggregate demand curve featured prominently in the aggregate demand and supply framework which will be examined in Chapter 26. From our analysis you will learn why economists focus so much attention on such topics as stability of the demand for money function and whether the demand for money is strongly influenced by interest rates.

First, however, let's examine the *ISLM* model in more detail to see how the *IS* and *LM* curves developed in Chapter 24 shift and the implications of these shifts. Remember, we are continuing to assume that the price level is fixed so that real and nominal quantities are the same.

FACTORS THAT CAUSE THE *IS* CURVE TO SHIFT

You have already learned that the *IS* curve describes equilibrium points in the goods market—the combinations of aggregate output and interest rate for which aggregate output produced equals aggregate demand. The *IS* curve shifts whenever a change in autonomous factors (independent of aggregate output) occurs that is unrelated to the interest rate. (A change in the interest rate that affects equilibrium aggregate output only causes a movement along the *IS* curve.) We have already identified five candidates for autonomous factors that can shift aggregate demand and hence affect the level of equilibrium output. We can now ask how changes in each of these factors affect the *IS* curve.

Changes in Autonomous Consumer Expenditure   A rise in autonomous consumer expenditure shifts up aggregate demand and shifts the *IS* curve to the right (see Figure 25.1). To see how this shift occurs, suppose the *IS* curve is initially at IS_1 in panel (a) and a huge oil field is discovered in Wyoming, perhaps containing more oil than in Saudi Arabia. Consumers now become more optimistic about the future health of the economy, and autonomous consumer expenditure rises. What happens to the equilibrium level of aggregate output as a result of this rise in autonomous consumer expenditure when the interest rate is held constant at i_A?

The IS_1 curve tells us that equilibrium aggregate output is at Y_A when the interest rate is at i_A (point A). Panel (b) shows that this point is an equilibrium in the goods market because the aggregate demand function (Y_1^{ad}) at an interest rate i_A crosses the 45°, $Y = Y^{ad}$ line at an aggregate output level of Y_A. When autonomous consumer expenditure rises because of the oil discovery, the aggregate demand function shifts up to Y_2^{ad} and equilibrium output rises to $Y_{A'}$. This rise in equilibrium output from Y_A to $Y_{A'}$ when the interest rate is i_A is plotted in panel (a) as a movement from point A to point A'. The same analysis can be applied to every point on the initial IS_1 curve; therefore, the rise in autonomous consumer expenditure shifts the *IS* curve to the right from IS_1 to IS_2 in panel (a).

A decline in autonomous consumer expenditure reverses the direction of the analysis. For any given interest rate, the aggregate demand function shifts down, the equilibrium level of aggregate output falls, and the *IS* curve shifts to the left.

Changes in Investment Spending Unrelated to the Interest Rate   In Chapter 24 you learned that changes in the interest rate affect planned investment spending and hence the equilibrium level of output, but *this* change in investment spending merely causes a movement along the *IS* curve and not a shift. A rise in planned investment spending unrelated to the interest rate

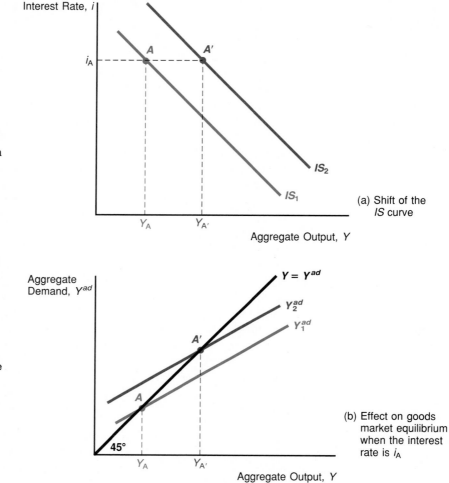

Figure 25.1
Shift in the *IS* Curve
The *IS* curve will shift out from IS_1 to IS_2 as a result of the following: (1) an increase in autonomous consumer spending; (2) an increase in planned investment spending due to business optimism; (3) an increase in government spending; (4) a decrease in taxes; or (5) an increase in net exports which is unrelated to interest rates. Panel (b) shows how changes in the above factors lead to the rightward shift in the *IS* curve using the Keynesian cross diagram. For any given interest rate (here i_A), these changes shift up the aggregate demand function and raise equilibrium output from Y_A to $Y_{A'}$.

shifts up the aggregate demand function, as in panel (b) of Figure 25.1 (say, companies become more confident about investment profitability after the Wyoming oil discovery). For any given interest rate, the equilibrium level of aggregate output rises and the *IS* curve will shift to the right, as in panel (a).

A decrease in investment spending because companies become more pessimistic about investment profitability shifts the aggregate demand function down for any given interest rate; the equilibrium level of aggregate output falls, shifting the *IS* curve to the left.

Changes in Government Spending An increase in government spending will also cause the aggregate demand function at any given interest rate to shift up, as in panel (b). The equilibrium level of aggregate output rises at any given interest rate, and the *IS* curve shifts to the right. Conversely, a decline in government spending shifts the aggregate demand function down and the equilibrium level of output falls, shifting the *IS* curve to the left.

Changes in Taxes   Unlike changes in other factors that directly affect the aggregate demand function, a decline in taxes shifts the aggregate demand function, by raising consumer expenditure and shifting up the aggregate demand function at any given interest rate. A decline in taxes raises the equilibrium level of aggregate output at any given interest rate and shifts the *IS* curve to the right (as in Figure 25.1). Recall, however, that a change in taxes has a smaller effect on aggregate demand than an equivalent change in government spending. So for a given change in taxes, the *IS* curve will shift less than for an equal change in government spending.

A rise in taxes lowers the aggregate demand function and reduces the equilibrium level of aggregate output at each interest rate. Therefore, a rise in taxes shifts the *IS* curve to the left.

Changes in Net Exports Unrelated to the Interest Rate   As with planned investment spending, changes in net exports arising from a change in interest rates merely causes a movement along the *IS* curve and not a shift. An autonomous rise in net exports unrelated to the interest rate, say because American-made jeans become more chic than French-made jeans, shifts up the aggregate demand function and causes the *IS* curve to shift to the right, as in Figure 25.1. Conversely, an autonomous fall in net exports shifts the aggregate demand function down and the equilibrium level of output falls, shifting the *IS* curve to the left.

FACTORS THAT CAUSE THE *LM* CURVE TO SHIFT

The *LM* curve describes the equilibrium points in the money market; that is, the combinations of aggregate output and interest rate for which the quantity of money demanded equals the quantity of money supplied. While five factors can cause the *IS* curve to shift (changes in autonomous consumer expenditure, planned investment spending unrelated to the interest rate, government spending, taxes, and net exports), only two factors can cause the *LM* curve to shift: autonomous changes in money demand and changes in money supply. How do changes in these two factors affect the *LM* curve?

Changes in the Money Supply   A rise in the money supply shifts the *LM* curve to the right, as shown in Figure 25.2. To see how this shift occurs, suppose the *LM* curve is initially at LM_1 in panel (a) and the Federal Reserve conducts open market purchases that increase the money supply. If we consider point A, which is on the initial LM_1 curve, we can examine what hap-

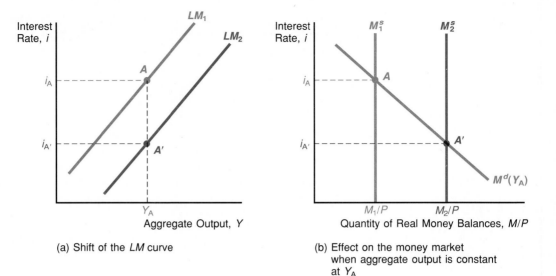

Figure 25.2

Shift in the *LM* Curve from an Increase in the Money Supply   The *LM* curve shifts to the right from LM_1 to LM_2 when the money supply increases because, as indicated in panel (b), at any given level of aggregate output (say, Y_A) the equilibrium interest rate falls (point A to A').

pens to the equilibrium level of the interest rate holding output constant at Y_A.

Panel (b), which contains a supply and demand diagram for the money market, depicts the equilibrium interest rate initially as i_A at the intersection of the supply curve for money (M_1^s) and the demand curve for money (M^d). The rise in the quantity of money supplied shifts out the supply curve to M_2^s and, holding output constant at Y_A, the equilibrium interest rate falls to $i_{A'}$. In panel (a) this decline in the equilibrium interest rate from i_A to $i_{A'}$ is shown as a movement from point A to point A'. The same analysis can be applied to every point on the initial LM_1 curve, with the conclusion that at any given level of aggregate output, the equilibrium interest rate falls when the money supply increases. Thus LM_2 is below and to the right of LM_1.

Reversing this reasoning—a decline in the money supply shifts the *LM* curve to the left. A decline in the money supply results in a shortage of money at points on the initial *LM* curve. This condition of excess demand for money can be eliminated by a rise in the interest rate, which reduces the quantity of money demanded until it again equals the quantity of money supplied.

Autonomous Changes in Money Demand   An autonomous rise in money demand (not caused by a change in the price level, aggregate output, or the interest rate) shifts the *LM* curve to the left, as shown in Figure 25.3. Con-

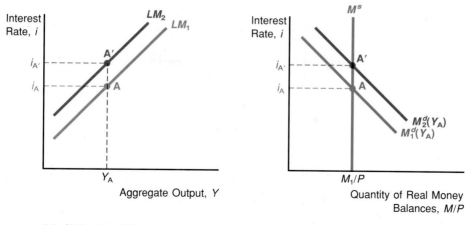

(a) Shift in the *LM* curve

(b) Effect on the money
market when aggregate
output is constant at Y_A

Figure 25.3
Shift in the *LM* Curve When Money Demand Increases   The *LM* curve shifts to the left
from LM_1 to LM_2 when money demand increases because, as is indicated in panel (b), at
any given level of aggregate output (say, Y_A) the equilibrium interest rate rises (point A to
A′).

sider point A on the initial *LM* curve, LM_1. Suppose that a massive financial
panic occurs, sending many companies into bankruptcy. Because bonds
have become a riskier asset, people want to shift from holding bonds to
holding money; they will hold more money at all interest rates and output
levels. The resulting increase in money demand at an output level of Y_A is
shown by the shift of the money demand curve from M_1^d to M_2^d in panel (b).
The new equilibrium in the money market now indicates that if aggregate
output is constant at Y_A, the equilibrium interest rate will rise to $i_{A'}$ and the
point of money market equilibrium moves from A to A′.

Conversely, an autonomous decline in money demand would lead to a
rightward shift in the *LM* curve. The fall in money demand would create an
excess supply of money, which is eliminated by a rise in the quantity of
money demanded from a decline in the interest rate.

CHANGES IN EQUILIBRIUM LEVEL OF THE
INTEREST RATE AND AGGREGATE OUTPUT

You can now use your knowledge of factors that cause the *IS* and *LM* curves
to shift for the purpose of analyzing how the equilibrium levels of the interest rate and aggregate output change in response to changes in monetary
and fiscal policies.

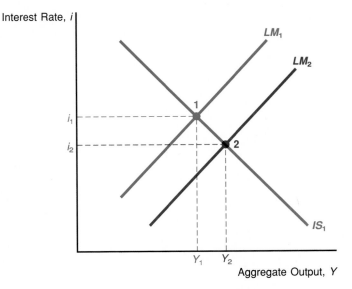

Figure 25.4
Response of Aggregate Output and the Interest Rate to an Increase in the Money Supply The increase in the money supply shifts the *LM* curve to the right from *LM*₁ to *LM*₂; the economy moves to point 2, where output has increased to Y_2 and the interest rate has declined to i_2.

Response to a Change in Monetary Policy

Figure 25.4 illustrates the response of output and interest rate to an increase in the money supply. Initially, the economy is in goods and money market equilibrium at point 1, the intersection of IS_1 and LM_1. Suppose that at the resulting level of aggregate output, Y_1, the economy is suffering from an unemployment rate of 20% and the Federal Reserve decides it should try to raise output and reduce unemployment by raising the money supply. Will the Fed's change in monetary policy have the intended effect?

The rise in the money supply causes the *LM* curve to shift out to LM_2 and the equilibrium point for both the goods and money market moves to point 2 (intersection of IS_1 and LM_2). As a result of an increase in money supply, the interest rate declines to i_2 and aggregate output rises to Y_2; the Fed's policy has been successful in improving the health of the economy.

For a clear understanding of why aggregate output rises and the interest rate declines, think about exactly what has happened in moving from point 1 to point 2. When the economy is at point 1, the increase in the money supply (rightward shift of the *LM* curve) creates an excess supply of money, resulting in a decline in the interest rate. The decline causes investment spending and net exports to rise, which, in turn, raises aggregate demand and causes aggregate output to rise. The excess supply of money is eliminated when the economy reaches point 2, because the rise in output and fall in the interest rate both have raised the quantity of money demanded until it equals the new higher level of the money supply.

A decline in the money supply reverses the process; it shifts the *LM* curve to the left, causing the interest rate to rise and output to fall. Accordingly, ***aggregate output is positively related to the money supply;*** aggregate output expands when the money supply is increased and falls when it is decreased.

Response to a Change in Fiscal Policy

Suppose the Federal Reserve is not willing to increase the money supply when the economy is suffering from a 20% unemployment rate at point 1. Can the federal government come to the rescue and manipulate government spending and taxes to raise aggregate output and reduce the massive unemployment?

The *ISLM* model demonstrates that it can. Figure 25.5 depicts the response of output and the interest rate to an expansionary fiscal policy (increase in government spending or decrease in taxes). An increase in government spending or a decrease in taxes causes the *IS* curve to shift out to IS_2, and the equilibrium point for both the goods and money market moves to point 2 (intersection of IS_2 with LM_1). The result of the change in fiscal policy is a rise in aggregate output to Y_2 and a rise in the interest rate to i_2. Note the difference in the effect on the interest rate of the expansionary fiscal policy from the expansionary monetary policy. In the case of the expansionary fiscal policy, the interest rate rises, while in the case of expansionary monetary policy, the interest rate falls.

Why does an increase in government spending or a decrease in taxes move the economy from point 1 to point 2, causing a rise in both aggregate output and the interest rate? An increase in government spending raises aggregate demand directly, while a decrease in taxes makes more income

Figure 25.5
Response of Aggregate Output and the Interest Rate to an Expansionary Fiscal Policy Expansionary fiscal policy (a rise in government spending or a decrease in taxes) shifts the *IS* curve to the right from IS_1 to IS_2; the economy moves to point 2 and aggregate output increases to Y_2, while the interest rate rises to i_2.

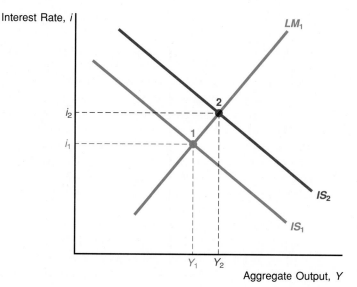

available for spending and raises aggregate demand by raising consumer expenditure. The resulting increase in aggregate demand causes aggregate output to rise. The higher level of aggregate output raises the quantity of money demanded, creating an excess demand for money, which in turn causes the interest rate to rise. At point 2 the excess demand for money created by a rise in aggregate output has been eliminated by a rise in the interest rate, which lowers the quantity of money demanded.

A contractionary fiscal policy (decrease in government spending or increase in taxes) reverses the process described in Figure 25.5; it causes aggregate demand to fall, which shifts the *IS* curve to the left and causes both aggregate output and the interest rate to fall. ***Aggregate output and the interest rate are positively related to government spending and are negatively related to taxes.***

Study Guide

As a study aid, Table 25.1 indicates the effect on aggregate output and interest rates of a change in the seven factors that shift the *IS* and *LM* curves. In addition the table provides schematics describing the reason for the output and interest rate response. *ISLM* analysis is best learned by practicing applications. To get this practice, you might try to develop the reasoning for your own Table 25.1 in which all the factors decrease rather than increase or answer problems at the end of this chapter.

APPLICATION
THE VIETNAM WAR BUILDUP AND THE RISE///////////////////// IN INTEREST RATES, 1965–1966

From early 1965 to the end of 1966, America dramatically increased its involvement in the Vietnam war by increasing the number of troops in Vietnam from under 25,000 to over 350,000. The troop buildup resulted in a substantial rise in military spending, which led to a \$46 billion (1982 dollars) increase in government spending from 1965 to 1966 (from \$487 billion to \$533 billion). What does our *ISLM* model predict should have happened to aggregate output and interest rates as a result?

Figure 25.6 shows that the increase in government spending would have shifted the *IS* curve to the right from IS_1 to IS_2, while the *LM* curve remained unchanged since the money supply (*M*1) remained almost constant in real terms: \$502 billion 1982 dollars in 1965 and \$500 billion 1982 dollars in 1966. The *ISLM* model then predicts that the economy moves from point 1 to point 2 in which both GNP and interest rates rise, and this is exactly what happened from 1965 to 1966: GNP rose by \$120 billion in 1982 dollars (a multiple of the \$46 billion increase in government spending), from \$2088

Table 25.1   Summary: Effects From Factors That Shift the *IS* and *LM* Curves

Factor and Change	Response	Reason	
$C \uparrow$	$Y \uparrow i \uparrow$	$C \uparrow \rightarrow Y^{ad} \uparrow \rightarrow$	*IS* shifts right
$I \uparrow$	$Y \uparrow i \uparrow$	$I \uparrow \rightarrow Y^{ad} \uparrow \rightarrow$	*IS* shifts right
$G \uparrow$	$Y \uparrow i \uparrow$	$G \uparrow \rightarrow Y^{ad} \uparrow \rightarrow$	*IS* shifts right
$T \uparrow$	$Y \downarrow i \downarrow$	$T \uparrow \rightarrow C \downarrow \rightarrow Y^{ad} \downarrow \rightarrow$	*IS* shifts left
$NX \uparrow$	$Y \uparrow i \uparrow$	$NX \uparrow \rightarrow Y^{ad} \uparrow \rightarrow$	*IS* shifts right
$M^s \uparrow$	$Y \uparrow i \downarrow$	$M^s \uparrow \rightarrow i \downarrow \rightarrow$	*LM* shifts right
$M^d \uparrow$	$Y \downarrow i \uparrow$	$M^d \uparrow \rightarrow i \uparrow \rightarrow$	*LM* shifts left

Note: Only increases ($\uparrow$) in the factors are shown. The effect of decreases in the factors would be the opposite of those indicated in the second column.

billion to $2208 billion, while the interest rate on three-month Treasury bills rose from 3.95 to 4.88%.[1]

Economists at the time agreed that taxes needed to be increased to keep the economy from overheating and to reduce interest rates by shifting the *IS* curve back to the left. Unfortunately, President Lyndon Johnson thought it politically infeasible to raise taxes to pay for what was rapidly becoming America's most unpopular war. Taxes were not increased until 1968, and by then the overheated economy had burst into inflation and record-high interest rates.

EFFECTIVENESS OF MONETARY VERSUS FISCAL POLICY

Our discussion of the effects of fiscal and monetary policy suggests that a government can easily lift an economy out of a recession by implementing any one of a number of policies (changing the money supply, government spending, or taxes). But how can policymakers decide which of these policies to use if faced with too much unemployment? Should they decrease taxes, increase government spending, raise the money supply, or do all three? And if they decide to increase the money supply, by how much? Economists do

---

[1]An alternative explanation of why interest rates rose from 1965 to 1966 is that expected inflation increased over this period, causing nominal interest rates to rise. (See Chapter 6 for an explanation of why a rise in expected inflation can raise nominal interest rates.) Note that this explanation and the *ISLM* explanation above are not inconsistent; both the rise in expected inflation and the rightward shift of the *IS* curve may have contributed to the rise in interest rates in this period.

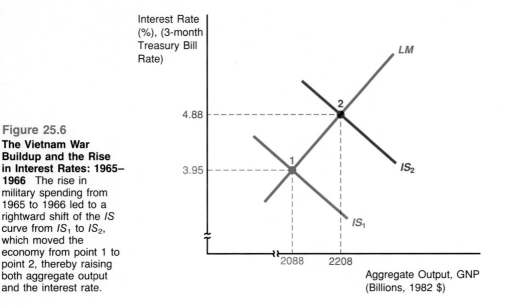

Figure 25.6
The Vietnam War Buildup and the Rise in Interest Rates: 1965–1966 The rise in military spending from 1965 to 1966 led to a rightward shift of the *IS* curve from IS_1 to IS_2, which moved the economy from point 1 to point 2, thereby raising both aggregate output and the interest rate.

not pretend to have all the answers, and although the *ISLM* model will not clear the path to aggregate economic bliss, it *can* help policymakers to decide which policies might be most effective under what circumstances.

When Is Monetary Policy More Effective Than Fiscal Policy? The Case of Complete Crowding Out

The *ISLM* model developed so far in this chapter shows that both monetary and fiscal policy affect the level of aggregate output. To understand when monetary policy is more effective than fiscal policy, we will examine a special case of the *ISLM* model in which money demand is unaffected by the interest rate (money demand is said to be "interest inelastic") so that monetary policy affects output but fiscal policy does not.

Consider the slope of the *LM* curve if the demand for money is unaffected by changes in the interest rate. If point 1 in panel (a) of Figure 25.7 is such that the quantity of money demanded equals the quantity of money supplied, then it is on the *LM* curve. If the interest rate rises to, say, i_2, the quantity of money demanded is unaffected, and it will continue to equal the *unchanged* quantity of money supplied only if aggregate output remains *unchanged* at Y_1 (point 2). Equilibrium in the money market will occur at the same level of aggregate output regardless of the value of the interest rate, and the *LM* curve will be vertical, as shown in both panels (a) and (b) of Figure 25.7.

Suppose the economy is suffering from a high rate of unemployment, which policymakers try to eliminate with either expansionary fiscal or mone-

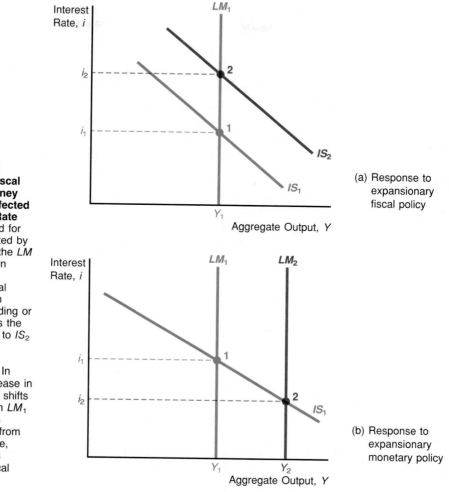

Figure 25.7
Effectiveness of Monetary and Fiscal Policy When Money Demand Is Unaffected by the Interest Rate
When the demand for money is unaffected by the interest rate, the *LM* curve is vertical. In panel (a), an expansionary fiscal policy (increase in government spending or cut in taxes) shifts the *IS* curve from IS_1 to IS_2 and leaves the aggregate output unchanged at Y_1. In panel (b), an increase in the money supply shifts the *LM* curve from LM_1 to LM_2 and raises aggregate output from Y_1 to Y_2. Therefore, monetary policy is effective while fiscal policy is not.

tary policy. Panel (a) depicts what happens when an expansionary fiscal policy (increase in government spending or cut in taxes) is implemented, which shifts the *IS* curve to the right from IS_1 to IS_2. As you can see in panel (a), the fiscal expansion has no effect on output; aggregate output remains at Y_1 when the economy moves from point 1 to point 2.

In our earlier analysis, expansionary fiscal policy always increased aggregate demand and raised the level of output. Why doesn't this happen in panel (a)? The answer is that because the *LM* curve is vertical, the rightward shift of the *IS* curve raises the interest rate to i_2, which causes investment spending and net exports to fall sufficiently to completely offset increased spending resulting from expansionary fiscal policy. Put another way, increased spending that results from expansionary fiscal policy has "crowded out" investment spending and net exports, which decrease because of the rise in the interest rate. This situation in which expansionary fiscal policy does not lead to a rise in output is frequently referred to as a case of **complete crowding out.**[2]

Panel (b) shows what happens when the Federal Reserve tries to eliminate high unemployment by an expansionary monetary policy (increase in the money supply). Here the LM curve shifts to the right from LM_1 to LM_2 because at each interest rate output must rise so that the quantity of money demanded rises to match the increase in the money supply. Aggregate output rises from Y_1 to Y_2 (the economy moves from point 1 to point 2) and expansionary monetary policy does affect aggregate output in this case.

We conclude from the analysis in Figure 25.7 that if the demand for money is unaffected by changes in the interest rate (money demand is "interest inelastic"), then monetary policy is effective, while fiscal policy is not. An even more general conclusion can be reached: ***The less interest sensitive is money demand, the more effective is monetary policy relative to fiscal policy.***

Because interest sensitivity of money demand is important to policymakers' decisions regarding the use of monetary or fiscal policy to influence economic activity, the subject has been studied extensively by economists and has been the focus of many debates. Refer back to Chapter 23 which discusses findings on the interest sensitivity of money demand.

APPLICATION
TARGETING ON MONEY SUPPLY/ VERSUS INTEREST RATES

The *ISLM* model has important implications for an issue discussed in Chapter 20: Should the Federal Reserve conduct monetary policy by using its policy tools to "hit" a money supply target (try to make the money supply equal to a target value) or should it try to "hit" an interest rate target instead? Our *ISLM* model will answer this question.[3]

---

[2]When the demand for money is affected by the interest rate, the usual case in which the *LM* curve slopes upward but is not vertical, some crowding out occurs. The rightward shift of the *IS* curve also raises the interest rate, which causes investment spending and net exports to fall somewhat. However, as Figure 25.5 indicates, the rise in the interest rate is not sufficient to reduce investment spending and net exports to the point where aggregate output does not increase. Thus expansionary fiscal policy increases aggregate output and only "partial" crowding out occurs.

[3]The classic paper on this topic is William Poole, "The Optimal Choice of Monetary Policy Instruments in a Simple Macro Model," *Quarterly Journal of Economics* 84 (May 1970), pp. 192–216. A less mathematical version of his analysis, which is far more accessible to students, is contained in William Poole, "Rules of Thumb for Guiding Monetary Policy," in *Open Market Policies and Operating Procedures—Staff Studies* (Washington, D.C.: Board of Governors of the Federal Reserve System, 1971).

As we saw in Chapter 19, when the Federal Reserve attempts to hit a money supply target, it cannot at the same time pursue an interest rate target, and vice versa; the Fed can hit one target or the other, but not both. Consequently, it needs to know which of these two targets will produce more accurate control of aggregate output.

In contrast to the textbook world you have been inhabiting, in which the *IS* and *LM* curves are assumed to be fixed, the real world is one of great uncertainty in which *IS* and *LM* curves shift unexpectedly because of unanticipated changes in autonomous spending and money demands. To understand whether the Fed should use a money supply target or an interest rate target, we need to look at two cases: first, one in which uncertainty about the *IS* curve is far greater than uncertainty about the *LM* curve, and second, one in which uncertainty about the *LM* curve is far greater than uncertainty about the *IS* curve.

The *ISLM* diagram in Figure 25.8 illustrates the outcome of the two targeting strategies for the case in which the *IS* curve is unstable and uncertain, while the *LM* curve is stable and certain. If the Fed expects that the *IS* curve will be at *IS** and desires aggregate output of *Y**, it will set its interest rate target at *i** so that the expected level of output is *Y**. This policy of targeting the interest rate at *i** is labeled "*interest rate target.*" (Recall from Chapter 20 that the Fed can hit its interest rate target by buying and selling bonds when the interest rate differs from *i**. When it is above *i**, the Fed buys bonds to raise the price and lower the interest rate back down to *i**. When the interest rate is below *i**, the Fed sells bonds to lower the price and raise the interest rate back up to *i**.)

Figure 25.8
Money Supply and Interest Rate Targets When the *IS* Curve Is Unstable and the *LM* Curve Is Stable   The unstable *IS* curve fluctuates between *IS'* and *IS"*. The money supply target produces smaller fluctuations in output (Y'_M to $Y"_M$) than the interest rate targets (Y'_i to $Y"_i$). Therefore, the money supply target is preferred.

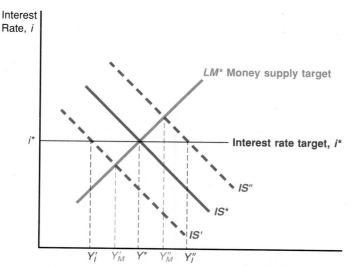

If, instead, the Fed pursues a money supply target, it will set the money supply so that the resulting *LM* curve, *LM**, intersects the *IS** curve at the desired output level of *Y**. This policy of targeting the money supply is labeled "*money supply target.*"

Because the *IS* curve is unstable, it fluctuates between *IS'* and *IS"*, causing aggregate output to fluctuate between Y'_I and Y''_I for the interest rate target policy, or between Y'_M and Y''_M for the money supply target policy. As you can see in the figure, the money supply target leads to smaller output fluctuations around the desired level than does the interest rate target. A rightward shift of the *IS* curve to *IS"*, for example, causes the interest rate to rise given a money supply target, and this rise in the interest rate leads to a lower level of investment spending and net exports, and hence to a smaller increase in aggregate output than occurs under an interest rate target. Since smaller output fluctuations are desirable, the conclusion is that **if the IS curve is more unstable than the LM curve, a money supply target is preferred.**

The outcome of the two targeting strategies for the case of a stable *IS* curve and an unstable *LM* curve is illustrated in Figure 25.9. Again, the interest rate and money supply targets are set so that the expected level of aggregate output equals the desired level *Y**. Because the *LM* curve is now unstable, it fluctuates between *LM'* and *LM"* even when the money supply is fixed, causing aggregate output to fluctuate between Y'_M and Y''_M. The interest rate target, on the other hand, is not affected by uncertainty about the *LM* curve because it is set by the Fed's adjusting the money supply whenever the interest rate tries to depart from *i**. The only effect of the fluctuating *LM* curve, then, is that the money supply fluctuates more as a result of the inter-

Figure 25.9
Money Supply and Interest Rate Targets When the *LM* Curve Is Unstable and the *IS* Curve Is Stable The unstable *LM* curve fluctuates between *LM'* and *LM"*. The money supply target then produces bigger fluctuations in output (Y'_M to Y''_M) than the interest rate target (which leaves output fixed at *Y**). Therefore, the interest rate target is preferred.

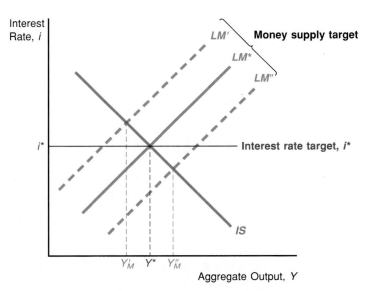

est rate target policy. The outcome of the interest rate target is that output will be exactly at the desired level with no fluctuations. Since smaller output fluctuations are desirable, the conclusion from Figure 25.9 is that *if the LM curve is more unstable than the IS curve, an interest rate target is preferred.*

Milton Friedman and his followers tend to believe that the money demand function and hence the *LM* curve is stable, and they conclude that a money supply target is always better than an interest rate target. Keynesians are much less confident in the stability of the money demand function and are more likely to support an interest rate target. This was especially true in the 1980s since the money demand function proved to be highly unstable—a result of the rapid proliferation of new financial instruments whose presence can affect the demand for money (see Chapter 23). It is important to recognize, however, that the crucial factor in deciding which target is preferred is the *relative* instability of the *IS* and *LM* curves. Although the *LM* curve has been unstable recently, the evidence supporting a stable *IS* curve is also weak. The recent instability in the money demand function does not automatically mean that money supply targets should be abandoned for an interest rate target.[4]

THE *ISLM* MODEL AND THE AGGREGATE DEMAND CURVE

So far in our *ISLM* analysis we have been assuming that the price level is fixed, causing nominal values and real values to be the same. In the real world, the price level is highly variable; so we need to ask how the *ISLM* analysis is affected when the price level changes. When we conduct the *ISLM* analysis with a changing price level, we find that as the price level falls, the level of aggregate output rises. Thus we obtain a relationship between the price level and quantity of aggregate output for which the goods and money markets are in equilibrium, called the **aggregate demand curve.** This aggregate demand curve is a central element in the aggregate supply and demand analysis of Chapter 26 which allows us to explain changes not only in aggregate output, but also in the price level.

---

[4]The analysis so far has been conducted assuming that the price level is fixed. More realistically, when the price level can change so that there is uncertainty about expected inflation, the case for an interest rate target is even weaker. As we learned in Chapters 4 and 6, the interest rate that is more relevant to investment decisions is the *real* interest rate (the nominal interest rate minus expected inflation) and not the nominal interest rate. Thus, when expected inflation rises, at each given nominal interest rate, the real interest rate falls and investment and net exports rise, shifting the *IS* curve to the right. Similarly, a fall in expected inflation raises the real interest rate at each given nominal interest rate, lowers investment and net exports, and shifts the *IS* curve to the left. Since, in the real world, expected inflation undergoes large fluctuations, the *IS* curve in Figure 25.9 will also have substantial fluctuations, making it less likely that the interest rate target is better than the money supply target.

Because we now want to examine what happens when the price level changes, we no longer can assume that real and nominal values are the same. The spending variables that affect the *IS* curve (consumer expenditure, investment spending, government spending, and net exports) describe the demand for goods and services and are in *real terms;* that is, they describe the physical quantities of goods that people want to buy. Since these quantities do not change when the price level changes, a change in the price level has no effect on the *IS* curve, which describes the combinations of the interest rate and aggregate output *in real terms* that satisfy goods market equilibrium.

On the other hand, the *LM* curve *is* affected by changes in the price level because liquidity preference theory states that the demand for money *in real terms* depends on real income and interest rates. This makes sense because money is valued in terms of what it can buy. However, the money supply that you read about in newspapers is not the money supply *in real terms,* but it is a nominal quantity. If the price level falls, say, by 50%, with the money supply unchanged, the value of the money supply in real terms increases (doubles) because it can be used to purchase more goods and services. The effect on the *LM* curve, then, is identical to the effect from an increase in the money supply holding the price level fixed. The higher value of the real money supply creates an excess supply of money, causing the interest rate to fall at any given level of aggregate output and the *LM* curve to shift to the right (see Figure 25.2).

Deriving the Aggregate Demand Curve

Now that you understand how a change in the price level affects the *IS* and *LM* curves, we can analyze what happens in the *ISLM* diagram when the price level changes. This exercise is carried out in Figure 25.10. Panel (a) contains an *ISLM* diagram for a given value of the nominal money supply. Let us first consider a price level of P_1. The *LM* curve at this price level is marked as $LM(P_1)$, and its intersection with the *IS* curve is at point 1, where output is Y_1. The equilibrium output level Y_1 that occurs when the price level is P_1 is also plotted in panel (b) as point 1. If the price level rises to P_2, then *in real terms* the money supply has fallen. The effect on the *LM* curve is identical to a decline in the nominal money supply when the price level is fixed; the *LM* curve will shift in to $LM(P_2)$. The new equilibrium level of output has fallen to Y_2 because planned investment and net exports fall when the interest rate rises. Point 2 in panel (b) plots this level of output for the price level of P_2. A further increase in the price level to P_3 causes a further decline in the real money supply, leading to a further decline in planned investment and net exports, and output declines to Y_3. Point 3 in panel (b) plots this level of output for the price level of P_3.

The line that connects the three points in panel (b) is the aggregate demand curve (*AD*), and it indicates the level of aggregate output consistent

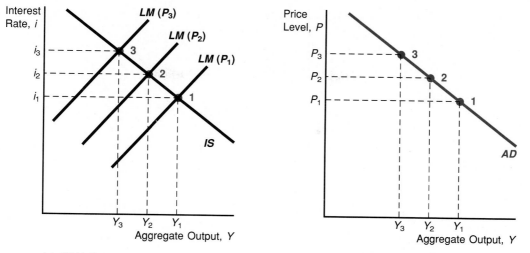

(a) *ISLM* diagram

(b) Aggregate demand curve

Figure 25.10

Deriving the Aggregate Demand Curve   The *ISLM* diagram in the panel (a) shows that as the price level rises from P_1 to P_2 to P_3, the *LM* curve shifts to the left and equilibrium output falls. The combinations of the price level and equilibrium output from panel (a) are then plotted in the panel (b), and the line connecting them is the aggregate demand curve, *AD*.

with goods and money market equilibrium at any given price level. This aggregate demand curve has the usual downward slope, since a higher price level reduces the money supply in real terms, raises interest rates, and lowers the equilibrium level of aggregate output.

What Causes the Aggregate Demand Curve to Shift?

The *ISLM* analysis demonstrates how the equilibrium level of aggregate output changes for a given price level. Thus a change in any factor that causes the *IS* or *LM* curves to shift (except a change in the price level) causes the aggregate demand curve to shift. To see how this works, let's first look at what happens to the aggregate demand curve when the *IS* curve shifts.

Factors That Cause the Aggregate Demand Curve to Shift by Shifting the IS Curve   Five factors cause the *IS* curve to shift: changes in autonomous consumer spending, changes in investment spending related to business confidence, changes in government spending, changes in taxes, and autonomous changes in net exports. How these factors lead to a shift in the aggregate demand curve is examined in Figure 25.11.

Suppose that initially the aggregate demand curve is at AD_1 and there is a rise, for example, in government spending. The *ISLM* diagram in the

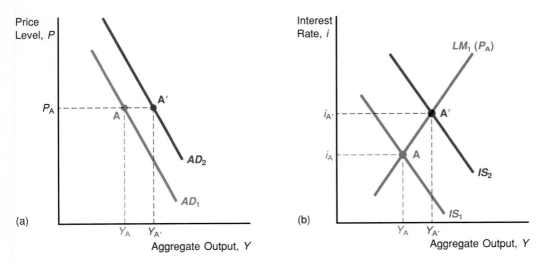

Figure 25.11
Shift in the Aggregate Demand Curve from a Shift in the *IS* Curve Expansionary fiscal policy, a rise in net exports, or more optimistic consumers and business firms shift the *IS* curve to the right in panel (b), and at a price level of P_A, equilibrium output rises from Y_A to $Y_{A'}$. This change in equilibrium output is shown as a movement from point A to point A' in panel (a); thus the aggregate demand curve shifts to the right from AD_1 to AD_2.

panel (b) shows what then happens to equilibrium output, holding the price level constant at P_A. Initially, equilibrium output is at Y_A at the intersection of IS_1 and LM_1. The rise in government spending (holding the price level constant at P_A) shifts the *IS* curve to the right and raises equilibrium output to $Y_{A'}$. In panel (a) this rise in equilibrium output is shown as a movement from point A to point A', and the aggregate demand curve shifts to the right (to AD_2).

The conclusion from Figure 25.11 is that ***any factor that shifts the IS curve also shifts the aggregate demand curve in the same direction.*** Therefore, "animal spirits" which encourage a rise in autonomous consumer spending or planned investment spending, a rise in government spending, a fall in taxes, or an autonomous rise in net exports—all of which shift the *IS* curve to the right—will also shift the aggregate demand curve to the right. On the other hand, a fall in autonomous consumer spending, a fall in planned investment spending, a fall in government spending, a rise in taxes or a fall in net exports will cause the aggregate demand curve to shift to the left.

Factors That Cause the Aggregate Demand Curve to Shift by Shifting the LM Curve Shifts in the *LM* curve are caused by either an autonomous change in money demand (not caused by a change in *P, Y,* or *i*) or a change in the money supply. Figure 25.12 shows how either of these changes leads to a shift in the aggregate demand curve. Again, we are initially at the AD_1 aggregate demand curve and we look at what happens to the level of equilibrium

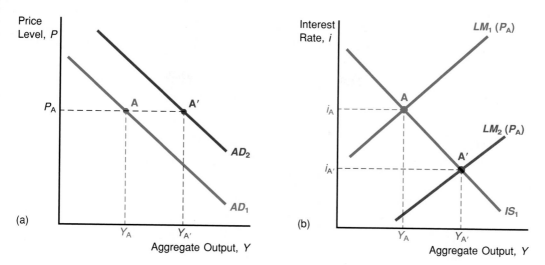

Figure 25.12

Shift in the Aggregate Demand Curve from a Shift in the *LM* Curve   A rise in the money supply or a fall in money demand shift the *LM* curve to the right in panel (b), and at a price level of P_A, equilibrium output rises from Y_A to $Y_{A'}$. This change in equilibrium output is shown as a movement from point A to point A' in panel (a); thus the aggregate demand curve shifts to the right from AD_1 to AD_2.

output when the price level is held constant at P_A. A rise in the money supply shifts the *LM* curve to the right and raises equilibrium output to $Y_{A'}$. This rise in equilibrium output is shown as a movement from point A to point A' in panel (a), and the aggregate demand curve thus shifts to the right.

Our conclusion from Figure 25.12 is similar to that of Figure 25.11: ***Any factor that shifts the LM curve also shifts the aggregate demand curve in the same direction.*** Therefore, a decline in money demand as well as an increase in the money supply, both of which shift the *LM* curve to the right, also shift the aggregate demand curve to the right. The aggregate demand curve will shift to the left, however, if money supply declines or money demand rises.

You have now derived and analyzed the aggregate demand curve—an essential element in the aggregate demand and supply framework that we will examine in Chapter 26. The aggregate demand and supply framework is particularly useful because it demonstrates how the price level is determined, and it enables us to examine factors that affect aggregate output when the price level varies.

SUMMARY

1. The *IS* curve is shifted to the right by a rise in autonomous consumer spending, a rise in planned investment spending related to business confidence, a rise in government spending, a fall in taxes, or an autonomous rise in net exports.

On the other hand, a movement in the opposite direction of these five factors will shift the *IS* curve to the left.

2. The *LM* curve is shifted to the right by a rise in the money supply or an autonomous fall in

money demand; it is shifted to the left by a fall in the money supply or an autonomous rise in money demand.

3. A rise in the money supply raises equilibrium output but lowers the equilibrium interest rate. Expansionary fiscal policy (a rise in government spending or a fall in taxes) also raises equilibrium output, but in contrast to expansionary monetary policy, raises the interest rate.

4. The less interest sensitive is money demand, the more effective is monetary policy relative to fiscal policy.

5. The *ISLM* model provides the following conclusion about the conduct of monetary policy: When the *IS* curve is more unstable than the *LM* curve, pursuing a money supply target provides smaller output fluctuations than pursuing an interest rate target and is preferred; when the

LM curve is more unstable than the *IS* curve, pursuing an interest rate target leads to smaller output fluctuations and is preferred.

6. The aggregate demand curve tells us the level of aggregate output that is consistent with goods and money market equilibrium for any given price level. It slopes downward because a lower price level creates a higher level of the real money supply, lowers the interest rate, and raises equilibrium output. The aggregate demand curve shifts in the same direction as a shift in the *IS* or *LM* curves; hence it shifts to the right when government spending increases, taxes decrease, "animal spirits" encourage consumer and business spending, autonomous net exports increase, the money supply increases, or money demand decreases.

KEY TERMS

complete crowding out
aggregate demand curve

QUESTIONS AND PROBLEMS

1. If taxes and government spending rise by equal amounts, what will happen to the position of the *IS* curve? Explain this with a Keynesian cross diagram.

* 2. What happened to the *IS* curve during the Great Depression when investment spending collapsed? Why?

3. What happens to the position of the *LM* curve if the Fed decides that it will decrease the money supply to fight inflation and if, at the same time, the demand for money falls?

* 4. Answer true, false, or uncertain: "An excess demand for money resulting from a rise in the demand for money can be eliminated only by a rise in the interest rate."

In the remaining problems, demonstrate your answers with an ISLM diagram.

5. In late 1969 the Fed reduced the money supply while the government raised taxes. What do you

think should have happened to interest rates and aggregate output?

* 6. "The high level of interest rates and the rapidly growing economy during the second two years of Ronald Reagan's first term as president can be explained by a tight monetary policy that was combined with an expansionary fiscal policy." Do you agree? Why or why not?

7. Suppose the Federal Reserve wants to keep interest rates from rising when the government sharply increases military spending. How can the Fed do this?

* 8. Evidence (Chapter 23) indicates that lately the demand for money has become quite unstable. Why is this finding important to Federal Reserve policymakers?

9. Answer true, false, or uncertain: "As the price level rises, the equilibrium level of output determined in the *ISLM* model also rises."

*10. What will happen to the position of the aggregate demand curve if the money supply is reduced when government spending increases?

11. An equal rise in government spending and taxes will have what effect on the position of the aggregate demand curve?

*12. If money demand is unaffected by changes in the interest rate, what effect will a rise in government spending have on the position of the aggregate demand curve?

Using Economic Analysis to Predict the Future

13. Predict what will happen to interest rates and output if a stock market crash occurs which causes autonomous consumer expenditure to fall.

*14. Predict what will happen to interest rates and aggregate output when there is an autonomous export boom.

15. If a series of defaults in the bond market make bonds riskier and as a result the demand for money rises, predict what will happen to interest rates and aggregate output.

CHAPTER 26

Aggregate Demand and Supply Analysis

PREVIEW In previous chapters we focused considerable attention on the money supply and monetary policy because they touch our everyday lives by affecting the prices of the goods we buy and the quantity of available jobs. In this chapter we develop a basic tool—aggregate demand and supply analysis—that will enable us to study the effects of money on output and prices. **Aggregate demand** is the total quantity demanded at different price levels of final goods and services produced in the economy. **Aggregate supply** is the total quantity of final goods and services that firms in the economy want to sell at different price levels. As with other supply and demand analyses, the actual quantity of output and the price level are determined by equating aggregate demand and aggregate supply.

Aggregate demand and supply analysis will enable us to explore how aggregate output and the price level are determined. Not only will it help us to interpret recent episodes in the business cycle, but it will enable us to understand the debates on how economic policy should be conducted.

AGGREGATE DEMAND

The first building block of aggregate supply and demand analysis is the **aggregate demand curve,** which describes the relationship between the quantity of aggregate output demanded and the price level, when all other variables are held constant. **Monetarists** (led by Milton Friedman) view the aggregate demand curve as downward sloping with one primary factor that causes it to shift—changes in the quantity of money. **Keynesians** (the followers of Keynes) also view the aggregate demand curve as downward sloping, but they believe that changes in government spending and taxes or in consumer and business willingness to spend can cause it to shift *as well as* changes in the money supply.

Monetarist View of Aggregate Demand

The monetarist view of aggregate demand links the quantity of money, M, with total nominal spending on goods and services, $P \times Y$ (P = the price level and Y = aggregate real output, or equivalently, aggregate real income). To do this it uses a concept called **velocity:** the average number of times per year that a dollar is spent on final goods and services. More formally, velocity (V) is calculated by dividing nominal spending ($P \times Y$) by the money supply (M); that is,

$$V = \frac{P \times Y}{M}$$

Suppose the total nominal spending in a year was $2000 billion and the money supply was $1000 billion; velocity would then be 2(= $2000b/ $1000b). On average, the money supply supports a level of transactions asso-

Following the Financial News

Aggregate Output, Unemployment, and the Price Level

Newspapers periodically report data that provide information on the level of aggregate output, unemployment, and the price level. The relevant data series, their frequency, and when they are published follow:

Aggregate Output and Unemployment

Real GNP:
  Quarterly, that is, Jan.–March, April–June, July–Sept., Oct.–Dec.; published about three weeks after the end of a quarter; a "flash" estimate is reported about a month earlier, just before the end of the quarter, but this estimate is much less accurate.

Industrial production:
  Monthly; industrial production is not as comprehensive a measure of aggregate output as real GNP because it only measures manufacturing output; the estimate for the previous month is reported in the middle of the following month.

Unemployment rate:
  Monthly; previous month's figure is usually published on Friday of the second week of the following month.

Price Level

GNP deflator:
  Quarterly; this comprehensive measure of the price level (described in the Appendix to Chapter 1) is published at the same time as the real GNP data.
CPI:
  Monthly; the consumer price index (CPI) is a measure of the price level facing consumers (also described in the Appendix to Chapter 1); the value for the previous month is published in the fourth week of the following month.
PPI:
  Monthly; the producers price index (PPI) is a measure of the average level of prices (wholesale) charged by producers, and is published at the same time as industrial production data.

ciated with 2 times its value in final goods and services in the course of a year. By multiplying both sides by M, we obtain the **equation of exchange,** which relates the money supply to aggregate spending:

$$M \times V = P \times Y \tag{26.1}$$

At this point our equation of exchange is nothing more than an identity; that is, it is true by definition. It does not tell us that when M rises, aggregate spending will rise as well. For example, the rise in M could be offset by a fall in V, with the result that $M \times V$ does not rise. However, Milton Friedman's analysis of the demand for money (discussed in detail in Chapter 23) suggests that velocity varies over time in a predictable manner unrelated to changes in the money supply. With this analysis, the equation of exchange is transformed into a theory of how aggregate spending is determined and is called the **modern quantity theory of money.**

To see how the theory works, let's look at an example. If velocity is predicted to be 2 and the money supply is $1000 billion, the equation of exchange tells us that aggregate spending will be $2000 billion (2 × $1000b). If the money supply doubles to $2000 billion, then Friedman's analysis suggests that velocity will continue to be 2 and aggregate spending will double to $4000 billion (2 × $2000b). Thus Friedman's modern quantity theory of money concludes that *changes in aggregate spending are primarily determined by changes in the money supply.*

Deriving the Aggregate Demand Curve   To learn how the modern quantity theory of money generates the aggregate demand curve, let's look at an example in which we measure aggregate output in billions of 1982 dollars, with the price level in 1982 having a value of 1.0. As shown, with a predicted velocity of 2 and a money supply of $1000 billion, aggregate spending will be $2000 billion. If the price level is given at 2.0, then the quantity of aggregate output demanded is $1000 billion (1982 dollars), because aggregate spending, $P \times Y$, then continues to equal 2.0 × 1000 = $2000 billion, the value of $M \times V$. This combination of a price level of 2.0 and aggregate output of 1000 is marked as point A in Figure 26.1. If the price level is given at 1.0 instead, then aggregate output demanded is 2000 (point B), so aggregate spending continues to equal $2000 billion = 1.0 × 2000. Similarly, at an even lower price level of 0.5, the quantity of output demanded rises to 4000, shown by point C. The curve connecting these points is the aggregate demand curve, given a money supply of $1000 billion, marked as AD_1, and as you can see, it has the usual downward slope of a demand curve, indicating that as the price level falls (everything else held constant), the quantity of output demanded rises.

Shifts in the Aggregate Demand Curve   In Friedman's modern quantity theory, changes in the money supply are the primary source of the changes in

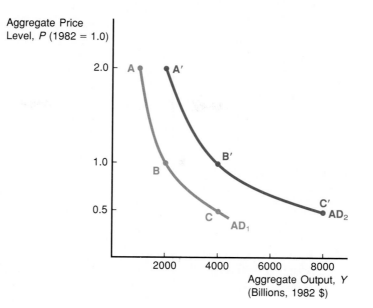

Figure 26.1
Aggregate Demand Curve The rise in the money supply from $1000 billion to $2000 billion leads to a shift in the aggregate demand curve from AD_1 to AD_2.

aggregate spending and shifts in the aggregate demand curve. To see how a change in the money supply shifts the aggregate demand curve, let's look at what happens when the money supply increases to $2000 billion. Now aggregate spending rises to $2 \times \$2000$ billion = $4000 billion, and at a price level of 2.0, the quantity of aggregate output demanded will rise to 2000 ($2.0 \times 2000 = \$4000$ billion). Therefore, at a price level of 2.0, the aggregate demand curve moves from point A to A'. At a price level of 1.0, the quantity of output demanded rises from 2000 to 4000 (from point B to B'), and at a price level of 0.5, output demanded rises from 4000 to 8000 (from point C to C'). The result is that the rise in the money supply to $2000 billion shifts the aggregate demand curve out to AD_2 in Figure 26.1.

Similar reasoning indicates that a decline in the money supply lowers aggregate spending proportionally and reduces the quantity of aggregate output demanded at each price level. Thus a decline in the money supply shifts the aggregate demand curve to the left.

Keynesian View of Aggregate Demand

Rather than determining aggregate demand from the equation of exchange, the Keynesian analysis analyzes aggregate demand in terms of its four component parts: **consumer expenditure,** the total demand for consumer goods and services; **planned investment spending,** the total planned spending by business firms on new machines, factories, and other inputs to production, plus the planned spending on new residential houses[1]; **government spending,** spending by all levels of government (federal, state, and local) on goods and services (paper clips, computers, computer programming, missiles, government workers, etc.); and **net exports,** the net foreign spending on domestic goods and services, equal to exports minus imports. Using the symbols C for consumer expenditure, I for planned investment spending, G for government spending, and NX for net exports, we can write the following expression for aggregate demand (Y^{ad}):

$$Y^{ad} = C + I + G + NX \tag{26.2}$$

Aggregate Demand Curve Keynesian analysis, like monetarist analysis, suggests that the aggregate demand curve is downward sloping because a lower price level ($P \downarrow$), holding the nominal quantity of money constant, leads to a larger quantity of money *in real terms* (that is, in terms of the goods and services that it can buy). The larger quantity of money in real terms ($M/P \uparrow$), which results from the *lower* price level, causes interest rates to fall ($i \downarrow$), as suggested in Chapter 6. The resulting lower cost of financing purchases of new physical capital makes investment more profitable and stimulates planned investment spending ($I \uparrow$). Since [as shown in Equation (26.2)] the increase in planned investment spending adds directly to aggregate demand ($Y^{ad} \uparrow$), the lower price level leads to a higher level of aggregate demand (that is, $P \downarrow \rightarrow Y^{ad} \uparrow$). Schematically, we can write the mechanism just described as follows. When $P \downarrow$,

$$\frac{M}{P} \uparrow \rightarrow i \downarrow \rightarrow I \uparrow \rightarrow Y^{ad} \uparrow$$

Another mechanism generating a downward-sloping aggregate demand curve operates through international trade. Since a lower price level ($P \downarrow$) leads to a larger quantity of money in real terms ($M/P \uparrow$) and lower interest rates ($i \downarrow$), U.S. dollar bank deposits become less attractive relative to deposits denominated in foreign currencies, thereby causing a fall in the value of dollar deposits relative to other currency deposits (a decline in the exchange rate, denoted by $E \downarrow$). The lower value of the dollar, which makes domestic goods cheaper relative to foreign goods, then causes net exports to rise, which, in turn, increases aggregate demand; that is,

$$M/P \uparrow \rightarrow i \downarrow \rightarrow E \downarrow \rightarrow NX \uparrow \rightarrow Y^{ad} \uparrow$$

The mechanisms described also indicate why Keynesian analysis suggests that changes in the money supply shift the aggregate demand curve.

---

[1]Recall that use of the word *investment* here is somewhat different from everyday usage. Economists restrict use of the word *investment* to a purchase of *new* physical capital such as a *new* machine or a *new* house that adds to expenditure. In contrast, in everyday speech *investment* can also refer to purchases of financial assets or used physical capital.

For a given price level, a rise in the money supply causes the real money supply to increase ($M/P \uparrow$), which leads to an increase in aggregate demand, as shown above. Thus an increase in the money supply shifts the aggregate demand curve to the right (as in Figure 26.1) because it lowers interest rates and stimulates planned investment spending and net exports. Similarly, a decline in the money supply shifts the aggregate demand curve to the left.[2]

In contrast to monetarists, Keynesians believe that other factors (manipulation of government spending and taxes, changes in net exports, and shifts in consumers' and businesses' spending) are also an important source of shifts in the aggregate demand curve. For instance, if the government spends more ($G \uparrow$) or net exports increase ($NX \uparrow$), aggregate demand rises and the aggregate demand curve shifts to the right. A decrease in government taxes ($T \downarrow$) leaves consumers with more income to spend, so consumer expenditure rises ($C \uparrow$). Aggregate demand also rises and the aggregate demand curve shifts to the right. Finally, if consumer and business optimism increases, consumer expenditure and planned investment spending rise ($C \uparrow$ and $I \uparrow$), again shifting the aggregate demand curve to the right. Keynes described these waves of optimism and pessimism as **"animal spirits"** and considered them a major factor affecting the aggregate demand curve and an important source of business cycle fluctuations.

The Crowding Out Debate

You have seen that both monetarists and Keynesians agree that the aggregate demand curve is downward sloping and shifts in response to changes in the money supply. However, monetarists see only one important source of movements in the aggregate demand curve—changes in the money supply—while Keynesians suggest that other factors—fiscal policy, net exports, and "animal spirits"—are equally important sources of shifts in the aggregate demand curve.

Since aggregate demand can be written as the sum of $C + I + G + NX$, it might appear as though any factor that affects one of its components must cause aggregate demand to change. Then it would seem as though a fiscal policy change such as a rise in government spending (holding the money supply constant) would necessarily shift the aggregate demand curve. Since the monetarist framework views changes in the money supply as the only important source of shifts in the aggregate demand curve, they must have an explanation as to why the above reasoning is invalid.

Monetarists agree that an increase in government spending will raise aggregate demand if the other components of aggregate demand, C, I, and NX, remained unchanged after the government spending rise. They con-

---

[2]A complete demonstration of the Keynesian analysis of the aggregate demand curve is found in Chapters 24 and 25.

tend, however, that the increase in government spending will "crowd out" private spending (C, I, and NX), which will fall by exactly the amount of the government spending increase. This phenomenon of an exactly offsetting movement of private spending to an expansionary fiscal policy, such as a rise in government spending, is called **complete crowding out.**

How might complete crowding out occur? When government spending increases ($G \uparrow$), the government has to finance this spending by competing with private borrowers for funds in the credit market. Interest rates will rise ($i \uparrow$), increasing the cost of financing purchases of both physical capital and consumer goods and lowering net exports. The result is that private spending will fall ($C \downarrow$, $I \downarrow$, and $NX \downarrow$) and so aggregate demand may remain unchanged. This chain of reasoning can be summarized as follows:

$$G \uparrow \rightarrow i \uparrow \rightarrow C \downarrow, I \downarrow, \text{ and } NX \downarrow$$

therefore,

$$C + I + G + NX = Y^{ad} \text{ is unchanged}$$

Keynesians do not deny the validity of the first set of steps. They agree that an increase in government spending raises interest rates, which in turn lowers private spending; indeed, this is a feature of the Keynesian analysis of aggregate demand (Chapters 24 and 25). However, they contend that only **partial crowding out** occurs, in which there is some decline in private spending that does not completely offset the rise in government spending.

The Keynesian crowding out picture suggests that when government spending rises, aggregate demand does increase and the aggregate demand curve shifts to the right. The *extent* to which crowding out occurs is the issue that separates monetarist and Keynesian views of the aggregate demand curve. We will discuss the evidence on this issue in Chapter 27.

AGGREGATE SUPPLY

The key feature of aggregate supply is that, as the price level increases, the quantity of output supplied increases *in the short run*. Figure 26.2 illustrates the positive relationship between quantity of output supplied and price level. Suppose initially that the quantity of output supplied at a price level of 1.0 is 4000, represented by point A. A rise in the price level to 2.0 leads, in the short run, to an increase in the quantity of output supplied to 6000 (point B). The line connecting points A and B (AS_1) describes the relationship between the quantity of output supplied in the short run and the price level and is called the **aggregate supply curve;** as you can see, it is upward sloping.

To understand why the aggregate supply curve is upward sloping, we have to look at the factors that cause the quantity of output supplied to change. Because the goal of business is to make profits, the quantity of out-

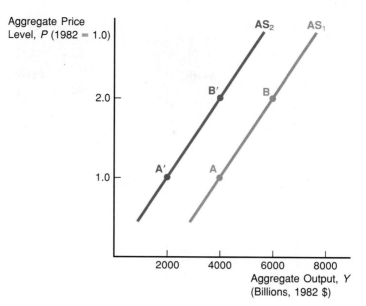

Figure 26.2
Aggregate Supply Curve in the Short Run A rise in the costs of production shifts the supply curve inward from AS_1 to AS_2.

put supplied is determined by the profit made on each unit of output. If profit rises, more output will be produced and the quantity of output supplied will increase; if it falls, less output will be produced and quantity of output supplied will fall.

Profit on a unit of output equals the price for the unit minus the costs of producing it. In the short run, costs of many factors that go into producing goods and services are fixed; wages, for example, are often fixed for periods of time by labor contracts (sometimes as long as three years), and raw materials are often bought by firms under long-term contracts that fix the price. Because these costs of production are fixed in the short run, when the overall price level rises, the price for a unit of output will be rising relative to the costs of producing it and the profit per unit will rise. Because the higher price level results in higher profits in the short run, firms increase production and the quantity of aggregate output supplied rises, resulting in an upward-sloping aggregate supply curve.

Frequent use of the phrase *short run* in the preceding paragraph hints that the aggregate supply curve (AS_1 in Figure 26.2) may not remain fixed as time passes. To see what happens over time, you need to understand what makes the aggregate supply curve shift.

Shifts in the Aggregate Supply Curve

You have seen that the profit on a unit of output determines the quantity of output supplied. If the cost of producing a unit of output rises, profit on a unit of output falls and the quantity of output supplied falls. To learn what this implies for the position of the aggregate supply curve, let's consider what happens at a price level of 1.0 when the costs of production increase. Now that firms are earning a lower profit per unit of output, they reduce production and the quantity of aggregate output supplied falls from 4000 (point A) to 2000 (point A′). Applying the same reasoning at point B indicates that aggregate output supplied falls to point B′. What we see is that *the aggregate supply curve shifts inward when costs of production increase. Similarly, the aggregate supply curve shifts out when costs decrease.*

EQUILIBRIUM IN AGGREGATE SUPPLY AND DEMAND ANALYSIS

The equilibrium level of aggregate output and the price level will occur at the point where the quantity of aggregate output demanded equals the quantity of aggregate output supplied. However, in the context of aggregate supply and demand analysis, there are two types of equilibria—equilibrium in the short and in the long run.

Equilibrium in the Short Run

Figure 26.3 illustrates an equilibrium in the short run in which the quantity of aggregate output demanded equals the quantity of output supplied, that is, where the aggregate demand curve (*AD*) and the aggregate supply curve (*AS*) intersect at point E. The equilibrium level of aggregate output equals *Y** and the equilibrium price level equals *P**.

Figure 26.3
Equilibrium in the Short Run Equilibrium occurs at point E at the intersection of the aggregate demand curve *AD* and the aggregate supply curve *AS*.

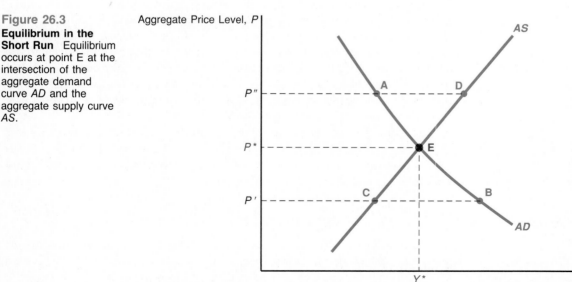

As in our earlier supply and demand analyses, equilibrium is a useful concept only if there is a tendency for the economy to head toward it. You can see that the economy heads into the equilibrium at point E by first looking at what happens when we are at a price level above the equilibrium price level P^*. If the price level is at P'', the quantity of aggregate output supplied at point D is greater than the quantity of aggregate output demanded at point A. Since people want to sell more goods and services than others want to buy (a condition of *excess supply*), the prices of goods and services will fall and the aggregate price level will fall. This decline in the price level will continue until it has reached its equilibrium level of P^* at point E.

When the price level is below the equilibrium price level, say, at P', then the quantity of output demanded is greater than the quantity of output supplied. Now the price level will rise, because people want to buy more goods than others want to sell (a condition of *excess demand*). This rise in the price level will continue until it has again reached its equilibrium level of P^* at point E.

Equilibrium in the Long Run

Usually in supply and demand analysis once we find the equilibrium in which the quantity demand equals the quantity supplied, no additional need for discussion exists. In *aggregate* supply and demand analysis, however, this is not the case. Even when the quantity of aggregate output demanded equals the quantity supplied, forces operate that can cause the equilibrium to move over time. To understand why, we must remember that if costs of production change, the aggregate supply curve will shift.

The most important component of production costs is wage cost (approximately 70% of production costs), which is determined in the labor market. If the economy is booming, employers will find that they have difficulty hiring qualified workers and may even have a hard time keeping their present employees. In this case, the labor market is tight because the demand for labor exceeds the supply, and employers will raise wages to attract needed workers which raises the cost of production. The higher costs of production now lower the profits per unit of output at each price level so that the aggregate supply curve shifts in to the left (see Figure 26.2).

On the other hand, if the economy enters a recession and the labor market is slack because demand for labor is less than supply, workers who cannot find jobs will be willing to work for lower wages. In addition, workers with jobs may be willing to make wage concessions to keep from losing them (as airline and steel workers did in the 1980s).[3] Therefore, in a slack labor market in which the demand for labor is less than the supply, wages and

---

[3] Airline and steel workers may have lost jobs because of other market forces besides overall high unemployment in the economy, specifically, airline deregulation and a change in the competitiveness of the American auto industry compared to the rest of the world.

hence costs of production will fall, profits per unit of output will rise, and the aggregate supply curve will shift out to the right.

Our analysis suggests that the aggregate supply curve will shift depending on whether the labor market is tight or slack. How do we decide which it is? One helpful concept is the **natural rate of unemployment,** the rate of unemployment when demand for labor equals supply (many economists believe the rate is currently around 6%). When unemployment at, say, 4% is below the natural rate of unemployment of 6%, then the labor market is tight; wages will rise and the aggregate supply curve will shift in. When unemployment at, say, 8% is above the natural rate of unemployment, then the labor market is slack; wages will fall and the aggregate supply curve will shift out. Only when unemployment is at the natural rate will no pressure exist from the labor market for wages to rise or fall, so the aggregate supply need not shift.

The level of aggregate output produced at the natural rate of unemployment is called the **natural rate level of output.** Because, as we have seen, the aggregate supply curve will not remain stationary when unemployment and aggregate output differ from their natural rate levels, we need to look at how the short-run equilibrium changes over time in response to two situations: when equilibrium is initially below the natural rate level and when it is initially above the natural rate level.

In panel (a) of Figure 26.4, the initial equilibrium occurs at point 1, the intersection of the aggregate demand curve (AD) and the initial aggregate supply curve (AS_1). Since the level of equilibrium output, Y_1, is greater than the natural rate level, marked as Y_n, unemployment is less than the natural rate and excessive tightness exists in the labor market. This tightness drives wages up, raises production costs, and shifts the aggregate supply curve in to AS_2. The equilibrium is now at point 2 and output falls to Y_2. Since aggregate output is still above the natural rate level ($Y_2 > Y_n$), wages continue to be driven up, eventually shifting the aggregate supply curve to AS_3. The equilibrium reached at point 3 is on the vertical line at Y_n and is a long-run equilibrium. Since output is at the natural rate level, there is no further pressure on wages to rise and thus no further tendency for the aggregate supply curve to shift.

The movements in panel (a) indicate that the economy will not remain at a level of output higher than the natural rate level because the aggregate supply curve will shift in, raise the price level, and cause the economy to slide up along the aggregate demand curve until it comes to rest at a point on the vertical line through the natural rate level of output, Y_n. Since the vertical line through Y_n is the only place at which the aggregate supply curve comes to rest, this vertical line indicates the quantity of output supplied in the long run for any given price level. We can characterize this as the **long-run aggregate supply curve.**

In panel (b), the initial equilibrium at point 1 is one at which output (Y_1) is below the natural rate level. Since unemployment is higher than the natu-

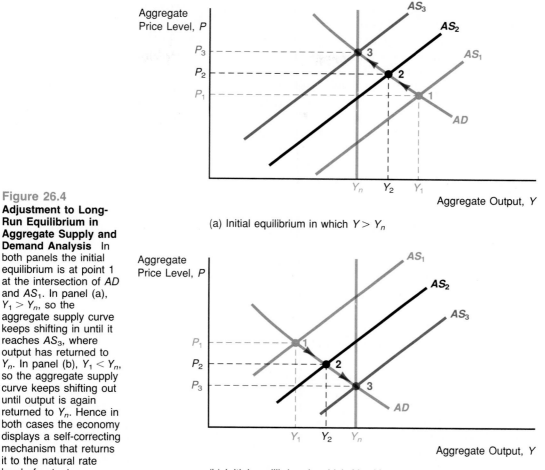

(a) Initial equilibrium in which $Y > Y_n$

(b) Initial equilibrium in which $Y < Y_n$

Figure 26.4
Adjustment to Long-Run Equilibrium in Aggregate Supply and Demand Analysis In both panels the initial equilibrium is at point 1 at the intersection of AD and AS_1. In panel (a), $Y_1 > Y_n$, so the aggregate supply curve keeps shifting in until it reaches AS_3, where output has returned to Y_n. In panel (b), $Y_1 < Y_n$, so the aggregate supply curve keeps shifting out until output is again returned to Y_n. Hence in both cases the economy displays a self-correcting mechanism that returns it to the natural rate level of output.

ral rate, wages will begin to fall, shifting the aggregate supply curve outward until it comes to rest at AS_3. The economy slides down along the aggregate demand curve until it reaches the long-run equilibrium point 3, the intersection of the aggregate demand curve (AD) and the long-run aggregate supply curve at Y_n. Here, as in panel (a), the economy comes to rest when output has again returned to the natural rate level.

A striking feature of both panels of Figure 26.4 is that regardless of where output is initially, it returns eventually to the natural rate level. This feature is described by saying that the economy has a **self-correcting mechanism.**

An important issue for policymakers is how rapidly this self-correcting mechanism works. Many economists, particularly Keynesians, believe that the self-correcting mechanism takes a long time, so that the approach to long-run equilibrium is slow. This view is reflected in John Maynard Keynes' often quoted remark, "In the long run, we are all dead." These economists view the self-correcting mechanism as slow because wages are inflexible, particularly in the downward direction when unemployment is high. The resulting slow wage and price adjustment means that the aggregate supply curve does not move quickly to restore the economy to the natural rate of unemployment. Hence, when unemployment is high, these economists (called **activists**) are more likely to see the need for active government policy to restore the economy to full employment.

On the other hand, other economists, particularly monetarists, believe that wages are sufficiently flexible, so that the wage and price adjustment process is reasonably rapid. As a result of this flexibility, adjustment of the aggregate supply curve to its long-run position and the economy's return to the natural rate level of output and unemployment will occur quickly. Thus these economists (called **nonactivists**) see much less of a need for active government policy to restore the economy to the natural rate level of output and unemployment when unemployment is high. Indeed, monetarists advocate the use of a "rule" in which the money supply or the monetary base grows at a constant rate in order to minimize fluctuations in aggregate demand which might lead to output fluctuations. We will return to the debate about whether active government policy to keep the economy near full employment is beneficial in Chapter 28.

Shifts in Aggregate Demand

You are now ready to analyze what happens when the aggregate demand curve shifts. Our discussion of the Keynesian and monetarist views of aggregate demand indicates that six factors can affect the aggregate demand curve: (1) the money supply, (2) government spending, (3) net exports, (4) taxes, (5) consumer optimism, and (6) business optimism—the last two affecting willingness to spend ("animal spirits"). The possible effect on the aggregate demand curve of these six factors is summarized in Table 26.1.

Figure 26.5 depicts the effect of an outward shift in the aggregate demand curve caused by any of the following events: an increase in the money supply ($M \uparrow$), an increase in government spending ($G \uparrow$), an increase in net exports ($NX \uparrow$), a decrease in taxes ($T \downarrow$), or an increase in willingness of consumers and businesses to spend because they become more optimistic ($C \uparrow$, $I \uparrow$). The figure has been drawn so that initially the economy is in long-run equilibrium at point 1, where the initial aggregate demand curve (AD_1) intersects the aggregate supply curve at Y_n. When the aggregate demand curve shifts out to AD_2, the economy moves to point $1'$, where both output and the price level rise. However, the economy will not remain at point $1'$ because output at $Y_{1'}$ is above the natural rate level. Wages will rise, eventually shifting the aggregate supply curve in to AS_2, where it finally comes to rest. The economy thus slides up the aggregate demand curve from

Table 26.1   Summary: Factors That Shift the Aggregate Demand Curve

Factor		Shift in the Aggregate Demand Curve
Money supply	↑	→
Government spending	↑	→
Taxes	↑	←
Net exports	↑	→
Consumer optimism	↑	→
Business optimism	↑	→

Note: Only increases (↑) in the factors are shown. The effect of decreases in the factors would be the opposite of those indicated in the second column. Note that monetarists do not view the other factors besides the money supply to be an important source of shifts in the aggregate demand curve.

point 1' to point 2, which is the point of long-run equilibrium at the intersection of AD_2 and Y_n. ***While the initial effect of the rightward shift in the aggregate demand curve is a rise in both the price level and output, the ultimate effect is only a rise in the price level.***

Shifts in Aggregate Supply

Not only can shifts in aggregate demand be a source of fluctuations in aggregate output (the business cycle), but shifts in aggregate supply can be as well.

Figure 26.5
Response of Output and the Price Level to a Shift in the Aggregate Demand Curve A shift in the aggregate demand curve from AD_1 to AD_2 moves the economy from point 1 to point 1'. Since $Y_{1'} > Y_n$ the aggregate supply curve begins to shift in eventually reaching AS_2, where output returns to Y_n and the price level has risen to P_2.

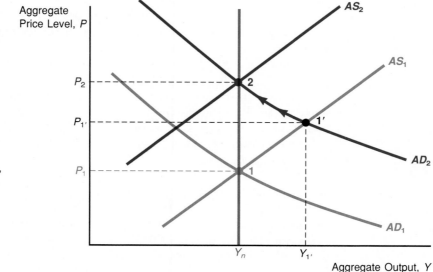

Factors that cause the aggregate supply curve to shift are factors that affect costs of production. They are (1) the tightness of the labor market, (2) expectations of inflation, (3) workers' attempts to push up their real wages, and (4) changes in the production costs that are unrelated to wages (such as energy costs). The first three factors shift the aggregate supply curve by affecting wage costs (approximately 70% of production costs) while the fourth affects other costs of production.

Tightness of the Labor Market   Our analysis of the approach to long-run equilibrium has shown us that when the labor market is tight ($Y > Y_n$), wages and hence production costs rise, while when the labor market is slack ($Y < Y_n$), wages and production costs fall. The effects on the aggregate supply curve are as follows: *When aggregate output is above the natural rate level ($Y > Y_n$), the aggregate supply curve shifts in; when aggregate output is below the natural rate level ($Y < Y_n$), aggregate supply curve shifts out.*

Expected Price Level   Workers and firms care about wages in real terms, that is, in terms of the goods and services that wages can buy. When the price level increases, a worker earning the same nominal wage will be able to buy fewer goods and services. A worker who expects the price level to rise will thus demand a higher nominal wage in order to keep his real wage from falling. If, for example, Chuck the Construction Worker expects prices to increase by 5%, he will want a wage increase of at least 5% (possibly more if he thinks he deserves an increase in real wages). Similarly, if Chuck's employer knows that the houses he is building will rise in value at the same rate as inflation (5%), his employer will be willing to pay Chuck 5% more. An increase in the expected price level leads to higher wages, which, in turn, raise the costs of production, lower the profits per unit of output at each price level, and shift the aggregate supply curve in (see Figure 26.2). Therefore, *a rise in the expected price level causes the aggregate supply curve to shift in; the greater the expected increase in price level (that is, the higher is expected inflation), the larger is the inward shift.*

Wage Push   Suppose Chuck and his fellow construction workers decide to strike and succeed in obtaining higher real wages. This "wage push" will then raise the costs of production and the aggregate supply curve will shift in. *A successful wage push by workers will also cause the aggregate supply curve to shift inward.*

Changes in Production Costs Unrelated to Wages   Changes in technology and the supply of raw material (called **supply shocks**) also can shift the aggregate supply curve. A negative supply shock, such as a reduction in the availability of raw materials (like oil), which raises their price, raises production costs and shifts the aggregate supply curve in. A positive supply shock such as unusually good weather, which leads to a bountiful harvest and low-

Table 26.2 **Summary: Factors That Shift the Aggregate Supply Curve**

Factor	Shift in the Aggregate Supply Curve
$Y > Y_n$	←
$Y < Y_n$	→
Expected price level ↑	←
Wage push	←
Positive supply shock	→
Negative supply shock	←

ers the cost of food, will reduce production costs and shift the aggregate supply curve out. Similarly, the development of a new technology that lowers production costs, perhaps by raising worker productivity, can also be considered a positive supply shock that shifts the aggregate supply curve outward.

The effect on the aggregate supply curve of changes in production costs unrelated to wages can be summarized as follows:[4] *A negative supply shock that raises production costs shifts the aggregate supply curve in, while a positive supply shock that lowers production costs shifts the aggregate supply curve out.*

As a study aid, factors that shift the aggregate supply curve are listed in Table 26.2.

Now that you know what factors can affect the aggregate supply curve, we can examine what occurs when they cause the aggregate supply curve to shift in, as in Figure 26.6. Suppose that the economy is initially at the natural rate level of output at point 1, when the aggregate supply curve shifts from AS_1 to AS_2 because of a negative supply shock (e.g., a sharp rise in energy prices). The economy will move from point 1 to point 2, where the price level rises but aggregate output *falls.* A situation of a rising price level but a falling level of aggregate output, as pictured in Figure 26.6, has been labeled "stagflation" (a combination of the words stagnation and inflation). Now at point 2 output is below the natural rate level, so wages fall and shift the aggregate supply curve back out to where it was initially at AS_1. The result is

---

[4]Developments in the foreign exchange market can also shift the aggregate supply curve by changing domestic production costs. As Chapter 21 discussed in more detail, when the dollar increases in value, it makes foreign goods cheaper in the United States. The decline in prices of foreign goods and hence foreign factors of production lowers U.S. production costs and thus raises the profit per unit of output at each price level in the United States. An increase in the value of the dollar, therefore, shifts the aggregate supply curve out. Conversely, a decline in the value of the dollar, which makes foreign factors of production more expensive, shifts the aggregate supply curve in.

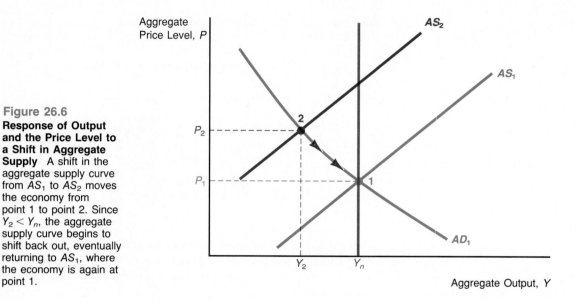

Figure 26.6
Response of Output and the Price Level to a Shift in Aggregate Supply A shift in the aggregate supply curve from AS_1 to AS_2 moves the economy from point 1 to point 2. Since $Y_2 < Y_n$, the aggregate supply curve begins to shift back out, eventually returning to AS_1, where the economy is again at point 1.

that the economy slides down the AD_1 aggregate demand curve (assuming the aggregate demand curve remains in the same position) and the economy returns to the long-run equilibrium at point 1. *While an inward shift in the aggregate supply curve initially raises the price level and lowers output, the ultimate effect is that output and price level are unchanged (holding the aggregate demand curve constant).*

Shifts in the Long-Run Aggregate Supply Curve: Real Business Cycle Theory and Hysteresis

Up to this point we have assumed that the natural rate level of output (Y_n) and hence the long-run aggregate supply curve (the vertical line through Y_n) are given. However, over time the natural rate level of output clearly increases as a result of economic growth. If the productive capacity of the economy is growing at a steady rate of 3% per year, for example, this means that every year Y_n will grow by 3% and the long-run aggregate supply curve at Y_n will shift to the right by 3%. To simplify the analysis when Y_n grows at a steady rate, Y_n and the long-run aggregate supply curve are drawn as fixed in the aggregate demand and supply diagrams. Keep in mind, however, that the level of aggregate output pictured in the aggregate demand and supply diagrams is actually best thought of as the level of aggregate output relative to its normal (trend) rate of growth.

The usual assumption when conducting aggregate demand and supply analysis is that shifts in either the aggregate demand or aggregate supply curves have no effect on the natural rate level of output (which grows at a steady rate). Movements of aggregate output around the Y_n level in the diagram then describe short-run (business cycle) fluctuations in aggregate output. However, some economists take issue with the assumption that Y_n is unaffected by aggregate demand and supply shocks.

One group, led by Edward Prescott of the University of Minnesota, has developed a theory of aggregate economic fluctuations called **real business cycle theory** in which aggregate supply (real) shocks do affect the natural rate level of output, Y_n. This theory views shocks to tastes (workers' willingness to work, for example) and technology (productivity) as the major driving forces behind short-run fluctuations in the business cycle, because these shocks lead to substantial short-run fluctuations in Y_n. Shifts in the aggregate demand curve, say as a result of changes in monetary policy, on the other hand, are not viewed as being particularly important to aggregate output fluctuations. Because real business cycle theory views most business cycle fluctuations as resulting from fluctuations in the natural rate level of output, it does not see much of a need for activist policy to eliminate high unemployment. Real business cycle theory is highly controversial and is currently the subject of intensive research.[5]

Another group of economists disagrees with the assumption that the natural rate level of output, Y_n, is unaffected by aggregate demand shocks. These economists contend that the natural rate level of unemployment and output are subject to **hysteresis,** a departure from full employment levels as a result of past high unemployment.[6] When unemployment rises because of a reduction of aggregate demand that shifts the AD curve inward, the natural rate of unemployment is viewed as rising above the full employment level. This could occur because the unemployed become discouraged and so look less hard for work or because employers may be reluctant to hire workers who have been unemployed for a long time, thinking that it is a signal that the worker is undesirable. The outcome is that the natural rate of unemployment shifts upward after unemployment has become high and so Y_n falls below the full employment level. In this situation, the self-correcting mechanism will only be able to return the economy to the natural rate level of output and unemployment—not to the full employment levels. Only with expansionary policy to shift the aggregate demand curve to the right and raise aggregate output can the natural rate of unemployment be lowered (Y_n raised) to the full employment level. Proponents of hysteresis are thus more likely to promote activist, expansionary policies to restore the economy to full employment.

---

[5]See Charles Plosser, "Understanding Real Business Cycles," *Journal of Economic Perspectives* 3 (Summer 1989), pp. 51–77, for a detailed review of the literature on real business cycle theory.

[6]For a further discussion of hysteresis, see Olivier Blanchard and Lawrence Summers, "Hysteresis in the Unemployment Rate," *NBER Macroeconomics Annual*, 1986.

Study Guide

Aggregate supply and demand analysis is best learned by practicing applications. In this section we have traced out what happens to aggregate output when there is an increase in the money supply or a negative supply shock. Make sure that you can also draw the appropriate shifts in the aggregate demand and supply curves, and analyze what happens when other variables such as taxes or the expected price level change.

Summary   Aggregate demand and supply analysis yields the following conclusions (under the usual assumption that the natural rate level of output is unaffected by aggregate demand and supply shocks):

1. A shift in the aggregate demand curve—which can be caused by changes in monetary policy (the money supply), fiscal policy (government spending or taxes), international trade (net exports), or in "animal spirits" (business and consumer optimism)—affects output only in the short run and has no effect in the long run. Furthermore, the initial change in the price level is less than is achieved in the long run, when the aggregate supply curve has fully adjusted.

2. A shift in the aggregate supply curve—which can be caused by changes in expected inflation, workers' attempts to push up real wages, or a supply shock—affects output and prices only in the short run and has no effect in the long run (holding the aggregate demand curve constant).

3. The economy has a self-correcting mechanism, which will return it to the natural rate levels of unemployment and aggregate output over time.

APPLICATION
EXPLAINING PAST BUSINESS CYCLE EPISODES /

Aggregate supply and demand analysis is an extremely useful tool for analyzing aggregate economic activity; we will apply it to several business cycle episodes. In addition, since a good economic model must be able to predict the future as well as explain the past, we will look at how aggregate supply and demand analysis can be used to predict the response of aggregate output and price level to events that might happen in the future. To simplify our analysis, we will assume that initially aggregate output is at the natural rate level in all of the following applications.

The Vietnam War Buildup: 1964–1970

America's involvement in Vietnam began to escalate in the early 1960s, and after 1964, the United States was fighting a full-scale war. Beginning in

1965, the resulting increases in military expenditure raised government spending, while at the same time the Federal Reserve increased the rate of money growth in an attempt to keep interest rates from rising. What does aggregate supply and demand analysis suggest should have happened to aggregate output and the price level as a result of the Vietnam war buildup?

The rise in government spending and the higher rate of money growth would shift the aggregate demand curve to the right (shown in Figure 26.5). As a result, aggregate output would rise, unemployment would fall, and the price level would rise. Table 26.3 demonstrates that this is exactly what happened: The unemployment rate fell steadily from 1964 to 1969, remaining well below what economists now think was the natural rate of unemployment during that period (around 5%), and inflation began to rise. As Figure 26.5 predicts, unemployment would eventually begin to return to the natural rate level because of the economy's self-correcting mechanism. This is exactly what we saw occurring in 1970, when the inflation rate rose even higher and unemployment increased.

Negative Supply Shocks: 1973–1975 and 1978–1980

In 1973, the economy was hit by a series of negative supply shocks. As a result of the oil embargo stemming from the Arab-Israeli war of 1973, the Organization of Petroleum Exporting Countries (OPEC) was able to engineer a quadrupling of oil prices by restricting oil production. In addition, a series of crop failures throughout the world led to a sharp increase in food prices. Another factor was the termination of wage and price controls in 1973 and 1974, which led to a push by workers to obtain wage increases that had been prevented by the controls. The triple thrust of these three events caused the aggregate supply curve to shift in sharply, and as the aggregate demand and supply diagram in Figure 26.6 predicts, both the price level and unemployment began to rise dramatically (see Table 26.4).

Table 26.3   Unemployment and Inflation During the Vietnam War Buildup: 1964–1970

Year	Unemployment Rate	Inflation (Year to Year)
1964	5.0%	1.3%
1965	4.4%	1.7%
1966	3.7%	2.9%
1967	3.7%	2.9%
1968	3.5%	4.2%
1969	3.4%	5.4%
1970	4.8%	5.9%

Source: *Economic Report of the President.*

Table 26.4 **Unemployment and Inflation During the Supply Shock Periods: 1973–1975 and 1978–1980**

Year	Unemployment Rate	Inflation (Year to Year)	Year	Unemployment Rate	Inflation (Year to Year)
1973	4.8%	6.2%	1978	6.0%	7.7%
1974	5.5%	11.0%	1979	5.8%	11.3%
1975	8.3%	9.1%	1980	7.0%	13.5%

Source: *Economic Report of the President.*

The 1978–1980 period is almost an exact replay of the 1973–1975 period. By 1978, the economy had just about fully recovered from the 1973–1974 supply shocks, when poor harvests and a doubling of oil prices (as a result of the overthrow of the Shah of Iran) again led to another sharp inward shift of the aggregate supply curve. The pattern predicted by Figure 26.6 played itself out again—inflation and unemployment both shot upward (see Table 26.4).

A Positive Supply Shock and a Decline in American Competitiveness: 1985–1986

At the beginning of 1986, a world oil glut encouraged by increased Saudi Arabian production caused the price of oil to drop by over 50%. Many forecasters expected a scenario opposite to that played out in 1973–1975 and 1978–1980; the positive supply shock was expected to shift out the aggregate supply curve, resulting in both a decline in inflation and a business cycle boom in 1986. As can be seen in Table 26.5, although the forecasters' predictions that inflation would fall were realized, a boom did not materialize—unemployment declined only slightly. What went wrong with their forecasts?

Table 26.5 **Unemployment and Inflation: 1985–1986**

Year	Unemployment Rate	Inflation (Year to Year)
1985	7.1%	3.6%
1986	6.9%	1.9%

Source: *Economic Report of the President,* 1987.

The forecasts went astray because the ability of American firms to compete with foreign firms unexpectedly continued to deteriorate in 1986, despite a decline in the value of the dollar. Net exports, which in 1985 were −$140 billion (1982 dollars), in 1986 fell to −$180 billion (1982 dollars), the most negative value in U.S. history. The large decline in net exports resulted in an inward shift of the aggregate demand curve that offset some of the expansionary impact of the outward shift in the aggregate supply curve. As our aggregate supply and demand analysis indicates, the outcome was only a mild improvement on the unemployment front with a substantial decline in inflation.

APPLICATION
PREDICTING FUTURE ECONOMIC ACTIVITY/ /

Now let's see what will happen to aggregate output and the price level if certain events happen that have a reasonable probability of occurring in the near future.

Elimination of Japanese Trade Barriers   The U.S. and Japanese governments have been engaged in talks about eliminating barriers to exports of U.S. goods to Japan. If the talks are successful in tearing down these barriers, what might we predict would happen to output and the price level in the United States?

Our aggregate supply and demand analysis of the elimination of Japanese trade barriers would be that pictured in Figure 26.5. The elimination of Japanese trade barriers would cause U.S. net exports to rise, leading to a rightward shift of the aggregate demand curve, which would initially raise aggregate output and the price level (increasing inflation) in the United States. In the long run, however, aggregate output would return to its natural rate level and the price level would stop rising so that the increase in inflation would be only temporary.

Reduction in U.S. Military Operations Overseas   If after the recent U.S. intervention in the Middle East, Americans decide that they no longer want to engage in overseas military operations in the future and so the government cuts military spending, what effect would this have on the economy?

The reduction in military spending would probably lead to less government spending and a leftward shift of the aggregate demand curve. The outcome would be opposite to that pictured in Figure 26.5; the price level would fall, lowering the inflation rate, and aggregate output would also fall at first; however, in the long run, aggregate output would return to the natural rate level.

Study Guide
Many examples of future events with implications for shifts in the aggregate demand and supply curves come to mind. Try to think of some yourself and then use aggregate supply and demand analysis to predict what will happen to the economy. Such exercises will help you master aggregate supply and demand analysis (and may even be fun).

SUMMARY

1. The aggregate demand curve indicates the quantity of aggregate output demanded at each price level and it is downward sloping. Monetarists view changes in the money supply as the primary source of shifts in the aggregate demand curve. Keynesians believe that not only are changes in the money supply important to shifts in the aggregate demand curve, but so also are changes in fiscal policy (government spending and taxes), net exports, and the willingness of consumers and businesses to spend ("animal spirits").

2. In the short run, the aggregate supply curve is upward sloping, because a rise in the price level raises the profit earned on each unit of production and the quantity of output supplied rises. Four factors can cause the aggregate supply curve to shift: (a) tightness of the labor market as represented by unemployment relative to the natural rate, (b) expectations of inflation, (c) workers' attempts to push up their real wages, and (d) supply shocks (unrelated to wages), which affect production costs.

3. Equilibrium in the short run occurs at the point where the aggregate demand curve intersects the aggregate supply curve. Although this is where the economy heads temporarily, it has a self-correcting mechanism, which leads it to settle permanently at the long-run equilibrium in which the aggregate output is at the natural rate level. Shifts in either the aggregate demand or aggregate supply curve can produce changes in aggregate output and the price level.

4. Aggregate supply and demand analysis is a useful tool because it can be used either to explain past business cycle episodes or to predict the response of aggregate output and the price level to future events.

KEY TERMS

aggregate demand and supply

aggregate demand curve

monetarists

Keynesians

velocity

equation of exchange

modern quantity theory of money

consumer expenditure

planned investment spending

government spending

net exports

"animal spirits"

complete crowding out

partial crowding out

aggregate supply curve

natural rate of unemployment

natural rate level of output

long-run aggregate supply curve

self-correcting mechanism

activists

nonactivists

supply shock

real business cycle theory

hysteresis

QUESTIONS AND PROBLEMS

1. Given that a monetarist predicts velocity to be 5, graph the aggregate demand curve that results if the money supply is $400 billion. If the money supply falls to $50 billion, what happens to the position of the aggregate demand curve?

* 2. Milton Friedman states that "money is all that matters to nominal income." How is this statement built into the aggregate demand curve in the monetarist framework?

3. Suppose government spending is raised at the same time that the money supply is lowered. What will happen to the position of the Keynesian aggregate demand curve? the monetarist aggregate demand curve?

* 4. Why does the Keynesian aggregate demand curve shift when "animal spirits" change, but the monetarist aggregate demand curve does not?

5. If the dollar increases in value relative to foreign currencies so that foreign goods become cheaper in the United States, what will happen to the position of the aggregate supply curve? to the aggregate demand curve?

* 6. Answer true, false, or uncertain: "Profit-maximizing behavior on the part of business firms explains why the aggregate supply curve is upward sloping."

7. If huge budget deficits cause the public to think that there will be higher inflation in the future, what is likely to happen to the aggregate supply curve when budget deficits rise?

* 8. If a pill were invented that, when taken by workers, made them twice as productive, and their wages did not change, what would happen to the position of the aggregate supply curve?

9. When aggregate output is below the natural rate level, what will happen to the price level over time if the aggregate demand curve remains unchanged? Why?

*10. Show how aggregate supply and demand analysis can explain why both aggregate output and the price level fell sharply when investment spending collapsed during the Great Depression.

11. Answer true, false, or uncertain: "An important difference between monetarists and Keynesians rests on how long they think the long run actually is."

Using Economic Analysis to Predict the Future

*12. Predict what will happen to aggregate output and the price level if the Federal Reserve increases the money supply at the same time the Congress implements an income tax cut.

13. Suppose the public believes that a newly announced anti-inflation program will work, and so lowers its expectations of future inflation. What will happen to aggregate output and the price level in the short run?

*14. Proposals have come before Congress that advocate the implementation of a national sales tax. Predict the effect of such a tax on both the aggregate supply and demand curves and on aggregate output and the price level.

15. With the decline in the value of the dollar since 1985, some experts predict a dramatic improvement in the ability of American firms to compete abroad. Predict what would happen to output and the price level in the United States as a result?

Aggregate Supply and the Phillips Curve: A Historical Perspective

In this appendix we examine how economists' view of aggregate supply has evolved over time and how a concept called the *Phillips curve*, which describes the relationship between unemployment and inflation, fits into the analysis of aggregate supply.

The classical economists, who predated Keynes, believed that wages and prices were extremely flexible, so the economy would always adjust quickly to the natural rate level of output (Y_n). In effect, this view is equivalent to assuming that the aggregate supply curve *even in the short run* is vertical at an output level of Y_n.

With the advent of the Great Depression in 1929 and the subsequent long period of high unemployment, the classical view of an economy that adjusts quickly to the natural rate level of output became less tenable. The teachings of John Maynard Keynes emerged as the dominant way of thinking about the determination of aggregate output, and the view that aggregate supply is vertical was abandoned. Instead, the early Keynesians in the 1930s, 1940s, and 1950s assumed that, for all practical purposes, the price level could be treated as fixed. Hence they viewed aggregate supply as a horizontal curve in which aggregate output could increase without an increase in the price level.[1]

In 1958, A. W. Phillips published his famous paper, which outlined a relationship between unemployment and inflation.[2] This relationship was popularized by Paul Samuelson and Robert Solow of the Massachusetts Institute of Technology in the early 1960s, and naturally enough, it became known as the Phillips curve after its discoverer. The Phillips curve indicates that the rate of change of wages ($\Delta w/w$, called *wage inflation*) is negatively related to the difference between the actual unemployment rate (U) and the natural rate of unemployment (U_n),

$$\Delta w/w = -h \times (U - U_n)$$

---

[1]The assumption of a fixed price level is an essential element of the *ISLM* model adhered to by the early Keynesians (Chapters 24 and 25).

[2]A. W. Phillips, "The Relationship Between Unemployment and the Rate of Change of Money Wages in the United Kingdom, 1861–1957," *Economica* 25 (November 1958).

where h is a constant that indicates how much wage inflation changes for a given change in $U - U_n$. If h were 2, for example, a one percentage point increase in the unemployment rate relative to the natural rate would result in a two percentage point decline in wage inflation.

The Phillips curve provides a view of aggregate supply, because it indicates that a rise in aggregate output that lowers the unemployment rate will raise wage inflation and thus lead to a higher level of wages and the price level. In other words, the Phillips curve implies that the aggregate supply curve will be upward sloping. In addition, it indicates that when $U > U_n$ (the labor market is easy), $\Delta w/w$ is negative and wages decline over time. Thus the Phillips curve supports the view of aggregate supply in Chapter 26 that when the labor market is easy, production costs will fall and the aggregate supply curve will shift out.[3]

Figure 26A.1 shows what the Phillips curve relationship looks like for the United States. As we can see from panel (a), the relationship works well until 1969 and seems to indicate an apparent trade-off between unemployment and wage inflation: If the public wants to have a lower unemployment rate, they can "buy" this by accepting a higher rate of wage inflation.

In 1967, however, Milton Friedman pointed out a severe flaw with the Phillips curve analysis because it left out an important factor that affects wage changes: workers' expectations of inflation.[4] Friedman noted that firms and workers are concerned with *real* wages, not nominal wages; they are concerned with the wage adjusted for any expected increase in the price level—that is, they look at the rate of change of wages minus expected inflation. When unemployment is high relative to the natural rate, *real* (not nominal) wages should fall ($\Delta w/w - \pi^e < 0$); when unemployment is low relative to the natural rate, *real* wages should rise ($\Delta w/w - \pi^e > 0$). The Phillips curve relationship thus needs to be modified by replacing $\Delta w/w$ by $\Delta w/w - \pi^e$. This results in an *expectations-augmented Phillips curve,* expressed as

$$\frac{\Delta w}{w} - \pi^e = -h \times (U - U_n) \quad \text{or} \quad \frac{\Delta w}{w} = -h \times (U - U_n) + \pi^e$$

---

[3]Because workers normally become more productive over time as a result of new technology and increases in physical capital, their real wages grow over time, even when the economy is at the natural rate of unemployment. To reflect this, the Phillips curve should include a term that reflects the growth in real wages due to higher worker productivity. We have left this term out of the equation in the text because higher productivity that results in higher real wages will not cause the aggregate supply curve to shift out. If, for example, workers become 3% more productive every year and their real wages grow at 3% per year, then the effective cost of workers to the firm (called *unit labor costs*) remains unchanged and the aggregate supply curve does not shift. Thus the $\Delta w/w$ term in the Phillips curve above is more accurately thought of as the change in the unit labor costs.

[4]This criticism of the Phillips curve was outlined in Milton Friedman's famous presidential address to the American Economic Association: Milton Friedman, "The Role of Monetary Policy," *American Economic Review* 58 (March 1968), 1–17.

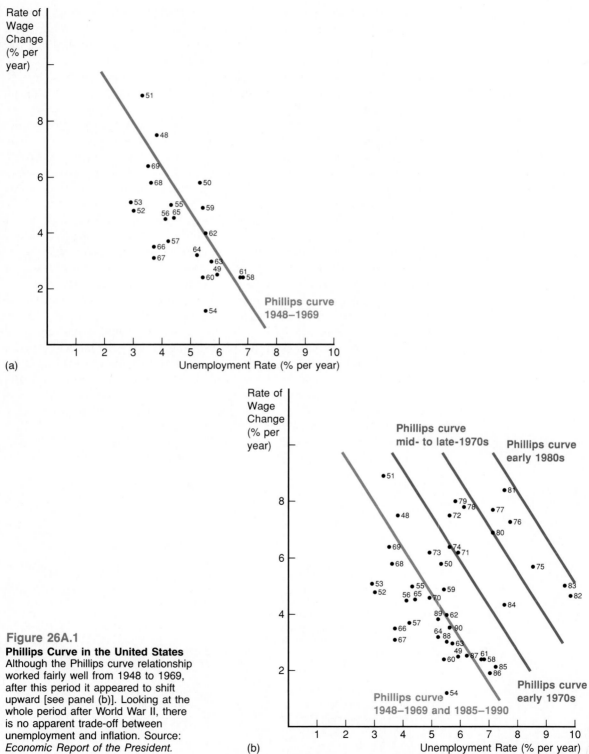

(a)

Figure 26A.1

Phillips Curve in the United States
Although the Phillips curve relationship worked fairly well from 1948 to 1969, after this period it appeared to shift upward [see panel (b)]. Looking at the whole period after World War II, there is no apparent trade-off between unemployment and inflation. Source: *Economic Report of the President.*

(b)

The expectations-augmented Phillips curve implies that as expected inflation rises, nominal wages will be increased to prevent real wages from falling; thus the Phillips curve will shift upward. The resulting rise in production costs would then shift the aggregate supply curve inward. The conclusion from Friedman's modification of the Phillips curve is therefore that the higher is expected inflation, the larger is the inward shift in the aggregate supply curve; this conclusion is built into the analysis of the aggregate supply curve in the chapter.

Friedman's modification of the Phillips curve analysis was remarkably clairvoyant: With the rising inflation in the late 1960s, the Phillips curve did indeed begin to shift upward, as we can see in panel (b). An important feature of panel (b) is that a trade-off between unemployment and wage inflation is no longer apparent; there is no clear-cut relationship between unemployment and wage inflation—a high rate of wage inflation does not mean that unemployment is low, or a low rate of wage inflation that unemployment is high. This is exactly what the expectations-augmented Phillips curve predicts: A rate of unemployment permanently below the natural rate of unemployment cannot be "bought" by accepting a higher rate of inflation, because no long-run trade-off between unemployment and wage inflation exists.[5]

A further refinement of the concept of aggregate supply came from research by Milton Friedman, Edmund Phelps, and Robert Lucas, who explored the implications of the expectations-augmented Phillips curve for the behavior of unemployment. Solving the expectations-augmented Phillips curve for U leads to the following expression:

$$U = U_n - \frac{(\Delta w/w - \pi^e)}{h}$$

---

[5]This prediction can be derived from the expectations-augmented Phillips curve as follows. When wage inflation is held at a constant level, inflation and expected inflation will eventually equal wage inflation. Thus in the long run,

$$\pi^e = \frac{\Delta w}{w}$$

Substituting the long-run value of π^e above into the expectations-augmented Phillips curve gives us

$$\frac{\Delta w}{w} = -h \times (U - U_n) + \frac{\Delta w}{w}$$

Subtracting $\Delta w/w$ from both sides of the equation results in the following equation:

$$0 = -h \times (U - U_n)$$

which implies that

$$U = U_n$$

This equation then tells us that in the long run, for any level of wage inflation unemployment will settle to its natural rate level: Hence the long-run Phillips curve is vertical and there is no long-run trade-off between unemployment and wage inflation.

Since wage inflation and price inflation are closely tied to each other, π can be substituted for $\Delta w/w$ in the above expression to obtain

$$U = U_n - \frac{(\pi - \pi^e)}{h}$$

This expression, often referred to as the "Lucas supply function," indicates that deviations of unemployment and aggregate output from the natural rate levels respond to unanticipated inflation (actual inflation minus expected inflation, $\pi - \pi^e$). When inflation is greater than anticipated, unemployment will be below the natural rate (and aggregate output above the natural rate). When inflation is below its anticipated value, unemployment will rise above the natural rate level. The conclusion from this view of aggregate supply is that only unanticipated policy can cause deviations from the natural rate of unemployment and output. The implications of this view are explored in detail in Chapter 30.

CHAPTER 27

Money and Economic Activity: The Empirical Evidence

PREVIEW   Since 1980, the U.S. economy has been on a roller coaster, with output and unemployment undergoing drastic fluctuations. The recession of 1980 was followed by one of the shortest economic expansions on record. After a year, the economy plunged into the 1981–1982 recession, the most severe economic contraction in the postwar era—the unemployment rate climbed to over 10%. The 1981–1982 recession was then followed by a long economic expansion that led to a decline of the unemployment rate below 6% in the 1987–1990 period. With Iraq's invasion of Kuwait and the rise in oil prices in the second half of 1990, the economy again plunged into recession. With large fluctuations in aggregate output and the economic instability that accompanies them, policymakers face the following dilemma: What policy or policies should be implemented to reduce output fluctuations in the future?

As you learned in Chapter 26, monetarists believe that there is only one major source of output fluctuations: changes in the money supply. Their solution to reducing output fluctuations is a constant money growth rate rule. Keynesians, on the other hand, believe that there are other sources of output fluctuations (fiscal policy, net exports, "animal spirits," supply shocks), and they doubt that controlling the money supply alone will eliminate them. As you can see, it is extremely important for policymakers to know how important money is as a factor in determining aggregate economic activity.

In this chapter we examine empirical evidence on the effect of money on aggregate output (real GNP) and aggregate spending (nominal GNP) and discuss the disagreement between monetarists and Keynesians on the importance of money to these variables. Amazingly, although there has been some convergence of views, after thirty years differences still exist! Debates in the physical sciences usually are resolved more quickly. Why is this not the case in economics?

This chapter provides an answer to this question by focusing on why empirical evidence in economics is much harder to interpret than evidence in the physical sciences. Debates in economics often remain unresolved because there are two different kinds of evidence which sometimes generate conflicting conclusions. The analysis in this chapter will not only help you understand the debate on the importance of money to economic activity, but more importantly, it will provide you with a perspective on how to evaluate other controversies in economics (as well as other scientific disciplines) that are hard to settle.

TWO TYPES OF EMPIRICAL EVIDENCE

We encounter two types of empirical evidence in economics and other scientific disciplines: **Structural model evidence** examines whether one variable affects another by using data to build a model that explains the channels through which this variable affects the other; **reduced form evidence** examines whether one variable has an effect on another simply by looking directly at the relationship between the two variables.

Suppose you were interested in whether drinking coffee leads to heart disease. Structural model evidence would involve developing an empirical model that analyzed data on how coffee is metabolized by the human body, how it affects the operation of the heart, and how its effects on the heart lead to heart attacks. Reduced form evidence would involve looking directly at whether coffee drinkers tend to experience heart attacks more frequently than noncoffee drinkers.

How you look at the evidence—whether you focus on structural model evidence or reduced form evidence—can lead to different conclusions. This is particularly true for the debate between monetarists and Keynesians: Monetarists tend to focus on reduced form evidence and find that changes in the money supply are more important to economic activity than do Keynesians, who focus on structural model evidence. To understand the differences in their views about the importance of monetary policy, we need to look at the nature of the two types of evidence and the advantages and disadvantages of each.

Structural Model Evidence

The Keynesian analysis discussed in Chapter 26 is specific about the channels through which the money supply affects economic activity (called the **transmission mechanisms of monetary policy**). Keynesians typically examine the effect of money on economic activity by building a **structural model**—a description of how the economy operates using a collection of equations that describe the behavior of business firms and consumers in many sectors of the economy. These equations then show the channels through which monetary and fiscal policy affect aggregate output and spending. A Keynesian structural model, for example, might have behavioral equations that describe the workings of monetary policy with the following schematic diagram:

$$M \dashrightarrow \boxed{i \dashrightarrow I \dashrightarrow} \dashrightarrow Y$$

The model describes the transmission mechanism of monetary policy as follows: The money supply (M) affects interest rates (i), which in turn affect investment spending (I), which in turn affects aggregate output or aggregate spending (Y). The Keynesians examine the relationship between M and Y by looking at empirical evidence (structural model evidence) on the specific channels of monetary influence, such as the link between interest rates and investment spending.

Reduced Form Evidence

Monetarists, on the other hand, do not describe specific ways that the money supply affects aggregate spending. Instead, they examine the effect of money on economic activity by looking at whether movements in Y are tightly linked to (have a high correlation with) movements in M. Using reduced form evidence, monetarists analyze the effect of M on Y as if the economy were a black box in which its workings cannot be seen. The monetarist way of looking at the evidence can be represented by the following schematic diagram, in which the economy is drawn as a black box with a question mark:

Now that we have seen how monetarists and Keynesians look at the empirical evidence on the link between money and economic activity, we can consider the advantages and disadvantages of a reduced form versus a structural model approach.

Advantages and Disadvantages of Structural Model Evidence

The structural model approach, used primarily by Keynesians, has the advantage of giving us an understanding of how the economy works. If the structure is correct, that is, if it contains all the transmission mechanisms and channels through which monetary and fiscal policy can affect economic activity, then the structural model approach has three major advantages over the reduced form approach.

1. Because we can separately evaluate each transmission mechanism to see whether it is plausible, we will obtain more pieces of evidence on whether money has an important effect on economic activity. If we find important effects of money on economic activity, for example, we will have more confidence that changes in money actually cause the changes in economic activity; that is, we will have more confidence on the direction of causation between M and Y.

2. Knowing how changes in money affect economic activity may help us to more accurately predict the effect of M on Y. Expansions in the money supply might be found to be less effective when interest rates are low. Then, when interest rates are higher, we would be able to predict that an expansion in the money supply would have a larger impact on Y than would otherwise be the case.

3. By knowing how the economy operates, we may be able to predict how institutional changes in the economy might affect the link between M and Y. For instance, before 1980 when Regulation Q was still in effect, restrictions of interest payments on savings deposits meant that the average consumer would not earn more on savings when interest rates rose. With the termination of Regulation Q, the average consumer now earns more on savings when interest rates rise. If we understand how earnings on savings affect consumer spending, we might be able to say that a change in the money supply, which affects interest rates, will have a different effect today than it would have had before 1980. Because of the rapid pace of financial innovation, the advantage of being able to predict how institutional changes affect the link between M and Y may be even more important now than in the past.

These three advantages of the structural model approach suggest that this approach is better than the reduced form approach *if we know the correct structure of the model*. Put another way, structural model evidence is only as good as the structural model it is based on; that is, it is best only if all the transmission mechanisms are fully understood. This is a big *if*, since failing to include one or two relevant transmission mechanisms for monetary policy in the structural model might result in a serious underestimate of the impact of M on Y.

Monetarists worry that many Keynesian structural models may ignore the transmission mechanisms for monetary policy that are most important. For example, if the most important monetary transmission mechanisms involve consumer spending rather than investment spending, the Keynesian structural model (such as the one on page 635), which focuses on investment spending for its monetary transmission mechanism, may underestimate the importance of money to economic activity. In other words, monetarists reject the interpretation of evidence from many Keynesian structural models because they believe the channels of monetary influence are too narrowly defined. In a sense they accuse Keynesians of wearing blinders that prevent them from recognizing the full importance of monetary policy.

Advantages and Disadvantages of Reduced Form Evidence

The main advantage of reduced form evidence over structural model evidence is that no restrictions are imposed on the way monetary policy affects the economy. Thus if we are not sure that we know what all the monetary transmission mechanisms are, we may be more likely to spot the full effect of M on Y by looking at whether movements in Y have a high correlation with movements in M. Monetarists favor reduced form evidence because they believe that the particular channel through which changes in the money supply affect Y are diverse and continually change. They contend that it may be too difficult to identify all the transmission mechanisms of monetary policy.

The most notable objection to reduced form evidence is that it may misleadingly suggest changes in M cause changes in Y when this is not the case. A basic principle applicable to all scientific disciplines, including economics, states that *correlation does not necessarily imply causation*. Because the movement on one variable is tightly linked to another doesn't necessarily mean that one variable causes the other.

Suppose you notice that wherever criminal activity abounds, more police patrol the street. Should you then conclude that police patrols cause criminal activity and recommend that pulling police off the street is the solution for lowering the crime rate? Clearly the answer is "no," because police patrols do not cause criminal activity; criminal activity causes police patrols. This situation is called **reverse causation** and can lead to misleading conclusions when interpreting correlations (see Box 27.1).

The reverse causation problem may be present when examining the link between money and aggregate output or spending. Our discussion of the

B o x   2 7 . 1

The Perils of Reverse Causation: A Russian Folk Tale

A Russian folk tale illustrates the problems that can arise from reverse causation. As the story goes, there once was a severe epidemic in the Russian countryside and many doctors were sent to the towns where the epidemic was at its worst. The peasants in the town noticed that wherever doctors went, many people were dying. So to reduce the death rate, they killed off all the doctors.

Were the peasants better off? Why or why not?

Box 2 7 . 2

The Perils of Ignoring a Third Driving Factor: How to Lose a Presidential Election

The political advisor to a presidential candidate discovers a little town in New Hampshire whose vote for president always exactly matches the national vote; that is, in every election there has been a perfect correlation between the town's vote and the national vote. The political advisor thus tells the candidate that his election will be assured if all his campaign funds are spent on this one town.

Should the presidential candidate promote or fire this advisor? Why or why not?

conduct of monetary policy in Chapter 20 suggested that when the Federal Reserve has an interest rate or a free reserves target, higher output may lead to a higher money supply. If most of the correlation between M and Y occurs because of the Fed's interest rate target, then controlling the money supply will not help control aggregate output, because it is actually Y that is causing M rather than the other way around.

Another facet of the correlation-causation question is that a third factor (yet unknown) could be the driving force behind two variables that move along together. Coffee drinking might be associated with heart disease not because coffee drinking causes heart attacks, but because coffee drinkers tend to be people who are under a lot of stress and the stress causes heart attacks. Getting people to stop drinking coffee, then, would not lower the incidence of heart disease. Similarly, if there is an unknown third factor that causes M and Y to move together, controlling M will not improve the control of Y. (The perils of ignoring a third driving factor are illustrated by Box 27.2.)

Summary   No clear-cut case can be made that reduced form evidence is preferable to structural model evidence, or vice versa. The structural model approach, used primarily by Keynesians, provides an understanding of how the economy works. If the structure is correct, it more accurately predicts the effect of monetary policy, allows predictions of how the effect of monetary policy will change when institutions change, and provides more confidence in the direction of causation between M and Y. If the structure of the model is not correctly specified because it leaves out important transmission mechanisms of monetary policy, then it could be very misleading regarding the effectiveness of monetary policy.

The reduced form approach, used primarily by monetarists, does not restrict the way monetary policy affects the economy and may be more likely to spot the full effect of M on Y. However, reduced form evidence cannot rule out the possibility of reverse causation in which changes in output cause changes in money, or that a third factor drives changes in both output and money. A high correlation of money and output might then be misleading, since controlling the money supply would not help control the level of output.

EARLY KEYNESIAN EVIDENCE ON THE IMPORTANCE OF MONEY

Although Keynes proposed his framework for analyzing aggregate economic activity in 1936, his views reached their peak of popularity among economists in the 1950s and early 1960s, when the majority of economists had accepted his framework. Although Keynesians currently believe that money has important effects on economic activity, the early Keynesians of the 1950s and early 1960s characteristically held the view that *monetary policy does not matter at all* to movements in aggregate output and hence to the business cycle.

Their belief in the ineffectiveness of monetary policy stemmed from three pieces of structural model evidence:

1. During the Great Depression, interest rates on U.S. Treasury securities fell to extremely low levels; the three-month Treasury bill rate, for example, declined to below 1%. Early Keynesians viewed monetary policy as affecting aggregate demand solely through its effect on nominal interest rates which, in turn, affect investment spending; they believed that low interest rates during the depression indicated that monetary policy was "easy" because it encouraged investment spending and so could not have played a contractionary role during this period. Since monetary policy was not capable of explaining why the worst economic contraction in U.S. history had taken place, they concluded that changes in the money supply have no effect on aggregate output—in other words, money doesn't matter.

2. Early empirical studies found no linkage between movements in nominal interest rates and investment spending. Because early Keynesians saw this link as the channel through which changes in the money supply affect aggregate demand, finding that the link was weak also led them to the conclusion that changes in the money supply have no effect on aggregate output.

3. Surveys of businesspeople revealed that their decisions on how much to invest in new physical capital were not influenced by market interest rates. This evidence added further confirmation that the link between interest rates and investment spending was weak, strengthening the conclusion that money doesn't matter.

The result of this interpretation of the evidence was that most economists paid only scant attention to monetary policy until the mid-1960s.

Study Guide

Before reading the next subsection, which discusses objections that were raised against early Keynesian interpretation of the evidence, use the ideas on the disadvantages of structural model evidence discussed earlier to see if you can think of some objections yourself. This will help you learn how to put into practice the principles of evaluating evidence discussed in the previous section.

Objections to Early Keynesian Evidence

While Keynesian economics was reaching its ascendancy in the 1950s and 1960s, a small group of economists at the University of Chicago, led by Milton Friedman, adopted what was then an unfashionable view—that money *does* matter to aggregate demand.[1] Friedman and his disciples, who later became known as monetarists, objected to the early Keynesian interpretation of the evidence on the grounds that the structural model used by the early Keynesians was severely flawed. Since structural model evidence is only as good as the structural model it is based on, the monetarist critique of this evidence needs to be taken seriously.

In 1963, Friedman and Anna Schwartz published their classic book, *A Monetary History of the United States, 1867–1960,* which showed that contrary to the early Keynesian beliefs, monetary policy during the Great Depression was not "easy"; indeed, it had never been more contractionary. Friedman and Schwartz documented the massive bank failures of this period and the resulting decline in the money supply—the largest ever experienced in the United States (see Chapter 16). Thus monetary policy could explain the worst economic contraction in U.S. history, and the Great Depression could not be singled out as a period that demonstrates the ineffectiveness of monetary policy.

A Keynesian could still counter Friedman and Schwartz's argument that money was contractionary during the Great Depression by citing the low level of interest rates. But were these interest rates really so low? Referring to Chapter 7, Figure 7.1 (page 133), you will note that while interest rates on U.S. Treasury securities and high-grade corporate bonds were low during the Great Depression, interest rates on lower-grade bonds, such as Baa corporate bonds, rose to unprecedented high levels during the sharpest part of the contraction phase (1930–1933). By the standard of these lower-grade bonds, then, interest rates were high and monetary policy was tight.

---

[1]Clark Warburton at the FDIC was one of the few economists not associated with the University of Chicago who actively supported this view.

There is a moral to this story. Although much aggregate economic analysis proceeds as though there is only *one* interest rate, we must always be aware that there are *many*—some of which may tell different stories. During normal times, most interest rates move in tandem, so lumping them all together and looking at one representative interest rate may not be too misleading. But this is not always so. Unusual periods (like the Great Depression) do occur, when interest rates on different securities begin to diverge. It is exactly this kind of situation in which a structural model (like the early Keynesians') that looks at only the interest rates on a low-risk security such as a U.S. Treasury bill or bond can be very misleading.

There is a second, and potentially more important, reason why the early Keynesian structural model's focus on nominal interest rates provides a misleading picture of the tightness of monetary policy during the Great Depression. In a period of deflation, when there is a declining price level, low *nominal* interest rates do not necessarily indicate that the cost of borrowing is low and that monetary policy is easy—in fact, the cost of borrowing could be quite high. If, for example, the public expects the price level to decline at a 10% rate, then even though nominal interest rates are at zero, the real cost of borrowing would be as high as +10%. [Recall from Chapter 4 that the real rate equals the nominal rate, 0, minus the expected rate of inflation, −10%, so the real rate = 0 − (−10%) = +10%.]

In Figure 27.1 you can see that this is exactly what happened during the Great Depression: Real interest rates on U.S. Treasury bills were far higher during the 1931–1933 contraction phase of the Great Depression than was the case throughout the next forty years.[2] As a result, movements of *real* interest rates indicate that contrary to the early Keynesians' beliefs, monetary policy was extremely tight during the Great Depression. Since an important role for monetary policy during this depressed period could no longer be ruled out, most economists were forced to rethink their position regarding whether money matters.

Monetarists also objected to the early Keynesian structural model's view that a weak link between nominal interest rates and investment spending indicates that investment spending is unaffected by monetary policy. A weak link between *nominal* interest rates and investment spending does not rule out a strong link between *real* interest rates and investment spending. As depicted in Figure 27.1, nominal interest rates are often a very misleading indicator of real interest rates—not only during the Great Depression but in

---

[2]In the 1980s, real interest rates rose to exceedingly high levels, approaching those of the Great Depression period. Much current research is trying to explain this phenomenon, some of which points to monetary policy as the source of high real rates in the 1980s. For example, see Oliver J. Blanchard and Lawrence H. Summers, "Perspectives on High World Interest Rates," *Brookings Papers on Economic Activity* 2 (1984), pp. 273–324; and John Huizinga and Frederic S. Mishkin, "Monetary Policy Regime Shifts and the Unusual Behavior of Real Interest Rates," *Carnegie-Rochester Conference Series on Public Policy* 24 (1986), pp. 231–274.

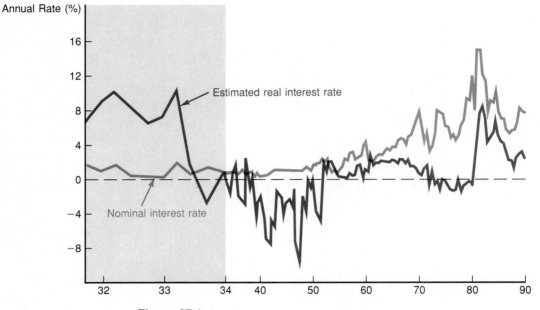

Annual Rate (%)

Figure 27.1
Real and Nominal Interest Rates (Three-Month Treasury Bills): 1931–1990 Source:
Frederic S. Mishkin, "The Real Interest Rate: An Empirical Investigation," *Carnegie-Rochester Conference Series on Public Policy* 15 (1981), pp. 151–200, and an update from the author.

later periods as well. Since real interest rates more accurately reflect the true cost of borrowing, they should be more relevant to investment decisions than nominal interest rates. Accordingly, the two pieces of early Keynesian evidence indicating that nominal interest rates have little effect on investment spending do not rule out a strong effect of changes in the money supply on investment spending and hence on aggregate demand.

Monetarists also assert that interest rate effects on investment spending might be only one of many channels through which monetary policy affects aggregate demand. Monetary policy could then have a major impact on aggregate demand even if interest rate effects on investment spending are small, as was suggested by the early Keynesians.

Study Guide
As you read the monetarist evidence presented in the next section, again try to think of objections to the evidence: This time use the ideas on the disadvantages of reduced form evidence.

EARLY MONETARIST EVIDENCE ON THE _____
IMPORTANCE OF MONEY

In the early 1960s, Milton Friedman and his followers published a series of studies based on reduced form evidence that promoted the case for a strong effect of money on economic activity. In general, reduced form evidence can be broken down into three categories: (1) timing evidence, which looks at whether the movements in one variable typically occur before another; (2) statistical evidence, which performs formal statistical tests on the correlation of the movements of one variable with another; and (3) historical evidence, which examines specific historical episodes to see whether movements in one variable appear to cause another. Now let's look at the monetarist evidence on the importance of money that falls into each of these three categories.

Timing Evidence

Monetarist timing evidence looks at how the rate of money supply growth moves relative to the business cycle. The evidence on this relationship was first presented by Friedman and Schwartz in their famous paper, "Money and Business Cycles," published in 1963.[3] Friedman and Schwartz found that in every business cycle they studied over nearly a hundred-year period, the rate at which the money supply is growing always decreases before output does. On average the peak in the rate of money growth occurs sixteen months before the peak in the level of output. However, this lead time is variable, ranging from a few months to over two years in length. The conclusion of Friedman and Schwartz from this evidence is that money growth causes business cycle fluctuations, but its effect on the business cycle operates with "long and variable lags."

Timing evidence is based on the philosophical principle first stated in Latin, _post hoc, ergo propter hoc,_ which means that if one event occurs after another, the second event must have been caused by the first. This principle is valid only if we know that the first event is an _exogenous event,_ that is, an event occurring as a result of an independent action that could not possibly be caused by the event following it or by some third factor that might affect both it and the event following. If the first event is exogenous, when the second event follows the first, we can be sure that it is the _first_ event that is causing the second.

An example of an exogenous event is a controlled experiment. A chemist mixes two chemicals—suddenly his lab blows up and he with it. We can be

---

[3]Milton Friedman and Anna Schwartz, "Money and Business Cycles," _Review of Economics and Statistics_ 45, Supplement (February 1963), pp. 32–64.

absolutely sure that the cause of his demise was the act of mixing the two chemicals together. The principle of *post hoc, ergo propter hoc* is extremely useful in scientific experimentation.

Unfortunately, economics does not enjoy the precision of the hard sciences like physics or chemistry. Often we cannot be sure that an economic event, such as a decline in the rate of money growth, is an exogenous event—it could have been caused, itself, by a third factor or by the event it is supposedly causing. When another event (such as a decline in output) typically follows the first event (a decline in money growth), we cannot be sure that it is the decline in money growth that caused the decline in output. Timing evidence is clearly of a reduced form nature because it looks directly at the relationship of the movements of two variables. Money growth could lead output, yet both could be driven by a third factor.

Because timing evidence is of a reduced form nature, there is also the possibility of reverse causation, in which output growth causes money growth. How can this reverse causation occur while money growth still leads output? There are several ways that this can happen, but we will deal with just one example.[4]

Suppose you are in a hypothetical economy with a very regular business cycle movement [plotted in panel (a) of Figure 27.2] that is four years long; that is, it is four years from peak to peak. Let's assume that in our hypothetical economy there is reverse causation from output to the money supply, so movements in the money supply and output are perfectly correlated; that is, the money supply (M) and output (Y) have upward and downward movements at the same time. The result is that the peaks and troughs of the M and Y series in panels (a) and (b) occur at exactly the same time; therefore, no lead or lag relationship exists between them.

Now let's construct the rate of money supply growth from the money supply series in panel (b). This is done below in panel (c). What is the rate of growth of the money supply when at its peaks in years 1 and 5? At these points it is not growing at all; thus the rate of growth is zero. Similarly, at the trough in year 3, the growth rate is zero. When the money supply is declining from its peak in year 1 to its trough in year 3, it has a negative growth rate, and its decline is fastest sometime between years 1 and 3 (year 2). Translating to panel (c), the rate of money growth is below zero from years 1 to 3, with its most negative value reached at year 2. By similar reasoning, you can see that the growth rate of money is positive in years 0 to 1 and 3 to 5, with the highest values reached in years 0 and 4. When we connect all these points together,

---

[4]A famous article by James Tobin, "Money and Income: Post Hoc, Ergo Propter Hoc," *Quarterly Journal of Economics* (May 1970), pp. 301–317 describes an economic system in which changes in aggregate output cause changes in the growth rate of money, but changes in the growth rate of money have no effect on output. Tobin shows that such a system with reverse causation could yield timing evidence similar to that found by Friedman and Schwartz.

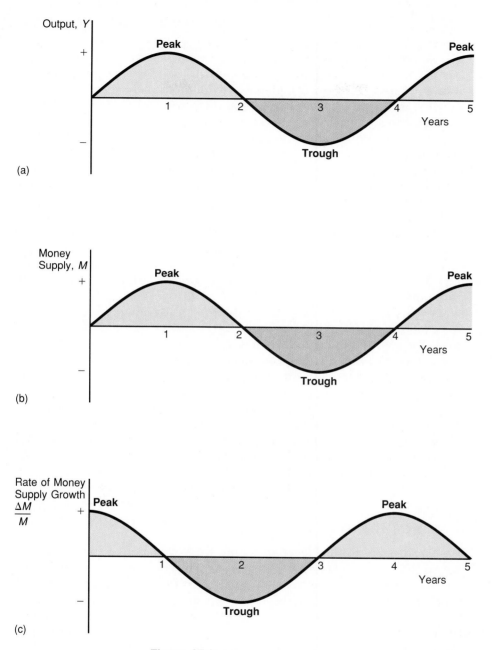

Figure 27.2
Hypothetical Example in Which Money Growth Leads Output Although neither M nor Y leads each other (that is, their peaks and troughs coincide), ΔM/M has its peaks and troughs one year ahead of M and Y, thus leading both series. (Note that M and Y in the panels are drawn as movements around a positive average value so that a + value means a value above the average and a − value means a value below the average, not a negative value.)

we get the money growth series in panel (c), in which the peaks are at years 0 and 4, with a trough in year 2.

Now let's look at the relationship of the money growth series of panel (c) with the level of output [panel (a)]. As you can see, the money growth series always has its peaks (and troughs) exactly one year before the peaks (and troughs) of the output series. What we then find is that our hypothetical economy is one in which the rate of money growth always decreases one year before output. This evidence does not, however, imply that money growth drives output. In fact, by assumption, we know that this economy is one in which causation actually runs from output to the level of money supply, and there is no lead or lag relationship between the two. Only by our judicious choice of using the *growth rate* of the money supply rather than its *level* have we found a leading relationship.

This example shows how easy it is to misinterpret timing relationships. Furthermore, by searching for what we hope to find, we might focus on a variable, such as a growth rate, rather than a level, which suggests a misleading relationship. Timing evidence can be a dangerous tool for deciding on causation.

Stated even more forcefully, "one person's lead is another person's lag." For example, you could just as easily interpret the relationship of money growth and output in Figure 27.2 to say the money growth rate lags output by three years. After all, the peaks in the money growth series occur three years after the peaks in the output series. In short, you could say that output leads money growth.

Overall we have seen that timing evidence is extremely hard to interpret. First, unless we can be sure that changes in the leading variable are exogenous events, we cannot be sure that the leading variable is actually causing the variable following. Second, it is all too easy to find what you seek when looking for timing evidence. Perhaps the best way of describing this danger is to say that "timing evidence may be in the eyes of the beholder."

Statistical Evidence

Monetarist statistical evidence examines the correlations between money and aggregate output or aggregate spending by performing formal statistical tests. Again in 1963 (obviously a vintage year for the monetarists), Milton Friedman and his coauthor David Meiselman published a paper that proposed the following test of a monetarist model against a Keynesian model.[5] In the Keynesian framework, investment and government spending are the sources of fluctuations in aggregate demand, so Friedman and Meiselman

---

[5]Milton Friedman and David Meiselman, "The Relative Stability of Monetary Velocity and the Investment Multiplier," ed. Commission on Money and Credit, in *Stabilization Policies* (Englewood Cliffs, N.J.: Prentice-Hall, 1963), pp. 165–268.

constructed a "Keynesian" autonomous expenditure variable (A) equal to investment spending plus government spending. They characterized the Keynesian model as saying that A should be highly correlated with aggregate spending (Y), while the money supply (M) should not. In the monetarist model, the money supply is the source of fluctuations in aggregate spending, and M should be highly correlated with Y, while A should not.

A logical way to find out which model is better would be to see which is more highly correlated with Y: M or A. When Friedman and Meiselman conducted this test for many different periods of U.S. data, they discovered that *the monetarist model wins!*[6] They concluded that monetarist analysis gives a better description of how aggregate spending is determined than does Keynesian analysis.

Several objections were raised against the Friedman-Meiselman evidence:

1. The standard criticisms of this reduced form evidence are the ones we have already discussed: Reverse causation could occur or a third factor might drive both series.

2. The test may not be fair because the Keynesian model has too simple a characterization. Keynesian structural models frequently include hundreds of equations. The one-equation Keynesian model that Friedman-Meiselman tested may not adequately capture the effects of autonomous expenditure. Furthermore, Keynesian models usually include the effects of other variables. By ignoring them, the effect of monetary policy might be overestimated, while the effect of autonomous expenditure is underestimated.

3. The Friedman-Meiselman measure of autonomous expenditure, A, might be constructed poorly preventing the Keynesian model from performing well. For example, orders for military hardware affect aggregate demand before they appear as spending in the autonomous expenditure variable that Friedman and Meiselman used. A more careful construction of the autonomous expenditure variable should take account of the placing of orders for military hardware. When the autonomous expenditure variable was constructed more carefully by critics of the Friedman-Meiselman study they found that the results were reversed: The Keynesian model won.[7] A more recent postmortem on the appropriateness of different ways of deter-

---

[6]Friedman and Meiselman did not actually run their tests using the Y variable because they felt that this gave an unfair advantage to the Keynesian model since A is included in Y. Instead, they subtracted off A from Y and tested for the correlation of $(Y - A)$ with M or A.

[7]See, for example, Albert Ando and Franco Modigliani, "The Relative Stability of Monetary Velocity and the Investment Multiplier," *American Economic Review* 55 (September 1965), pp. 693–728.

mining autonomous expenditure does not give a clear-cut victory to either the Keynesian or monetarist model.[8]

Historical Evidence

The monetarist historical evidence, found in the Friedman and Schwartz volume, *A Monetary History of the United States: 1867–1960,* has been very influential in gaining support for the monetarist position. You have already seen that the book was extremely important as a criticism of early Keynesian thinking, because it showed that the Great Depression was not a period of easy monetary policy; rather, the depression could be attributed to the sharp decline in the money supply from 1930 to 1933 resulting from bank panics. In addition, *A Monetary History* documents in great detail that the growth rate of money leads business cycles because it declines before every recession. This timing evidence is, of course, subject to all the criticisms raised earlier.

The historical evidence, however, contains one feature that makes it different from other monetarist evidence we have discussed so far. Several episodes occur in which changes in the money supply appear to be exogenous events. These episodes are almost like controlled experiments, so the *post hoc, ergo propter hoc* principle is far more likely to be valid: If the decline in the growth rate of the money supply is soon followed by a decline in output in these episodes, much stronger evidence is presented that money growth is the driving force behind the business cycle.

One of the best examples of such an episode is the increase in reserve requirements in 1936–1937 (discussed in Chapter 20) that led to a sharp decline in the money supply and in its rate of growth. The increase in reserve requirements was implemented because the Federal Reserve wanted to improve its control of monetary policy; it certainly was not implemented in response to economic conditions. We can thus rule out reverse causation from output to the money supply. Also, it is hard to think of a third factor that could have driven the Fed to increase reserve requirements and that could also have directly affected output. Therefore, the decline in the money supply in this episode can probably be classified as an exogenous event with the characteristics of a controlled experiment. Soon after this "controlled experiment," the very severe recession of 1937–1938 occurred. The conclusion: In this episode, the change in the money supply due to the Fed's increase in reserve requirements was indeed the source of the business cycle contraction that followed.

A Monetary History also documents other historical episodes, such as the banking panic in 1907 and other years in which the decline in money growth

---

[8]See William Poole and Edith Kornblith, "The Friedman-Meiselman CMC paper: New Evidence on an Old Controversy," *American Economic Review* 63 (December 1973), pp. 908–917.

again appears to be an exogenous event. The fact that recessions frequently followed apparently exogenous declines in money growth is very strong evidence that changes in the growth rate of the money supply do have an impact on aggregate output.

Overview of the Monetarist Evidence

Where does this discussion of the monetarist evidence leave us? You have seen that because of reverse causation and third factor possibilities, there are some serious doubts about the conclusions that can be drawn from timing and statistical evidence alone. However, some of the historical evidence in which exogenous declines in money growth are followed by business cycle contractions does provide stronger support for the monetarist position. When historical evidence is combined with timing and statistical evidence, the conclusion that money does, indeed, matter seems warranted.

As you can imagine, the economics profession was quite shaken by the appearance of the monetarist evidence, since up to that time the majority of the profession believed that money does not matter at all. Monetarists had demonstrated that this early Keynesian position was probably wrong, and it won them a lot of converts. Recognizing the falsehood of the position that money does not matter does not necessarily mean that we must accept the position that money is *all* that matters. Many Keynesian economists shifted their views toward the monetarist position, but did not shift them all the way. Instead, they adapted an intermediate position compatible with the Keynesian aggregate supply and demand analysis described in Chapter 26: They believed that money was extremely important, but that fiscal policy as well as net exports and "animal spirits" also contributed to fluctuations in aggregate demand.

Economic research went in two directions after the successful monetarist attack against the early Keynesian position. One direction was to improve on the Keynesian structural models. Two important lessons were learned from the monetarist evidence. One was the need to be very careful in specifying how fiscal policy variables affect economic activity in a Keynesian framework. An example is the use of orders for military hardware, rather than military spending figures, in evaluating the impact of fiscal policy on aggregate demand. The other lesson was that there were likely to be other channels of monetary influence on aggregate demand than merely interest rate effects on investment.

The monetarist evidence thus encouraged Keynesian economists to search for new channels of monetary influence. One leader in this movement was Nobel Prize winner Franco Modigliani of MIT, who in the late 1960s helped push forward the development of the structural model now used by the Federal Reserve Board to forecast economic activity and analyze policy. This model has been known as the FRB–MIT (Federal Reserve

Board–Massachusetts Institute of Technology) or more recently as the MPS (MIT–Penn–SSRC) model.

The second direction was to improve on the monetarist reduced form evidence by using more sophisticated reduced form models. Specifically, reduced form models were constructed that allowed for measurement of the relative impact of both monetary and fiscal policy, while allowing policies to affect economic activity with long lags. This research culminated in the St. Louis model, which was developed at the Federal Reserve Bank of St. Louis in the late 1960s and early 1970s.

MORE SOPHISTICATED MONETARIST EVIDENCE: ————————————— THE ST. LOUIS MODEL

In 1968, Leonall Andersen and Jerry Jordan, economists at the Federal Reserve Bank of St. Louis, published the first version of the St. Louis model.[9] Their intent was to test three commonly held Keynesian positions using a more sophisticated reduced form approach. These positions are that the response of economic activity to fiscal policy relative to monetary policy is (1) stronger, (2) more predictable, and (3) faster. Andersen and Jordan suggested the following reduced form model:

$$\Delta Y_t = f(\Delta M_t, \Delta M_{t-1}, \Delta M_{t-2}, \ldots, \Delta F_t, \Delta F_{t-1}, \Delta F_{t-2}, \ldots)$$

where ΔY_t = change in nominal aggregate spending at time t
$f(\ldots)$ = means that ΔY_t is a function of the variables inside the parentheses
ΔM_t = change in the money supply at time t
ΔF_t = change in fiscal policy at time t
$\Delta M_{t-i}, \Delta F_{t-i}$ = change in money supply and fiscal policy at time $t - i$, that is, i quarters earlier

This model is a variant of the Friedman-Meiselman approach, which allows for effects on aggregate spending from both monetary and fiscal policy simultaneously. In addition, the effects for both types of policy are not viewed as immediate, rather they can affect aggregate spending with some delay. When Andersen and Jordan estimated this model using several measures of fiscal policy, they found that the three Keynesian positions were not supported. Monetary policy, as represented by the change in the money supply, had (1) a more powerful impact, (2) a more predictable impact, and (3) a faster impact than fiscal policy.

————————
[9]Leonall Andersen and Jerry Jordan, "Monetary and Fiscal Actions: A Test of Their Relative Importance in Economic Stabilization," Federal Reserve Bank of St. Louis, *Review* 50 (November 1968), pp. 11–23.

The criticisms of this evidence are not different from those raised previously against the Friedman-Meiselman evidence. First is the objection that the causation might run from ΔY to ΔM rather than the other way around. Second, a third factor could be driving both ΔM and ΔY, so that changes in the money supply do not cause changes in aggregate spending. Third, the measures that Andersen and Jordan used to represent fiscal policy may not be accurate, which could lead to an understatement of the effect of fiscal policy. Fourth, the characterization of the effects of fiscal policy might be too simple. For example, Keynesian structural models allow for fiscal policy effects to differ depending on at what stage of the business cycle the policy is implemented. Fifth, there might be other variables left out of the model that, if included, would alter the estimates of the effectiveness of monetary policy versus fiscal policy.

At the same time, the St. Louis model does indicate that the monetarist statistical evidence holds up in a more sophisticated reduced form framework that includes the effects of both monetary and fiscal policy and allows these policies to affect economic activity with long lags. However, the criticisms of reduced form evidence in general are not resolved by the St. Louis approach.

THE SEARCH FOR NEW MONETARY TRANSMISSION MECHANISMS: THE MPS MODEL

The traditional Keynesian view of the monetary transmission mechanism can be characterized as follows:

$$M \uparrow \rightarrow i \downarrow \rightarrow I \uparrow \rightarrow Y \uparrow$$

However, as we have seen, the interest rate (i) effect on investment spending (I) is usually fairly small. We have mentioned that in response to monetarist evidence that money matters, many Keynesian economists began to search for new channels of monetary influence on economic activity. These transmission mechanisms, most of which are incorporated into Franco Modigliani's MPS model, a version of which is currently used for policy analysis by the Federal Reserve, fall into three categories: those operating through investment spending, through consumer expenditure, and through international trade.

Investment Spending

Because Keynes emphasized the role of investment in business cycle fluctuations, the earliest work on new monetary transmission mechanisms first focused on investment spending.

The Availability Hypothesis Starting in the late 1950s, economists began to recognize that interest rates may not fully represent the cost of financing investment spending. When monetary policy is restrictive, bankers might start to ration loans to their customers instead of allowing the interest rates on these loans to rise; that is, they would not make loans available at the stated interest rate. This phenomenon, which was described in Chapter 8, is known as *credit rationing*. An expansionary monetary policy might then increase the quantity of available loans, causing investment spending to rise, even though interest rates do not have much of a measurable decline. Schematically, the monetary policy effect is

$$M \uparrow \rightarrow \text{loans} \uparrow \rightarrow I \uparrow \rightarrow Y \uparrow$$

One way to look for this monetary transmission mechanism is to see whether there is a high correlation between investment spending and business loans. If you find that the correlation is high, would you necessarily conclude that the amount of loans outstanding is the driving force behind investment spending? You should have your doubts because of the reverse causation argument. The quantity of loans could rise because businesses want to invest more and thus demand more loans. As a result, causation could run from investment to loans rather than the other way around, and some economists have doubted the importance of the availability hypothesis for commercial (business) lending.

The availability hypothesis received far wider support in its application to the residential housing market of the 1960s. When market interest rates rose above the Regulation Q ceiling (which put a limit on the maximum interest rate that savings and loans, and mutual savings banks could pay on their deposits), these institutions began to lose deposits because of disintermediation (Chapter 13). Because banks issued most of the residential mortgages in the 1960s, the drop in their deposits reduced the availability of these mortgages. Potential home buyers could not then obtain mortgages and buy the house they wanted, and the demand for residential housing fell.

The sharp drop in housing purchases in 1966 and 1969, when market interest rates rose above Regulation Q ceilings, is consistent with the preceding analysis. Changes in the regulatory environment—the elimination of the Regulation Q ceilings and the entrance of other financial intermediaries into the residential mortgage market—have diminished the importance of this channel of monetary influence. Why? Because it is now less likely that disintermediation will occur, since mortgage-issuing institutions can pay higher interest on their deposits when market interest rates rise; therefore they do not lose deposits.

This is an excellent example of how an understanding of the workings of the mechanisms inside the black box can help predict how the effect of monetary policy might change when the institutional environment changes.

Tobin's q Theory Economists have suggested that monetary policy can also affect investment spending through its effect on the prices of common stock.

James Tobin developed a theory of the link between stock prices and investment spending, referred to as Tobin's q theory. Tobin defines q as follows:

$$q = \frac{\text{market value of firms}}{\text{replacement cost of capital}}$$

If q is high, the market price of firms is high relative to the replacement cost of capital, and new plant and equipment capital is cheap relative to the market value of business firms. Companies can then issue stock and get a high price for it relative to the cost of the plant and equipment they are buying. Thus investment spending will rise because firms can buy a lot of new investment goods with only a small issue of stock.

On the other hand, when q is low, firms will not purchase new investment goods because the market value of firms is low relative to the cost of capital. If companies want to acquire capital when q is low, they can buy another firm cheaply and acquire old capital instead. Investment spending, the purchase of new investment goods, will then be very low. The Tobin q theory gives a good explanation for the extremely low rate of investment spending during the Great Depression. In that period stock prices collapsed and by 1933 were worth only one-tenth of their value in late 1929; q fell to unprecedented low levels.

The crux of this discussion is that a link exists between Tobin's q and investment spending. But how might monetary policy affect stock prices? Quite simply, when money supply increases, the public finds it has more money than it wants and so gets rid of it through spending. One place the public spends is in the stock market, increasing the demand for stocks and consequently raising their prices.[10] Combining this with the fact that higher stock prices (P_s) will lead to a higher q and thus higher investment spending (I) leads to the following transmission mechanism of monetary policy:[11]

$$M \uparrow \rightarrow P_s \uparrow \rightarrow q \uparrow \rightarrow I \uparrow \rightarrow Y \uparrow$$

Asymmetric Information Effects   In our discussion of the impact of asymmetric information on financial markets in Chapter 8, we saw that the higher is the net worth of business firms, the less severe are adverse selection and moral hazard problems. Higher net worth means that lenders in effect have more collateral for their loans, and so losses from adverse selection are re-

---

[10]A somewhat more Keynesian story with the same outcome is that the increase in the money supply lowers interest rates on bonds so that the yields on alternatives to stocks fall. This makes stocks more attractive relative to bonds, so the demand for them increases, raises their price, and thereby lowers their yield.

[11]An alternative way of looking at the link between stock prices and investment spending is that higher stock prices lower the yield on stocks and reduce the cost of financing investment spending through issuing equity. This way of looking at the link between stock prices and investment spending is formally equivalent to the Tobin q approach; see Barry Bosworth, "The Stock Market and the Economy," *Brookings Papers on Economic Activity* 2 (1975), pp. 257–290.

duced. A rise in net worth, which reduces the adverse selection problem, thus encourages increased lending to finance investment spending. Higher net worth of business firms also reduces the moral hazard problem because it means that owners have a higher equity stake in their firms. With more of an equity stake in their firms, owners have less incentive to engage in risky investment projects or to spend the firms' funds on items that benefit them personally but that do not add to profits. Since taking on less risky investment projects and spending less for personal benefits make it more likely that lenders will be paid back, an increase in business firms' net worth leads to an increase in lending and hence in investment spending.

A rise in stock prices raises the net worth of firms and so leads to higher investment spending because of the reduction in adverse selection and moral hazard problems. Since, as we have noted, monetary policy affects stock prices, our asymmetric information analysis provides the following additional monetary transmission mechanism:

$$M \uparrow \rightarrow P_s \uparrow \rightarrow \text{adverse selection} \downarrow \rightarrow \text{loans} \uparrow \rightarrow I \uparrow \rightarrow Y \uparrow$$
$$\text{\& moral hazard} \downarrow$$

Consumer Expenditure

Monetarist reduced form evidence also suggests that there might be a more direct link between monetary policy and consumer expenditure. The earliest work along these lines focused on possible interest rate effects on one component of consumer spending, **consumer durable expenditure,** the spending by consumers on durable items such as automobiles and refrigerators.

Interest Rate Effects on Consumer Durable Expenditure Because consumer spending on durable items such as automobiles is often financed by borrowing, early Keynesian structural model builders looked for some effect of interest rates on consumer durable expenditure. They reasoned that lower interest rates, which lowered the cost of financing these purchases, would encourage consumers to increase their consumer durable expenditure. The resulting channel of monetary influence on aggregate demand is the following:

$$M \uparrow \rightarrow i \downarrow \rightarrow \text{consumer durable expenditure} \uparrow \rightarrow Y \uparrow$$

However, the size of this effect was found to be small. Some other channel of monetary influence on consumer spending was needed to explain why monetary policy might affect consumer expenditure.

Wealth Effects In their search for new monetary transmission mechanisms researchers looked at how the balance sheet of consumers might affect their spending decisions. Franco Modigliani was the first to take this tack, using his famous life-cycle hypothesis of consumption. **Consumption** is spending by consumers on nondurable goods and services.[12] It differs from consumer expenditure because it does not include spending on consumer durables. The basic premise of Modigliani's theory is that consumers smooth out their consumption over time. Therefore, what determines consumption spending is the lifetime resources of consumers, not just today's income. An important component of consumers' lifetime resources is financial wealth, a major component of which is common stocks. When stock prices rise, the value of financial wealth increases, thus increasing the lifetime resources of consumers, and consumption should rise. Since we have already seen that expansionary monetary policy can lead to a rise in stock prices, we then have another monetary transmission mechanism:

$$M \uparrow \rightarrow P_s \uparrow \rightarrow \text{wealth} \uparrow \rightarrow \text{lifetime resources} \uparrow \rightarrow \\ \text{consumption} \uparrow \rightarrow Y \uparrow$$

Modigliani's research has found this to be an extremely powerful mechanism, which adds substantially to the potency of monetary policy.[13]

Liquidity Effects   The stock market also affects consumer durable expenditure. The argument for this effect concentrates on the illiquid nature of consumer durables such as automobiles or household appliances. If all of a sudden you needed cash and tried to sell your consumer durables to raise it, you would expect to take a big loss, because you could not get their full value in a distress sale. In contrast, if you held financial assets (such as money in the bank, stocks, or bonds), you could easily sell them quickly for their full market value and raise the cash. Now ask yourself this question: If you expected to find yourself in financial distress, would you rather be holding illiquid consumer durables or more liquid financial assets? Naturally you would rather hold the financial assets. Therefore, if the possibility of financial distress increases, consumers will spend less on consumer durables; if the possibility of financial distress becomes less likely, consumers will spend more on consumer durables.

A consumer's balance sheet should be an important influence on his or her estimate of the likelihood of suffering financial distress. Specifically, when consumers have a lot of financial assets relative to their debts, their estimate of the probability of financial distress is low, and they will be more willing to purchase consumer durables. When stock prices rise, the value of financial assets rises as well; consumer durable expenditure will also rise, because consumers have a more secure financial position and a lower esti-

---

[12]Consumption also includes another small component which is the services that a consumer receives from the ownership of housing and consumer durables.

[13]See Franco Modigliani, "Monetary Policy and Consumption," in *Consumer Spending and Money Policy: The Linkages* (Federal Reserve Bank of Boston, 1971), pp. 9–84.

B o x   2 7 . 3

Consumers' Balance Sheets and the Great Depression

The years between 1929 and 1933 witnessed the worst deterioration in consumers' balance sheets ever seen in the United States. The stock market crash in 1929, which continued until 1933, reduced the value of consumers' wealth by $311 billion (1982 dollars) and, as expected, consumption dropped sharply (by over $70 billion). Because of the decline in the price level in that period, the level of real debt consumers owed also increased sharply (over 20%). The result: The value of financial assets relative to the amount of debt declined sharply, helping to add to the likelihood of financial

distress. Not surprisingly, spending for consumer durables and residential housing fell precipitously: From 1929 to 1933, consumer durable expenditure declined by over 50%, while expenditure on residential housing declined by 80%.*

---

*For a further discussion of the effect of consumers' balance sheets on spending during the Great Depression, see Frederic S. Mishkin, "The Household Balance Sheet and the Great Depression," *Journal of Economic History* 38 (December 1978), pp. 918–937.

mate of the likelihood of suffering financial distress. We now have another powerful transmission mechanism for monetary policy because of the link between money and stock prices:[14]

$$M \uparrow \rightarrow P_s \uparrow \rightarrow \text{value of financial assets} \uparrow \rightarrow \text{likelihood of financial distress} \downarrow \rightarrow \text{consumer durable expenditure} \uparrow \rightarrow Y \uparrow$$

The liquidity argument can also be applied to the demand for residential houses, because like consumer durables, they are very illiquid. A rise in stock prices, which improves the health of consumers' balance sheets, will lower the likelihood of financial distress and increase willingness of consumers to buy new houses. So another channel of monetary influence is

$$M \uparrow \rightarrow P_s \uparrow \rightarrow \text{value of financial assets} \uparrow \rightarrow \text{likelihood of financial distress} \downarrow \rightarrow \text{spending on new residential housing} \uparrow \rightarrow Y \uparrow$$

The three monetary transmission mechanisms suggest that monetary policy effects on consumers' balance sheets can have large effects on aggregate demand. One period where these effects might have been extremely important was during the Great Depression (see Box 27.3).

International Trade

With the growing internationalization of the economy and the advent of flexible exchange rates, an exchange rate effect on net exports has become an important monetary transmission mechanism.

---

[14]See Frederic S. Mishkin, "What Depressed the Consumer? The Household Balance Sheet and the 1973–1975 Recession," *Brookings Papers on Economic Activity* 1 (1977), pp. 123–164.

Exchange Rate Effect on Net Exports   As was discussed in more detail in Chapter 21, when domestic interest rates fall (with inflation unchanged), domestic deposits become less attractive relative to deposits denominated in foreign currencies. The result is a fall in the value of dollar deposits relative to other currency deposits, that is, a fall in the exchange rate (denoted by $E \downarrow$). The lower value of the domestic currency makes domestic goods cheaper than foreign goods, thereby causing a rise in net exports and hence in aggregate output. The monetary transmission mechanism operating through international trade is thus

$$M \uparrow \rightarrow i \downarrow \rightarrow E \downarrow \rightarrow NX \uparrow \rightarrow Y \uparrow$$

Effect of All the Monetary Transmission Mechanisms Combined

You have now seen that the search for additional channels of monetary influence has led to the discovery of many monetary transmission mechanisms (summarized in the schematic diagram in Figure 27.3).

Can the combined effect of all of these mechanisms produce a Keynesian structural model that indicates changes in the money supply have a major impact on aggregate spending and output? Modigliani's MPS model, which incorporates most of the mechanisms described, does just that. Figure 27.4 illustrates the response of aggregate spending (nominal GNP) to a decrease of $1 billion of demand deposits for the (Keynesian) MPS model and the (monetarist) St. Louis model. Notice that both models display a strong effect on aggregate spending from the change in the money supply.

OVERVIEW OF THE MONETARIST-KEYNESIAN DEBATE ON MONEY AND ECONOMIC ACTIVITY

The monetarist reduced form evidence presented a major challenge to the Keynesian view that money does not matter. This led to a more open-minded search for new monetary transmission mechanisms, and the result has been a convergence of the Keynesian and monetarist views (as seen in Figure 27.4) on the importance of money to economic activity. There is now general agreement among Keynesians that monetary policy is indeed an extremely important source of business cycle fluctuations. However, proponents of a new theory of aggregate fluctuations called the *real business cycle theory* do not accept the monetarist reduced form evidence that money is important to business cycle fluctuations because they believe there is reverse causation from the business cycle to money (Box 27.4).

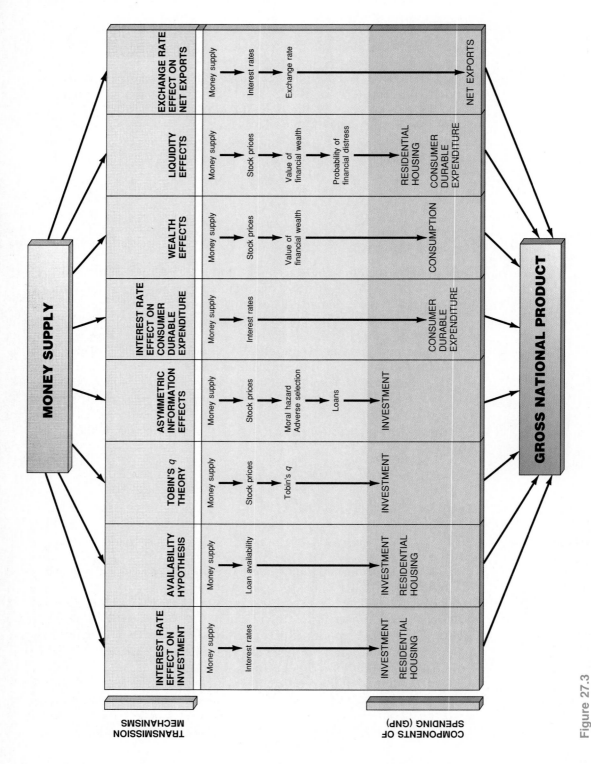

Figure 27.3
The Link Between Money and GNP: Monetary Transmission Mechanisms

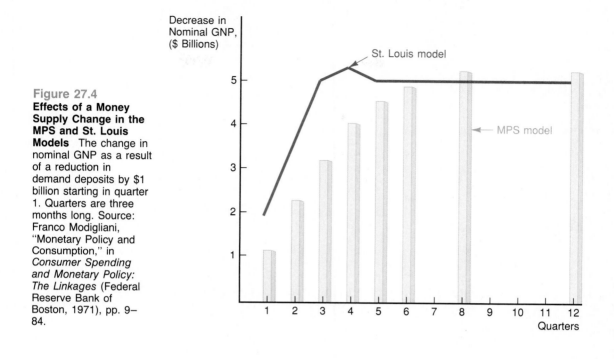

Figure 27.4
Effects of a Money Supply Change in the MPS and St. Louis Models The change in nominal GNP as a result of a reduction in demand deposits by $1 billion starting in quarter 1. Quarters are three months long. Source: Franco Modigliani, "Monetary Policy and Consumption," in *Consumer Spending and Monetary Policy: The Linkages* (Federal Reserve Bank of Boston, 1971), pp. 9–84.

B o x   2 7 . 4

Real Business Cycle Theory and the Debate on Money and Economic Activity

New entrants to the debate on money and economic activity are advocates of *real business cycle theory*. This theory states that real shocks to tastes and technology (rather than monetary shocks) are the driving forces behind business cycles. Proponents of this theory do not accept the monetarist view that money matters to business cycles, because they believe that the correlation of output with money reflects reverse causation; that is, it is the business cycle that drives money rather than the other way around. An important piece of evidence they offer to support the reverse causation argument is that almost none of the correlation between money and output comes from the monetary base, which is controlled by the monetary authorities.* Instead, the money-output correlation stems

from other sources of money supply movements that, as we saw in Chapters 15 and 16, are affected by the actions of banks, depositors, and borrowers from banks and that are more likely to be influenced by the business cycle.

Although real business cycle theory sees no role for money in the business cycle, it does view money as an important determinant of inflation. Thus monetary policy still plays a crucial role in the economy.

Robert King and Charles Plosser, "Money, Credit and Prices in a Real Business Cycle," *American Economic Review* 74 (June 1984), pp. 363–380.

Figure 27.5
Effects of a Government Expenditure Change in the MPS and St. Louis Models: Response of Nominal GNP to a $1 Billion Increase in Government Expenditure Sources: See Figure 27.4 and L. Anderson and K. Carlson, "A Monetarist Model for Economic Stabilization," Federal Reserve Bank of St. Louis, *Review* (April 1980), pp. 7–25.

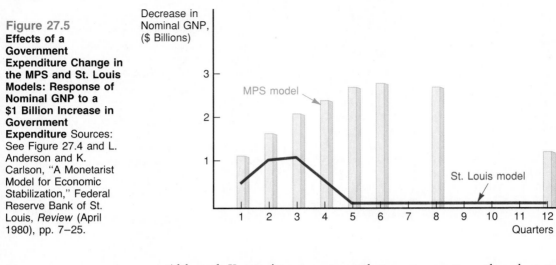

Although Keynesians now agree that money matters, they do not agree with the monetarist statement that money is *all* that matters. Their structural models still provide strong evidence that fiscal policy has powerful effects. This can be seen in Figure 27.5, which shows a large response of output to an increase of $1 billion of government spending for the MPS model, but only a small response for the St. Louis model. Reduced form evidence and structural model evidence, then, do not yield similar conclusions on the effectiveness of fiscal policy, and so the monetarist-Keynesian debate on the determinants of aggregate demand is not yet fully resolved.

SUMMARY

1. Monetarists tend to focus on reduced form evidence and find that changes in the money supply are more important to economic activity than do Keynesians, who focus on structural model evidence. There is no clear-cut case to be made that one type of evidence is preferred: Both have their advantages and disadvantages. The main advantage of structural model evidence is that it provides us with an understanding of how the economy works and gives us more confidence in the direction of causation between money and output. However, if the structure is not correctly specified because it ignores important monetary transmission mechanisms, it could seriously underestimate the effectiveness of monetary policy. Reduced form evidence has the advantage of not restricting the way monetary policy affects economic activity and so may be more likely to capture the full effects of monetary policy. However, reduced form evidence cannot rule out the possibility of reverse causation or a third driving factor, which could lead to misleading conclusions about the importance of money.

2. The early Keynesians believed that money does not matter because they found weak links between interest rates and investment, and because low interest rates on Treasury securities convinced them that monetary policy was "easy" during the worst economic contraction in U.S. history, the Great Depression. Monetarists objected to this interpretation of the evidence on the grounds that (1) the focus on nominal rather than real interest rates may have obscured any link between interest rates and investment, (2) interest rate effects on investment might be only one of many channels through which mone-

tary policy affects aggregate demand, and (3) by the standards of real interest rates and interest rates on lower grade bonds, monetary policy was extremely contractionary during the Great Depression.

3. Early monetarist evidence falls into three categories: timing, statistical, and historical. Because of reverse causation and third-factor possibilities, some serious doubts exist regarding conclusions that can be drawn from timing and statistical evidence alone. However, some of the historical evidence in which exogenous declines in money growth are followed by recessions provides stronger support for the monetarist position that money matters.

4. The monetarist evidence stimulated two directions of empirical research. One direction, represented by the St. Louis model, improved on the monetarist reduced form evidence by using more sophisticated reduced form models. The second direction, represented by Modigliani's MPS model, improved upon the Keynesian structural models by searching for new monetary transmission mechanisms, which include the availability thesis, Tobin's q theory, asymmetric information effects, interest rate effects on consumer durable expenditure, wealth effects, liquidity effects, and exchange rate effects on net exports.

5. As a result of empirical research, there has been a convergence of Keynesian and monetarist opinion to the view that money does matter. However, Keynesians do not agree with the monetarist position that money is *all* that matters.

KEY TERMS

structural model
  evidence

reduced form evidence

transmission
  mechanisms
  of monetary policy

structural model

reverse causation

consumer durable
  expenditure

consumption

QUESTIONS AND PROBLEMS

1. Suppose that a researcher is trying to determine whether jogging is good for your health. She examines this question in two ways. In method A she looks to see whether joggers live longer than nonjoggers. In method B she looks to see whether jogging reduces cholesterol in the bloodstream and lowers blood pressure; then she asks whether lower cholesterol and blood pressure prolong life. Which of these two methods will produce reduced form evidence and which produces structural model evidence?

2. If research indicates that joggers do not have lower cholesterol and blood pressure than nonjoggers, is it still possible that jogging is good for your health? Give a concrete example.

3. If research indicates that joggers live longer than nonjoggers, is it possible that jogging is not good for your health? Give a concrete example.

* 4. Suppose you plan to buy a car and want to know whether a General Motors car is more reliable than a Ford. One way to find out is to ask owners of both cars how often their cars go into the shop for repairs. The other way is to visit the factory producing the cars and see which one is built better. Which procedure will provide reduced form evidence and which structural model evidence?

* 5. If the GM car you plan to buy has a better repair record than a Ford, does this mean that the GM car is necessarily more reliable? (GM car owners might, for example, change their oil more frequently than Ford owners.)

* 6. Suppose when you visit the Ford and GM car

factories to examine how the cars are built, you only have time to see how well the engine is put together. If Ford engines are better built than GM engines, does that mean that the Ford will be more reliable than the GM car?

7. How might bank behavior (described in Chapter 16) lead to causation running from output to the money supply? What does this say about evidence that finds a strong correlation between money and output?

* 8. What operating procedures of the Fed (described in Chapter 20) might explain how movements in output might cause movements in the money supply?

9. "In every business cycle in the last hundred years, the rate at which the money supply is growing always decreases before output does. Therefore, the money supply causes business cycle movements." Do you agree? What objections can you raise against this argument?

*10. How did the research strategies of Keynesian and monetarist economists differ after they were exposed to the earliest monetarist evidence?

11. In the 1973–1975 recession, the value of common stocks in real terms fell by nearly 50%. How might this decline in the stock market have affected aggregate demand and thus contributed to the severity of this recession? Be specific about the mechanisms through which the stock market decline affected the economy.

*12. Answer true, false, or uncertain: "The cost of financing investment is related only to interest rates. Therefore, the only way that monetary policy can affect investment spending is through its effects on interest rates."

13. Predict what will happen to stock prices if the money supply rises. Explain why you are making this prediction.

*14. Franco Modigliani has found that the most important transmission mechanisms of monetary policy involve consumer expenditure. Describe how at least two of these mechanisms work.

15. "The monetarists have demonstrated that the early Keynesians were wrong in saying that money doesn't matter at all to economic activity. Therefore we should accept the monetarist position that money is all that matters." Do you agree? Why or why not?

CHAPTER 28

Money and Inflation

Since the early 1960s when the inflation rate hovered between 1% and 2%, the economy has suffered from higher and more variable rates of inflation. By the late 1960s, the inflation rate climbed to over 5%, and by 1974, it reached the double-digit level. After moderating somewhat during the 1975–1978 period, it skyrocketed above 10% in 1979 and 1980, only to slow down to around the 5% level from 1982 to 1990. Inflation, the condition of a continually rising price level, has become a major concern of politicians and the public, and how to control it frequently dominates the discussion of economic policy.

How do we prevent the inflationary fire from igniting and stop the roller coaster ride in the inflation rate of the past thirty years? Milton Friedman provides an answer in his famous proposition, "Inflation is always and everywhere a monetary phenomenon." He postulates that the source of all inflations is a high growth rate of the money supply: Simply by reducing the growth rate of the money supply to low levels, inflation can be prevented.

In this chapter we use the aggregate demand and supply analysis (Chapter 26) to understand the role of monetary policy in creating inflation. You will find that as long as inflation is defined to be a condition of a continually, rapidly rising price level, monetarists and Keynesians both agree with Friedman's proposition that inflation is a monetary phenomenon.

But what *causes* inflation? Why does an inflationary monetary policy occur? You will see that inflationary monetary policy is an offshoot of other government policies: the attempt to hit high employment targets or the running of large budget deficits. Understanding how these policies lead to inflation will provide us with some idea of how to prevent it at a minimum cost in terms of unemployment and output loss.

MONEY AND INFLATION: THE EVIDENCE

The evidence for Friedman's statement is straightforward. ***In every case in which a country's inflation rate is extremely high for any sustained period of time, its rate of money supply growth is extremely high.***

Consider the inflation experienced in Latin America from 1980 to 1990: A popular belief exists that something structural in the Latin American economies (militant labor unions, unstable political systems) causes high inflation. In reality, inflation experience in Latin America is varied; some Latin American countries, such as Honduras, have had average annual inflation rates below 10% during this period, while others, such as Argentina, Brazil, and Peru, have suffered from inflation rates exceeding 200%.

Box 28.1, which plots the inflation rates for Latin American countries against the growth rates of their money supplies, reveals that the countries with very high inflation also have the highest rates of money growth. Evidence for the Latin American countries as well as other countries throughout the world (Figure 1.2 in Chapter 1) seems to support the proposition that extremely high inflation is the result of a high rate of money growth. Keep in mind, however, that you are looking at reduced form evidence, which focuses solely on the correlation of two variables: money growth and the inflation rate. As with all reduced form evidence, reverse causation (inflation causing money supply growth) or a third factor that drives both money growth and inflation could be present.

How might you rule out these possibilities? First, you might look for historical episodes in which an increase in money growth appears to be an exogenous event; then a high inflation rate for a sustained period following the increase in money growth would provide strong evidence that high money growth is the driving force behind the inflation. Luckily, such clear-cut historical episodes—hyperinflations (extremely rapid inflations with inflation rates exceeding 50% per month)—do exist. The most notorious example is the German hyperinflation in 1921–1923.

The German Hyperinflation: 1921–1923

The German hyperinflation started in 1921 when the need to make reparations and reconstruct the economy after World War I caused government expenditures to greatly exceed revenues. The German government could have raised revenues to pay for this increased expenditure by raising taxes, but this solution was, as always, politically unpopular and would have taken much time to implement. The government could also have financed the expenditure by borrowing from the public, but the amount needed was far in excess of its capacity to borrow. There was only one route left: the printing press. The government could pay for its expenditures simply by printing more currency (increasing the money supply) and using it to make payments to those individuals and companies that were providing it with goods and services. As shown in Figure 28.1, this is exactly what the German government did; in late 1921, the money supply began to grow rapidly and so did the price level.

In 1923, the budgetary situation of the German government deteriorated even further. In early 1923 the French invaded the Ruhr because Germany failed to make its scheduled reparations payments. A general

B o x   2 8 . 1   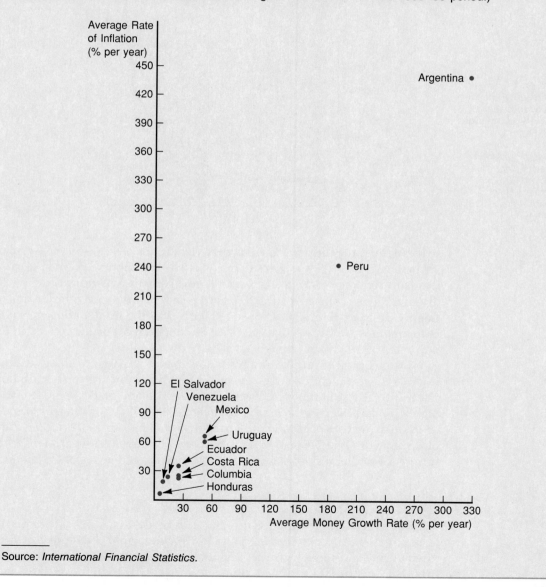   **A Global Perspective**

Inflation and Money Growth Rates in Latin America: 1980–1990

This graph plots for a group of Latin American countries the average inflation rate over the ten-year period 1980–1990 against the average money growth rate over the same period (at an annual rate in percent). It demonstrates that high inflation in these countries is generally associated with a high rate of money growth. (Countries such as Brazil, Chile, Nicaragua, and Bolivia do not appear in the graph because their data were unavailable for the entire 1980–90 period.)

Source: *International Financial Statistics*.

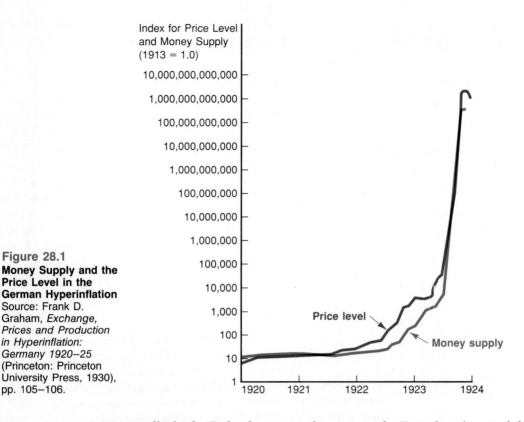

Figure 28.1
**Money Supply and the
Price Level in the
German Hyperinflation**
Source: Frank D.
Graham, *Exchange,
Prices and Production
in Hyperinflation:
Germany 1920–25*
(Princeton: Princeton
University Press, 1930),
pp. 105–106.

strike in the Ruhr then ensued to protest the French action, and the German government actively supported this "passive resistance" by making payments to striking workers. As a result, government expenditures climbed dramatically and the government printed currency at an even faster rate to finance this spending. As displayed in Figure 28.1 the result of the explosion in the money supply was that the price level blasted off, leading to an inflation rate for 1923 that exceeded 1,000,000%.

The invasion of the Ruhr and the printing of currency to pay striking workers fit the characteristics of an exogenous event. Reverse causation (meaning the rise in the price level caused the French to invade the Ruhr) is highly implausible, and it is hard to imagine a third factor that could have been a driving force behind both inflation and explosion in the money supply. Therefore, the German hyperinflation is a "controlled experiment" that supports Friedman's proposition that inflation is a monetary phenomenon.

Recent Examples of Rapid Inflation

Although recent rapid inflations are not as dramatic as the German hyperinflation, many countries in the 1980s experienced rapid inflations in which the high rates of money growth can also be classified as exogenous events. Box 28.1 illustrates that of all Latin American countries in the decade from

1980 to 1990, Argentina had both the highest rate of money growth and the highest average inflation rates. Indeed, the inflation problem in Argentina worsened later in the decade, with the inflation rate rising above 10,000%. [Bolivia had an even higher inflation rate in 1985 (see Chapter 30, Box 30.2) but it is not included in the group of countries in Box 28.1 because Bolivian data on money growth and inflation were not available for the entire 1980–1990 period.] The explanation for the high rate of money growth is similar to the explanation for Germany during its hyperinflation: The unwillingness of Argentina to finance its government expenditures by raising taxes led to large budget deficits (sometimes over 15% of GNP), which were financed by money creation.

That the inflation rate is high in all cases in which the high rate of money growth can be classified as an exogenous event (including episodes in Argentina and in Germany) is strong evidence that high money growth causes high inflation.

THE MEANING OF "INFLATION"

You may have noticed that all the empirical evidence on the relationship of money growth and inflation discussed so far looks only at cases in which the price level is continually rising at a rapid rate. It is this definition of the word *inflation* that Friedman and other economists use when they make statements such as "Inflation is always and everywhere a monetary phenomenon." This is not what your friendly newscaster means when she reports the monthly inflation rate on the nightly news. She is only telling you how much, in percentage terms, the price level has changed from the previous month. For example, when you hear that the monthly inflation rate is 1% (12% annual rate), this merely indicates that the price level has risen by 1% in that month. This could be a one-shot change, in which the high inflation rate is merely temporary, not sustained. Only if the inflation rate remains high for a substantial period of time (greater than 1% per month for several years) will economists say that inflation has been high.

Accordingly, Milton Friedman's proposition actually says that upward movements in the price level are a monetary phenomenon *only* if the upward movement is a continuing process. Be careful about defining the word *inflation,* because with it defined to be a continuing, rapidly rising price level, most economists, whether monetarist or Keynesian, agree with Friedman's proposition.

VIEWS OF INFLATION

Now that you understand what Milton Friedman's proposition means, we can use the aggregate supply and demand analysis learned in Chapter 26 to show that large continuing upward movements in the price level (high inflation) can only occur if there is a continually increasing money supply.

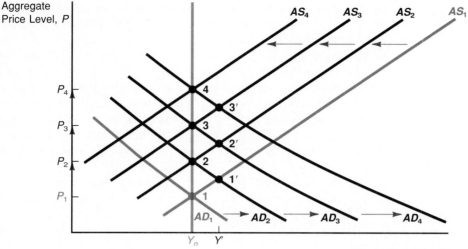

Figure 28.2

Response to a Continually Rising Money Supply   The continually rising money supply shifts the aggregate demand curve to the right from AD_1 to AD_2 to AD_3 to AD_4, while the supply curve shifts in from AS_1 to AS_2 to AS_3 to AS_4. The result is that the price level rises continually from P_1 to P_2 to P_3 to P_4.

The Monetarist View

First, let us look at the outcome of a continually increasing money supply using monetarist analysis (Figure 28.2). Initially, the economy is at point 1 with output at the natural rate level and the price level at P_1 (the intersection of the aggregate demand curve, AD_1 and the aggregate supply curve, AS_1). If the money supply increases steadily in the course of the year, the aggregate demand curve shifts right to AD_2. At first, for a very brief time, the economy may move to point 1' and output may increase above the natural rate level to Y', but the resulting decline in unemployment below the natural rate level will cause wages to rise and the aggregate supply curve will quickly begin to shift in. It will stop shifting only when it reaches AS_2, at which time the economy has returned to the natural rate level of output on the long-run aggregate supply curve.[1] At the new equilibrium, point 2, the price level has increased from P_1 to P_2.

   If the money supply increases the next year, the aggregate demand curve will shift to the right again to AD_3 and the aggregate supply curve will

<hr />

[1] In monetarist analysis, the aggregate supply curve may immediately shift in toward AS_2 because workers and firms may expect the increase in the money supply, so that expected inflation will be higher. In this case, the movement to point 2 will be very rapid, and output need not rise above the natural rate level. (Chapter 30 discusses how the theory of rational expectations provides further support for this scenario.)

shift in from AS_2 to AS_3; the economy will then move to point 2' and then 3, where the price level has risen to P_3. If the money supply continues to grow in subsequent years, the economy will continue to move to higher and higher price levels. As long as the money supply grows, this process will continue and inflation will occur.

Do monetarists believe that a continually rising price level can be due to any other source besides money supply growth? The answer is "no." In monetarist analysis, the money supply is viewed as the only source of shifts in the aggregate demand curve, so there is nothing else that can move the economy from points 1 to 2 to 3 and beyond. ***Monetarist analysis indicates that rapid inflation must be driven by high money supply growth.***

The Keynesian View

Keynesian analysis indicates that the continually increasing money supply will have the same effect on the aggregate demand and supply curves that we see in Figure 28.2; the aggregate demand curve will keep on shifting to the right and the aggregate supply curve will keep shifting inward.[2] The conclusion is the same one the monetarists find: A rapidly growing money supply will cause the price level to rise continually at a high rate, thus generating an inflation.

Could a factor other than money generate high inflation in the Keynesian analysis? The answer is "no." This result probably surprises you, since in Chapter 26 you learned that Keynesian analysis allows other factors besides changes in the money supply to affect the aggregate demand and supply curves (such as fiscal policy and supply shocks). To see why Keynesians also view high inflation as a monetary phenomenon, let's examine whether their analysis allows other factors to generate high inflation in the absence of a high rate of money growth.

Can Fiscal Policy by Itself Produce Inflation? To examine this question let us look at Figure 28.3, which demonstrates the effect of a one-shot permanent increase in government expenditure (say, from $500 billion to $600 billion) on aggregate output and the price level. Initially we are at point 1, where output is at the natural rate level and the price level is P_1. The increase in government expenditure shifts the aggregate demand curve out to AD_2 and we move to point 1', where output is above the natural rate level at $Y_{1'}$. The aggregate supply curve will begin to shift inward, eventually reaching AS_2, where it intersects the aggregate demand curve AD_2 at point 2, at which output is again at the natural rate level and the price level has risen to P_2.

---

[2]The only difference in the two analyses is that Keynesians believe that the aggregate supply curve would shift in more slowly than do monetarists. Thus Keynesian analysis suggests that output might tend to stay above the natural rate longer than monetarist analysis does.

Figure 28.3
Response to a One-Shot Permanent Increase in Government Expenditure The one-shot permanent increase in government expenditure shifts the aggregate demand curve out from AD_1 to AD_2, moving the economy from point 1 to point 1'. Because output now exceeds the natural rate level Y_n, the aggregate supply curve eventually shifts in to AS_2 and the price level rises from P_1 to P_2, a one-shot permanent increase, but not a continuing increase.

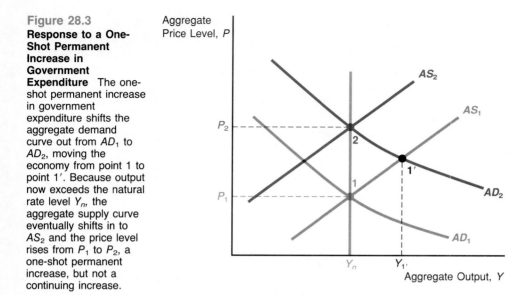

The net result of a one-shot permanent increase in government expenditure is a one-shot permanent increase in the price level. What happens to the inflation rate? When we move from point 1 to 1' to 2, the price level rises and we have a positive inflation rate. But when we finally get to point 2, the inflation rate returns to 0. We see that the one-shot increase in government expenditure leads to only a *temporary* increase in the inflation rate, not to an inflation in which the price level is continually rising.

If, however, government spending increased continually, we *could* get a continuing rise in the price level. It appears, then, that Keynesian analysis could reject the Friedman proposition that inflation is always a result of money growth. The problem with this argument is that a continually increasing level of government expenditure is not a feasible policy. There is a limit on the total amount of possible government expenditure; the government cannot spend more than 100% of GNP. In fact, well before this limit is reached, the political process would stop the increases in government spending. As revealed in the continual debates in Congress over balanced budgets and government spending, both the public and politicians have a particular target level of government spending they deem appropriate; although small deviations from this level might be tolerated, large deviations would not. Indeed, public and political perceptions impose tight limits on the degree to which government expenditures can increase.

What about the other side of fiscal policy, taxes? Could continual tax cuts generate an inflation? Again the answer is "no." The analysis in Figure 28.3 also describes the price and output response to a one-shot decrease in taxes. There will be a one-shot increase in the price level, but the increase in the inflation rate will be only temporary. We can increase the price level by

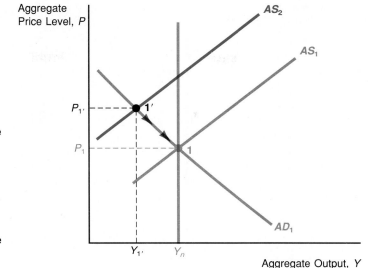

Figure 28.4
Response to a Supply Shock   A negative supply shock (or a wage push) shifts the aggregate supply curve in to AS_2 and results in high unemployment at point 1'. As a result the aggregate supply curve shifts back out to AS_1 and the economy returns to point 1, where the price level has returned to P_1.

cutting taxes even more, but this process would have to stop—when taxes are at zero, they can't be reduced further. We must conclude, then, that ***Keynesian analysis indicates that high inflation cannot be driven by fiscal policy alone.***[3]

Can Supply-Side Phenomena by Themselves Produce Inflation?   Since supply shocks and workers' attempts to increase their wages can shift the aggregate supply curve inward, you might suspect that these supply-side phenomena by themselves could stimulate inflation. Again, we can show that this suspicion is incorrect.

Suppose that there is a negative supply shock—for example, an oil embargo—that raises oil prices (or workers could have successfully pushed up their wages). As displayed in Figure 28.4, the negative supply shock shifts in the aggregate supply curve from AS_1 to AS_2. If the money supply remains unchanged, leaving the aggregate demand curve at AD_1, we move to point 1', where output is below the natural rate level ($Y_{1'}$) and the price level is higher ($P_{1'}$). The aggregate supply curve will now shift back out to AS_1, because unemployment is above the natural rate, and the economy slides down AD_1 from point 1' to point 1. The net result of the supply shock is that

---

[3]The argument here demonstrates that "animal spirits" also cannot be the source of inflation. Although consumer and business optimism which stimulates their spending can produce a one-shot shift in the aggregate demand curve and a *temporary* inflation, it cannot produce continuing shifts in the aggregate demand curve and inflation in which the price level continually rises. The reasoning is the same as that above: Consumers and businesses cannot continue to raise their spending without limit because their spending cannot exceed 100% of GNP.

we return to full employment at the initial price level and an inflation does not result. Additional negative supply shocks that again shift the aggregate supply curve inward will lead to the same outcome: The price level will temporarily rise, but inflation will not result. The conclusion we have reached is the following: ***Supply-side phenomena can also not be the source of high inflation.***[4]

Summary   Our aggregate demand and supply analysis shows that Keynesian and monetarist views of the inflation process are not very different. Both believe that high inflation can occur only with a high rate of money growth. Recognizing that by inflation we mean a continuing increase in the price level at a rapid rate, most economists agree with Milton Friedman that "inflation is always and everywhere a monetary phenomenon."

WHY DOES INFLATIONARY MONETARY POLICY OCCUR? _____

Although we now know *what* must occur to generate a rapid inflation—a high rate of money growth—we still don't know *why* high inflation occurs until we understand why inflationary monetary policies occur. If everyone agrees that inflation is not a good thing for an economy, why do we see so much of it? Why do governments pursue inflationary monetary policies? Since there is nothing intrinsically desirable about inflation and since we know that a high rate of money growth doesn't happen of its own accord, it must follow that in trying to achieve other goals, governments end up with a high money growth rate and high inflation. In this section we will examine the government policies that are the most common sources of inflation.

High Employment Targets and Inflation

The first goal most governments pursue that often results in inflation is high employment. The U.S. government is committed by law (the Employment Act of 1946 and the Humphrey-Hawkins Act of 1978) to promoting high employment. While it is true that both laws require a commitment to a high level of employment consistent with a stable price level, in practice our government has often pursued a high employment target with little concern about the inflationary consequences of its policies. This was true especially in the mid-1960s and 1970s when the government began to take a more active role in attempting to stabilize unemployment.

----

[4]Supply-side phenomena, which alter the natural rate level of output (and shift the long-run aggregate supply curve at Y_n), can produce a permanent one-shot change in the price level. However, this resulting one-shot change results in only a *temporary* inflation, not a continuing rise in the price level.

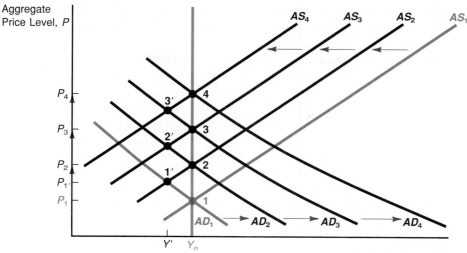

Figure 28.5
Cost-Push Inflation with an Activist Policy to Promote High Employment In a cost-push inflation the inward shifts of the aggregate supply curve from AS_1 to AS_2 to AS_3 and so on cause a government with a high employment target to shift the aggregate demand curve to the right continually to keep unemployment and output at their natural rate levels. The result is a continuing rise in the price level from P_1 to P_2 to P_3 and so on.

There are two types of inflation that can result from an activist stabilization policy to promote high employment: a **cost-push inflation,** which occurs because of negative supply shocks or a push by workers to get higher wages, and a **demand-pull inflation,** which results when policymakers pursue policies that shift out the aggregate demand curve. We will now use our aggregate demand and supply analysis to examine how a high employment target can lead to cost-push and demand-pull inflations.

Cost-Push Inflation In Figure 28.5 the economy is initially at point 1, the intersection of the aggregate demand curve AD_1 and the aggregate supply curve AS_1. Suppose workers decide to raise wages either because (1) they want to increase their real wages (wages in terms of the goods and services they can buy), or (2) they expect inflation to be high and so they demand and get increases in their wages in order to keep up with inflation. The effect of such an increase (similar to a negative supply shock) is to shift the aggregate supply curve in to AS_2.[5] If government fiscal and monetary policy remains unchanged, the economy would move to point $1'$ at the intersection of the

---

[5]The cost-push inflation we describe here might also occur as a result of firms' attempts to get higher prices or negative supply shocks.

new aggregate supply curve AS_2 and the aggregate demand curve AD_1. Output would decline to below its natural rate level (Y'), while the price level would rise to $P_{1'}$.

What would activist policymakers with a high employment target do if this situation developed? Because of the drop in output and resulting increase in unemployment, they would implement policies to raise the aggregate demand curve to AD_2 so that we would return to the natural rate level of output at point 2 and price level P_2. The workers who have raised their wages have not fared too badly. The government has stepped in to make sure that there is no excessive unemployment and they have achieved their goal of higher wages. Because the government has, in effect, given in to the demands of workers for higher wages, an activist policy with a high employment target is often referred to as an **accommodating policy.**

The workers, having eaten their cake and had it too, might be encouraged to raise their wages again. In addition, other workers might now realize that their wages have fallen relative to their fellow workers, and because they don't want to be left behind, these workers will raise *their* wages. The result—the aggregate supply curve shifts in again to AS_3. Unemployment develops again when we move to point $2'$, and the activist policies will once more be used to shift the aggregate demand curve out to AD_3 and return the economy to full employment at a price level of P_3. If this process continues, the result will be a continuing increase in the price level, that is, a cost-push inflation.

What role does monetary policy play in a cost-push inflation? A cost-push inflation can only occur if the aggregate demand curve is shifted out continually. In Keynesian analysis, the first shift of the aggregate demand curve to AD_2 could certainly be achieved by a one-shot increase in government expenditure or a one-shot decrease in taxes. But what about the next required outward shift of the aggregate demand curve to AD_3, and the next, and the next? The limits on the maximum level of government expenditure and the minimum level of taxes would prevent the use of this expansionary fiscal policy for very long. Thus it cannot be used to continually shift out the aggregate demand curve. On the other hand, the aggregate demand curve *can* be shifted out continually by continually increasing the money supply; that is, by going to a higher rate of money growth. Therefore, *a cost-push inflation is also a monetary phenomenon because it cannot occur without the accommodating policy of an acquiescence by the monetary authorities to a higher rate of money growth.*

Demand-Pull Inflation There is another way that the goal of high employment can lead to inflationary monetary policy. Even at full employment, unemployment is always present because of frictions in the labor market, which make it difficult to match workers with employers. An unemployed auto worker in Detroit may not know about a job opening in the electronics industry in California and, even if he did, may not want to move or be re-

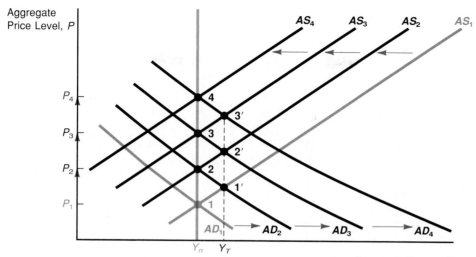

Figure 28.6
Demand-Pull Inflation: The Consequence of Setting Too Low an Unemployment Target
Too low an unemployment target (too high an output target of Y_T) causes the government to
shift out the aggregate demand curve from AD_1 to AD_2 to AD_3 and so on, while the
aggregate supply curve shifts in from AS_1 to AS_2 to AS_3 and so on. The result is a
continuing rise in the price level known as a demand-pull inflation.

trained. So the unemployment rate when there is full employment (the natural rate of unemployment) will be greater than zero. If policymakers set a
target for unemployment that is too low because it is less than the natural
rate of unemployment, this can set the stage for a higher rate of money
growth and a resulting inflation. Again we can show how this can happen
using an aggregate supply and demand diagram (Figure 28.6).

If policymakers have an unemployment target (say, at 4%) which is
below the natural rate (estimated to be around 6% currently), then they will
try to achieve an output target greater than the natural rate level of output.
This target level of output is marked as Y_T in Figure 27.6. Suppose that we
are initially at point 1; the economy is at the natural rate level of output, but
is below the target level of output, Y_T. In order to hit the unemployment
target of 4%, policymakers enact policies to increase aggregate demand, and
the effects of these policies shift the aggregate demand curve until it reaches
AD_2 and the economy moves to point 1'. Output is at Y_T, and the 4% unemployment rate goal has been reached.

If the targeted unemployment rate was at the natural rate level of 6%,
there would be no problem. However, since at Y_T the 4% unemployment
rate is below the natural rate level, wages will rise and the aggregate supply
curve will shift in to AS_2, moving the economy from point 1' to point 2. The
economy is back at the 6% natural rate of unemployment but at a higher

price level of P_2. We could stop there, but because unemployment is again higher than the target level, policymakers would shift out the aggregate demand curve again to AD_3 to hit the output target at point 2′, and the whole process would continue to drive the economy to point 3 and beyond. The overall result? A steadily rising price level, an inflation.

How will policymakers be able to continually shift the aggregate demand curve outward? You have already seen that they cannot do it through fiscal policy because of the limits on raising government expenditures and reducing taxes. Instead they will have to resort to expansionary monetary policy: that is, a continuing increase in the money supply and hence a high money growth rate.

Pursuing too high an output target, or equivalently, too low an unemployment rate, is the source of inflationary monetary policy in this situation, but it seems senseless for policymakers to do this. They have not gained the "good" of a permanently higher level of output but have generated the "bad" of an inflation. If, however, they do not realize that the target rate of unemployment is below the natural rate, the process that we see in Figure 28.6 will be well under way before they realize their mistake.

Since the inflation described results from policymakers pursuing policies that shift the aggregate demand curve out, it is called a demand-pull inflation. In contrast, a cost-push inflation occurs when workers push up their wages. Is it easy to distinguish between them in practice? The answer is "no." We have seen that both types of inflation will be associated with higher money growth, so we cannot distinguish them on this basis. Yet, as Figures 28.5 and 28.6 demonstrate, a demand-pull inflation will be associated with periods when unemployment is below the natural rate level, while a cost-push inflation is associated with periods when unemployment is above the natural rate level. In order to decide which type of inflation has occurred we can look at whether unemployment has been above or below its natural rate level. This would be easy if economists and policymakers actually knew how to measure the natural rate of unemployment, but unfortunately this very difficult research question is still not fully resolved by the economics profession. In addition, the distinction between a cost-push and demand-pull inflation is blurred, because a cost-push inflation can be initiated by a demand-pull inflation. When a demand-pull inflation produces higher inflation rates, expected inflation will eventually rise and cause workers to demand higher wages so that their real wages do not fall. Thus, eventually, the demand-pull inflation can trigger a cost-push inflation.

Budget Deficits and Inflation

Our discussion of the evidence on money and inflation suggested that another possible source of inflationary monetary policy is budget deficits. In Chapter 18 you learned that the government can finance its budget deficits in either one of two ways: by selling bonds to the public or by money creation, also called "printing money" (in the United States this is done by Treasury sales of bonds to the public which are then bought by the Fed). Selling bonds to the public has no direct effect on the monetary base (and therefore on the money supply), so it will have no obvious effect on aggregate demand and should have no inflationary consequences. On the other hand, money creation *does* have an impact on aggregate demand and can create inflation.

In our earlier analyses you saw that inflation can develop only when the stock of money grows continually. Can a budget deficit financed by printing money do this? The answer is "yes," if the budget deficit persists for a substantial period of time. In the first period, if the deficit is financed by money creation, the money supply will rise, shifting the aggregate demand curve to the right, and leading to a rise in the price level (Figure 28.2). If the budget deficit is still present in the next period, it has to be financed all over again. The money supply will rise again and the aggregate demand curve will again shift out to the right, causing the price level to rise further. As long as the deficit persists and the government resorts to printing money to pay for it, this process will continue. ***Financing a persistent deficit by money creation will lead to a sustained inflation.***

A critical element in this process is that the deficit is persistent. If temporary, it would not produce an inflation because the situation would then be similar to Figure 28.3, in which there is a one-shot increase in government expenditure. In the period when the deficit occurs, there will be an increase in money to finance it and the resulting shift out of the aggregate demand curve will raise the price level. If the deficit disappears next period, there is no longer a need to print money. The aggregate demand curve will not shift further and the price level will not continue to rise. Hence the one-shot increase in the money supply from the temporary deficit only generates a one-shot increase in the price level, and no inflation develops.

To summarize: ***A deficit can be the source of a sustained inflation only if (1) it is persistent and not temporary and (2) the government finances it by creating money rather than by issuing bonds to the public.***

If inflation is the result, then why do governments frequently finance persistent deficits by creating money? The answer to this question is the key to understanding how budget deficits may lead to inflation.

Budget Deficits and Money Creation in Countries Besides the United States
Although the United States has a well-developed capital market in which huge quantities of its government bonds can be sold, this is not the situation in many developing countries. If developing countries run budget deficits, they cannot finance them by issuing bonds and must resort to their only other alternative, printing money. As a result, when they run large deficits relative to their GNP, the money supply grows at substantial rates and an inflation results.

Earlier we cited Latin American countries with high inflation rates and high money growth as evidence that inflation is a monetary phenomenon.

Those Latin American countries with high money growth are exactly the ones that have persistent, extremely large budget deficits relative to GNP. The only way to finance the deficits is to print more money, so the ultimate source of their high inflation rates is their large budget deficits.

In all episodes of hyperinflations, huge government budget deficits are also the ultimate source of inflationary monetary policies. The budget deficits during hyperinflations are so large that even if a capital market exists to issue government bonds, it does not have sufficient capacity to handle the quantity of bonds that the government wishes to sell. In this situation, the government must also resort to the printing press to finance the deficits.

Budget Deficits and Money Creation in the United States So far you have seen why budget deficits in some countries must lead to money creation and inflation. Either the deficit is huge or the country does not have sufficient access to capital markets in which it can sell government bonds. But neither of these situations seems to describe the situation in the United States. Recently the United States has been experiencing deficits much larger than in the past. Even so, the magnitude of these deficits relative to GNP is small compared to the deficits of countries that have experienced hyperinflations; the U.S. deficit as a percent of GNP reached a peak of 6% in 1983, while Argentina's budget deficit has often exceeded 15% of GNP. Furthermore, since the United States has the best-developed government bond market of any country in the world, it can issue large quantities of bonds to finance its deficit.

Although it appears that moderate deficits in the United States need not lead to inflation, you should not assume that deficits in the United States present *no* inflationary danger. To understand why moderate budget deficits might be inflationary, recall that the Fed might have a goal of preventing high interest rates (Chapter 18). When the government issues bonds to finance a deficit, this might put upward pressure on interest rates, and the Fed may buy bonds to prop their price up and prevent interest rates from rising. Since the Fed's open market purchases lead to an increase in high-powered money, the net effect of government financing of the deficit by issuing bonds is an increase in the money supply. If the budget deficit persists so that the quantity of bonds supplied keeps on growing, the upward pressure on interest rates will continue, the Fed will purchase bonds again and again, and the money supply will continually rise, resulting in inflation.

Not all economists agree that deficits in and of themselves lead to continuing upward pressure on interest rates. Much research is now being done to assess the importance of budget deficits to the inflation process. Many economists, however, do worry that large deficits in the United States may lead to higher inflation.

Summary Although high inflation is "always and everywhere a monetary phenomenon" in the sense that it cannot occur without a high rate of money growth, there are reasons *why* this inflationary monetary policy occurs. The two underlying reasons are the adherence of policymakers to a high employment target and the presence of persistent government budget deficits.

APPLICATION
EXPLAINING THE RISE IN U.S. INFLATION: 1960–1980 / / / / / / / / / / / / / / /

Now that we have examined the underlying sources of inflation, let us apply this knowledge to understanding the underlying causes of the rise in U.S. inflation from 1960 to 1980.

Figure 28.7 documents the rise in inflation from 1960 to 1980. At the beginning of the period the inflation rate is close to 1% at an annual rate, while in the late 1970s it is averaging around 8%. How does the analysis of this chapter explain this rise in inflation?

The conclusion that inflation is a monetary phenomenon is given a fair amount of support by the period from 1960 through 1980. In this period there is a close correspondence between movements in the inflation rate and the monetary growth rate from two years earlier (Figure 28.7). (The money growth rates are from two years earlier because research indicates that a change in money growth takes that long to affect the inflation rate.) The rise in inflation from 1960 to 1980 can be attributed to the rise in the money growth rate over this period; but you have probably noticed that in 1974–1975 and 1979–1980 the inflation rate is well above the money growth rate

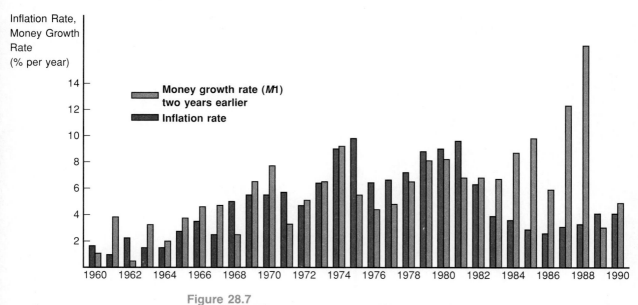

Figure 28.7
Inflation and Money Growth: 1960–1990 Source: *Economic Report of the President.*

from two years earlier. You may recall from Chapter 26 that temporary upward bursts of the inflation rate in those years can be attributed to supply shocks from oil and food price increases that occurred in 1973–1975 and 1978–1980.

However, the linkage between money growth and inflation after 1980 is not at all evident in Figure 28.7. This is the result of substantial gyrations in velocity in the 1980s (documented in Chapter 23). Indeed, the early 1980s are a period of rapid disinflation (a substantial fall in the inflation rate) and yet the money growth rates in Figure 28.7 do not display a visible downward trend until after the disinflation is over. (The disinflationary process in the 1980s will be discussed in another application later in this chapter.) Although some economists see the 1980s as evidence against the money and inflation link, others view the 1980s as an unusual period with large fluctuations in interest rates and rapid financial innovation that has made the correct measurement of money a difficult task (see Chapter 2). In their view the 1980s are an aberration and they believe that the close correspondence of money and inflation will reassert itself.

What is the underlying cause of increased rate of money growth that we see occurring from 1960 to 1980? We have identified two possible sources of inflationary monetary policy: government adherence to a high employment target and budget deficits. In Figure 28.8 let us see if budget deficits can explain the move to an inflationary monetary policy by plotting the ratio of government debt to GNP. This ratio provides a reasonable measure of whether government budget deficits put upward pressure on interest rates. Only if this ratio is rising might there be tendency for budget deficits to raise interest rates, since the public is then being asked to hold more government bonds relative to their capacity to buy them. Surprisingly, over the course of

Figure 28.8
Government Debt to GNP Ratio: 1960–1990
Source: *Economic Report of the President.*

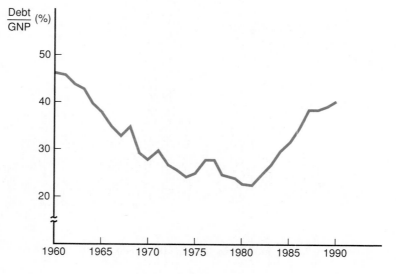

the twenty-year period from 1960 to 1980, this ratio was falling, not rising. Thus U.S. budget deficits in this period did not raise interest rates and so could not have encouraged the Fed to expand the money supply by buying bonds. Therefore, Figure 28.8 tells us that we can rule out budget deficits as a source of the rise in inflation in this period.

Since politicians were frequently bemoaning the budget deficits in this period, why did deficits not lead to an increase in the debt-GNP ratio? The reason is that in this period U.S. budget deficits were sufficiently small that the increase in the stock of government debt in this twenty-year period was still slower than the growth in nominal GNP, and the ratio of debt to GNP declined. You can see that interpreting budget deficit numbers is a tricky business.[6]

Since we have ruled out budget deficits as the instigator, what else could be the underlying cause of the higher rate of money growth and more rapid inflation in the 1960s and 1970s? Figure 28.9, which shows the unemployment rate relative to the natural rate of unemployment, shows that the economy was experiencing unemployment below the natural rate in all but one year throughout the 1965–1973 period. This suggests that in 1965–1973 the American economy was experiencing the demand-pull inflation described in Figure 28.6.

Apparently policymakers pursued policies that continually shifted the aggregate demand curve to the right in trying to achieve an output target that was too high, thus producing the continuing rise in the price level outlined in Figure 28.6. This occurred because policymakers, economists, and politicians had become committed in the mid-1960s to a target unemployment rate of 4%, the level of unemployment they thought was consistent with price stability. In hindsight, most economists today agree that the natural rate of unemployment was substantially higher in this period, ranging from 5 to 6% (see Figure 28.9). The result of the inappropriate 4% unemployment target was the beginning of the most sustained inflationary episode in American history.

After 1975, the unemployment rate was regularly above the natural rate of unemployment, yet inflation continued. It appears that we have the phenomenon of a cost-push inflation described in Figure 28.5 (but whose impetus was the earlier demand-pull inflation). The persistence of inflation can be explained by the public's knowledge that government policy continued to

---

[6]Another way of understanding the decline in the debt-GNP ratio is to recognize that a rise in the price level reduces the value of the outstanding government debt *in real terms,* that is, in terms of the goods and services it can buy. Thus even though budget deficits did lead to a somewhat higher *nominal* amount of debt in this period, the continually rising price level (inflation) produced a lower *real* value of the government debt. The decline in the real amount of debt at the same time that real GNP was rising in this period then resulted in the decline in the debt-GNP ratio. For a fascinating discussion of how tricky it is to interpret deficit numbers, see Robert Eisner and Paul J. Pieper, "A New View of the Federal Debt and Budget Deficits," *American Economic Review* 74 (March 1984), pp. 11–29.

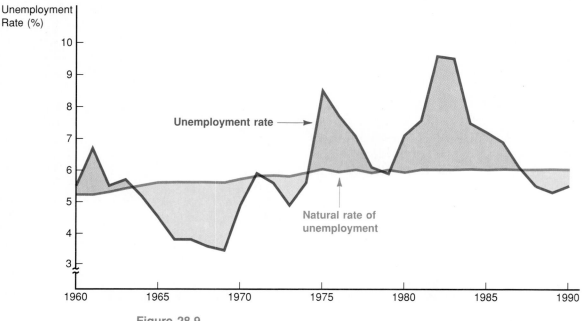

Figure 28.9
Unemployment and the Natural Rate of Unemployment: 1960–1990 Sources:
Unemployment rate: *Economic Report of the President;* natural rate of unemployment:
Robert Gordon, *Macroeconomics,* Fifth Edition (Chicago: Scott, Foresman, 1990).

be concerned with achieving high employment. With a higher rate of expected inflation arising initially from the demand-pull inflation, the aggregate supply curve in Figure 28.5 continued to shift inward, causing a rise in
unemployment which policymakers would try to eliminate by shifting the
aggregate demand curve to the right. The result was a continuation of the
inflation that had started in the 1960s.

THE ACTIVIST/NONACTIVIST POLICY DEBATE

All economists have similar policy goals—they want to promote high employment and price stability—and yet they often have very different views of
how policy should be conducted. Activists view the self-correcting mechanism through wage and price adjustment to be very slow and hence see the
need for the government to pursue active, accommodating, discretionary
policy to eliminate high unemployment whenever it develops. Nonactivists,
on the other hand, believe that the performance of the economy would be
improved if the government avoided active policy to eliminate unemployment. Here we will explore the activist/nonactivist policy debate by first looking at what their policy responses might be when the economy suffers high
unemployment.

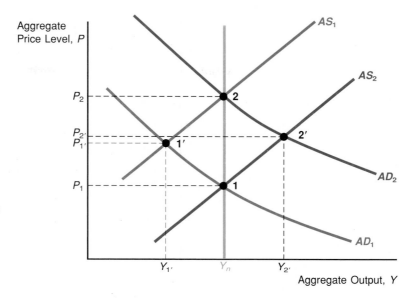

Figure 28.10
The Choice Between Activist and Nonactivist Policy
When the economy has moved to point 1′, the policymaker has two choices of policy: the nonactivist policy of doing nothing and letting the economy return to point 1 or the activist policy of shifting the aggregate demand curve to AD_2 to move the economy to point 2.

Responses to High Unemployment

Suppose policymakers are confronted with an economy that has moved to point 1′ in Figure 28.10. At this point, aggregate output ($Y_{1'}$) is lower than the natural rate level and the economy is suffering from high unemployment. Policymakers have two viable choices: If they do nothing (are nonactivists) the aggregate supply curve will eventually shift out over time, driving the economy from point 1′ to point 1, where full employment is restored. The accommodating, activist alternative is to try to eliminate the high unemployment by attempting to shift the aggregate demand curve out to AD_2 by pursuing expansionary policy (an increase in the money supply, increase in government spending, or lowering of taxes). If policymakers could shift the aggregate demand curve to AD_2 instantaneously, then the economy would immediately move to point 2 where there is full employment. However, several types of lags exist that prevent this immediate movement from occurring:

1. The *data lag* is the time it takes for policymakers to obtain the data that tell them what is happening in the economy. Accurate data on GNP, for example, are not available until several months after a given quarter is over.

2. The *recognition lag* is the time it takes for policymakers to be sure of what the data are signaling about the future course of the economy. For example, to minimize errors, the National Bureau of Economic Research (the organization that officially dates business cycles) will not declare the economy to be in recession until at least six months after it has determined the recession has begun.

3. The *legislative lag* represents the time it takes to pass legislation to implement a particular policy. The legislative lag does not exist for most monetary policy actions such as open market operations. It can, however, be quite important for the implementation of fiscal policy when it sometimes can take six months to a year to get legislation passed to change taxes or government spending.

4. The *implementation lag* is the time it takes for policymakers to change policy instruments once they have decided on the new policy. Again, this lag is unimportant for the conduct of open market operations because the Fed's trading desk can almost immediately purchase or sell bonds once it is told to do so by the Federal Open Market Committee. Actually implementing fiscal policy may take time, however; for example, getting government agencies to change their spending habits takes time, as does changing tax tables.

5. The *effectiveness lag* is the time it takes for the policy to actually have an impact on the economy. An important element of the monetarist viewpoint is that the effectiveness lag for changes in the money supply is long and variable (from several months to several years). Keynesians usually view fiscal policy as having a shorter effectiveness lag than monetary policy (fiscal policy takes approximately a year until it has its full effect), but there is substantial uncertainty about how long this lag is.

Activist and Nonactivist Positions

Now that you understand the considerations that affect decisions by policymakers on whether to pursue an activist or nonactivist policy, we can examine when each of these policies would be preferable.

The Case for an Activist Policy   Activists, such as the Keynesians, view the wage and price adjustment process as being extremely slow. Thus they see a high cost for a nonactivist policy, because the slow movement of the economy back to full employment results in a large loss of output. On the other hand, even though the five lags described result in a year or two delay in order to shift the aggregate demand curve to AD_2, the aggregate supply curve moves very little during this time. The appropriate path for policymakers to pursue is thus an activist policy of moving the economy to point 2 in Figure 28.10.

The Case for a Nonactivist Policy   Nonactivists, such as the monetarists, view the wage and price adjustment process as being more rapid than do activists and see a lower cost to a nonactivist policy because output is soon back at the natural rate level. On the other hand, they suggest that an activist, accommodating policy of shifting the aggregate demand curve to AD_2 will be costly because it produces more volatility in both the price level and output. The reason for this volatility is that the time it takes to shift the aggregate demand curve out to AD_2 is substantial, while the wage and price adjustment process is more rapid. Hence before the aggregate demand curve shifts out, the aggregate supply curve will have shifted out to AS_2 and the economy will have moved from point 1′ to point 1, where it has returned to the natural rate level of output, Y_n. After adjustment to the AS_2 curve is complete, the shift of the aggregate demand curve to AD_2 finally takes effect, leading the economy to point 2′ at the intersection of AD_2 and AS_2. Aggregate output at $Y_{2'}$ is now greater than the natural rate level ($Y_{2'} > Y_n$) and so the aggregate supply curve will now shift inward back to AS_1, moving the economy to point 2 where output is again at the natural rate level.

Although the activist policy eventually moves the economy to point 2 as policymakers intended, it has led to a sequence of equilibrium points—1′, 1, 2′, and 2—in which both output and the price level have been highly variable: Output overshoots its target level of Y_n and the price level falls from $P_{1'}$ to P_1 and then rises to $P_{2'}$ and eventually to P_2. Since this variability is undesirable, policymakers would be better off pursuing the nonactivist policy, which moved the economy to point 1 and left it there.

Expectations and the Activist/ Nonactivist Debate

Our analysis of inflation in the middle to late 1970s (in the application starting on page 679) demonstrates that expectations about policy can be an important element in the inflation process. Allowing for expectations about policy to affect how wages are set (the wage-setting process) provides an additional reason for pursuing a nonactivist policy.

Does the Possibility that Expectations About Policy Matter to the Wage-Setting Process Strengthen the Case for a Nonactivist Policy? The case for an activist policy states that with slow wage and price adjustment, the activist policy returns the economy to full employment at point 2 far more quickly than it takes to get to full employment at point 1 under nonactivist policy. However, the activist argument does not allow for (1) the possibility that expectations about policy matter to the wage-setting process and (2) that the economy might initially have moved from point 1 to point 1′ because an attempt by workers to raise their wages or a negative supply shock shifted the aggregate supply curve from AS_2 to AS_1. We therefore need to ask the following question about activist policy: Will the aggregate supply curve continue to shift inward after the economy has reached point 2, leading to a cost-push inflation?

The answer to this question is "yes" *if* expectations of policy matter. Our discussion of cost-push inflation in Figure 28.5 suggests that if workers know policy will be accommodating in the future, they will continue to push their wages up and the aggregate supply curve will keep on shifting inward. As a result, policymakers are forced to accommodate the cost push by continuing to shift the aggregate demand curve to the right in order to eliminate the unemployment that develops. The accommodating, activist policy with its high employment target has the hidden cost or disadvantage that it may well lead to inflation.[7]

The main advantage of a nonaccommodating, nonactivist policy, in which policymakers do not try to shift out the aggregate demand curve in response to the cost push, is that it will prevent inflation. As depicted in Figure 28.4, the result of an upward push on wages in the face of a nonaccommodating, nonactivist policy will be a period of unemployment above the natural rate level, which will eventually shift the aggregate supply curve and the price level back to their initial positions. The main criticism of this nonactivist policy is that the economy will suffer protracted periods of unemployment when the aggregate supply curve shifts inward. Workers, however, would probably not push for higher wages to begin with if they knew that policy would be nonaccommodating, because their wage gains will lead to a protracted period of unemployment. A nonaccommodating, nonactivist policy may have not only the advantage of preventing inflation, but also have the hidden benefit of discouraging inward shifts in the aggregate supply curve that lead to excessive unemployment.

In conclusion: *If workers' opinions about whether policy is accommodating or nonaccommodating matter to the wage-setting process, then the case for a nonactivist policy is much stronger and the case for an activist policy is much weaker.*

Do Expectations About Policy Matter to the Wage-Setting Process? The answer to this question is crucial to deciding whether activist or nonactivist policy is preferred and so has become a major topic of current research for economists; but the evidence is not yet conclusive. We can ask, however, whether expectations about policy do affect people's behavior in other contexts. This information will help us to know if expectations regarding whether or not policy is accommodating are important to the wage-setting process.

As any good negotiator knows, convincing your opponent that you will be nonaccommodating is crucial to getting a good deal. If you are bargaining with a car dealer over price, for example, you must convince him that you can just as easily walk away from the deal and buy a car from a dealer on the other side of town. This principle also applies to conducting foreign policy—it is to your advantage to convince your opponent that you will go to war (be nonaccommodating) if your demands are not met. Similarly, if your oppo-

---

[7]The issue that is being described here is the "dynamic inconsistency of policy" described by Finn Kydland and Edward Prescott, "Rules Rather than Discretion: The Inconsistency of Optimal Plans," *Journal of Political Economy* 85 (June 1977), pp. 473–491. A much less technical discussion of this subject can be found in Edward Prescott, "Should Control Theory Be Used for Economic Stabilization?" in Karl Brunner and Allan H. Meltzer, eds., *Optimal Policies, Control Theory and Technology Exports, Carnegie-Rochester Conference Series on Public Policy* 7 (1977), pp. 13–38.

The Perils of Accommodating Policy: The Terrorism Dilemma

A major dilemma confronting our foreign policy in recent years is whether to cave in to the demands of terrorists when they are holding American hostages. Since our hearts go out to the hostages, we might be tempted to pursue an accommodating policy of giving in to the terrorists to bring the hostages safely back home. However, pursuing this accommodating policy is likely to encourage terrorists to take additional hostages in the future.

The terrorism dilemma illustrates the principle that opponents are more likely to take advantage of you in the future if you accommodate them now. Recognition of this principle, which demonstrates the perils of accommodating policy, explains why governments in countries such as the United States and Israel have been reluctant to give in to terrorist demands even though it has sometimes resulted in the death of hostages.

nent thinks that you will be accommodating, he will almost certainly take advantage of you. (For an example, see Box 28.2.) Finally, anyone who has dealt with a two-year-old child knows that the more you give in (pursue an accommodating policy), the more demanding the child becomes. In conclusion, people's expectations about policy *do* affect their behavior. Consequently, it is quite plausible that expectations about policy also affect the wage-setting process.[8]

Rules versus Discretion: The Conclusions

The following conclusions can be generated from our analysis: Activists believe in the use of discretionary policy to eliminate excessive unemployment whenever it develops, because they view the wage and price adjustment process to be sluggish and unresponsive to expectations about policy. Nonactivists, on the other hand, believe that a discretionary policy that reacts to excessive unemployment is counterproductive, because wage and price adjustment is rapid and because expectations about policy can matter to the wage-setting process. Nonactivists thus advocate the use of a policy rule to keep the aggregate demand curve from fluctuating away from the trend rate of growth of the natural rate level of output. Monetarists, who adhere to the nonactivist position and who also see money as the sole source of fluctuations

---

[8]A recent development in monetary theory, the new classical macroeconomics, strongly suggests that expectations about policy are crucial to the wage-setting process and the movements of the aggregate supply curve. We will explore why the new classical macroeconomics comes to this conclusion when we discuss the implications of the rational expectations hypothesis (Chapters 29 and 30), which states that expectations are formed using all available information, including expectations about policy.

in the aggregate demand curve, therefore advocate the use of policy rule in which the Federal Reserve keeps the money supply growing at a constant rate. This monetarist rule is referred to as a **constant-money-growth-rate rule.**

As our analysis indicates, an important element for the success of a non-accommodating policy rule is that it be *credible;* that is, the public must believe that policymakers will be tough and not accede to a cost push by shifting the aggregate demand curve out to eliminate unemployment. In other words, government policymakers need to have credibility in the eyes of the public as inflation fighters. Otherwise, workers will be more likely to push for higher wages, which will shift the aggregate supply curve inward after the economy reaches full employment at a point like 2 in Figure 28.10 and lead to unemployment or inflation or both. Alternatively, a credible, nonaccommodating policy rule has the benefit that it makes a cost push less likely and thus helps prevent inflation and potential increases in unemployment because of a cost push. The following application suggests that recent historical experience is consistent with the importance of credibility to successful policy-making.

APPLICATION
THE IMPORTANCE OF CREDIBILITY TO VOLCKER'S/ / / / / / / / / / / / / / / VICTORY OVER INFLATION

In the period from 1965 through the 1970s, policymakers had little credibility as inflation fighters—a well-deserved reputation, since they pursued an accommodating policy to achieve high employment. As we have seen, the outcome was not a happy one. Inflation soared to double-digit levels, while the unemployment rate remained high. In order to wring inflation out of the system, the Federal Reserve under Chairman Volcker put the economy through two back-to-back recessions in 1980 and 1981–1982 (Chapter 20). (The data on inflation, money growth, and unemployment in this period are shown in Figures 28.7 and 28.9.) Only after the 1981–1982 recession, the most severe in the postwar period with unemployment above the 10% level, did Volcker establish credibility for the Fed's anti-inflation policy. By the end of 1982, inflation was running at a rate of less than 5%.

An indication of Volcker's credibility arose in 1983 when the money growth rate accelerated dramatically and yet inflation did not rise. Workers and firms were convinced that if inflation reared its head, Volcker would pursue a nonaccommodating policy of squashing it. They thus did not raise wages and prices, which would have shifted the aggregate supply curve inward and would have led to both inflation and unemployment. The success of Volcker's anti-inflation policy continued throughout the rest of his term as chairman, which ended in 1987; unemployment fell steadily while the inflation rate remained below 5%. Volcker's triumph over inflation was achieved because he obtained credibility the hard way; he earned it.

SUMMARY

1. Milton Friedman's famous proposition that "inflation is always and everywhere a monetary phenomenon" is supported by the following evidence: Every country that has experienced a sustained, high inflation has also experienced a high rate of money growth.
2. Aggregate demand and supply analysis shows that Keynesian and monetarist views of the inflation process are not very different. Both believe that high inflation can occur only if there is a high rate of money growth. As long as we recognize that by inflation we mean a rapid continuing increase in the price level, then almost all economists agree with Milton Friedman's proposition.
3. Although high inflation is "always and everywhere a monetary phenomenon" in the sense that it cannot occur without a high rate of money growth, there are reasons *why* this inflationary monetary policy occurs. The two underlying reasons are the adherence of policymakers to a high employment target and the presence of persistent government budget deficits.
4. Activists believe in the use of discretionary policy to eliminate excessive unemployment whenever it occurs, because they view wage and price adjustment to be sluggish and unresponsive to expectations about policy. Nonactivists take the opposite view and believe that discretionary policy is counterproductive. In addition, they regard the credibility of a nonaccommodating (nonactivist) anti-inflation policy to be crucial to its success.

KEY TERMS

cost-push inflation

demand-pull inflation

accommodating policy

constant-money-growth-
   rate rule

QUESTIONS AND PROBLEMS

1. "There are frequently years when the inflation rate is high and yet money growth is quite low. Therefore, the statement that inflation is a monetary phenomenon cannot be correct." Comment.
* 2. Why do economists focus on historical episodes of hyperinflation to decide whether inflation is a monetary phenomenon?
3. Answer true, false, or uncertain: "Since increases in government spending raise the aggregate demand curve in Keynesian analysis, fiscal policy by itself can be the source of inflation."
* 4. Answer true, false, or uncertain: "A cost-push inflation occurs as a result of workers' attempts to push up their wages. Therefore, inflation does not have to be a monetary phenomenon."
5. Answer true, false, or uncertain: "Since government policymakers do not consider inflation to be desirable, their policies cannot be the source of inflations."
* 6. Answer true, false, or uncertain: "A budget deficit that is only temporary cannot be the source of inflation."
7. How can the Fed's desire to prevent high interest rates lead to inflation?
* 8. Answer true, false, or uncertain: "If the data and recognition lags could be reduced, activist policy would more likely be beneficial to the economy."
9. Answer true, false, or uncertain: "The more sluggish is wage and price adjustment, the more variable are output and the price level when an activist policy is pursued."
10. Answer true, false, or uncertain: "If the public believes that the monetary authorities will pursue an accommodating policy, a cost-push inflation is more likely to develop."

11. Why are activist policies to eliminate unemployment more likely to lead to inflation than nonactivist policies?

*12. Answer true, false, or uncertain: "The less important expectations about policy are to movements of the aggregate supply curve, the stronger is the case for activist policy to eliminate unemployment."

13. If the economy's self-correcting mechanism works slowly, should the government necessarily pursue an activist policy to eliminate unemployment?

*14. "In order to prevent inflation, the Fed should follow Teddy Roosevelt's advice: 'Speak softly and carry a big stick.'" What is the Fed's "big stick" referred to in this statement? What is the statement trying to say?

15. In a speech early in the Iraq-Kuwait crisis, President George Bush stated that although his heart went out to the hostages held by Sadaam Hussein, he would not let this hostage taking deter the United States from insisting on the withdrawal of Iraq from Kuwait. Do you think that Bush's position made sense? Explain why or why not.

CHAPTER 29

The Theory of Rational Expectations and Efficient Capital Markets

PREVIEW   Throughout our discussion of the many facets of money, banking, and financial markets, you may have noticed that the subject of expectations keeps cropping up over and over again. If consumers expect that they will be richer in the future, for example, they spend more today and aggregate output will increase; if banks expect deposit outflows to occur, they increase their holdings of excess reserves, which causes the money supply to fall; and if participants in the capital markets expect interest rates to rise and expect capital losses on long-term bonds, they will decrease their demand for long-term bonds and their prices will fall. Expectations influence the behavior of all participants in the economy and have a major impact on economic activity.

With the development of a new theory, the theory of rational expectations, the importance of expectations to economic behavior has come to the fore in discussions of monetary policy. The theory of rational expectations attempts to explain how the various economic agents form their expectations. It is at the center of many recent debates about how monetary policy and fiscal policy should be conducted (Chapter 30). In addition, when this theory is applied to financial markets, where it is called the theory of efficient capital markets (or, more simply, efficient markets theory), it has important implications about what factors determine securities' prices and how these prices move over time.

In the present chapter we shall examine the basic reasoning behind the theory of rational expectations and apply it to financial markets. In addition to helping us understand the factors that influence the formation of business and consumer expectations, rational expectations theory explains some puzzling features of the operation and behavior of financial markets. You will see, for example, that it explains why changes in stock prices are unpredictable and why listening to a stock broker's hot tips may not be advisable.

On a theoretical basis, rational expectations is a powerful tool for analyzing behavior. But in order to establish that it is *in reality* a useful tool, we must compare the theory with the data. Does the empirical evidence support it? Although the verdict is not yet in, the available evidence indicates that, for many purposes, this theory is a good starting point for analyzing expectations.

THE ROLE OF EXPECTATIONS IN ECONOMIC ACTIVITY

It is difficult to think of any sector of the economy in which expectations do not matter to the effects of policy and the way markets behave. To see the critical role of expectations in influencing economic activity, it might be useful to list the various avenues in which they have come into play in our study of money, banking, and financial markets.

Study Guide

Before you read on, try to write down a list of examples from this book in which expectations influence economic behavior and then compare your list to the examples that follow. This is an excellent way for you to review how the material we have studied so far fits together.

---

1. Asset Demand and the Determination of Interest Rates. Because expectations of returns are an important factor in determining the quantity of an asset people demand, expectations are central to the behavior of asset prices in a financial market (Chapters 5 and 6). For example, we have seen that expectations of inflation have a major impact on bond prices and interest rates through the Fisher effect. The speed with which expectations of inflation respond to a higher rate of money growth is an important factor determining whether interest rates rise or fall when money growth increases.

2. The Risk and Term Structure of Interest Rates. Expectations are also central in the determination of the risk and term structure of interest rates (Chapter 7). Expectations about the likelihood of bankruptcy are probably the most important factors in determining the risk structure of interest rates. Expectations of future short-term interest rates play a central role in the determination of long-term interest rates.

3. Asymmetric Information and Financial Structure. Expectations are what make the asymmetric information problems of adverse selection and moral hazard we encountered in Chapters 8, 10, 11, and 12 important in determining financial structure. Financial intermediaries engage in the important task of information collection because they have expectations that adverse selection will occur; that is, the least desirable credit risks will be the most likely ones to seek out loans. Similarly, expectations that borrowers will commit moral hazard by taking on too much risk is what drives financial institutions to take steps to limit moral hazard through monitoring and enforcement of restrictive covenants. The greater are expectations of adverse selection and moral hazard, the greater will be the efforts of financial institutions to engage in activities to reduce these asymmetric information problems; hence, the greater will be the impact of asymmetric information on our financial structure.

4. Bank Asset and Liability Management. Banks' decisions about which assets to hold are influenced by their expectations about the returns, risk, and liquidity of different assets (Chapter 9). Their decisions about which liabilities to acquire are influenced by their expectations about the future cost of issuing different liabilities. In addition, because banks must manage liquidity to remain solvent, expectations about deposit outflows will affect their decisions about whether to hold more or less liquid assets.

5. Financial Innovation. Because financial institutions are concerned with the future profitability of the new financial instruments they issue, expectations about interest rate movements and the nature of the regulatory environment in the future affect financial innovation (Chapter 13). Furthermore, regulators, in deciding on which regulations to impose on financial markets, must guess what the behavior of financial institutions will be in response to new regulation. The result can be a complicated game between regulators and regulated in which each tries to outguess the other.

6. The Money Supply Process. As you should recall from Chapters 14 to 16, depositor behavior and bank behavior are important in the money supply process. Depositors' decisions to hold currency versus demand or time deposits are affected primarily by expectations of the relative returns of these assets. Banks' decisions about excess reserves and borrowing from the Fed are influenced by their expectations of the returns they can earn on loans. In addition, the amount of excess reserves is affected by bankers' expectations concerning depositor outflows.

The role of expectations in bank panics and the resulting declines in the money supply are especially important (Chapter 16). Depositors' expectations that a bank or banks are in trouble cause them to withdraw deposits, which in turn causes banks to fail, which causes more banks to fail. Bankers' expectations of deposit outflows make the situation even worse because their scramble for liquidity and the resulting increase in excess reserves can lead to more bank failures. The net result of this process is that the currency-checkable deposits ratio and excess reserves rise, causing a sharp drop in the money supply.

7. The Federal Reserve. The Fed's expectations of inflation and the state of the economy affect the targets it sets for monetary policy. Its expectations of short-term interest rates can be a factor in the procedures it uses to control the money supply (Chapter 20).

8. Foreign Exchange Rates. Recall that the exchange rate is the price of one asset (deposits denominated in the domestic currency) in terms of another (deposits denominated in the foreign currency). Thus the expected returns of foreign deposits relative to domestic deposits is a central element in the determination of foreign exchange rates (Chapter 21). Since expected appreciation or depreciation of the domestic currency affects the expected return on foreign deposits relative to domestic deposits, expectations about the price level, inflation, tariffs and quotas, import and export demand, and the money supply play an important role in determining the exchange rate. In addition, expectations that a central bank is about to devalue or revalue its domestic currency are a key feature of a speculative attack on a currency (Chapter 22).

9. The Demand for Money. Because money is just another asset, its expected return relative to other assets is an important factor in determining its demand (Chapter 23). Expectations about the level of lifetime resources (usually represented by permanent income) are frequently thought to be another major determinant of the demand for money.

10. Aggregate Demand. Expectations play a prominent role in determining aggregate demand. Our discussion of the *ISLM* model (Chapters 24 and 25) and the transmission mechanisms of monetary policy (Chapter 27) reveals that consumer expenditure is related to consumers' expectations of the future resources available to them and of the likelihood of financial distress. Investment spending depends on business firms' expectations of future profits from investment projects as well as expectations about the cost of financing the project. It is no wonder that Keynes emphasized "animal spirits"—in other words, expectations—as a major factor driving aggregate demand and the business cycle.

11. Aggregate Supply and Inflation. Analysis of the aggregate supply curve (Chapter 26) indicated that workers' expectations about inflation and the likely response of government policy to unemployment affect the position of the aggregate supply curve. It influences workers' willingness to push wages higher. These expectations play a central role in cost-push inflation whereby the aggregate supply curve shifted further and further inward (Chapter 28). The public's expectations of government policy, which are affected by the credibility of government policymakers, have implications for the desirability of pursuing activist or nonactivist policies.

In conclusion, expectations are important in every sector of the economy through their effects on policy and market behavior. In the next section, we will outline the theory of rational expectations—currently the most widely used theory to describe the formation of business and consumer expectations.

THEORY OF RATIONAL EXPECTATIONS

In the 1950s and 1960s, economists regularly viewed expectations as formed from past experience only. Expectations of inflation, for example, were typically viewed as being an average of past inflation rates. This view of expectations formation, called **adaptive expectations,**[1] suggests that changes in expectations will occur slowly over time as past data change. So if inflation had formerly been steady at a 5% rate, expectations of future inflation would be 5% too. If inflation rose to a steady rate of 10%, expectations of future inflation would rise toward 10%, but slowly: In the first year expected inflation might rise only to 6%; in the second year, to 7%; and so on.

Adaptive expectations have been faulted on the grounds that people use more information than just past data on a single variable to form their expectations of that variable. Their expectations of inflation will almost surely be affected by their predictions of future monetary policy as well as by current and past monetary policy. In addition, people often change their expectations quickly when faced with new information. To meet these objections to adaptive expectations, John Muth developed an alternative theory of expectations (called **rational expectations**) which can be stated as follows.[2] *Expectations will not differ from optimal forecasts (the best guess of the future) using all available information.* What exactly does this mean?

To explain more clearly, let's use the theory of rational expectations to examine how expectations are formed in a situation that most of us encounter at some point in our lifetime: our drive to work. Suppose that when Joe Commuter does not travel during rush hour, it takes an average of 30 minutes for his trip. Sometimes it takes him 35 minutes, other times 25 minutes, but the average non-rush-hour driving time is 30 minutes. If, however, Joe leaves for work during rush hour, it takes him, on average, an additional 10 minutes to get to work. Given that he leaves for work during the rush hour, the best guess of the driving time (the **optimal forecast**) is 40 minutes.

If the only information available to Joe before he leaves for work that would have a potential effect on his driving time is that he is leaving during rush hour, what does rational expectations theory allow you to predict about

---

[1]More precisely, adaptive expectations, say of inflation, are written down as a weighted average of past inflation rates; that is,

$$\pi_t^e = (1 - \lambda) \sum_{i=0}^{\infty} \lambda^i \pi_{t-i}$$

where π_t^e = adaptive expectation of inflation at time t
π_{t-i} = inflation at time $t - i$
λ = a constant between the values of 0 and 1

[2]John Muth, "Rational Expectations and the Theory of Price Movements," *Econometrica* 29 (1961), pp. 315–335.

Joe's expectations of his driving time? Since the best guess of his driving time using all available information is 40 minutes, Joe's expectation should also be the same. Clearly, an expectation of 35 minutes would not be rational because it is not equal to the optimal forecast, the best guess of the driving time.

Suppose the next day, given the same conditions and the same expectations, it takes Joe 45 minutes to drive, and the day after suppose it takes Joe only 35 minutes. Do these variations mean that Joe's 40-minute expectation is irrational? No, an expectation of 40 minutes of driving time is still a rational expectation. In both cases, the forecast is off by 5 minutes, so the expectation has not been perfectly accurate. However, the forecast does not have to be perfectly accurate to be rational—it only need be the *best possible* given the available information; that is, it has to be correct *on average,* and that the 40-minute expectation is. Since there is bound to be some randomness in Joe's driving time, no matter what the driving conditions are like, an optimal forecast will not be completely accurate.

The example makes the following important point about rational expectations: ***Even though a rational expectation equals the optimal forecast using all available information, the prediction represented by the expectation may not always be perfectly accurate.***

What if an item of information relevant to predicting driving time is unavailable or ignored? Suppose on Joe's usual route to work there is an accident which causes a two-hour traffic jam. If Joe has no way of ascertaining this information, his rush-hour expectation of 40 minutes driving time is still rational because the accident information is not available to him for making his optimal forecast. On the other hand, if there is a radio or TV traffic report about the accident that Joe did not hear or that he heard but ignored, his 40-minute expectation is no longer rational. With the availability of this information Joe's optimal forecast should have been 2 hours and 40 minutes!

Accordingly, there are two reasons why an expectation may fail to be rational:

1. People might be aware of all available information, but they are too lazy to make their expectation the best guess possible.
2. People might be unaware of some *available* relevant information, so their best guess of the future will not be correct on average.

Nonetheless, it is important to recognize that if an additional factor is important but information about it is *not* available, an expectation that does not take account of it can still be rational.

A More Formal Statement of the Theory

Let us make our discussion of the theory of rational expectations somewhat more formal by using the following symbols:

X = the variable that is being forecast (in the above example, it is Joe Commuter's driving time)

X^e = the expectation of this variable (Joe's expectation of his driving time)

X^{of} = the optimal forecast of X using all available information (the best guess possible of the driving time)

The theory of rational expectations then simply says

$$X^e = X^{of} \qquad\qquad (29.1)$$

That is, the expectation of X equals the optimal forecast using all available information.

Why Does the Theory of Rational Expectations Make Sense?

Why do people try to make their expectations equal to their best guess possible of the future using all available information? The simplest explanation is that it is costly for people not to do so. Joe Commuter has a strong incentive to make his expectations of the time it takes him to drive to work as accurate as possible. If he underpredicts his driving time, he will often be late to work and his boss may fire him. If he overpredicts, he will, on average, get to work too early and will have given up his "beauty sleep" unnecessarily. Accurate expectations are desirable and there are strong incentives for people to try to make them equal to optimal forecasts by using all available information.

The same principle applies to business firms. Suppose that an appliance manufacturer, say General Electric, knows that interest rate movements are important to the sales of appliances. If General Electric makes poor forecasts of interest rates, it will earn less profit because it might either produce too many appliances or too few. There are strong incentives for General Electric to acquire all available information to help it to forecast interest rates and use the information to make the best guess possible of future interest rate movements.

The incentives for equating expectations with optimal forecasts are especially strong in financial markets. In these markets people with better forecasts of the future get rich quickly. The application of rational expectations theory to financial markets (where it is called efficient markets theory) is thus particularly useful.

Implications of the Theory

Rational expectations theory leads to two commonsense implications for the way expectations are formed that are important in the analysis of the aggregate economy.

1. If there is a change in the way a variable moves, the way expectations of this variable are formed will change as well. This tenet of rational expectations theory can be most easily understood by a concrete example.

Suppose that, as Keynes thought (Chapter 23), interest rates move in such a way that they tend to return to a "normal" level in the future. If today's interest rate is high relative to the normal level, then an optimal forecast of the interest rate in the future is that it will decline to the normal level. Rational expectations theory would imply that when today's interest rate is high, the expectation is that it will fall in the future.

Suppose, on the other hand, the way in which the interest rate moves changes so that when the interest rate is high, it stays high. Now, when today's interest rate is high, the optimal forecast of the future interest rate, and hence the rational expectation, is that it will stay high. Expectations of the future interest rate no longer will indicate the interest rate will fall. The change in the way the interest rate variable moves has therefore led to a change in the way that expectations of future interest rates are formed. The rational expectations analysis here is generalizable to expectations of any variable. Hence, when there is a change in the way any variable moves, the way expectations of this variable are formed will change too.

2. The forecast errors of expectations will on average be zero and cannot be predicted ahead of time. The forecast error of an expectation is $X - X^e$, the difference between the realization of a variable X and the expectation of the variable; that is, if Joe Commuter's driving time on a particular day is 45 minutes and his expectation of the driving time is 40 minutes, the forecast error is 5 minutes.

Suppose that in violation of the rational expectations tenet, Joe's forecast error is not, on average, equal to zero; instead, it equals 5 minutes. The forecast error is now predictable because Joe will soon notice that he is, on average, 5 minutes late for work and can improve his forecast by increasing it by 5 minutes. Rational expectations theory implies that this is exactly what Joe will do because he will want his forecast to be the best guess possible. When Joe has revised his forecast upwards by 5 minutes, on average, the forecast error will equal zero and it cannot be predicted ahead of time. Rational expectations theory implies that forecast errors of expectations cannot be predicted.

EFFICIENT MARKETS THEORY: RATIONAL EXPECTATIONS IN FINANCIAL MARKETS

While the theory of rational expectations was being developed by monetary economists, financial economists were developing a parallel theory of expectations formation in financial markets. It led them to the same conclusion as the rational expectations theorists: Expectations in financial markets are equal to optimal forecasts using all available information.[3] Although finan-

---

[3]The development of efficient markets theory was not completely independent of the development of rational expectations theory since financial economists were aware of Muth's work.

cial economists gave their theory another name, calling it the *theory of efficient capital markets* or *efficient markets theory,* in fact their theory is just an application of rational expectations to the pricing of securities.

Efficient markets theory is based on the assumption that prices of securities in financial markets fully reflect all available information. You may recall (Chapter 4) that the rate of return from holding a security equals the sum of the capital gain on the security (the change in the price) plus any cash payments, divided by the initial purchase price of the security:

$$RET = \frac{P_{t+1} - P_t + C}{P_t} \tag{29.2}$$

where RET = the rate of return on the security held from time t to $t + 1$
(say, the end of 1991 to the end of 1992)
P_{t+1} = the price of the security at time $t + 1$, the end of the holding period
P_t = the price of the security at time t, the beginning of the holding period
C = cash payment (coupon or dividend payments) made in the period t to $t + 1$

Let us look at the expectation of this return at time t, the beginning of the holding period. Since the current price P_t and the cash payment C are known at the beginning, the only variable in the definition of the return that is uncertain is the price next period (P_{t+1}).[4] Denoting the expectation of the security's price at the end of the holding period as P_{t+1}^e, the expected return (RET^e) is

$$RET^e = \frac{P_{t+1}^e - P_t + C}{P_t}$$

Efficient markets theory also views expectations of future prices as equal to optimal forecasts using all currently available information. In other words, the market's expectations of future security prices are rational, so that

$$P_{t+1}^e = P_{t+1}^{of}$$

which in turn implies that the expected return on the security will equal the optimal forecast of the return:

$$RET^e = RET^{of} \tag{29.3}$$

Unfortunately, we cannot observe either RET^e or P_{t+1}^e, so the rational expectations equations by themselves do not tell us much about how the finan-

---

[4]There are cases where C might not be known at the beginning of the period, but this does not make a substantial difference to the analysis. The only modification is that we would assume that not only price expectations but also the expectations of C are optimal forecasts using all available information.

cial market behaves. However, if we can devise some way to measure the value of RET^e, these equations will have important implications for how prices of securities change in financial markets.

The supply and demand analysis of the bond market developed in Chapter 6 shows us that the expected return on a security (the interest rate in the case of the bond examined) will have a tendency to head toward the equilibrium return that equates the quantity demanded to the quantity supplied. Supply and demand analysis enables us to determine the expected return on a security with the following equilibrium condition: The expected return on a security (RET^e) equals the equilibrium return (RET^*), which equates the quantity demanded of the security to the quantity supplied; that is,

$$RET^e = RET^* \tag{29.4}$$

The academic field of finance explores the factors (risk and liquidity, for example) that influence the equilibrium returns on securities. For our purposes, it is sufficient to know that we can determine the equilibrium return and thus determine the expected return with the equilibrium condition.

We can derive an equation to describe pricing behavior in an efficient market by using the equilibrium condition above to replace RET^e with RET^* in the rational expectations equation ($RET^{of} = RET^e$). By doing this, we obtain,

$$RET^{of} = RET^* \tag{29.5}$$

This equation tells us: ***Current prices in a financial market will be set so that the optimal forecast of a security's return using all available information equals the security's equilibrium return.*** Financial economists state it more simply: A security's price fully reflects all available information in an efficient market.

Why Does the Efficient Markets Theory Make Sense?

Let us see what the efficient markets condition means in practice and why it is a sensible characterization of pricing behavior. Suppose the equilibrium return of a security, say Exxon common stock, is 10% at an annual rate and its current price (P_t) is lower than the optimal forecast of tomorrow's price (P_{t+1}^{of}) so that the optimal forecast of the return at an annual rate is 50%, a return that is greater than the equilibrium return of 10%. One is now able to predict that, on average, Exxon's return would be abnormally high. This situation is called an **unexploited profit opportunity** because, on average, people would be earning more than they should, given the characteristics of that security. Knowing that, on average, you can earn such an abnormally high rate of return on Exxon because $RET^{of} > RET^*$, you would buy more, which in turn would drive up its current price (P_t) relative to the expected future price (P_{t+1}^{of}), thus lowering RET^{of}. When the current price had risen sufficiently so that RET^{of} equals RET^* and the efficient markets condition [Equation (29.5)] is satisfied, the buying of Exxon will stop and the unexploited profit opportunity will disappear.

Similarly, a security for which the optimal forecast of the return is -5% while the equilibrium return is 10% ($RET^{of} < RET^*$) would be a poor investment because, on average, it earns less than the equilibrium return. In such a case, you would sell the security and drive down its current price relative to the expected future price until RET^{of} rose to the level of RET^* and the efficient markets condition is again satisfied. What we have shown can be summarized:

$$\text{If } RET^{of} > RET^* \rightarrow P_t \uparrow \rightarrow RET^{of} \downarrow$$
$$\text{If } RET^{of} < RET^* \rightarrow P_t \downarrow \rightarrow RET^{of} \uparrow$$
$$\text{until}$$
$$RET^{of} = RET^*$$

Another way to state the efficient markets condition is: ***In an efficient market, all unexploited profit opportunities will be eliminated.***

An extremely important factor in this reasoning is that ***not everyone in a financial market must be well informed about a security or have rational expectations for its price to be driven to the point at which the efficient markets condition holds.*** Financial markets are structured so that many participants can play the market. As long as a few keep their eyes open for unexploited profit opportunities, they will eliminate any of the profit opportunities that appear because, in so doing, they make a profit. The theory of efficient markets makes sense because it does not require everyone in a market to be cognizant of what is happening to every security.

APPLICATION
A PRACTICAL GUIDE TO INVESTING IN THE / STOCK MARKET

Efficient markets theory is not esoteric without applications to the real world. It is extremely valuable because it can be applied directly to an issue that concerns many of us—how to get rich (or at least not get poor) in the stock market. (The "Following the Financial News" box shows how stock prices are reported daily.) A practical guide to investing in the stock market, which we will develop here, will provide us with a better understanding of the use and implications of efficient markets theory. In addition, we will examine evidence concerning these implications. Eugene Fama, a prominent financial economist, states in a well-known survey of the empirical data on efficient markets theory, "In short, the evidence in support of the effi-

Following the Financial News

Stock Prices

Stock prices are published daily, and in the *Wall Street Journal* they are reported in the sections "NYSE-Composite Transactions," "Amex-Composite Transactions," and "Over-the-Counter Markets." The New York Stock Exchange (NYSE) and American Stock Exchange (Amex) stocks have their prices quoted under the following format:

	52 Weeks Hi	52 Weeks Lo	Stock	Sym	Div	Yld %	PE	Vol 100s	Hi	Lo	Close	Net Chg	
	14	2¾	Intlake	IK		...	12	60	4⅛	4	4	− ⅛	
▶	139¾	96¼	IBM	IBM	4.84	4.4	11	22147	111⅞	110⅛	110⅝	− ⅝	◀
	87⅜	57	IntFlavor	IFF	2.40	3.0	20	512	81⅜	80½	81¼	+ ⅝	
s	34¾	9	IntGameTech	IGT		...	23	1119	32⅜	29½	31½	− ¾	
	45	27¼	IntMultfood	IMC	1.18a	2.7	18	159	43⅜	42⅝	43	+ ¼	

Source: *Wall Street Journal* (Friday, April 12, 1991).

The following information is included in each column. [International Business Machines (IBM) common stock is used as an example.]

52 Weeks
Hi = highest price of a share in the past 52 weeks: 139¾ for IBM stock.

52 Weeks
Lo = lowest price of a share in the past 52 weeks: 96¼ for IBM stock.

Stock = company name; IBM for International Business Machines.

Sym = symbol that identifies company.

Div = annual dividends: $4.84.

Yld % = yield for stock expressed as annual dividends divided by today's closing price; 4.4% = 4.84 ÷ 110⅝ for IBM stock.

PE = price-earnings ratio; the stock price divided by the annual earnings per share: 11 for IBM stock.

Vol. 100s = number of shares (in 100s) traded that day: 2,214,700 shares for IBM.

Hi = highest price of a share that day: 111⅞.

Lo = lowest price of a share that day: 110⅛.

Close = closing price (the last price) that day: 110⅝.

Net Chg = change in the closing price from the previous day: −⅝.

Prices quoted for shares traded over-the-counter (that is, through dealers rather than on an organized exchange) are sometimes quoted with the same information, but in many cases only the bid price (the price the dealer is willing to pay for the stock) and the asked price (the price the dealer is willing to sell the stock for) are quoted.

cient markets model is extensive, and (somewhat uniquely in economics) contradictory evidence is sparse."[5]

How Valuable Are Published Reports of Financial Analysts?

You have just read in the "Heard on the Street" column of the *Wall Street Journal* that financial analysts are predicting there will be a boom in oil stocks

[5]Eugene Fama, "Efficient Capital Markets: A Review of Theory and Empirical Work," *Journal of Finance* (May 1970), pp. 383–416.

because an oil shortage is developing. Should you proceed to withdraw all your hard-earned savings from the bank and invest it in oil stocks?

Efficient markets theory tells us that by purchasing a security we cannot expect to earn an abnormally high return, a return greater than the equilibrium return. Information in newspapers and in the published reports of financial analysts is readily available to many market participants and it is already reflected in market prices. So acting on this information will not yield abnormally high returns on average. How valuable, then, are published reports of financial analysts? The answer is "not very."

The Evidence: Do Financial Analysts Beat the Market?　The implication of efficient markets theory that published reports of financial analysts are not valuable indicates that their published recommendations cannot help us to outperform the general market. There are many studies that shed light on whether financial analysts and mutual funds (some of which charge steep sales commissions to people who purchase them) beat the market.[6] One common test that has been performed is to take buy and sell recommendations from a group of analysts or mutual funds and compare the performance of the resulting selection of stocks with the market as a whole. Sometimes the financial analysts' choices have even been compared to a group of stocks that has been chosen by putting a copy of the financial page of the newspaper on a dartboard and choosing the stocks by a throw of darts. The *Wall Street Journal,* for example, has a regular feature called "Investment Dartboard," which compares how well stocks picked by financial analysts do relative to stocks picked by a dartboard. Do the analysts win? To their embarrassment, on average they do not. The dartboard or the overall market does just as well even when the comparison includes only analysts who have been successful in the past in predicting the stock market.[7]

In studies of mutual fund performance, mutual funds are separated into different groups depending on whether they had the highest or lowest profits in a chosen period. When their performance is compared to a subsequent period, the mutual funds that did well in the first period do not beat the market in the second.

The conclusion from the study of financial analysts and mutual fund performance is: ***Having performed well in the past does not indicate that a financial analyst or a mutual fund will perform well in the future.*** It is not pleasing news to financial analysts, but it is exactly what efficient markets theory predicts. It says that some financial analysts will be lucky (and some will be unlucky). Being lucky does not mean that a forecaster actually has the

---

[6]For a survey of these studies, see Eugene Fama, *Foundations of Finance* (New York: Basic Books, 1976), Chapter 5.

[7]There is one exception to the usual finding that financial analysts do not beat the market: the Value Line Survey. See Fischer Black, "Yes Virginia, There Is Hope: Tests of the Value Line Ranking System," *Financial Analysts Journal* 29 (September/October 1973), pp. 10–14.

Box 29.1

An Exception that Proves the Rule: Ivan Boesky

Efficient market theory indicates that financial analysts should not have the ability to beat the market. Yet this is exactly what Ivan Boesky was able to do until 1986, when he was charged by the SEC with making unfair profits (rumored to be in the hundreds of millions) by trading on inside information. In an out-of-court settlement, Boesky was banned from the securities business, fined $100 million, and sentenced to three years in jail. If the stock market is efficient, can the SEC legitimately claim that Boesky was able to beat the market? The answer is "yes."

Ivan Boesky was the most successful of the so-called arbs (short for arbitrageurs) who made hundreds of millions in profits for himself and his clients by investing in the stocks of firms that were about to be taken over by other firms at an above market price. Boesky's continuing success was assured by an arrangement in which he paid cash (sometimes in a suitcase) to Dennis Levine, an investment banker who had inside information about when a takeover was to take place because his firm was arranging the financing of the deal. When Levine found out that a firm was planning a takeover, he would inform Boesky, who would then buy the stock of the company being taken over and sell it after the stock had risen.

Boesky's ability to make millions year after year in the 1980s is an exception that proves the rule that financial analysts cannot continually outperform the market; yet it supports the efficient markets claim that only information *unavailable* to the market enables an investor to do so. Boesky profited from knowing about takeovers *before* the rest of the market so that this information was unavailable to the market.

ability to continually beat the market. (An exception that proves the rule is discussed in Box 29.1.)

Probably no other conclusion is met with more skepticism by students than this when they first hear it. We all know or have heard of somebody who has been successful in the stock market for a period of many years. We wonder, how could someone be so consistently successful if he or she did not really know how to predict when returns would be abnormally high? The following story, reported in the press, illustrates why such anecdotal evidence is not reliable.

A get-rich-quick artist invented the following clever scam. Every week he wrote two letters. In letter A he would pick team A to win a particular football game, and in letter B he would pick the opponent (B). Certain persons would then be separated into two groups, and he would send letter A to one and letter B to the other. The following week he would do the same thing, but would send *these* letters only to the group who had received the first letter with the correct prediction. After doing this for some ten games, he had a small cluster who had received letters with the correct winning team for every game. He then mailed a final letter to them. He declared that since he, after all, was obviously an expert predictor of the outcome of football games (he had picked winners ten weeks in a row!), and since his predictions were profitable for the recipients who bet on the games, he would continue to send his predictions only if he were paid a substantial amount of money. When one of his clients figured out what he was up to, the con man was prosecuted and thrown in jail!

What is the lesson of the story? Even if no forecaster is an accurate predictor of the market, there will always be a group of consistent winners. A person who has done well regularly in the past cannot guarantee that he will do well in the future. Note that there will also be a group of persistent losers, but you rarely hear about them because no one brags about a poor forecasting record.

Should You Be Skeptical of Hot Tips?

Suppose your broker phones you with a hot tip to buy stock in the Happy Feet Corporation (HFC) because it has just developed a product that is completely effective in curing athlete's foot. The stock price is sure to go up. Should you follow her advice and buy HFC stock?

Efficient markets theory indicates that you should be skeptical of such news. If the stock market is efficient, it has already priced HFC stock so that its expected return will equal the equilibrium return. The hot tip is not particularly valuable and will *not* enable you to earn an abnormally high return.

You might wonder, though, if the hot tip is based on new information and would give you an edge on the rest of the market. If other market participants have gotten this information before you, the answer is "no." As soon as the information hits the street, the unexploited profit opportunity it creates will be quickly eliminated. The stock's price will already reflect the information and you should expect to realize only the equilibrium return. On the other hand, if you are one of the first to know the new information (as Ivan Boesky was; see Box 29.1), it can do you some good. Only then can you be one of the lucky ones who, on average, will earn an abnormally high return by helping to eliminate the profit opportunity by buying HFC stock.

The Evidence   Because most hot tips are whispered from ear to ear, it is not possible to collect data on the frequency with which they allow people to earn abnormally high returns. Since it is unlikely that financial analysts' hot tips are any better than their published recommendations, the evidence we have presented indicates financial analysts do not beat the market and hot tips are unlikely to be very valuable.

Do Stock Prices Follow a Random Walk?

The term **random walk** describes the movements of a variable whose future changes cannot be predicted (are random) because, given today's value, the variable is just as likely to fall as to rise. An important implication of efficient markets theory is that stock prices should approximately follow a random walk; that is, *future changes in stock prices should, for all practical purposes, be unpredictable.* The random walk implication from efficient markets theory is one that is most commonly mentioned in the press because it is the most readily comprehensible to the public. In fact, when people mention the "random walk theory of stock prices," what is actually being referred to is efficient markets theory.

The case for random walk stock prices can be demonstrated. Suppose that people could predict that the price of HFC stock would rise 1% in the coming week. The predicted rate of capital gains and rate of return on HFC stock would then be over 50% at an annual rate. Since this is very likely to be far higher than the equilibrium rate of return on HFC stock ($RET^{of} > RET^*$), efficient markets theory indicates that people would immediately buy this stock and bid up its current price. The action would stop only when the predictable change in the price dropped to near zero so that $RET^{of} = RET^*$.

Similarly, if people could predict that the price of HFC stock would fall by 1%, the predicted rate of return would be quite negative ($RET^{of} < RET^*$) and people would immediately sell. The current price would fall until the predictable change in the price rose back to near zero, where the efficient markets condition again holds. Efficient markets theory suggests that the predictable change in stock prices will be near zero, leading to the conclusion that stock prices will generally follow a random walk.[8]

The Evidence   There are two types of tests that economists have used to explore the hypothesis that stock prices follow a random walk. In the first, economists examine stock market records to see if changes in stock prices could have been predicted utilizing past changes. Specifically, they explore whether changes in stock prices are systematically related to past changes. The second type of test examines the data to see if other publicly available information besides past stock prices could have been used to predict changes. These tests are somewhat more stringent because other information besides past stock price data (for example, money supply growth, government spending, interest rates, corporate profits) might be used to help forecast stock returns. The results of both types of tests generally confirm

---

[8]Note that the random walk behavior of stock prices is only an *approximation* derived from efficient markets theory. It would hold exactly only for a stock for which an unchanged price leads to its having the equilibrium return. Then, when the predictable change in the stock price is exactly zero, $RET^{of} = RET^*$.

the efficient markets view that stock prices are not predictable and follow a random walk.[9]

Do Stock Prices Always Rise When There Is Good News?

If you follow the stock market, you might have noticed the following puzzling phenomenon. When good news about a stock is announced (for example, a particularly favorable earnings report), the price of the stock frequently does not rise. Efficient markets theory and the random walk behavior of stock prices explain this phenomenon.

Because changes in stock prices are unpredictable, when information is announced that has already been expected by the market, the stock price will remain unchanged. The announcement does not contain any new information that should lead to a change in stock prices. If this were not the case and the announcement led to a change in stock prices, it would mean that the change was predictable. Since this is ruled out in an efficient market, **stock prices will respond to announcements only when the information in these announcements is new;** that is, it is unexpected. If an announcement is expected, there will be no stock price response.

Sometimes a stock price declines when good news is announced. Although this seems somewhat peculiar, it is completely consistent with the workings of an efficient market. Suppose that although the announced news is good, it is not as good as the market *expected*. HFC's earnings may have risen 15%, but if the market expected the earnings to rise by 20%, the new

[9]The first type of test using only stock market data is referred to as a test of "weak-form efficiency" because the information set that can be used to predict stock prices is restricted solely to the past price data. The second type of test is referred to as a test of "semistrong-form efficiency" because the information set is expanded to include all publicly available information and not just past stock prices. There is a third type of test called a test of "strong-form efficiency" because the information set includes insider information, that is, information only known to the owners of the corporation such as when they plan to declare a high dividend. These strong-form tests do sometimes indicate that insider information could have been used to predict changes in stock prices. This finding, however, does not contradict efficient markets theory because this information was not made available to the market and therefore could not be reflected in market prices. In fact, there are strict laws against using insider information to trade in financial markets. Recent evidence does find some departures from random walk stock market behavior, but the size of these departures is small. See James M. Poterba and Lawrence H. Summers, "Mean Reversion in Stock Prices: Evidence and Implications," *Journal of Financial Economics* 22 (1988), pp. 27–59; Eugene F. Fama and Kenneth R. French, "Permanent and Temporary Components of Stock Prices," *Journal of Political Economy* 96 (1988), pp. 246–273; and Andrew W. Lo and A. Craig MacKinlay, "Stock Market Prices Do Not Follow Random Walks: Evidence from a Simple Specification Test," *Review of Financial Studies* 1 (1988), pp. 41–66. However, Myung Jig Kim, Charles R. Nelson, and Richard Startz, "Mean Reversion in Stock Prices? A Reappraisal of the Evidence," *Review of Financial Studies* 4 (1991), question whether some of these findings are valid.

information contained in the announcement is actually unfavorable and the stock price declines.

The Evidence   The evidence cited that stock prices follow a random walk suggests that stock prices will frequently not rise when good news is announced. The evidence that this occurs is even more straightforward. We often see news articles of the type featured in the "Following the Financial News" box or headlines like the following one in *The New York Times* on October 15, 1987 (just shortly before the Black Monday crash):

TRADE GAP SHRINKS LESS THAN
HOPED: MARKETS PLUNGE

DOW FALLS RECORD 95.46

Is Technical Analysis Worthwhile?

A popular technique used to predict stock prices is to study past stock price data and search for patterns such as trends and regular cycles in stock prices. Depending on what patterns appear, rules for when to buy and sell stocks are then established. This forecasting procedure is called "technical analysis," and it once (some twenty years ago) had a very large following in the financial community. It now has a smaller following because the development of efficient markets theory suggests that technical analysis is a waste of time. The simplest way to understand why is to use the random walk result derived from efficient markets theory that holds that past stock price data cannot help predict changes. Therefore, technical analysis, which relies on such data to produce its forecasts, cannot successfully predict changes in stock prices.

The Evidence   There are two types of tests that bear directly on the value of technical analysis. The first performs the empirical analysis described earlier to evaluate the performance of any financial analyst, technical or otherwise. The results are exactly what efficient markets theory predicts: Technical analysts fare no better than other financial analysts; on average they do not outperform the market, and successful past forecasting records do not indicate their forecasts will outperform the market in the future. The second type of tests (first performed by Sidney Alexander) takes the rules developed in technical analysis for when to buy and sell stocks and applies them to new data.[10] The performance of these rules is then evaluated by the profits

---

[10]Sidney Alexander, "Price Movements in Speculative Markets: Trends or Random Walks," *Industrial Management Review* 2 (May 1961), pp. 7–26 and "Price Movements in Speculative Markets: Trends or Random Walks, No. 2," in Paul Cootner, ed., *The Random Character of Stock Prices* (Cambridge, Mass.: MIT Press, 1964).

Following the Financial News

The Stock Market

Besides the information on stock prices traded on the New York Stock Exchange, the American Stock Exchange, other regional markets and over-the-counter, the *Wall Street Journal* publishes daily two columns that provide an analysis of the stock market. The "Heard on the Street" column reports what financial analysts are saying about individual stocks, while the "Abreast of the Market" column

(see example below) appraises what is happening to the overall market. These two columns always appear on the first or second page of the third section, C, of the *Journal*.

Is what this article says about the relation of bullish earnings reports and stock prices consistent with efficient markets theory?

Industrial Average Climbs 64.85, Its Second-Largest Rise This Year

ABREAST OF THE MARKET

By Craig S. Smith
Staff Reporter of The Wall Street Journal

NEW YORK — Stock prices rocketed higher yesterday, largely on relief that corporate profits weren't as bad as many had feared.

The Dow Jones Industrial Average soared in the final half-hour of trading, to end with a 64.85-point gain at 2452.72. That was its second-largest daily advance this year, following a rise of 78.71 on Aug. 27.

Traders said a string of earnings reports that were either benign or better than expected encouraged bargain hunters to buy shares while scaring short sellers into covering their loans.

Short sellers sell borrowed stock to profit from the decline in share prices. When they sense that the market has bottomed out, they will buy stocks to pay back the loans.

"This is a technical rally that has a long way to go," said Thomas Gallagher, managing director of capital commitment

at Oppenheimer. "There is a tremendous amount of [short sellers] out there."

Big Board advancers led decliners, 1,116 to 436, with 431 stocks ending unchanged. Volume on the New York Stock Exchange surged to 204,120,000 shares from Wednesday's 161.3 million shares.

Dow Chemical, Caterpillar and **Waste Management** were among the big companies whose earnings pleasantly surprised investors.

"There was a fear that there would be a lot of disasters among third-quarter earnings, and so there is some comfort in the fact that earnings haven't fallen apart completely," said James M. Meyer, director of research at Janney Montgomery Scott.

Even mediocre profits brought an enthusiastic response. **Digital Equipment** surged 4¼ to 51 after reporting that it earned 21 cents a share in its fiscal first quarter, down from $1.20 a share in the year-earlier quarter.

"I wouldn't characterize those as good earnings," Mr. Meyer said. However, some analysts had expected the company to lose money in the quarter.

Source: *Wall Street Journal* (Friday, October 19, 1990).

that would have been made using them. The results of these tests are also unfavorable to technical analysis. Technical analysis does not outperform the overall market.

The Efficient Markets Prescription for the Investor

What is efficient markets theory's general recommendation for how an investor should invest in the stock market? It tells us that hot tips, financial analysts' published recommendations, and technical analysis—all of which make use of publicly available information—cannot help the investor to outperform the market. Indeed, it indicates that any investor without better information than other market participants cannot expect to beat the market. So what is he or she to do?

Efficient markets theory leads to the conclusion that such an investor (and almost all of us fit into this category) should not try to outguess the market by constantly buying and selling securities. The only outcome of this process is that the investor will make his or her broker richer by paying a substantial amount for brokerage commissions.[11] Instead, the investor should pursue a "buy and hold strategy," that is, purchase stocks and hold them for long periods of time. This will lead to the same returns, on average, but the investor's net profits will be higher because there will be fewer brokerage commissions.[12]

It is frequently a sensible strategy for a small investor, whose costs of managing a portfolio may be high relative to its size, to buy into a mutual fund rather than individual stocks. Since efficient markets theory indicates that no mutual fund can consistently outperform the market, an investor should not buy into one that has high management fees or that pays sales commissions to brokers. He or she should purchase a mutual fund without any sales commissions (called a no-load fund) which also has low management fees.

As we have seen, the evidence, almost without exception, strongly supports efficient markets theory in the stock market. Outlined here, the basic prescription for the investor is one that receives much scientific support.[13] (See Box 29.2.)

---

[11]The investor may also have to pay Uncle Sam capital gains taxes on any profits that are realized when a security is sold—an additional reason why continual buying and selling does not make sense.

[12]As we saw in Chapter 5, the investor can also minimize risk by holding a diversified portfolio. The investor will be better off by pursuing a buy and hold strategy with a diversified portfolio, or equivalently with a mutual fund that has a diversified portfolio.

[13]Some research has found results that are not fully consistent with efficient markets theory [see Michael Jensen, ed., "Symposium on Some Anomalous Evidence Regarding Market Efficiency," *Journal of Financial Economics* 6 (June/September 1978)], but the magnitudes of the deviations from the efficient markets condition are sufficiently small that the basic prescription outlined requires little modification.

Box   2 9 . 2

What Does the Stock Market Crash of 1987 Tell Us About Rational Expectations and Efficient Markets?

Some economists have suggested that the October 19, 1987, stock market crash should make us question the validity of efficient markets and rational expectations. They do not believe that a rational marketplace could have produced such a massive swing in share prices. To what degree should the stock market crash make us doubt the validity of rational expectations and efficient markets theory?

Nothing in rational expectations and efficient markets theory rules out large one-day changes in stock prices. A large change in stock prices can result from a dramatic change in optimal forecasts of the future valuation of firms. There are many possible explanations for why rational expectations of the future value of firms dropped dramatically on October 19, 1987: the moves in Congress to restrict corporate takeovers, the disappointing performance of the trade deficit, congressional failure to substantially reduce the budget deficit, increased fears of inflation, the decline of the dollar, and in-

creased fears of financial distress in the banking industry. There is, however, a lingering suspicion that factors other than market fundamentals (items that have a direct impact on future earnings prospects for the firms) may have had an impact on stock prices. Analysts often attribute a large role to market psychology, for example.

One lesson from the crash might be that the stock market is not entirely driven by market fundamentals and that market psychology or the institutional structure of the marketplace can influence stock prices. However, nothing in this view precludes the basic rationale for efficient markets or rational expectations theory—that market participants eliminate unexploited profit opportunities. Thus, even though stock market prices may not always solely reflect market fundamentals, the basic implications of rational expectations and efficient markets theory stressed in the text are still likely to hold.

EVIDENCE ON RATIONAL EXPECTATIONS IN OTHER MARKETS

Evidence in other financial markets also supports efficient markets theory and hence the rationality of expectations. For example, there is little evidence that financial analysts are able to outperform the bond market.[14] The returns on bonds appear to conform to the efficient markets condition of Equation (29.5).

Rationality of expectations is, however, much harder to test in markets other than financial markets because price data that reflect expectations are not as readily available. The most common tests of rational expectations in these markets make use of survey data on the forecasts of market partici-

---

[14]See the discussion in Frederic S. Mishkin, "Efficient Markets Theory: Implications for Monetary Policy," *Brookings Papers on Economic Activity* 3 (1978), pp. 707–768, of the results in Michael J. Prell, "How Well Do the Experts Forecast Interest Rates?" Federal Reserve Bank of Kansas City, *Monthly Review* (September/October 1973).

pants. For example, one well-known study by James Pesando used a survey of inflation expectations that were collected from prominent economists and inflation forecasters.[15] In that survey, these people were asked what they predicted the inflation rate would be over the next six months and over the next year. Since rational expectations theory implies that forecast errors should on average be zero and cannot be predicted, tests of the theory involve asking whether the forecast errors in a survey could be predicted ahead of time using publicly available information. The evidence from Pesando's and other subsequent studies is rather mixed. Sometimes the forecast errors cannot be predicted and at other times they can. The evidence is not as supportive of rational expectations theory as is the evidence from financial markets.

Does the fact that forecast errors from surveys are often predictable suggest that we should reject rational expectations theory in these other markets? The answer is "not necessarily." One problem with this evidence is that the expectations data are obtained from surveys rather than from actual economic decisions of market participants. It is a serious criticism of this evidence. Survey responses are not always reliable because there is little incentive for the participants to tell the truth. For example, when people are asked in surveys how much television they watch, it is well known that responses greatly underestimate the actual time spent. Neither are people very truthful about the shows they watch. Often they say they watch ballet on public television. We actually know they are watching Vanna White turn letters on the "Wheel of Fortune" instead, because it, not ballet, has high Nielsen ratings. Truly, how many people will admit to being regular watchers of the "Wheel of Fortune"?

A second problem with the survey evidence is that a market's behavior may not be equally influenced by the expectations of all the survey participants, making survey evidence a poor guide to market behavior. For example, we have already seen that prices in financial markets *behave* as if expectations are rational even though many of the market participants do not have rational expectations.[16]

Proof is not yet conclusive on the validity of rational expectations theory in markets besides financial markets. One important conclusion, however, that *is* supported by the survey evidence, is that ***if there is a change in the way a variable moves, the way expectations of this variable are formed will change as well.***

---

[15]James Pesando, "A Note on the Rationality of the Livingston Price Expectations," *Journal of Political Economy* 83 (August 1975), pp. 845–858.

[16]There is some fairly strong evidence for this proposition. For example, Frederic S. Mishkin, "Are Market Forecasts Rational?" *American Economic Review* 71 (June 1981), pp. 295–306, finds that although survey forecasts of short-term interest rates are not found to be rational, the bond market *behaves* as if the expectations of these interest rates are rational.

SUMMARY

1. A review of the topics covered in the study of money, banking, and financial markets shows that expectations are important to almost all economic behavior.

2. The theory of rational expectations states that expectations will not differ from optimal forecasts (the best guesses of the future) using all available information. Rational expectations theory makes sense because it is costly for people not to have the best forecast of the future. Two important implications of the theory are (1) if there is a change in the way a variable moves, the way expectations of this variable are formed will change too, and (2) the forecast errors of expectations are unpredictable.

3. Efficient markets theory is the application of rational expectations to the pricing of securities in financial markets. Current security prices will fully reflect all available information because in an efficient market all unexploited profit opportunities are eliminated. The elimination of unex-

ploited profit opportunities necessary for a financial market to be efficient does not require that all market participants be well informed and have rational expectations.

4. Efficient markets theory indicates that hot tips, financial analysts' published recommendations, and technical analysis cannot help the investor to outperform the market. The prescription for investors is to pursue a buy and hold strategy, that is, purchase stocks and hold them for long periods of time. Empirical evidence generally supports efficient markets theory in the stock market.

5. Although the evidence supporting rational expectations in the financial markets is strong, the evidence in other markets is more mixed. However, even for these other markets, there is support for the rational expectations conclusion that a change in the way a variable moves will change the way that expectations of the variable are formed.

KEY TERMS

adaptive expectations

rational expectations

optimal forecast

unexploited profit
  opportunity

random walk

QUESTIONS AND PROBLEMS

* 1. Answer true, false, or uncertain: "Forecasters' predictions of inflation are notoriously inaccurate. So their expectations of inflation cannot be rational."

2. "Whenever it is snowing when Joe Commuter gets up in the morning, he misjudges how long it will take him to drive to work. Otherwise, his expectations of the driving time are perfectly accurate. Since it snows once every ten years where Joe lives, Joe's expectations are almost always perfectly accurate." Are Joe's expectations rational? Why or why not?

* 3. If a forecaster spends hours every day studying data to forecast interest rates but his expecta-

tions are not as accurate as predicting that tomorrow's interest rates will be identical to today's interest rate, are his expectations rational?

4. Answer true, false, or uncertain: "If stock prices did not follow a random walk, there would be unexploited profit opportunities in the market."

* 5. In Chapter 27 you studied why stock prices might rise when the money supply rises. Does this mean that when you see that the money supply has had a sharp rise in the past week that you should go out and buy stocks? Why or why not?

6. If the public expects a corporation to lose $5 a share this quarter and it actually loses $4, which is still the largest loss in the history of the com-

pany, what does efficient markets theory say will happen to the price of the stock when its $4 loss is announced?

* 7. If I read in the *Wall Street Journal* that the "smart money" on Wall Street expects stock prices to fall, should I take their advice and sell all my stocks?

8. If my broker has been right in her five previous buy and sell recommendations, should I start listening to her advice?

* 9. Can a person expect the price of IBM to rise by 10% in the next month if his or her expectations are rational?

10. Answer true, false, or uncertain: "If most participants in the stock market do not follow what is happening to the monetary aggregates, prices of common stocks will not fully reflect information about them."

*11. Answer true, false, or uncertain: "An efficient market is one in which no one ever profits from having better information than the rest."

12. If higher money growth is associated with higher future inflation, and if announced money growth turns out to be extremely high but is still less than the market expected, what do you think would happen to long-term bond prices?

CHAPTER 30

Rational Expectations: Implications for Policy

PREVIEW

After World War II, economists, armed with Keynesian models (the *ISLM* model, for example) that described how government policies could be used to manipulate employment and output, felt that activist policies could reduce the severity of business cycle fluctuations without creating inflation. In the 1960s and 1970s, these economists got their chance to put their policies into practice (see Chapter 28), but the results were not what they had anticipated. The economic record from that period was not a happy one: Inflation accelerated, with the inflation rate often climbing above 10%, while the unemployment performance deteriorated from the performance of the 1950s.[1]

In the 1970s and 1980s economists such as Robert Lucas and Thomas Sargent, now both at the University of Chicago, applied rational expectations theory to examine why activist policies appear to have performed so poorly. Their analysis casts doubt on whether macroeconomic models can be used to evaluate the potential effects of policy or whether policy can be effective if the public *expects* that it will be implemented. Because the analysis of Lucas and Sargent has such strong implications for the way policy should be conducted, it has been labeled the "rational expectations revolution."[2]

The present chapter examines the analysis behind the rational expectations revolution. We start first with the "Lucas critique," which indicates that because expectations are important in economic behavior, it may be quite difficult to know what the outcome of an activist policy will be. We then discuss the effect of rational expectations on the aggregate demand and

----

[1]Some of the deterioration can be attributed, however, to the supply shocks in 1973–1975 and 1978–1980.

[2]Other economists who have been active in promoting the rational expectations revolution are Robert Barro of Harvard University, Bennett McCallum of Carnegie-Mellon University, and Edward Prescott and Neil Wallace of the University of Minnesota.

supply analysis developed in Chapter 26 by exploring three models that incorporate expectations in different ways.

A comparison of all three models indicates that the existence of rational expectations makes activist policies less likely to be successful and raises the issue of credibility as an important element affecting policy outcomes. With rational expectations, an essential ingredient to a successful anti-inflation policy is the credibility of the policy in the eyes of the public. The rational expectations revolution is now at the center of many of the current debates in monetary theory that have major implications for how monetary and fiscal policy should be conducted.

THE LUCAS CRITIQUE OF POLICY EVALUATION

In his famous paper, "Econometric Policy Evaluation: A Critique," Robert Lucas presented an argument that had devastating implications for the usefulness of conventional **econometric models** (models whose equations are estimated with statistical procedures).[3] Economists developed these models (for example, the St. Louis and MPS models described in Chapter 27) for two purposes: (1) to forecast economic activity and (2) to evaluate the effects of different policies. While Lucas' critique had nothing to say about the usefulness of these models as forecasting tools, he argued that they could not be relied on to evaluate the potential impact of particular policies on the economy.

To understand Lucas' argument, we must first understand econometric policy evaluation, that is, how econometric models are used to evaluate policy. As an example, we can examine how the Federal Reserve uses its econometric model (the MPS model) in making decisions about the future course of monetary policy. The MPS model contains equations that describe the relationships among hundreds of variables. These relationships are assumed to remain constant and are estimated using past data. Let's say that the Fed wants to know the effect on unemployment and inflation of an increase in the rate of money growth from 5 to 10%. It feeds the new higher rate of money growth into the model (actually into a computer that contains the model) and the model then provides an answer about how much unemployment will fall as a result of the higher money growth and how much the inflation rate will rise. Other possible policies such as a decline in money growth to 1% might also be fed into the model. After a series of these policies have been tried out, the policymakers at the Fed can see which policies produce the most desirable outcome for unemployment and inflation.

---

[3]Robert Lucas, Jr., "Econometric Policy Evaluation: A Critique," in Karl Brunner and Allan H. Meltzer, eds., *The Phillips Curve and Labor Markets, Carnegie-Rochester Conference Series on Public Policy* 1 (1976), pp. 19–46.

Lucas' challenge to this procedure for evaluating policies is based on a simple principle of rational expectations theory: *The way expectations are formed (the relationship of expectations to past information) changes when the behavior of forecasted variables changes.* So when policy changes, the relationship between expectations and past information will change, and since expectations affect economic behavior, the relationships in the econometric model will change. The econometric model which has been estimated with past data is then no longer the correct model for evaluating the response to this policy change and it may prove to be highly misleading.

An Example of the Lucas Critique: The Term Structure of Interest Rates

The best way to understand Lucas' argument is to look at a concrete example involving only one equation typically found in econometric models: the term-structure equation. The equation relates the long-term interest rate to current and past values of the short-term interest rate. It is one of the most important equations in Keynesian econometric models because it is the long-term interest rate that is typically viewed as having an impact on aggregate demand, not the short-term rate.

In Chapter 7 you learned that the long-term interest rate is related to an average of expected future short-term interest rates. Suppose that in the past when the short-term rate rose, it quickly fell back down again; that is, any increase was typically temporary. Since rational expectations theory suggests that any rise in the short-term interest rate is expected to be only temporary, a rise should have only a minimal effect on the average of expected future short-term rates. It will cause the long-term interest rate to rise by a negligible amount. The term-structure relationship estimated using past data will then show only a weak effect of changes in the short-term interest rate on the long-term rate.

Suppose the Fed wants to evaluate what will happen to the economy if it pursues a policy that is likely to raise the short-term interest rate from a current value of 10% to a permanently higher level of 12%. The term-structure equation that has been estimated using past data will indicate that there will be just a small change in the long-term interest rate. However, if the public recognizes that the short-term rate is rising to a permanently higher level, then rational expectations theory indicates that they will no longer expect a rise in the short-term rate to be temporary. Instead, when they see the interest rate rise to 12%, they will expect the average of future short-term interest rates to rise substantially and so the long-term interest rate will rise greatly, not minimally as the estimated term-structure equation suggests. You can see that evaluating the likely outcome of the change in Fed policy with an econometric model can be highly misleading.

The term-structure example also demonstrates another aspect of the Lucas critique. The effects of a particular policy depend critically on the public's expectations about the policy. If the public expects the rise in the short-term interest rate to be merely temporary, then we have seen that the response of long-term interest rates will be negligible. If, on the other hand, the public expects the rise to be more permanent, the response of long-term rates will be far greater. ***The Lucas critique not only points out that conventional econometric models cannot be used for policy evaluation, but it shows that the public's expectations about a policy will influence the response to the policy.***

The term-structure equation discussed here is only one of many equations in econometric models to which the Lucas critique applies. In fact, Lucas uses the examples of consumption and investment equations in his classic paper on econometric policy evaluation. One attractive feature of the term-structure example is that it deals with expectations in a financial market, a sector of the economy for which the theory and empirical evidence supporting rational expectations is very strong. The Lucas critique should still apply, however, to sectors of the economy for which rational expectations theory is more controversial, because the basic principle of the Lucas critique is not that expectations are always rational, but that the formation of expectations changes when the behavior of a forecasted variable changes. This less stringent principle is supported by the evidence in other sectors of the economy besides financial markets.

THE NEW CLASSICAL MACROECONOMIC MODEL

We now turn to the implications of rational expectations for the aggregate demand and supply analysis we studied in Chapter 26. The first model we examine that views expectations as rational is the new classical macroeconomic model developed by Lucas and Sargent, among others. In the new classical model, all wages and prices are completely flexible with respect to expected changes in the price level; that is, a rise in the expected price level results in an immediate and equal rise in wages and prices because workers try to keep their *real* wages from falling when they expect the price level to rise.

This view of how wages and prices are set indicates that a rise in the expected price level causes an immediate inward shift in the aggregate supply curve, which leaves real wages unchanged and aggregate output at the natural rate (full employment) level if expectations are realized. This model then suggests that anticipated policy has no effect on aggregate output and unemployment; only unanticipated policy has an effect.

Effect of Unanticipated and Anticipated Policy

First, let us look at the short-run response to an unanticipated (unexpected) policy such as an unexpected increase in the money supply.

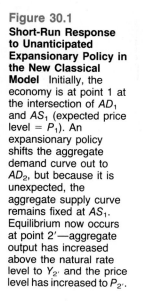

Figure 30.1
Short-Run Response to Unanticipated Expansionary Policy in the New Classical Model Initially, the economy is at point 1 at the intersection of AD_1 and AS_1 (expected price level = P_1). An expansionary policy shifts the aggregate demand curve out to AD_2, but because it is unexpected, the aggregate supply curve remains fixed at AS_1. Equilibrium now occurs at point 2'—aggregate output has increased above the natural rate level to $Y_{2'}$ and the price level has increased to $P_{2'}$.

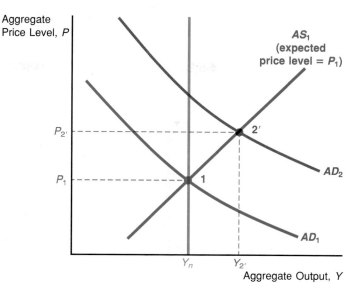

In Figure 30.1 the aggregate supply curve (AS_1) is drawn for an expected price level P_1. The initial aggregate demand curve (AD_1) intersects the AS_1 at point 1, where the realized price level is at the expected price level (P_1) and aggregate output is at the natural rate level (Y_n). Because point 1 is also on the long-run aggregate supply curve at Y_n, there is no tendency for the aggregate supply to shift. The economy remains in long-run equilibrium.

Suppose the Fed suddenly decides that the unemployment rate is too high and so makes a large bond purchase which is unexpected by the public. Then the money supply increases and the aggregate demand curve shifts out to AD_2. Because this shift is unexpected, the expected price level remains at P_1 and the aggregate supply curve remains at AS_1. Equilibrium is now at point 2', the intersection of AD_2 and AS_1. Aggregate output increases above the natural rate level to $Y_{2'}$ and the realized price level increases to $P_{2'}$.

If, on the other hand, the public expects that the Fed will make these open market purchases in order to lower unemployment because they have seen this done in the past, the expansionary policy will be anticipated. The outcome of such anticipated expansionary policy is illustrated in Figure 30.2. Because expectations are rational, workers and firms recognize that an expansionary policy will shift out the aggregate demand curve and they will expect the aggregate price level to rise to P_2. Workers will demand higher wages so that their real wage will remain the same when the price level rises. The aggregate supply curve then shifts in to AS_2, where it intersects AD_2 at point 2, an equilibrium point for which aggregate output is at the natural rate level (Y_n) and the price level has risen to P_2.

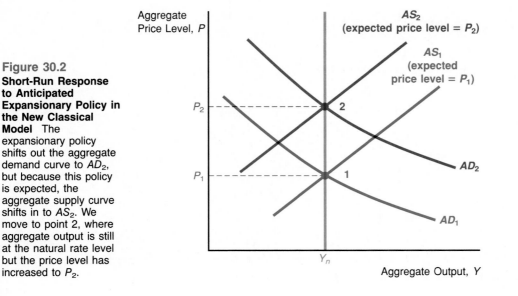

Figure 30.2
Short-Run Response to Anticipated Expansionary Policy in the New Classical Model The expansionary policy shifts out the aggregate demand curve to AD_2, but because this policy is expected, the aggregate supply curve shifts in to AS_2. We move to point 2, where aggregate output is still at the natural rate level but the price level has increased to P_2.

The new classical macroeconomic model demonstrates that aggregate output does not increase as a result of anticipated expansionary policy and that the economy immediately moves to a point of long-run equilibrium (point 2) in which aggregate output is at the natural rate level. Although Figure 30.2 suggests why this occurs, we have not yet proved why an anticipated expansionary policy shifts in the aggregate supply curve to exactly AS_2 (corresponding to an expected price level of P_2) and thus why aggregate output *necessarily* remains at the natural rate level. The proof is, unfortunately, somewhat difficult and is dealt with in Box 30.1.

The new classical model has the word *classical* associated with it because when policy is anticipated, the new classical model has a property that is associated with the classical economists of the nineteenth and early twentieth centuries: Aggregate output remains at the natural rate level. On the other hand, the new classical model allows aggregate output to fluctuate away from the natural rate level as a result of *unanticipated* movements in the aggregate demand curve. The conclusion from the new classical model is a striking one: ***Anticipated policy has no effect on the business cycle; only unanticipated policy matters.***[4]

This conclusion has been given the name the **policy ineffectiveness proposition** because it implies that one anticipated policy is just like any

---

[4]Note that the new classical view in which anticipated policy has no effect on the business cycle does not imply that anticipated policy has no effect on the overall health of the economy. The new classical analysis, for example, does not rule out possible effects of anticipated policy on the natural rate of output, Y_n, which can benefit the public.

B o x   3 0 . 1

A Proof of the Policy Ineffectiveness Proposition

The proof that in the new classical macroeconomic model aggregate output *necessarily* remains at the natural rate level when there is anticipated expansionary policy is as follows. In the new classical model, the expected price level for the aggregate supply curve occurs at its intersection with the long-run aggregate supply curve (see Figure 30.2). The optimal forecast of the price level is given by the intersection of the aggregate supply curve with the anticipated aggregate demand curve, AD_2. If the aggregate supply curve is to the right of AS_2 in Figure 30.2, it will intersect AD_2 at a price level higher than the expected level (at the intersection of this aggregate supply curve and the Y_n line). The

optimal forecast of the price level will then not equal the expected price level, thereby violating the rationality of expectations. A similar argument can be made to show that when the aggregate supply curve is to the left of AS_2, the assumption of rational expectations is violated. Only when the aggregate supply curve is at AS_2 (corresponding to an expected price level of P_2) are expectations rational, because the optimal forecast equals the expected price level. As we see in Figure 30.2, the AS_2 curve implies that aggregate output remains at the natural rate level as a result of the anticipated expansionary policy.

other; it has no effect on output fluctuations. You should recognize that this proposition does not rule out output effects from policy changes. If the policy is a surprise (unanticipated) then it will have an effect on output.[5]

Can an Expansionary Policy Lead to a Decline in Aggregate Output?

Another important feature of the new classical model is that an expansionary policy, such as an increase in the rate of money growth, can lead to a *decline* in aggregate output if the public expects an even more expansionary policy than the one actually implemented. There will be a surprise in the policy, but it will be negative and drive down output. Policymakers cannot be sure if their policies will work in the intended direction.

To see how an expansionary policy can lead to a decline in aggregate output, let us turn to the aggregate supply and demand diagram in Figure 30.3. Initially we are at point 1, the intersection of AD_1 and AS_1; output is Y_n and the price level is P_1. Now suppose that the public expects the Fed will increase the money supply in order to shift the aggregate demand curve to AD_2. As we saw in Figure 30.2, the aggregate supply curve shifts in to AS_2

---

[5]Thomas Sargent and Neil Wallace, "'Rational' Expectations, The Optimal Monetary Instrument, and the Optimal Money Supply Rule," *Journal of Political Economy* 83 (April 1975), pp. 241–254, first demonstrated the full implications of the policy ineffectiveness proposition.

Figure 30.3
Short-Run Response to an Expansionary Policy Which Is Less Expansionary Than Expected in the New Classical Model
Because the public expects the aggregate demand curve to shift to AD_2, the aggregate supply curve shifts in to AS_2 (expected price level = P_2). When the actual expansionary policy falls short of the public's expectation (the aggregate demand curve merely shifts to $AD_{2'}$), the economy ends up at point 2', at the intersection of $AD_{2'}$ and AS_2. Despite the expansionary policy, aggregate output falls to $Y_{2'}$.

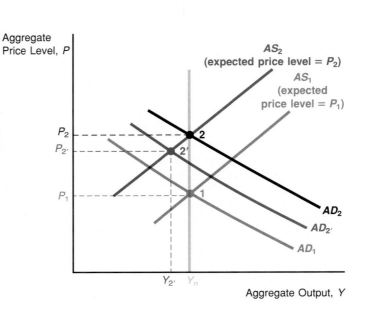

because the price level is expected to rise to P_2. Suppose that the expansionary policy engineered by the Fed actually falls short of what was expected, so that the aggregate demand curve only shifts out to $AD_{2'}$. The economy will move to point 2', the intersection of the aggregate supply curve AS_2 and the aggregate demand curve $AD_{2'}$. The result of the mistaken expectations is that output falls to $Y_{2'}$, while the price level rises to $P_{2'}$ rather than to P_2. The expansionary policy that is less expansionary than anticipated leads to an output movement directly opposite to that intended.

Study Guide
Mastering the new classical macroeconomic model, as well as the nonclassical, rational expectations model in the next section, requires practice. Make sure you can draw the aggregate demand and supply curves that explain what happens in each model when there is a contractionary policy that is (1) unanticipated, (2) anticipated, and (3) less countractionary than anticipated.

Implications for Policymakers

The new classical model with its policy ineffectiveness proposition has two important lessons as to how policymakers should conduct policy: (1) It illuminates the distinction between the effects of anticipated versus unanticipated policy actions, and (2) it demonstrates how policymakers cannot know the outcome of their decisions without knowing the public's expectations regarding them.

At first you might think policymakers can still use policy to stabilize the economy. Once they figure out the public's expectations, they can know what effect their policies will have. There are two catches to such a conclusion: First, it may be nearly impossible to find out what *the public's* expectations are, given that the public equals over 250 million U.S. citizens. Second, even if it was possible, policymakers run into further difficulties because, since the public has rational expectations, it will try to guess what policymakers plan to do. Public expectations do not remain fixed when policymakers are trying to surprise it—the public will revise its expectations, and policies will have no predictable effect on output.[6]

Where does this lead us? Should the Fed and other policy-making agencies pack up, lock the doors, and go home? In a sense, yes. The new classical model implies that discretionary stabilization policy cannot be effective and might have undesirable effects on the economy. Policymakers' attempts to use discretionary policy may create a fluctuating policy stance that leads to unpredictable policy surprises, which, in turn, cause undesirable fluctuations around the natural rate level of aggregate output. In order to eliminate these undesirable fluctuations, the Fed and other policy-making agencies should abandon discretionary policy and generate as few policy surprises as possible.

As we have seen in Figure 30.2, even though anticipated policy has no effect on aggregate output in the new classical model, it *does* have an effect on the price level. The new classical macroeconomists care about anticipated policy and suggest that policy rules be designed so that the price level will remain stable. One natural suggestion for achieving this goal, as well as for reducing uncertainty about policy, is for the monetary authorities to follow a constant money growth rule in which the rate of money growth is consistent with price stability. Many adherents of the new classical macroeconomics in the end support this monetarist policy prescription.

THE NONCLASSICAL RATIONAL EXPECTATIONS MODEL

Many economists do not accept the characterization of wage and price flexibility in the new classical model. In it all wages and prices are completely flexible with respect to expected changes in the price level; that is, a rise in the expected price level results in an immediate and equal rise in wages and

---

[6]This result follows from one of the implications of rational expectations: The forecast error of expectations about policy (the deviation of actual policy from expectations of policy) must be unpredictable. Since output is only affected by unpredictable (unanticipated) policy changes in the new classical model, policy effects on output must be unpredictable as well.

prices. The critics of the new classical model object to complete wage and price flexibility because of the existence of long-term contracts in the economy which prevent some wages and prices from rising fully with a rise in the expected price level.

Long-term labor contracts are one source of rigidity that prevents wages and prices from fully responding to changes in the expected price level (called "wage-price stickiness"). Workers might, for example, find themselves at the end of the first year of a three-year wage contract that specifies the wage rate for the coming two years. Even if new information appeared that would make them raise their expectations of the inflation rate and future price level, they could not do anything about it because they are locked into a wage agreement. Even with a high expectation about the price level, the wage rate will not adjust. In two years, when the contract is renegotiated, both workers and firms may build the expected inflation rate into their agreement, but they cannot do so immediately.

Another source of rigidity is that firms may be reluctant to change wages frequently even when there are no explicit wage contracts. Many workers have no explicit wage contracts, yet they still find that their wages are not raised more than once a year. Price stickiness may also occur because firms engage in fixed-price contracts with their suppliers. All of these rigidities (which diminish wage and price flexibility), even if they are not present in all wage and price arrangements, suggest that an increase in the expected price level might not translate into *an immediate and complete* adjustment of wages and prices.

Economists such as Stanley Fischer of MIT, Edmund Phelps of Columbia University, and John Taylor of Stanford University do not agree with the complete wage and price flexibility of the new classical macroeconomics. However, they still recognize the importance of expectations to the determination of aggregate supply and are willing to accept rational expectations theory as a reasonable characterization of how expectations are formed. The model they have developed, the "nonclassical rational expectations model" assumes that expectations are rational, but does not assume complete wage and price flexibility; instead, it assumes that wages and prices are sticky. Its basic conclusion is that unanticipated policy has a larger effect on aggregate output than anticipated policy (as in the new classical model). However, in contrast to the new classical model, the policy ineffectiveness proposition does not hold: Anticipated policy *does* affect aggregate output and the business cycle.

Effects of Unanticipated and Anticipated Policy

In panel (a) of Figure 30.4 we look at the short-run response to an unanticipated expansionary policy for the nonclassical rational expectations model. The analysis is identical to that of the new classical model. We again start at point 1, where the aggregate demand curve AD_1 intersects the aggregate

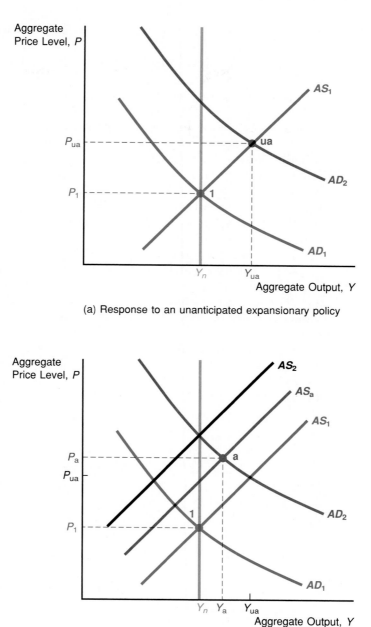

(a) Response to an unanticipated expansionary policy

Figure 30.4
Short-Run Response to Expansionary Policy in a Nonclassical Rational Expectations Model The expansionary policy which shifts aggregate demand to AD_2 has a bigger effect on output when it is unanticipated than when it is anticipated. When the expansionary policy is unanticipated in panel (a), the short-run aggregate supply curve does not shift and the economy moves to point ua so that aggregate output increases to Y_{ua}. When the policy is anticipated in panel (b), the short-run aggregate supply curve shifts in to AS_a (but not all the way to AS_2 because rigidities prevent complete wage and price adjustment) and the economy moves to point a so that aggregate output rises to Y_a (which is less than Y_{ua}).

(b) Response to an anticipated expansionary policy

supply curve AS_1 at the natural rate level of output and price level P_1. When the Fed pursues its expansionary policy of purchasing bonds and raising the money supply, the aggregate demand curve shifts out to AD_2. Because the expansionary policy is unanticipated, the expected price level remains unchanged, leaving the aggregate supply curve unchanged. Thus the economy moves to point ua, where aggregate output has increased to Y_{ua} and the price level has risen to P_{ua}.

In panel (b) we see what happens when the Fed's expansionary policy that shifts the aggregate demand curve from AD_1 to AD_2 is anticipated. Because the expansionary policy is anticipated and expectations are rational, the expected price level increases, causing wages to increase and the aggregate supply curve to shift in. Since there are rigidities that do not allow *complete* wage and price adjustment, the aggregate supply curve does not shift all the way in to AS_2 as it does in the new classical model. Instead, it moves to AS_a and the economy settles at point a, the intersection of AD_2 and AS_a. Aggregate output has risen above the natural rate level to Y_a, while the price level has increased to P_a. *Unlike in the new classical model, anticipated policy does have an effect on aggregate output in the nonclassical rational expectations model.*

We can see in Figure 30.4 that Y_{ua} is greater than Y_a so that the output response to unanticipated policy is larger than it is to anticipated policy. It is larger because the aggregate supply curve does not shift when policy is unanticipated, causing a lower price level and hence a higher level of output. We see that *like the new classical model, the nonclassical rational expectations model distinguishes between the effects of anticipated versus unanticipated policy, with unanticipated policy having a greater effect.*

Implications for Policymakers

Because the nonclassical rational expectations model indicates that anticipated policy has an effect on aggregate output, it does not rule out beneficial effects from activist stabilization policy, in contrast to the new classical model. It does warn the policymaker that designing such a policy will not be an easy task because the effects from anticipated versus unanticipated policy can be quite different. As in the new classical model, in order for policymakers to predict the outcome of their actions, they must be aware of the public's expectations about them. Policymakers are presented with similar difficulties in achieving successful policies in both the new classical and nonclassical rational expectations model.

A COMPARISON OF THE TWO RATIONAL EXPECTATIONS MODELS WITH THE TRADITIONAL MODEL

To obtain a clearer picture of the impact of the rational expectations revolution on our analysis of the aggregate economy, we can compare the two rational expectations models (the new classical macroeconomic model and the nonclassical rational expectations model) to a model we call, for lack of a better name, the "traditional model." In it expectations are *not* rational. The traditional model has the adaptive expectations mentioned in the previous chapter; that is, expectations are formed from past experience only. The traditional model views expected inflation as an average of past inflation rates. This average is not affected by the public's predictions of future policy; hence predictions of future policy do not affect the aggregate supply curve.

First, we will examine the short-run output and price responses in the three models. We will then examine the implications of these models for both stabilization and anti-inflation policies.

Study Guide

As a study aid, the comparison of the three models is summarized in Table 30.1. You may want to refer to the table as we proceed with the comparison.

Table 30.1   Summary: The Three Models

	Response to Unanticipated Expansionary Policy	Response to Anticipated Expansionary Policy	Can Activist Policy Be Beneficial?	Response to Unanticipated Anti-Inflation Policy	Response to Anticipated Anti-Inflation Policy	Is Credibility Important to Successful Anti-Inflation Policy?
Traditional model	$Y\uparrow\ P\uparrow$	$Y\uparrow\ P\uparrow$ by same as when policy is unanticipated	Yes	$Y\downarrow\ \pi\downarrow$	$Y\downarrow, \pi\downarrow$ by same as when policy is unanticipated	No
New classical macro-economic model	$Y\uparrow\ P\uparrow$	Y unchanged, $P\uparrow$ by more than when policy is unanticipated	No	$Y\downarrow\ \pi\downarrow$	Y unchanged, $\pi\downarrow$ by more than when policy is unanticipated	Yes
Nonclassical rational expectations model	$Y\uparrow\ P\uparrow$	$Y\uparrow$ by less than when policy is unanticipated; $P\uparrow$ by more than when policy is unanticipated	Yes, but is hard to design a beneficial policy	$Y\downarrow\ \pi\downarrow$	$Y\downarrow$ by less than when policy is unanticipated; $\pi\downarrow$ by more than when policy is unanticipated	Yes

Note: π represents the inflation rate.

Short-Run Output and Price Responses

Figure 30.5 carries out a comparison of the way aggregate output and the price level respond to an expansionary policy in the three models. Initially, the economy is at point 1, the intersection of the aggregate demand curve AD_1 with the aggregate supply curve AS_1. When the expansionary policy occurs, the aggregate demand curve shifts to AD_2. If the expansionary policy is *unanticipated,* all three models show the same short-run output response. The traditional model views the aggregate supply curve as given in the short run, while the other two view it as remaining at AS_1 because there is no change in the expected price level when the policy is a surprise. Thus *when policy is unanticipated,* all three models indicate a movement to point 1′, where the AD_2 and AS_1 curves intersect and where aggregate output and the price level have risen to $Y_{1'}$ and $P_{1'}$, respectively.

The response to the *anticipated* expansionary policy is, however, quite different in the three models. In the traditional model [panel (a)], the aggregate supply curve remains at AS_1 even when the expansionary policy is anticipated because adaptive expectations imply that anticipated policy has no effect on aggregate supply. It indicates that the economy moves to point 1′, which is where it moved when the policy was unanticipated. The traditional model does not distinguish between the effects of anticipated versus unanticipated policy: Both have the same effect on output and prices.

In the new classical model [panel (b)], the aggregate supply curve shifts in to AS_2 when policy is anticipated because when expectations of the higher price level are realized, aggregate output will be at the natural rate level. Thus it indicates that the economy moves to point 2; aggregate output does not rise, but prices do to P_2. This outcome is quite different from the move to point 1′ when policy is unanticipated. The new classical model distinguishes between the short-run effects of anticipated and unanticipated policies: Anticipated has no effect on output, while unanticipated does. Anticipated policy, however, has a bigger impact on price level movements than does unanticipated policy.

The nonclassical rational expectations model [panel (c)] is an intermediate position between the traditional and new classical models. It recognizes that anticipated policy affects the aggregate supply curve, but, because of rigidities such as long-term contracts, wage and price adjustment is not as complete as in the new classical model. Thus the aggregate supply curve only shifts in to $AS_{2'}$ in response to anticipated policy, and the economy moves to point 2′, where output at $Y_{2'}$ is lower than the $Y_{1'}$ level reached when the expansionary policy is unanticipated. On the other hand, the price level at $P_{2'}$ is higher than the level of $P_{1'}$ that resulted from the unanticipated policy. Like the new classical model, the nonclassical rational expectations model distinguishes between the effects of anticipated and unanticipated policies; anticipated has a smaller effect on output than unanticipated, while it has a larger effect on the price level. However, in contrast to the new classical model, anticipated policy does affect output fluctuations.

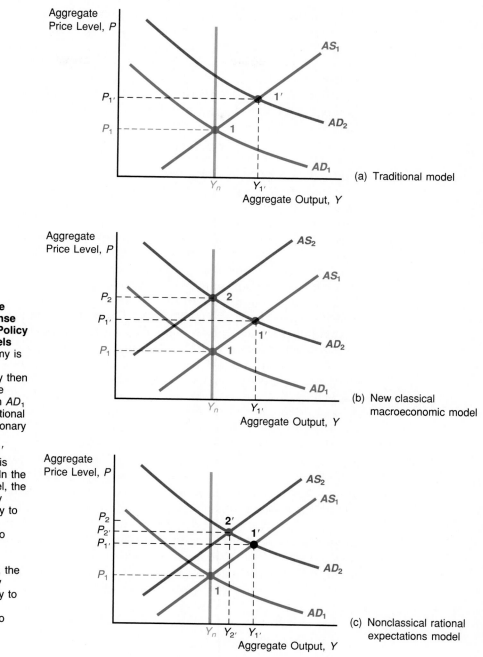

Figure 30.5
Comparison of the Short-Run Response to Expansionary Policy in the Three Models
Initially, the economy is at point 1 and the expansionary policy then shifts the aggregate demand curve from AD_1 to AD_2. In the traditional model, the expansionary policy moves the economy to point 1′ whether the policy is anticipated or not. In the new classical model, the expansionary policy moves the economy to point 1′ if it is unanticipated and to point 2 if it is anticipated. In the nonclassical model, the expansionary policy moves the economy to point 1′ if it is unanticipated and to point 2′ if it is anticipated.

(a) Traditional model

(b) New classical macroeconomic model

(c) Nonclassical rational expectations model

Stabilization Policy

The three models have different views of the effectiveness of stabilization policy; that is, policy intended to reduce output fluctuations. Because the effects of anticipated versus unanticipated policy are identical in the traditional model, policymakers do not have to concern themselves with the public's expectations. This makes it easier for them to predict the outcome of their policy, an essential matter if their policies are to have the intended effect. In the traditional model it is possible for an activist policy to stabilize output fluctuations.

The new classical model takes the extreme position that activist stabilization policy serves to aggravate output fluctuations. In this model, only unanticipated policy affects output; anticipated policy does not matter. Policymakers can affect output only by surprising the public with their policies. Because the public is assumed to have rational expectations, they will always try to guess what policymakers plan to do.

In the new classical model, the conduct of policy can be viewed as a game in which the public and the policymakers are always trying to outfox each other by guessing what the other's intentions and expectations are. The sole possible outcome of this process is that an activist stabilization policy will have no predictable effect on output and it cannot be relied upon to stabilize economic activity. Instead it may create a lot of uncertainty about policy that will increase random output fluctuations around the natural rate level of output. Such an undesirable effect is exactly the opposite of what the activist stabilization policy is trying to achieve. The outcome in the new classical view is that policy should follow a nonactivist rule in order to promote as much certainty about policy actions as possible.

The nonclassical rational expectations model again takes an intermediate position between the traditional and the new classical models. Contrary to the new classical model, it indicates that anticipated policy *does* matter to output fluctuations. Policymakers can count on some output response from their anticipated policies and can use them to stabilize the economy.

In contrast to the traditional model, however, the nonclassical rational expectations model recognizes that the effects of anticipated and unanticipated policy will not be the same. Policymakers will encounter more uncertainty about the outcome of their actions because they cannot be sure to what extent the policy is anticipated or not. Thus an activist policy is less likely to operate always in the intended direction and it is less likely that it will successfully achieve its goals. The nonclassical model with rational expectations raises the possibility that an activist policy could be beneficial, but the uncertainty about the outcome of policies in this model may make the design of such a beneficial policy extremely difficult.

Anti-Inflation Policies

So far we have focused on the implications of these three models for policies whose intent is to eliminate fluctuations in output. By the end of the 1970s, the high inflation rate (which exceeded 10%) helped shift the primary concern of policymakers to the reduction of inflation. What do these models have to say about anti-inflation policies designed to eliminate upward move-

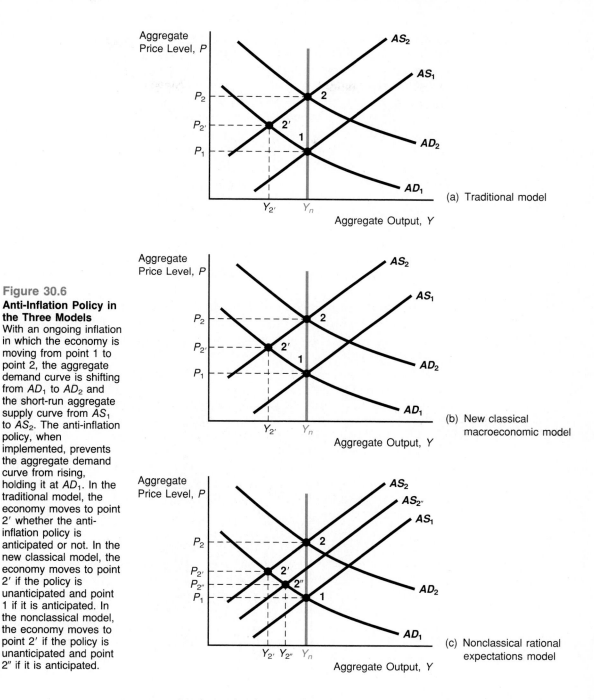

Figure 30.6
Anti-Inflation Policy in the Three Models
With an ongoing inflation in which the economy is moving from point 1 to point 2, the aggregate demand curve is shifting from AD_1 to AD_2 and the short-run aggregate supply curve from AS_1 to AS_2. The anti-inflation policy, when implemented, prevents the aggregate demand curve from rising, holding it at AD_1. In the traditional model, the economy moves to point 2' whether the anti-inflation policy is anticipated or not. In the new classical model, the economy moves to point 2' if the policy is unanticipated and point 1 if it is anticipated. In the nonclassical model, the economy moves to point 2' if the policy is unanticipated and point 2" if it is anticipated.

(a) Traditional model

(b) New classical macroeconomic model

(c) Nonclassical rational expectations model

ments in the price level? The aggregate demand and supply diagrams in Figure 30.6 will help us answer the question.

Suppose that the economy had settled into a sustained 10% inflation rate caused by a high rate of money growth that shifts the aggregate demand curve so that it moves up by 10% every year. If this inflation rate has been built into wage and price contracts, then the aggregate supply curve shifts so that it rises at the same rate. We see this in Figure 30.6 as a shift in the aggregate demand curve from AD_1 in year 1 to AD_2 in year 2, while the aggregate supply curve moves from AS_1 to AS_2. (Note that in making the figure easier to read, it is not drawn to scale where the AD_2 and AS_2 are 10% higher than the AD_1 and AS_1 curves.) In year 1 the economy is at point 1 (intersection of AD_1 and AS_1), while in the second year the economy moves to point 2 (intersection of AD_2 and AS_2) and the price level has risen 10% from P_1 to P_2.

Suppose that a new Federal Reserve chairman is appointed who decides that inflation must be stopped. He convinces the Board of Governors to stop the high rate of money growth so that the aggregate demand curve will not rise from AD_1. The policy of halting money growth immediately could be costly if it led to a fall in output. Let's use our three models to explore the degree to which aggregate output will fall as a result of an anti-inflation policy.

First, look at the outcome of this policy in the traditional model's view of the world [panel (a)]. In it the movement of the aggregate supply curve to AS_2 is already set in place and is unaffected by the new policy of keeping the aggregate demand curve at AD_1 (whether it is anticipated or not). The economy moves to point $2'$ (the intersection of the AD_1 and AS_2 curves), and the inflation rate slows down because the price level increases only to $P_{2'}$ rather than P_2. The reduction in inflation has not been without cost: Output has declined to $Y_{2'}$, which is well below the natural rate level.

The late Arthur Okun of the Brookings Institution estimated that in the traditional model the cost in terms of lost output for each one percentage point reduction in the inflation rate is 9% of a year's real GNP. The high cost of reducing inflation in the traditional model is one reason why some economists are reluctant to advocate an anti-inflation policy of the sort tried here. They question whether the cost of high unemployment is worth the benefits of a reduced inflation rate.

If you adhere to the new classical philosophy, you would not be as pessimistic about the high cost of reducing the inflation rate. If the public *expects* the monetary authorities to stop the inflationary process by ending the high rate of money growth, it will occur without any output loss. In panel (b), the aggregate demand curve will remain at AD_1, but since this is expected, wages and prices can be adjusted so that they will not rise and the aggregate supply curve will remain at AS_1 instead of moving to AS_2. The economy will continue to stay at point 1 (the intersection of AD_1 and AS_1), and aggregate output remains at the natural rate level while the inflation is stopped because the price level is unchanged.

An important element in the story is that the anti-inflation policy be anticipated by the public. If the policy is *not* expected, the aggregate demand curve remains at AD_1, but the aggregate supply curve continues its shift to

AS_2. The outcome of the unanticipated anti-inflation policy is a movement of the economy to point $2'$. Although the inflation rate slows in this case, it is not entirely eliminated as it was when the anti-inflation policy was anticipated. Even worse, aggregate output falls below the natural rate level to $Y_{2'}$. An anti-inflation policy that is unanticipated, then, is far less desirable than one that is.

The nonclassical rational expectations model [panel (c)] also leads to the conclusion that an anti-inflation policy that is unanticipated is less desirable than if it is anticipated. If the policy of keeping the aggregate demand curve at AD_1 is *not* expected, then the aggregate supply curve will continue its shift to AS_2 and the economy moves to point $2'$ at the intersection of AD_1 and AS_2. The inflation rate slows, but output declines to $Y_{2'}$, well below the natural rate level.

If, on the other hand, the anti-inflation policy is *expected,* then the aggregate supply curve will not move all the way to AS_2. Instead it will shift only to $AS_{2''}$ because some wages and price contracts (but not all) can be adjusted so that wages and price will not rise at their previous rates. Instead of moving to point $2'$ (as occurred when the anti-inflation policy was not expected), the economy moves to point $2''$, the intersection of the AD_1 and $AS_{2''}$ curves. The outcome is more desirable than when the policy is unanticipated—the inflation rate is lower (the price level only rises to $P_{2''}$ and not $P_{2'}$) and the output loss is smaller as well ($Y_{2''}$ is higher than $Y_{2'}$).

The Role of Credibility in Fighting Inflation

Both the new classical and nonclassical rational expectations models indicate that for an anti-inflation policy to be successful in reducing inflation at the lowest output cost, the public must believe (expect) that it will be implemented. In a new classical view of the world, the best anti-inflation policy (when it is credible) is to go "cold turkey." The rise in the aggregate demand curve from AD_1 should be stopped immediately. Inflation would be eliminated at once with no loss of output *if the policy were credible.* In a nonclassical world, the "cold turkey" policy, *even if credible,* is not as desirable because it will produce some output loss.

John Taylor, a proponent of the nonclassical rational expectations view, has demonstrated that a more gradual approach to reducing inflation may be able to eliminate inflation without producing a substantial output loss.[7] An important catch here is that this gradual policy must somehow be made credible, which may be harder to achieve for it than for a "cold turkey" anti-inflation policy which immediately demonstrates that the policymakers

---

[7]John Taylor, "The Role of Expectations in the Choice of Monetary Policy," in *Monetary Policy Issues in the 1980s* (Federal Reserve Bank of Kansas City, 1982), pp. 47–76.

are serious about fighting inflation. Taylor's contention that inflation can be reduced with little output loss may be overoptimistic.

Incorporating rational expectations into aggregate supply and demand analysis indicates that a successful anti-inflation policy must be credible. Evidence that credibility plays an important role in successful anti-inflation policies is provided by the dramatic end of the Bolivian hyperinflation in 1985 (see Box 30.2). Establishing credibility is easier said than done. You might think that an announcement by policymakers at the Federal Reserve that they plan to pursue an anti-inflation policy might do the trick. The public would expect this policy and would act accordingly. However, it implies that the public will believe the announcement of the policymakers.

Unfortunately, this is not the way the real world works.

Our historical review of Federal Reserve policymaking in Chapter 20 suggests that the Fed has never exercised tight control over the money supply. In fact, during the 1970s, the chairman of the Federal Reserve Board, Arthur Burns, repeatedly announced that the Fed would pursue a vigorous anti-inflation policy. The actual policy pursued, however, had quite a differ-

---

Box 30.2   **A Global Perspective**

Ending the Bolivian Hyperinflation: A Case Study of a Successful Anti-Inflation Program

The most remarkable anti-inflation program in the 1980s was that of Bolivia. In the first half of 1985, Bolivia's inflation rate was running at 20,000% and was rising. Indeed, the inflation rate was so high that the price of a movie ticket often rose while people waited in line to buy it. In August 1985, Bolivia's new president announced his anti-inflation program, the "New Economic Policy." In order to rein in money growth and establish credibility, the new government took drastic actions to slash the budget deficit by shutting down many state-owned enterprises, eliminating subsidies, freezing public-sector salaries, and collecting a new wealth tax. The finance ministry was run on a new footing; the budget was balanced on a day-by-day basis. Without exceptions, the finance minister would not authorize spending in excess of the amount of tax revenue that had been collected the day before.

Arthur Okun's rule of thumb that a reduction of 1% in the inflation rate requires a 9% loss of a year's aggregate output indicates that ending the Bolivian hyperinflation would have required halving Bolivian aggregate output for 400 years! Instead, the Bolivian inflation was stopped in its tracks within one month and the output loss was minor (less than 5% of GNP).

Other hyperinflations before World War II also were ended with small losses of output using policies similar to Bolivia's,[*] and a more recent anti-inflation program in Israel that also involved substantial reductions in budget deficits has sharply reduced inflation, indeed, without any clear loss of output. Credible anti-inflation policies have been highly successful in eliminating inflation.

---

[*]See Thomas Sargent, "The Ends of Four Big Inflations," in Robert E. Hall, ed., *Inflation, Causes and Consequences* (Chicago: University of Chicago Press for the NBER, 1982), pp. 41–98, for an excellent discussion of the end of four hyperinflations in the 1920s.

ent outcome as the rate of growth of the money supply increased rapidly during the period. Such episodes have reduced the credibility of the Federal Reserve in the eyes of the public and, as predicted by the new classical and nonclassical rational expectations models, have had serious consequences. The reduction of inflation that occurred from 1981 to 1984 was bought at a very high cost; the 1981–1982 recession that helped bring the inflation rate down was the most severe recession in the post-World War II period. Unless some method of restoring credibility to anti-inflation policy is achieved, eliminating inflation will be a costly affair because such policy will be unanticipated.

The U.S. government can play an important role in establishing credibility of anti-inflation policy. We have seen that large budget deficits may help stimulate inflationary monetary policy, and when the government and the Fed announce that they will pursue a restrictive anti-inflation policy, it is less likely they will be believed *unless* the federal government demonstrates fiscal responsibility. Another way to say this is to use the old cliche "actions speak louder than words." When the government takes actions that will help the Fed adhere to anti-inflation policy, then anti-inflation policy will have more credibility. Unfortunately, as the next section indicates, this lesson has sometimes been ignored by politicians in the United States and in other countries.

APPLICATION
CREDIBILITY AND THE REAGAN BUDGET DEFICITS/ / / / / / / / / / / / / / / /

The Reagan administration was strongly criticized for creating huge budget deficits by cutting taxes in the early 1980s. In the Keynesian framework we usually think of tax cuts as stimulating aggregate demand and increasing aggregate output. Could the expectation of large budget deficits have helped create a more severe recession in 1981–1982 after the Federal Reserve implemented an anti-inflation monetary policy?

Some economists answer "yes," using diagrams like panels (b) and (c) of Figure 30.6. They claim that the prospect of large budget deficits made it harder for the public to believe that an anti-inflationary policy would actually be pursued when the Fed announced that is what it intended to do. Consequently the aggregate supply curve would continue to rise from AS_1 to AS_2 as in panels (b) and (c). When the Fed actually kept the aggregate demand curve from rising to AD_2 by slowing the rate of money growth in 1980–1981 and allowing interest rates to rise, the economy moved to a point like 2′ in panels (b) and (c) and much unemployment resulted. As our analysis in panels (b) and (c) of Figure 30.6 predicts, the inflation rate did slow down substantially, falling below 5% by the end of 1982, but this was very costly: Unemployment reached a peak of 10.7%.

If the Reagan administration had actively tried to reduce deficits instead of raising them by cutting taxes, what might have been the outcome of the anti-inflation policy? Instead of moving to point 2', the economy might have moved to point 2'' in panel (c) (or even to point 1 in panel (b) if the new classical macroeconomists are right!). We would have had an even more rapid reduction in inflation and a smaller loss of output. No wonder some economists were so hostile to Reagan's budget policies!

Ronald Reagan is not the only head of state who ran large budget deficits while espousing an anti-inflation policy. Britain's Margaret Thatcher preceded Reagan in this activity, and economists such as Thomas Sargent assert that the reward for her policy was a climb of unemployment in Britain to unprecedented levels.[8]

Although many economists agree that the Fed's anti-inflation program lacked credibility, especially in its initial phases, not all of them agree that the Reagan budget deficits were the cause of the lack of credibility. The conclusion that the Reagan budget deficits helped create a more severe recession in 1981–1982 is controversial.

IMPACT OF THE RATIONAL EXPECTATIONS REVOLUTION

Rational expectations theory has caused a revolution in the way most economists now think about the conduct of monetary and fiscal policies and their effects on economic activity. One result of this revolution is that economists are now far more aware of the importance of expectations to economic decision making and to the outcome of particular policy actions. Although the rationality of expectations in all markets is still controversial, most economists now accept the following principle suggested by rational expectations: Expectations formation will change when the behavior of forecasted variables changes. As a result, the Lucas critique of policy evaluation using conventional econometric models is now taken seriously by the majority of the economics profession. The Lucas critique also demonstrates that the effect of a particular policy depends critically on the public's expectations about the policy. This observation has made economists much less certain that policies will have their intended effect. An important result of the rational expectations revolution is that economists are no longer as confident in the success of activist stabilization policies as they once were.

---

[8]Thomas Sargent, "Stopping Moderate Inflations: The Methods of Poincaré and Thatcher," in Rudiger Dornbusch and M. H. Simonsen, *Inflation, Debt and Taxation* (MIT Press, 1983), discusses the problems that Thatcher's policies caused and contrasts them with more successful anti-inflation policies pursued by the Poincaré government in France during the 1920s.

Has the rational expectations revolution convinced economists that there is no role for activist stabilization policy? Those who adhere to the new classical macroeconomics think so. Because anticipated policy does not affect aggregate output, activist policy can lead only to unpredictable output fluctuations. Pursuing a nonactivist policy in which there is no uncertainty about policy actions is then the best that we can do. Such a position is not accepted by many economists because the empirical evidence on the policy ineffectiveness proposition is quite mixed. Some studies find that only unanticipated policy matters to output fluctuations, while other studies find a significant impact of anticipated policy on output movements.[9] In addition, some economists question whether the degree of wage and price flexibility required in the new classical model actually exists.

The result is that many economists take an intermediate position that recognizes the distinction between the effects of anticipated versus unanticipated policy, but believe that anticipated policy can affect output. They are still open to the possibility that activist stabilization policy can be beneficial, but they recognize the difficulties of designing it.

The rational expectations revolution has also highlighted the importance of credibility to the success of anti-inflation policies. Economists now recognize that if an anti-inflation policy is not believed by the public, it may be less effective in reducing the inflation rate when it is actually implemented and may lead to a larger loss of output than is necessary. Achieving credibility (not an easy task since policymakers often say one thing then do another) should then be an important goal for policymakers. To achieve credibility, policymakers need to pursue consistency in their course of action.

The rational expectations revolution has caused major rethinking about the way economic policy should be conducted and has forced economists to recognize that we may have to accept a more limited role for what policy can do for us. Rather than attempting to fine-tune the economy so all output fluctuations are eliminated, we may have to settle for policies that create less uncertainty and thereby promote a more stable economic environment.

---

[9]Studies with findings that only unanticipated policy matters include Thomas Sargent, "A Classical Macroeconometric Model for the United States," *Journal of Political Economy* 84 (1976), pp. 207–237; Robert J. Barro, "Unanticipated Money Growth and Unemployment in the United States," *American Economic Review* 67 (1977), pp. 101–115; and Robert J. Barro and Mark Rush, "Unanticipated Money and Economic Activity," in Stanley Fischer, ed., *Rational Expectations and Economic Policy* (University of Chicago Press, 1980), pp. 23–48. Studies that find a significant impact of anticipated policy are Frederic S. Mishkin, "Does Anticipated Monetary Policy Matter? An Econometric Investigation," *Journal of Political Economy* 90 (February 1982), pp. 22–51; and Robert J. Gordon, "Price Inertia and Policy Effectiveness in the United States, 1890–1980," *Journal of Political Economy* 90 (December 1982), pp. 1087–1117.

SUMMARY

1. The simple principle (derived from rational expectations theory) that expectations formation changes when the behavior of forecasted variables changes leads to the famous Lucas critique of econometric policy evaluation. Lucas argued that when policy changes, expectations formation changes, hence the relationships in an econometric model will change. An econometric model that has been estimated with past data will no longer be the correct model for evaluating the effects of this policy change and may prove to be highly misleading. The Lucas critique also points out that the effects of a particular policy depend critically on the public's expectations about the policy.

2. The new classical macroeconomic model assumes that expectations are rational and that wages and prices are completely flexible with respect to the expected price level. It produces the policy ineffectiveness proposition that anticipated policy has no effect on output; only unanticipated policy matters.

3. The nonclassical rational expectations model also assumes that expectations are rational but views wages and prices as sticky. Like the new classical model, the nonclassical rational expectations model distinguishes between the effects from anticipated versus unanticipated policy: Anticipated policy has a smaller effect on aggre-

gate output than unanticipated policy. However, unlike results from the new classical model, anticipated policy does matter to output fluctuations.

4. The new classical model indicates that activist policy can only be counterproductive, while the nonclassical rational expectations model suggests that activist policy might be beneficial. However, since both indicate that there is uncertainty about the outcome of a particular policy, the design of a beneficial activist policy may be very difficult. A traditional model in which expectations about policy have no effect on the aggregate supply curve does not distinguish between the effects of anticipated versus unanticipated policy. This model favors activist policy because the outcome of a particular policy is less uncertain.

5. If expectations about policy affect the aggregate supply curve, as they do in the new classical and nonclassical rational expectations models, then an anti-inflation policy will be more successful (will produce a faster reduction in inflation with smaller output loss) if it is credible.

6. The rational expectations revolution has forced economists to be less optimistic about the effective use of activist stabilization policy and has made them more aware of the importance of credibility to successful policy-making.

KEY TERMS

econometric models

policy ineffectiveness
 proposition

QUESTIONS AND PROBLEMS

1. If the public expects the Fed to pursue a policy that is likely to raise short-term interest rates permanently to 12% and then the Fed does not go through with this policy change, what will happen to long-term interest rates? Why?

* 2. If consumer expenditure is related to consumers' expectations of their average income in the future, will an income tax cut have a larger effect

on consumer expenditure if the public expects the tax cut to last for one year or for ten years?

In all the following questions, use an aggregate supply and demand diagram to illustrate your answer.

3. Having studied the new classical model, the new chairman of the Federal Reserve Board has

thought up a sure-fire plan for reducing inflation and lowering unemployment. He announces that the Fed will lower the rate of money growth from 10 to 5%, and then persuades the FOMC to keep the rate of money growth at 10%. If the new classical view of the world is correct, can his plan achieve the goals of lowering inflation and unemployment? How? Do you think his plan will work? If the traditional model's view of the world is correct, will the Fed chairman's sure-fire plan work?

* 4. Answer true, false, or uncertain: "The costs of fighting inflation in the new classical and nonclassical rational expectations models are lower than in the traditional model."

5. The new classical model is sometimes characterized as an offshoot of the monetarist model because they have similar views of aggregate supply. What are the differences and similarities between the monetarist and the new classical view of aggregate supply?

* 6. Answer true, false, or uncertain: "The new classical model does not eliminate policymakers' ability to reduce unemployment because they can always pursue policies that are more expansionary than the public expects."

7. What principle of rational expectations theory is used to prove the proposition that stabilization policy can have no predictable effect on aggregate output in the new classical model?

* 8. Answer true, false, or uncertain: "The Lucas critique by itself casts doubt on the ability of activist stabilization policy to be beneficial."

9. Answer true, false, or uncertain: "Anti-inflation policy will be more successful, the more credible are the policymakers who pursue this policy."

*10. Many economists are worried that a high level of budget deficits may lead to inflationary monetary policies in the future. Could these budget deficits have an effect on the current rate of inflation?

Using Economic Analysis to Predict the Future

11. Suppose that a treaty limiting the number of nuclear weapons is signed with the Russians. The result of the treaty is that the public expects military and hence government spending to be reduced. If the new classical view of the economy is correct and government spending does affect the aggregate demand curve, predict what will happen to aggregate output and the price level when government spending is reduced in line with the public's expectations.

12. How would your prediction differ in Problem 11 if the nonclassical rational expectations model provides a more realistic description of the economy? What if the traditional model provides the most realistic description of the economy?

*13. The chairman of the Federal Reserve Board announces that over the next year the rate of money growth will be reduced from its current rate of 10% to a rate of 2%. If the chairman is believed by the public but the Fed actually reduces the rate of money growth to 5%, predict what will happen to the inflation rate and aggregate output if the new classical view of the economy is correct.

*14. How would your prediction differ in Problem 13 if the nonclassical rational expectations model provides a more accurate description of the economy? What if the traditional model provides the most realistic description of the economy?

Models of Capital Market Asset Pricing

In Chapter 5 we demonstrated the benefits of diversification. In this appendix, we examine diversification and the relationship between risk and returns in more detail. As a result we obtain an understanding of two basic theories of asset pricing: the capital asset pricing model (CAPM) and arbitrage pricing theory (APT).

DIVERSIFICATION AND BETA

We start our analysis by considering a portfolio of n assets whose return is

$$R_p = x_1 R_1 + x_2 R_2 + \cdots + x_n R_n \qquad \text{(MA5.1)}$$

where

R_p = the return on the portfolio of n assets
R_i = the return on asset i
x_i = the proportion of the portfolio held in asset i

The expected return on this portfolio, $E(R_p)$, equals

$$\begin{aligned} E(R_p) &= E(x_1 R_1) + E(x_2 R_2) + \cdots + E(x_n R_n) \\ &= x_1 E(R_1) + x_2 E(R_2) + \cdots + x_n E(R_n) \end{aligned} \qquad \text{(MA5.2)}$$

An appropriate measure of the risk for this portfolio is the standard deviation of the portfolio's return (σ_p) or its squared value, the variance of the portfolio's return (σ_p^2) which can be written as

$$\begin{aligned} \sigma_p^2 = E[R_p - E(R_p)]^2 &= E[\{x_1 R_1 + \cdots + x_n R_n\} - \{x_1 E(R_1) + \cdots + x_n E(R_n)\}]^2 \\ &= E[x_1\{R_1 - E(R_1)\} + \cdots + x_n\{R_n - E(R_n)\}]^2 \end{aligned}$$

This expression can be rewritten as

$$\begin{aligned} \sigma_p^2 &= E[\{x_1[R_1 - E(R_1)]\} + \cdots + x_n[R_n - E(R_n)]\} \times \{R_p - E(R_p)\}] \\ &= x_1 E[\{R_1 - E(R_1)\} \times \{R_p - E(R_p)\}] + \cdots + x_n E[\{R_n - E(R_n)\} \times \{R_p - E(R_p)\}] \end{aligned}$$

This gives us the following expression for the variance of the portfolio's return:

$$\sigma_p^2 = x_1 \sigma_{1p} + x_2 \sigma_{2p} + \cdots + x_n \sigma_{np} \qquad \text{(MA5.3)}$$

where

$$\sigma_{ip} = \text{the covariance of the return on asset } i$$
$$\text{with the portfolio's return} = E[\{R_i - E(R_i)\} \times \{R_p - E(R_p)\}]$$

Equation (MA5.3) tells us that the contribution to risk of asset i to the portfolio is $x_i\sigma_{ip}$. By dividing this contribution to risk by the total portfolio risk (σ_p^2), we have the proportionate contribution of asset i to the portfolio risk:

$$x_i\sigma_{ip}/\sigma_p^2$$

The ratio σ_{ip}/σ_p^2 tells us about the sensitivity of asset i's return to the portfolio's return. The higher the ratio is the more the value of the asset moves with changes in the value of the portfolio and the more asset i contributes to portfolio risk. Our algebraic manipulations have thus led to the following important conclusion: ***The marginal contribution of an asset to the risk of a portfolio depends not on the risk of the asset in isolation, but rather on the sensitivity of that asset's return to changes in the value of the portfolio.***

If the total of all risky assets in the market is included in the portfolio, then it is called the **market portfolio.** If we suppose that the portfolio, p, is the market portfolio, m, then the ratio σ_{im}/σ_m^2 is called the asset i's **beta,** that is,

$$\beta_i = \sigma_{im}/\sigma_m^2 \tag{MA5.4}$$

where

$$\beta_i = \text{the beta of asset } i$$

An asset's beta then is a measure of the asset's marginal contribution to the risk of the market portfolio. A higher beta means that an asset's return is more sensitive to changes in the value of the market portfolio and that the asset contributes more to the risk of the portfolio.

Another way to understand beta is to recognize that the return on asset i can be considered as being made up of two components—one that moves with the market's return (R_m) and the other a random factor with an expected value of zero that is unique to the asset (ϵ_i) and so is uncorrelated with the market return:

$$R_i = \alpha_i + \beta_i R_m + \epsilon_i \tag{MA5.5}$$

The expected return of asset i can then be written as

$$E(R_i) = \alpha_i + \beta_i E(R_m)$$

It is easy to show that β_i in the above expression is the beta of asset i we defined before by calculating the covariance of asset i's return with the market return using the two equations above:

$$\sigma_{im} = E[\{R_i - E(R_i)\} \times \{R_m - E(R_m)\}] = E[\{\beta_i[R_m - E(R_m)] + \epsilon_i\} \times \{R_m - E(R_m)\}]$$

However, since ϵ_i is uncorrelated with R_m, $E[\{\epsilon_i\} \times \{R_m - E(R_m)\}] = 0$. Therefore,

$$\sigma_{im} = \beta_i \sigma_m^2$$

Dividing through by σ_m^2 gives us the following expression for β_i:

$$\beta_i = \sigma_{im}/\sigma_m^2$$

which is the same definition for beta we found in Equation (MA5.4).

The reason for demonstrating that the β_i in Equation (MA5.5) is the same as the one we defined before is that Equation (MA5.5) provides better intuition about how an asset's beta measures its sensitivity to changes in the market return. Equation (MA5.5) tells us that when the beta of an asset is 1.0, its return on average increases by 1 percentage point when the market return increases by 1 percentage point; when the beta is 2.0, the asset's return on average increases by 2 percentage points when the market return increases by 1 percentage point; and when the beta is 0.5, the asset's return only increases by 0.5 percentage point on average when the market return increases by 1 percentage point.

Equation (MA5.5) also tells us that we can get estimates of beta by comparing the average return on an asset with the average market return. For those of you who know a little econometrics, this estimate of beta is just an ordinary least squares regression of the asset's return on the market return. Indeed, the formula for the ordinary least squares estimate of $\beta_i = \sigma_{im}/\sigma_m^2$ is exactly the same as the definition of β_i above.

SYSTEMATIC AND NONSYSTEMATIC RISK

We can derive another important idea about the riskiness of an asset using Equation (MA5.5). The variance of asset i's return can be calculated from Equation (MA5.5) as

$$\sigma_i^2 = E[R_i - E(R_i)]^2 = E[\beta_i\{R_m - E(R_m)\} + \epsilon_i]^2$$

and since ϵ_i is uncorrelated with the market return,

$$\sigma_i^2 = \beta_i^2 \sigma_m^2 + \sigma_\epsilon^2$$

The total variance of the asset's return can thus be broken up into a component that is related to market risk, $\beta_i^2 \sigma_m^2$, and a component that is unique to the asset, σ_ϵ^2. The $\beta_i^2 \sigma_m^2$ component related to market risk is referred to as **systematic risk** and the σ_ϵ^2 component unique to the asset is called **nonsystematic risk.** We can thus write the total risk of an asset as being made up of systematic risk and nonsystematic risk:

$$\text{Total Asset Risk} = \text{Systematic Risk} + \text{Nonsystematic Risk} \quad \text{(MA5.6)}$$

Systematic and nonsystematic risk each have another feature that makes the distinction between these two types of risk important. Systematic risk is the part of an asset's risk that cannot be eliminated by holding the asset as part of a diversified portfolio, whereas nonsystematic risk is the part of an asset's risk that can be eliminated in a diversified portfolio. Understanding these features of systematic and nonsystematic risk leads to the following important conclusion: ***The risk of a well-diversified portfolio depends only on the systematic risk of the assets in the portfolio.***

We can see that this conclusion is true by considering a portfolio of n assets, each of which has the same weight in the portfolio of $(1/n)$. Using Equation (MA5.5), the return on this portfolio is

$$R_p = (1/n) \sum_{i=1}^{n} \alpha_i + (1/n) \sum_{i=1}^{n} \beta_i R_m + (1/n) \sum_{i=1}^{n} \epsilon_i$$

which can be rewritten as

$$R_p = \overline{\alpha} + \overline{\beta} R_m + (1/n) \sum_{i=1}^{n} \epsilon_i$$

where

$$\overline{\alpha} = \text{the average of the } \alpha_i\text{'s} = (1/n) \sum_{i=1}^{n} \alpha_i$$

$$\overline{\beta} = \text{the average of the } \beta_i\text{'s} = (1/n) \sum_{i=1}^{n} \alpha_i$$

If the portfolio is well diversified so that the ϵ_i's are uncorrelated with each other, then using this fact and the fact that all the ϵ_i's are uncorrelated with the market return, the variance of the portfolio's return is calculated as

$$\sigma_p^2 = \overline{\beta}^2 \sigma_m^2 + (1/n)(\text{average variance of } \epsilon_i)$$

As n gets large the second term, $(1/n)$(average variance of ϵ_i), becomes very small, so that a well-diversified portfolio has a risk of $\overline{\beta}^2 \sigma_m^2$, which is only related to systematic risk. As the previous conclusion indicated, nonsystematic risk can be eliminated in a well-diversified portfolio. This reasoning also tells us that the risk of a well-diversified portfolio is greater than the risk of the market portfolio if the average beta of the assets in the portfolio is greater than one; however, the portfolio's risk is less than the market portfolio if the average beta of the assets is less than one.

THE CAPITAL ASSET PRICING MODEL (CAPM)

We can now use the ideas we developed about systematic and nonsystematic risk and betas to derive one of the most widely used models of asset pricing—

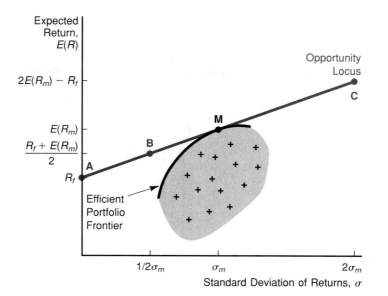

Figure MA5.1

Risk Expected Return Trade-off   The crosses show the combination of standard deviation and expected return for each risky asset. The efficient portfolio frontier indicates the most preferable standard deviation-expected return combinations that can be achieved by putting risky assets into portfolios. By borrowing and lending at the risk-free rate and investing in portfolio M, the investor can obtain standard deviation-expected return combinations that lie along the line connecting A, B, M, and C. This line, the opportunity locus, contains the best combinations of standard deviations and expected returns available to the investor; hence the opportunity locus shows the trade-off between expected returns and risk for the investor.

the capital asset pricing model (CAPM) developed by William Sharpe, John Litner, and Jack Treynor.

Each cross in Figure MA5.1 shows the standard deviation and expected return for each risky asset. By putting different proportions of these assets into portfolios, we can generate a standard deviation and expected return for each of the portfolios using Equations (MA5.2) and (MA5.3). The shaded area in the figure shows these combinations of standard deviation and expected return for these portfolios. Since risk-averse investors always prefer to have a higher expected return and a lower standard deviation of the return, the most attractive standard deviation-expected return combinations are the ones that lie along the heavy line, which is called the **efficient portfolio frontier.** These are the standard deviation-expected return combinations risk-averse investors would always prefer.

The capital asset pricing model assumes that investors can borrow and lend as much as they want at a risk-free rate of interest, R_f. By lending at the risk-free rate, the investor earns an expected return of R_f and his investment has a zero standard deviation because it is risk free. The standard deviation-expected return combination for this risk-free investment is marked as point

A in Figure MA5.1. Suppose an investor decides to put half of his total wealth in the risk-free loan and the other half in the portfolio on the efficient portfolio frontier with a standard deviation-expected return combination marked as point M in the figure. Using Equation (MA5.2) you should be able to verify that the expected return on this new portfolio is half way between R_f and $E(R_m)$, that is, $[R_f + E(R_m)]/2$. Similarly, because the covariance between the risk-free return and the return on portfolio M must necessarily be zero since there is no uncertainty about the return on the risk-free loan, you should also be able to verify, using Equation (MA5.3), that the standard deviation of the return on the new portfolio is half way between zero and σ_m, that is, $(1/2)\sigma_m$. The standard deviation-expected return combination for this new portfolio is marked as point B in the figure, and as you can see it lies on the line between point A and point M. Similarly, if an investor borrows the total amount of her wealth at the risk-free rate of R_f and invests the proceeds plus her wealth (that is, twice her wealth) in portfolio M, then the standard deviation of this new portfolio will be twice the standard deviation of return on portfolio M, $2\sigma_m$. On the other hand, using Equation (MA5.2), the expected return on this new portfolio is $E(R_m)$ plus $E(R_m) - R_f$, equals $2E(R_m) - R_f$. This standard deviation-expected return combination is plotted as point C in the figure.

You should now be able to see that both point B and point C are on the line connecting point A and point M. Indeed, by choosing different amounts of borrowing and lending, an investor can form a portfolio with a standard deviation-expected return combination that lies anywhere on the line connecting points A and M. You may have noticed that point M has been chosen so that the line connecting points A and M is tangent to the efficient portfolio frontier. The reason for choosing point M in this way is that it leads to standard deviation-expected return combinations along the line that are the most desirable for a risk-averse investor. This line can be thought of as the *opportunity locus* which shows the best combinations of standard deviations and expected returns available to the investor.

The capital asset pricing model makes another assumption: All investors have the same assessment of the expected returns and standard deviations of all assets. In this case, portfolio M is the same for all investors. Thus when all investors' holdings of portfolio M are added together, they must equal all of the risky assets in the market, which is just the market portfolio. The assumption that all investors have the same assessment of risk and return for all assets thus means that portfolio M is the market portfolio. Therefore, the R_m and σ_m in Figure MA5.1 are identical to the market return, R_m, and the standard deviation of this return, σ_m, referred to earlier in this appendix.

The conclusion that the market portfolio and portfolio M are one and the same means that the opportunity locus in Figure MA5.1 can be thought of as showing the trade-off between expected returns and increased risk for the investor. This trade-off is given by the slope of the opportunity locus,

$E(R_m) - R_f$, and it tells us that when an investor is willing to increase the risk of his portfolio by σ_m, then he can earn an additional expected return of $E(R_m) - R_f$. The market price of a unit of market risk, σ_m, is $E(R_m) - R_f$. $E(R_m) - R_f$ is therefore referred to as the **market price of risk.**

We now know that market price of risk is $E(R_m) - R_f$ and we also have learned that an asset's beta tells us about systematic risk, because it is the marginal contribution of that asset to a portfolio's risk. Therefore the amount an asset's expected return exceeds the risk-free rate, $E(R_i) - R_f$, should equal the market price of risk times the marginal contribution of that asset to portfolio risk, $[E(R_m) - R_f]\beta_i$. This reasoning yields the CAPM asset pricing relationship:

$$E(R_i) = R_f + \beta_i[E(R_m) - R_f] \qquad (MA5.7)$$

This CAPM asset pricing equation is represented by the upward sloping line in Figure MA5.2, which is called the **security market line.** It tells us the expected return that the market sets for a security given its beta. For example, it tells us that if a security has a beta of 1.0 so that its marginal contribution to a portfolio's risk is the same as the market portfolio, then it should be priced to have the same expected return as the market portfolio, $E(R_m)$.

To see that securities should be priced so that their expected return-beta combination should lie on the security market line, consider a security like S in the figure which is below the security market line. If an investor makes an investment in which half is put into the market portfolio and half into a risk-free loan, then the beta of this investment will be 0.5, the same as security S. However, this investment will have an expected return on the security market line which is greater than that for security S. Hence investors will not want to hold security S and its current price will fall, thus raising its expected

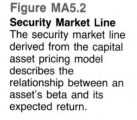

Figure MA5.2
Security Market Line
The security market line derived from the capital asset pricing model describes the relationship between an asset's beta and its expected return.

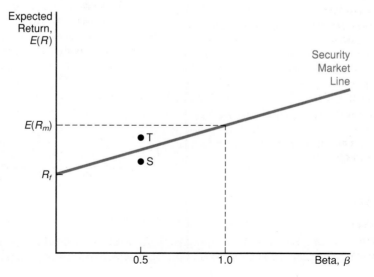

return until it equals the amount indicated on the security market line. On the other hand, suppose there is a security like T which has a beta of 0.5 but whose expected return is above the security market line. By including this security in a well-diversified portfolio with other assets with a beta of 0.5, none of which can have an expected return less than that indicated by the security line (as we have shown), investors can obtain a portfolio with a higher expected return than that obtained by putting half into a risk-free loan and half into the market portfolio. This would mean that all investors would want to hold more of security T, and so its price would rise, thus lowering its expected return until it equaled the amount indicated on the security market line.

The capital asset pricing model formalizes the following important idea: *An asset should be priced so that it has a higher expected return not when it has a greater risk in isolation, but rather when its systematic risk is greater.*

ARBITRAGE PRICING THEORY

Although the capital asset pricing model has proved to be very useful in practice, deriving it does require the adoption of some unrealistic assumptions, for example, the assumption that investors can borrow and lend freely at the risk-free rate, or the assumption that all investors have the same assessment of expected returns and standard deviations of returns for all assets. An important alternative to the capital asset pricing model is arbitrage pricing theory (APT) developed by Stephen Ross of Yale University.

In contrast to CAPM which has only one source of systematic risk, the market return, APT takes the view that there can be several sources of systematic risk in the economy which cannot be eliminated through diversification. These sources of risk can be thought of as factors that may be related to such items as inflation, aggregate output, default risk premiums, and/or the term structure of interest rates. The return on an asset i can thus be written as being made up of components that move with these factors and a random component that is unique to the asset (ϵ_i):

$$R_i = \beta_i^1(\text{factor 1}) + \beta_i^2(\text{factor 2}) + \cdots + \beta_i^k(\text{factor } k) + \epsilon_i \quad (MA5.8)$$

Since there are k factors, this model is called a k-factor model. The $\beta_i^1, \ldots, \beta_i^k$ describe the sensitivity of the asset i's return to each of these factors.

Just as in the capital asset pricing model, these systematic sources of risk should be priced. The market price for each factor j can be thought of as $E(R_{\text{factor } j}) - R_f$, and hence the expected return on a security can be written as:

$$E(R_i) = R_f + \beta_i^1[E(R_{\text{factor } 1}) - R_f] + \cdots + \beta_i^k[E(R_{\text{factor } k}) - R_f] \quad (MA5.9)$$

This asset pricing equation indicates that all the securities should have the same market price for the risk contributed by each factor. If the expected return for a security were above the amount indicated by the APT pricing equation, then it would provide a higher expected return than a portfolio of other securities with the same average sensitivity to each factor. Hence investors would want to hold more of this security and its price would rise until the expected return fell to the value indicated by the APT pricing equation. On the other hand, if the security's expected return were less than the amount indicated by the APT pricing equation, then no one would want to hold this security because a higher expected return could be obtained with a portfolio of securities with the same average sensitivity to each factor. As a result, the price of the security would fall until its expected return fell to the value indicated by the APT pricing equation.

As this brief outline of arbitrage pricing theory indicates, the theory supports a basic conclusion from the capital asset pricing model: An asset should be priced so that it has a higher expected return not when it has a greater risk in isolation, but rather when its systematic risk is greater. There is still substantial controversy about whether a variant of the capital asset pricing model or the arbitrage pricing theory is a better description of reality. At the present time, both frameworks are considered valuable tools for understanding how risk affects the prices of assets.

A Mathematical Treatment of the Baumol-Tobin and the Tobin Mean-Variance Models

THE BAUMOL-TOBIN MODEL OF TRANSACTIONS DEMAND FOR MONEY

The basic idea behind the Baumol-Tobin model was laid out in the chapter. Here we explore the mathematics that underlie their model. The assumptions of the model are:

1. An individual receives income of T_0 at the beginning of every period.
2. An individual spends his income at a constant rate, and so at the end of the period he has spent all his income T_0.
3. There are only two assets—cash and bonds. Cash earns a nominal return of zero, and bonds earn an interest rate i.
4. Every time an individual buys or sells bonds to raise cash he incurs a fixed brokerage fee of b.

Let us denote the amount of cash that the individual raises each time he buys or sells bonds as C, and n = the number of times he conducts a transaction in bonds. As we saw in Figure 23.3, where $T_0 = 1000$, $C = 500$, and $n = 2$,

$$n = T_0/C$$

Because the brokerage cost of each bond transaction is b, the total brokerage costs for a period are

$$nb = \frac{bT_0}{C}$$

Not only are there brokerage costs but there is also an opportunity cost to holding cash rather than bonds. This opportunity cost is the bond interest rate, i, times average cash balances held during the period, which, from the discussion in the chapter, we know is equal to $C/2$. The opportunity cost is then

$$\frac{iC}{2}$$

Combining these two costs, we have the total costs for an individual equal to

$$COSTS = \frac{bT_0}{C} + \frac{iC}{2}$$

The individual wants to minimize his costs by choosing the appropriate level of C. He does so by taking the derivative of costs with respect to C and setting it to zero.[1] That is,[2]

$$\frac{d\ COSTS}{dC} = \frac{-bT_0}{C^2} + \frac{i}{2} = 0$$

Solving for C yields the optimal level of C

$$C = \sqrt{\frac{2bT_0}{i}}$$

Because money demand, M^d, is the average desired holding of cash balances, $C/2$,

$$M^d = \frac{1}{2}\sqrt{\frac{2bT_0}{i}} = \sqrt{\frac{bT_0}{2i}} \qquad \text{(MA23.1)}$$

---

[1] In order to minimize costs, the second derivative must be greater than zero. We find that it is, because

$$\frac{d^2 COSTS}{dC^2} = \frac{-2}{C^3}(-bT_0) = \frac{2bT_0}{C^3} > 0$$

[2] An alternative way to get Equation (MA23.1) is to have the individual maximize his profits, which equal the interest on bonds minus the brokerage costs. The average holding of bonds over a period is just

$$\frac{T_0}{2} - \frac{C}{2}.$$

Thus profits are

$$PROFITS = \frac{i}{2}[T_0 - C] - \frac{bT_0}{C}$$

Then

$$\frac{d\ PROFITS}{dC} = \frac{-i}{2} + \frac{bT_0}{C^2} = 0$$

This equation yields the same square root rule as in (MA23.1).

This is the famous square root rule. It has these implications for the demand for money:

1. The transactions demand for money is negatively related to the interest rate i.

2. The transactions demand for money is positively related to income, but there are economies of scale in money holdings—that is, the demand for money rises less than proportionally with income. For example, if T_0 quadruples in Equation (MA23.1), the demand for money only doubles.

3. A lowering of the brokerage costs due to technological improvements would increase the demand for money.

4. There is no money illusion in the demand for money. If the price level doubles, then both T_0 and b will double. Equation (MA23.1) then indicates that M will double as well. Thus the demand for real money balances remains unchanged, which makes sense because neither the interest rate nor real income has changed.

THE TOBIN MEAN-VARIANCE MODEL

Tobin's mean-variance analysis of money demand is just an application of the basic ideas in the theory of asset demand outlined in Chapter 5. Tobin assumes that the utility people derive from their assets is positively related to the expected return on their portfolio of assets and is negatively related to the riskiness of this portfolio as represented by the variance (or standard deviation) of its returns. This framework implies that an individual has indifference curves that can be drawn as in Figure MA23.1. Notice that these

Figure MA23.1
Indifference Curves in a Mean-Variance Model
The indifference curves are upward sloping, and higher indifference curves indicate that utility is higher. In other words, $U_3 > U_2 > U_1$.

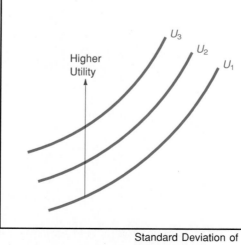

indifference curves are upward sloping because an individual is willing to accept more risk if he is offered a higher expected return. In addition, as we go to higher indifference curves utility is higher, because for the same level of risk the expected return is higher.

Tobin looks at the choice of holding money, which earns a certain zero return, or bonds, whose return R_B is

$$R_B = i + g$$

where

$$i = \text{the interest rate on the bond}$$
$$g = \text{the capital gain}$$

Tobin also assumes that the expected capital gain is zero[3] and its variance is σ_g^2. That is,

$$E(g) = 0 \text{ and so } E(R_B) = i + 0 = i$$
$$Var\,(g) = E[g - E(g)]^2 = E(g^2) = \sigma_g^2$$

where

$$E(.\,.\,.) = \text{the expectation of the variable inside the parentheses}$$
$$Var(.\,.\,.) = \text{the variance of the variable inside the parentheses}$$

If A is the fraction of the portfolio put into bonds ($0 \leq A \leq 1$) and $1 - A$ is the fraction of the portfolio held as money, then the return on the portfolio, R, can be written as

$$R = AR_B + (1 - A) \times 0 = AR_B = A(i + g)$$

Then the mean and variance of the return on the portfolio, denoted respectively as μ and σ^2, can be calculated as

$$\mu = E(R) = E(AR_B) = AE(R_B) = Ai$$
$$\sigma^2 = E[R - \mu]^2 = E[A(i + g) - Ai]^2 = E(Ag)^2 = A^2 E(g^2) = A^2 \sigma_g^2$$

Taking the square root of both sides of the equation directly above and solving for A yields

$$A = \frac{1}{\sigma_g}\sigma \qquad \text{(MA23.2)}$$

Substituting in for A in the equation $\mu = Ai$ using the preceding equation gives us

$$\mu = \frac{i}{\sigma_g}\sigma \qquad \text{(MA23.3)}$$

---

[3]This assumption is not critical to the results. If $E(g) \neq 0$ then it can be added to the interest term i and the analysis proceeds as above.

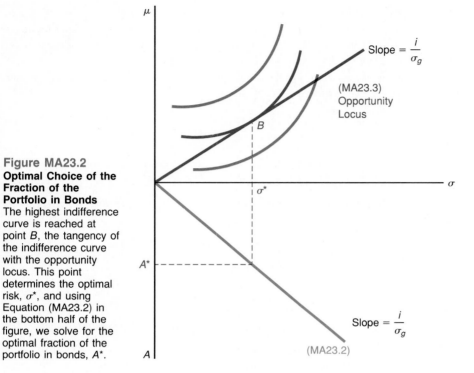

Figure MA23.2
Optimal Choice of the Fraction of the Portfolio in Bonds
The highest indifference curve is reached at point B, the tangency of the indifference curve with the opportunity locus. This point determines the optimal risk, σ^*, and using Equation (MA23.2) in the bottom half of the figure, we solve for the optimal fraction of the portfolio in bonds, A^*.

In figure: $\text{Slope} = \dfrac{i}{\sigma_g}$

(MA23.3) Opportunity Locus

B

σ^*

μ

σ

A^*

$\text{Slope} = \dfrac{i}{\sigma_g}$

(MA23.2)

A

Equation (MA23.3) is known as the *opportunity locus* because it tells us the combinations of μ and σ that are feasible for the individual. This equation is written in a form in which the μ variable corresponds to the Y axis and the σ to the X axis. The opportunity locus is a straight line going through the origin with a slope of i/σ_g. It is drawn in the top half of Figure MA23.2 along with the indifference curves from the previous figure.

The highest indifference curve is reached at point B, the tangency of the indifference curve and the opportunity locus. This point determines the optimal level of risk, σ^* in the figure. As Equation (MA23.2) indicates, the optimal level of A, A^*, is

$$A^* = \frac{\sigma^*}{\sigma_g}$$

This equation is solved in the bottom half of Figure MA23.2. The (MA23.2) equation for A is a straight line through the origin with a slope of

$$\frac{1}{\sigma_g}$$

Given σ^*, the value of A read off this line is the optimal value A^*. Notice that the bottom part of the figure is drawn so that as we move down, A is increasing.

Figure MA23.3
Optimal Choice of the Fraction of the Portfolio in Bonds as the Interest Rate Rises
The interest rate on bonds rises from i_1 to i_2, thus rotating the opportunity locus upward. The highest indifference curve is now at point C, where it is tangent to the new opportunity locus. The optimal level of risk rises from σ_1^* to σ_2^* and then Equation (MA23.2), in the bottom half of the figure, shows that the optimal fraction of the portfolio in bonds rises from A_1^* to A_2^*.

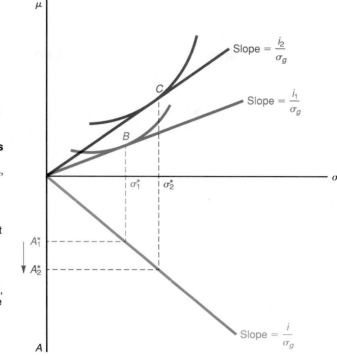

Now let's ask ourselves what happens when the interest rate increases from i_1 to i_2. This situation is shown in Figure MA23.3. Because σ_g is unchanged, the Equation (MA23.2) line in the bottom half of the figure does not change. However, the slope of the opportunity locus does increase as i increases. Thus the opportunity locus rotates up and we move to point C at the tangency of the new opportunity locus and the indifference curve. As you can see, the optimal level of risk increases from σ_1^* to σ_2^* and the optimal fraction of the portfolio in bonds rises from A_1^* to A_2^*. Thus we have the result that as the interest rate on bonds rises, the demand for money falls; that is, $1 - A$, the fraction of the portfolio held as money, declines.[4]

---

[4]The indifference curves have been drawn so that the usual result is obtained that as i goes up, A^* goes up as well. However, there is a subtle issue of income versus substitution effects. If, as people get wealthier, they are willing to bear less risk, and if this income effect is larger than the substitution effect, then it is possible to get the opposite result that as i increases, A^* declines. This set of conditions is unlikely, which is why the figure is drawn so that the usual result is obtained. For a discussion of income versus substitution effects, see David Laidler, *The Demand for Money: Theories and Evidence*, 3rd ed. (New York: Harper & Row, 1985).

Tobin's model then yields the same result as Keynes' analysis of the speculative demand for money: It is negatively related to the level of interest rates. This model, however, makes two important points that Keynes' model does not:

1. Individuals diversify their portfolio and hold money *and* bonds at the same time.

2. Even if the expected return on bonds is greater than the expected return on money, individuals will still hold money as a store of wealth because its return is more certain.

Algebra of the *ISLM* Model

The use of algebra to analyze the *ISLM* model allows us to extend the multiplier analysis in Chapter 24 and to obtain many of the results of Chapters 24 and 25 very quickly.

BASIC CLOSED-ECONOMY *ISLM* MODEL

The goods market can be described by the following equations, where

$C = \overline{C} + mpc\,(Y - T)$	Consumption Function	(MA25.1)
$I = \overline{I} - di$	Investment Function	(MA25.2)
$T = \overline{T}$	Taxes	(MA25.3)
$G = \overline{G}$	Government Spending	(MA25.4)
$Y = Y^{ad} = C + I + G$	Goods Market Equilibrium Condition	(MA25.5)

The money market is described by these equations

$M^d = \overline{M}^d + eY - fi$	Money Demand Function	(MA25.6)
$M^s = \overline{M}$	Money Supply	(MA25.7)
$M^d = M^s$	Money Market Equilibrium Condition	(MA25.8)

The uppercase terms are the variables of the model; $\overline{G}$, $\overline{T}$, and $\overline{M}$ are the values of the policy variables that are set exogenously (i.e., outside the model); and $\overline{C}$, $\overline{I}$, and $\overline{M}^d$ are autonomous components of consumer expenditure, investment spending, and money demand that are also determined exogenously (i.e., outside the model). Except for the interest rate, i, the lowercase terms are the parameters, the givens of the model, and all are assumed to be positive. The definitions of these variables and parameters are

$$C = \text{consumer spending}$$
$$I = \text{investment spending}$$
$$G = \overline{G} = \text{government spending}$$
$$Y = \text{output}$$
$$T = \overline{T} = \text{taxes}$$
$$M^d = \text{money demand}$$

$$M^s = \overline{M} = \text{money supply}$$
$$i = \text{interest rate}$$
$$\overline{C} = \text{autonomous consumer spending}$$
$$d = \text{interest sensitivity of investment spending}$$
$$\overline{I} = \text{autonomous investment spending related to business confidence}$$
$$\overline{M}^d = \text{autonomous money demand}$$
$$e = \text{income sensitivity of money demand}$$
$$f = \text{interest sensitivity of money demand}$$
$$mpc = \text{marginal propensity to consume}$$

IS and *LM* Curves

Substituting for C, I, and G in the goods market equilibrium condition and then solving for Y we obtain the *IS* curve,

$$Y = \frac{1}{1 - mpc} \times [\overline{C} + \overline{I} - mpc\,\overline{T} + \overline{G} - di] \qquad \text{(MA25.9)}$$

Solving for i from Equations (MA25.6) through (MA25.8), we obtain the *LM* curve

$$i = \frac{\overline{M}^d - \overline{M} + eY}{f} \qquad \text{(MA25.10)}$$

Solution of the Model

The solution to the model occurs at the intersection of the *IS* and *LM* curves, which involves solving for Y and i simultaneously, using both (MA25.9) and (MA25.10). The solutions for Y and i are

$$Y = \frac{1}{1 - mpc + \dfrac{de}{f}} \times \left[\overline{C} + \overline{I} - mpc\,\overline{T} + \overline{G} - \frac{d\overline{M}^d}{f} + \frac{d\overline{M}}{f}\right] \qquad \text{(MA25.11)}$$

$$i = \frac{1}{f(1 - mpc) + de} \times \{e(\overline{C} + \overline{I} - mpc\,\overline{T} + \overline{G}) \qquad \text{(MA25.12)}$$
$$+ \overline{M}^d(1 - mpc) - \overline{M}(1 - mpc)\}$$

Implications

The conclusions that are reached with these algebraic solutions are the same as those reached in Chapters 24 and 25. For example:

1. Because all the coefficients are positive, (MA25.11) indicates that a rise in $\overline{C}$, $\overline{I}$, $\overline{G}$, and $\overline{M}$ leads to a rise in Y, and a rise in $\overline{T}$ or $\overline{M}^d$ leads to a fall in Y.

2. (MA25.12) indicates that a rise in $\overline{C}, \overline{I}, \overline{G}$, and $\overline{M}^d$ leads to a rise in i, and a rise in $\overline{M}$ or $\overline{T}$ leads to a fall in i.

3. As f, the interest sensitivity of money demand, increases, the multiplier term

$$\frac{1}{1 - mpc + \dfrac{de}{f}}$$

increases, and so fiscal policy $(\overline{G}, \overline{T})$ has more effect on output; on the other hand, the term multiplying $\overline{M}$,

$$\frac{d}{f}\left(\frac{1}{1 - mpc + \dfrac{de}{f}} \right) = \frac{d}{f(1 - mpc) + de},$$

declines, so that monetary policy has less effect on output.

4. By similar reasoning, as d (the interest sensitivity of investment spending) increases, monetary policy has more effect on output and fiscal policy has less effect on output.

OPEN-ECONOMY *ISLM* MODEL

To make the basic *ISLM* model into an open-economy model we need to include net exports in the goods market equilibrium condition so that (MA25.5) becomes (MA25.5′):

$$Y = Y^{ad} = C + I + G + NX \qquad\qquad \text{(MA25.5′)}$$

As the discussion in Chapter 25 suggests, the net exports and exchange rate relations can be written

$$\begin{aligned} NX &= \overline{NX} - hE & \text{(MA25.13)} \\ E &= \overline{E} + ji & \text{(MA25.14)} \end{aligned}$$

where

$$\begin{aligned} NX &= \text{net exports} \\ \overline{NX} &= \text{autonomous net exports} \\ h &= \text{exchange rate sensitivity of net exports} \\ E &= \text{exchange rate (value of domestic currency)} \\ \overline{E} &= \text{autonomous exchange rate} \\ j &= \text{interest sensitivity of exchange rate} \end{aligned}$$

Substituting for net exports in the (MA25.5′) goods market equilibrium condition using the net exports and exchange rate relations, and then solving for Y as in the basic model, we obtain the open economy *IS* curve:

$$Y = \frac{1}{1 - mpc} \times [\overline{C} + \overline{I} - mpc\,\overline{T} + \overline{G} + \overline{NX} - h\overline{E} - (d + hj)i] \qquad \text{(MA25.15)}$$

The *LM* curve is the same as in the basic model, and so the solutions for *Y* and *i* are

$$Y = \frac{1}{1 - mpc + \dfrac{(d + hj)e}{f}} \qquad \text{(MA25.16)}$$

$$\times [\overline{C} + \overline{I} - mpc\,\overline{T} + \overline{G} - \frac{(d + hj)}{f}\,\overline{M}^d + \frac{(d + hj)}{f}\,\overline{M} + \overline{NX} - h\overline{E}]$$

$$i = \frac{1}{f(1 - mpc) + (d + hj)e} \qquad \text{(MA25.17)}$$

$$\times \{e(\overline{C} + \overline{I} - mpc\,\overline{T} + \overline{G} + \overline{NX} - h\overline{E}) + \overline{M}^d(1 - mpc) - \overline{M}(1 - mpc)\}$$

Implications

1. As the *IS* curve in (MA25.15) indicates, including net exports in aggregate demand provides an additional reason for the negative relationship between *Y* and *i* (the downward slope of the *IS* curve). This additional reason for the negative relationship of *Y* and *i* is represented by *hj* in the term $-(d + hj)i$.

2. (MA25.16) and (MA25.17) indicate that all the results we found for the basic model still hold.

3. (MA25.16) indicates that a rise in $\overline{NX}$ leads to a rise in *Y*, and an autonomous rise in the value of the domestic currency, $\overline{E}$, leads to a decline in *Y*.

4. (MA25.17) indicates that a rise in $\overline{NX}$ leads to a rise in *i*, and a rise in $\overline{E}$ leads to a decline in *i*.

Glossary

accommodating policy An activist policy in which a high employment target is pursued. **674**

acquisitions A purchase of a corporation by another corporation or a group of investors. **185**

activist An economist who views the self-correcting mechanism through wage and price adjustment to be very slow and hence sees the need for the government to pursue active, discretionary policy to eliminate high unemployment whenever it develops. **616**

adaptive expectations A view of expectations formation in which expectations of a variable are viewed as being an average of past values of the variable. **695**

adverse selection The problem created by asymmetric information *before* the transaction occurs in which the people who are the *most undesirable* from the other party's point of view are the ones who are most likely to want to engage in the financial transaction. **164, 250**

aggregate demand The total quantity of output demanded in the economy at different price levels. **555, 604**

aggregate demand curve A relationship between the price level and the quantity of aggregate output demanded when the goods and money markets are in equilibrium. **597, 604**

aggregate demand function The relationship between aggregate output and aggregate demand that shows the quantity of aggregate output demanded for each level of aggregate output. **560**

aggregate income The total income payments to households in the economy. **17**

aggregate output The total production of final goods and services in the economy. **6**

aggregate price level The average price of goods or services in an economy. **4**

aggregate supply The quantity of aggregate output supplied by the economy at different price levels. **604**

aggregate supply curve The relationship between the quantity of output supplied in the short run and the price level. **610**

"animal spirits" Waves of business and consumer optimism and pessimism that affect consumers' and businesses' willingness to spend. **609**

appreciation A situation in which a currency increases in value. **469**

asset A piece of property that is a store of value. **21**

asymmetric information The inequality of the information that each party to a transaction knows. **163**

autonomous consumer expenditure The amount of consumer expenditure that is independent of disposable income. **556**

balance of payments A bookkeeping system for recording all payments that have a direct bearing on the movement of funds between a country and foreign countries. **500**

balance sheet A list of the assets and liabilities of a bank (or firm) that balances (that is, total assets equal total liabilities plus capital). **198**

bank failure A situation in which a bank cannot satisfy its obligations to pay its depositors and thus goes out of business. **211**

bank holding companies Companies that own one or more banks. **230**

bank panic The simultaneous failure of many banks. **180, 362**

banks Financial institutions that accept deposits and make loans (such as commercial banks, savings and loan associations, and credit unions). **9**

beta A measure of the sensitivity of an asset's return to changes in the value of the market portfolio, which is also a measure of the asset's marginal contribution to the risk of the market portfolio. **MA-1–3**

Board of Governors of the Federal Reserve System A board with seven governors (including the chairman) that plays an essential role in decision making within the Federal Reserve System. **388**

bond A security that promises to make payments periodically for a specified period of time. **39**

branches Additional offices of banks that conduct banking operations. **237**

Bretton Woods system The international monetary system in use from 1945 to 1971 in which exchange rates were fixed and the U.S. dollar was freely convertible into gold (by foreign governments and central banks only). **506**

brokerage firms Firms that engage in all three securities markets as brokers, dealers, and investment bankers. **289**

brokered deposits Deposits that enable depositors to circumvent the $100,000 limit on federal deposit insurance by breaking up a large deposit into smaller packages of less than $100,000 at each bank so the total amount deposited is fully insured. **254**

budget deficit The excess of government expenditure over tax revenues. **9**

business cycles The upward and downward movement of aggregate output produced in the economy. **6**

call option An option contract that provides the right to buy a security at a specified price. **302**

capital account An account that describes the flow of capital between the United States and other countries. **408**

capital market A financial market in which longer-term debt and equity instruments are traded. **43**

capital mobility A situation in which foreigners can easily purchase a country's assets and the country's residents can easily purchase foreign assets. **479**

central bank The government agency that oversees the banking system and is responsible for the conduct of monetary policy; in the United States, the Federal Reserve System. **321**

closed-end fund A mutual fund structure in which a fixed number of nonredeemable shares are sold at an initial offering, then traded in the over-the-counter market like common stock. **283**

coinsurance A situation in which only a portion of losses are covered by insurance, so that the insured suffers a percentage of the losses along with the insurance agency. **275**

collateral Property that is pledged to the lender if a borrower cannot make his or her debt payment. **160**

compensating balances A required minimum amount of funds that a firm receiving a loan must keep in a checking account at the bank. **218**

complete crowding out The situation in which expansionary fiscal policy, such as an increase in government spending, does not lead to a rise in output because there is an exactly offsetting movement of private spending. **610**

consol A perpetual bond with no maturity date and no repayment of principal that periodically makes fixed coupon payments. **75**

constant-money-growth-rate rule A policy rule advocated by monetarists in which the Federal Reserve keeps the money supply growing at a constant rate. **688**

consumer durable expenditure Spending by consumers on durable items such as automobiles and household appliances. **654**

consumer expenditure The total demand (spending) for consumer goods and services. **555, 607**

consumption Spending by consumers on nondurable goods and services (including services related to the ownership of houses and consumer durables). **655**

consumption function The relationship between disposable income and consumer expenditure. **556**

costly state verification The fact that the monitoring process is expensive in terms of time and money. **173**

cost-push inflation Inflation that occurs because of the push by workers to get higher wages. **673**

coupon bond A credit market instrument that pays the owner of the bond a fixed interest payment every year until the maturity date, when a specified final amount is repaid. **68**

coupon rate The dollar amount of the yearly coupon payment expressed as a percentage of the face value of the coupon bond. **68**

credit rationing A situation in which a lender refuses to make a loan, even though borrowers are willing to pay the stated interest rate or even a higher rate. **218**

currency Paper money (such as dollar bills) and coins. **20**

current account An account that shows international transactions involving currently produced goods and services. **502**

current yield An approximation of the yield to maturity that equals the yearly coupon payment divided by the price of a coupon bond. **78**

debt-deflation A situation in which a substantial decline in the price level sets in, leading to a further deterioration in firms' net worth because of the increased burden of indebtedness. **182**

deductible The fixed amount that is deducted from the insured's loss when a claim is paid off. **275**

default A situation in which the party issuing the debt instrument is unable to make interest payments or pay off the amount owed when the instrument matures. **51**

default-free bonds Bonds with no default risk, such as U.S. government bonds. **133**

default risk The chance that the issuer of a bond will default, that is, be unable to make interest payments or pay off the face value when the bond matures. **133**

defensive open market operations Open market operations intended to offset movements in other factors that affect the monetary base (such as changes in Treasury deposits at the Fed or in float). **425**

demand curve The relationship between the quantity demanded and the price when all other economic variables are held constant. **103**

demand-pull inflation Inflation that results when policymakers pursue policies that shift the aggregate demand curve. **673**

deposit outflows The loss of deposits when depositors make withdrawals or demand payment. **206**

deposit rate ceilings Restrictions on the maximum interest rates payable on deposits. **308**

depreciation A situation in which a currency falls in value. **469**

devaluation A situation in which the par value of a currency is reset at a lower level. **509**

discount bond A credit market instrument that is bought at a price below its face value, and whose face value is repaid at the maturity date; it does not make any interest payments. **68**

discount loans A bank's borrowing from the Federal Reserve System; also called an "advance." **201**

discount rate The interest rate charged banks on discount loans. **209, 324**

discount window The Federal Reserve facility at which discount loans are made to banks. **428**

disintermediation A reduction in the flow of funds into the banking system so that the amount of financial intermediation declines. **308**

disposable income Total income available for spending, equal to aggregate income minus taxes. **556**

diversification The holding of many risky assets. **98**

dividends Periodic payments made by equities to shareholders. **41**

dual banking system The system in the United States in which banks supervised by the federal government and by the states operate side by side. **229**

duration analysis A measurement of the sensitivity of the market value of the bank's assets and liabilities to changes in interest rates. **222**

dynamic open market operations Open market operations that are intended to change the level of reserves and the monetary base. **425**

econometric model A model whose equations are estimated with statistical procedures. **716**

economies of scale The decrease in transactions costs per dollar of transaction as the size (scale) of transactions increases. **162**

Edge Act Corporation A special subsidiary of U.S. banks that is engaged primarily in international banking. **244**

efficient portfolio frontier The most preferable combinations of standard deviation and expected return that can be achieved by putting risky assets into portfolios. **744**

equation of exchange The equation $MV = PY$, which relates nominal income to the quantity of money. **524, 606**

equities Claims to share in the net income and the assets of a business firm (such as common stock). **41**

equity capital The difference between a firm's assets (what it owns or is owed) and its liabilities (what it owes). **170**

Eurobonds Bonds denominated in a currency other than that in which they are sold. **62**

Eurodollars U.S. dollars that are deposited in foreign banks outside of the United States or in foreign branches of U.S. banks. **54**

excess demand A condition in which quantity demanded is greater than quantity supplied. **106**

excess reserves Reserves in excess of required reserves. **202, 324**

excess supply A situation in which the quantity supplied exceeds the quantity demanded. **106**

exchange rate The price of one country's currency in terms of another. **467**

exchange rate overshooting A phenomenon in which the exchange rate changes by more in the short run than it does in the long run when the money supply changes. **489**

exchanges Secondary markets in which buyers and sellers of securities (or their agents or brokers) meet in one central location to conduct trades. **42**

expectations hypothesis The proposition that the interest rate on a long-term bond will equal an average of short-term interest rates that people expect to occur over the life of the long-term bond. **142**

expenditure multiplier The ratio of the change in aggregate output to a change in investment spending (or autonomous spending). **562**

face or par value A specified final amount paid to the owner of a coupon bond at the maturity date. **68**

federal funds rate The interest rate on overnight loans of deposits at the Federal Reserve. **54**

Federal Open Market Committee (FOMC) The committee that makes decisions regarding the conduct of open market operations; composed of the seven members of the Board of Governors and the Federal Reserve System, the president of the Federal Reserve Bank of New York, and the presidents of four other Federal Reserve banks. **388**

Federal Reserve banks The twelve district banks that are entities in the Federal Reserve System. **388**

Federal Reserve System (Fed) The central banking authority responsible for monetary policy in the United States. **30, 322**

fiat money Paper currency that governments make legal tender and yet is not convertible into coins or precious metal. **26**

financial crisis A major disruption in financial markets that is characterized by sharp declines in asset prices and the failures of many financial and nonfinancial firms. **178**

financial futures contract A futures contract in which the standardized commodity is a particular type of financial instrument. **300**

financial intermediaries Institutions that borrow funds from those who have saved and then, in turn, make loans to others (such as banks, insurance companies, mutual funds, pension funds, and finance companies). **10**

financial intermediation The process of indirect finance by which financial intermediaries link lender-savers and borrower-spenders. **43**

financial markets Markets in which funds are transferred from those who have surplus funds available to those who have a shortage of available funds. **11**

Fisher effect Named after economist Irving Fisher; the outcome that when expected inflation occurs, interest rates will rise. **114**

fixed exchange rate regime The international financial environment from after World War II up until 1971 in which central banks bought and sold their own currencies to keep their exchange rates fixed at a certain level. **506**

fixed investment spending Spending by business firms on equipment (computers, airplanes) and structures (factories, office buildings) and planned spending on residential houses. **558**

fixed payment loan A credit market instrument that provides a borrower with an amount of money that is repaid by making a fixed payment periodically (usually monthly) for a set number of years. **68**

float Cash items in process of collection at the Fed minus deferred availability cash items. **409**

foreign bonds Bonds sold in a foreign country which are denominated in that country's currency. **61**

foreign exchange market The market in which exchange rates are determined. **467**

forward exchange rate The exchange rate for the forward transaction. **13–14, 469**

forward premium The percentage difference between the forward and spot exchange rates.

forward transaction An exchange rate transaction that involves the exchange of bank deposits denominated in different currencies at some specified future date. **469**

free cash flow Cash flow is the difference between cash receipts and cash expenditures (which includes interest and dividends), while free cash flow is the amount of cash flow that exceeds the amount of profitable investment opportunities open to the firm. **188**

free reserves Excess reserves in the banking system minus the volume of discount loans. **454**

free rider problem The problem that occurs when people who do not pay for information can take advantage of the information that other people have paid for. **167**

fully funded A pension plan is *fully funded* if the contributions to the plan and their earnings over the years are sufficient to pay out the defined benefits when they come due. **279**

futures contract A contract in which the seller agrees to provide a certain standardized commodity to the buyer on a specified future date at an agreed upon price. **299**

gap analysis A measurement of the sensitivity of bank profits to changes in interest rates: calculated by subtracting the amount of rate-sensitive liabilities from rate-sensitive assets. **221**

gold standard A regime under which the currency of most countries is directly convertible into gold. **505**

government budget constraint The constraint that the government budget deficit must equal the sum of the change in the monetary base and the change in government bonds held by the public. **416**

government spending Spending by all levels of government on goods and services (e.g., typewriters, aircraft carriers). **555, 608**

gross national product (GNP) The value of all final goods and services produced in the economy during the course of a year. **17**

hedge Protection against risk. **300**

high-powered money Another name for the monetary base. **337**

hyperinflation An extreme inflation in which the inflation rate exceeds 50% per month. **25**

hysteresis A departure from full employment levels as a result of past high unemployment. **621**

incentive compatible When a contract aligns the incentives of both parties to the contract. **175–176**

income A flow of earnings per unit time. **21**

inflation The condition of a continually rising price level. **4**

inflation rate The rate of change of the price level, usually measured as a percentage change per year. **5**

insolvent A situation in which the value of a firm's or bank's assets fall below its liabilities so that it is bankrupt. **211**

interest parity condition A condition which states that the domestic interest rate equals the foreign interest rate plus the expected appreciation in the foreign currency. **480**

interest rate The cost of borrowing or the price paid for the rental of funds (usually expressed as a percentage per year). **7**

interest-rate risk The riskiness of returns that is associated with changes in interest rates. **207, 298**

intermediate target Any of a number of variables, such as monetary aggregates or interest rates, that have a direct effect on employment and the price level and that the Fed seeks to influence. **444**

intermediate term Referring to a debt instrument with a maturity of between one and ten years. **41**

international banking facilities (IBFs) Facilities within the United States that can accept time deposits from foreigners but are not subject to either reserve requirements or any restrictions on interest payments. **245**

International Monetary Fund (IMF) The international organization created by the Bretton Woods agreement whose objective is to promote the growth of world trade by making loans to countries experiencing balance of payments difficulties. **506**

international policy coordination Agreements among countries to enact policies cooperatively. **461**

international reserves Central bank holdings of assets denominated in foreign currencies. **493**

inventory investment spending Spending by business firms on additional holdings of raw materials, parts, and finished goods. **558**

investment banks Firms that assist in the initial sale of securities in the primary market. **286**

IS curve The relationship that describes the combinations of aggregate output and interest rates for which the total quantity of goods produced equals the total quantity demanded (goods market equilibrium). **571**

junk bonds Bonds with ratings below Baa (or BBB) that have a high default risk. **135**

Keynesian A follower of John Maynard Keynes who believes that movements in the price level and aggregate output are driven by changes not only in the money supply but also in government spending and fiscal policy and who does not regard the economy as inherently stable. **604**

L A measure of highly liquid assets that adds to *M3* short-term Treasury securities, commercial paper, long-term Eurodollars, savings bonds, and bankers' acceptances. **32**

law of one price The principle that if two countries produce an identical good, then the price of this good should be the same throughout the world no matter which country produces it. **472**

lender of last resort　A provider of reserves to banks when no one else would provide them in order to prevent bank failures. **379**

leverage　The firm's ratio of debt to equity. **190**

leveraged buyout (LBO)　A corporate restructuring in which equity is replaced by debt. **190**

liabilities　An IOU or a debt. **39**

line of credit　A bank's commitment (for a specified future period of time) to provide a firm with loans up to a given amount at an interest rate that is tied to some market interest rate. **216, 225**

liquidity　The relative ease and speed with which an asset can be converted into a medium of exchange. **24**

liquidity management　The decisions made by a bank in order to maintain sufficient liquid assets to meet the bank's obligations to depositors. **207**

liquidity preference framework　A model developed by John Maynard Keynes that predicts the equilibrium interest rate on the basis of the supply and demand for money. **118**

liquidity preference theory　Keynes' theory of the demand for money. **530**

LM curve　The relationship that describes the combinations of interest rates and aggregate output for which the quantity of money demanded equals the quantity of money supplied (money market equilibrium). **571**

load funds　Open-end mutual funds sold by salespeople who receive a commission that is paid at the time of purchase and is immediately subtracted from the redemption value of the shares. **283**

loanable funds　The quantity of loans. **107**

loanable funds framework　A framework that determines the equilibrium interest rate using the supply and demand for bonds (loanable funds). **109**

loan sale　A contract (also called a secondary loan participation) that sells all or part of the cash stream from a specific loan and thereby removes the loan from the bank's balance sheet. **225**

long-run aggregate supply curve　The quantity of output supplied in the long run for any given price level. **614**

long term　Referring to a debt instrument with a maturity of ten years or more. **41**

luxury　An asset whose wealth elasticity is greater than one. **96**

M1　A measure of money that includes currency, traveler's checks, and checkable deposits. **31**

M2　A measure of money that adds to M1 money market deposit accounts, money market mutual fund shares, small denomination time deposits, savings deposits, overnight repurchase agreements, and overnight Eurodollars. **32**

M3　A measure of money that adds to M2 large-denomination time deposits, long-term repurchase agreements, and institutional money market fund shares. **32**

managed float regime (dirty float)　The current international financial environment in which exchange rates fluctuate from day to day, but central banks attempt to influence their countries' exchange rates by buying and selling currencies. **492**

marginal propensity to consume (mpc)　The slope of the consumption function line that measures the change in consumer expenditure resulting from an additional dollar of disposable income. **556**

market equilibrium　A situation occurring when the quantity that people are willing to buy (demand) equals the amount that people are willing to sell (supply). **106**

market portfolio　A portfolio that includes the total of all risky assets. **740**

market price of risk　The market price of a unit of market risk, $E(R_m) - R_f$. **746**

matched sale-purchase transaction　An arrangement in which the Fed sells securities and the buyer agrees to sell them back to the Fed in the near future; sometimes called a "reverse repo." **427–428**

maturity　Time (term) to the expiration date (maturity date) of a debt instrument. **41**

medium of exchange　Something that is used to pay for goods and services. **21**

mergers　An arrangement in which two corporations combine to make one larger corporation. **185**

modern quantity theory of money　The theory that changes in aggregate spending are primarily determined by changes in the money supply. **606**

monetarist　A follower of Milton Friedman who sees changes in the money supply as the primary source of movements in the price level and aggregate output and who views the economy as inherently stable. **604**

monetary aggregates　The various measures of money used by the Federal Reserve System (M1, M2, M3, and L). **31**

monetary base　The sum of the Fed's monetary liabilities (currency in circulation and reserves) and the U.S. Treasury's monetary liabilities (Treasury currency in circulation, primarily coins). **323**

monetary neutrality　A proposition that in the long run a percentage rise in the money supply is matched by the same percentage rise in the price level, leaving unchanged the real money supply and all other economic variables such as interest rates. **488**

monetary policy The management of the money supply and interest rates. **8**

monetary theory The theory that relates changes in the quantity of money to changes in economic activity. **6, 523**

monetizing the debt A method of financing government spending by which the government debt issued to finance government spending is removed from the hands of the public and is replaced by high-powered money instead. **421**

money (or money supply) Anything that is generally accepted in payment for goods or services or in the repayment of debts. **3**

money center banks Large banks in key financial centers. **213**

money market A financial market in which only short-term debt instruments (maturity less than one year) are traded. **43**

money multiplier A ratio that relates the change in the money supply to a given change in the monetary base. **336**

moral hazard A situation that occurs after a transaction in which one party to the transaction has incentives to engage in behavior that is undesirable from the other party's point of view. **164, 249**

multiple deposit creation A process by which the Fed supplies the banking system with $1 of additional reserves, and deposits increase by a multiple of this amount. **324**

national banks Federally chartered banks. **229**

natural rate level of output The level of aggregate output produced at the natural rate of unemployment. **441, 614**

natural rate of unemployment The rate of unemployment consistent with full employment at which the demand for labor equals the supply of labor. **614**

necessity An asset is a *necessity* if as wealth grows, the percentage increase in the demand for the asset is less than the percentage increase in wealth—in other words, its wealth elasticity is less than one. **96**

net exports The net foreign spending on domestic goods and services, equal to exports minus imports. **555, 608**

net worth The difference between a firm's assets (what it owns or is owed) and its liabilities (what it owes). **170**

no-load funds Mutual funds sold directly to the public with no sales commissions. **283**

nominal interest rate An interest rate that does not take inflation into account. **88**

nonactivist An economist who believes that the performance of the economy would be improved if the government avoids active policy to eliminate unemployment. **616**

nonbank banks Limited service banks that either do not make commercial loans or alternatively do not take in deposits. **239**

nonborrowed monetary base The monetary base minus discount loans. **343**

nonsystematic risk The component of an asset's risk that is unique to the asset and so can be eliminated by diversification. **742**

off-balance-sheet activities Bank activities which involve trading financial instruments and the generation of income from fees and loan sales, all of which affect bank profits but are not visible on bank balance sheets. **224**

official reserve transactions balance The current account balance plus items in the capital account. **503**

open-end fund The most common structure of mutual fund in which shares can be redeemed at any time at a price that is tied to the asset value of the fund. **283**

open market operations The Fed's buying (or selling) of bonds in the open market. **325**

open market purchase A purchase of bonds by the Fed. **337**

open market sale A sale of bonds by the Fed. **337**

operating target Any of a set of variables, such as reserve aggregates or interest rates, that the Fed seeks to influence and that are responsive to its policy tools. **444**

opportunity cost The amount of interest (expected return) sacrificed by not holding the alternative asset. **119**

optimal forecast The best guess of the future using all available information. **695**

over-the-counter (OTC) market A secondary market in which dealers at different locations who have an inventory of securities stand ready to buy and sell securities "over the counter" to anyone who comes to them and is willing to accept their prices. **42**

partial crowding out The situation in which an increase in government spending leads to a decline in private spending that does not completely offset the rise in government spending. **610**

payments system The method of conducting transactions in the economy. **25**

Phillips curve A relationship between unemployment and inflation discovered by A. W. Phillips. **628**

planned investment spending Total planned spending by business firms on new physical capital (e.g., machines, computers, apartment buildings) plus planned spending on new residential houses. **555, 607**

policy ineffectiveness proposition The conclusion from the new classical model that anticipated policy has no effect on output fluctuations. **720**

preferred habitat theory The theory that the interest rate on a long-term bond will equal an average of short-term interest rates expected to occur over the life of the long-term bond, plus a risk premium that responds to supply and demand conditions for that bond. **146**

present value or present discounted value (PV) Today's value of a payment to be received in the future when the interest rate is i. **69–70**

primary market A financial market in which new issues of a security are sold to initial buyers. **41**

principal-agent problem A moral hazard problem that occurs when the manager in control (the agent) acts in his or her own interest rather than in the interest of the owners (the principals) because his or her incentives differ from theirs. **171, 259**

printing money A method of financing government spending through the creation of high-powered money. **421, 677**

pure flexible exchange rate regime (or clean float) An exchange rate system that has no central bank intervention in the foreign exchange market. **41**

put option Option contract that provides the right to sell a security at a specified price. **302**

quantity theory of money The theory that nominal income is determined solely by movements in the quantity of money. **525**

quotas Restrictions on the quantity of foreign goods that can be imported. **475**

random walk The movements of a variable whose future changes cannot be predicted (are random) because, given today's value, the variable is just as likely to fall as to rise. **705**

rate of capital gains The change in a security's price relative to the initial purchase price.

rational expectations A view of expectations formation that holds that expectations will not differ from optimal forecasts (the best guess of the future) using all available information. **695**

real bills doctrine A guiding principle (now discredited) for the conduct of monetary policy that states that as long as loans are made to support the production of goods and services, providing reserves to the banking system to make these loans will not be inflationary. **451**

real business cycle theory A theory that views real shocks to tastes and technology as the major driving force behind short-run, business cycle fluctuations. **621**

real interest rate The interest rate adjusted for expected changes in the price level (inflation) so that it more accurately reflects the true cost of borrowing. **88**

real money balances The quantity of money in real terms. **533**

real terms A valuation in terms of real goods and services one can buy. **88, 598**

recession A period when aggregate output is declining. **6**

reduced form evidence Evidence that examines whether one variable has an effect on another by simply looking directly at the relationship between the two variables. **634**

Regulation Q The regulation under which the Federal Reserve System has the power to set maximum interest rates that banks can pay on savings and time deposits. **60**

regulatory forbearance A refraining by regulators from engaging in their right to put an insolvent bank out of business. **255**

repurchase agreement (repo) An arrangement in which the Fed purchases securities with an agreement that the seller will repurchase them in a short period of time, usually less than a week. **427**

required reserves Reserves that are held because the Fed requires that for every dollar of deposits at a bank, a certain fraction must be kept as reserves. **202, 324**

required reserves ratio The fraction of deposits that the Fed requires be kept as reserves. **202, 324**

reserve currency A currency, like the U.S. dollar, that is used by other countries to denominate the assets they hold as international reserves. **507**

reserves Banks' holding of deposits in accounts at the Fed, plus currency that is physically held by banks (vault cash). **202, 323**

restrictive covenants Provisions that restrict and specify certain activities that the borrower can engage in. **161**

return, or rate of return For any security, the *rate of return* equals the payments to the owner plus the change in the security's value, expressed as a fraction of its purchase price. **84**

revaluation The resetting of the par value of a currency at a higher level. **509**

reverse causation A situation in which one variable is said to cause another variable when, in reality, the reverse is true. **637**

reverse repo A transaction (sometimes called a matched sale-purchase) in which the Fed sells securities and the buyer agrees to sell them back to the Fed in the near future. **428**

risk-based premiums An insurance premium that is charged on the basis of how much risk a policyholder poses for the insurance company. **274**

risk premium The spread between the interest rate on bonds with default risk and the interest rate on default-free bonds. **134**

risk structure of interest rates The relationship among the various interest rates on bonds with the same term to maturity. **132**

secondary market A financial market in which securities that have previously been issued (and are thus secondhand) can be resold. **41**

secondary reserves U.S. government and agency securities held by banks. **202**

securities Claims on the borrower's future income or assets that are sold by the borrower to the lender (also called financial instruments). **39**

securitization The process of transforming illiquid financial assets into marketable capital market instruments. **305**

security market line A line derived from the capital asset pricing model which describes the relationship between an asset's beta and its expected return. **746**

segmented markets theory A theory of term structure that sees markets for different maturity bonds as completely separated and segmented, so that the interest rate for each maturity bond is determined solely by supply and demand for that maturity bond. **145**

self-correcting mechanism A characteristic of the economy that causes output to return eventually to the natural rate level regardless of where it is initially. **615**

share draft accounts Accounts at credit unions that are similar to NOW accounts. **310**

short term Referring to a debt instrument with a maturity of one year or less. **41**

simple deposit multiplier The multiple increase in deposits generated from an increase in the banking system's reserves in a simple model in which the behavior of depositor and bank plays no role. **330**

simple loan A credit market instrument providing the borrower with an amount of funds that must be repaid to the lender at the maturity date along with an additional payment (interest). **68**

sources of the base The factors that determine the monetary base. **408**

Special Drawing Rights (SDRs) An IMF-issued paper substitute for gold that functions as international reserves. **514**

specialist A dealer-broker operating in an exchange who maintains orderly trading of the set of securities for which he is responsible. **290**

spot exchange rate The exchange rate for a spot transaction. **469**

spot transaction The predominant type of exchange rate transaction that involves the immediate exchange of bank deposits denominated in different currencies. **469**

state banks State chartered banks. **229**

sterilization A central bank strategy for offsetting the effects of changes in international reserves. In the case of an increase in international reserves, it involves open market sales of domestic securities in order to prevent the monetary base from rising. **514**

sterilized foreign exchange intervention A foreign exchange intervention with an offsetting open market operation that leaves the monetary base unchanged. **494**

store of value A store of purchasing power over time. **24**

structural model A description of how the economy operates using a collection of equations that describe the behavior of business firms and consumers in many sectors of the economy. **634**

structural model evidence Evidence that examines whether one variable affects another by using data to build a model illustrating the channels through which this variable affects the other. **634**

supply curve The relationship between the quantity supplied and the price when all other economic variables are held constant. **105**

supply shocks   Changes in technology and the supply of raw materials that can shift the aggregate supply curve. **618**

systematic risk   The component of an asset's risk that is related to market risk and so cannot be eliminated by diversification. **742**

T-account   A simplified balance sheet in the form of a T that lists only the changes that occur in balance sheet items starting from some initial balance sheet position. **204**

takeover   A purchase of a corporation by another corporation or a group of investors. **185**

tariffs   Taxes on imported goods. **475**

term structure of interest rates   The relationship among interest rates on bonds with different terms to maturity. **132**

theory of asset demand   The theory that the quantity demanded of an asset is (1) usually positively related to wealth; (2) positively related to its expected return relative to alternative assets; (3) negatively related to the risk of its return relative to alternative assets; and (4) positively related to its liquidity relative to alternative assets. **98**

theory of purchasing power parity (PPP)   The theory that exchange rates between any two currencies will adjust to reflect changes in the price levels of the two countries. **472**

trade balance   The difference between merchandise exports and imports. **502**

transactions cost   The time and money spent trying to exchange goods and services. **22**

transmission mechanisms of monetary policy   The channels through which the money supply affects economic activity. **634**

underfunded   If the contributions to a pension plan and their earnings are not sufficient to pay out the defined benefits, the plan is *underfunded*. **279**

underground economy   Unreported economic activity, also called the "subterranean economy." **364**

underwriters   Investment banks that guarantee prices on securities to corporations and then sell the securities to the public. **286**

unemployment rate   The percentage of the labor force unemployed. **6**

unexploited profit opportunity   A situation in which someone can earn a higher than normal return. **700**

unit of account   Something used to measure value in the economy. **23**

unsterilized foreign exchange intervention   A foreign exchange intervention in which a central bank allows the purchase or sale of domestic currency to have an effect on the monetary base. **494**

uses of the base   The items describing how the base is used (Federal Reserve notes, reserves, and Treasury currency outstanding not held at the Fed). **408**

vault cash   Currency that is physically held by banks and stored in vaults overnight. **202**

velocity (of money)   The rate of turnover of money; the average number of times per year that a dollar is spent in buying the total amount of final goods and services produced in the economy. **524, 605**

venture capital firm   Financial intermediaries that pool the resources of their partners and use the funds to help budding entrepreneurs start up new businesses. **173**

wealth   The total collection of pieces of property that are a store of value. **21**

wealth elasticity of demand   The *wealth elasticity of demand* measures how much, with everything else unchanged, demand for an asset changes in percentage terms in response to a percentage change in wealth. **95**

World Bank (The International Bank for Reconstruction and Redevelopment)   An international organization that provides long-term loans to assist developing countries in building dams, roads, and other physical capital that would contribute to their economic development. **506**

yield curve   A plot of the yields on default-free government bonds with different terms to maturity. **140**

yield on a discount basis or discount yield   The measure of interest rates by which dealers in bill markets quote the interest rate on U.S. Treasury bills [formally defined in Equation (4.8)]. **79**

yield to maturity   The interest rate that equates the present value of payments received from a credit market instrument with its value today. **71**

Answers to Selected Questions and Problems

Chapter 1

2. The data in Figures 1.1, 1.2, 1.3, and 1.4 suggest that real output, the inflation rate, and interest rates would fall.

4. You might be more likely to buy a house or a car because the cost of financing them would fall, or you might be less likely to save because you earn less on your savings.

6. No. It is true that people who borrow to purchase a house or car are worse off because it costs them more to finance their purchase; however, savers benefit because they can earn higher interest rates on their savings.

8. In the mid to late 1970s the value of the dollar was low, making travel abroad relatively more expensive; thus is was a good time to vacation in the United States and see the Grand Canyon. With the rise of the dollar's value in the early 1980s, travel abroad became relatively cheaper and it was a good time to visit the Tower of London.

Chapter 2

2. Since the apple-orchard owner only likes bananas but the banana grower doesn't like apples, the banana grower will not want apples in exchange for his bananas and they will not trade. Similarly, the chocolatier will not be willing to trade with the banana grower because he does not like bananas. The orchard owner will not trade with the chocolatier because he doesn't like chocolate. Hence in a barter economy, trade between these three people may well not take place because in no case is there a double coincidence of wants. However, if money is introduced into the economy, the orchard owner can sell his apples to the chocolatier and then use the money to buy bananas from the banana grower. Similarly, the banana grower can use the money he receives from the orchard owner to buy chocolate from the chocolatier, and the chocolatier can use the money to buy apples from the orchard owner. The result is that the necessity of a double coincidence of wants is eliminated, and everyone is better off because our three producers are now able to eat what they each like best.

4. Because money was losing value at a slower rate (the inflation rate was lower) in the 1950s than in the 1970s, it was then a better store of value and you would have been willing to hold more of it.

6. Money loses its value at an extremely rapid rate in hyperinflation, so you want to hold it for as short a time as possible. Thus, money is like a hot potato that is quickly passed from one person to another.

8. Not necessarily. Although the total amount of debt has predicted inflation and the business cycle better than $M1$, $M2$, or $M3$, it may not be a better predictor in the future. Without some theoretical reason for believing that the total amount of debt will continue to predict well in the future, we may not want to define money as the total amount of debt.

10. $M1$ contains the most liquid assets, while $M3$ is the largest measure.

12. Revisions are not a serious problem for long-run movements of the money supply because revisions for short-run (one-month) movements tend to cancel out. Revisions for long-run movements, such as one-year growth rates, are thus typically quite small.

14. Because a check was so much easier to transport than gold, people would frequently rather be paid by check even if there were a possibility that the check might bounce. In other words, the lower transactions costs when people were paid by checks made them more willing to accept them.

Chapter 3

1. The share of IBM stock is an asset for its owner because it entitles her to a share of the earnings and assets of IBM. The share is a liability for IBM because it is a claim on its earnings and assets by the owner of the share.

3. Yes, because the absence of financial markets means that funds cannot be channeled to those who have the most productive use for them. Entrepreneurs then cannot acquire funds to set up businesses that would help the economy grow rapidly.

5. Because the costs of making the loan to your neighbor are high (e.g., legal fees, fees for a credit check, etc.), you will probably not be able to earn 5% on the loan after your expenses even though it has a 10% interest rate. You are better off depositing your savings with a financial intermediary and earning 5% interest.

7. Since private gains from selling information by private firms may not be as large as overall gains to society from this activity, less information than is socially optimal is supplied in the marketplace.

9. Restricting the assets that financial intermediaries may hold can be beneficial because it prevents them from taking on too much risk, thus ensuring their soundness. However, these regulations can also be costly because they may keep funds from flowing to those who can most productively use them.

11. Competition is considered to be an important force that promotes efficiency in financial markets. Restricting competition in the financial industry is likely to increase inefficiency in the economy, leading to a less healthy economy.

13. This statement is false. Prices in secondary markets determine the prices that firms issuing securities receive in primary markets. In addition, secondary markets make securities more liquid and thus easier to sell in the primary markets. Therefore, secondary markets are if anything more important than primary markets.

15. Increased discussion of foreign financial markets in the U.S. press and the growth in markets for international financial instruments such as Eurodollars and Eurobonds.

Chapter 4

1. Less. It would be worth $1/(1 + .20) = \$.83$ when the interest rate is 20%, rather than $1/(1 + .10) = \$.91$ when the interest rate is 10%.

3. $\$3000 = \$1100/(1 + .10) + \$1210/(1 + .10)^2 + \$1331/(1 + .10)^3$

5. $\$2000 = \$100/(1 + i) + \$100/(1 + i)^2 + \cdots + \$100/(1 + i)^{20} + \$1000/(1 + i)^{20}$

7. 14.9%. This answer is derived as follows: The present value of the $2 million payment five years from now is $\$2/(1 + i)^5$ million which equals the $1 million loan. Thus $1 = 2/(1 + i)^5$. Solving for i, $(1 + i)^5 = 2$, so that $i = \sqrt[5]{2} - 1 = .149 = 14.9\%$.

9. If the one-year bond did not have a coupon payment, its yield to maturity would be ($1000 − $800)/$800 = $200/$800 = .25 = 25%. Since it does have a coupon payment, its yield to maturity must be greater than 25%. On the other hand, because the current yield is a good approximation of the yield to maturity for a twenty-year bond, we know that the yield to maturity on this bond is approximately 15%. Therefore, the one-year bond has a higher yield to maturity.

11. You would rather own the Treasury bill because it has a higher yield to maturity. As the example in the text indicates, the discount yield's understatement of the yield to maturity for a one-year bond is substantial, exceeding one percentage point. Thus, the yield to maturity on the one-year bill would be greater than 9%, the yield to maturity on the one-year Treasury bond.

13. No. If interest rates rise sharply in the future, long-term bonds may suffer such a sharp fall in price that their return might be quite low, possibly even negative.

15. The economists are right. They reason that nominal interest rates were below expected rates of inflation in the late 1970s, making real interest rates negative. The expected inflation rate, however, fell much faster than nominal interest rates in the mid-1980s, so nominal interest rates were above the expected inflation rate and real rates became positive.

Chapter 5

2. (a) More, because your wealth has increased; (b) more, because it has become more liquid; (c) less, because its expected return has fallen relative to Polaroid stock; (d) more, because it has become less risky relative to stocks; (e) less, because its expected return has fallen.

4. (a) More, because they have become more liquid; (b) more, because their expected return has risen relative to stocks; (c) less, because they have become less liquid relative to stocks; (d) less, be-

cause their expected return has fallen; **(e)** more, because they have become more liquid.

6. Purchasing shares in the pharmaceutical company is more likely to reduce your overall risk because the correlation of returns on your investment in a football team with the returns on the pharmaceutical company should be low. On the other hand, the correlation of returns on an investment in a football team and an investment in a basketball team are probably pretty high, so in this case there would be little risk reduction if you invested in both.

Chapter 6

1. When the Fed sells bonds to the public it increases the supply of bonds, thus shifting the supply curve (B^s) to the right. The result is that the intersection of the supply and demand curves (B^s and B^d) occurs at a higher equilibrium interest rate, and the interest rate rises. With the liquidity preference framework, the decrease in the money supply shifts the money supply curve (M^s) to the left, and the equilibrium interest rate rises. The answer from the loanable funds framework is consistent with the answer from the liquidity preference framework.

3. When the price level rises, the quantity of money in real terms falls (holding the nominal supply of money constant); in order to restore their holdings of money in real terms to their former level, people will want to hold a greater nominal quantity of money. Thus the money demand curve (M^d) shifts to the right, and the interest rate rises.

6. Interest rates rise. The sudden increase in people's expectations of future real estate prices raises the expected return on real estate relative to bonds, so the demand for bonds falls. The demand curve (B^d) shifts to the left, and the equilibrium interest rate rises.

8. In the loanable funds framework, the increased riskiness of bonds lowers the demand for bonds. The demand curve (B^d) shifts to the left, and the equilibrium interest rate rises. The same answer is found in the liquidity preference framework. The increased riskiness of bonds relative to money increases the demand for money. The money demand curve (M^d) shifts to the right, and the equilibrium interest rate rises.

10. Yes, interest rates will rise. The lower commission on stocks makes them more liquid than bonds, and the demand for bonds will fall. The demand curve (B^d) will therefore shift to the left, and the equilibrium interest rate will rise.

12. The interest rate on the AT&T bonds will rise. Because people now expect interest rates to rise, the expected return on long-term bonds such as the 8⅝ s of 2007 will fall, and the demand for these bonds will decline. The demand curve (B^d) will therefore shift to the left, and the equilibrium interest rate will rise.

14. Interest rates will rise. When bond prices become volatile and bonds become riskier, the demand for bonds will fall. The demand curve (B^d) will shift to the left, and the equilibrium interest rate will rise.

Chapter 7

2. U.S. Treasury bills have lower default risk and more liquidity than negotiable CDs. Thus the demand for Treasury bills is higher, and they have a lower interest rate.

4. True. When bonds of different maturities are close substitutes, a rise in interest rates on one bond causes the interest rates on others to rise because the expected returns on bonds of different maturities cannot get too far out of line.

6. **(a)** The yield to maturity would be 5% for a one-year bond, 6% for a two-year bond, 6.33% for a three-year bond, 6.5% for a four-year bond, and 6.6% for a five-year bond. **(b)** The yield to maturity would be 5% for a one-year bond, 4.5% for a two-year bond, 4.33% for a three-year bond, 4.25% for a four-year bond, and 4.2% for a five-year bond. The upward-sloping yield curve in **(a)** would be even more steep if people preferred short-term bonds over long-term bonds because long-term bonds would then have a positive risk premium. The downward-sloping yield curve in **(b)** would be less steep and might even have a slight positive upward slope when the long-term bonds have a positive risk premium.

8. The flat yield curve at shorter maturities suggests that short-term interest rates are expected to fall moderately in the near future, while the steep upward slope of the yield curve at longer maturities indicates that interest rates further into the future are expected to rise. Since interest rates and expected inflation move together, the yield curve suggests that the market expects inflation to fall moderately in the near future but to rise later on.

10. The reduction in income tax rates would make the tax-exempt privilege for municipal bonds less valuable, and they would be less desirable than taxable Treasury bonds. The resulting decline in the demand for municipal bonds and increase in demand for Treasury bonds would raise interest rates on municipal bonds while causing interest rates on Treasury bonds to fall.

12. Lower brokerage commissions for corporate bonds would make them more liquid and thus increase their demand, which would lower their risk premium.

14. Abolishing estate taxes would make flower bonds less attractive than Treasury bonds. The resulting decline in the demand for flower bonds and increase in demand for Treasury bonds would raise the interest rates on flower bonds while causing the interest rates on Treasury bonds to fall.

Chapter 8

2. Financial intermediaries develop expertise in such areas as computer technology so that they can inexpensively provide liquidity services such as checking accounts which lower transactions costs for depositors. Financial intermediaries also can take advantage of economies of scale and engage in large transactions that have a lower cost per dollar per transaction.

4. Standard accounting principles make profit verification easier, thereby reducing adverse selection and moral hazard problems in financial markets and thus making them operate better. Standard accounting principles make it easier for investors to screen out good firms from bad firms, thereby reducing the adverse selection problem in financial markets. In addition, they make it harder for managers to understate profits, thereby reducing the principal-agent (moral hazard) problem.

6. Smaller firms that are not well known are the most likely to use bank financing. Since it is harder for investors to acquire information about these firms, it will be hard for the firms to sell securities in the financial markets. Banks that specialize in collecting information about smaller firms will then be the only outlet these firms have for financing their activities.

8. Yes. The person who is putting her life savings into her business has more to lose if she takes on too much risk or engages in personally beneficial activities that don't lead to higher profits. So she will act more in the interest of the lender, making it more likely that the loan will be paid off.

10. True. If the borrower turns out to be a bad credit risk and goes broke, the lender loses less because the collateral can be sold to make up any losses on the loan. Thus adverse selection is not as severe a problem.

12. The separation of ownership and control creates a principal-agent problem. The manager (the agent) does not have as strong an incentive to maximize profits as the owners (the principals). Thus the managers might not work hard, might engage in wasteful spending for personal perks, or might pursue business strategies that enhance their personal power but do not increase profits.

14. A stock market crash reduces the net worth of firms and so increases the moral hazard problem. With less of an equity stake, owners have a greater incentive to take on risky projects and spend corporate funds on items that benefit them personally. A stock market crash which increases the moral hazard problem thus makes it less likely that lenders will be paid back. So lending and investment will decline, thus creating a financial crisis in which financial markets do not work well and the economy suffers.

Chapter 9

2. The rank from most to least liquid is **(c)**, **(b)**, **(a)**, and **(d)**.

4. Reserves drop by $500. The T-account for the First National Bank is as follows:

FIRST NATIONAL BANK

Assets	Liabilities
Reserves −$500	Checkable deposits −$500

6. The bank would rather have the balance sheet listed in this problem because after it loses $50 million due to deposit outflow, the bank would still have excess reserves of $5 million ($50 million in reserves minus required reserves of $45 million (10% of the $450 million of deposits)). Thus the bank would not have to alter its balance sheet further and would not incur any costs as a result of the deposit outflow. On the other hand, with the balance sheet in the problem above, the bank would have a shortfall of reserves of $20

million ($25 million in reserves minus the required reserves of $45 million). In this case the bank will incur costs when it raises the necessary reserves through the methods described in the text.

8. No. When you turn a customer down, you may lose his business forever—which is extremely costly. Instead, you might go out and borrow from other banks, corporations, or the Fed to obtain funds so that you can make the customer the loans. Alternatively, you might sell negotiable CDs or some of your securities to acquire the necessary funds.

10. Compensating balances can act as collateral. They also help establish long-term customer relationships, which make it easier for the bank to collect information about prospective borrowers, thus reducing the adverse selection problem. Compensating balances help the bank monitor the activities of a borrowing firm, so that it can prevent the firm from taking on too much risk, thereby not acting in the interest of the bank.

12. False. Although diversification is a desirable strategy for a bank, it may still make sense for a bank to specialize in certain types of lending. For example, a bank may have developed expertise in screening and monitoring a particular kind of loan, thus improving its ability to handle problems of adverse selection and moral hazard.

14. The assets fall in value by 8% (= −2% × 4 years), while the liabilities fall in value by 12% (= −2% × 6 years). Since the liabilities fall in value by 4% more than the assets do, the net worth of the bank rises by 4%, that is, by $3 million (= 4% × $75 million). The interest rate risk can be reduced by shortening the maturity of the liabilities to a duration of four years or lengthening the maturity of the assets to a duration of six years. Alternatively, you could engage in an interest-rate swap, in which you swap the interest earned on your assets with the interest on another bank's assets that have a duration of six years.

Chapter 10

1. (a) Office of the Controller of the Currency; (b) the Federal Reserve; (c) state banking authorities and the FDIC; (d) the Federal Reserve.

3. Bank chartering may set up a barrier to entry that keeps firms and individuals out of banking, making the industry less competitive. On the other hand, bank chartering has the benefit of preventing dishonest firms and individuals from entering banking.

5. Without help, the FDIC would not be able to pay off all insured depositors because its insurance fund is too small. However, the existence of the FDIC still helps prevent bank failures because the public knows that the Fed and the federal government will stand behind the FDIC to provide banks and the FDIC with adequate funds in a crisis.

7. False. Although banks have incentives to hold bank capital, they may not hold enough because the private costs to them of bank failure are less than the social costs.

9. New technologies such as electronic banking facilities are frequently shared by several banks, so these facilities are not classified as branches. Thus they can be used by banks to escape limitations to offering services in other states and, in effect, to escape limitations from restrictions on branching.

11. Because restrictions on branching are stricter for commercial banks than for savings and loans. Thus, small commercial banks have greater protection from competition and are more likely to survive than are small savings and loans.

13. International banking has been encouraged by giving special tax treatment and relaxed branching regulations to Edge Act corporations and to International Banking Facilities (IBFs), IBFs and Edge Act corporations have been given this favorable treatment in order to make American banks more competitive with foreign banks. The hope is that this will create more banking jobs in the United States.

15. No, because the Saudi-owned bank is subject to the same regulations as the American-owned bank.

Chapter 11

2. There would be adverse selection because people who might want to burn their property for some personal gain would actively try to obtain substantial fire insurance policies. Moral hazard could also occur because a person with a fire insurance policy has less incentive to take measures to prevent a fire.

4. Regulations that restrict banks from holding risky assets directly decrease the moral hazard of

risk taking by the bank. Requirements that force banks to have a large amount of capital also decrease the banks' incentives for risk taking because banks now have more to lose if they fail. Such regulations will not completely eliminate the moral hazard problem because bankers have incentives to hide their holdings of risky assets from the regulators and to overstate the amount of their capital.

6. The S&L crisis did not occur until the 1980s because interest rates stayed low before then, so S&Ls were not subjected to losses from high interest rates. Also, the opportunities for risk taking were not available until the 1980s when legislation and financial innovation made it easier for S&Ls to take on more risk, thus greatly increasing the adverse selection and moral hazard problems.

8. The FIRREA legislation provided funds for the S&L bailout, created the Resolution Trust Corporation to manage the resolution of insolvent thrifts, eliminated the Federal Home Loan Bank Board and gave its regulatory role to the Office of Thrift Supervision, eliminated the FSLIC whose insurance role and regulatory responsibilities were taken over by the FDIC, imposed restrictions on thrift activities similar to those in effect before 1982, increased the capital requirements to those adhered to by commercial banks, and increased the enforcement powers of thrift regulators.

10. If political candidates receive campaign funds from the government and are restricted in the amount they spend, they will have less need to satisfy lobbyists to win elections. As a result, they may have greater incentives to act in the interest of the taxpayer (the principal) and so the political process might improve.

12. Eliminating or limiting the amount of deposit insurance would help reduce the moral hazard of excessive risk taking on the part of banks. It would, however, make bank failures and panics more likely, so it might not be a very good idea.

14. The economy would benefit from reduced moral hazard; that is, banks would not want to take on too much risk because doing so would increase their deposit insurance premiums. The problem is, however, that it is difficult to monitor the degree of risk in bank assets since, frequently, only the bank making loans knows how risky they are.

Chapter 12

1. Because there would be more uncertainty about how much they would have to pay out in any given year, life insurance companies would tend to hold shorter-term assets that are more liquid.

3. Because benefits paid out are set to equal contributions to the plan and their earnings.

5. Because the greater the amount of the policy, the greater is the incentive for the policyholder to commit moral hazard and engage in activities that make the insurance payoff more likely. Since these payoffs will be costly, the insurance company will want to reduce moral hazard by limiting the amount of insurance.

7. Because interest rates on loans are typically lower at banks than at finance companies.

9. Because you do not have to pay a commission on a no-load fund, it is in effect cheaper than a load fund, which does require a commission.

11. Government loan guarantees may be very costly because like any insurance they lead to moral hazard. Since the banks and other institutions making the guaranteed loans do not suffer any losses if the loans default, they have little incentive not to make bad loans. The resulting losses to the government can be substantial, as has been the case in recent years.

13. No. Investment banking is a risky business because if the investment bank cannot sell a security it is underwriting for the price it promised to pay the issuing firm, the investment bank can suffer substantial losses.

15. Because by keeping banks from securities underwriting, they have less competition and thus can earn higher profits.

Chapter 13

1. Financial innovation is driven by the search for profits—in other words, by greed. Since financial innovation is usually beneficial, greed can be viewed as a positive force in our society.

3. You can sell a contract that delivers three-month CDs or T-bills in nine months' time. Then if the interest rate rises, the price of the contract will fall and the profits you make will offset the higher interest payments on your loan.

5. Probably not, because the costs of servicing these credit cards would not have been as high, thus enabling the banks to earn a profit on them.

7. True. Banks have increased their borrowing in the Eurodollar market, causing it to grow faster, because it allowed them to avoid the restrictions on raising funds arising from Regulation Q and because the funds acquired in the Eurodollar market were not initially subject to reserve requirements.

9. Not very. The net result of bank regulations such as Regulation Q, which was supposed to help channel low-cost funds into the mortgage market, has been that it is now harder for mortgage-issuing institutions to obtain funds that could then be lent out as mortgages. In addition, regulations that restrict thrifts to making mortgage loans may have hurt their financial health so that they have been ultimately unable to make as many mortgage loans.

11. If the Fed pays an interest rate of i_{Fed} on reserves, the tax on deposits imposed by reserve requirements will fall to $(i - i_{Fed}) \times r_d$. The result of the lower tax on deposits would be that banks could now pay a higher interest rate on deposits and so make them more competitive with money market funds. Depositors would now find deposits more attractive relative to money market funds so that deposits would rise while money market funds would decline.

13. If inflation became more variable, interest rates would also probably become more variable and interest-rate risk would increase. Trading in financial futures and options markets would then increase because it enables people to avoid some of the increased interest-rate risk.

15. If Regulation Q ceilings were reimposed, banks would not be able to compete as effectively for funds, causing funds to flow from banks into money market mutual funds. In addition, it would stimulate the commercial paper market because banks would then try to obtain funds by having their holding companies issue commercial paper on which there are no interest-rate ceilings.

Chapter 14

1. False. A bank's cash holdings are already counted as reserves, so depositing them in the Fed leaves the bank's reserves unchanged.

3. Reserves at the First National Bank remain unchanged as the following T-accounts indicate:

FIRST NATIONAL BANK

Assets		Liabilities	
Reserves	0	Discount loans	+ $1 million
Securities	+ $1 million		

FEDERAL RESERVE SYSTEM

Assets		Liabilities
Securities	− $1 million	
Discount loans	+ $1 million	

5. The T-accounts are identical to those in the section Deposit Creation: The Single Bank and the section Deposit Creation: The Banking System except that all the entries are multiplied by 10,000 (that is, $100 becomes $1 million). The net result is that checkable deposits rise by $10 million.

7. The $1 million Fed purchase of bonds increases reserves in the banking system by $1 million, and the total increase in checkable deposits is $10 million. The fact that banks buy securities rather than make loans with their excess reserves makes no difference in the multiple deposit creation process.

9. Reserves in the banking system fall by $1000 and a multiple contraction occurs, reducing checkable deposits by $10,000.

11. The level of checkable deposits falls by $50 million. The T-account of the banking system in equilibrium is as follows:

BANKING SYSTEM

Assets		Liabilities	
Reserves	− $5 million	Checkable deposits	−50 million
Securities	+ $5 million		
Loans	− $50 million		

Chapter 15

2. Reserves are unchanged, but the monetary base falls by $2 million as indicated by the following T-accounts:

IRVING THE INVESTOR

Assets		Liabilities
Currency	− $2 million	
Securities	+ $2 million	

FEDERAL RESERVE SYSTEM

Assets	Liabilities
Securities − $2 million	Currency − $2 million

4. Uncertain. As the formula in Equation 15.4 indicates, if $r_D + \{ER/D\}$ is greater than one, the money multiplier can be less than one. In practice, however, $\{ER/D\}$ is so small that $r_D + \{ER/D\}$ is less than one and the money multiplier is greater than one.

6. The money supply fell sharply because when $\{C/D\}$ rose there was a shift from one component of the money supply (checkable deposits) with more multiple expansion to another (currency) with less. Overall multiple deposit expansion fell, leading to a decline in the money supply.

8. There is a shift from one component of the money supply (checkable deposits) with less multiple expansion to another (traveler's checks) with more. Multiple expansion therefore increases and the money supply increases.

10. Yes, because with no reserve requirements on time deposits, a shift from checkable deposits (with less multiple expansion) to time deposits (with more multiple expansion) increases the total amount of deposits and raises $M2$. On the other hand, if reserve requirements were equal for both types of deposits, they would both undergo the same amount of multiple expansion, and a shift from one to the other would have no effect on $M2$. Thus control of $M2$ would be better because random shifts from time deposits to checkable deposits or vice versa would not affect $M2$.

12. Both the Fed's purchase of $100 million of bonds (which raises the monetary base) and the lowering of r_D (which increases the amount of multiple expansion and raises the money multiplier) lead to a rise in the money supply.

14. The Fed's sale of $1 million of bonds shrinks the monetary base by $1 million, while the reduction of discount loans also lowers the monetary base by another $1 million. The resulting $2 million decline in the monetary base leads to a decline in the money supply.

Chapter 16

2. The rise in interest rates in a boom increases the cost of holding excess reserves and the incentives to borrow from the Fed. Therefore, $\{ER/D\}$ falls, which increases the amount of reserves available to support checkable deposits, and the volume of discount loans increases, which raises the monetary base. The result is a higher money supply during a boom. Similarly, when interest rates fall during a recession, the money supply also has a tendency to fall because $\{ER/D\}$ rises and the volume of discount loans falls.

4. Using deposits for illegal transactions would no longer increase the probability of being caught by the government. The expected return on checkable deposits relative to currency would therefore rise, and the currency-checkable deposits ratio would fall.

6. Since the wealth elasticity of currency is lower than that of checkable deposits, the demand for currency will rise less than the demand for checkable deposits and the currency-checkable deposits ratio will fall.

8. The level of $\{ER/D\}$ would rise because excess reserves would now be more attractive to hold because of the interest they would earn.

10. A rise in expected inflation would increase interest rates (through the Fisher effect), which would in turn cause $\{ER/D\}$ to fall and the volume of discount loans to rise. As the answer to Problem 2 suggests, the result would be an increase in the money supply.

12. The money supply would fall because if the discount window were eliminated, banks would need to hold more excess reserves, making less reserves available to support deposits. Moreover, abolishing discounting would reduce the volume of discount loans, which would also cause the monetary base and the money supply to fall.

14. The Congressional action would probably lead to more check forgery, which leads to losses for depositors with checking accounts. The expected return on checkable deposits relative to currency falls and the currency-checkable deposits ratio would rise. Now because there has been a movement toward currency which does not undergo multiple deposit expansion, overall multiple deposit expansion would decrease and the money supply would fall.

Chapter 17

1. Because of traditional American hostility to a central bank and centralized authority, the sys-

tem of twelve regional banks was set up to diffuse power along regional lines.

3. Like the U.S. Constitution, the Federal Reserve System, originally established by the Federal Reserve Act, has many checks and balances and is a peculiarly American institution. The ability of the twelve regional banks to affect discount policy was viewed as a check on the centralized power of the Board of Governors, just as states' rights are a check on the centralized power of the federal government. The provision that there be three types of directors (A, B, and C) representing different groups (professional bankers, businesspeople, and the public) was again intended as a check or balance to prevent any group from dominating the Fed. The Fed's independence of the federal government and the setting up of the Federal Reserve banks as incorporated institutions were further intended to restrict government power over the banking industry.

5. The Board of Governors sets reserve requirements and the discount rate; the FOMC directs open market operations. In practice, however, the FOMC helps to make decisions about reserve requirements and the discount rate.

7. The Board of Governors has clearly gained power at the expense of the regional Federal Reserve banks. This trend toward ever more centralized power is a general one in American government, but in the case of the Fed it was a natural outgrowth of the Fed having been given the responsibility for promoting a stable economy. This responsibility has required greater central direction of monetary policy, the role taken over the years by the Board of Governors and by the FOMC, which the Board controls.

9. The threat that Congress will acquire greater control over the Fed's finances and budget.

11. False. Maximizing one's welfare does not rule out altruism. Operating in the public interest is clearly one objective of the Fed. The theory of bureaucratic behavior only points out that other objectives, such as maximizing power, also influence Fed decision making.

13. False. The Fed is still subject to political pressure because Congress can pass legislation limiting the Fed's power. If the Fed is performing badly, Congress can therefore make the Fed accountable by passing legislation that the Fed does not like.

Chapter 18

2. In both cases, the monetary base declines by $200 billion. The T-accounts when the bonds are sold to banks are as follows:

FEDERAL RESERVE

Assets	Liabilities
Securities − $200 billion	Reserves − $200 billion

BANKS

Assets	Liabilities
Securities + $200 billion Reserves − $200 billion	

The T-accounts when the bonds are sold to private investors are as follows:

FEDERAL RESERVE

Assets	Liabilities
Securities − $200 billion	Currency − $200 billion

IRVING THE INVESTOR

Assets	Liabilities
Securities + $200 billion Currency − $200 billion	

5. The Fed would not be able to present checks for payment to California banks as quickly as it normally would, so float would go up. As the T-accounts in the text indicate, this would lead to a rise in the monetary base.

7. When contractors receive $100 million from the Fed for the new building, they will deposit their checks in local banks. The resulting T-accounts for the Fed and the local banks are as follows:

FEDERAL RESERVE

Assets	Liabilities
New building + $100 million	Reserves + $100 million

LOCAL BANK

Assets	Liabilities
Reserves	Deposits
+ $100 million	+ $100 million

The result is that reserves and hence the monetary base will rise by $100 million.

9. Because the Treasury is better able to predict when it needs to make payments, it can keep fewer deposits at the Fed. The result of a decline in Treasury deposits at the Fed would be a rise in reserves and hence in the monetary base (see in the text the fourth T-account in the section Treasury Deposits with the Fed).

11. When the $200 billion deficit is financed by selling bonds to the public or to banks, the monetary base will remain unchanged. However, when the bonds are sold to the Fed, the monetary base rises by $200 billion. The T-accounts are the same as those in the text in the sections Debt Financing ($\Delta BONDS$) and Financing with Money Creation (ΔMB), in which the entries have been multiplied by 2000 (that is, $100 million becomes $200 billion).

13. The monetary base need not be affected because the Fed is not required to help the Treasury finance deficits by buying Treasury bonds. However, if deficits cause interest rates to rise and the Fed tries to prevent higher interest rates by buying bonds, a higher deficit might lead to a higher monetary base. The fall in the deficit from $200 billion to $100 billion might then cause a smaller increase in the monetary base than would otherwise occur.

Chapter 19

1. The snowstorm would cause float to increase, which would increase the monetary base. To counteract this effect, the manager will undertake a defensive open market sale.

3. As we saw in Chapter 18, when the Treasury's deposits at the Fed fall, the monetary base increases. In order to counteract this increase the manager would undertake an open market sale.

5. It suggests that defensive open market operations are far more common than dynamic operations, because repurchase agreements are used primarily to conduct defensive operations in order to counteract temporary changes in the monetary base.

7. The monetary base and the money supply would increase indefinitely. Banks could borrow at the lower discount rate and then lend the proceeds at a higher interest rate. Hence banks would make a profit on every dollar borrowed from the Fed, so they would continue to borrow indefinitely—which, in turn, would increase the monetary base indefinitely.

9. This statement is incorrect. The FDIC would not be effective in eliminating bank panics without Fed discounting to troubled banks in order to keep bank failures from spreading.

11. Usually not, since most declines in the Fed discount rate occur because market interest rates have fallen and the Fed does not want to let the discount rate get too far out of line with market rates. Thus a fall in the discount rate frequently says nothing about the future direction of Fed policy.

13. Abolishing discounting would provide tighter control over the money supply because no fluctuation in the volume of discount loans would be possible. On the other hand, the proposal to tie the discount rate to market interest rates may be more desirable because it has the advantage that the Fed could still perform its role as lender of last resort.

15. Open market operations are more flexible, reversible, and faster to implement than are the other two tools. Discount policy is more flexible, reversible, and faster to implement than changing reserve requirements, but it is less effective than either of the other two tools.

Chapter 20

1. The statement is incorrect. Some unemployment is beneficial to the economy because the availability of vacant jobs makes it more likely that a worker will find the right job and that the employer will find the right worker for the job.

3. True. In such a world, hitting a monetary target would mean that the Fed would also hit its interest target, or vice versa. Thus the Fed could pursue both a monetary and an interest rate target at the same time.

5. The Fed can control the interest rate on three-month Treasury bills by buying and selling them in the open market. When the bill rate rises above the target level, the Fed would buy bills, which would bid up their price and lower the interest rate to its target level. Similarly, when

the bill rate falls below the target level, the Fed would sell bills to raise the interest rate to the target level. The resulting open market operations would of course affect the money supply and cause it to change. Thus, the Fed would be giving up control of the money supply in order to pursue the interest rate target.

7. Not necessarily. Although *nominal* interest rates are measured more accurately and quickly than the money supply, the interest rate variable that is probably of more concern to policymakers is the *real* interest rate. Because the measurement of real interest rates requires estimates of inflation, it is not true that real interest rates are necessarily measured more accurately and quickly than the money supply. Interest rate targets are therefore not necessarily better than money supply targets.

9. Because the Fed did not lend to troubled banks during this period, massive bank failures occurred, which led to a decline in the money supply when depositors increased their holdings of currency relative to deposits and banks increased their excess reserves to protect themselves against runs. As our money supply model presented in Chapters 14–16 indicates, these decisions by banks and depositors led to a sharp contraction of the money supply.

11. When the economy enters a recession, interest rates usually fall. If the Fed is targeting interest rates, it tries to prevent a decline in interest rates by selling bonds, thus lowering their prices and raising interest rates to the target level. The open market sale would then lead to a decline in the monetary base and in the money supply. The decline in interest rates would also cause excess reserves to rise and the volume of discount loans to fall, thereby raising free reserves. With a free reserve target, the Fed would find monetary policy easy and would pursue contractionary policy. Therefore, neither interest rate nor free reserve targets are very satisfactory because both can lead to a slower rate of money supply growth during a recession, just when the Fed would not want to slow money supply growth.

13. A borrowed reserves target will produce smaller fluctuations in the federal funds rate. In contrast to when there is a nonborrowed reserves target, when the federal funds rate rises with a borrowed reserves target, the Fed prevents the tendency of discount borrowings to rise by buying bonds to lower interest rates. The result is smaller fluctuations in the federal funds rate with a borrowed reserves target.

15. In actuality the Fed may prefer to control interest rates rather than the money supply because it wishes to avoid the conflict with Congress that occurs when interest rates rise. The Fed might also believe that interest rates are actually a better guide to what will happen to economic activity.

Chapter 21

2. False. Although a weak currency has the negative effect of making it more expensive to buy foreign goods or to travel abroad, it may help domestic industry. Domestic goods become cheaper relative to foreign goods, and the demand for domestically produced goods increases. The resulting higher sales of domestic industry may lead to higher employment, a beneficial effect on the economy.

4. It predicts that the value of the French franc will fall 5% in terms of dollars.

6. Even though the Japanese price level rose relative to the American, the yen appreciated because the increase in Japanese productivity relative to American productivity made it possible for the Japanese to continue to sell their goods at a profit at a high value of the yen.

8. The pound depreciates but overshoots, declining by more in the short run than in the long run. Consider Britain to be the domestic country. The rise in the money supply leads to a higher domestic price level in the long run, which leads to a higher expected future exchange rate. The resulting expected depreciation of the pound raises the expected return on foreign deposits, shifting RET^f out to the right. The rise in the money supply lowers the interest rate on pound deposits in the short run, which shifts $RET^£$ in to the left. The short-run outcome is a lower equilibrium exchange rate. However, in the long run the domestic interest rate returns to its previous value and $RET^£$ shifts back to its original position. The exchange rate rises to some extent, although it still remains below its initial position.

10. The dollar will depreciate. A rise in nominal interest rates but a decline in real interest rates implies a rise in expected inflation that produces an expected depreciation of the dollar that is larger than the increase in the domestic interest rate. As a result, the expected return on foreign

deposits rises by more than the expected return on domestic dollar deposits. RET^f shifts out more than $RET^\$$, so the equilibrium exchange rate falls.

12. The dollar depreciates. An increased demand for imports would lower the expected future exchange rate and result in an expected appreciation of the foreign currency. The higher resulting expected return on foreign deposits shifts the RET^f schedule out to the right and the equilibrium exchange rate falls.

14. The purchase of dollars involves a sale of foreign assets which means that international reserves fall. However, the offsetting open market purchase means that the monetary base and the money supply will remain unchanged. If dollar and foreign deposits are perfect substitutes, then there is no effect on the exchange rate because neither the RET^f or $RET^\$$ schedules shift since there is no change in the money supply. If dollar and foreign deposits are not perfect substitutes, then there might be an effect on the exchange rate if the purchase of dollars leads to a decline in the risk premium on holding dollars. Then $RET^f + \delta$ shifts in to the right and the equilibrium exchange rate rises, the opposite scenario depicted in Figure 21.9.

Chapter 22

2. Because other countries often intervene in the foreign exchange market when the United States has a deficit, so that U.S. holdings of international reserves do not change. When the Netherlands has a deficit, on the other hand, it must intervene in the foreign exchange market and buy guilders, which results in a loss of international reserves for the Netherlands.

4. 2 francs per dollar.

6. Because under the Bretton Woods system, speculators knew that they could not lose once a speculative attack began. If they were selling a central bank its currency, the central bank would buy it up, losing international reserves. When it had depleted its international reserves, the central bank eventually had to allow the currency to depreciate and the speculators get rich. In a managed float system, the central bank can let its exchange rate fluctuate, and therefore speculators can't keep selling a central bank its currency knowing that it will soon depreciate.

8. A large balance of payments surplus may require a country to finance the surplus by selling its currency in the foreign exchange market, thereby gaining international reserves. The result is that the central bank will have supplied more of its currency to the public, and the monetary base will rise. The resulting rise in the money supply can cause the price level to rise, leading to a higher inflation rate.

10. Countries may implement contractionary monetary policy because they may decide to intervene in the foreign exchange market and buy their currency in order to finance the deficit. The result is that they lose international reserves and their monetary base falls, leading to a decline in the money supply.

12. When other countries buy U.S. dollars to keep their exchange rates from changing vis-á-vis the dollar because of the U.S. deficits, they gain international reserves and their monetary base increases. The outcome is that the money supply in these countries grows faster and leads to higher inflation throughout the world.

14. There are no direct effects on the money supply because there is no central bank intervention in a pure flexible exchange rate regime; thus changes in international reserves which affect the monetary base do not occur. However, monetary policy can be affected by the foreign exchange market because monetary authorities may want to manipulate exchange rates by changing the money supply and interest rates.

Chapter 23

1. Velocity in 1992, 1993, and 1994 is approximately 10, 11, and 12, respectively. The rate of velocity growth is approximately 10% per year.

3. Nominal GNP declines by approximately 10%.

5. The price level quadruples.

7. False. The two approaches differ in that Fisher's rules out any possible effect of interest rates on the demand for money while the Cambridge approach does not.

9. The demand for money would decrease. People would be more likely to expect interest rates to fall and therefore more likely to expect bond prices to rise. The increase in the expected return on bonds relative to money will then mean that people would demand less money.

11. Money balances should average one-half of Grant's monthly income because he would hold

no bonds, since holding them would entail additional brokerage costs but would not provide him with any interest income.

13. True. Because bonds are riskier than money, risk-averse people would be likely to want to hold both.

15. In Keynes' view velocity is unpredictable because interest rates, which have large fluctuations, affect the demand for money and hence velocity. In addition, Keynes' analysis suggests that if people's expectations of the "normal" level of interest rates change, the demand for money changes. Since Keynes thought that these expectations move unpredictably, money demand and velocity are also unpredictable. Friedman, on the other hand, sees the demand for money as stable, and since he also believes that changes in interest rates have only small effects on the demand for money, his position is that the demand for money and hence velocity is predictable.

Chapter 24

2. Companies cut production when their unplanned inventory investment is greater than zero because they are then producing more than they can sell. If they continue not to cut production, profits will suffer because they are building up unwanted inventory, which is costly to store and finance.

4. The equilibrium level of output is 1500. When planned investment spending falls by 100, the equilibrium level of output falls by 500 to 1000.

6. Nothing. The \$100 billion increase in planned investment spending is exactly offset by the \$100 billion decline in autonomous consumer expenditure, and autonomous spending and aggregate output remain unchanged.

8. Equilibrium output of 2000 occurs at the intersection of the 45°, $Y = Y^{ad}$ line and the aggregate demand function, $Y^{ad} = C + I + G = 500 + .75Y$. If government spending rises by 100, then equilibrium output will rise by 400 to 2400.

10. Taxes should be reduced by \$400 billion because the increase in output for a \$$T$ decrease in taxes is \$$T$; that is, it equals the change in autonomous spending ($mpc \times T$) × the multiplier $[1/(1 - mpc)] = mpc \times T \times 1/(1 - mpc) = .5T \times 1/(1 - .5) = .5T/.5 = T$.

12. Rise. The fall in autonomous spending from an increase in taxes is always less than the change in taxes because the marginal propensity to consume is less than one. On the other hand, autonomous spending rises one for one with a change in autonomous consumer expenditure. Thus, if taxes and autonomous consumer expenditure rise by the same amount, autonomous spending must rise and aggregate output also rises.

14. When aggregate output falls, the demand for money falls, shifting the money demand curve to the left, which causes the equilibrium interest rate to fall. Because the equilibrium interest rate falls when aggregate output falls, there is a positive association between aggregate output and the equilibrium interest rate, and the *LM* curve slopes up.

Chapter 25

2. When investment spending collapsed, the aggregate demand function in the Keynesian cross diagram fell, leading to a lower level of equilibrium output for any given interest rate. The fall in equilibrium output for any given interest rate implies that the *IS* curve shifted to the left.

4. False. It can also be eliminated by a fall in aggregate output, which lowers the demand for money and brings it back into equality with the supply of money.

6. The *ISLM* model gives exactly this result. The tax cuts shifted the *IS* curve to the right, while tight money shifted the *LM* curve to the left. The interest rate at the intersection of the new *IS* and *LM* curves is necessarily higher than at the initial equilibrium and aggregate output can be higher.

8. Because it suggests that an interest rate target is better than a money supply target. The reason is that unstable money demand increases the volatility of the *LM* curve relative to the *IS* curve, and as demonstrated in the text, this makes it more likely that an interest rate target is preferred to a money supply target.

10. The effect on the aggregate demand curve is uncertain. A rise in government spending would shift the *IS* curve to the right, raising equilibrium output for a given price level. On the other hand, the reduction in the money supply would shift the *LM* curve to the left, lowering equilibrium output for a given price level. Depending on which of these two effects on equilibrium output is stronger, the aggregate demand curve could shift either to the right or to the left.

12. No effect. The *LM* curve would be vertical in this case, meaning that a rise in government spend-

ing and a rightward shift in the *IS* curve would not lead to higher aggregate output but rather only to a rise in the interest rate. For any given price level, therefore, equilibrium output would remain the same and the aggregate demand curve would not shift.

14. The increase in net exports shifts the *IS* curve to the right, and the equilibrium level of interest rates and aggregate output will rise.

Chapter 26

2. Since the position of the aggregate demand curve is fixed if nominal income (*PY*) is fixed, Friedman's statement implies that the position of the aggregate demand curve is completely determined by the quantity of money. This is built in to the monetarist aggregate demand curve because it shifts only when the money supply changes.

4. The Keynesian aggregate demand curve shifts because a change in "animal spirits" causes consumer expenditure or planned investment spending to change, which then causes the quantity of aggregate output demanded to change at any given price level. In the monetarist view, on the other hand, a change in "animal spirits" has little effect on velocity, and aggregate spending (*PY*) remains unchanged; hence the aggregate demand curve does not shift.

6. True. Given fixed production costs, firms can earn higher profits by producing more when prices are higher. Profit-maximizing behavior on the part of firms thus leads them to increase production when prices are higher.

8. The aggregate supply curve would shift out because production costs would fall.

10. The collapse in investment spending during the Great Depression reduced the quantity of output demanded at any given price level and shifted the aggregate demand curve to the left. In an aggregate demand and supply diagram the equilibrium price level and aggregate output would then fall, which explains the decline in aggregate output and the price level that occurred during the Great Depression.

12. Both the increase in the money supply and the income tax cut would increase the quantity of output demanded at any given price level and so would shift the aggregate demand curve out to the right. The intersection of the aggregate demand and aggregate supply curve would be at a higher level of both output and the price level in the short run. However, in the long run, the aggregate supply curve would shift inward, leaving output at the natural rate level, but the price level would be even higher.

14. Because goods would cost more, the national sales tax would raise production costs, and the aggregate supply curve would shift inward. The intersection of the aggregate supply curve with the aggregate demand curve would then be at a higher level of prices and a lower level of aggregate output; aggregate output would fall and the price level would rise.

Chapter 27

4. Seeing which car is built better produces structural model evidence because it explains why one car is better than the other (that is, how the car is built). Asking owners how often their cars undergo repairs produces reduced form evidence because it looks only at the correlation of reliability with the manufacturer of the car.

5. Not necessarily. If GM car owners change their oil more frequently than Ford owners, GM cars would have better repair records even though they are not more reliable cars. In this case, it is a third factor (the frequency of oil changes) that leads to the better repair record for GM cars.

6. Not necessarily. Although the Ford engine might be built better than the GM engine, the rest of the GM car might be better made than the Ford. The result could be that the GM car is more reliable than the Ford.

8. If the Fed has interest rate targets, a rise in output that raises interest rates might cause the Fed to buy bonds and bid up their price in order to drive interest rates back down to their target level (see Chapter 6). The result of these open market purchases would be that the increase in output would cause an increase in the monetary base and hence an increase in the money supply. In addition, a rise in output and interest rates would cause free reserves to fall (because excess reserves would fall and the volume of discount loans would rise). If the Fed has a free reserves target, the increase in aggregate output will then cause the Fed to increase the money supply because it believes that money is tight.

10. Monetarists went on to refine their reduced form models with more sophisticated statistical procedures—one outcome of which was the St.

Louis model. Keynesians began to look for transmission mechanisms of monetary policy that they may have ignored, culminating in models like the MPS model.

12. False. Monetary policy can affect stock prices, which affect Tobin's q, thereby affecting investment spending. In addition, monetary policy can affect loan availability, which may also influence investment spending.

14. There are three mechanisms involving consumer expenditure. First, a rise in the money supply lowers interest rates and reduces the cost of financing purchases of consumer durables, and consumer durables expenditure rises. Second, a rise in the money supply causes stock prices and wealth to rise, leading to greater lifetime resources for consumers and causing them to increase their consumption. Third, a rise in the money supply that causes stock prices and the value of financial assets to rise also lowers people's probability of financial distress, and so they spend more on consumer durables.

Chapter 28

2. Because hyperinflations appear to be examples in which the increase in money supply growth is an exogenous event, the fact that hyperinflation occurs when money growth is high is powerful evidence that a high rate of money growth causes inflation.

4. False. Although workers' attempts to push up their wages can lead to inflation if the government has a high employment target, inflation is still a monetary phenomenon because it cannot occur without accommodating monetary policy.

6. True. If financed with money creation, a temporary budget deficit can lead to a one-time rightward shift in the aggregate demand curve and hence to a one-time increase in the price level. However, once the budget deficit disappears, there is no longer any reason for the aggregate demand curve to shift. Thus a temporary deficit cannot lead to a continuing rightward shift of the aggregate demand curve and therefore cannot produce inflation, a continuing increase in the price level.

8. True. The monetarist objection to activist policy would no longer be as serious. The aggregate demand curve could be quickly moved to AD_2 in Figure 28.10, and the economy would move quickly to point 2 because the aggregate supply curve would not have time to shift. The scenario of a highly variable price level and output would not occur, making an activist policy more desirable.

10. True, if expectations about policy affect the wage-setting process. In this case, workers and firms are more likely to push up wages and prices because they know that if they do so and unemployment develops as a result, the government will pursue expansionary policies to eliminate the unemployment. Therefore, the cost of pushing up wages and prices is lower and workers and firms will be more likely to do it.

12. True. If expectations about policy have no effect on the aggregate supply curve, then a cost-push inflation is less likely to develop when policymakers pursue an activist accommodating policy. Furthermore, if expectations about policy do not matter, then pursuing a nonaccommodating, nonactivist policy does not have the hidden benefit of making it less likely that workers will push up their wages and create unemployment. The case for an activist policy is therefore stronger.

14. The Fed's big stick is the ability to let unemployment develop as a result of a wage push by not trying to eliminate unemployment with expansionary monetary policy. The statement proposes that the Fed should pursue a nonaccommodating policy because this will prevent cost-push inflation and make it less likely that unemployment develops because of workers' attempts to push up their wages.

Chapter 29

1. False. Expectations can be highly inaccurate and still be rational because optimal forecasts are not necessarily accurate: A forecast is optimal if it is the best possible even if the forecast errors are large.

3. No, because he could improve the accuracy of his forecasts by predicting that tomorrow's interest rates will be identical to today's. His forecasts are thus not optimal and he does not have rational expectations.

5. No, you shouldn't buy stocks because the rise in the money supply is publicly available information that will be already incorporated into stock prices. Thus you cannot expect to earn more than the equilibrium return on stocks by acting on the money supply information.

7. No, because this is publicly available information and is already reflected in stock prices. The optimal forecast of stock returns will equal the equilibrium return, and so there is no benefit from selling your stocks.

9. No, if the person has no better information than the rest of the market. An expected price rise of 10% over the next month implies over a 100% annual return on IBM stock, which certainly exceeds its equilibrium return. This would mean that there is an unexploited profit opportunity in the market, which would have been eliminated in an efficient market. The only time that the person's expectations could be rational is if she had information unavailable to the market which allows her to beat the market.

11. False. The people with better information are exactly those who make the market more efficient by eliminating unexploited profit opportunities. These people can profit from their better information.

Chapter 30

2. A tax cut that is expected to last for ten years will have a larger effect on consumer expenditure than the one that is expected to last only one year. The reason is that the longer the tax cut is expected to last, the greater its effect on expected average income and consumer expenditure.

4. True, if the anti-inflation policy is credible. As is shown in Figure 30.6, if anti-inflation policy is believed (and hence expected), then there is no output loss in the new classical model [the economy stays at point 1 in panel (b)] and there is a smaller output loss than would otherwise be the case in the nonclassical rational expectations model [the economy goes to point 2″ rather than point 2′ in panel (c)].

6. Uncertain. It is true that policymakers can reduce unemployment by pursuing a more expansionary policy than the public expects. However, the rational expectations assumption indicates that the public will attempt to anticipate policymakers' actions. Policymakers cannot be sure whether expansionary policy will be more or less expansionary than the public expects and thus cannot use policy to make a predictable impact on unemployment.

8. True, because the Lucas critique indicates that the effect of policy on the aggregate demand curve depends on the public's expectations about that policy. The outcome of a particular policy is thus less certain in Lucas's view than if expectations about it do not matter, and it is harder to design a beneficial activist stabilization policy.

10. Yes, if budget deficits lead to an inflationary monetary policy and expectations about monetary policy affect the aggregate supply curve. In this case, a large budget deficit would cause the aggregate supply curve to shift in more because expected inflation would be higher. The result is that the increase in the price level (the inflation rate) would be higher.

13. The aggregate supply curve would shift in less than the aggregate demand curve shifts out; hence, at their intersection, aggregate output would rise and the price level would be higher than it would have been if money growth had been reduced to a rate of 2%.

14. Using the traditional model, the aggregate supply curve would continue to shift in at the same rate, and the smaller rightward shift of the aggregate demand curve because money supply growth has been reduced would mean a smaller increase in the price level and a reduction of aggregate output. In the nonclassical model, the effect of this anti-inflation policy on aggregate output is uncertain. The aggregate supply curve would not shift in by as much as in the traditional model because the anti-inflation policy is expected, but it would shift in by more than would occur in the new classical model. Thus inflation falls, but aggregate output may rise or fall depending on whether the aggregate supply curve shifts in more or less than the aggregate demand curve shifts out.

Credits

Page 141: **Following the Financial News: Yield Curves.** "Treasury Yield Curve" from THE WALL STREET JOURNAL, March, 1991. Reprinted by permission of The Wall Street Journal, © 1991 Dow, Jones and Company, Inc. All Rights Reserved Worldwide.

Page 158: **Figure 8.1:** "Sources of External Funds for Nonfinancial Businesses in the United States" from ASYMMETRIC INFORMATION, CORPORATE FINANCE AND INVESTMENT by R. Glenn Hubbard. Copyright © 1990 by The University of Chicago Press. Reprinted by permission of the University of Chicago Press.

Page 287: **Figure 12.1:** Advertisement for the UAL Corporation from THE WALL STREET JOURNAL, March 20, 1991. Copyright © 1991 by United Airlines. Reprinted by permission of United Airlines.

Page 709: **Following The Financial News: The Stock Market.** "Industrial Average Climbs 64.85, Its Second-Largest This Year" by Craig S. Smith from THE WALL STREET JOURNAL, October, 1990. Reprinted by permission of The Wall Street Journal, © 1990 Dow, Jones and Company, Inc. All Rights Reserved Worldwide.

Index

The page numbers followed by "n" signify information included in a footnote on that page.

ratio of excess reserves to, 349–350, 357–358

ratio of money market funds to, 357–358

ratio of time deposits to, 357–358
and money supply, 373
required reserve ratio on, 372–373

shifts from, into currency, 341

Chemical Bank Corp., 236, 244

Chicago Board of Trade (CBT), 42, 300–301, 303

Chicago Mercantile Exchange (CME), 301, 303

CHIPS (Clearing House Inter-bank Payment System), 28

Christiano, Lawrence, 531n

Chrysler Corp., default risk of, 133

Churchill, Winston, 261

Citibank, 239
introduction of negotiable CDs by, 51

Citicorp, 214, 236, 239, 244, 246

Civil Aeronautics Board, 544n

Clearing House Inter-bank Payment System (CHIPS), 28

Clift, Eleanor, 260n

Closed-end funds, 283

Coelho, Tony, 261

Coins:
minting of, 413, 421n
in monetary base, 407, 408, 413n

Coinsurance:
in insurance policies, 276
proposed, for federal deposit insurance, 263

Collateral, 160–161
defined, 160
loan management and, 218

Collateralized debt, 160–161
as solution to adverse selection problem, 170

Collateralized mortgage obligations (CMOs), 306–307

Columbia Savings and Loan, 261

Commercial banks, 203, 234–240
branching restrictions on, 237–240
chartering of, 391
as financial intermediaries, 47
foreign, 294
number of, in U.S., 234
regulation of, 234–240
separation of, from securities industry, 291–294
size distribution of, in 1989, 235
ten largest U.S., in 1990, 236

Commercial loans, 203
as capital market instruments, 56
as simple loans, 68

Commercial paper, 52, 309

Commodities Futures Trading Commission (CFTC), 58

Compensating balances, 218

Competitive Equality Banking Act of 1987, 257, 261

Complete crowding out, 592–594, 610

Comptroller of the Currency, 48, 229, 230–231, 252, 257, 268, 391

Computers, payments system and, 27–28, 239–240

Congress, and Federal Reserve system, 396–399, 401, 403–404

Consol, 75–76, 83

Constant-money-growth-rate rule, 688

Consumer debt, collateralized, 160–161

Consumer durable expenditure, 654–657

Consumer expenditure, 555
autonomous, 556–557
aggregate output and, 563–564, 569, 570n
defined, 556
Friedman-Meiselman measure of, 645, 647–648, 650–651
and IS curve, 482, 582
and consumption function, 556–559
defined, 555, 607
as monetary transmission mechanism, 654–657

Consumer finance companies, 282

Consumer loans, 56, 203

Consumer optimism, 617

Consumer Price Index (CPI), 605

Consumption:
defined, 655
Modigliani's theory of, 654–655

Consumption function:
consumer expenditure and, 556–559
defined, 556
example of, 557

Continental Illinois National Bank, 252, 376, 431, 434

Contracts:
debt, 161, 171–174
equity, 171–174

Contractual savings institutions, 48–49

Cooley, Thomas F., 553n

Cootner, Paul, 708n

Corporate bonds:
as capital market instruments, 55
default risk on, 133–136
percentage of corporate financing by, 158, 160
yield on, 132–133

Corporate financing:
access to securities markets and, 160
external sources of, 158–161
stock issuance and, 158
through collateralized debt, 160–161

Corporate indebtedness:
growth in, 185, 186, 193–196
principal-agent problem and, 187–190

Corporate restructuring:
costs and benefits of, 193–197
economic analysis of, 185–197
through mergers or acquisitions (takeovers), 185–191
of oil industry in the 1980s, 192–193
principal-agent problem in, 187–190
reasons for, 190–191

Correlation-causation question, 637–638

Corrigan, E., Gerald, 433

Cost, transactions, 22, 161–163

Cost-push inflation, 673–674
expectations and, 694

Costly state verification, 173

Coupon bond, defined, 68
consol, 75–76
yield on, 72–76

Coupon rate, 68

Covenants, restrictive, 161, 176–177, 215–216, 251n

CPI (Consumer Price Index), 605

Cranston, Alan, 260

Credibility, and inflation, 688, 733–737

Credit:
adjustment, 429
extended, 429
lines of, long-term customer relationships and, 216–218
seasonal, 429

Credit agencies, federal, 284–285

Credit cards, bank, 303–305

Average Inflation Rate Versus Average Rate of Money Growth for a Number of Countries: 1980–1990

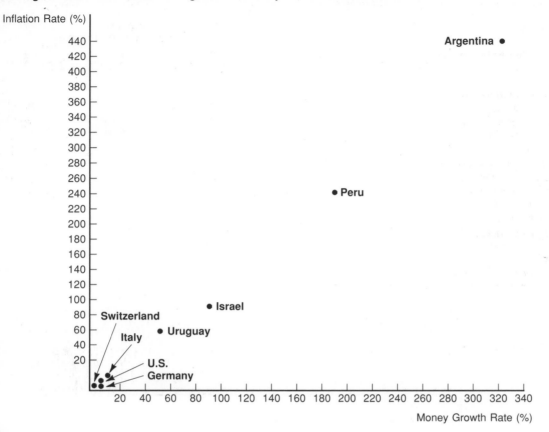

Business Cycle and Interest Rates (Three-Month Treasury Bills): 1951–1990 (Shaded Areas Are Recessions)

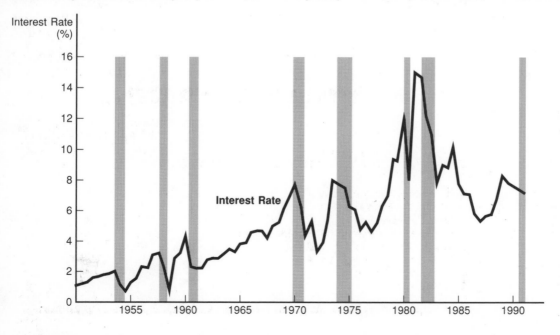

Symbol	Page where introduced	Term
M	343	quantity of money
M^d	118	demand for money
M^s	118	supply of money
MB	337	monetary base (high-powered money)
MB_n	343	nonborrowed monetary base
mpc	556	marginal propensity to consume
$M1$	31	$M1$ monetary aggregate
$M2$	32	$M2$ monetary aggregate
$M3$	32	$M3$ monetary aggregate
MMF	356	money market mutual fund shares
NX	555	net exports
P	524	price level
P_t	85	price of a security at time t
RET	85	return
$RET^\$$	478	expected return on dollar deposits
RET^F	479	expected return on foreign deposits
R	332	reserves
RR	332	required reserves
r_D	308	reserve requirement for checkable deposits
r_T	348	reserve requirement ratio on time deposits
S	105	supply curve
T	356	time deposits
T	416	taxes
V	524	velocity
Y	454	aggregate output, national income
Y^{ad}	555	aggregate demand
Y_n	614	natural rate level of output